Macroeconomics

Macroeconomics

Graeme Chamberlin and Linda Yueh

THOMSON

Australia • Canada • Mexico • Singapore • Spain • United Kindom • United States

THOMSON

Macroeconomics
Graeme Chamberlin and Linda Yueh

Publishing Director
John Yates

Publisher
Patrick Bond

Development Editor
Anna Carter

Production Editor
Stuart Giblin

Manufacturing Manager
Helen Mason

Marketing Manager
Katie Thorn

Typesetter
Saxon Graphics Ltd, Derby

Production Controller
Maeve Healy

Printer
Canale, Italy

Cover Design
Jackie Wrout

Text Design
Design Deluxe, Bath, UK

For more information, contact Thomson Learning, High Holborn House; 50-51 Bedford Row, London WC1R 4LR or visit us on the World Wide Web at: http://www.thomsonlearning.co.uk

ISBN-13: 978-1-84480-042-1
ISBN-10: 1-84480-042-3

This edition published 2006 by Thomson Learning.

British Library Cataloguing-in-Publication Data
A catalogue record for this book is available from the British Library

Contents

Preface

Unlike microeconomics, macroeconomics is informed by the economic context. There is no clear division between theory and empirics; indeed much of the theory is driven by empirical observations which cause a modification of existing approaches. For students beginning the study of economics, macroeconomics can be a challenge due to both of the above respects. On the basic concepts, the standard models are generally applicable – those pertaining to the real side of the macroeconomy and the monetary side, the IS-LM framework, AS-AD, to name a few. However, as the basic frameworks progress to more complicated concepts, such as fiscal and monetary policies, growth models, the new global economy and certainly the international financial architecture, the context and examples that inform our understanding become tremendously important. Indeed, some of these phenomena, such as the great success of the East Asian economies in achieving double-digit growth through an export-oriented strategy, and the numerous financial crises from Mexico to Asia to Europe which rippled through emerging and developed markets alike, have informed the most important developments in macroeconomics in our time. This context, therefore, is worthy of study by students interested in both the global economy and the recent developments in macroeconomics.

This book is a general textbook in macroeconomics and meets the demand for examples from the international context. Our materials, therefore, encompass standard introductory macroeconomic topics and also the latest concepts arising from the international context. Examples that require mature economies will relate to Europe and the US upon which most macroeconomic theories are based. We will cover issues spanning the US 'twin deficits', as well as the euro and EMU, plus many other issues in the UK economy. We will also cover the changing international economic order, including the WTO, the growth model of Latin America in contrast to East Asia, the transition of China and other recently marketized economies, and the financial crises of the past two decades which fundamentally overhauled the theories surrounding liquidity crises, exchange rates and structural reforms related to liberalization.

The textbook is suited for at least four different levels of instruction. The first is one that includes a good review of some concepts from principles, such as the determinants of national income. This textbook does this so that students with a less comprehensive background can have the required resources in one text. The second is a standard intermediate treatment of macroeconomics. The textbook starts with a detailed derivation of the Keynesian cross and components of aggregate demand, which leads to the general equilibrium models of IS-LM and AS-AD and the external sector. Finally, the textbook is suitable for more advanced teaching of macroeconomics as the standard models are followed by rigorous treatment of international policy coordination, financial crises, long-run economic growth and even development and transition economics. In some chapters where suitable, there are technical sections and appendices to support mathematical teaching of these materials. At the same time, the course is also suited to non-specialist students in economics as the topics are covered without a reliance on mathematical derivations, but rather technically with diagrams and with a large number of examples that explain the concepts intuitively. The topics of interest to non-specialist students in particular are also stand-alone topics, which include consumption theory, investment theory, fiscal policy, inflation and monetary policy, economic growth, development economics and international financial architecture issues. The case studies of countries and topics such as the new economy would also be of interest to business, political science and students of other disciplines.

Structure and plan of the book

Road map

One of the hardest things for students to grasp about macroeconomics is the manipulation of the models because there are usually a number of variables that interact and affect each other. In essence, this is the nature of macroeconomics which is about the interaction among elements in a circular flow of income. Therefore, this textbook is designed to present the building blocks of the models piece by piece. Part of the difficulty encountered by students is indeed the confusing array of variables that need to be considered in the general equilibrium models. We therefore give instructors the option of introducing the models in a closed economy context and then tackling the open economy versions. The book is also flexible in allowing instructors to start with the Keynesian cross and cover the differences between neoclassical and Keynesian economics, which some may find useful. Alternatively, some may choose to start with the IS-LM model or AS-AD, an approach that is catered for in this textbook as they are presented in clearly demarcated chapters. We also allow scope for more advanced topics to be covered in this textbook. Namely, we dedicate the last two parts to models of long-run economic growth and the international financial architecture, which are not usually covered in this degree of detail in a standard macroeconomic textbook. The four chapters (one appears on the companion website only) encompass international policy coordination, which includes optimal currency areas, three generations of currency and financial crises with examples, models of economic growth that range from neoclassical to endogenous growth theory, and also development economics, which includes WTO issues.

This brings us to the final aspect of this textbook. The treatment of the materials is dealt with step-by-step so that the first parts deal with a closed economy, with reference to several major economies as examples. Since most macro models are developed in the context of industrialized economies, we follow the history of these developments but widely in that the coverage spans the US, UK and Europe. The latter parts cover a broad international context. The open economy versions of the general equilibrium models are presented and the examples encompass Latin America, East and South Asia, and sub-Saharan Africa, in addition to examples drawn from the developed economies. The international focus of the latter parts of the textbook also provide in-depth treatment of the approaches to growth of the major emerging economies today, namely, China, India, Brazil and Russia. This is done by reference to, but not depending on a technical treatment of, the models of growth and concepts covered earlier. Chapter 15, on currency and financial crises, is similarly constructed. This allows these sections to be used as stand-alone, additional topics of study. Therefore, the latter chapters comprise topics that can be incorporated into a macroeconomics course or can be used as part of a course that covers major developments in the global economy in the past few decades.

Structure of the book

The textbook is clearly laid out in several parts which follow the general structure of national income determination, real macroeconomy, money and financial markets, general equilibrium models, short-run fluctuations and stabilization, the open economy, international policy and long-run economic growth. The structure demarcates closed economy followed by open economy treatment. We start with the circular flow of income and review the determinants of national income. These components of national income then go on to form the Keynesian cross and are used later to derive the aggregate demand curve. By understanding the theories of consumption, investment and government spending, the students will have a good grasp of the real side of the macroeconomy, as well as having the basics with which to build more complex general equilibrium models. With this, we move to the nominal side of the macroeconomy and cover not only money markets, but also provide a treatment of modern financial markets. With the components of the macroeconomy covered, we introduce a general equilibrium model, IS-LM. We then introduce prices and present the AS-AD model. This is presented in the short, medium and long run. These constitute the main models of the economy. We then move to consider two aspects of short-run macroeconomic fluctuations, that is, real business cycles, and inflation and unemployment in the form of the Phillips curve.

The next part covers the open economy, in which we tackle the balance of payments, exchange rates and the open economy versions of the general equilibrium models. This is followed by two chapters on international policy coordination and financial crises. The textbook concludes with two chapters on models of long-run economic growth and approaches to growth, which continues the international focus to the end. With this structure we will have presented the major models of macroeconomics followed by coverage of a number of the most exciting developments in the recent literature, such as currency and financial crises, and the prospects of economic growth in the evolving international economic system. Although the earlier parts of the textbook focus on developed economies, this is a result of most of models fitting industrialized economies as they were derived in that context. By contrast, the latter chapters include many emerging economies which are beginning to shape macroeconomic debates and models with their growth experience. We have covered both in the hope of bringing the students up to date with the evolution of macroeconomic theories, which are very much shaped by empirical developments and contexts.

Key features in the text

International focus

The book covers the basic macroeconomic models using the UK or US as the context both for simplification and because the models were primarily developed for industrialized economies. The latter parts of the book then use models developed for Europe, Latin America, Asia and the transition economies to explain international growth and crises. Nevertheless, throughout the book, there are numerous examples drawn from the global context to highlight and illustrate the concepts. The strong international focus of the book is particularly underscored by the second half of the book, which is entirely international in focus and which matches the interests and requirements of macroeconomics today.

'Global applications'

Throughout the book are 'Global applications', which are text boxes, case studies and detailed explanations. These are intended to bring out the empirical relevance of macroeconomic topics and keep the ideas topical, as well as provide in-depth treatment of certain topics.

Assessment material

There are review questions and more advanced question at the end of every chapter. Further questions will be available on the website. These are intended for self-assessment and answers are provided on the website.

Recommended reading

We have listed a number of references that would make for useful additional reading if students wish to pursue a topic in more depth. The contributions of these authors to macroeconomics are often incorporated in the textbook, but original materials are always valuable.

Supplementary material

Additional supplementary material can be found on the supporting website at www.thomsonlearning.co.uk/chamberlin_yueh.

Course sequences

Macroeconomics is a relevant subject not only to students of economics, but also business, management, international relations and political science, among others. As such, this textbook can be used in a course in at least five different ways, depending on the level, focus and length of the course.

- For a course in intermediate macroeconomics, that is, after the principles level, this textbook provides a straightforward path through the major short-run and long-run models.
- For a course that is geared toward a more international focus, this textbook can also be taught in a sequence that introduces open economy factors first.
- For a shorter course that aims to cover the technical materials, this textbook can be used to teach the building blocks of the major macroeconomic models.
- For courses that survey or cover advanced topics in macroeconomics, this textbook has stand-alone chapters which can serve to cover specific topics, such as economic growth and development or international financial architecture and currency crises.
- For a postgraduate or advanced undergraduate course that includes macroeconomics as a module or topic for non-specialist students, this text can be used to provide an introduction to the main issues and examples in an international context.

The two main proposed course structures are detailed in the following sections. The alternative structures can be found on the companion website.

Course in intermediate macroeconomics

For a lecture course that follows on from an introductory or principles of economics course, we would recommend the following sequence through the chapters.

Part I would provide a review of the main determinants of national income and introduce technical concepts used throughout the book, which are useful as a reminder of the circular flow of income. Part I could be covered in one lecture.

Part II would follow, covering the main theories and evidence surrounding the real economy. The use of the Keynesian cross framework will provide a technical basis of analysis, which may also be a review for some students. Even so, we suggest that each of the main components of aggregate demand covered in this part be covered in an integrated fashion using the Keynesian cross when possible. Two lectures on consumption, one on investment and one on government spending would be recommended.

Part III introduces money into the macroeconomy. There are two chapters on the money market and financial markets. One lecture on each of these should cover the nominal side of the economy.

Part IV covers the models of the economy. The first is the IS-LM model, which is partitioned as developing the model, and then the use of fiscal and monetary policy within the framework, moving on to the debate between Keynesians and classicists and then concluding with the neoclassical version. There is a significant amount of technical materials in this chapter, which will warrant four lectures. The second chapter covers the AS-AD model. The first part of the chapter develops the aggregate demand curve, drawing from the earlier Part II. This could comprise one lecture. The AS curve is then derived in both the short run and long run, which comprises one lecture. This, plus hysteresis and the medium run, would comprise three lectures.

Part V covers short-run fluctuations and stabilization. There are two chapters covering real business cycles and the Phillips curve. Real business cycles and stabilization policies would warrant one lecture, while the Phillips curve chapter would take two to provide sufficient time to cover inflation, unemployment, monetary policy and output fluctuations.

Part VI then introduces the open economy. The first chapter covers the basics of the balance of payments and exchange rate determination. Although this chapter is not the most technically challenging, typically students struggle with some of these concepts. It would be worthwhile to spend two lectures on these two topics, one on trade and capital flows, and a second on exchange rates. The second chapter on the IS-LM-BP model becomes more technical and warrants two lectures to cover the construction and use of this framework. The final chapter is on the AS-AD open economy model and warrants two lectures to cover the materials.

There are 25 suggested lectures at this point. There may be room for more or less in your course. Obviously, these are our suggested guidelines and actual number of hours will differ depending on the duration of the lectures and semester length. In any event, this should provide coverage of the main topics in macroeconomics. Depending on the direction of your course and time, there are at least two paths at this point in terms of topics.

Part VII could be the final set of lectures in your course, especially if industrialized countries are the main focus. There are two chapters on international policy coordination and financial crises. Each or parts of these chapters could be covered in one lecture each.

Or, you may opt for Part VIII, which covers models of long-run growth. The chapter here includes models of growth. An additional chapter is available on the companion website and covers topics in development and transition economics. The more technical chapter on growth will probably take two lectures to cover, while the development economics chapter would take one.

You may also opt for a combination of coverage of international financial architecture and growth. It would be possible to cover long-run growth models and then development and financial crises in four lectures. Alternatively, you may want to have a final lecture on international policy coordination and exchange rate regimes, which follow on neatly from Part VI. This could be done in one lecture. Depending on your preferences, the course would have 26 lectures in this case or a bit longer if you cover more topics.

Open economy approach to intermediate macroeconomics

For those who wish to start with an open economy version based on a standard lecture course, we recommend the following sequence.

Part I introducing the macroeconomy would be followed by Part II covering the determinants of aggregate demand. This would take five lectures, as before. Part III on money and financial markets would follow, warranting two lectures. The first chapter of Part VI covering the final component of aggregate demand would follow. This chapter could be covered in two lectures, one on the balance of payments and the other on exchange rates. This will provide a complete picture of the open economy version of the macroeconomy before turning to the general equilibrium models.

Part IV covering IS-LM in two lectures would be followed by two lectures covering the second chapter in Part VI, which is the IS-LM-BP model. The second chapter in Part IV covering AS-AD in two lectures would again be followed by two lectures on the third chapter in Part VI, which is the open economy version. We have reduced the number of recommended lectures on the IS-LM and AS-AD models since students will be covering the open economy versions straight afterward, giving reinforcement to the materials in the closed economy context. Part V on real business cycles and the Phillips curve would come next in the form of three lectures, as before.

At this point, we would recommend a longer international section and would suggest covering all of Part VII in two lectures, as it encompasses the international financial architecture and currency crises. We would also recommend the additional chapter on the companion website as it deals with the evidence of cross-country growth and the evolving international economic system's influence on economic development. This would leave the chapter on long-run economic growth models in Part VIII as an optional lecture.

This sequence is comparable to the first version with a rearrangement of chapters so that the open economy versions of the models follow from the closed economy ones. As the final two parts of the book are particularly relevant to a course with an open economy focus, we strongly recommend including them in the sequence of lectures and have made suggestions as to how this might be done. But, of course, this again depends on the number of lecture hours and the level of students. We have written the chapters in such a way that this sequence is as viable as the first one, and hope that our strong international focus comes through in this recommended course structure.

Acknowledgements

Thomson would like to thank the following for their reviews:

Marta Aloi, University of Nottingham
Klas Fregert, Lund University
Manto Gotsi, University of Aberdeen
Dave Higgins, University of York
Yoonbai Kim, National University of Singapore/University of Kentucky
Paul Mizen, University of Nottingham
Ilmakunnas Pekka, Helsinki School of Economics
Chris Reid, University of Portsmouth
Tom van veen, Maastricht University
Koen Vermeylen, University of Amsterdam
Chong K Yip, The Chinese University of Hong Kong

Walk-through tour

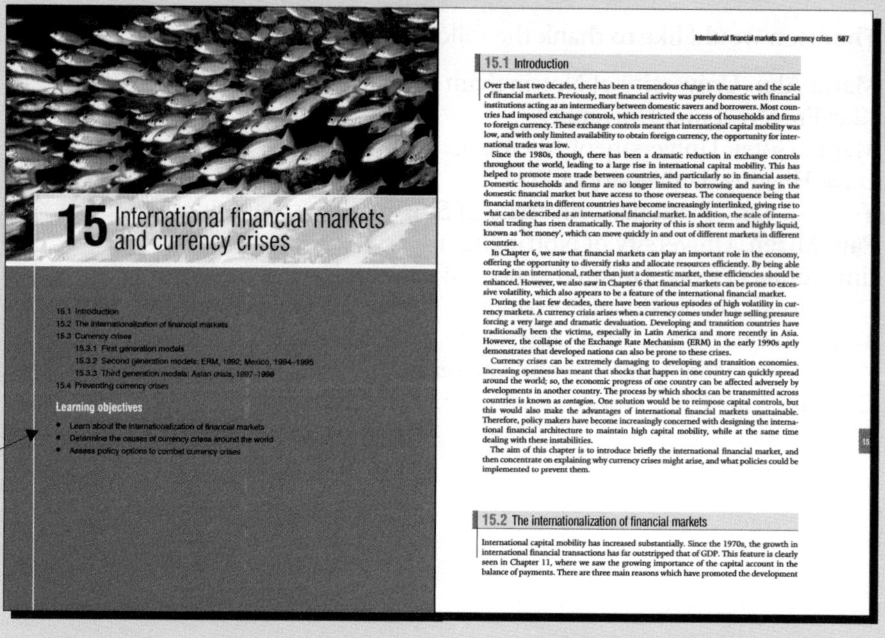

Learning objectives

Appear at the start of every chapter to help you monitor your understanding and progress through the chapter. Each chapter also begins with a list of the main headings within the text.

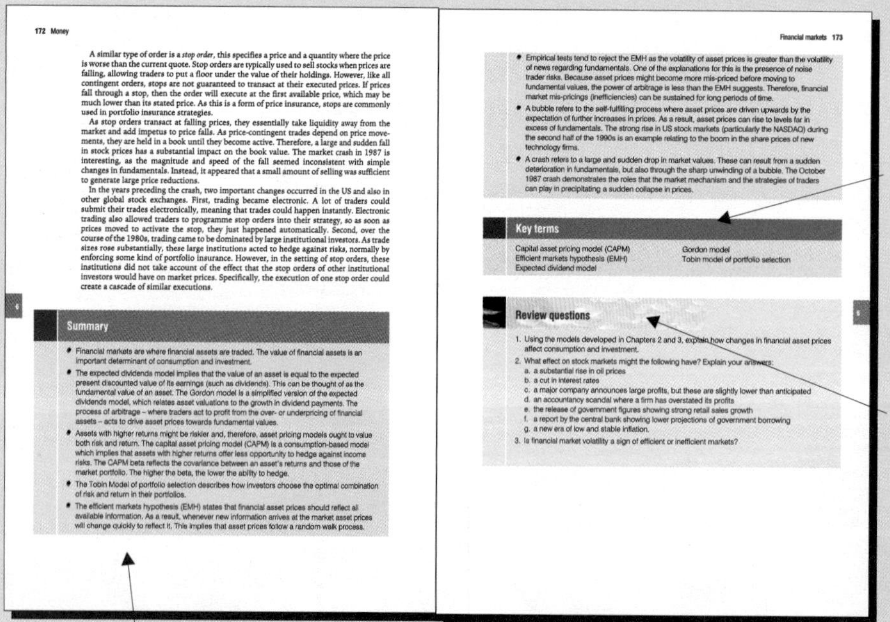

Key terms

Highlighted in colour throughout and explained in full in a glossary on the website, enabling you to find explanations of key terms quickly.

Review questions

Provided at the end of each chapter, these help reinforce and test your knowledge and understanding, and provide a basis for group discussions and activities.

Summary

Each chapter ends with a comprehensive summary that provides a thorough recap of the key issues in each chapter, helping you to assess your understanding and revise key content.

Global applications

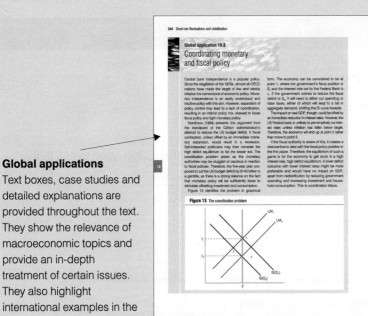

Text boxes, case studies and detailed explanations are provided throughout the text. They show the relevance of macroeconomic topics and provide an in-depth treatment of certain issues. They also highlight international examples in the text.

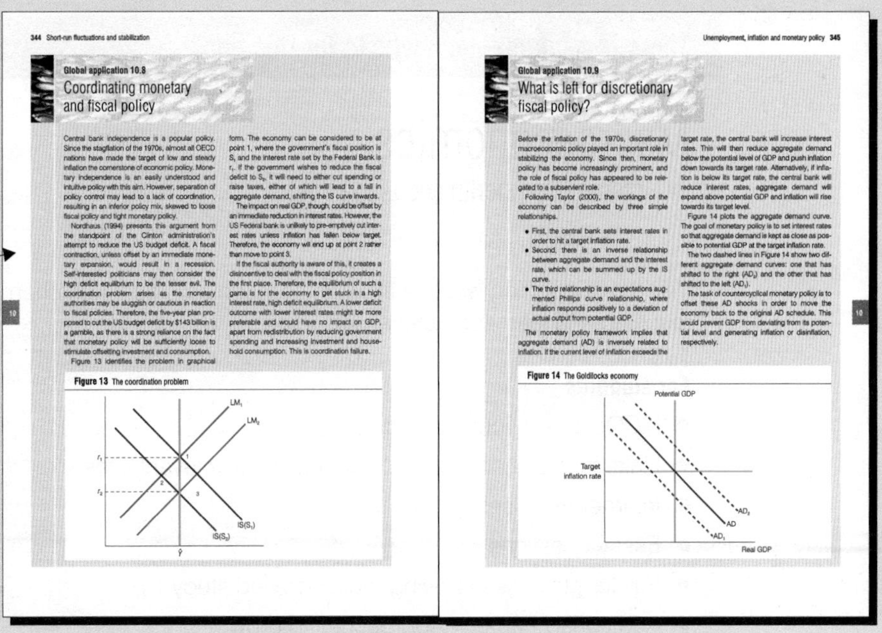
344 Short-run fluctuations and stabilization

Global application 10.8

Coordinating monetary and fiscal policy

Central bank independence is a popular policy. Since the stagflation of the 1970s, almost all OECD nations have made the target of low and steady inflation the cornerstone of economic policy. Monetary independence is an easily understood and intuitive policy with this aim. However, separation of policy control may lead to a lack of coordination, resulting in an inferior policy mix, skewed to loose fiscal policy and tight monetary policy.

Nordhaus (1994) presents this argument from the standpoint of the Clinton administration's attempt to reduce the US budget deficit. A fiscal contraction, unless offset by an immediate monetary expansion, would result in a recession. Self-interested politicians may then consider the high deficit equilibrium to be the lesser evil. The coordination problem arises as the monetary authorities may be sluggish or cautious in reaction to fiscal policies. Therefore, the five-year plan proposed to cut the US budget deficit by $143 billion is a gamble, as there is a strong reliance on the fact that monetary policy will be sufficiently loose to stimulate offsetting investment and consumption.

Figure 13 identifies the problem in graphical form. The economy can be considered to be at point 1, where the government's fiscal position is S_1 and the interest rate set by the Federal Bank is r_1. If the government wishes to reduce the fiscal deficit to S_2, it will need to either cut spending or raise taxes, either of which will lead to a fall in aggregate demand, shifting the IS curve inwards.

The impact on real GDP, though, could be offset by an immediate reduction in interest rates. However, the US Federal bank is unlikely to pre-emptively cut interest rates unless inflation has fallen below target. Therefore, the economy will end up at point 2 rather than move to point 3.

If the fiscal authority is aware of this, it creates a disincentive to deal with the fiscal policy position in the first place. Therefore, the equilibrium of such a game is for the economy to get stuck in a high interest rate, high deficit equilibrium. A lower deficit outcome with lower interest rates might be more preferable and would have no impact on GDP, apart from redistribution by reducing government spending and increasing investment and household consumption. This is coordination failure.

Figure 13 The coordination problem

Unemployment, inflation and monetary policy 345

Global application 10.9

What is left for discretionary fiscal policy?

Before the inflation of the 1970s, discretionary macroeconomic policy played an important role in stabilizing the economy. Since then, monetary policy has become increasingly prominent, and the role of fiscal policy has appeared to be relegated to a subservient role.

Following Taylor (2000), the workings of the economy can be described by three simple relationships.

- First, the central bank sets interest rates in order to hit a target inflation rate.
- Second, there is an inverse relationship between aggregate demand and the interest rate, which can be summed up by the IS curve.
- The third relationship is an expectations augmented Phillips curve relationship, where inflation responds positively to a deviation of actual output from potential GDP.

The monetary policy framework implies that aggregate demand (AD) is inversely related to inflation. If the current level of inflation exceeds the target rate, the central bank will increase interest rates. This will then reduce aggregate demand below the potential level of GDP and push inflation down towards its target rate. Alternatively, if inflation is below its target rate, the central bank will reduce interest rates, aggregate demand will expand above potential GDP and inflation will rise towards its target level.

Figure 14 plots the aggregate demand curve. The goal of monetary policy is to set interest rates so that aggregate demand is kept as close as possible to potential GDP at the target inflation rate.

The two dashed lines in Figure 14 show two different aggregate demand curves: one that has shifted to the right (AD_2) and the other that has shifted to the left (AD_1).

The task of countercyclical monetary policy is to offset these AD shocks in order to move the economy back to the original AD schedule. This would prevent GDP from deviating from its potential level and generating inflation or disinflation, respectively.

Figure 14 The Goldilocks economy

More advanced problems

More advanced problems are provided at the end of each chapter to test your understanding further.

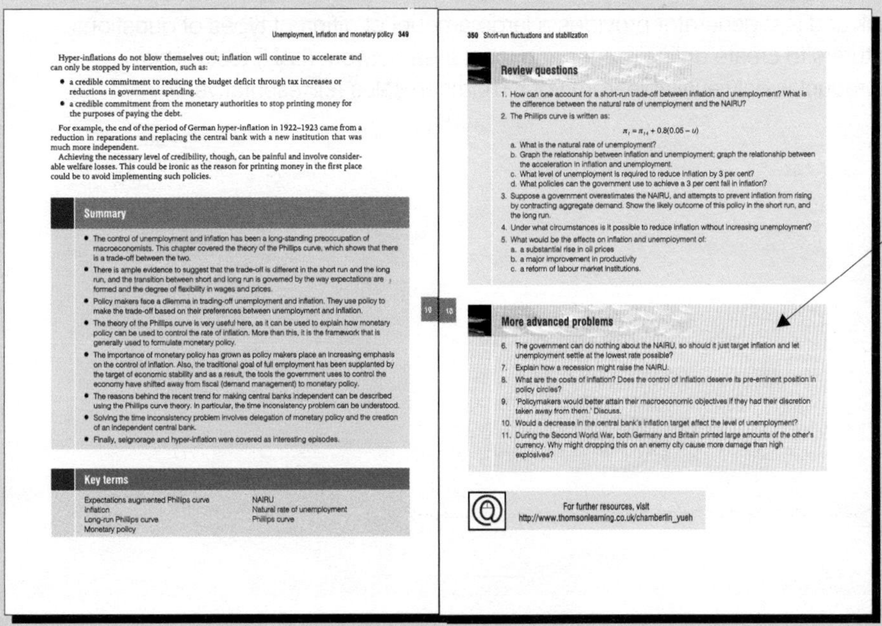
Unemployment, inflation and monetary policy 349

Hyper-inflations do not blow themselves out; inflation will continue to accelerate and can only be stopped by intervention, such as:

- a credible commitment to reducing the budget deficit through tax increases or reductions in government spending.
- a credible commitment from the monetary authorities to stop printing money for the purposes of paying the debt.

For example, the end of the period of German hyper-inflation in 1922–1923 came from a reduction in reparations and replacing the central bank with a new institution that was much more independent.

Achieving the necessary level of credibility, though, can be painful and involve considerable welfare losses. This could be ironic as the reason for printing money in the first place could be to avoid implementing such policies.

Summary

- The control of unemployment and inflation has been a long-standing preoccupation of macroeconomists. This chapter covered the theory of the Phillips curve, which shows that there is a trade-off between the two.
- There is ample evidence to suggest that the trade-off is different in the short run and the long run, and the transition between short and long run is governed by the way expectations are formed and the degree of flexibility in wages and prices.
- Policy makers face a dilemma in trading-off unemployment and inflation. They use policy to make the trade-off based on their preferences between unemployment and inflation.
- The theory of the Phillips curve is very useful here, as it can be used to explain how monetary policy can be used to control the rate of inflation. More than this, it is the framework that is generally used to formulate monetary policy.
- The importance of monetary policy has grown as policy makers place an increasing emphasis on the control of inflation. Also, the traditional goal of full employment has been supplanted by the target of economic stability and as a result, the tools the government uses to control the economy have shifted away from fiscal (demand management) to monetary policy.
- The reasons behind the recent trend for making central banks independent can be described using the Phillips curve theory. In particular, the time inconsistency problem can be understood.
- Solving the time inconsistency problem involves delegation of monetary policy and the creation of an independent central bank.
- Finally, seignorage and hyper-inflation were covered as interesting episodes.

Key terms

Expectations augmented Phillips curve
Inflation
Long-run Phillips curve
Monetary policy
NAIRU
Natural rate of unemployment
Phillips curve

350 Short-run fluctuations and stabilization

Review questions

1. How can one account for a short-run trade-off between inflation and unemployment? What is the difference between the natural rate of unemployment and the NAIRU?
2. The Phillips curve is written as:

$$\pi_t = \pi_{t-1} + 0.8(0.05 - u)$$

   a. What is the natural rate of unemployment?
   b. Graph the relationship between inflation and unemployment; graph the relationship between the acceleration in inflation and unemployment.
   c. What level of unemployment is required to reduce inflation by 3 per cent?
   d. What policies can the government use to achieve a 3 per cent fall in inflation?
3. Suppose a government overestimates the NAIRU, and attempts to prevent inflation from rising by contracting aggregate demand. Show the likely outcome of this policy in the short run, and the long run.
4. Under what circumstances is it possible to reduce inflation without increasing unemployment?
5. What would be the effects on inflation and unemployment of:
   a. a substantial rise in oil prices
   b. a major improvement in productivity
   c. a reform of labour market institutions.

More advanced problems

6. The government can do nothing about the NAIRU, so should it just target inflation and let unemployment settle at the lowest rate possible?
7. Explain how a recession might raise the NAIRU.
8. What are the costs of inflation? Does the control of inflation deserve its pre-eminent position in policy circles?
9. 'Policymakers would better attain their macroeconomic objectives if they had their discretion taken away from them.' Discuss.
10. Would a decrease in the central bank's inflation target affect the level of unemployment?
11. During the Second World War, both Germany and Britain printed large amounts of the other's currency. Why might dropping this on an enemy city cause more damage than high explosives?

For further resources, visit http://www.thomsonlearning.co.uk/chamberlin_yueh

There is a companion website for this book

Macroeconomics
by Graeme Chamberlin and Linda Yueh

Visit the supporting website at www.thomsonlearning.co.uk/chamberlin_yueh to find further teaching and learning material, including:

For students

- MCQs to test your learning
- Links to useful company, news and other relevant sites
- Internet exercises
- Essay questions
- Full-length cases allowing more detailed study
- Additional chapter – Approaches to growth
- Glossary
- References and further reading

For lecturers

- Further case studies
- Instructor's manual – including how to teach from this text, suggested answers to the review questions and more advanced problems
- Downloadable PowerPoint slides
- Further questions to be used in tutorials and seminars, with suggested answers

Supplementary resources

Exam View®
This testbank and test generator provides a large amount of different types of questions, allowing lecturers to create online, paper and local area network (LAN) tests. This CD-based product is only available from your Thomson sales representative.

Part I

Defining the macroeconomy

Chapter 1 Macroeconomics and the circular flow of income

The macroeconomy is defined and introduced in this section. The concept of the circular flow of income is covered and how it serves as the foundation for the macroeconomy.

1 Macroeconomics and the circular flow of income

Learning objectives

- Understand what macroeconomics is about
- Represent the macroeconomy by the circular flow of income
- Use the circular flow of income to measure national income/output
- Understand the usefulness of macroeconomic models in analysing the economy and forming economic policy

1.1 Introduction

Economics is a social science; this means that it is a study of the choices and actions that members of society make. Microeconomics does this at the individual level. For example, it is concerned with the choices that consumers make between different goods and services, or whether firms produce output using capital or labour. One perception is that macroeconomics is just the aggregation of all the decisions that are taken at the micro level. For example, total employment is found by just adding up all the employment decisions of firms. Total consumer expenditure is found by just adding up all the choices made by households. Therefore, macroeconomics would appear to be built firmly on micro foundations.

However, macroeconomics is really the study of the economy as a whole. Macroeconomists accept that the decisions taken at the micro level are important, but do not necessarily agree that an economy is simply the sum of its parts. If this were the case, it would be tantamount to saying that all economic decisions taken by firms and households were independent of each other, effectively made in isolation. Instead, they realize that there are important interactions among firms, consumers and the government. For example, a household's consumption decision will depend on its income, but this income is derived from employment, which in turn is the result of the hiring and investment decisions made by firms. However, a firm's decision to invest and hire labour will depend upon their projected sales which will be determined largely by household consumption.

These interactions mean that the economy as a whole – something we describe as the macroeconomy – may be something different than the sum of its parts. The economy can be viewed as a system where there are actions and interactions between households, firms, the government, financial institutions and the foreign sector. This system has come to be known as the **circular flow of income**.

An important aspect of macroeconomics is the role of government policies. As the government is part of the circular flow of income, it is in a position to take measures to try to influence parts of it to achieve certain goals. These objectives are usually the promotion of economic growth, low unemployment, the control of inflation and trade balance. If we think of the economy as a central heating system that pumps hot water around a house, then the use of government policy can be viewed as the thermostat. If it is too cold, then action must be taken to make things warmer, more hot water must circulate. Likewise, if it is too warm, action must be taken to cool things down. Policy making at the macro level is mainly about influencing the circular flow of income.

1.2 The circular flow of income

Figure 1.1 depicts the circular flow of income. It is a simple description of how a modern economy can be viewed as a system with five main players all linked by the actions and reactions of each other.

Households

Households have two main functions: they are workers and consumers. As workers they provide labour to firms for which they are compensated with wages. As consumers they purchase goods and services from firms which constitutes consumer expenditure. Although these are considered to be the two main functions of the household sector, it can be seen from Figure 1.1 that households are also investors and taxpayers. The counterpart

Figure 1.1 The circular flow of income

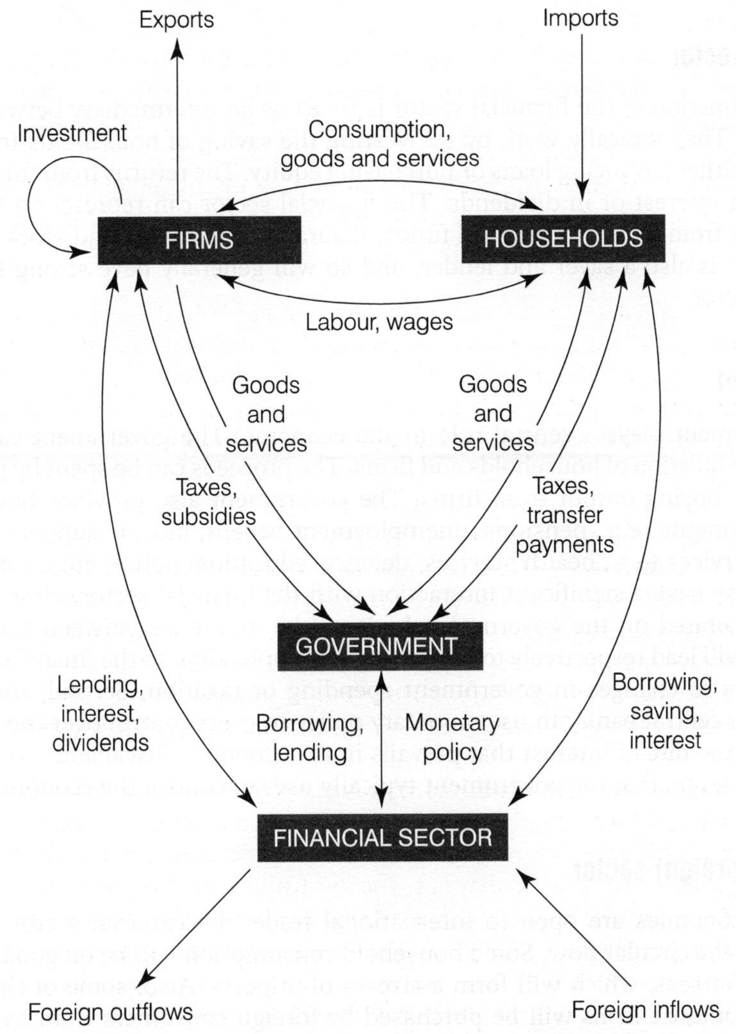

to consumer expenditure is saving, which represents income that the household sector decides not to spend. This saving can be invested by making deposits at financial institutions, such as banks. The government will also levy taxes on the households, but in return supply them with public services, such as education and defence, and provide transfer payments, such as pensions and unemployment benefits.

Firms

Firms are producers of goods or services. The production process requires inputs of labour and capital. Labour is hired from the household sector for which wages are paid, and capital investment can be funded either through retained profits or by borrowing from the financial sector. There are principally two ways in which the firm can borrow. First, they can take out bank loans, on which interest payments are levied. Alternatively, they could sell equity in the form of stocks and shares to raise funds. The equity holders then own a stake in the company and so will be entitled to a share of the firm's earnings, which are paid in the form of dividends. Firms also have interactions with the government, which is a customer, a levier of taxes and a provider of subsidies.

Financial sector

The main function of the financial sector is to act as an intermediary between borrowers and savers. They typically work by reinvesting the saving of households in firms, which they do by either advancing loans or purchasing equity. The returns from this are then paid to savers in interest or in dividends. The financial sector can represent a broad array of institutions from banks to pension funds, insurance companies and stock markets. The government is also a saver and lender, and so will generally have strong links with the financial sector.

Government

The government plays a central role in the economy. The government can raise funds through the taxation of households and firms. The proceeds can be spent by providing subsidies to or buying output from firms. The government also provides households with transfer payments (e.g., pensions, unemployment benefit, income support, child benefit, etc.) and services (e.g., health services, defence, education, police, etc.). Finally, the government may have a significant interaction with the financial sector. First, any deficit or surplus generated on the government budget (the difference between tax revenue and spending) will lead respectively to borrowing from or lending to the financial sector. Fiscal policy refers to changes in government spending or taxation. Second, the government through the central bank can use monetary policy to exert control over the level of credit creation or the rate of interest that prevails in the economy. Fiscal and monetary policies are the two levers that the government typically uses to control the economy.

External (foreign) sector

As most economies are open to international trade, the external sector must also be included in the circular flow. Some household consumption will be on goods and services produced overseas, which will form a stream of imports. Also, some of the output produced by domestic firms will be purchased by foreign consumers from overseas, which constitutes exports. Economies are not just open to trade in goods and services, but also to financial flows. Due to continuing deregulation and liberalization of financial markets, there are strong linkages between the financial sectors in different countries and an international market for saving and borrowing. Domestic residents can invest in financial institutions overseas, and foreigners can invest in domestic financial institutions.

Injections and leakages

The circular flow of income shows the economy as a system. We have already used the analogy that this is not unlike a central heating system pumping hot water around a house. As more hot water enters the system it gets warmer. In terms of the economy, this would correspond to larger income flows circulating. Therefore, an important question would ask what factors determine the size of income flows in an economy.

Injections are items which add to the circular flow of income. These are investment (I), government spending (G) and exports (X). Correspondingly, **leakages** from the circular flow are those items which lead to lower income flows; these are saving (S), taxes (T) and imports (M). For example, if households were to increase their level of saving – but this was not associated with a rise in investment – then we would expect income flows to fall as

Some players in the circular flow of income: households, workers, financial institutions...
Source: Getty Images

unused savings build up in financial institutions. The same outcome would result if the government increased taxes, but did not use the proceeds to fund higher government spending.

It is often queried why consumption is not also counted as an injection. The reason why this is so is because consumption is the counterpart to savings. So, an increase in consumption would imply a fall in savings, which is a leakage. As the effects of an increase in injections should be the same as a fall in leakages, it would be double counting to also include consumption in the set of injections.

When injections exceed leakages the circular flow of income will increase, and likewise will fall when leakages exceed injections. The economy will be in equilibrium when leakages are equal to injections.

$$I + G + X = S + T + M$$

Therefore, the level of national income in an economy will be determined by the factors that account for injections and leakages. Much of the study of macroeconomics is concerned with this issue. If the government wished to increase the level of national income, its response would be to use policies (monetary or fiscal) that either increase injections or reduce leakages. Likewise, if the economy was seen to be overheating, then the government might wish to introduce policies (monetary or fiscal) that reduce injections or increase leakages.

1.3 National income accounting and the circular flow of income

Gross Domestic Product (GDP) is a measure of the total output produced by an economy. There are three different ways of calculating the level of national output; these are the expenditure method, income method and output method.

National income accounting has a direct relationship to the circular flow of income. First of all, the level of GDP is an indicator of the strength of the circular flow of income. Second, due to the circular flow, the three methods of calculating GDP should all produce the same measure. This can be seen by using the UK national accounts as an example.

Expenditure method

This calculates national income by adding together all expenditures on domestic goods and services. These include consumption, investment, government spending and also net exports (exports minus imports). Exports represent expenditures on domestic goods from

Figure 1.2 UK GDP measured by components Source: UK Office for National Statistics (ONS)

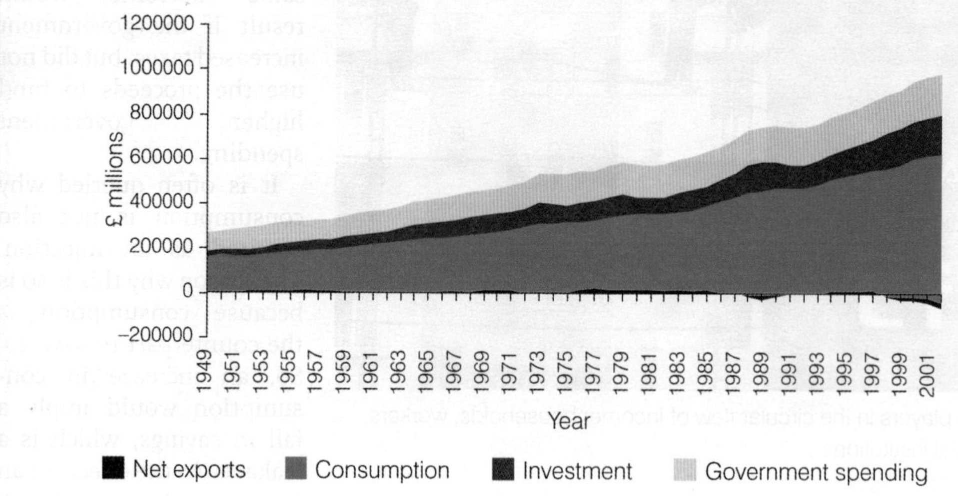

the foreign sector, whereas imports represent expenditures on foreign goods by domestic consumers. Net exports represent the overall effect on total domestic expenditure.

Therefore, GDP (Y) can be calculated using the rule:

$$Y = C + G + I + X - M$$

Figure 1.2 shows the history of both total expenditure and its components. Consumption has traditionally represented the largest part of GDP, averaging around 65 per cent of the total. Investment and government spending represent around 15 per cent and 20 per cent, respectively, of the total. Net exports make up a very small component, usually because exports and imports tend largely to net each other out.

Simply adding all expenditures together is argued to overestimate national income. This is because expenditures are usually undertaken at market prices, which have in turn been distorted by government taxes and subsidies. As taxes normally exceed subsidies, market prices will tend to be higher than the factor cost of producing them, and therefore GDP would be overstated. This can be corrected by accounting for the presence of these taxes and subsidies.

$$\text{GDP (factor cost)} = \text{GDP (market prices)} - \text{Taxes} + \text{Subsidies}$$

Figure 1.3 reflects the adjustment of GDP from market prices to factor cost for the UK economy.

Income method

A measure of GDP can be calculated by simply adding up the total income earned by all domestic households and firms.

$$Y = \text{Other Income} + \text{Corporate Profits} + \text{Wages and Salaries}$$

Other income principally includes rental and interest income. Figure 1.4 shows the total and the composition of UK national income on this definition. It can be seen that wages and salaries represent the largest proportion of total income.

Figure 1.3 UK GDP measured by factor cost and market prices Source: ONS

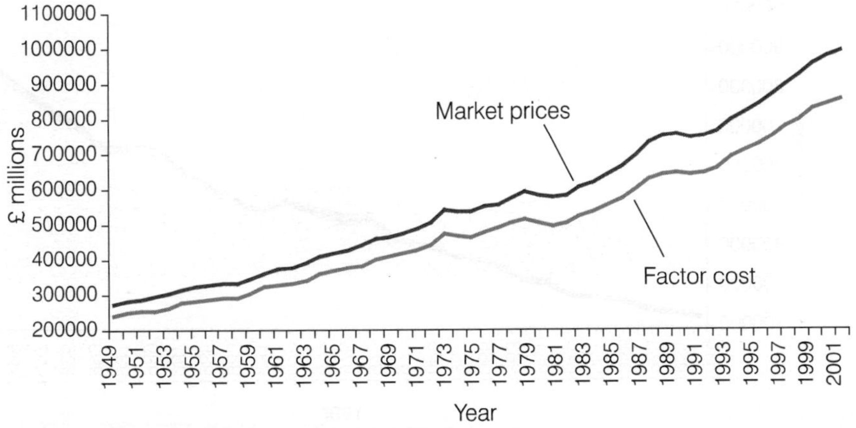

Figure 1.4 UK GDP by sources of income Source: ONS

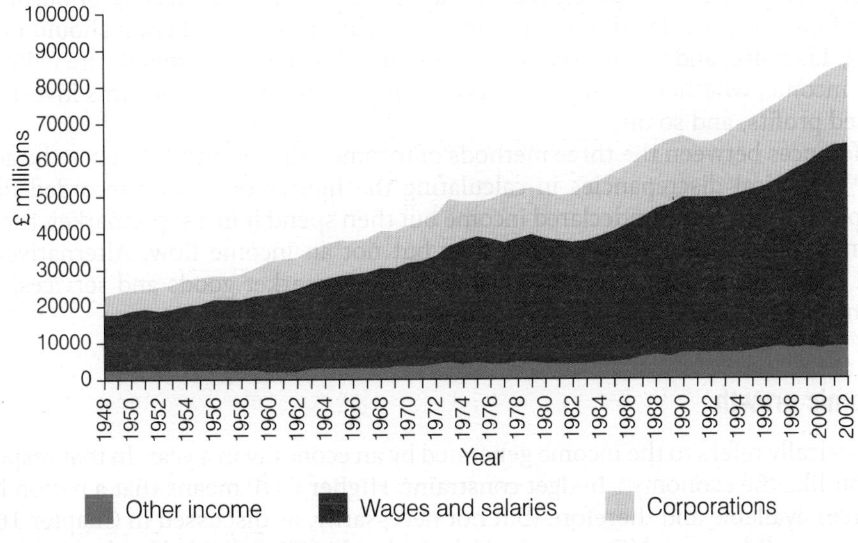

Output method

As the output of some firms forms part of the inputs into others, summing the output of every firm would imply double counting and lead to an overstatement of the figures. The output method avoids this by just totalling instead the value added by each firm at each stage of the production process.

The three alternative measures of GDP are plotted in Figure 1.5. It is clear that the three methods produce fairly consistent estimates of national income. This is unexpected as

Figure 1.5 Measuring UK GDP Source: ONS

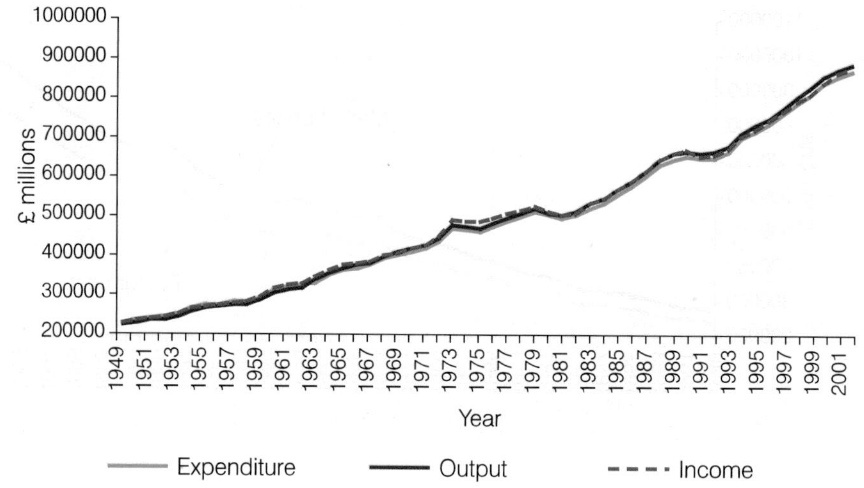

according to the circular flow of income the three estimates should in fact be identical to one another. As all flows of expenditure are related to the purchasing of output, and all flows of income are related to the producing of output, this prediction should not be surprising. Likewise, and just to complete the circular linkages, all expenditure will be funded out of income, whether it is households consuming out of wages or firms investing out of retained profits, and so on.

Differences between the three methods of income calculation are likely to be accounted for by statistical discrepancies in calculating the figures or by non-recorded flows. For example, if I earn some undeclared income but then spend it in a supermarket, the national accounts will record an expenditure flow but not an income flow. Alternatively, I may spend some legitimately declared income on black market goods and services, in which case income flows will exceed expenditure flows.

Economic growth

GDP basically refers to the income generated by an economy in a year. In that respect, it is a little bit like the economy's budget constraint. Higher GDP means that a nation has more resources available and therefore (but not necessarily, as discussed in Chapter 16) higher welfare or well-being. **GDP per capita** is the level of GDP divided by the country's population, and is a widely used indicator of the material standard of living in a country.

Economic growth is the change in GDP and is the main concern for governments and policy makers. High and sustained economic growth means that a nation's economy is generating more and more income, which allows the continual improvement of living standards. Figure 1.6 plots the recent history of economic growth in the UK economy.

There are two aspects of this graph that make for interesting comment. First, the trend rate shows that GDP grows consistently over time, implying that people become increasingly richer and enjoy improving living standards. The second aspect is an important one in that the GDP does not grow steadily. In fact, the actual level of GDP fluctuates quite considerably around the trend path, which is a sign that the rate of economic growth is not constant in the short run.

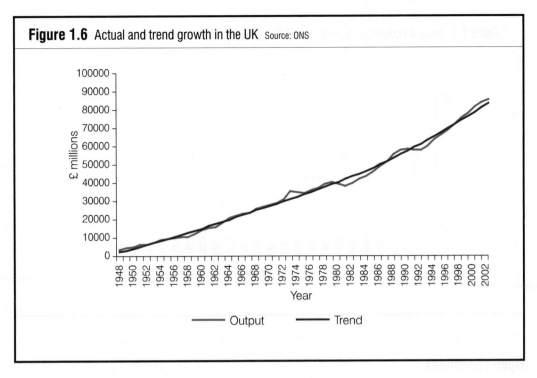

Figure 1.6 Actual and trend growth in the UK Source: ONS

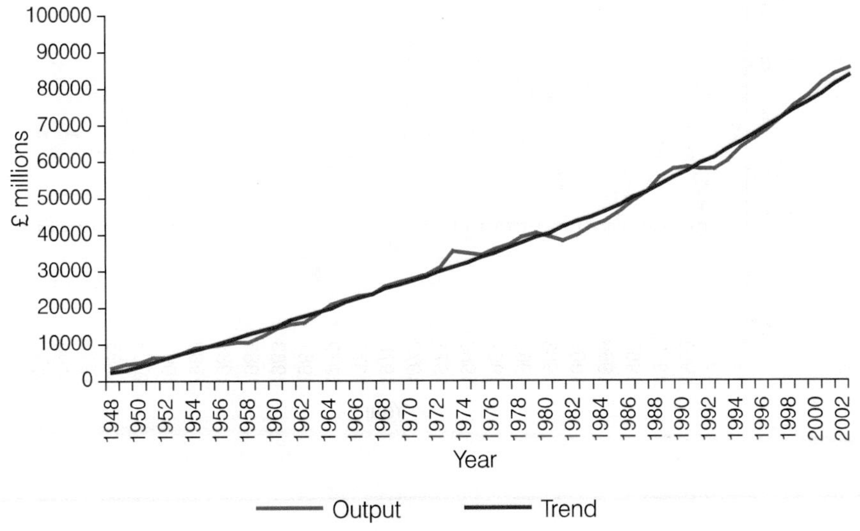

This is confirmed in Figure 1.7, where the annual rate of economic growth in the UK economy is seen to vary considerably. The cyclical nature of growth in the short run is marked by alternating booms and recessions. This is also of concern to policy makers for a number of reasons. Although recessions might be relatively short-lived, they can have very painful welfare effects, particularly in generating unemployment. However, if the economy grows too fast then the effect might be to bid up prices and generate inflation. The cyclical nature of growth, as will be discussed later in this book, is argued to have a detrimental effect on the rate of long-term or trend growth in the economy. The processes that drive this might be interrupted by the stop-start nature of growth in the short run. For example, periods of volatile growth might act as an impediment to long-term investments in new technologies because firms are uncertain over the state of demand for their products.

Economic growth in the short and long run is the key target for macroeconomic policy making. The aim is to maximize long-run growth to maintain continual improvements in living standards, and stabilize growth in the short run to avoid the painful consequences of business cycles – notably episodes of high unemployment.

As a central player in the circular flow of income, the government can use policy to lever the economy in a desirable direction. In terms of stabilizing the business cycle, this could be achieved by influencing the level of injections and leakages in the circular flow. This, though, is easier said than done! Countless policy makers have declared victory over the cycle of boom and bust only to be embarrassed subsequently.

Promoting long-run growth has been a global challenge throughout history. Looking at the circular flow it is less obvious as to where the government can be influential, mainly because the drivers of economic growth are perceived to be a little more specific than just controlling leakages and injections. The main drivers of growth in the long run are usually an increase in the available factors of production or improvements in productivity, meaning that more output can be produced from the same inputs. In the circular flow, the firm sector is particularly important here. Growth arises because they receive better quality factors of production (such as more skilled labour) or because firm investment is successful in fuelling productivity (perhaps by developing more advanced technologies). Later in this book various models of long run economic growth will be discussed in more detail.

Figure 1.7 Annual economic growth in the UK Source: ONS

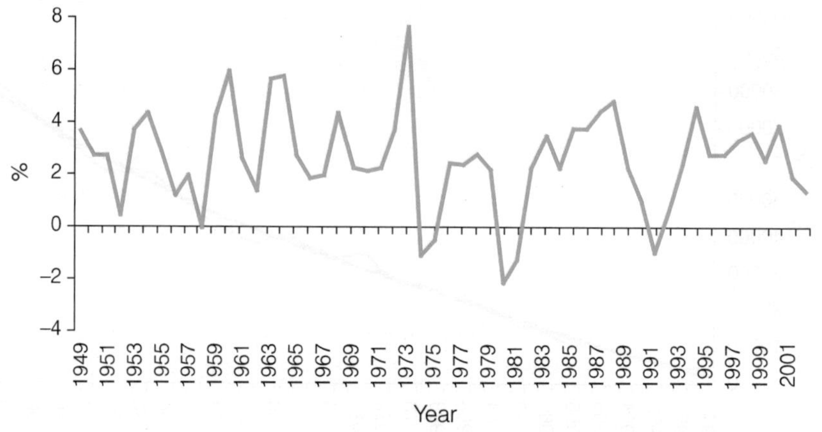

Open economies

Openness refers to the influences that overseas factors exert on the domestic economy. A completely closed economy is one that is entirely self-sufficient and has no economic links with any others. Modern day economies are open to the international economy in two ways, both of which are clearly shown as part of the circular flow of income in Figure 1.1.

The first is through the trade of goods and services. Exports are injections and imports are leakages from the circular flow. Figure 1.8 shows the sum of exports and imports as a proportion of GDP. It is clear that this proportion has risen continuously since the beginning of the 1970s. In recent decades, the growth in world trade has exceeded the growth in output, showing the increasing importance of the foreign sector on the domestic economy. Growth in world trade has averaged over 9 per cent, while global economic growth has grown at 3.8 per cent since the Second World War.

The trade of physical goods and services is in reality just one element of the increasing openness of economies. The second element is shown as capital flows to and from the financial sector, which reflects the globalization of financial markets. Domestic investors increasingly have the opportunity to borrow and invest abroad, as does the foreign sector to borrow from and invest in the domestic economy.

Open for trade: Yantian container terminal, South China.
Source: Panorama Stock Photos Co Ltd/Alamy

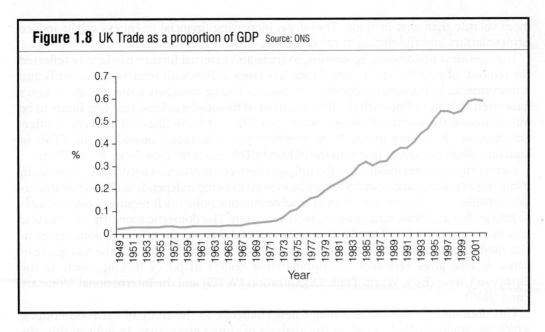

Figure 1.8 UK Trade as a proportion of GDP Source: ONS

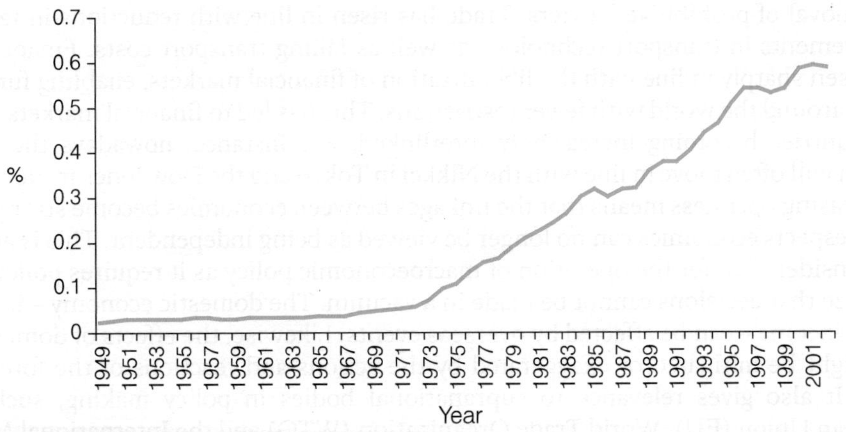

Figure 1.9 External assets and liabilities as a proportion of GDP Source: ONS

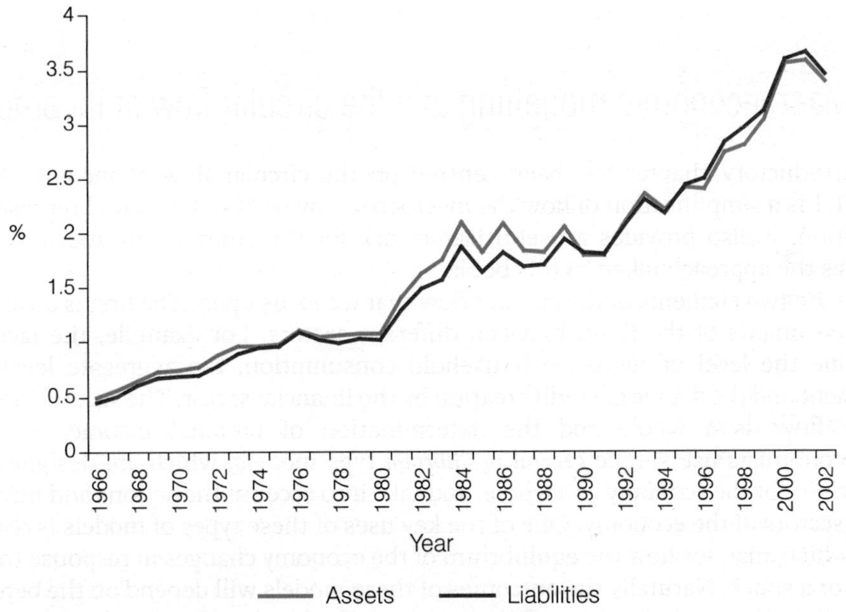

These investments typically take one of two forms. The first is direct investment which relates to the purchase of overseas physical capital, such as machinery and factories. The second is portfolio capital, which represents purchases of financial assets, such as bonds and equities. Figure 1.9 plots the UK's external assets and liabilities as a proportion of GDP. The stock of assets represents the value of overseas investment made by domestic residents, whereas liabilities represent the value of domestic investment held by foreign residents. It is clear that both these measures have risen substantially, particularly since the beginning of the 1980s. What is also clear is that the growth in financial flows has been more volatile than that in trade. Therefore, increasing financial openness might induce extra volatility into the circular flow of income.

The openness of domestic economies to trade and external finance has largely reflected the removal of prohibitive barriers. Trade has risen in line with reductions in tariffs and improvements in transport technology as well as falling transport costs. Financial flows have risen sharply in line with the liberalization of financial markets, enabling funds to be moved around the world with fewer restrictions. This has led to financial markets in different countries becoming increasingly interlinked. For instance, nowadays the FTSE in London will often move in line with the Nikkei in Tokyo and the Dow Jones in New York.

Increasing openness means that the linkages between economies become stronger, so in many respects economies can no longer be viewed as being independent. This is an important consideration for the operation of macroeconomic policy as it requires policy makers to realize that decisions cannot be made in a vacuum. The domestic economy – its circular flow of income – can be affected by overseas events. Likewise, the effects of domestic policies might be mitigated or exaggerated by the actions and reactions of the foreign residents. It also gives relevance to supranational bodies in policy making, such as the European Union (EU), World Trade Organization (WTO) and the International Monetary Fund (IMF).

This undoubtedly represents a major new challenge to the study of macroeconomics, which has traditionally focused on the analysis of closed economies. In light of this, the approach taken in this book is to place a strong emphasis on the modelling of open economies.

1.4 Macroeconomic modelling and the circular flow of income

This introductory chapter has been centred on the circular flow of income. Although Figure 1.1 is a simplification of how the macroeconomy works, it is a good representation. In addition, it also provides a useful framework for the study of macroeconomics and underlies the approach taken in this book.

There are two elements of the circular flow that we focus upon. The first is an analysis of the determinants of the flows between different sectors. For example, the factors that determine the level of aggregate household consumption, the aggregate level of firm investment and the degree of credit creation by the financial sector. The second looks at the circular flow as a whole and the determination of national income. To do this macroeconomists use simple *general equilibrium* type models, which are designed to find equilibrium for the economy as a whole, and take into account the actions and interactions among sectors of the economy. One of the key uses of these types of models is *comparative statics*, which analyses how the equilibrium of the economy changes in response to a policy change or a shock. Naturally the outcomes of these models will depend on the behavioural assumptions that underlie them. This leads to a further justification for understanding things like the determination of consumption, investment, and so on.

The models we use here are fairly simple, but larger and more complicated models based on the same principle of the circular flow of income are actively used in policy circles around the world. The large-scale macroeconomic models are usually constructed by defining all the behavioural relationships, such as a consumption function, investment function, frameworks for monetary and fiscal policies, and so on, and then finding a general equilibrium for the economy based on these relationships. The effects of policy changes and shocks can then be deduced by analysing their consequences for the equilibrium of the economy.

An example of these types of models is the Bank of England Quarterly Model (BEQM) and a full model listing can be found on the Bank of England website. There are over 4000 equations in this model! This model is widely used to forecast movements in the economy and plays a particularly important role in the setting of monetary policy. Similar models are used by the European Central Bank and the US Federal Reserve Bank, as well as by other central banks around the world. Macroeconomic models are also used by HM Treasury and by finance ministries in many countries. Advances in computer power have made solving and manipulating these large models feasible, and forecasts and simulations can be produced quickly.

The grandfather of macroeconomic modelling, has to be the Phillips machine, designed by William (Bill) Phillips in 1949. This was described as a hydraulic computer and worked by pumping water through pipes which collected in reservoirs, each measuring key macroeconomic variables. This is a clear description of the circular flow of income, where economics are represented by hydraulics and the workings of the economy are represented by the flow of water. Changes in behaviour (such as the saving ratio), policies and shocks could all be modelled by controlling valves which affected the flow of water between reservoirs. The Phillips machine measured changes in national income to an impressive 4 per cent accuracy! By linking two Phillips machines together it was even possible to model an international economy by allowing water to flow between them representing trade flows.

During its time, the Phillips machine was the only macroeconomic simulation tool in existence. Demand came from governments who used the machine to try to aid policy design to achieve full employment. Several universities also demanded versions to use in policy analysis work, and even private corporations purchased machines to use as a forecasting tool. The fact that modern macroeconomic modelling is built on the same principles is a testament to Phillips' original work. However, it also placed the circular flow of income at the centre of macroeconomic thinking which remains just as relevant today.

Summary

- This first chapter has introduced the subject of macroeconomics, which differs from microeconomics as it analyses the economy as a whole.
- The workings of the macroeconomy can be summarized neatly by the circular flow of income, which describes how the various players in an economy such as households, firms, etc. are linked together. These linkages and interactions suggest that the economy should be considered as being more than the sum of its parts.
- The relevance of the circular flow is demonstrated in national income accounting where the expenditure, income and output methods should each produce the same measure of national income/output.
- Macroeconomic policy making has largely focused on promoting high and stable economic growth. High growth over the long run produces sustained improvements in material living standards.
- The relevance of the circular flow is demonstrated in national income accounting where the expenditure, income and output methods should each produce the same measure of national income/output.
- Macroeconomic policy making has largely focused on promoting high and stable economic growth. High growth over the long run produces sustained improvements in material living standards.

- In the short run, the goal of policy makers is to smooth out cyclical movements in the economy to avoid episodes of high unemployment or inflation. To this end, the government with its central position in the circular flow of income can use monetary and fiscal policies to influence the economy.
- Over the last four decades economies have become increasingly open to each other through international trade and capital flows. This has meant that the study of open economies is increasingly relevant.
- The formulation of policy is greatly aided by the use of macroeconomic models. These are heavily based on the circular flow of income and can be used to analyse the effects of policies or shocks on the economy.
- The first of these was the Phillips machine, a hydraulic computer which represented the circular flow with water. Over time, macro modelling has evolved and advances in computer power have enabled more complicated models to be used with relative ease. However, despite a higher level of complexity, the underlying principle behind the models has remained unchanged.

Key terms

Circular flow of income
Economic growth
Gross Domestic Product (GDP)
GDP per capita
Injections
Leakages
National income accounting

Review questions

1. Explain the difference between microeconomics and macroeconomics. How are the two related?
2 Why are economists interested in macroeconomic models?

More advanced problems

'Gross Domestic Product (GDP) is a good measure of a country's standard of living.' Discuss.

For further resources, visit
http://www.thomsonlearning.co.uk/chamberlin_yueh

Part II

The real macroeconomy

The real side of the macroeconomy is introduced and discussed in this section. The components of aggregate demand; namely, consumption, investment and government spending, are covered. The one element of the real macroeconomy that is not included is exports and imports, which is covered as part of the open economy section.

2 Consumption

Learning objectives

- Define consumption, consumer expenditure and saving
- Understand the link between consumption and income as described by the Keynesian consumption function
- Use the optimal consumption model to describe how consumption decisions are related to rational utility maximizing behaviour
- Show how the permanent income hypothesis and life cycle hypothesis base consumption decisions on future as well as current income
- Explain how changes in expectations, interest rates, wealth, credit constraints and uncertainty can account for recent changes in consumption and saving

2

2.1 Introduction

Consumer expenditure by households on goods and services represents the largest part of **aggregate demand**. Since 1980, this has on average accounted for 63 per cent of total aggregate demand in the UK, and similar figures would be expected for other developed countries. The size of total consumer expenditure is the result of choices made by private households. The counterpart to the **consumption** decision is saving, which is typically any income a household chooses not to spend. Savings, though, can of course be used to fund future consumption.

The household decision to spend or save plays a critical part in the circular flow of income and therefore on the performance of the economy. Because of this, theories that can account for and predict consumer expenditure are very important and of great interest to economists and policy makers. The aim of this chapter is to set out the main theories of consumer behaviour and, with the use of empirical evidence, show how they are relevant.

Consumption and consumer expenditure

Before we proceed, it is vitally important that the distinction between consumption and consumer expenditure is made clear. Consumer expenditure is the act of purchasing a good or service. Consumption, on the other hand, is the act of deriving a flow of benefits from the usage of those goods or services. Considering these definitions, the two concepts would be identical only if goods and services were consumed at the same time they are purchased. However, if a good can be stored and used repeatedly over a period of time, then the good continues to be consumed after the act of purchasing it. In this case, consumption and consumer expenditure do not occur at the same time.

Consumer expenditure can be further broken down into spending on services and on durable and non-durable goods. A durable good is one that can be used many times, such as a washing machine, a television, a car, and so on. By contrast, a non-durable good is one that is used up in its consumption; for example, food, energy and public transport. Services

Figure 2.1 Components of UK consumer expenditure Source: ONS and authors' calculations

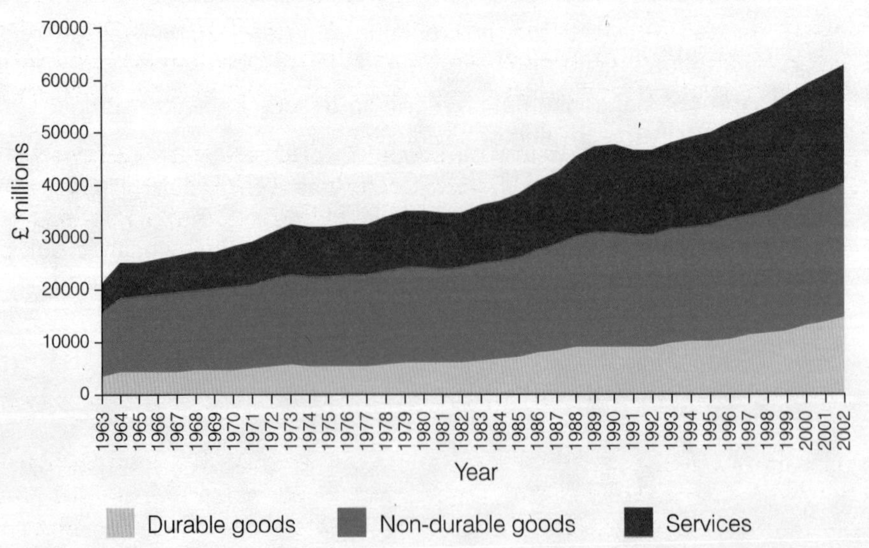

obviously share the same characteristics as non-durable goods. In Figure 2.1 household consumption in the UK is broken down into these three categories.

Consumer expenditure on non-durable goods and services can be treated as consumption. However, spending on durable goods is harder to classify. If a household buys a washing machine for £200 which is expected to last for ten years, then the annual consumer expenditure on washing machines is £200 but the annual consumption is only £20. The remaining £180 must be considered as **saving**; this is the value of washing services that will be consumed in the future.

Despite the presence of durable goods, many economists do not worry about using consumer expenditure and consumption interchangeably. There are two main reasons for this. First, durable goods represent a relatively small proportion of total household expenditure. This can be seen from Figure 2.1, where in 2002 the relative proportion is only 23 per cent. This means that the vast majority of consumer expenditure can also be thought of as consumption.

Second, consumer expenditure, and not consumption, plays the central role in the circular flow of income. When a firm sells a washing machine for £200, this is the figure that enters its balance sheets and determines its annual profits. These profits then form the basis of how much investment the firm needs to undertake, how much labour it should hire, what tax it owes to the government, and so on. When economists and policy makers consider the importance of consumption in the operation of the economy, they are actually just concerned with the role consumer expenditure plays in the circular flow of income.

In the next section, we will discuss some of the theories that economists have developed to explain consumption behaviour by households.

2.2 Theories of consumption behaviour

Many alternative theories have been offered to explain consumer behaviour. The two most prominent are the **Keynesian consumption function** and the **permanent income hypothesis (PIH)**. Another influential theory which shares very similar foundations to the permanent income hypothesis is the **life cycle hypothesis** (LCH). The main difference between these two competing theories is the view that households take of their income. In the Keynesian consumption function, households base consumption decisions solely on current income. The permanent income/life cycle hypothesis argues that households take a much longer-term view of income. Consumption choices will therefore be forward-looking, depending not just on current income, but also on expectations about future income.

Both models make plausible arguments about what factors determine household expenditure. However, the models make different predictions about the pattern of consumption. Policy makers wishing to control consumption would then take different actions depending on their view on which theory best represents the real picture.

2.3 The Keynesian consumption function

This is also known as the **absolute income hypothesis** (AIP). John Maynard Keynes, in his book *The General Theory* (1936), argued that the main determinant of a household's consumption is its current income. This best represents a household's resources or budget constraint. In response to the criticism that expectations about future income may also be important, a simple answer was offered. In forming expectations about the future,

2

households are likely to base their predictions on their current income. Whenever people are asked to make forecasts they often do so against a point of reference – with this reference point being current income. In addition, basing consumption on current income seems consistent with other theories in other social sciences which are based on psychology or rules of thumb. Therefore, it would be extremely difficult to justify a model of consumption that is not largely based on current income.

Following this reasoning, and aggregating over all households, this would mean that aggregate consumption (C) is just a simple function of aggregate income.

$$C = a + cY \tag{2.1}$$

where

a = autonomous consumption
c = marginal propensity to consume
Y = aggregate income.

The Keynesian consumption function is shown graphically in Figure 2.2.

Autonomous consumption, a, is consumption which is undertaken independently of income. Regardless of income, a household would need to make certain subsistence expenditures simply to survive. Also, consuming out of wealth would count as autonomous consumption. If a household owned a stock of financial assets, these could be used to support consumption regardless of the amount of current income (i.e., autonomous consumption is equal to a proportion of wealth (W), $a = \gamma W$). The level of autonomous consumption determines where the consumption function intersects the vertical axis.

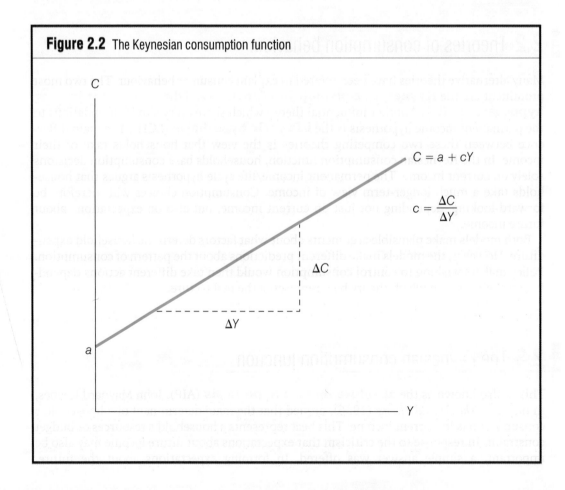

Figure 2.2 The Keynesian consumption function

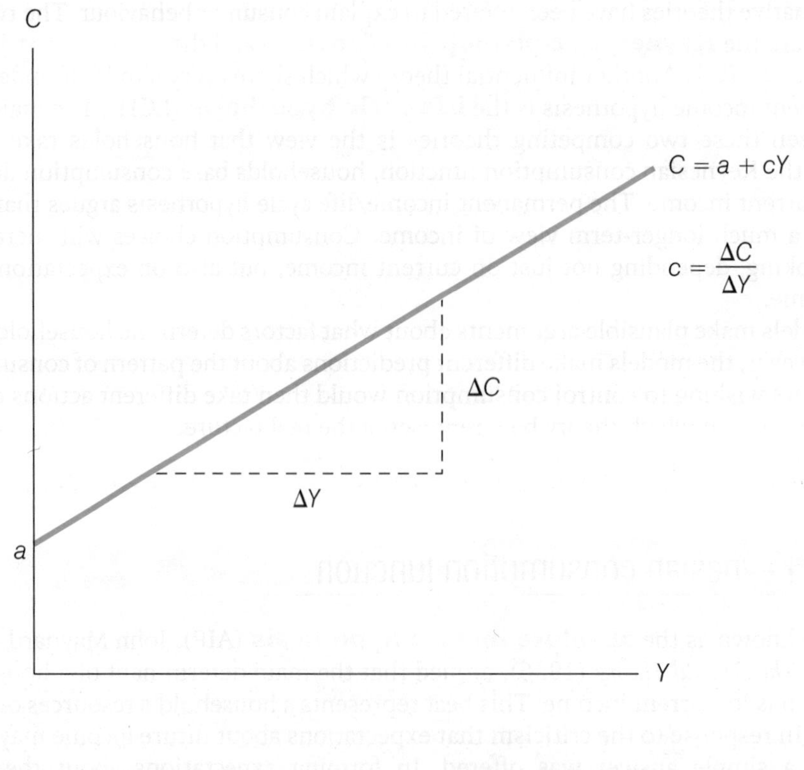

Anything that leads to a change in this would lead to a shift in the consumption function. For example, if wealth increased, the entire function would shift upwards meaning more consumption at every level of income.

The **marginal propensity to consume** (*mpc*) gives the relationship between changes in consumption (ΔC) and changes in income (ΔY). Simply put, it is the change in consumption that would result from a £1 change in income.

The marginal propensity to consume will determine the slope of the consumption function:

$$c = \frac{\Delta C}{\Delta Y}$$

If the *mpc* were to rise, then the entire consumption function would pivot upwards, reflecting the change in the slope.

Therefore, the change in consumption following a change in income is simply:

$$\Delta C = c\Delta Y$$

Conventionally, the *mpc* lies between 0 and 1 (although not necessarily), meaning that consumption moves less than one-to-one with changes in income. This is because saving acts as a counterpart to consumption. When income increases, households will typically save a proportion of their extra income. Likewise, when income falls, households would be expected to reduce saving as well as consumption.

In a similar vein, the relationship between changes in saving and income are given by the **marginal propensity to save** (*mps*). This simply tells us how much saving will change when income varies by £1:

$$\Delta S = s\Delta Y$$

Therefore, the marginal propensity to save is defined as $s = \frac{\Delta S}{\Delta Y}$.

Given that all income is either consumed or saved, it must be the case that any change in income is equal to the sum of the changes in consumption and saving:

$$\Delta Y = \Delta C + \Delta S$$

Dividing both sides by the change of income results in a very simple rule:

$$\frac{\Delta Y}{\Delta Y} = \frac{\Delta C}{\Delta Y} + \frac{\Delta S}{\Delta Y}$$

So, we can conclude that: $1 = c + s$.

The marginal propensity to consume and the marginal propensity to save should add up to 1. This does not preclude the marginal propensity to consume from exceeding 1, but in this case it would imply that the marginal propensity to save is negative. This is possible if there is borrowing or dis-saving, as this could fund extra consumption in excess of the change in income.

Income and disposable income

Household income can come from various sources (look back at the circular flow of income outlined in Chapter 1). The main source is labour income, but income from financial assets (e.g., interest from savings, dividends from equities, rent from property) should also be included. When the economy performs well, household income is expected to rise simply because unemployment falls and more people are working. However, it must also be

Global application 2.1

The marginal propensity to consume and aggregate consumption

The marginal propensity to consume (*mpc*) describes how consumption changes when income changes by one unit. If the *mpc* is constant, then the consumption function will be linear. An extra unit of income will have the same effect on consumption regardless of the initial level of income.

This is clearly seen in Figure 1. Here it is the case that the same changes in income, $\Delta Y = Y_2 - Y_1 = Y_4 - Y_3$, produce the same changes in consumption, $\Delta C = C_2 - C_1 = C_4 - C_3$, regardless of the initial level of income. The $mpc = \Delta C/\Delta Y$, is then unchanged along the entire length of the consumption function.

If we take Figure 1 to represent the common household consumption function, then one of the important consequences of the constant *mpc* is that aggregate consumption will be invariant to the distribution of income in the economy. If there are two households, one with income of Y_1 and the other with higher income of Y_4, then transferring income from the rich to the poor household will have no effect on aggregate consumption. For example, if the rich household sees its income reduced to Y_3 and this is transferred to the poor household which sees its income rise to Y_2, then aggregate consumption is left unchanged because $C_1 + C_4 = C_2 + C_3$. The linear household consumption function ensures that aggregate consumption is simply the same linear function of aggregate income.

The situation changes when the marginal propensity to consume is no longer independent of the level of income. There is a strong rationale for suggesting that the *mpc* actually falls as income rises. Richer households would be expected to

Figure 1 Linear consumption function

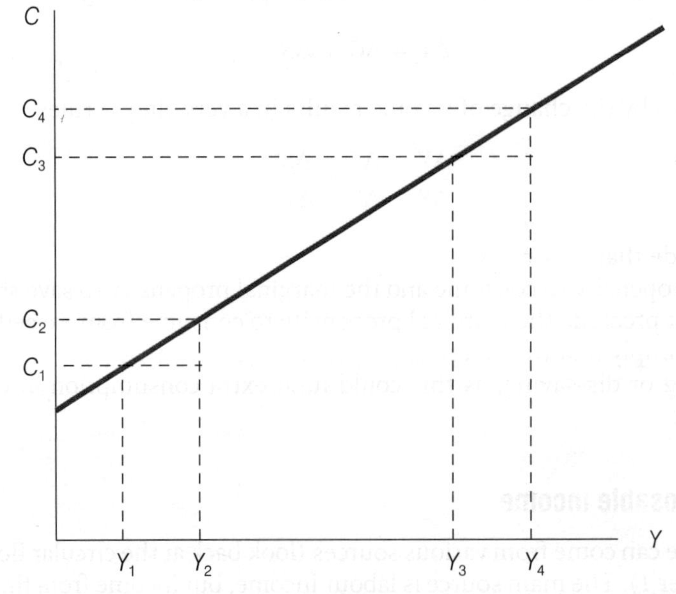

Global application 2.1 (continued)

have already purchased the goods and services they desire, so any extra income is likely to be saved. This fits in with the law of diminishing marginal utility of consumption, which states that the extra utility or welfare gained from an additional unit of consumption falls as consumption increases. Later in the chapter, it will be shown that this is an important concept with major implications for the determination of consumption. For now though, assume that it justifies a falling *mpc* as income rises, in which case the consumption function is no longer linear.

In Figure 2, it is once again the case that $\Delta Y = Y_2 - Y_1 = Y_4 - Y_3$, but now $C_2 - C_1 > C_4 - C_3$, implying that $mpc = \Delta C/\Delta Y$ falls as income rises. As a result, the consumption function is concave, so the same change in income produces smaller changes in consumption at higher levels of income.

If Figure 2 is the representative household consumption function, then the level of aggregate consumption is no longer independent of the distribution of income. Transferring income from the rich to poor household will increase aggregate consumption, while transferring income from poor to rich would reduce it. Breaking the assumption of a linear household consumption function means that we can no longer draw a simple aggregate consumption function as a function of aggregate income. The same level of aggregate income can clearly have different levels of aggregate consumption depending on how it is distributed.

This gives the government scope to alter the level of consumption through the tax and benefits system. An increase in taxes on the rich to fund benefits payments will increase overall consumption because the poor have a higher *mpc*. However, the result would be that the level of saving in the economy would fall. If the government wished to increase the saving ratio (perhaps so that there are more funds for the financial system to lend to business for investment), then it would seek to redistribute income towards richer households because the rich save a higher proportion of any extra income.

Figure 2 Non-linear consumption function

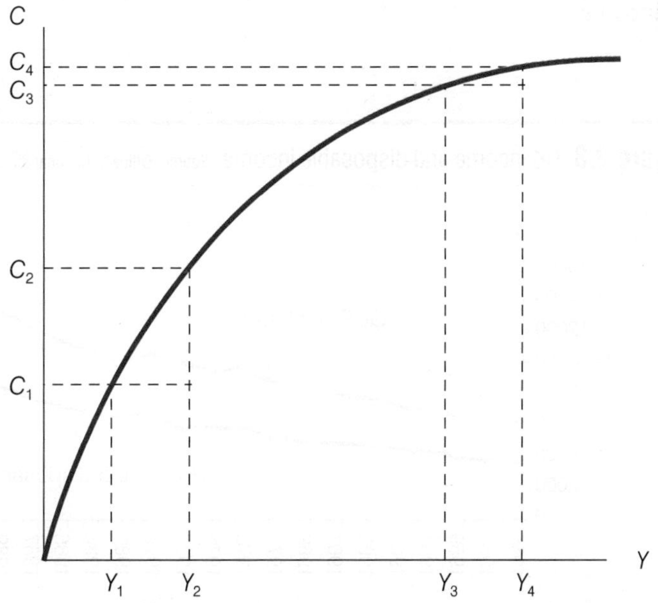

accepted that a well-performing economy is likely to have increased income from other sources. For example, firms making larger profits may be able to distribute higher dividends to their shareholders. Rising house prices may increase the rental yields of property, and so on.

2

For consumption decisions, though, households would be more concerned not so much about income, but *disposable income*. Disposable income is the income that a household can actually use to either save or spend. Therefore, the Keynesian consumption function in (2.1) should be rewritten as:

$$C = a + cY^d \tag{2.2}$$

where Y^d is disposable income.

It is the role of government that accounts for disposable income differing from actual household income. This is achieved in two ways. First, household income is transferred to the government in taxes. Second, household income can be supplemented by receiving welfare and other benefits from the government, such as pensions. These benefits are collectively known as transfer payments.

The link between disposable and actual income can be written as follows:

Disposable Income = Actual Income – Taxes + Transfer Payments

This can be simplified further. As the government is taking with one hand (taxation) and giving with the other (transfer payments), the flows to and from the household sector can just be netted out:

Net Taxes = Taxes – Transfer Payments

Leaving us with:

Disposable Income = Actual Income – Net Taxes

Net taxes are usually positive meaning that taxation exceeds transfer payments. As a result, household disposable income should be lower than actual income. Figure 2.3 plots the history of GDP per head and household disposable income per head for the UK. Over the past two decades, disposable income typically represents between 60–70 per cent of total income.

Figure 2.3 UK income and disposable income Source: Office of National Statistics (ONS)

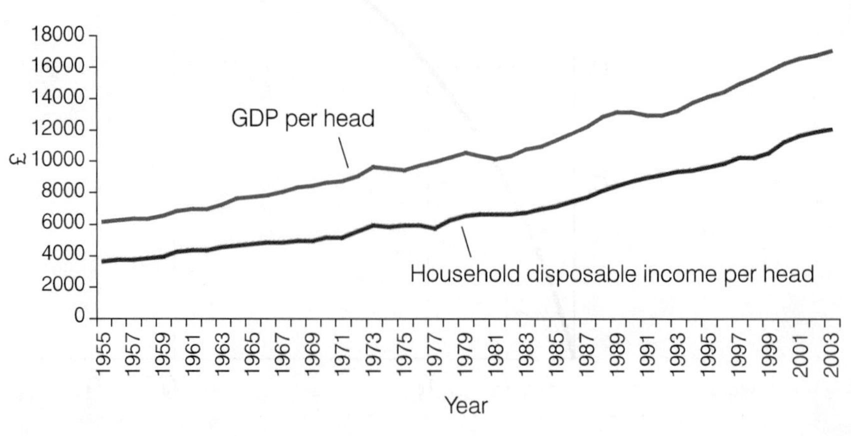

A simple way of representing the difference between actual and disposable income is through the use of *lump sum taxes*. These are often referred to as poll taxes, and consist of a fixed payment that is levied independently of income. A lump sum tax means that everybody pays the same amount regardless of their income. From this perspective, the tax is a charge for being a citizen of a particular country or region.

Disposable income can now be written simply in terms of actual income as:

$$Y^d = Y - T$$

where T is the lump sum tax. Using this definition of disposable income, the consumption function can be rewritten in the following way:

$$C = a + c(Y - T) \tag{2.3}$$

This new consumption function is plotted in Figure 2.4. It should be fairly clear that changes in taxes will lead to changes in consumption through their effects on disposable income. Higher taxes will lead to a downward shift in the consumption function, meaning that at every level of actual income the level of consumption will be correspondingly lower.

In asserting a positive linear relationship between disposable income and consumption, the Keynesian consumption function is both relatively simple and intuitively pleasing. Figure 2.5 is a scatter plot of household consumption and disposable income (both in terms of per person) for the UK. The positive correlation predicted by the Keynesian consumption function seems to very much hold true. This offers some evidence that over time changes in consumption are driven by changes in disposable income.

However, despite its basic logic and apparent ability to fit the data, objections to this model have been raised. These pointed to the Keynesian model being an incomplete theory of consumer behaviour. This is because first it is not clear that consumer behaviour is

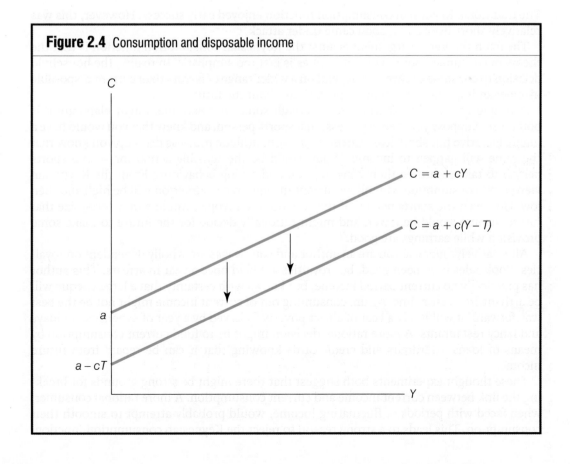

Figure 2.4 Consumption and disposable income

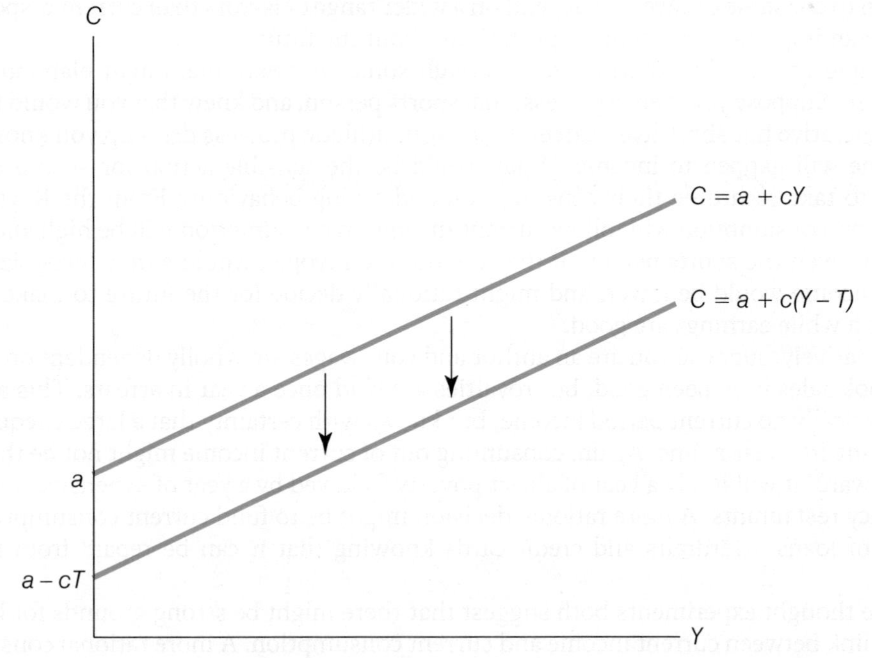

2

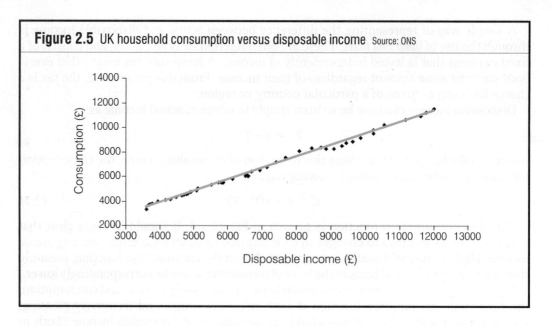

Figure 2.5 UK household consumption versus disposable income Source: ONS

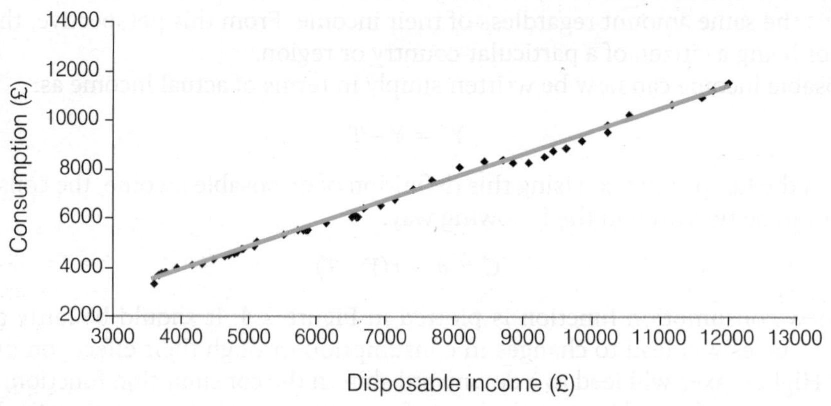

consistent with rational behaviour, and second there is a need for models that allow a much richer set of factors to be determinants other than current disposable income.

Objections to the Keynesian consumption function

The traditional Keynesian consumption function enjoyed early success. However, this was relatively short-lived and it soon came under attack.

The main theoretical argument against the Keynesian consumption function is that the theory of consumer choice which it implies is just too simplistic. In reality, the household decision to consume or save will depend on a wider range of factors than current disposable income; an important one being expectations about the future.

A couple of thought experiments, although somewhat extreme, might elaborate this point well. Suppose you were a professional sports person, and knew that you would have a highly lucrative but short-lived career. Once your athletic prowess dries up you know that the same will happen to income. What would be the sensible action for such a sports person to take regarding their consumption and saving behaviour? From the Keynesian viewpoint, consumption will follow current income so consumption will be high and then low. However, the sports person, if they are not too myopic, would surely recognize that future income would be lower, and might rationally decide for the future to make some provision while earnings are good.

Alternatively, suppose you are an author and your wages are wholly dependent on royalties. Book sales have been good, but royalties are paid once a year in arrears. This author has practically no current period income, but knows with certainty that a large cheque will be arriving in a year's time. Again, consuming out of current income might not be the best way forward; it will imply a year of abject poverty followed by a year of expensive holidays and fancy restaurants. A more rational decision might be to fund current consumption by means of loans, overdrafts and credit cards knowing that it can be repaid from future income.

These thought experiments both suggest that there might be strong grounds for breaking the link between current income and current consumption. A more rational consumer, when faced with periods of fluctuating income, would probably attempt to smooth their consumption. This leads to a strong reason to reject the Keynesian consumption function.

As it is not consistent with maximizing lifetime utility or welfare, it would imply households make irrational decisions. The theories of the permanent income hypothesis and the life cycle hypothesis answer this criticism by reintroducing the theory of rational choice decision making into consumer behaviour.

2.4 The permanent income and life cycle hypotheses

The permanent income hypothesis (PIH) and life cycle hypothesis (LCH) were developed by Milton Friedman and Franco Modigliani, respectively. Both these theories share similar foundations, arguing that consumption decisions will be based on a longer-term view of income. This result is just the outcome of households trying to maximize their lifetime utility (welfare). Therefore, to gain an understanding of the consumption-smoothing nature of the LCH and the PIH, it is first necessary to outline the *optimal consumption model*.

The optimal consumption model describes how consumers should choose the path of consumption over time, subject to the resource constraints they face in order to maximize their lifetime utility. Not only can this model be used to account for the main predictions of the LCH and PIH, but can also be used to show how a range of different factors can influence consumption and saving.

Optimal consumption

Applying utility-maximizing behaviour to consumption choices over time can be demonstrated in a simple two-period model. These two periods represent the total lifetime of a household, where period 1 can be thought of as the current period, and period 2 as the future. The objective of the household is to choose a consumption plan for each period (C_1,C_2) that maximizes its total lifetime utility. This decision will consist of two parts, and we shall look at each in turn. First, the **intertemporal budget constraint** defines all the feasible consumption patterns that a household can choose. Second, household preferences will decide which one of these feasible plans is optimal.

Intertemporal budget constraint

A household budget constraint can no longer be viewed in terms of just current income (intertemporal means across different time periods). Instead, if households can save and borrow, income can be transferred across time periods. Therefore, future income should form part of the resources that households can use for current consumption, and current income can form part of the resources a household can use for future consumption.

The three characteristics of the intertemporal budget constraint are:

1. Income in each period is given by Y_1 and by Y_2, respectively.
2. The household can transfer income across periods by borrowing and lending freely at an interest rate of r.
3. Finally, the household must reach the end of period 2 without leaving debts, otherwise households would consume an infinite amount.

Given this information, it is possible to write down the two-period budget constraint that this household faces. In period 1, the household receives income of Y_1, if it chooses to consume a level of C_1; the difference is savings, S.

$$S = Y_1 - C_1$$

Savings, of course, can be either positive or negative. Negative saving is just borrowing, enabling the household to consume more than their current income. However, given that the household must reach the end of period 2 without leaving debts, second period consumption (C_2) will be constrained. The maximum second period consumption must not exceed the total amount of second period resources.

$$C_2 \leq (1 + r)\, S + Y_2 \tag{2.4}$$

Second period resources consist of period 2 income and the returns from the saving decision taken in period 1. If savings is positive ($C_1 < Y_1$), then these savings, plus the interest that is gained at the rate r, will be also be available. However, if savings is negative ($C_1 > Y_1$), then this borrowing and the interest fees (also charged at a rate of r) would have to be repaid in period 2, reducing the resources available for consumption.

Substituting in for saving, we can write the period 2 constraint in (2.4) as:

$$C_2 \leq (1 + r)(Y_1 - C_1) + Y_2 \tag{2.5}$$

This highlights the trade-off that households face. Given their income stream (Y_1, Y_2), a household can increase current consumption if it is prepared to consume less in the future. Likewise, accepting lower current consumption enables more to be consumed in the future.

Finally, an interesting way of writing the intertemporal budget constraint can be found by rearranging (2.5) one final time by dividing both sides by $(1 + r)$ and collecting the consumption and income terms together on different sides of the equation:

$$C_1 + \frac{C_2}{(1+r)} \leq Y_1 + \frac{Y_2}{(1+r)} \tag{2.6}$$

This simply states that the present discounted value of consumption cannot exceed the present discounted value of income. The concept of present discounted value is very important and will be used extensively throughout the book. From (2.6) you can see that future values are divided by the interest rate. This is because the same unit of income is worth different amounts in different time periods as income cannot be transferred costlessly over time.

For example, income derived in period 1 can be transferred to later periods by saving in interest bearing assets such as bank accounts. As a result of interest being accrued, the initial investment is worth more in later periods, so current income is worth more in the future. This works the other way around too. If income in the future is to be brought into the present it can be borrowed, but in order to do so interest must be paid. This acts to reduce the current value of future income. In defining the current budget constraint that the household faces, future income must therefore be expressed in terms of its current value, or its present discounted value. This concept is explained in more detail in Global application 2.2.

The intertemporal budget constraint (2.6), defined by Y_1, Y_2 and r, is shown in Figure 2.6.

The area defined by the budget constraint is known as the budget set, and represents all the possible points at which the household can consume over the two periods. The slope of the budget line is given by $-(1 + r)$. The interest rate reflects the cost of transferring consumption over time, whether it is the rate of return on savings or the cost of borrowing. When the household is free to borrow and save there is no reason for consumption to be tied to current income.

The points where the budget constraint meets the axes represent the maximum possible consumption in each period.

In period 1, the maximum the household can spend is $Y_1 + Y_2/(1 + r)$. This is the present discounted value of all its lifetime income – the household spends all of its period 1 income, and borrows all of its period 2 income to spend now.

Global application 2.2

Present discounted values

If you were offered the choice between £1000 today or £1000 in one year's time, which would you choose? Most people would choose the former. The reason is not because people are impatient, but because interest rates are usually positive – £1000 in a year's time is worth less than £1000 today.

The interest rate can be thought of as the cost of transferring money over time. Suppose the interest rate was 5 per cent, then investing £1000 in the bank would mean that next period we would have £1050. This represents the value of £1000 today in one year's time and because of the positive interest rate it is clearly more than £1000.

To turn this calculation around, what would be the current value of £1000 received in a year's time? This is the same as asking, how much would we have to invest today at a rate of 5 per cent to obtain £1000 one year in the future? This amount is known as the **present discounted value**. If £PDV is the present discounted value (PDV) of £1000 one year in the future, then

$$\pounds PDV \times 1.05 = \pounds 1000$$

$$\pounds PDV = \frac{1000}{1.05} = \pounds 952.38$$

At an interest rate of 5 per cent, £1000 in a year's time is worth only £952.38 today. This represents the amount a household could borrow from a bank if it wished to consume against this future income. That is, a bank loan of £952.38 paid back a year later with interest of 5 per cent means that the total repaid is £952.38 × 1.05 = £1000.

The PDV is a way of giving a current value to a stream of future cash flows (income, profits, rents, etc.). This is done by discounting future income by the rate of interest. The higher the interest rate, the lower the present discounted value of future income. For example, if the interest rate was 10 per cent then the PDV of £1000 in the future is:

$$\pounds PDV = \frac{1000}{1.1} = \pounds 909.09$$

The higher the interest rate, the lower the PDV of future cash flows.

The PDV of £1000 received in two years' time would be calculated by discounting twice. This is because the interest rate is applied each year, so:

$$\pounds PDV \times 1.05 \times 1.05 = \pounds 1000$$

$$\pounds PDV = \frac{1000}{1.05^2} = \pounds 907.03$$

So, income of £1000 to be received in two year's time is worth only £907.03 today.

In general terms, suppose at time t there is a future stream of income given by the following cash payments: $X_t, X_{t+1}, X_{t+2}, X_{t+3}, \ldots\ldots, X_{t+n}$ and the interest rate is r. The PDV of this income stream is:

$$PDV = X_t + \frac{X_{t+1}}{(1+r)} + \frac{X_{t+2}}{(1+r)^2} + \frac{X_{t+3}}{(1+r)^3} + \ldots\ldots + \frac{X_{t+n}}{(1+r)^n}$$

Note that because the first cash payment (X_t) is received straight away this does not need to be discounted.

It is reasonable to suggest that future income flows are unlikely to be known with certainty, therefore it might be more accurate to think in terms of expected future income, $E(X_t), E(X_{t+1}), E(X_{t+2}), E(X_{t+3}), \ldots\ldots E(X_{t+n})$. In this case, the *expected present discounted value* (EPDV) of the future uncertain stream of income is given by:

$$EPDV = E(X_t) + \frac{E(X_{t+1})}{(1+r)} + \frac{E(X_{t+2})}{(1+r)^2} + \frac{E(X_{t+3})}{(1+r)^3} + \ldots\ldots + \frac{E(X_{t+n})}{(1+r)^n}$$

In period 2, the maximum the household can spend is simply $(1 + r)Y_1 + Y_2$. By spending nothing in the first period, the household can deposit all its income in the bank, meaning that after interest there will be an amount of $(1 + r)Y_1$ available in addition to the second period income.

2

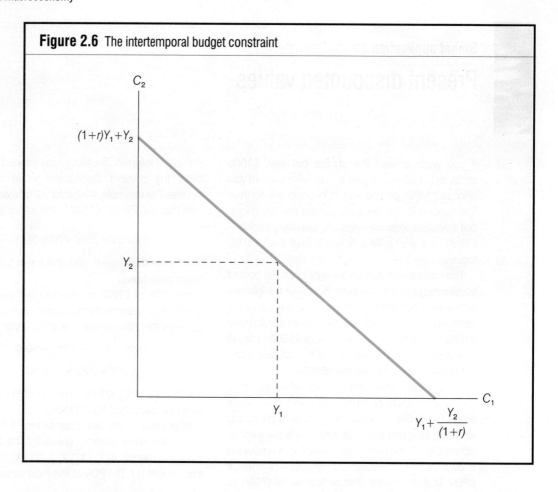

Figure 2.6 The intertemporal budget constraint

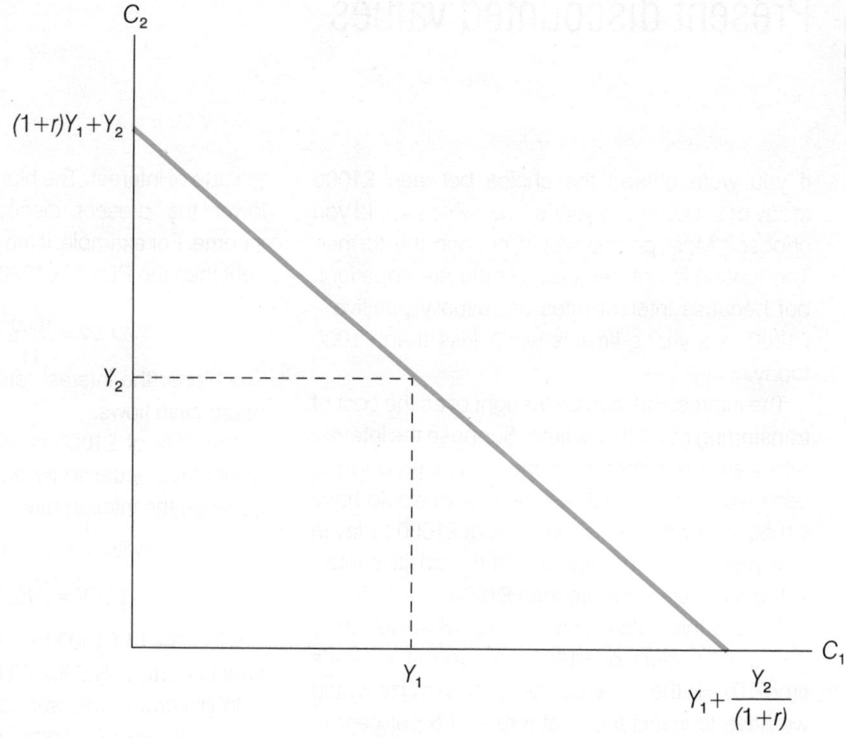

Consumer preferences

Now that we know all the feasible consumption decisions a household can undertake, which will prove to be the optimal decision in terms of welfare? A **lifetime utility function** tells us how much happiness or satisfaction a household will achieve from its lifetime pattern of consumption. This is given by:

$$U = U(C_1,C_2) \tag{2.7}$$

It is easier to understand the properties of the lifetime utility function if we first look at how total utility would change with respect to consumption in a one-period only model, such as $U = U(C)$. This is shown in Figure 2.7.

The shape of the utility function is interesting; it can be described as a concave function. As consumption rises, total utility rises; but, it does so at a diminishing rate. This outcome is due to the law of diminishing marginal utility of consumption. The marginal utility of consumption (MU_C) explains how total utility changes when consumption changes by one unit. It is therefore given by the ratio of the change in total utility and the change in consumption:

$$MU_C = \frac{\Delta U}{\Delta C} \tag{2.8}$$

From Figure 2.7, it is clear that this ratio gets smaller and smaller as consumption gets larger. Therefore, the marginal utility from an extra unit of consumption is much lower at high levels of consumption than at low levels.

Figure 2.7 Total utility function: one period model

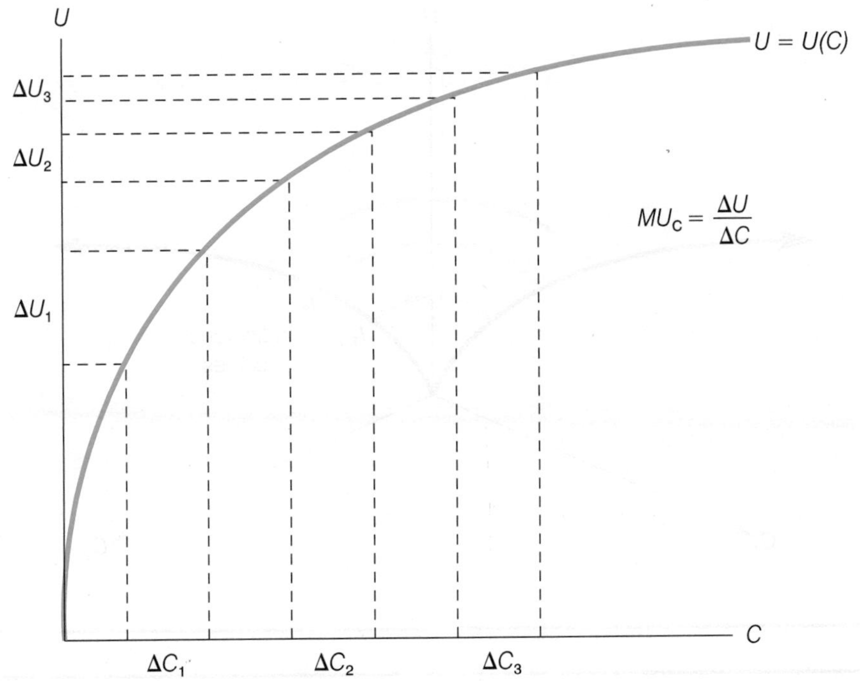

There is a strong rationale for imposing the law of diminishing marginal utility. Households will typically order their expenditures so that they purchase the goods and services that provide the highest utility first. As consumption increases further, the household starts consuming goods and services that it has lower preferences for, and therefore the additions to total utility are correspondingly less. At very high levels of consumption, the extra utility from an additional unit of consumption would be expected to be fairly small, as the household is purchasing goods for which it has a relatively low preference.

If the law of diminishing marginal utility of consumption continues to hold, then the total utility function in a two-period model would have similar concave properties. Total utility will rise if consumption in either period increases, but again, the marginal utility of consumption will diminish within each period. This is shown in Figure 2.8.

Figure 2.8 is a diagram in three dimensions. Total utility is plotted on the vertical axis, and the two inputs into the utility function, C_1 and C_2, are also both plotted on their own axes. As consumption in either, or both, periods rises, total utility will rise; but, again, it will do so at a decreasing rate. However, every level of total utility can be generated by a range of different consumption plans. These combinations can be joined together to form *indifference curves*, which identify all the combinations of C_1 and C_2 and that generate the same level of total utility.

In Figure 2.9 these indifference curves are plotted in two dimensions. The way to think about Figure 2.9 is to imagine that you are simply looking down on Figure 2.8 from above.

The set of indifference curves has two important features. First, there is a separate indifference curve for every level of total utility. Moving to a higher indifference curve ($I_1 \rightarrow I_2 \rightarrow I_3$) is associated with moving to a higher level of total utility.

2

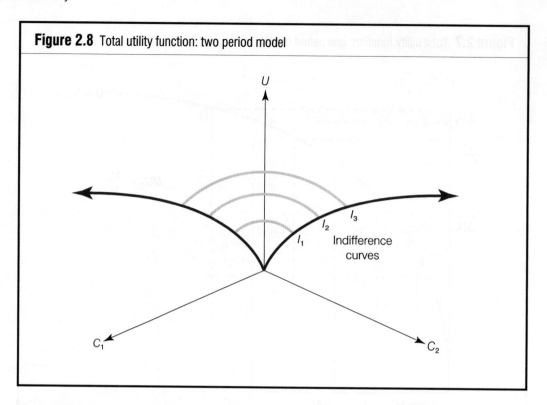

Figure 2.8 Total utility function: two period model

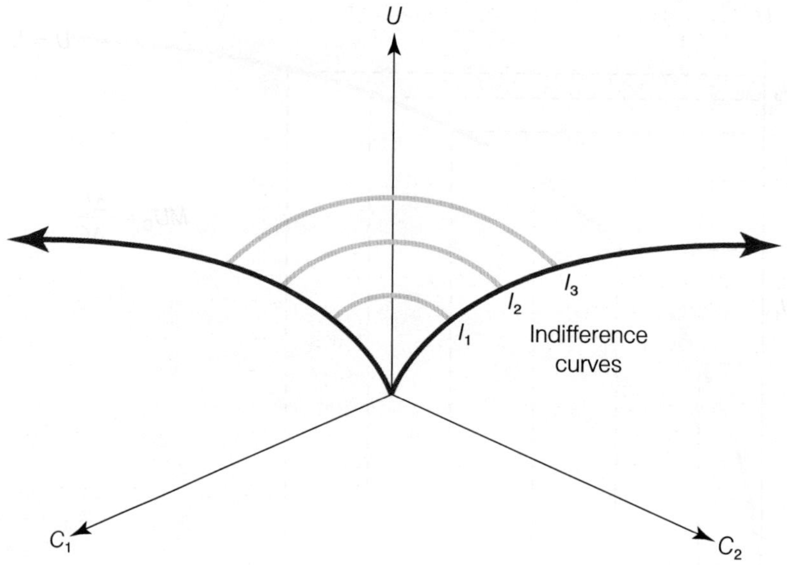

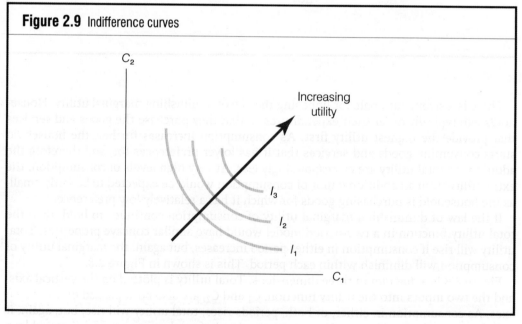

Figure 2.9 Indifference curves

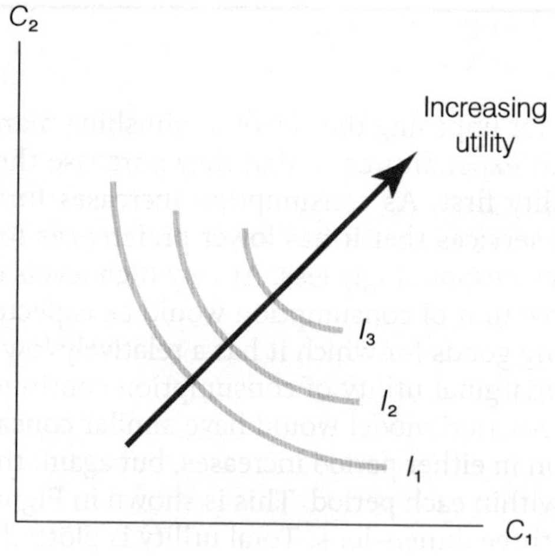

Second, because of the law of diminishing marginal utility of consumption, the indifference curves are convex in shape. This is important because it means that households will generally prefer average patterns of consumption over extremes. As we shall see later, this is the central feature of both the PIH and LCH. To understand why, consider Figure 2.10. Suppose a household were offered two choices of consumption plans. The first (C_1',C_2') offers a large amount of period 2 consumption, and a fairly low amount of period 1 consumption. The second (C_1'',C_2'') gives the opposite pattern: a large amount of period 1 consumption and a small amount in period 2. As both these points are on the same

Global application 2.3

How's life? Is consumption the key to happiness?

The concept of utility has been at the centre of economic thinking for over two centuries. As a subjective/notional measure of well-being, it has occupied a position of unrivalled importance with the *raison d'être* of economics to organize society so as to maximize utility. The traditional approach is to assume that utility is a function of income or consumption. This is a materialistic approach to measuring well-being, arguing that the more goods and services we can consume, the happier we become.

Recently, this view has been challenged. A paper by John Helliwell (2002) based on successive waves of the World Values Survey (WVS) attempts to measure international and interpersonal differences in subjective well-being. This work is potentially important, and fits into a wider literature on the economics of happiness. If the goal of policy makers is to maximize the well-being or utility of society, then the solution may actually be broader than just seeking to enhance prosperity. In essence, people's utility may depend on more things than just consumption.

Health status
Based on an individual's self-assessed state of health it was reported that a 1 per cent increase in reported average health status is associated with a greater than 1 per cent increase in subjective well-being. Health is usually the most significant of all the variables, but its effect is liable to be overstated. This is because, like well-being, its measure is somewhat subjective. Personal responses to the survey are therefore likely to be biased in the same way.

Employment status
The survey found that individuals report large well-being reductions from being unemployed. The survey, though, does not measure how long individuals have been or expect to be unemployed. As this increases, one would expect the build up in terms of debt, despair and the associated obsolescence of job-related human capital to increase. These habituation effects of unemployment could be important.

Family status
Married people are found to be the happiest, followed in turn by the 'living as married', widows or widowers, the divorced and finally the separated. The difference in subjective well-being between being married and separated is greater than the effect of being employed or unemployed. Once again, habituation effects that are not picked up in the survey might be important. For example, as divorce usually follows separation, the average divorced person has been separated or divorced for longer than the average separated person has been separated.

Education
Surprisingly, this effect turns out to be small and insignificant, as many studies have shown that education levels have been linked to participation in social activities as well as an indicator of health and wealth. One explanation is that the perceived benefits of education are largely picked up through higher incomes. However, it is certainly not inconceivable that once allowing for the effects of higher incomes and access to social activities and connections the effect of education on well-being is minor.

Age
The World Value Survey plots a U-shaped curve between well-being and age. The base group consists of those in the 18–24 bracket. However, those in the next three categories become progressively less happy reaching a low point in the 35–44 year-old age group. From then onwards, subjective well-being rises systematically and significantly. Those in the 55–64 year-old age group are equally as happy as those in the 18–24 group. The over-65 group is the happiest of the lot – with the difference between the well-being of this group and that of the lowest (35–44 group) being almost the same as the difference between employed and unemployed.

Global application 2.3 (continued)

Religious activity

There is a strong relationship between measures of religious activity and subjective well-being. There has been debate as to whether this is the due to the support provided by religious beliefs and convictions, or due to the social and community networks provided by such religious participation. The WVS attempts to differentiate between these two effects by asking respondents different questions about the importance of God in their lives and how frequently they attend church. The results show that both these variables have strong and easily distinguished linkages to life satisfaction.

Voluntary organizations

Individual participation in voluntary organizations is found to have a positive effect on self-reported well-being and is valued at about a tenth as much as marriage. The measure does not include participation in religious activities, which is counted by the measure above. There is an argument that this measure could be affected by optimism bias, with those who give optimistic measures of well-being likely to be outgoing people who are more likely to get involved in organizations. However, this effect still remains when comparing across countries where you would expect personality differences among individuals to average out at the national level.

Trust

The WVS asks a question along the lines of whether or not it is ever justifiable to cheat on taxes. This is taken to be an indicator of the degree of trust that prevails in a given society, and therefore used to assess the impact of living in a high-trust society on well-being. It is found that slightly more than half the respondents answered that it is never justifiable to cheat on taxes, and that they correspondingly report themselves to be more satisfied with their lives.

Governance measures

Looking across countries, a World Bank measure on the quality of governance is found to be an important measure of well-being. This measure is based on indicators, such as accountability, stability, lack of violence, government effectiveness, the regulatory framework, rule of law and control of corruption. It is not surprising that higher levels of this variable are found to be associated with higher levels of well-being. Many services crucial to individuals and families, ranging from health, education, justice and transportation are provided and regulated by governments. The quality of the services is likely to be higher where the quality of the government is greater.

Individual and national incomes

The link between income and well-being is normally found to be positive in these types of analyses. It is usual to find a link between income and well-being amongst individuals in the same country, and also a positive cross-country correlation between GDP per capita and well-being measures. There is, however, some ambiguity over the size and significance of the income effects on well-being, with different studies reporting different levels of magnitude.

The WVS is based on a large and international sample, and finds that the effects of national and personal incomes may be non-linear in nature. It is found that moving from the fourth to the fifth decile in the distribution of family incomes raises well-being by 10 per cent, whereas moving from the ninth to the tenth decile only raises well-being by 1 per cent. This is despite the fact that moving from the ninth to the tenth deciles involves much larger increases in absolute income in most countries than any other movements across deciles. This is evidence of diminishing returns to higher incomes, and justifies the law of diminishing marginal utility of consumption used in the optimal consumption models.

John Helliwell's study using the World Values Survey provides an interesting analysis of the factors that determine well-being. It is clear that income (and therefore consumption) is important. It is also interesting that the relationship between income and well-being is found to be non-linear and in tune with the predictions of the law of diminishing marginal utility of consumption. However, it must also be acknowledged that well-being depends on a broader set of factors, with health, family and employment statuses being equally, if not more, important than income itself.

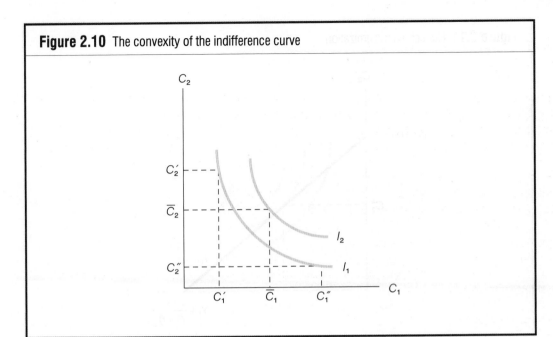

Figure 2.10 The convexity of the indifference curve

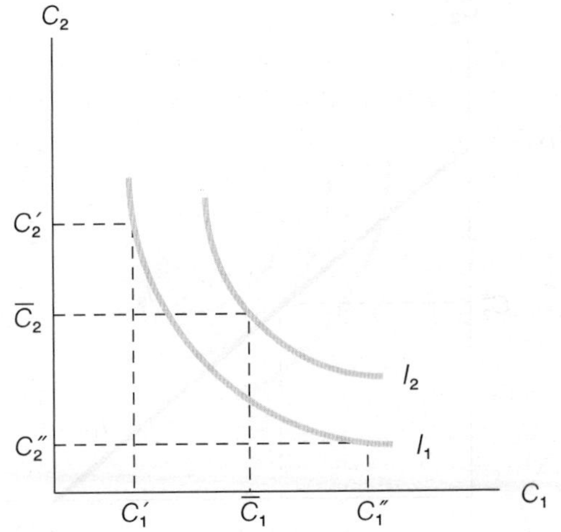

indifference curve (I_1), the household would be indifferent in choosing between them. The total utility gained from either of these two patterns of consumption will be the same.

Now, think about what would happen to total utility if we were to move away from these extreme consumption patterns to one such as ($\overline{C}_1$,$\overline{C}_2$), which offers an average amount of consumption in both periods. Due to the law of diminishing marginal utility, at (C_1',C_2'), the marginal utility lost by giving up a unit of C_2' will be less than the extra utility gained by gaining an extra unit of C_1'. Therefore, moving consumption from period 2 to period 1 would increase total utility.

Exactly the same logic, but in reverse, holds for the consumption pattern (C_1'',C_2''). Total utility will be increased by switching consumption from period 1 (where the marginal utility of consumption is low) to period 2 (where the marginal utility of consumption is high). This reasoning clearly demonstrates why a household would prefer an average consumption plan, ($\overline{C}_1$,$\overline{C}_2$). Moving away from the extremes and towards the average would move the household on to a higher indifference curve (I_2) associated with a larger amount of lifetime utility.

Household maximization

The objective of the household must therefore be to find the pattern of consumption which delivers the highest level of total utility, and is feasible given lifetime resources. Or, put another way, to find the pattern of consumption that enables the highest indifference curve to be reached while staying within the budget set.

In Figure 2.11, the optimal consumption plan for this household is at C_1^*, C_2^*. This is where the indifference curve I_2 forms a tangent to the budget constraint. Any other consumption plan will involve moving to an indifference curve which is either:

- feasible, but makes the household worse off in terms of utility, such as I_1;

or

- offers a higher level of utility, but is infeasible given the intertemporal budget constraint, such as I_3.

2

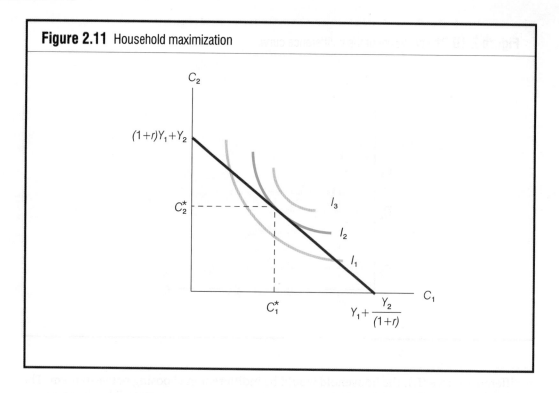

Figure 2.11 Household maximization

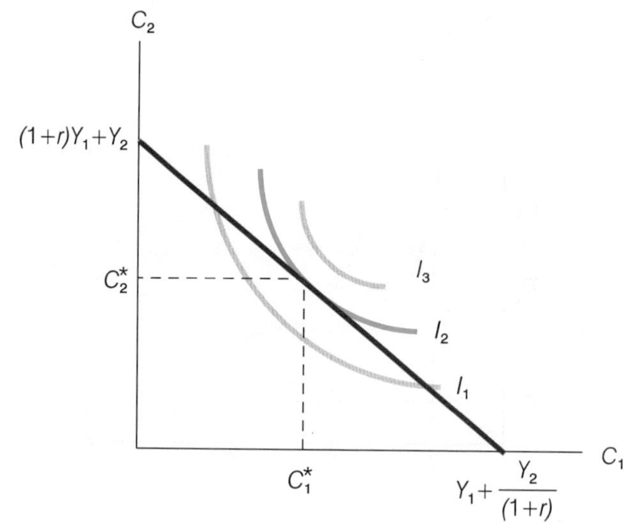

Consumption smoothing

What are the predictions of the utility maximizing household model for aggregate consumption? First, the link between current income and consumption strongly advocated by the Keynesian consumption function is broken. The maximizing household would base its consumption decisions on a longer-term view of lifetime resources instead. Consumption choices are no longer constrained by current income, but by the present discounted value of lifetime income. In addition, future consumption forms part of the household's present decision.

Second, we expect to see evidence of *consumption smoothing*. This is a consequence of the law of diminishing marginal utility of consumption which pushes the household to prefer averages over extremes. The household would find it optimal to use borrowing and saving to achieve this end.

Figure 2.12 shows the case for a household with very high period 1 income, and correspondingly low income in period 2. If this household were to consume out of current income, it would achieve the total utility commensurate with the indifference curve, I_1. However, this household can achieve a higher level of total utility while still satisfying its intertemporal budget constraint by moving consumption to (C_1^*, C_2^*). This household is a net saver, deciding to save a total of $S = Y_1 - C_1^*$ in the first period, to achieve higher consumption in the future.

This situation may account for why people invest during their working lives in pensions for their retirement.

Figure 2.13 highlights the opposite scenario. This household has relatively low first period income, but relatively high second period income. The same issues still apply; by smoothing consumption the household can move to a higher indifference curve ($I_1 \rightarrow I_2$) and be made better off in terms of utility. Smoothing consumption in this case requires the household to borrow an amount, $C_1^* - Y_1$.

This household is a net borrower. Such a situation may describe students or young professionals. These are households that will start with relatively low income but are likely to

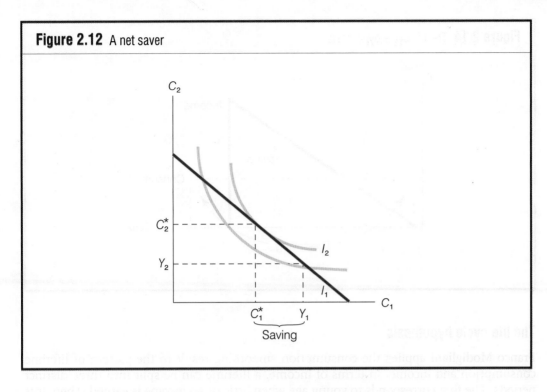

Figure 2.12 A net saver

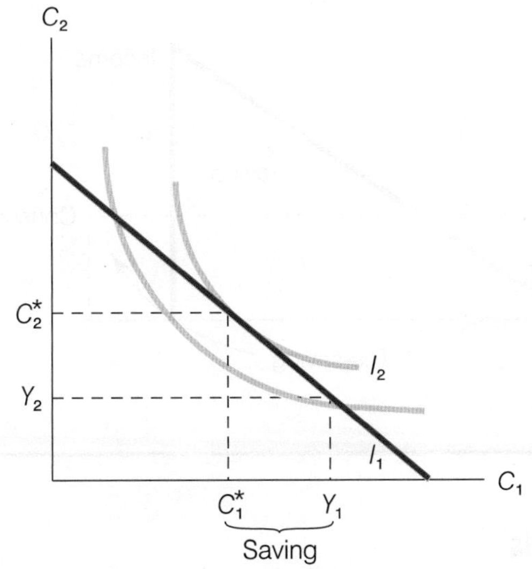

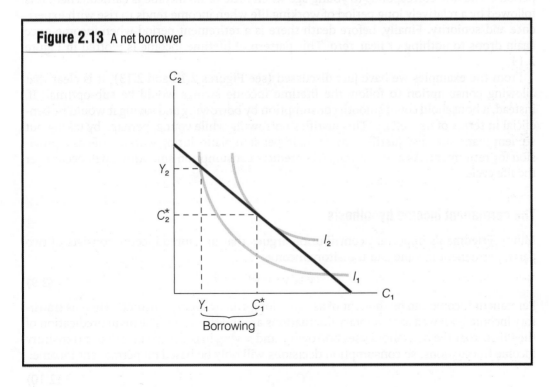

Figure 2.13 A net borrower

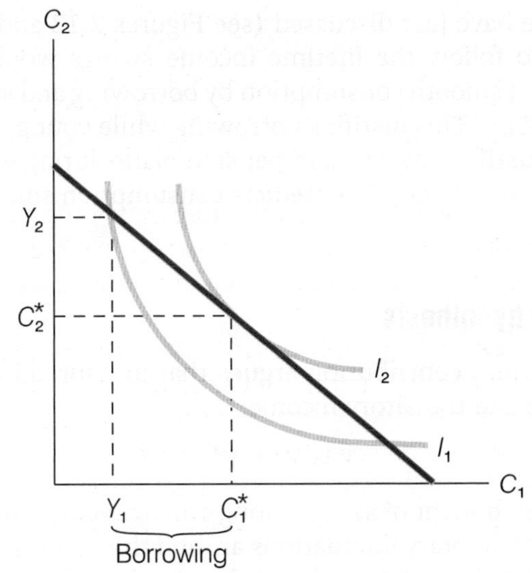

achieve much higher income in the future. Therefore, maintaining current consumption by borrowing against this higher future income is just a consequence of rational behaviour.

These predictions, basing consumption on lifetime rather than current income and smoothing consumption, form the basis of the LCH and PIH which we consider next.

2

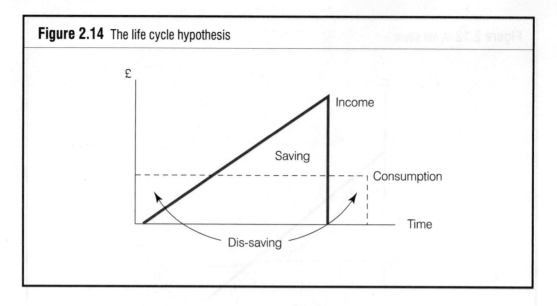

Figure 2.14 The life cycle hypothesis

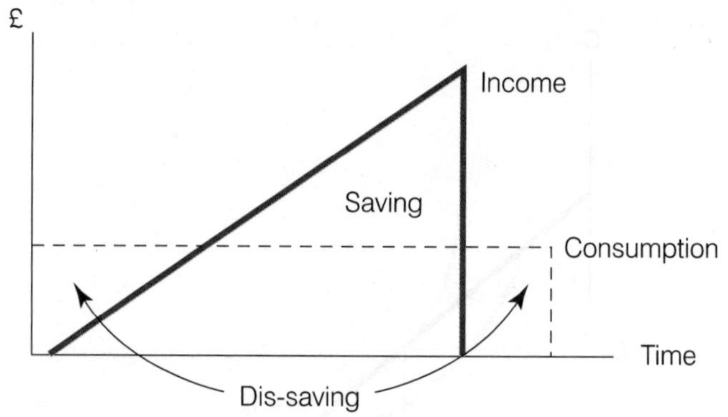

The life cycle hypothesis

Franco Modigliani applies the consumption smoothing result to the pattern of lifetime consumption and income. In terms of income, a lifetime can be split into three distinct periods. The first corresponds to young age when little or no income is earned. Then, it is followed by a relatively long period of working life when income tends to rise with experience and seniority. Finally, before death there is a retirement period when income once again drops to nothing or near zero. This pattern of lifetime income is plotted in Figure 2.14.

From the examples we have just discussed (see Figures 2.12 and 2.13), it is clear that allowing consumption to follow the lifetime income swings would be sub-optimal. If, instead, a household could smooth consumption by borrowing and saving it would be beneficial in terms of its welfare. This justifies borrowing while young, perhaps by taking out student loans, and also justifies investing in pension plans during working life as a provision for retirement. As a result, the LCH predicts consumption smoothing will occur over the life cycle.

The permanent income hypothesis

Milton Friedman's important contribution argues that measured income consists of two parts, permanent income and transitory income:

$$Y = Y^P + Y^T \tag{2.9}$$

Permanent income can be thought of as some long-run or average income, whereas transitory income is viewed as temporary fluctuations around this level. The main predication of the PIH is that the household uses borrowing and saving in order to smooth out transitory income fluctuations, so consumption decisions will only be based on permanent income:

$$C = c_p Y^P \tag{2.10}$$

The theory predicts that the marginal propensity to consume out of permanent income (c_p) will be much higher than the marginal propensity to consume out of measured income, with empirical estimates suggesting that $c_p \approx 1$. This is shown in Figure 2.15, where the short-run consumption function (C_{SR} – based on measured income) is much flatter than the long-run consumption function (C_{LR} – based on permanent income).

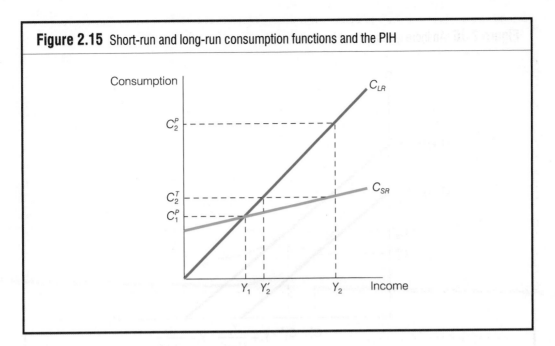

Figure 2.15 Short-run and long-run consumption functions and the PIH

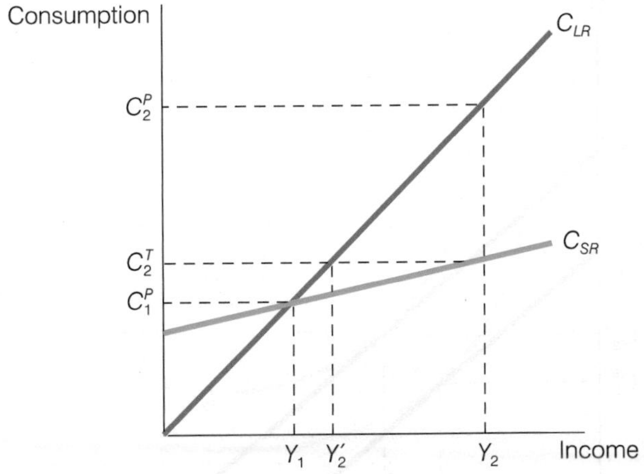

Suppose initially that measured income and permanent income coincide at Y_1, where consumption is C_1^P. If income rises to Y_2, then consumption will only increase to the extent that permanent income has risen. In the short run, it is assumed that households are unable to ascertain whether the rise in measured income is permanent or transitory so consumption will only increase to C_2^T. This reflects the small increase in permanent income (Y_2') from spreading the transitory increase in income over the long run. If, however, the increase in income is permanent, then estimates of permanent income will also increase to Y_2 and consumption to C_2^P.

One of the strong features of the PIH is that it forms a link between the Keynesian consumption function and the optimal consumption model. Basing consumption decisions on permanent income implies that the marginal propensity to consume out of short-run transitory shocks will be low, reflecting the consumption-smoothing behaviour implied by the optimal consumption model. However, it also fosters a long-run relationship between consumption and income similar to the Keynesian consumption function and the empirical evidence offered in Figure 2.5. Over time, we would anticipate the trend in permanent income to reflect the trend in measured income due to underlying economic growth.

2.5 Explaining consumption patterns

The optimal consumption model provides a good framework for analysing changes in consumption. As households are always looking to maximize their utility, anything which moves the position of the intertemporal budget constraint is likely to have an effect on consumption.

In this section we shall look at several factors which might account for changes in consumption in the UK. First of all though, we shall investigate what effects changes in current income would have in the optimal consumption model. This will also emphasize the differences between the predictions of the PIH and LCH compared to the predictions of the Keynesian consumption function.

2

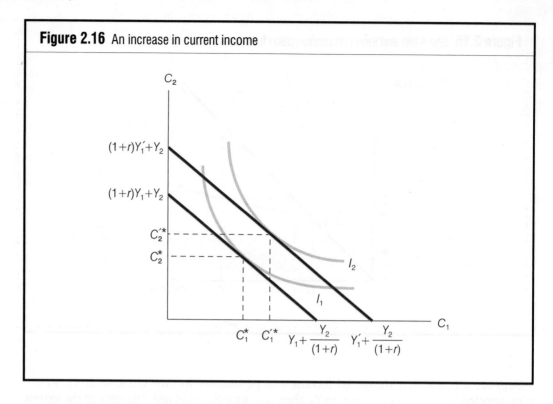

Figure 2.16 An increase in current income

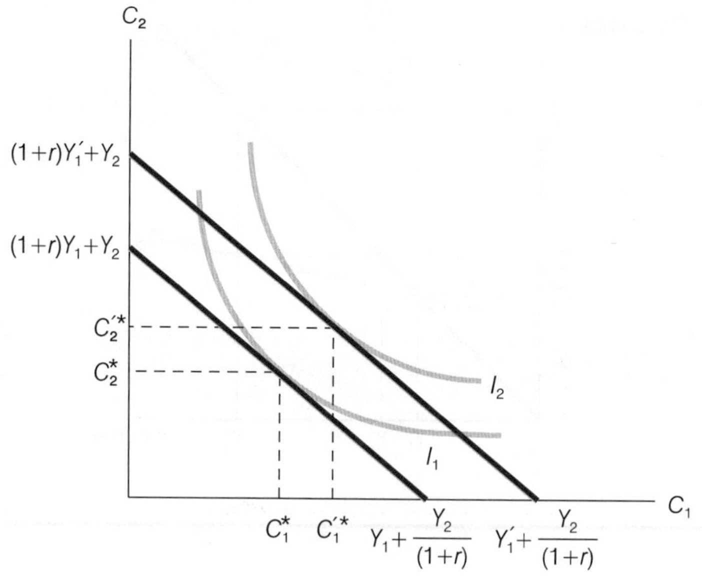

Changes in current income

As Figure 2.16 shows, an increase in current income from Y_1 to Y_1' would lead to an outward shift in the intertemporal budget constraint. It is now possible to consume more in both periods. The household will then choose its new consumption plan by maximizing its utility subject to the new constraint.

Following a change in period 1 income, consumption in both periods will rise. Consumption-smoothing behaviour would imply that the household will save some of the increase in income for the future. This represents the main difference between the Keynesian consumption function and the PIH. Under the PIH, current consumption will only respond to the degree that permanent income changes. As this refers to long-run average income, the change in current income will be spread over the total lifetime. Consumption will then only change by a smaller amount, but will be higher in every period.

Other factors determining consumption

Unlike the Keynesian consumption function, the optimal consumption model suggests that many factors other than current income may be important. In this section we identify some of these factors in relation to recent consumption trends in the UK economy.

An interesting, and often used, statistic for analysing consumer behaviour is the *saving ratio*. The saving ratio is simply the proportion of income that is saved, or S/Y. If it assumed that all income is either consumed or saved, then it must be true that:

$$C + S = Y$$

Dividing everything by income gives:

$$\frac{C}{Y} + \frac{S}{Y} = \frac{Y}{Y}$$

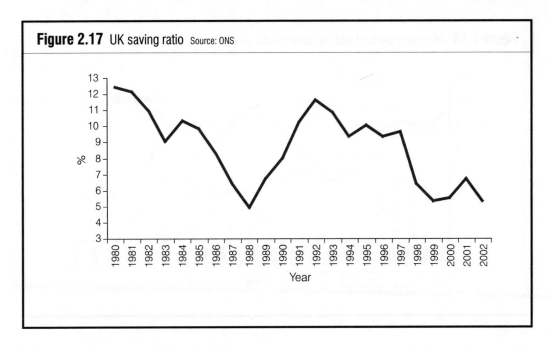

Figure 2.17 UK saving ratio Source: ONS

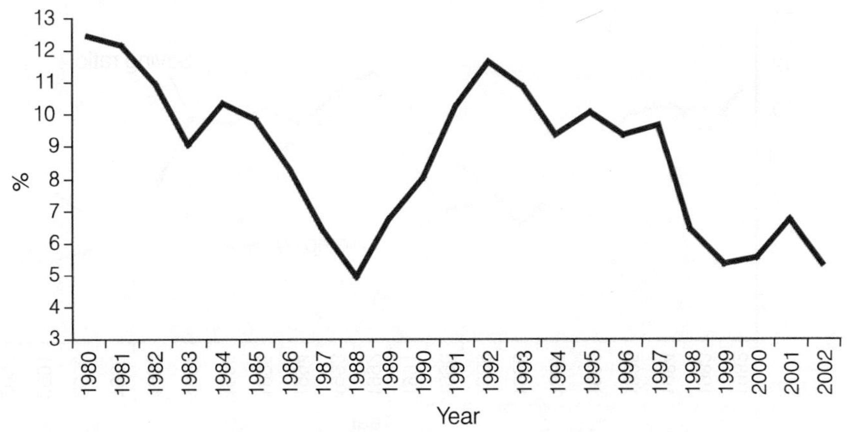

Therefore, the saving ratio is simply:

$$\frac{S}{Y} = 1 - \frac{C}{Y} \tag{2.11}$$

An analysis of the saving ratio enables us to observe changes in consumption other than those generated by changes in current income. For example, if consumption rises with no change in the level of income, then it is clear that the saving ratio will fall. Obviously, the opposite holds true, a rise in the saving ratio would see a fall in consumption that is independent of a change in current income. The recent history of the UK saving ratio is plotted in Figure 2.17. Next, we will attempt to use the optimal consumption model to explain what factors might be responsible for the observed trends.

Changes in future income

Changes in future income will have exactly the same effects on the intertemporal budget constraint as changes in current income. Following the PIH, if consumption decisions are based on a longer-term view of the average level of income, it does not matter what actual path income takes. Whether it was current or future income that rose, the effects would be the same. An increase in expected future income would shift the intertemporal budget constraint outwards and raise current consumption. Therefore, Figure 2.16 is equally applicable here.

A good indicator of expected future income may be the unemployment rate. High unemployment might signify a higher likelihood of being made unemployed and would worsen job market prospects. Both would tend to tend to reduce expectations of future income. Low unemployment would have entirely the opposite effect. Households will feel more secure in their future income and more optimistic about achieving better job prospects.

In Figure 2.18 there appears to be a clear relationship between the unemployment rate and the saving ratio. Movements in the saving ratio seem to pre-empt movements in unemployment, which might suggest that consumption falls in response to expectations of higher future unemployment.

Figure 2.18 UK unemployment and the saving ratio Source: ONS

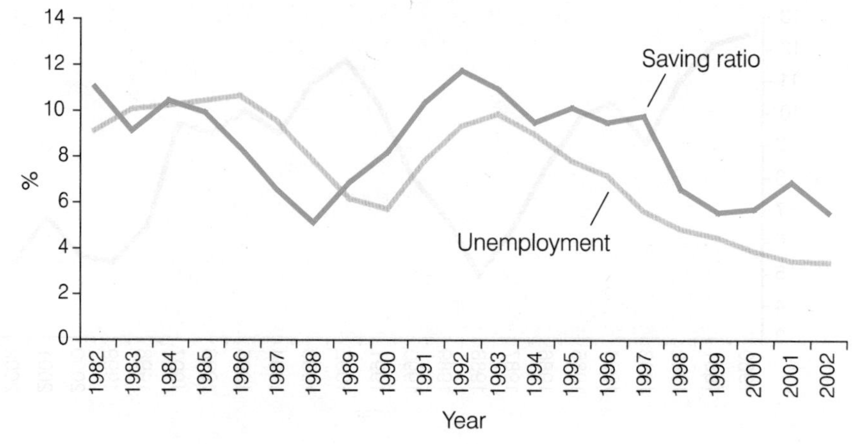

Figure 2.19 Consumer confidence and the growth in consumer expenditure Source: GfK and ONS

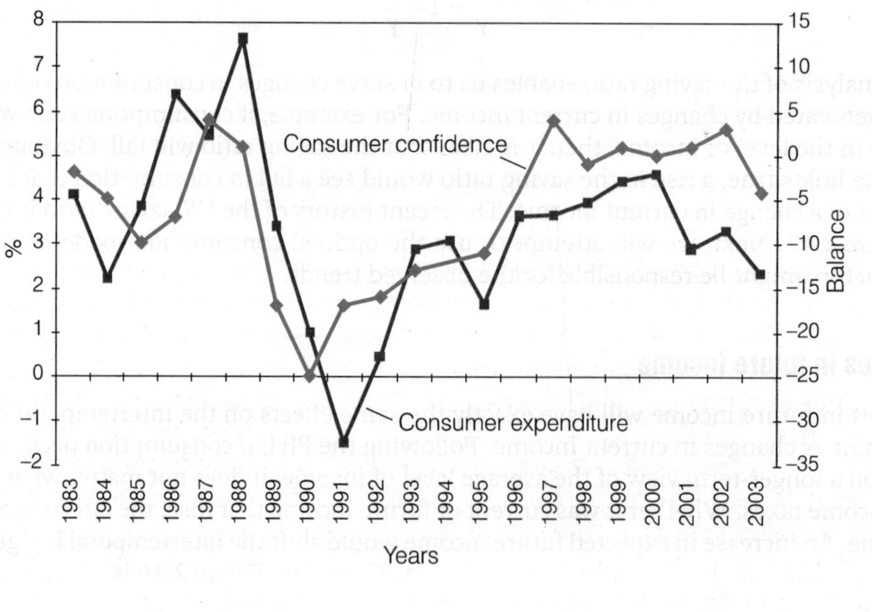

Further evidence is presented in Figure 2.19, which plots a clear relationship between consumer confidence and the growth rate of consumer expenditure in the UK. As measures of consumer confidence are likely to be heavily influenced by expectations of the future, this too draws a link between current consumption and expectations of future income.

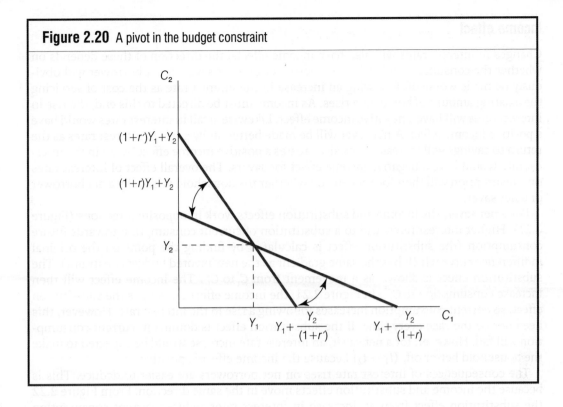

Figure 2.20 A pivot in the budget constraint

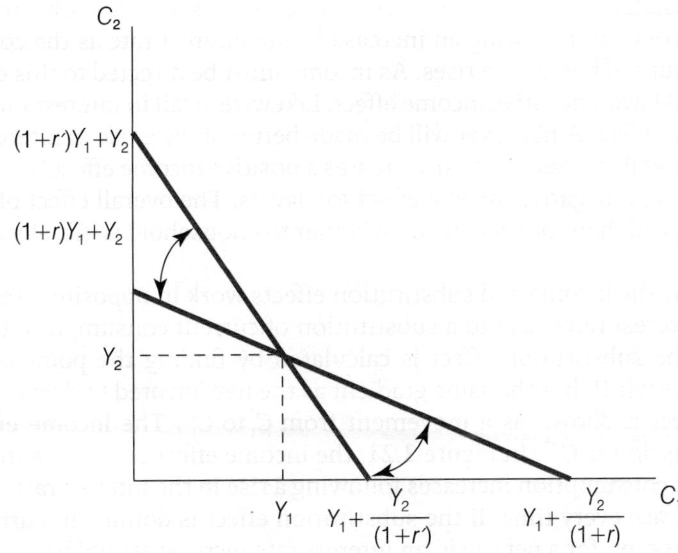

Interest rates

The effect of interest rate changes is easily predicted using our two-period consumption model. Interest rates represent the costs of borrowing and the returns to saving, and can be thought of as the price of moving income or resources over time.

An increase in interest rates from r to r' makes borrowing more expensive and reduces the present discounted value of future income. Therefore, the maximum amount that can be consumed in the first period will fall. However, higher interest rates will generate higher returns from saving, so the potential for second period consumption will rise. Falls in the interest rate would have the opposite effect. Therefore, changes in the interest rate create pivots in the intertemporal budget constraint. This is shown in Figure 2.20.

At which point, though, will the constraint pivot? The answer is through the original income point, Y_1,Y_2. This is where the consumer is neither borrowing or saving but simply consuming out of their current income, so changes in the interest rate will have no effect on this point. Increases in the cost of borrowing are irrelevant if you are not borrowing, and likewise the higher returns to savers if you are not saving. This point will always be part of the budget constraint regardless of what the prevailing interest rate happens to be.

When analysing the effects of interest rate changes, the impact on consumption can be split into two parts: the substitution effect and the income effect.

Substitution effect

The household decides how much to consume, and how much to save for the future. The interest rate represents the price of current consumption in terms of future consumption. As the interest rate rises, future consumption becomes relatively cheaper than current consumption because the costs of borrowing and the returns to saving are both greater. Therefore, it would encourage households to substitute current for future consumption.

2

Income effect

Changes in interest rates will also have income effects; the direction of these depends on whether the consumer is initially a net borrower or a net saver. A net borrower will obviously be made worse off following an increase in the interest rate as the cost of servicing the existing amount of borrowing rises. As income must be directed to this end, the rise in interest rates will have a negative income effect. Likewise, a fall in interest rates would have a positive income effect. A net saver will be made better off by a rise in interest rates as the return to savings will increase. This also creates a positive income effect. A fall in the interest rate would have a negative income effect for savers. The overall effect of interest rates on consumption will therefore depend on whether the household is initially a net borrower or a net saver.

For a net saver, the income and substitution effects work in opposite directions (Figure 2.21). Higher interest rates lead to a substitution of current consumption towards future consumption (the substitution effect is calculated by finding the point on the original indifference curve which has the same gradient as the new pivoted budget constraint). The substitution effect is shown as a movement from C_1^* to C_1^S. The income effect will then increase consumption to $C_1'^*$. In Figure 2.21, the income effect outweighs the substitution effect, so current consumption increases following a rise in the interest rate. However, this need not be the case every time. If the substitution effect is dominant, current consumption will fall. However, for a net saver, an interest rate increase would be expected to make the household better off, ($I_1 \rightarrow I_2$) because the income effect is positive.

The consequences of interest rate rises on net borrowers are easier to deduce. This is because the income and substitution effects move in the same direction. From Figure 2.22 the substitution effect from an increase in interest rates reduces current consumption ($C_1^* \rightarrow C_1^S$). The income effect ($C_1^S \rightarrow C_1'^*$) reinforces this movement and reduces current consumption further. Because the income effect is negative, the net borrower household will always be made worse off ($I_1 \rightarrow I_2$) following an increase in interest rates.

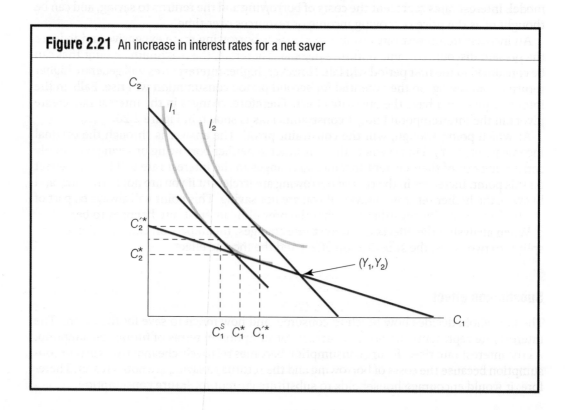

Figure 2.21 An increase in interest rates for a net saver

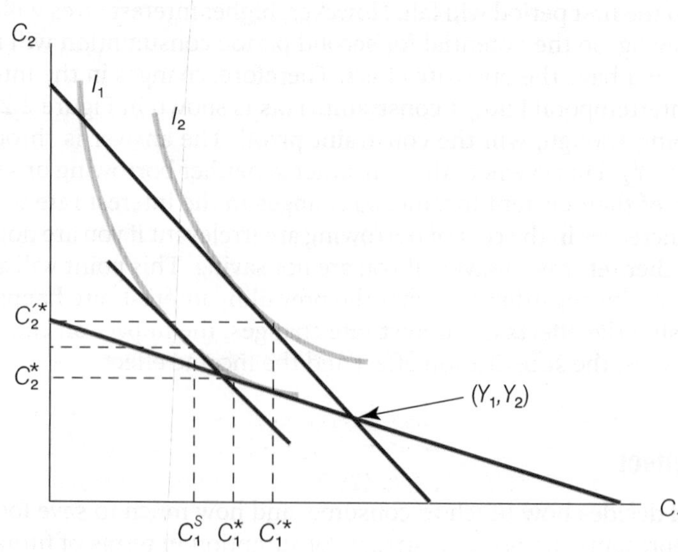

Figure 2.22 An increase in interest rates for a net borrower

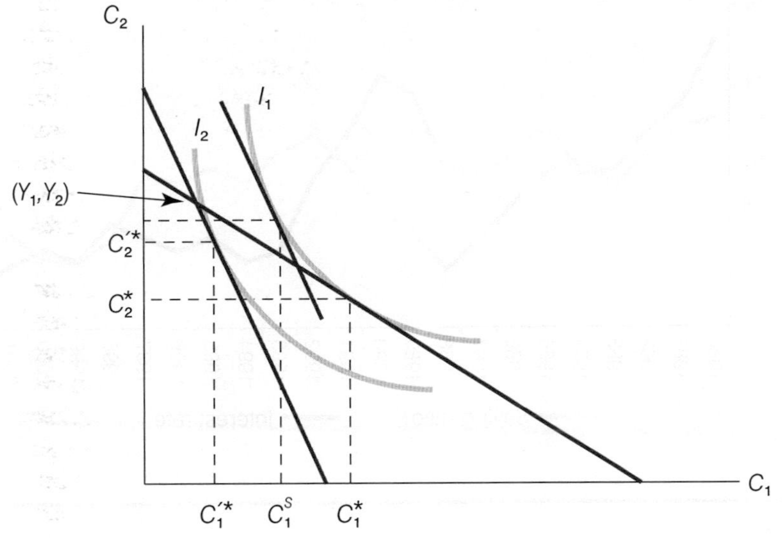

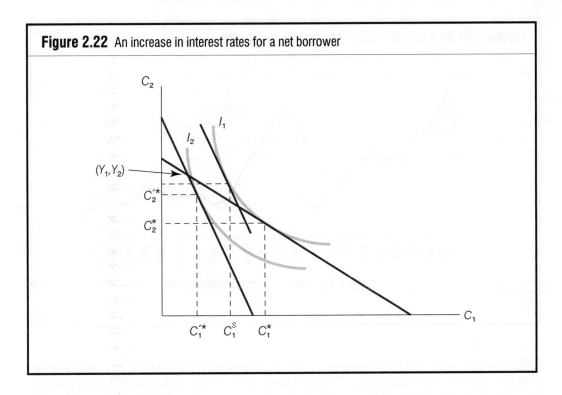

Empirical evidence tends to suggest that interest rate changes have small substitution effects on the timing of consumption, and therefore the income effect is usually dominant. Therefore, a rise in interest rates would increase the current consumption of net savers but reduce that of net borrowers.

The evidence from Figure 2.23 indicates that the saving ratio and the interest rate share a positive association. This would tend to suggest that most households are in fact net borrowers, so current consumption will respond inversely to interest rate changes. This is fairly easy to justify as most households are mortgage holders, incurring relatively significant debts to buy their houses. Changes in the Bank of England base rate usually lead to the same movement in mortgage rates. The low interest rates in the UK over the last decade would have reduced the costs of servicing mortgage debts freeing up extra income for consumption. This could be an important factor in accounting for the fall in the saving ratio over this period.

Financial market constraints

The consumption-smoothing model at the heart of the LCH and the PIH depends crucially on the ability to use saving and borrowing to offset changes in current income. Households, though, are likely to face constraints and will be unable to save, and in particular borrow, in an unlimited way.

Imagine a household with low current income, but expectations of fairly high future income. From Figure 2.13 being constrained to the low current income is clearly sub-optimal. This household would ideally be a net borrower. However, the household could face constraints in its ability to borrow.

First, financial institutions may be unwilling or at best very cautious about advancing loans on expected future income. This is because it is highly uncertain and unsecured. Second, there are institutional constraints. Even if financial institutions are willing to advance loans, they may have limitations on their ability to create credit. Policy makers

Figure 2.23 Bank of England base rates and the saving ratio Source: ONS

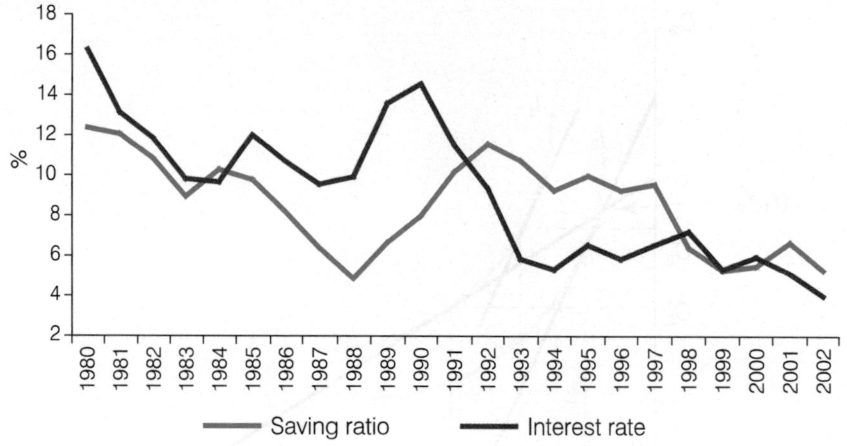

could impose constraints for various reasons. Controlling credit would be a way for the government to control aggregate demand. Also, by limiting credit creation, the government could ensure the capital adequacy of financial institutions. Over-lending could make these institutions susceptible to bank runs and financial panics if loans are defaulted on.

The presence of borrowing constraints has two interesting implications for the determination of consumption. The first is that even though households may be rational optimizers, the pattern of consumption will follow the predictions of the Keynesian model in being fairly tied to current income. Credit-constrained households may wish to borrow against future income to increase current consumption but cannot. They will only be able to consume more when their current income increases. The second is that changes in the laws and regulations governing credit creation may lead to sudden large jumps in consumption.

Financial market deregulation in the UK

One of the significant explanations for the large fall in the savings ratio in the second half of the 1980s may have been the deregulation of financial markets in 1986 – an event known as the *Big Bang*. This led to a proliferation in the availability of credit, which until then had been relatively tightly controlled.

If households are optimal consumers, but face restrictions on their ability to borrow, then current consumption is likely to be constrained. In Figure 2.24 the household is forced to consume at the restricted level, $C_1^{R^*}$. Ideally, it could borrow and consume at a level of C_1^*; however, credit restrictions make this point unattainable.

However, removing these constraints suddenly extends the budget constraint to include the dashed segment of the line in Figure 2.24. This would then allow these previously constrained households to move towards their preferred consumption plans. This jump in consumption would happen quickly and result in a sharp fall in the saving ratio.

Figure 2.24 Removing credit constraints

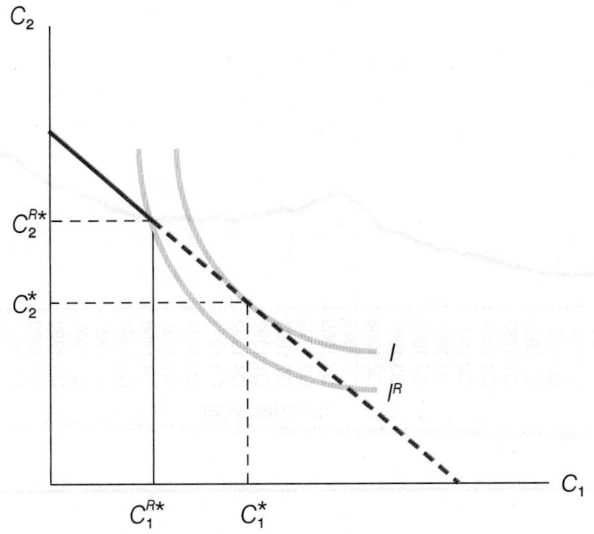

Wealth

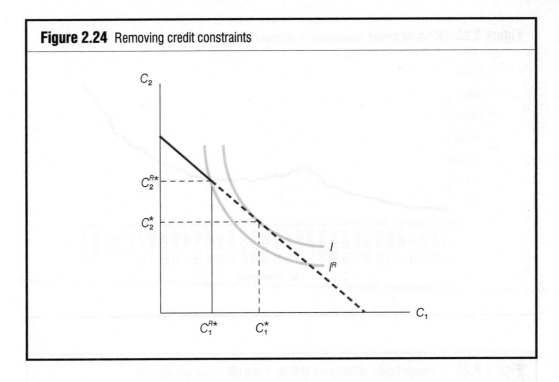

If a household, in addition to its income, also has some initial wealth, W_1, this can be added to the intertemporal constraint:

$$C_1 + \frac{C_2}{(1+r)} \leq W_1 + Y_1 + \frac{Y_2}{(1+r)}$$

Again, the current discounted value of consumption cannot exceed the current discounted value of lifetime resources, but these resources now also include wealth. Changes in wealth would have exactly the same effects on consumption as changes in income.

The housing market and consumption in the UK

The recent boom in UK house prices is easy to see from Figure 2.25. As property is the major asset of most households, these high prices increase household wealth. In addition, following two decades of financial liberalization, it is increasingly easy for households to borrow against this property wealth – a process known as mortgage equity withdrawal (MEW). As these loans are secured on the value of the property, they are considered to be fairly safe for loan providers. Therefore, households can borrow at relatively low levels of interest. Total MEW is shown in Figure 2.26 and provides the direct link between the rise in house prices and the fall in the saving ratio.

This suggests that the future path of consumption in the UK might be heavily influenced by whether or not there is a downturn in the housing market. First, if prices stabilize or fall, households will no longer see the value of their housing equity rise, providing them with no asset value from which to borrow. If house prices fall, the impact on consumption could be quite significant as the equity used to secure loans would disappear. Consequently, households would have to pay back equity into their houses, diminishing the resources available for consumption.

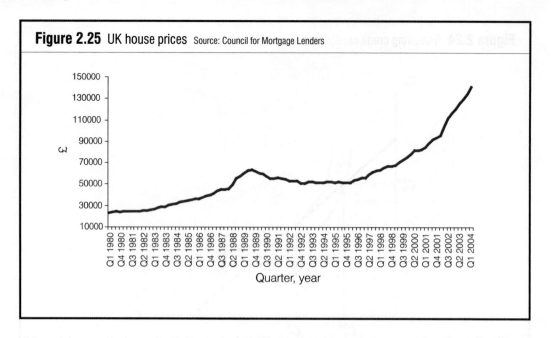

Figure 2.25 UK house prices Source: Council for Mortgage Lenders

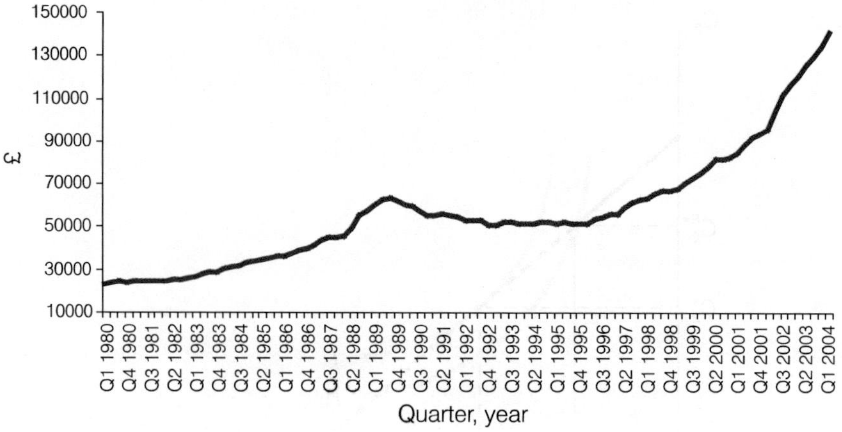

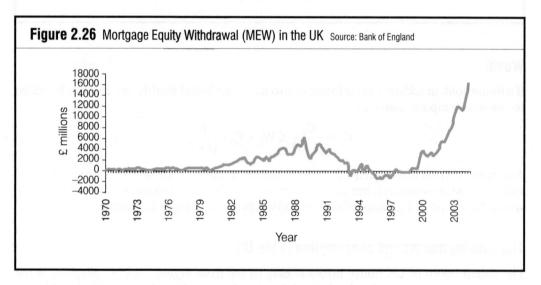

Figure 2.26 Mortgage Equity Withdrawal (MEW) in the UK Source: Bank of England

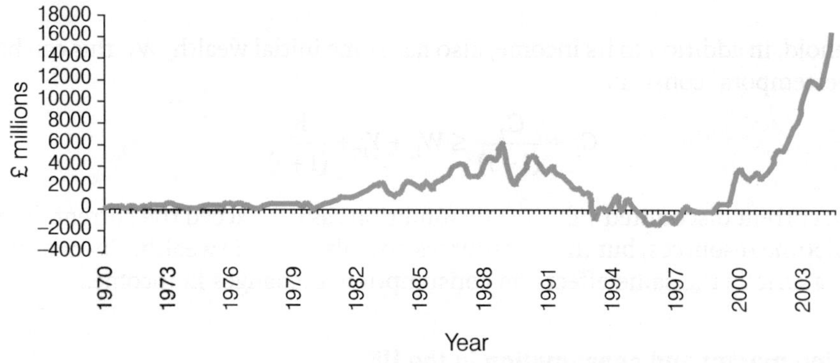

UK stock market performance and pension funds

Despite wider share ownership in recent years, UK consumption does not appear to be highly sensitive to stock market values. Therefore, changes in asset prices are not considered to be an important factor in determining current consumption or the saving ratio. Figure 2.27 plots the recent history of the UK stock market.

During the second half of the 1990s, stock prices rose substantially. This was predominately linked to the emergence of 'New Economy' firms and technologies, particularly in Information and Communication Technologies (ICT). However, since 2000 these have been largely reversed. This reflects the fact that part of the dramatic increase in equity values was related to a stock market bubble and therefore was not sustainable (this episode of boom and bust in stock markets is covered in some detail in Chapter 6). The saving ratio, though, does not seem to have been affected by the collapse in asset prices, but it may be premature to say that there will be no long-lasting effect on consumption.

Figure 2.27 UK Stock Market Source: ONS

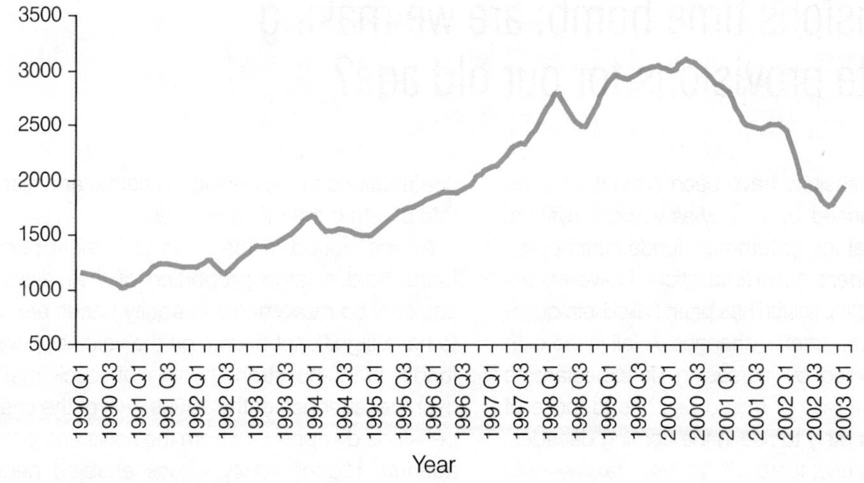

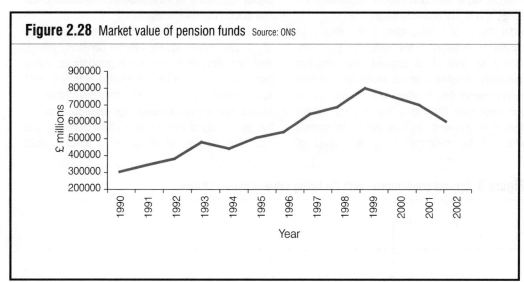

Figure 2.28 Market value of pension funds Source: ONS

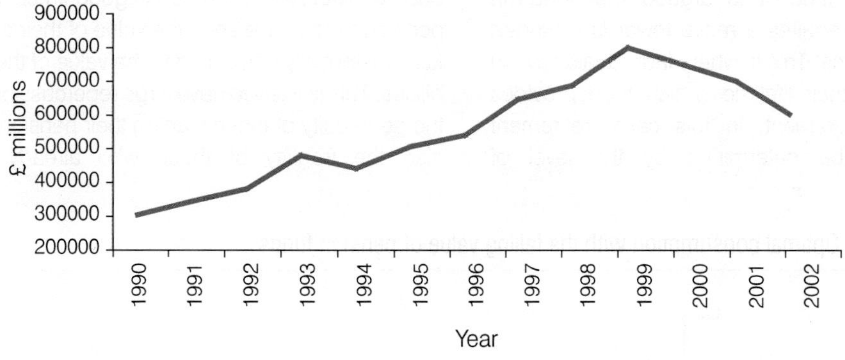

Most pension funds hold sizeable amounts of equities in their portfolios. Figure 2.28 plots the market value of pension funds and, unsurprisingly, it shares a very similar trend to the stock market. According to the LCH, the fall in stock prices, and therefore the value of pension funds, means that retirement income will be lower. People must save more today or work longer in order to build up a sufficient amount of pension reserves to fund their retirement consumption. The consequences of this so far have largely been seen in fewer people taking early retirement rather than an increase in saving.

Uncertainty and precautionary saving

This brings us to consider uncertainty in more detail. One of the most powerful motivations for saving is in order to take precautions against uncertain future events. The 'saving

2

Global application 2.4

The pensions time bomb: are we making adequate provisions for our old age?

Traditionally, pensions have been provided by the state and financed by a 'pay-as-you-go' system. This means that the government funds current pensions from current general taxation. However, the future of the state pension has been called into question due to demographic changes. A fall in the birth rate accompanied by increasing life-expectancies implies that the ratio of retired persons to those of working age is likely to rise in the coming decades. As a consequence, there will be fewer taxpayers to support each person of retirement age. Maintaining the value of the state pension would then become increasingly expensive and require significant tax increases or a higher retirement age.

Under these circumstances, it is rational to anticipate an erosion of the value of the state pension over time. It is argued that long-run sustainability requires a move towards a funded pension scheme. This is where individuals save in a fund over their lifetime, which then provides income in retirement. In this case, retirement income will be determined by the level of contributions to the pension scheme, and also the rate of return the funds generate.

As mentioned in the main text, most pension funds hold a large proportion of their assets in equities, so movements in equity prices are likely to have significant effects on the value of pension funds. With the strengthening of stock markets over the latter half of the 1990s, talk of the crisis in pensions disappeared from the news and political agenda. Higher equity values enabled pension funds to offer fairly lucrative terms, and many people were able to take early retirement. The high equity valuations saw the assets of pensions funds rise above their liabilities.

The subsequent fall in equity prices has had a significant impact on the funded pension system. Saddled with liabilities made in good times, many pension funds have seen the value of their assets fall substantially compared to the value of their liabilities. This is likely to have large repercussions on the generosity of those starting their pension, and also the fragility of those who already hold

Figure 3 Optimal consumption with the falling value of pension funds

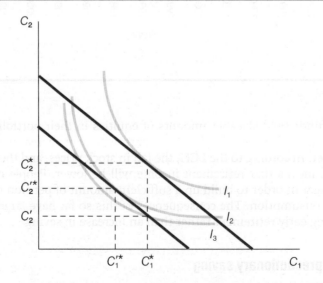

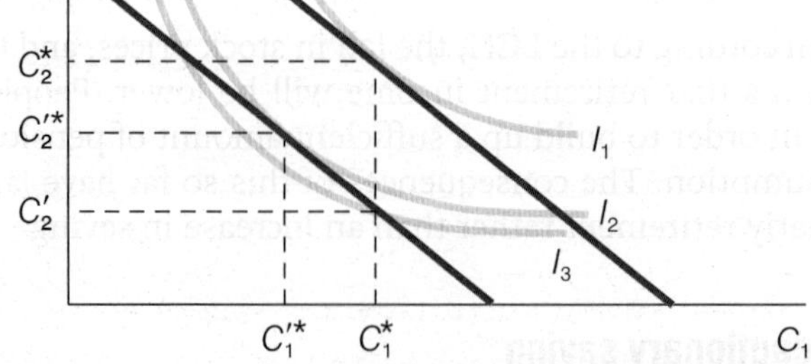

Global application 2.4 (continued)

pensions. The upshot is that the level of contributions required for maintaining retirement income has increased – implying that higher saving rates or longer working lives are necessary.

Under the predictions of the optimal consumption model, the effects of the fall in the stock market are shown in Figure 3. In early 2000, the representative consumer can be thought of as consuming the current and future bundle consumption bundle (C_1^*, C_2^*). This where the representative household is on the highest indifference curve (I_1), subject to its lifetime resource constraint.

Following the fall in stock market values and the diminishing value of pension fund assets, the wealth of the representative household falls. The optimal response would be to maximize utility subject to the new, lower, lifetime resources constraint, giving consumption levels (C_1', C_2'). As the household is now on a lower indifference curve (I_2), the fall in wealth has clearly reduced lifetime utility/well-being. Present consumption falls, as households realize they must save more in order to preserve adequate consumption levels in the future.

Living in denial might be extremely harmful in terms of welfare. If the representative household continues to consume at the level C_1^*, they would only have adequate resources to consume at C_2'in retirement. This combination of lifetime consumption would lower welfare even further, moving the representative household on to the lower indifference curve, I_3.

Failing to respond to the recent developments in the pensions situation is clearly sub-optimal. The real fear is that if households are myopic and do not make adequate provisions, this outcome is a distinct reality. The worry for policy makers is the difficulty in encouraging young people to start saving for their retirement in 30 to 40 years' time. Given that their myopia is likely to harm their and society's welfare, is there a need for government policy to enforce adequate savings?

Global application 2.5

Empirical evidence on consumption and stock markets in the US

The dramatic movements in the stock market during the second half the 1990s and the beginning of the new millennium have ignited policy makers' interest in the link between consumption and wealth, and particularly consumption and stock market prices.

Figure 4 plots the recent history of real personal disposable income, consumer expenditure, and net wealth of the household sector in the US. There is a clear long-run association between consumer expenditure and disposable income, but the trends in these series have been dwarfed by recent movements in household net wealth.

Net wealth is simply the difference between the financial assets and liabilities of the household sector. The sharp rise during the later part of the 1990s, and the subsequent fall during the first two years of the new millennium, coincide with movements in the stock market. This period represents the technology bubble and its unwinding. The value of equity markets during this period was largely driven by new technology firms. Advances in Information and Communication Technologies (the ICT Revolution) were expected to usher in a new golden economic era for the US economy characterized by high productivity growth. This justified a rise in equity prices, but a bubble arises when price increases develop a momentum of their own and prices rise for no other reason than investors expecting them to rise further in the future. The bubble manifested itself particularly in internet companies, giving rise to an episode

2

Global application 2.5 (continued)

Figure 4 Real personal disposable income, consumer expenditure and net wealth of the US household sector

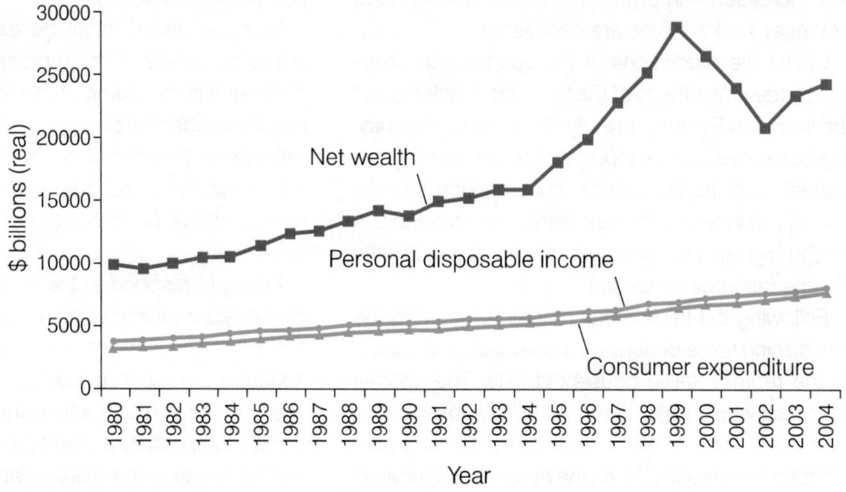

known as *dot com mania*. The consequence of bubbles is that stock markets became overvalued compared to fundamentals such as corporate earnings and eventually a correction will occur. In Figure 5 it is obvious that there is a high correlation between household net wealth and household equity wealth.

Despite the large swings in equity prices, the impact on consumption was less marked. Although that is not to say it wasn't significant. It is difficult to make out in Figure 5, but it is the case that household consumption grew relatively robustly during the late 1990s. Estimates by Ludvigson and Steindel (1999) suggest that in the US the household marginal propensity to consume out of net wealth is approximately 0.05. This seems fairly small but when we are considering trillion dollar changes in equity values, this amounts to a significant effect on consumer expenditure. However, the low responsiveness of consumer expenditure to wealth is puzzling considering that the propensity to consume out of disposable income has been calculated to be around 0.7.

The low propensity to consume out of wealth, and particularly to stock market movements, is not uncommon throughout the world. This is mainly because share ownership by households is not that significant, so a strong link is not to be expected. However, in the US, share ownership is relatively widespread, so other factors must be accountable.

One explanation is that stock markets are notoriously volatile, which makes it hard for households to judge the permanency of price movements. This would justify a cautious response in consumer expenditures. It could even be the case (although unlikely) that the household sector realized that the bubble had over-inflated asset prices and their long-run true value was considerably lower than currently stated. As consumption decisions under the PIH are based on long-run values, this too would generate a more moderate response in consumer expenditures.

The final reason why consumption may be fairly unresponsive to equity price movements is related to the way households hold equity wealth. The composition of different types of assets is broken down in Figure 6.

First, a large proportion of household equity wealth is held in pension and life insurance funds. This wealth is highly illiquid, meaning that a household cannot easily consume out of it. This should be obvious for life insurance reserves, and cashing out pension funds normally involves financial penalties.

Global application 2.5 (continued)

Figure 5 Real net wealth and equity wealth of the household sector in the US

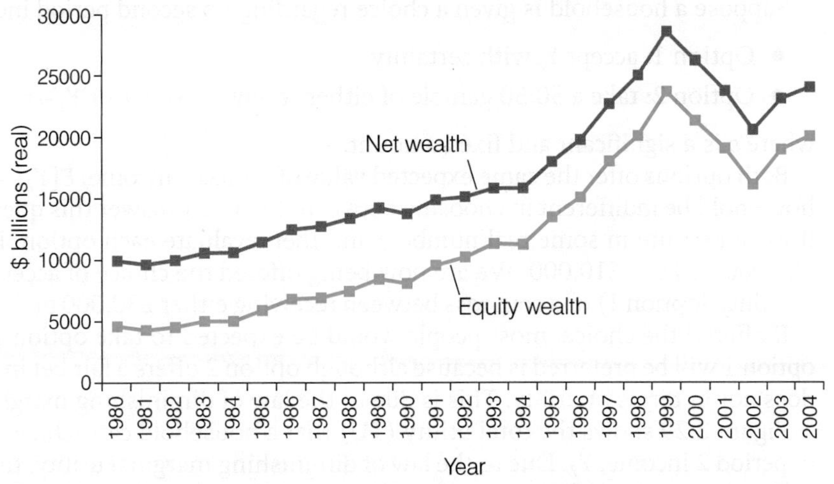

The other forms of household equity holdings are more liquid. Bank personal trusts and mutual funds both represent indirect holdings of equities, in the sense that a household deposits funds at a financial institution, which then invests on behalf of the household. Direct holdings of equities represent the assets directly held by the household sector in its own portfolios, and in Figure 6 it is clearly the case that this has been an important part of movements in equity wealth. These are fairly liquid so there should be little barrier to using this wealth to fund consumption.

Households may be unwilling to use their private portfolios to fund consumption as they are seen as investments or savings for long-term purposes. Specifically, this is most likely to be for retirement, but also for the college education of children. In this case, equity holdings are inherently ring-fenced from the resources available for consumption.

Figure 6 Composition of household equity wealth in the US

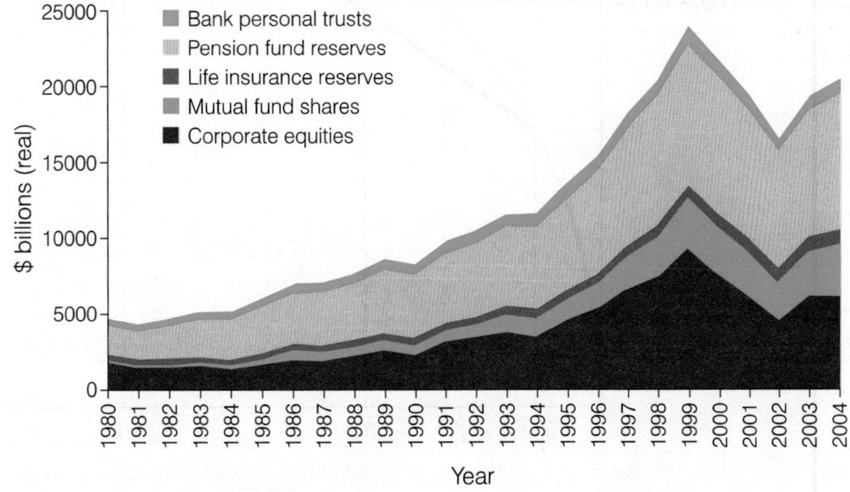

2

for a rainy day' argument is at the heart of the theory of **precautionary saving**. Up until now, it has been argued that households either know their future income with certainty, or if it is uncertain, they just evaluate it according to its expected value. In other words, the uncertainty itself has no consequence whatsoever. In actuality, we may beg to disagree and a simple example might explain why.

Suppose a household is given a choice regarding its second period income:

- Option 1: accept Y_2 with certainty
- Option 2: take a 50:50 gamble of either receiving $Y_2 + \varepsilon$ or $Y_2 - \varepsilon$

where ε is a significant and fixed amount.

Both options offer the same expected value of period 2 income, $E[Y_2] = Y_2$, so should the household be indifferent in choosing between them? To answer this question it might help if we substitute in some real numbers and then evaluate each option. For example, $Y_2 =$ £20,000 and $\varepsilon =$ £10,000. We are now being offered the choice of accepting £20,000 with certainty (option 1) or a coin toss between receiving either £30,000 or £10,000 (option 2).

If offered the choice, most people would be expected to take option 1. The reason why option 1 will be preferred is because although option 2 offers a fair bet in terms of money, it does not in terms of utility. This is due to the law of diminishing marginal utility.

Figure 2.29 shows the total utility (TU) that a household can achieve from a given level of period 2 income, Y_2. Due to the law of diminishing marginal utility, the extra (marginal) utility that is gained from an extra ε of income is less than the utility that would have been lost if this amount were taken away. For this reason, the total utility from consuming at Y_2 exceeds the average total utility gained from a 50 per cent chance of consuming at either $Y_2 + \varepsilon$ or $Y_2 - \varepsilon$.

Figure 2.29 Certainty equivalence

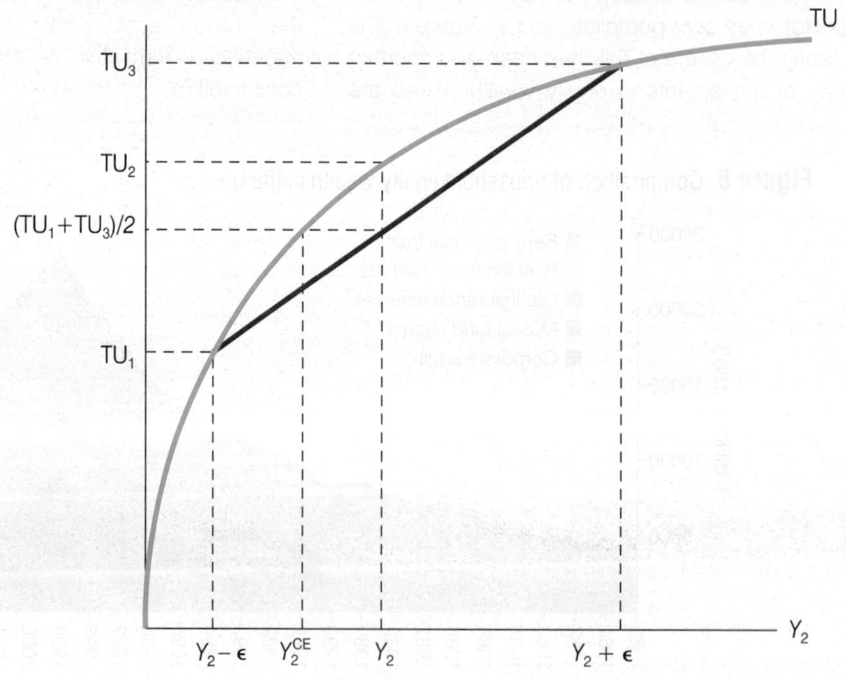

The *certainty equivalence* of the gamble presented as option 2 is the certain amount of income where the household is indifferent between accepting or undertaking the gamble. It is clear that the certainty equivalent of a gamble is less than the expected value of the gamble, $Y_2^{CE} < Y_2$. The difference between the two reflects the amount of money that the household would be willing to pay to avoid facing the uncertainty. This principle has a clear application in insurance markets where people are prepared to pay premiums to avoid certain risks.

An increase in uncertainty about future income by reducing its certainty equivalence would have the same effect as a fall in its expected future value. Current consumption will fall and the saving ratio will rise, as households transfer resources to the future in order to cover the effects of uncertainty. Precautionary saving may provide an additional reason as to why the saving ratio may share a similar trend to the rate of unemployment (see Figure 2.18). Higher unemployment not only leads to lower expectations of future income, it may also increase its uncertainty.

Global application 2.6

The econometrics of the permanent income hypothesis

The permanent income hypothesis (PIH) argues that households are rational in choosing the pattern of consumption over their lifetime in order to maximize their total lifetime utility. As a result, the path of consumption reflects the household's expectations of current and future resources, not just current income. If the household's preferences obey the law of diminishing marginal utility of consumption, then the optimal consumption path will involve using saving and borrowing to smooth consumption over the life cycle.

In a seminal paper by Robert Hall (1978), he argues that if the PIH is correct, then changes in consumption over time should be unpredictable. This is because at any instance the future path of consumption already reflects the household's complete information, so the only thing that will lead to a change in consumption is the arrival of new information that was previously unknown. Therefore, consumption should follow a process known as a *random walk*:

$$C_t = C_{t-1} + \varepsilon_t$$

This states that consumption this period is equal to consumption last period plus a random error term, ε_t. The change in consumption ($\Delta C_t = C_t - C_{t-1}$)is then simply equal to this unpredictable random error process:

$$\Delta C_t = \varepsilon_t$$

It is a fairly undisputable fact that measures of permanent income and consumption rise over time (see Figures 2.5 and 2.15), so a more accurate description of consumption might be a *random walk* with drift process:

$$\Delta C_t = \mu + \varepsilon_t$$

This states that the change in consumption is equal to a constant μ plus the random error term, so consumption will move in a random manner around a trend line. Empirically, this is more believable and fits in with the idea of the short- and long-run consumption functions in Figure 2.15. The bottom line is that consumption will rise over time in line with the trend growth in permanent income, but in the short run there will be transitory fluctuations around this trend growth rate reflecting the arrival of new information on factors that determine lifetime resources.

Robert Hall's argument is that testing for the existence of the PIH simply involves testing consumption for the presence of a random walk. More specifically, changes in consumption should be unpredictable so other factors such as interest rates and the change in disposable income should be insignificant. The common approach is to test whether or not consumption responds to known changes in income (ΔY_t):

2

Global application 2.6 (continued)

$$\Delta C_t = \mu + \beta \Delta Y_t + \varepsilon_t$$

If the above equation is estimated econometrically, and the coefficient β is found to be statistically different from zero, then this prompts a rejection of the PIH. Consumption is proved to respond to predictable changes in income, but under the PIH this cannot be the case because consumption decisions should already incorporate this information, so β should be zero.

Empirical evidence tends to imply that $\beta > 0$, leading to a rejection of the PIH. This is known as the *excess sensitivity* puzzle, as consumption is responding to more than it should if households were rational maximizers of lifetime utility. There have been many hypotheses for the empirical breakdown of the PIH, and Muellbauer (1994) is a good reference on this discussion. However, despite there being many possible explanations for the excess sensitivity puzzle, the presence of borrowing constraints and precautionary saving motives have been widely accepted as the prominent reasons behind the failure of the PIH.

For the predictions of the PIH to hold true, then households must be able to borrow and save in an unconstrained way in order to smooth consumption. If, though, there are borrowing constraints, then households may find it hard to borrow against future income, in which case consumption becomes inherently tied to current income. For example, if households anticipate higher future income, but are unable to borrow sufficiently to smooth consumption, then they will only be able to increase current consumption once the future increase in income comes to fruition.

Following Campbell and Mankiw (1989), the excess sensitivity puzzle can be accounted for by arguing that there are two types of households: those that are constrained and those that are unconstrained in credit markets. The unconstrained households can borrow and save at will so the pattern of their consumption (ΔC_t^U) will follow the random walk with drift process implied by the PIH:

$$\Delta C_t^U = \mu + \varepsilon_t$$

The constrained households, though, will see the pattern of their consumption (ΔC_t^C) defined by changes in their income (ΔY_t^C):

$$\Delta C_t^C = \Delta Y_t^C$$

Therefore, in the economy the total change in consumption will reflect the total changes in the consumption of the constrained and unconstrained households:

$$\Delta C_t = \Delta C_t^C + \Delta C_t^U$$

Substituting in the consumption functions of the constrained and unconstrained households into the above then:

$$\Delta C_t = \Delta Y_t^C + \mu + \varepsilon_t$$

It is assumed that the proportions of constrained and unconstrained households are λ and $(1 - \lambda)$, respectively. If the constrained households hold the proportion λ of total income, then it is the case that $\Delta Y_t^C = \lambda \Delta Y_t$. If we substitute this relationship into the above:

$$\Delta C_t = \mu + \lambda \Delta Y_t + \varepsilon_t$$

There is a very obvious relationship between this equation and the test for the PIH. All that is required to explain excess sensitivity and a rejection of the PIH is for $\lambda > 0$, that is, the presence of credit-constrained households in the economy.

The precautionary saving motive is also a factor that accounts for the empirical breakdown of the PIH. It is a fair assumption that a household's degree of risk aversion falls with their wealth, which can be financial wealth, but also human wealth, such as income. It would therefore be expected that as income increases, risk aversion falls. As a result, the level of precautionary saving will fall and consumption increases. This restores a link between changes in consumption and changes in current income, so $\beta > 0$.

Carroll (1997) offers an interesting description as to how the precautionary saving motive leads to a rejection of the PIH. In his theory of *buffer stock saving*, he argues that households with low wealth are unwilling to borrow as the effects of unexpected income shocks could lead to very low consumption. That is because the household could face the chance of both low income and loan repayments. Therefore, if λ represents the proportion of these households in the economy, the PIH will fail as long as $\lambda > 0$. Households choose to behave as if they are credit-constrained, even though they might not face formal credit constraints.

Summary

- This chapter has outlined and applied the main theories accounting for consumer behaviour.
- The traditional model is the Keynesian consumption function which suggests that aggregate consumption is a linear function of the aggregate income. The empirical evidence tends to support a strong link between consumption and disposable income, especially over time.
- Shifts in the consumption function can result from any factor that changes autonomous consumption. These will predominately include wealth changes, implying a higher level of consumption at every level of income.
- Objections to the Keynesian consumption function arose because it was at odds with the theory of rational choice. This argues that consumption decisions should be consistent with households maximizing lifetime utility, with the main result being that households will base consumption decisions not just on current income but a longer-term view of income. It also opens up an appealing role for expectations to play in determining consumption.
- Due to the law of diminishing marginal utility of consumption, the optimal consumption model suggests that households will save and borrow in order to smooth consumption over their lifetimes. This is the main prediction behind the permanent income hypothesis and the life cycle hypothesis.
- The optimal consumption model can also be applied to analyse a multitude of factors that might produce changes in consumption. These include: changes in expected future income; changes in interest rates, which produce income and substitution effects and have different consequences for savers and borrowers; and changes in wealth, which might arise from movement in house or financial assets prices.
- The impact of uncertainty on the precautionary saving motive was introduced, which showed that the effects of greater uncertainty over income can have similar effects as lower expectations.

Key terms

Aggregate demand
Autonomous consumption
Consumption
Intertemporal budget constraint
Keynesian consumption function/absolute income hypothesis
Lifetime utility function
Marginal propensity to consume (*mpc*)
Marginal propensity to save (*mps*)
Permanent income hypothesis/life cycle hypothesis
Precautionary saving
Present discounted value
Saving

2

Review questions

1. Suppose that instead of a lump sum tax the government introduced a proportional income tax such that:

$T = tY$, where t is the marginal tax rate.

   a. What is the new relationship between income and disposable income?
   b. Draw the new consumption function and describe what happens when the tax rate changes. How will changes in the marginal tax rate affect the savings ratio (S/Y)?
   c. The government decides that a uniform tax rate is unfair. Incomes below $\bar{Y}$ are to be taxed at the rate t_l and incomes above are to be taxed at the higher rate t_h: what effect will this have on the shape of the household consumption function? How might the progressiveness of the tax system affect the level of aggregate consumption?

2 A household with a life expectancy of five years expects to receive the following income stream at the end of the year.

Year	Income
1	£20,000
2	£25,000
3	£25,000
4	£30,000
5	£40,000

The prevailing interest rate is 10 per cent.

   a. What is the expected present discounted value of the household's income?
   b. The interest rate falls to 5 per cent, what is the new present discounted value of the household's income?
   c. The interest rate starts off at 10 per cent, but after two years falls to 5 per cent. Then, during the final year the interest rate rises sharply to 15 per cent. Recalculate the expected present discounted value of the income stream with this path of interest rates.

3. Using the optimal consumption model, explain what effect the following will have on current and future consumption:
   a. a severe recession is expected with 100 per cent certainty
   b. a severe recession is expected with a small likelihood of 10 per cent
   c. a cut in interest rates
   d. an announcement that building societies intend to convert to banks and make windfall payments to depositors
4. Explain why a net borrower might become a net lender, but a net lender will never become a net borrower, following a rise in interest rates.
5. Why might spending on durable goods be more closely related to current income than spending on non-durable goods and services?

More advanced problems

6. Suppose a household's preferences over consumption in two periods can be represented in a utility function of the following form:

$$U(C_1,C_2) = U(C_1) + \rho U(C_2)$$

   a. What interpretation can be given to the parameter ρ? If the law of diminishing marginal utility of consumption holds, how will the parameter ρ affect the shape of the household's indifference curves?
   b. A household has income in each period of Y_1 and Y_2, and faces an interest rate of zero? Show the intertemporal pattern of consumption when:

$$\rho = 0.1$$
$$\rho = 1$$
$$\rho = 5$$

   c. Does the inadequacy of personal saving for retirement undermine the personal income and life cycle hypotheses?

7. A household receives income in period 1 of Y_1 and income in period 2 of Y_2. A bank, however, charges a different interest rate on savings (r_s) and loans (r_l).
   a. Why might a bank charge a higher rate of interest on loans than it pays on savings accounts?
   b. Draw the intertemporal budget constraint when $r_l > r_s$.
   c. In an attempt to attract new savers, the bank raises the interest rate on saving accounts to r_s', so that $r_s < r_s' < r_l$. What will the new intertemporal budget constraint look like? What effect will this have on the intertemporal consumption pattern of households? Will it depend on whether the household was initially a net saver or a net borrower?

8. As an election approaches, the government wishes to stimulate the economy by boosting current consumption. In order to achieve this, it has proposed an immediate and one-off tax cut. Explain how the following factors might affect the success of the policy:
   a. households are permanent income consumers
   b. the economy consists of a large number of credit-constrained households
   c. the tax cut produces a 'feel good' factor leading to a change in preferences towards current consumption
   d. the general public are aware that the government has financed the tax cut through borrowing, which must be repaid with interest after the election.

9. 'Different theories of consumption behaviour mainly reflect different assumptions about the quality of capital markets.' Discuss.

10. Explain why households pay insurance premiums. What effect might a reduction in social security payments have on the saving ratio?

For further resources, visit
http://www.thomsonlearning.co.uk/chamberlin_yueh

3 Investment

Learning objectives

- Define investment and its three main components
- Use the optimal capital stock model to explain changes in business investment
- Construct Tobin's q as a forward-looking model of business investment
- Identify the factors that are responsible for inventory investment
- Understand the main determinants of residential investment
- Explain how the supply of investment finance can determine aggregate investment

3.1 Introduction

Private investment represents additions to the nation's **capital stock**. Investment is important because it plays a dual role in the economy. First, it is part of **aggregate demand**, so it enters the circular flow of income and determines output movements in the short run. Second, by augmenting the nation's stock of productive assets, investment is central to the determination of long-run economic growth.

Although investment expenditures constitute a much smaller part of aggregate demand than consumption, the pace and pattern of business investment is central to the understanding of economic activity. As Figure 3.1 shows, investment is much more volatile than both consumption and GDP. Also, investment is often seen to be a leading indicator of GDP, meaning that changes in investment predict future movements in output. Empirical evidence leads us to believe that investment may be an important factor in accounting for business cycles.

Components of private investment

The three main components of private investment are fixed business investment, residential investment, and changes in the stock of inventories. The relative size and recent trends of each of these components are shown in Figure 3.2.

Fixed business investment This represents expenditure by firms on additions to their capital stock. A firm's stock of capital is all the physical assets at its disposal which can be used to produce output, including items such as machinery and computer hardware. In terms of size, this is the most important component of private investment, so its analysis will be the main focus of this chapter.

Inventory investment Inventories are stocks of inputs, semi-completed and finished goods that firms hold in storage. There are many reasons why firms may hold these, which will be

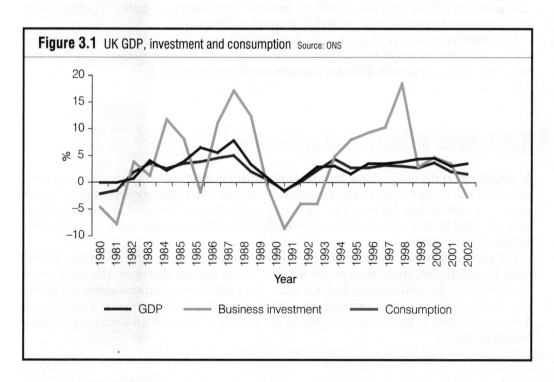

Figure 3.1 UK GDP, investment and consumption Source: ONS

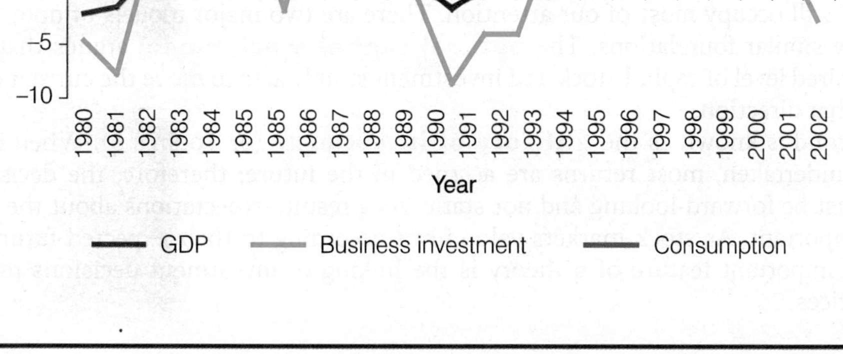

Figure 3.2 Components of private investment Source: ONS

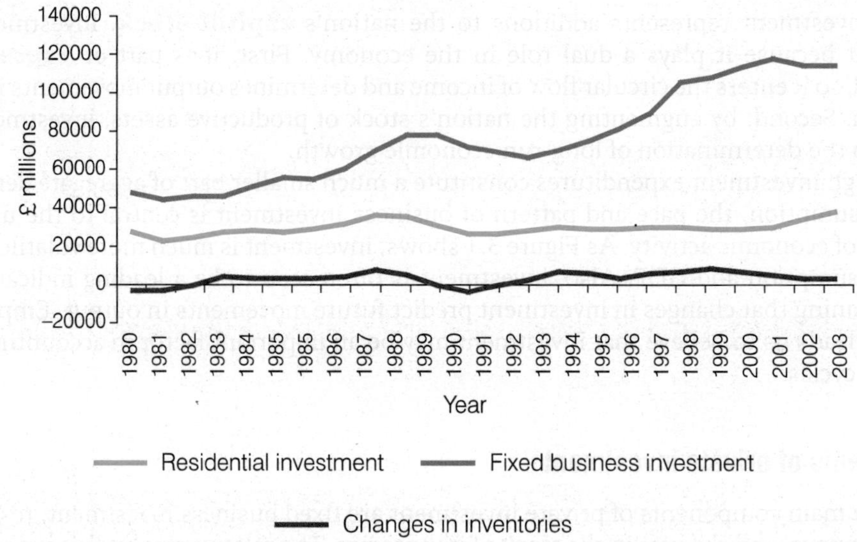

discussed briefly in the chapter. Although changes in inventories are only a small component of total investment expenditures, they are believed to be highly pro-cyclical and may account for much of the volatility that is seen in investment expenditures.

Residential investment This refers to investment on improving or building residential property. This is slightly different from the previous two components as it is not strictly undertaken by private business. However, because it represents a significant proportion of total investment expenditures, we feel it deserves some analysis.

The main focus of this chapter is to introduce the major models of investment, and explain what factors might be important in determining private investment. The best way to do this is to analyse each different component of investment in turn.

3.2 Theories of fixed business investment

As mentioned at the outset, fixed business investment is the most important part of investment and will occupy most of our attention. There are two major models of note, which share very similar foundations. The **optimal capital stock model** argues that firms have a desired level of capital stock and investment simply acts to move the current capital stock in that direction.

The second is known as the **q theory of investment** (or Tobin's q). When investment is undertaken, most returns are accrued in the future; therefore, the decision to invest must be forward-looking and not static. As a result, expectations about the future will be important. As stock markets value firms according to their expected future cash flows, an important feature of q theory is the linking of investment decisions to stock market prices.

3.2.1 Optimal capital stock model

This is also referred to as the **neoclassical model of investment**. The model argues that firms will settle on an **optimal level of capital stock**, which is where profits are maximized. Investment is then determined implicitly; it is the required additions or reductions to the capital stock that move it from its current to its optimal level.

Profit maximization is the key to the investment decision. Firm profits are calculated in the conventional way – as total revenue minus total costs:

$$\Pi = TR - TC \tag{3.1}$$

Total revenue is found by multiplying the output of the firm (Y) by the price at which it is sold (P).

$$TR = PY \tag{3.2}$$

The relationship between a firm's output and its inputs of capital is described by a production function: $Y = F(K)$. The production function simply states how much output can be produced at each level of capital stock. A common assumption is that the production function experiences *diminishing returns* to capital. This means that as a firm installs more and more capital, output will rise but at a declining rate. Consequently, the production function will have a concave shape as shown in Figure 3.3. The typical justification would be that the firm installs the most productive capital first, so as the capital stock gets larger the added capital is relatively less productive. Also, as the capital stock gets larger it may become harder to integrate and install new capital, or to manage it effectively so its marginal addition to total output falls.

Figure 3.3 The production function

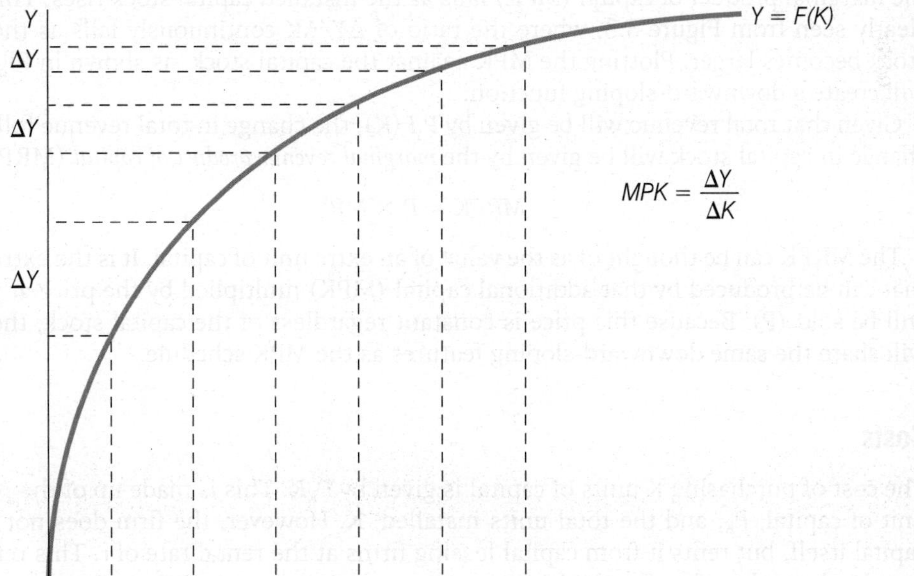

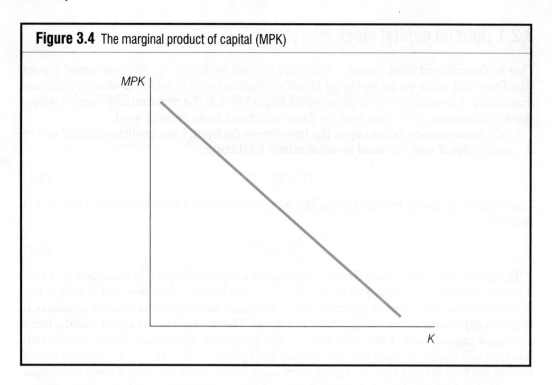

Figure 3.4 The marginal product of capital (MPK)

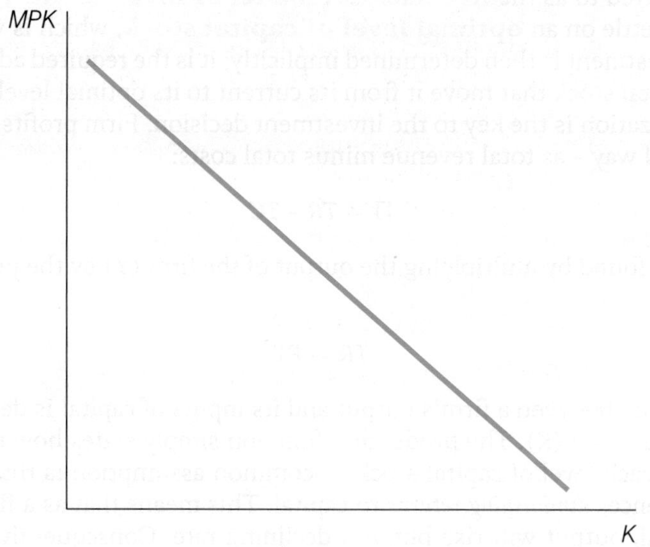

The **marginal product of capital** (MPK) tells us how total output changes when the capital stock changes by one unit:

$$MPK = \frac{\Delta Y}{\Delta K} \qquad (3.3)$$

As the production function displays diminishing returns to capital, it must be the case that the marginal product of capital (MPK) falls as the installed capital stock rises. This can be clearly seen from Figure 3.3, where the ratio of $\Delta Y/\Delta K$ continuously falls as the capital stock becomes larger. Plotting the MPK against the capital stock, as shown in Figure 3.4, will create a downward-sloping function.

Given that total revenue will be given by $P.F(K)$, the change in total revenue following a change in capital stock will be given by the *marginal revenue product of capital* (MRPK):

$$MRPK = P \times MPK \qquad (3.4)$$

The MRPK can be thought of as the value of an extra unit of capital. It is the extra output that can be produced by that additional capital (MPK) multiplied by the price at which it will be sold (P). Because this price is constant regardless of the capital stock, the MRPK will share the same downward-sloping features as the MPK schedule.

Costs

The cost of purchasing K units of capital is given by $P_K K$. This is made up of the price of a unit of capital, P_K, and the total units installed, K. However, the firm does not buy the capital itself, but rents it from capital leasing firms at the rental rate of r. This rental rate can simply be thought of as the interest rate.

Let us explain this a little more. An investor can always deposit its funds in a financial institution, such as a bank, and earn a rate of return determined by the interest rate. Alternatively, the investor could purchase some capital and rent it to a firm. If credit markets are competitive, so no excess profits can be earned by lenders, the rental rate charged would be equal to the opportunity cost of investing those funds elsewhere, which is the rate of interest. Even if the investor deposited its funds in the bank, the bank would then need to reinvest these funds in order to earn a return sufficient to pay the interest they owe to depositors. This could be done again by investing in capital and renting it to firms. If the bank were to break even, then the rental rate on capital would be equal to the interest rate.

The rental rate of capital would differ from the interest rate if the capital stock was non-durable, meaning that it was prone to wearing out. If a proportion, δ, of the capital stock were to depreciate every period, these costs would be passed on to the firm. In this case, the rental rate of capital in competitive financial markets would be $(r + \delta)$. In what follows, we assume away these depreciation costs so the rental rate of capital is just equal to the interest rate.

Therefore, the total cost of installing K units of capital is:

$$TC = rP_K K \tag{3.5}$$

The *marginal cost* of capital is the cost of installing one extra unit of capital stock:

$$MC = rP_K \tag{3.6}$$

This cost is constant and does not change with the amount of capital stock already installed.

Profit maximization

Given the costs and revenues involved in installing capital, the firm can work out the size of the capital stock that would maximize its profits:

$$\Pi = PF(K) - rP_K K \tag{3.7}$$

The solution to this problem is most easily shown by using the diagram in Figure 3.5.

In panel (a) of Figure 3.5, the total revenue and total cost at each level of capital stock is plotted. Profits will be maximized at K^*, where the vertical distance between these two is the greatest. This will be where the slopes of the two functions are equal to each other.

When the slope of the total revenue and total cost functions are equal, it is the same as saying the marginal revenue product is equal to the marginal cost. In panel (b) of Figure 3.5, it can be seen that the profit maximizing capital stock, K^*, is where these two schedules intersect one another.

Therefore, profits will be maximized at the level of capital stock where the marginal revenue product of capital is equal to the marginal cost, or

$$P.MPK = rP_K \tag{3.8}$$

The intuition behind this result is simple. Suppose the marginal revenue product exceeds the marginal cost: $(P.MPK < rP_K)$. Increasing the capital stock by one unit would increase revenues by more than costs, so total profits will rise. From Figure 3.5, if $K < K^*$, then increasing the capital stock would raise total profits.

Likewise, suppose the marginal revenue product of capital were less than the marginal cost $(P.MPK < rP_K)$. Increasing the capital stock by one unit would reduce profits as the additional revenues gained would be exceeded by the costs. In fact, reducing the capital stock would lead to an improvement in profits because the total revenues lost would be lower than the total costs saved. From Figure 3.5, if $K > K^*$, then reducing the capital stock would raise profits.

It is only at the level of capital stock, K^* $(P.MPK = rP_K)$, where there is no incentive for the firm to invest or disinvest. Having established the optimal capital stock, this model predicts that firm investment will be given by a simple relationship:

$$I = K^* - K \tag{3.9}$$

Figure 3.5 Optimal capital stock

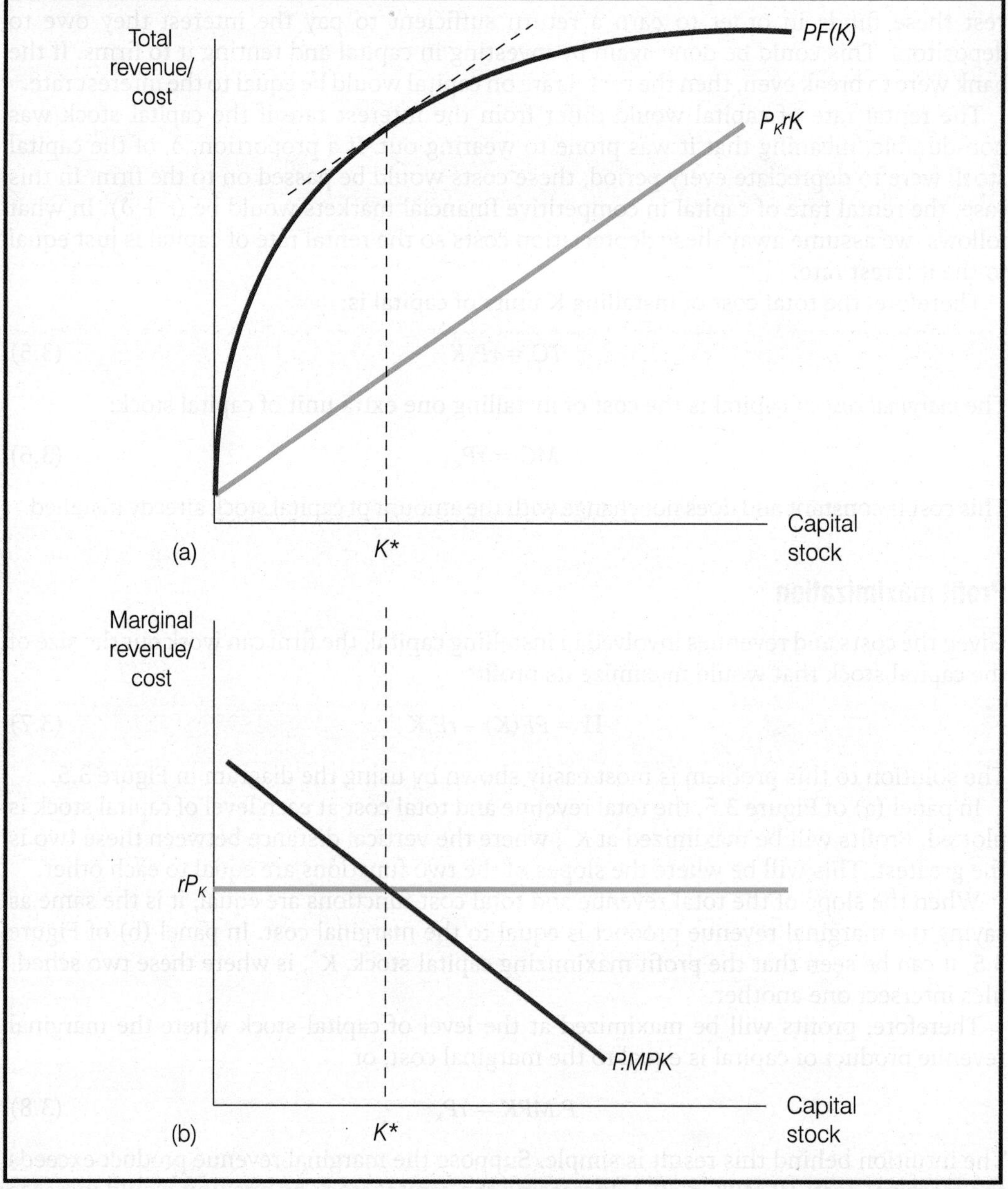

Investment is determined implicitly by the firm seeking to move its capital stock towards its optimal level.

What factors affect investment?

If all firms were at their optimal (profit maximizing) level of capital stock, then what factors would lead to a change in investment? This simple model argues that anything which leads to a change in the level of the optimal capital stock will induce investment. There are several factors that may be of interest here.

Productivity shocks

An increase in productivity, through either a technological advance or an improvement in efficiency, means that a higher level of output can be produced at each level of capital stock. This is shown graphically in panel (a) of Figure 3.6. The entire production function, and therefore the revenue function, will simply shift upwards.

As a consequence, the MPK and MRPK schedules will also shift outwards (panel (b) of Figure 3.6), reflecting the fact that each additional unit of capital will now produce more output and revenue, respectively. The positive productivity shock would therefore increase the optimal level of capital stock ($K_1^* \rightarrow K_2^*$) and stimulate investment ($I = K_2^* - K_1^*$). Of course, a negative productivity shock would be expected to have entirely the opposite effect.

Figure 3.6 An increase in prices or productivity

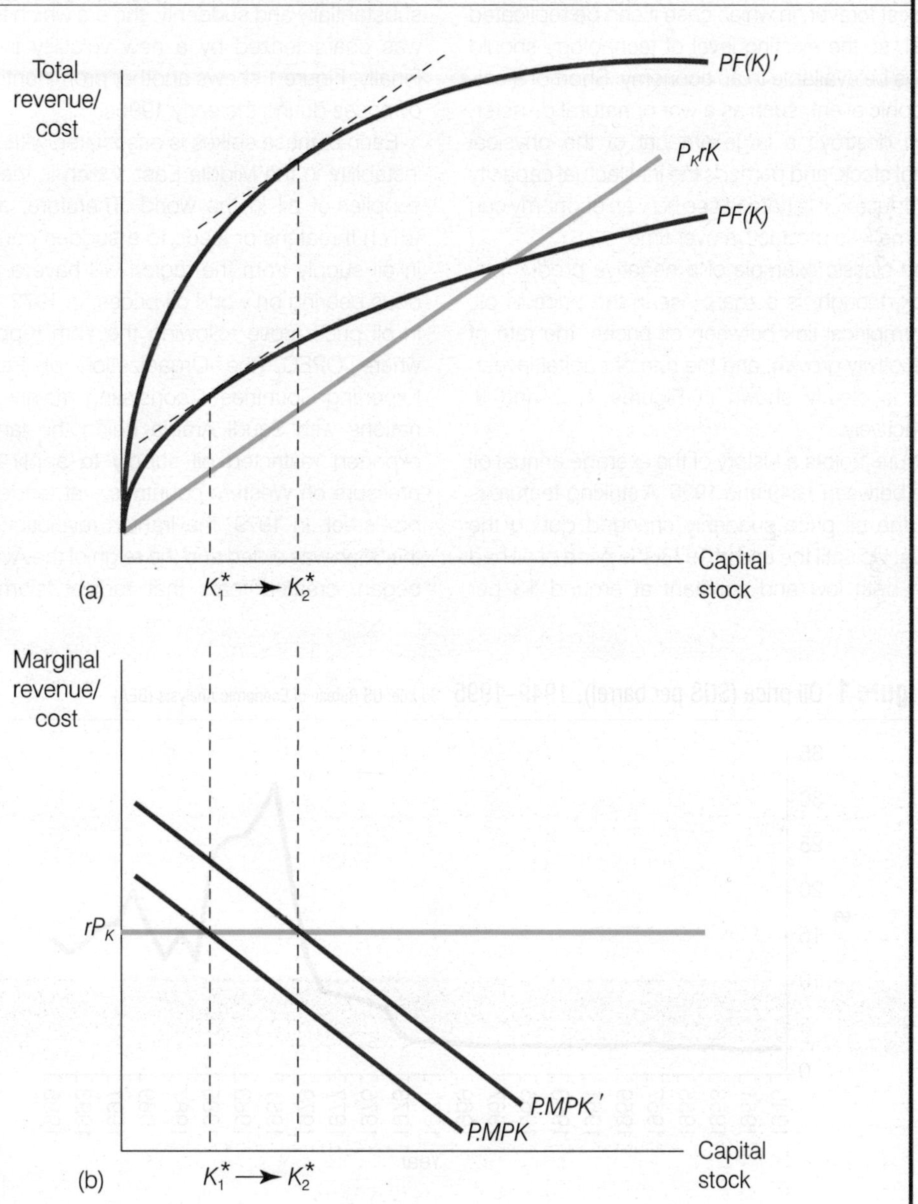

3

Global application 3.1

Oil prices, productivity and capital investment

It is hard to think of what might cause a negative productivity shock. We usually think of an increase in productivity as being associated with technological advance, so a negative productivity shock implies that technology has regressed. However, once a new technology is developed, its blueprints will exist forever, in which case it can be replicated at will, so the existing level of technology should always be available to an economy. Short of a catastrophic event, such as a war or natural disaster, which destroys a large amount of the physical capital stock, and perhaps the intellectual capacity to produce it, it is hard to see how an economy can become less productive over time.

The classic example of a negative productivity shock, though, is a sharp rise in the price of oil. The empirical link between oil prices, the rate of productivity growth, and the rate of capital investment is clearly shown in Figures 1, 2 and 3, respectively.

Figure 1 plots a history of the average annual oil price between 1949 and 1995. A striking feature is how the oil price suddenly changed during the 1970s. Up until the end of 1973, the price of oil had been both low and constant at around $3 per barrel. However, during the latter months of 1973, oil prices doubled to around $7 per barrel. Another dramatic increase in oil price occurred in 1979, when prices jumped to over $20 per barrel, and continued to rise to in excess of $30 per barrel over the next two years. Not only did the oil price rise substantially and suddenly, the era which followed was characterized by a new volatility in prices. Finally, Figure 1 shows another prominent spike in oil prices during the early 1990s.

Each of these spikes is associated with political instability in the Middle East, which is the largest supplier of oil in the world. Therefore, anything which threatens or leads to a sudden contraction in oil supply from the region will have a tremendous bearing on world oil prices. In 1973, the rise in oil price arose following the Yom Kippur war, where OPEC (the Organization of Petroleum Exporting Countries – consisting mainly of Arab nations with Saudi Arabia being the largest oil exporter) restricted oil supply to apply political pressure on Western countries that tended to be pro-Israel. In 1979, the Iranian revolution, where the Shah was exiled and the reign of the Ayatollahs began, created fears that radical Islam would

Figure 1 Oil price ($US per barrel), 1949–1995 Source: US Bureau of Economic Analysis (BEA)

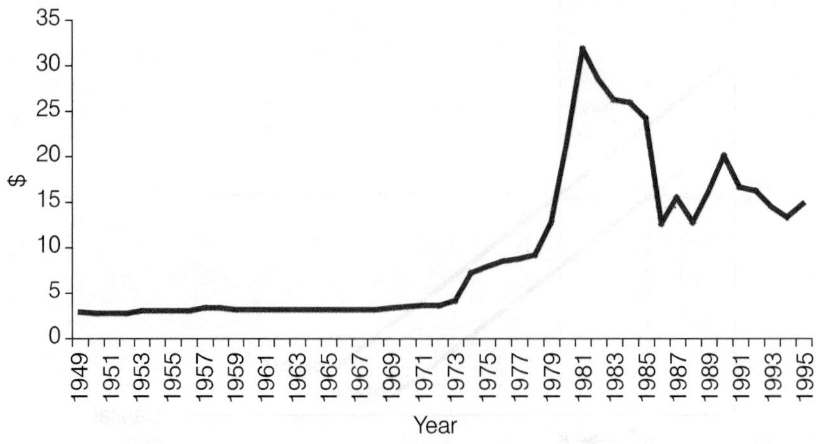

Global application 3.1 (continued)

come to control the gulf region and with it the world's oil supply. This was compounded by the start of the Iran-Iraq war, with Iraq being one of the largest oil producers in the region. Finally, the peak in the early 1990s reflects the period leading up to and during the first Gulf War. The Iraqi invasion of Kuwait and the accompanying threat of invading Saudi Arabia once again meant that instability led to a very insecure supply of oil.

In Figures 2 and 3, these three periods of sharp oil price rises are associated with negative rates of capital productivity growth and investment. How can we explain this possible linkage?

For capital to operate efficiently, it requires a cheap and stable source of energy. If energy suddenly becomes very expensive, then capital which could previously have been run efficiently may now be too expensive to run. In this case, the firm which owns the capital will limit its use. This implies that the same stock of capital is now effectively producing less, which will show up as a fall in capital productivity. And because firms are using less

Figure 2 Productivity growth of capital in the UK, 1970–1995

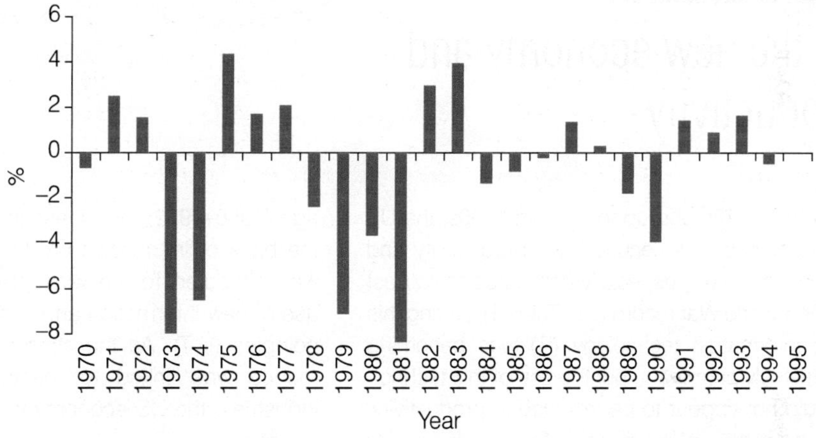

Figure 3 Rate of growth in the capital stock in the UK, 1970–1995

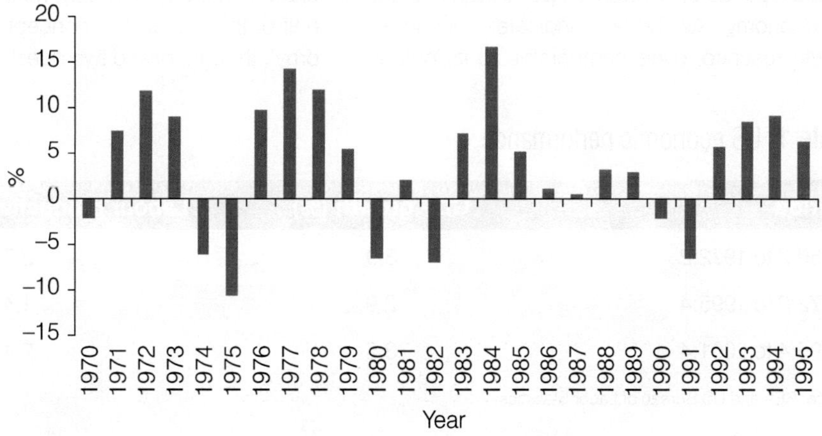

3

Global Application 3.1 (continued)

capital, they are unlikely to invest in new capital stock. In fact, they will just let their stocks run down through depreciation or through premature scrapping, which explains the negative capital investment growth rates in Figure 3.

Therefore, the productivity of the capital stock is largely driven by the cost of energy, of which the oil price is typically the main driving force. The post-Second World War period of 1950–1973 is seen historically as a golden economic era – marked by high productivity and output growth. Cheap and readily available oil was certainly one of the contributing factors. However, the profitability of much of the capital stock installed over this period was dependent on this trend continuing. The sudden hikes in oil prices in the 1970s brought an end to the years of impressive economic performance and brought in a new era of stagflation, which was characterized both by high inflation and high unemployment.

Global application 3.2

IT, the new economy and productivity

Since the 1970s and up to the mid-1990s, the US economy had experienced poor productivity and economic growth, especially compared to its post Second World War record (see Table 1). During this time, information technology (IT) was becoming increasingly prominent, but the use of this technology did not appear to be reflected in productivity. This gave rise to the famous Solow productivity paradox which stated that 'computers can be seen everywhere apart from the productivity figures'.

In contrast, the second half of the 1990s represented a period of spectacular performance of the US economy. As Table 1 indicates, economic growth reached levels comparable to its golden age (1950–1972), and these in turn were built on the back of impressive productivity figures. This was attributed to the widespread adoption and use of new information and communication technologies (ICT). As the strong economic performance was linked to these new technology industries, the US economy was dubbed a 'new economy'.

Figure 4 plots an index of equipment and software investment in the US economy, clearly showing that the improvement in productivity coincided with a surge in investment during the second half of the 1990s. The concept of the 'new economy', though, raised two questions. First, why did

Table 1 US economic performance

Period	GDP growth (%)	Labour productivity growth (%)
1950:2 to 1972:2	3.9	2.7
1972:2 to 1995:4	2.9	1.4
1995:4 to 2001:4	3.5	2.4

Source: BEA and US Bureau of Labor Statistics

3

Global application 3.2 (continued)

Figure 4 Index of US equipment and software investment Source: BEA

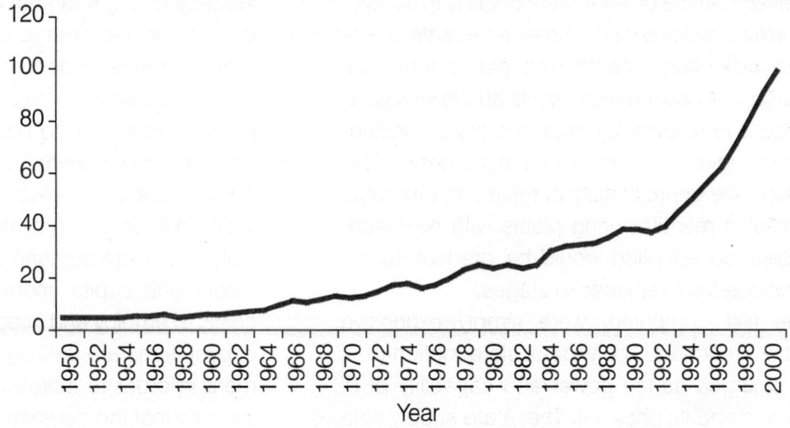

it take so long for IT to impact on productivity? Second, how sustainable will the improvement in productivity be?

IT and firm productivity: general purpose technologies

General purpose technologies (GPT) can be described as enabling technologies that open up new opportunities rather than providing complete, final solutions. As they have wide applications and can promote a high degree of complimentary innovations, the contribution of a GPT is much larger than simply the cost of the capital investment multiplied by its rate of return. For this reason GPTs are considered to be drivers of economic growth, with examples including power delivery systems, such as the waterwheel, steam, electricity, internal combustion; and also organizational technologies, such as the factory system and mass production.

A paper by Paul David (1990) likens the effect of information technology to that of the electric dynamo. First, it is a general purpose technology that is likely to lead to a surge in productivity growth and second, like the electric dynamo, there was a considerable time lag between developing the technology and its impact on productivity measures.

The electric dynamo had two main effects on productivity. The first was a direct effect in reducing power requirements in factories that had previously relied on steam or water power. The second, and perhaps more significant, was that the dynamo enabled more efficient organization structures for factories. Previous factory designs based on steam- or water-powered belt and shaft systems had to build in a compact fashion as large power losses were experienced over long belts; however, the dyanamo enabled each machine to be powered individually. Therefore, factories could be organized to take advantage of mass production techniques, particularly by taking advantage of economies of scale through breaking down the production of goods into specialized stages over an assembly/production line.

Computers have the capabilities to achieve the same type of things. As computers become cheaper and more powerful, their value is enhanced by managers inventing new processes, procedures and organizational structures to take advantage of these capabilities.

The adoption of IT and its effect on productivity follows a similar lag to the process of electrification to factories. Fifty per cent diffusion rates of electrification in manufacturing came four decades after the first power station opened. This largely

3

Global application 3.2 (continued)

reflected supply side issues. The first power plants were regionally isolated and small in scale. However, with the development of grids to transfer electricity over longer distances, it became possible to build large, centralized plants that took advantage of economies of scale and lower costs. The lag also reflects demand-side issues, including the regime transformation hypothesis. This points to the unprofitability of replacing otherwise serviceable manufacturing plants with new technologies, so adoption would be gradual as old technologies are replaced in stages.

The first computers were simply expensive number crunchers. The wide-scale adoption of IT only emerged as the power and capability of IT improved and its price fell. These are supply side issues, but demand side factors are also likely to be important. The demand for IT is likely to arise through the development of complimentary technologies, with perhaps the best example of this being the Internet. If the adoption of new technologies is partly dependent on the emergence of these complimentary technologies, then it is unsurprising that there are significant lags between the emergence of a GPT and its effect on the economy.

The case against the IT miracle

The belief in the existence of a 'new economy' and optimism that it would lead to a sustained surge in productivity growth was not uniformly held. In particular, Robert Gordon (2000) believes that it is unlikely to have a long-term effect on productivity growth and is only a transitory phenomenon.

His argument takes three strands:

1) **Productivity growth is cyclical**: Standard measures of productivity are usually calculated by taking a ratio of output and inputs. A productivity increase is recorded if the same value of inputs leads to an increase in output. However, because over the economic cycle output and inputs do not move in a perfectly synchronized manner, recorded levels of productivity are also likely to change.

   When economic growth takes off, firms typically meet extra demand by using their current labour and capital more intensively. As it is costly to employ and integrate new labour and capital, firms are unlikely to undertake investment in order to increase capacity until they are sure that the increase in demand is permanent. In addition, increasing capacity cannot be done instantaneously, so input changes tend to lag behind output changes. Likewise, when demand and output fall, firms will not scrap capital or make employees redundant straight away.

   Therefore, it is natural for productivity to be pro-cyclical. The upturn in measured productivity in the US during the second half of the 1990s coincides with stronger growth in the economy (see Table 2). Gordon's argument partially makes the case for output driving productivity rather than the other way around.

2) **Limited spillover effects**: The IT sector has had limited spillover effects on the rest of the economy. Gordon's second point is that the impact of IT on the productivity figures largely consists of a gain in productivity in the computer hardware sector itself (e.g., production

Table 2 US multifactor productivity and output growth

Period	Annual % growth of multifactor productivity	Output %
1870–1913	0.47	4.42
1913–1972	1.08	3.14
1972–1995	0.02	2.75
1995–1999	1.25	4.90

Global application 3.2 (continued)

of computers) and from capital deepening (e.g., firm investment in IT elsewhere in the economy). Accounting for this, the impact of IT on productivity on the rest of the economy is limited. Without evidence of large spillover effects on productivity, it is hard to attribute IT with the status of a GPT.

3) **The IT revolution fails to measure up to the great inventions of the past**. Table 2 reports the annual average percentage increase in productivity in the US during several intervals between 1870 and 1999. The improvement in multifactor productivity (productivity of labour and capital) in the 'new economy' era of 1995–1999 is marked compared to the dismal performance during 1972–1995. However, the period 1913–1972 represented a long, sustained period of high productivity growth and has been termed the Golden Economic Era.

Gordon's theory is that this long period of economic growth was driven by a cluster of technological changes that appeared during the last decade of the nineteenth century. The five major inventions were: the generation of electricity; the internal combustion engine; growth of transportation; chemicals, the entertainment and communication industries; and finally improved domestic health and sanitation. The 1913–1972 years represented an extraordinary period, and the slow growth rates from 1972–1995 simply represent a return to normality. Whether or not the IT revolution can drive such a persistent increase in productivity is debatable in Gordon's view. Quite simply, it doesn't measure up to the great inventions of the past.

In Gordon's figures, growth in the non-farm private business sector of the US economy was 1.35 per cent higher per annum during 1995–1999 than 1972–1995. Out of this, 0.54 per cent can be attributed to a cyclical effect, 0.33 per cent to capital deepening from computers and 0.29 per cent to an improvement in multifactor productivity in the computer hardware sector. The remaining 0.19 per cent represents only a small improvement in the structural growth of multifactor productivity. Therefore, the impact of the new economy is much smaller than estimated and is unlikely to have a sustained effect on productivity or economic growth.

Price of output Changes in the price of output would have a similar effect as changes in productivity. The implication of an increase in prices could also be demonstrated using Figure 3.6. The total revenue curve would shift upwards and the marginal revenue product of capital schedule will shift outwards. The consequence will once again be that the optimal capital stock will be higher, thereby encouraging firm investment.

With a positive productivity shock, this occurs because at every level of capital stock more can be produced. With a price rise, the same amount is produced, but it is sold at a higher price. Therefore, the revenues generated from a given level of capital stock will also be higher.

This might account for some of the pro-cyclical nature of investment. When the economy is performing well, aggregate demand may be strong, which supports higher prices and encourages investment. Likewise, in a recession, low demand could lead to poor sales and discounted prices, discouraging investment.

Price of capital goods

The price of capital goods directly affects the cost of the capital stock. Figure 3.7 demonstrates the consequences of an increase in the price of capital, P_K. As every unit of capital is more expensive, the total cost schedule will pivot upwards as seen in panel (a). The marginal cost schedule will also shift upwards because the cost of installing an extra unit of capital is greater (see panel (b) of Figure 3.7). Consequentially, the optimal capital stock and thus investment will fall.

Once it is accepted that the price of capital goods is important, there becomes a role for government policy to influence investment through the use of taxes and subsidies. The cost of capital can be adjusted to reflect the presence of taxes and subsidies:

$$P_K' = (1+\varphi)P_K \tag{3.10}$$

A tax on capital implies that $\varphi > 0$. Consequently, the optimal capital stock and investment will both fall following an increase in these taxes. However, a subsidy, ($\varphi < 0$), would have the opposite effect and could be used to encourage investment.

3

Figure 3.7 Changes in the price or rental of capital goods

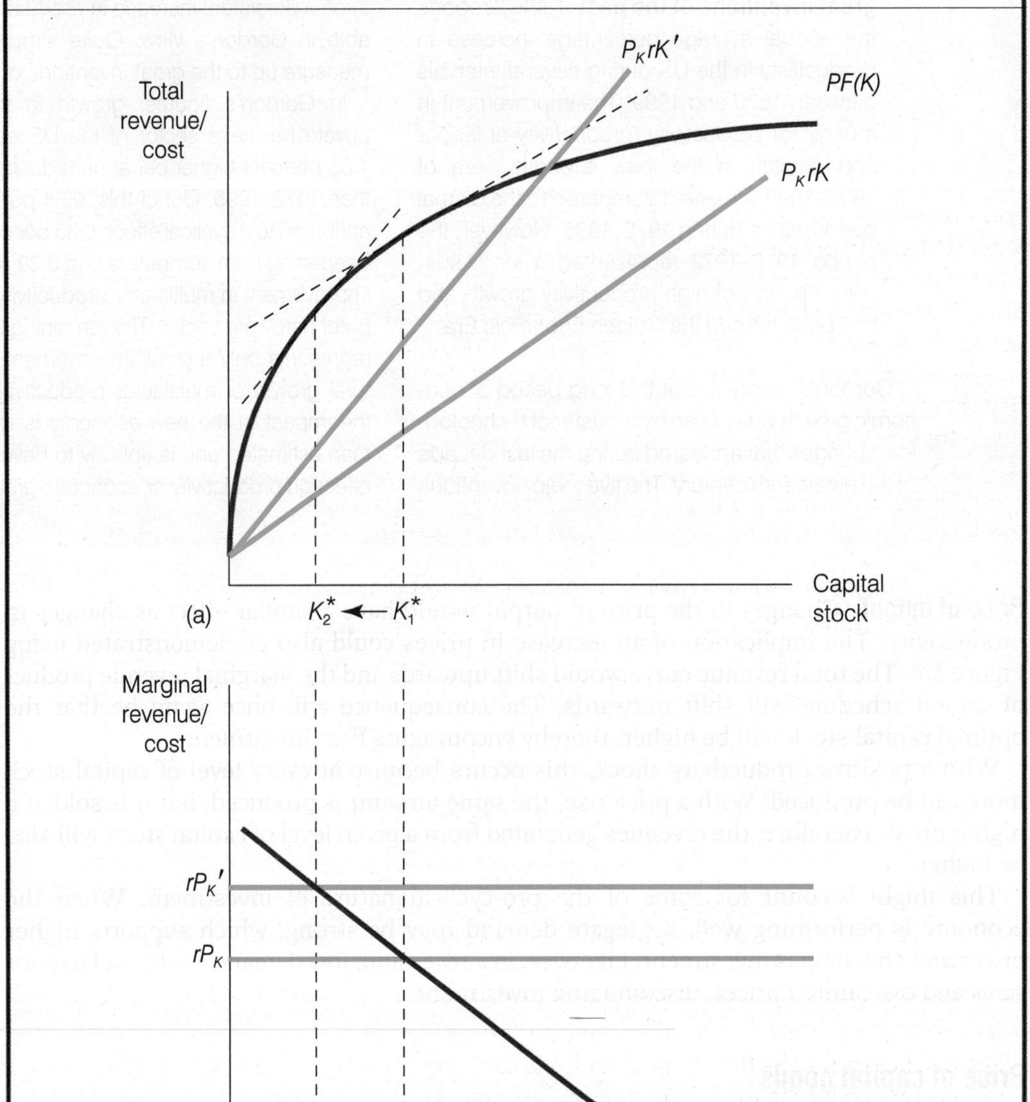

Interest rate changes

Interest rates will affect capital in entirely the same way as changes in the prices of capital goods (see Figure 3.7). The interest rate is seen as the opportunity cost of capital, instead of investing in capital goods there is always the possibility of saving in the bank. Therefore, changes in the interest rate will imply changes in the rental rate of capital.

3.2.2 Tobin's q

The optimal capital stock model offers numerous intuitions as to what might determine investment. However, there are several criticisms that can be made of the model, which may lead us to question its plausibility.

First, the model is not forward-looking, so it does not allow any room for investment to be determined by expectations. Given that investments tend to offer returns over a future period, it appears sensible that investment appraisal would have to be forward-looking. If the value of investments is linked to their expected future returns, then the stock market becomes important. The stock market valuation of a firm depends on the expected future cash flows it will generate. A high stock market value will be indicative of strong investor belief that the firm can make profitable investments.

Second, the capital stock is assumed to always change instantaneously to its new optimal level. This means that investment is exceedingly rapid, even a very large change in the capital stock would be installed very quickly. This does not hold well with actual experience, which suggests that changes in a firm's capital stock are gradual and that investments are implemented over a sustained period of time.

The logic for this is simple: firms cannot change their capital stocks without incurring costs. For example, installing new capital may require staff to be retrained. Making new capital stock compatible with the existing stock could require adjustment costs, and so on. The faster capital is installed, the more likely it is that these installation costs will be higher. Therefore, taking these also into account would justify a slower but more sustained rate of investment.

These two additions are incorporated into a theory known as **Tobin's q**, to which we now turn.

Stock markets and investment

In its most simple of guises, Tobin's q can be written as follows:

$$q = \frac{\text{Market Value of Firm}}{\text{Replacement Cost of Installed Capital}}$$

The market value of a firm is determined by the expected discounted future cash flows that it will generate. The replacement cost of installed capital is simply the price of purchasing that firm's capital stock. Tobin's q is just the ratio of the two.

The market value of a firm may differ from the cost of its physical capital due to intangible assets owned by the firm. These intangible assets might include things such as its technological know-how, reputation, marketing and distribution networks, and management structure. Combining these intangible assets with the tangible assets, that is the firm's stock of physical capital, could create value in excess of the cost of physical capital.

Therefore, changes in q will lead to changes in investment. If $q > 1$, then every £1 of installed capital would create more than £1 in market value. Installed capital is more valuable than uninstalled capital so investment would be positive.

Figure 3.8 q and investment

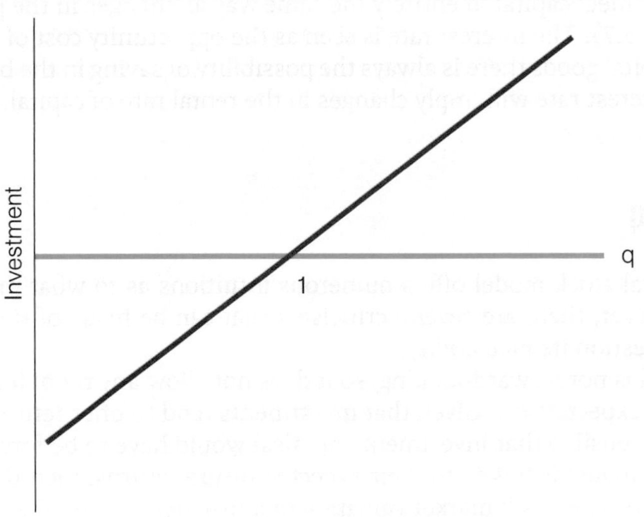

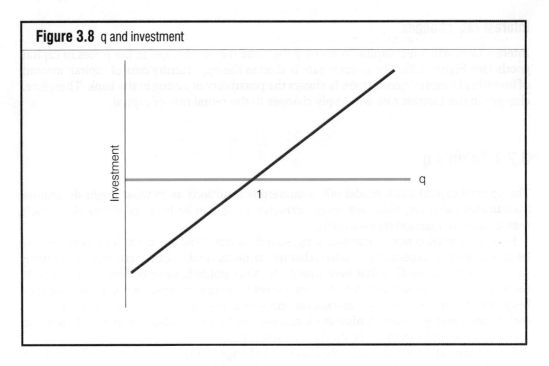

When $q = 1$, every £1 of installed capital will create an additional £1 of market value. In this case, installed and uninstalled capital has the same value and investment would be zero.

Finally, if $q < 1$, then uninstalled capital is more valuable than installed capital. Investment would be negative; a firm would be able to achieve more by selling its physical capital than it would lose in market value. The relationship between q and investment is summarized in Figure 3.8.

Tobin's q argues for a link between investment and the stock market. Owning a share in a company means that you own a fraction of the company, and are hence entitled to a share of any profits in the form of dividend payments. Therefore, the value of a company is determined by the total number of shares and the price of each share. These share prices are in turn determined by demand and supply in stock markets. For example, if investors are confident about the future prospects of a firm

Trading floor of the London Stock Exchange: creating market value.
Source: Kim Sayer/CORBIS

Figure 3.9 Annual changes in investment and stock prices in the UK Source: ONS

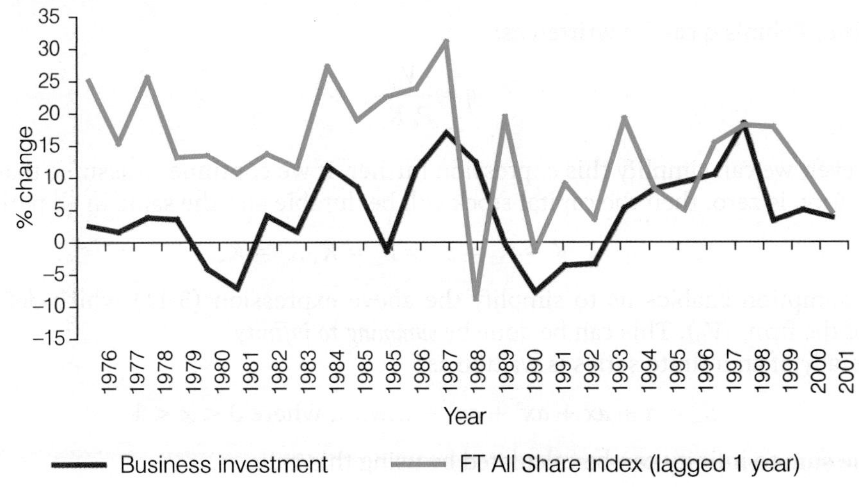

they will anticipate that owning shares in that firm would entitle them to high dividend payments. Therefore, the demand for that company's shares would rise, pushing up its share price and thus increasing its market value.

If it is the stock market that represents the value of a firm, then it is not surprising to expect a linkage between the stock market and investment. Changes in the value of stock markets should be positively correlated with future changes in investment. In Figure 3.9 annual changes of investment and stock prices lagged one year between 1976 and 2001 are plotted for the UK.

This chart shows some evidence supporting Tobin's q. There does appear to be some correlation between movements in the stock market and investment. However, the evidence supporting this relationship is by no means clear cut. This may be for a number of reasons.

First, not all firms are quoted on the stock market. A significant amount of investment is undertaken by these firms, so this would dilute any potential relationship between stock prices and investment.

Second, stock market valuations may be determined by factors other than fundamentals related to a firm's future cash flows. These will be discussed in more detail in Chapter 6, but it is widely recognized that stock markets tend to be fairly volatile. Such an example is clearly evident in Figure 3.9. The large fall in stock market prices in 1988 refers to the 1987 stock market crash (remember that in Figure 3.9 changes in stock market prices are lagged one year).

Tobin's q and the market value of the firm

The market value of the firm is given by the sum of its expected discounted future cash flows. The revenue the firm generates in each period is given as before:

$$P.F(K_t)$$

where K_t is the capital stock in period t.

The value of the firm at the present time (V_0) is given by the present discounted value of all future revenues:

$$V_0 = \frac{P.F(K_1)}{(1+r)} + \frac{P.F(K_2)}{(1+r)^2} + \frac{P.F(K_3)}{(1+r)^3} + \ldots \qquad (3.11)$$

The cost of the initially installed capital stock (K_0) is also as before:

$$P_K K_0$$

Therefore, Tobin's q can be written as:

$$q = \frac{V_0}{P_K K_0} \tag{3.12}$$

However, we can simplify this expression further. If we continue to assume that capital depreciation is zero, then the capital stock will be durable and the same in all periods, so:

$$K = K_0 = K_1 = K_2 = K_3 \ldots = K_\infty$$

This assumption enables us to simplify the above expression (3.11) which defines the value of the firm, (V_0). This can be done by *summing to infinity*.

Generally, if an infinite series is written as

$$S_\infty = a + ax + ax^2 + ax^3 + \ldots\ldots\ldots, \text{ where } 0 < x < 1$$

then the sum to infinity can be calculated by using this rule:

$$S_\infty = a\left(\frac{1}{1-x}\right)$$

For the series describing the discounted future cash flows of the firm, (V_0):

$$a = \frac{P.F(K)}{(1+r)} \quad x = \frac{1}{(1+r)}$$

Therefore,

$$\frac{1}{1-x} = \frac{1}{1-\frac{1}{1+r}} = \frac{1}{\frac{1+r}{1+r} - \frac{1}{1+r}} = \frac{1}{\frac{r}{1+r}} = \frac{1+r}{r}$$

Hence,

$$V_0 = \frac{P.F(K)}{(1+r)} \times \frac{(1+r)}{r} = \frac{P \cdot F(K)}{r} \tag{3.13}$$

Substituting for this in the definition of q, (3.12) results in:

$$q = \frac{P.F(K)}{rP_K K} \tag{3.14}$$

The same factors that cause a change in investment in the optimal capital stock model are likely to cause a change in investment in the q-based model. Investment is likely to rise if productivity or output prices rise, or the interest rate falls – these factors will lead to an increase in the market value of the firm. A fall in the cost of capital goods would also encourage investment.

The main feature added by q-based models is that current investment will also be influenced by the future values of these variables. For example, an expected future technological breakthrough will raise future cash flows and the current market value of the firm. In this way, current investment can be driven by expectations about the future.

Adjustment costs

It is assumed that firms will invest or disinvest depending on whether q is greater or less than 1. However, what factors might account for the speed at which this investment takes place?

The analysis so far has assumed that the marginal cost of changing the capital stock is simply given by the price of a unit of physical capital, P_K. This may not be entirely accurate. The firm may also face costs in installing or uninstalling capital. For example, any new additions would have to be made compatible with the existing stock, and this may incur costs.

It is plausible to argue that these installation costs increase with the size of the investment. It is much more expensive to make large wholesale changes to the capital stock then just small fine-tuning changes. Therefore, installation costs will increase with the rate of investment. Also, installation costs are transitory; once the capital is installed no further installation costs are levied.

The presence of these installation or adjustment costs suggests that it would be optimal to make small changes to the capital stock. Adding this insight to the q theory enables us to write down a rule that determines investment:

$$I = \frac{1}{\theta}(q - 1) \tag{3.15}$$

Investment will increase when $q > 1$ and fall when $q < 1$. The parameter θ reflects installation costs. As these rise, investment will respond more gradually.

3.3 Inventory investment

There are several reasons why firms may hold inventories. First, holding stocks of inventories would allow firms to smooth production. Changes in inventories act as a shock absorber to fluctuations in demand. In times of high demand, stocks of inventories will be run down, and in times of low demand stocks of inventories will rise. Production smoothing would be the most efficient way of organizing production. If output were to simply follow the pattern of demand, then the firm would have to incur costs from having to continuously alter their employment of labour and capital. Production smoothing would act to minimize these costs.

Second, holding inventories would enable the firm to avoid stock outs. This is where the firm has to turn away customers because it has no stock to sell. Clearly, stock outs would be poor for revenue.

Production smoothing and the pro-cyclicality of inventory investment

The main rationale for smoothing production is to reduce average total cost over time/the economic cycle. A firm's total cost function is assumed to be convex as shown in Figure 3.10. Convexity implies that the marginal cost of an extra unit of output increases with the level of output. There are many justifications for this. Firms will generally employ the most productive factors of production first, so as output increases, less efficient capital and labour might be used in the production process. If labour inputs cannot be easily adjusted, then producing high levels of output may require existing workers to be employed at more expensive overtime rates. Finally, as the firm grows in size it might become progressively harder to manage, leading to growing inefficiencies.

The convexity of the total costs curve is sufficient reason to use inventories to smooth production. Using Figure 3.10, a firm which sees alternating periods of high and low output, Q_H and Q_L respectively, will also see total cost alternating between TC_H and TC_L. On average, total cost will be given by $(TC_L + TC_H)/2$. However, producing at the average output level $\overline{Q} = (Q_H + Q_L)/2$ would achieve a lower average cost of $\overline{TC}$. Maintaining the average level of output in a fluctuating economy requires the use of inventories. In times of low output, the firm would acquire inventory stocks of $\overline{Q} - Q_L$, which are then run down by $Q_H - \overline{Q}$ in times of high output.

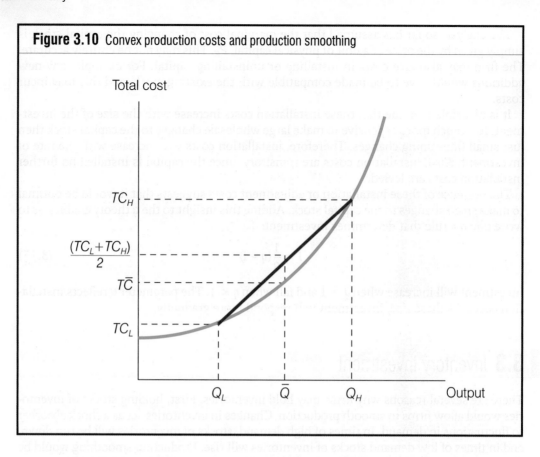

Figure 3.10 Convex production costs and production smoothing

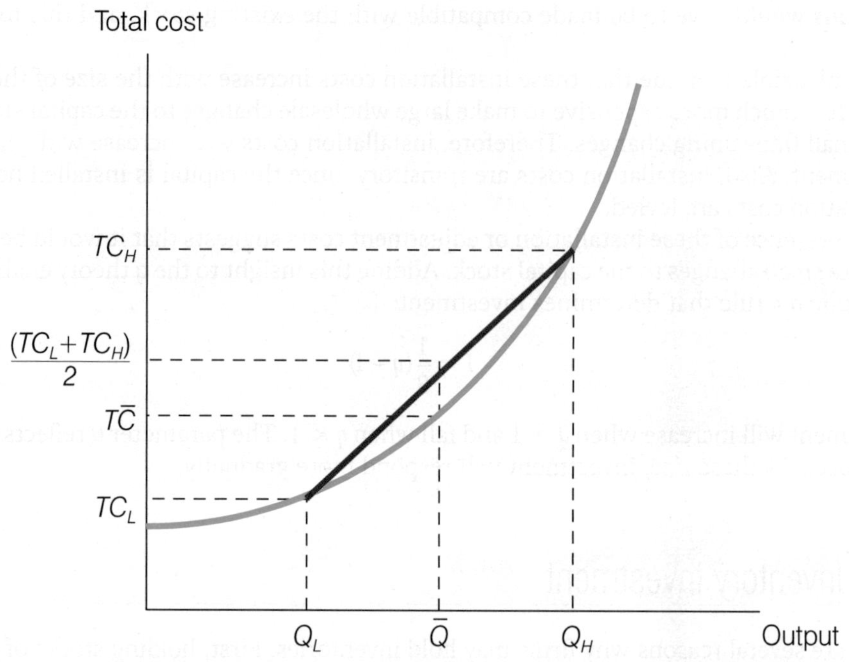

The production-smoothing model implies that inventory investment is constant over the economic cycle. When output is low inventory investment is greater than production demands, so stocks increase. However, when output is high inventory demand can be met by the same level of inventory investment and the use of acquired inventory stocks.

The benefits of production smoothing are directly related to the convexity of the total cost curve. The more convex, the larger the gains from production smoothing. However, as the total cost curve becomes less convex the benefits of production smoothing disappear. In fact, if the total cost function was linear (so it is no longer strictly convex), then the gains from production smoothing would completely disappear. Linear total costs imply constant marginal costs at all levels, so there are no gains to smoothing production.

The cost gains from smoothing production need to be weighed against the costs of storing inventories. As storage costs become more significant, the pro-cyclicality of inventory investment will increase. This is because the cost gains from production smoothing are low because marginal costs are fairly constant, or because storage costs are relatively high so as to offset the cost savings from smoothing production.

Accelerator model of investment

The **accelerator model of investment** could apply to most types of investment, but it is particularly relevant to inventory investment. It states that inventory investment is likely to be highly pro-cyclical. If firms hold stocks of inventories (K_{inv}) proportional to output, then:

$$K_{inv} = \nu Y \quad (3.16)$$

Changes in output would lead to proportional changes in the stock of inventories:

$$\Delta K_{inv} = v\Delta Y \quad (3.17)$$

Therefore, inventory investment (I_{inv}) will respond positively to changes in output:

$$I_{inv} = v\Delta Y \quad (3.18)$$

Workers construct a building in central Bangkok, Thailand
Source: Getty Images

Empirical evidence in support of the accelerator model is offered in Figure 3.11. This is a scatter plot of economic growth and inventory investment, and a clear positive correlation exists. The observed pro-cyclicality of investment tends to reject the production smoothing model.

It is argued that inventory investment fits the accelerator model better than the other components of investment. The reason for the stronger pro-cyclical movement of inventories is most likely due to the fact that there are few installation costs involved with adding to the stock of inventories. Therefore, this investment will respond much more spontaneously to changes in output than fixed business investment.

Figure 3.11 Changes in GDP and inventories in the UK Source: ONS

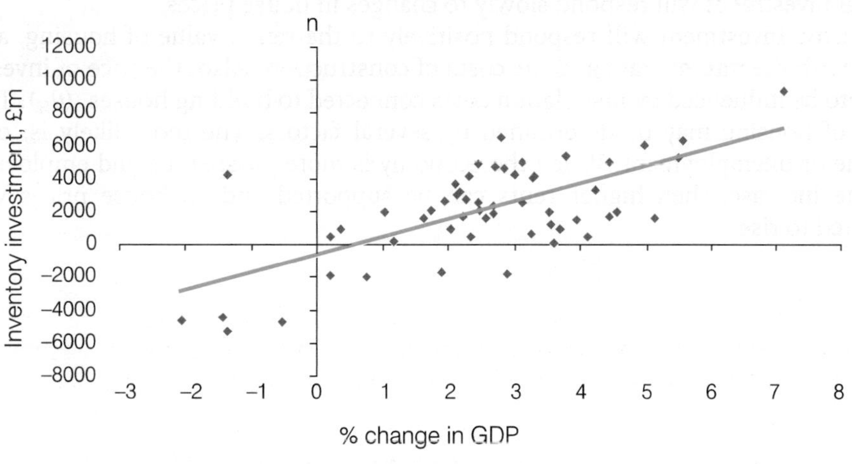

3

3.4 Residential investment

Residential investment refers to expenditure on improving existing dwellings or building new ones. The factors which determine residential investment should conceivably share a common structure with the q theory explaining fixed business investment. From the earlier discussion, we established that according to the q theory, a firm will invest if expected discounted value of the cash flows generated by that investment exceeds the cost of the physical capital required. This maxim should also apply to residential investment.

A house is an asset, so its value should reflect the future discounted value of rents that it earns. Just because a house might be owner-occupied does not mean that this principle no longer applies. Strictly speaking, the owner is also the tenant, so would in effect just be paying rent to himself or herself which would be a needless transaction. However, there is still an implicit rental value involved.

The current value of a house, V_0^H, should be determined by the discounted value of the future rents (R_1,R_2,R_3,...) that it will earn:

$$V_0^H = \frac{R_1}{(1+r)} + \frac{R_2}{(1+r)^2} + \frac{R_3}{(1+r)^3} + \ldots \tag{3.19}$$

If the rent is the same in all periods, $R = R_1 = R_2 = R_3 = \ldots$, then applying the same maths as used to derive equations (3.13) and (3.14) this will simplify to:

$$V_0^H = \frac{R}{r} \tag{3.20}$$

The physical cost of building a house is given by the construction price, P_H. Therefore, a q theory for housing investment (I_H) would take the following form:

$$q_H = \frac{R}{rP_H} \tag{3.21}$$

$$I_H = \frac{1}{\theta_H}(q_H - 1) \tag{3.22}$$

Where q theory fits residential investment quite well is incorporating adjustment costs. Adding to the stock of houses is a timely business and, therefore, it is expected that residential investment will respond slowly to changes in house prices.

Housing investment will respond positively to the rental value of housing, and negatively with the interest rate and the costs of construction. Also, the pace of investment is likely to be influenced by installation costs connected to building houses, (θ_H). The rental value of housing may be determined by several factors. The most likely is, of course, income or unemployment. When the economy is more prosperous and employment and income increase, then higher rents can be supported and so house prices would be expected to rise.

3

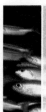

Global application 3.3

Is the UK building enough houses?

As Figure 5 will testify, the UK housing market has been experiencing a long and sustained boom in prices during the late 1990s. Strong economic conditions leading to low unemployment, coupled with historically low interest rates, have supported this large demand-led increase in price. Also, there have been no reported reasons as to why construction costs might have risen, implying that the house price rise has been driven by cost push on the supply side. Therefore, taking these things into consideration and looking at evidence, the value of q for housing investments in the UK should be very high. This would suggest that housing investment would be quite strong.

However, the evidence tends to point an entirely different picture. As Figure 6 shows, new housing construction is extremely low. Despite the large increases in house prices over the period, new housing completions have remained stagnant. What factors might account for this state of affairs?

One explanation is that developers would prefer to build new properties but are constrained by severe planning restrictions. High planning costs would imply that the costs of adjusting the size of the housing stock θ_H are also high. This would explain why residential investment is low even though the q on housing investment exceeds 1.

An alternative, but linked idea, is that housing developers are acting strategically. If planning restrictions have been tight, then the future supply of land for development may be low. Therefore, the most profitable way of developing current sites would be gradually. If all developers were to react to the high prices by rushing through all their development opportunities, the influx of supply would drive prices down. Then with few development opportunities in the future, total profits will be lower. By releasing new builds on to the market slowly and keeping supply low, then higher prices and profits can be achieved over time.

Figure 5 Average UK house prices Source: Council for Mortgage Lenders

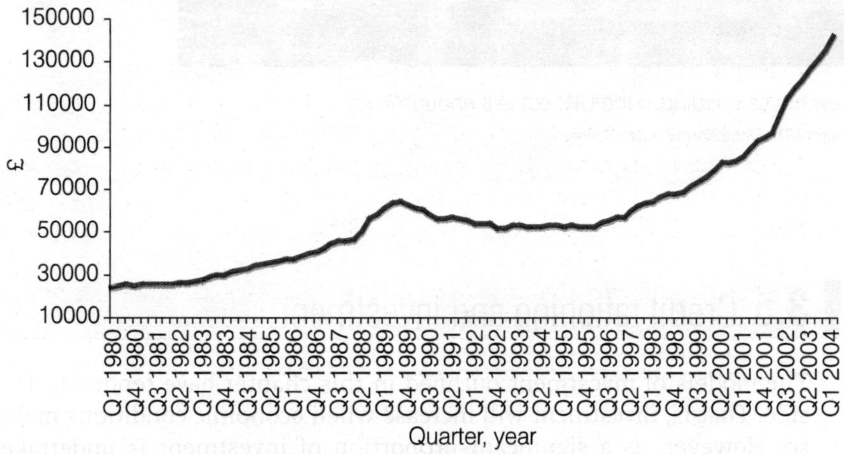

3

Global application 3.3 (continued)

Figure 6 Private sector housing completions in the UK Source: ONS

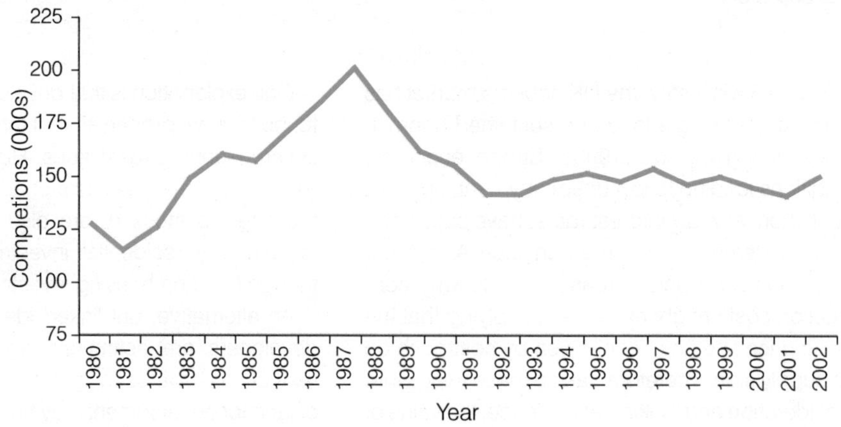

New house building in the UK: but is it enough?
Source: The Photolibrary Wales/Alamy

3.5 Credit rationing and investment

The models of investment outlined in this chapter have tended to focus on the demand side. That is, investment will increase when economic conditions make it profitable to do so. However, as a significant proportion of investment is undertaken using borrowed funds, this view implies that financial markets are always prepared to lend sufficient funds to satisfy investment demand. Once it is accepted that the supply of investment loans might not be perfectly elastic, the supply side might become an important determinant of aggregate investment. For example, if a firm wished to invest but no financial institution was prepared to advance the necessary loans, then investment would be constrained.

Financial markets aim to intermediate between savers and borrowers, but this role is beset with problems of *imperfect information*. A firm borrowing to invest knows far more about the risks and returns of the investment project than the financial institution providing the finance. This scenario where one party in a debt contract has superior information to the other is known as *asymmetric information*.

Asymmetric information can have an important effect on credit markets. Interest rates determine the cost of finance, but are not the only indicator of how financial markets affect investment. The availability of finance is also an important factor. Firms may be prepared to borrow to invest at the prevailing market interest rate but are unable to due to *credit rationing*. There are two reasons why asymmetric information may lead to credit rationing.

- **Moral hazard**: When a debt contract between borrowers and lenders allows for bankruptcy, it increases the incentive of the borrower to undertake risky investments. If high-risk investments come to fruition, they offer high returns to the borrower; but if they fail, then the borrower can avoid repayment by declaring bankruptcy.
- **Adverse selection**: This explains why a lender may prefer to ration credit rather than increase the interest rate. Risk-averse investors who undertake relatively safe but lower-return projects will be driven out of the loans market by an increase in interest rate. Therefore, as the interest rate increases, the lender is left with a higher proportion of riskier investments in their loan portfolios.

The combination of moral hazard and adverse selection can have an important effect on the supply of loans. The first order effect of an increase in interest rates is to increase the supply of loans. This is because every loan made by a financial institution achieves a higher rate of return so the credit supply curve is upward sloping.

However, the second order effect considers the impact of an increase in interest rates on the quality of loans. First, moral hazard implies that as the interest rate increases, the marginal investment project undertaken becomes more risky. In order to accept a loan at a higher interest rate, the project undertaken needs to offer a higher rate of return and therefore is likely to be riskier. Adverse selection implies that as the interest rate continues to increase, those undertaking safer but lower-return investments will be driven out of the market. Consequently, a point is reached where interest rate increases reduce the expected returns from loans due to deterioration in the quality of loans made.

Figure 3.12 plots the supply of credit by financial institutions against the domestic interest rate. At low rates of interest the first order effect dominates, so an increase in interest rates leads to an increase in the supply of loans. In this case, the supply of credit is upward sloping. However, there is a critical level of interest rates where the second order effect begins to dominate and further increases in interest rates reduce loan supply. This is because at higher rates the quality of the loan portfolio declines as it is made up of increasingly risky loans. As a result, the expected returns of the loan portfolio will fall (reflecting higher risks of default) when the interest rate surpasses this critical level and the loan supply curve becomes backward-bending.

Financial institutions would therefore be unwilling to advance loans beyond the level $\bar{S}$. This shows how asymmetric information produces the credit rationing result. This is potentially important as it implies that firms with otherwise profitable investment opportunities will be denied investment finance, and so this supply constraint can lean on the level of investment in the economy. The availability of finance can be just as important as the cost of finance as a determinant of investment.

3

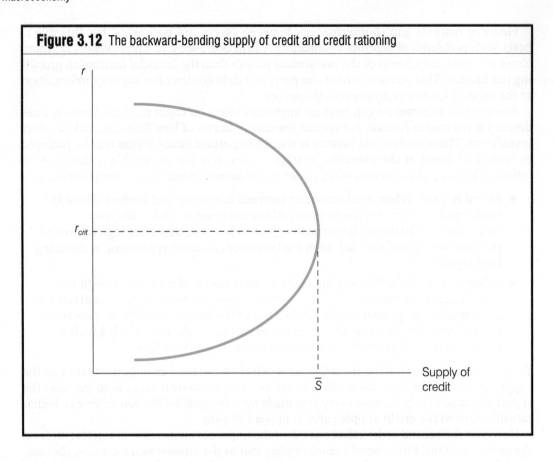

Figure 3.12 The backward-bending supply of credit and credit rationing

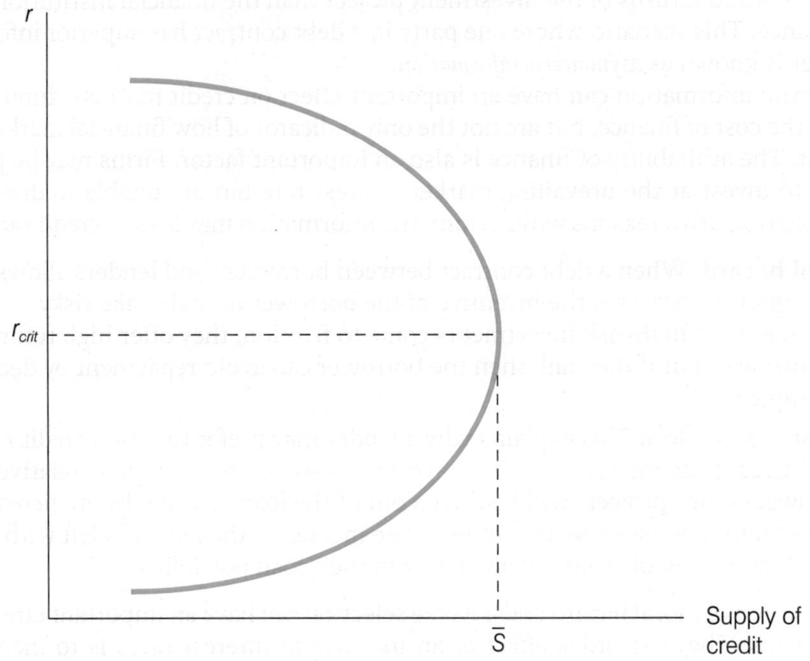

What factors affect the availability of credit?

Looking at Figure 3.12, the supply constraint ($\bar{S}$) is determined by the critical level of interest rate (r_{crit}), where the credit supply schedule becomes backward bending. Therefore, anything which alters the shape of the supply curve is likely to have an effect on the level at which credit rationing becomes relevant.

There are strong grounds for arguing that the availability of finance will be driven in large part by the same factors that determine the demand for investment. Adverse changes in the investment climate, due to any of the factors mentioned previously in this chapter, will lead to a corresponding adverse shift in the risk and return structure of the investment projects in the economy. The supply of loans curve will therefore shift in a manner such as that shown in Figure 3.13. Here, the interest rate at which the quality of the loan portfolio deteriorates falls to (r'_{crit}), so the new rationed level of credit shifts from $\bar{S}_1$ to $\bar{S}_2$.

The relationship between firm profit levels and investment

There is traditionally a link between firm profit levels and investment. First, high current profits might be an indicator of high future profits and therefore encourage investment. Second, high profits breed strong optimism which makes entrepreneurs more likely to undertake investment because they are more confident about the stream of future cash flows their business will generate. Finally, retained profits are a cheap source of investment funds and so enable investments to be made when otherwise the cost of finance would be prohibitive. This is due to the fact that internal funds will not be subject to the fees and service charges, implicit profit margin and repayment schedules that would be imposed if borrowing at commercial rates from financial institutions.

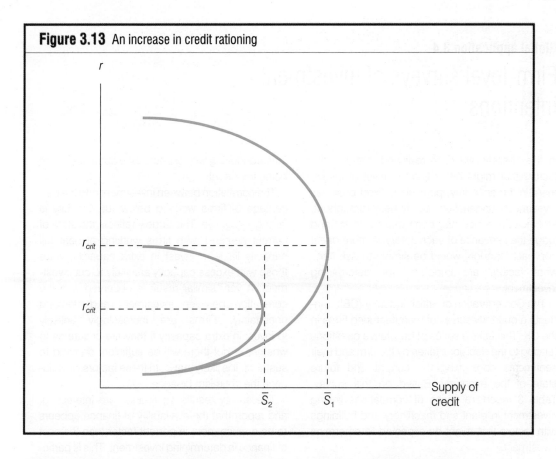

Figure 3.13 An increase in credit rationing

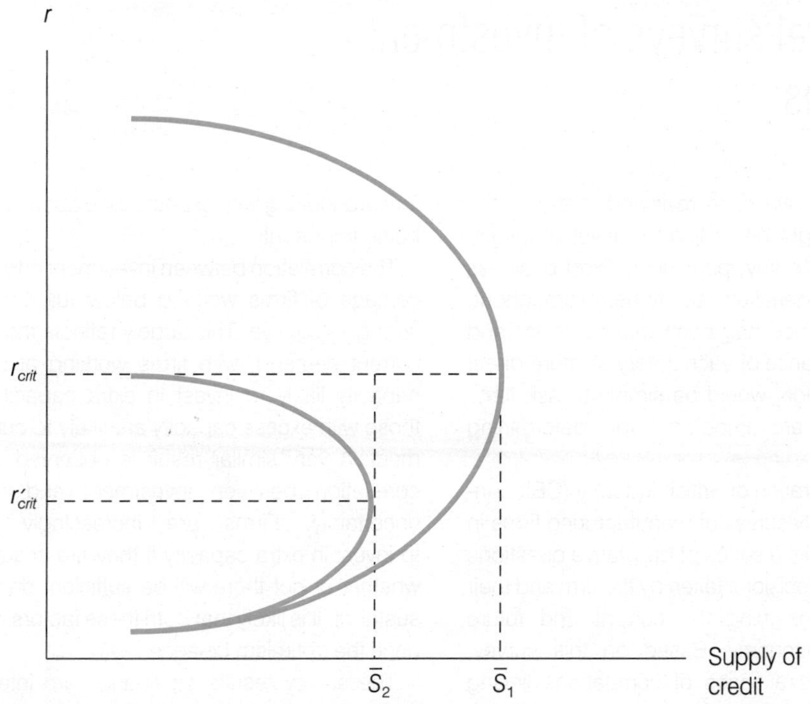

The theory of credit constraints suggest two further reasons why investment might be strongly related to profit levels. The first is that if firms are able to fund investment sufficiently through retained profits, then the supply constraints from financial markets become less binding. The credit rationing result implies that at any point in time there may be profitable investment opportunities that are not funded by financial institutions. The reason comes down to imperfect information, although the firm knows the project to be worthy, financial institutions do not have the same level of information about the financial merits and are thus unwilling to invest.

The credit rationing equilibrium suggests that there are investment projects which are not undertaken under conditions of imperfect information, but which would be undertaken if information was perfect. Therefore, these projects can only be undertaken when firms can build up sufficient internal funds through retained profits to reduce the need for external finance.

The second reason why profits might increase investment is that they reduce the moral hazard problem that helps to create the credit constraint in the first place. If a firm partially funds an investment project through retained earnings it has a greater stake in the project and more to lose if bankruptcy results. Therefore, moral hazard is mitigated and financial institutions would be more prepared to lend.

3

Global application 3.4

Firm-level surveys of investment intentions

In this chapter, we have reviewed many of the factors that might determine the level of investment in the economy, particularly fixed business investment undertaken by firms. Throughout, empirical evidence has been offered to try and judge the relevance of each theory. A more direct approach, though, would be simply to ask firms what factors are important for determining investment.

The Confederation of British Industry (CBI) conducts a quarterly survey of manufacturing firms in the UK. This asks a series of qualitative questions relating to the decisions taken by the firm and their sentiments concerning the current and future state of the economy. Based on this survey, Table 3 reports a series of correlations linking investment in plant and machinery and buildings with factors that might be expected to determine investment.

There is a high positive correlation between investment and optimism. As optimism refers to expectations over the next four months, this provides evidence that investment decisions are forward-looking with expectations about the future being important.

The correlation between investment and the percentage of firms working below full capacity is strongly negative. This largely reflects the state of current demand, with firms working at near full capacity likely to invest in extra capacity, while those with excess capacity are likely to cut investment. A very similar result is observed with the correlation between investment and demand uncertainty. Firms are increasingly unlikely to invest in extra capacity if they are unsure as to whether or not there will be sufficient demand to sustain it. It is likely that both these factors will influence the optimism balance.

The survey results on finance are interesting, and report that the availability of finance appears to be a much more important factor than the cost of finance in determining investment. This is particularly the case with the ability to raise external finance, which suggests that the supply of investment funds and the issue of credit rationing is also an important factor in determining investment.

Table 3 CBI Quarterly Industrial Trends Survey (1982–2005)

Factor	Plant and machinery	Buildings
Optimism balance (next 4 months)	0.66	0.57
% of firms working below capacity	–0.70	–0.76
Uncertainty of demand	–0.71	–0.76
Shortage of internal finance	–0.25	–0.37
Inability to raise finance	–0.68	–0.63
Cost of finance	0.00	–0.03

Summary

- Investment plays a dual role in the economy. As part of aggregate demand it can explain short-run cycles in economic growth, and by adding to the stock of productive capital it might explain long-run economic growth.
- Fixed business investment is the most significant part of investment expenditures. The two main theories accounting for this are the optimal capital stock and Tobin's q models.
- The optimal capital stock model explains investment as the change in the capital stock towards its profit maximization level. Investment will be positively related to the price of output and productivity, and negatively related to interest rates and the cost of capital goods.
- Tobin's q implies that fixed business investment is driven by expectations about the future. If expected future discounted cash flows rise then investment will increase; however, because of adjustment costs, this investment will be spread over time. Tobin's q suggests that there is a direct link between stock markets and investment.
- Inventories are stocks of inputs or semi-finished goods held by firms. Inventory investment is a small part of total investment, but important because it is highly pro-cyclical.
- The accelerator model suggests that investment is driven by changes in output and that inventory investment is highly pro-cyclical.
- Residential investment, particularly in new houses, is a significant part of total investment. If property provides a flow of rents, then it can be treated as an asset with its value determined by the level of its expected future discounted rental payments. For this reason, it is easy to adapt the Tobin's q model to explain this part of private investment.
- Finally, aggregate investment may be determined as much by the availability of investment finance as by the demand for investment. Due to problems of asymmetric information, financial markets have imperfect information about the quality of individual investment projects.
- Although an increase in interest rates implies that the returns from lending finance increase, it might also have a detrimental effect on the quality of loans.
- If the credit supply curve becomes backward bending, then investment finance might be rationed. If these constraints are binding, then it opens up a new channel for investment to be driven by internal finance such as retained profits.

Key terms

Accelerator model of investment
Capital stock
Marginal product of capital (MPK)
Optimal capital stock model or neoclassical theory of investment
q theory of investment or Tobin's q

Review questions

1. What are the three main components of private investment?
2. Using the optimal capital stock model, explain how fixed private investment undertaken by a firm might be influenced by the following:
   a. an increase in productivity
   b. a fall in the demand for the firm's output
   c. a fall in interest rates
   d. a tax on the purchase of new capital goods
   e. an increase in the rate of depreciation.
3. Using the different models of investment, explain why investment may be highly correlated with the business cycle.
4. A firm faces two potential cash flows connected with a new investment. If the project is successful, the investment will generate high future cash flows in the following years. However, if the project is unsuccessful, then the future cash flows will be low.
   a. If the firm believes that the investment project will be successful with probability *p*, (hence unsuccessful with probability *1-p*), how will it evaluate the present discounted value of the investment?
   b. Keynes believed that investment was driven by 'animal spirits' – waves of optimism and pessimism. Explain how this model can be used to show Keynes' idea.
   c. Over time, information concerning the likely success of an investment project becomes increasingly available. How might this affect the path investment takes in the economy? Why might it be significant whether or not there are high sunk costs in making investments?
5. A firm's production technology implies that the production function has a zone in which there are increasing returns to capital. Everywhere else the production function exhibits decreasing returns to scale with respect to capital.
   a. Sketch both the production function described above and the corresponding marginal productivity of capital schedule.
   b. What happens to investment once the capital stock falls within the range of increasing returns to capital?
   c. What explanations might account for a zone of increasing returns to capital in a firm production function?
6. Tobin's q implies a linkage between firm investment and stock prices. How might the following affect the value of q, stock prices and the level of investment?
   a. an increase in the current interest rate paid on bonds
   b. an expected increase in future interest rates
   c. increasing uncertainty about the path the economy will take
   d. an announcement that a competitor firm is experiencing financial difficulties
   e. a government announcement of lower corporation taxes in the future.
7. Two different firms each undertake an identical investment project that yields positive profits. Firm 1 intends to distribute these as dividend payments to its shareholders, whereas firm 2 decides that the profit stream will be used to fund further investment. How might the share prices of the two firms differ?
8. What are the advantages and disadvantages for a firm in holding inventories? What factors might determine the size of the inventory stock that firms decide to hold? What factors determine the sensitivity of inventory investment?
9. Explain how the following might affect residential investment:
   a. increased availability of mortgage credit
   b. an increase in the supply of land for development
   c. new legislation that increases the time for planning decisions to be taken.

3

More advanced problems

10. A firm faces a production function of the form, $Y = AK^{\alpha}$, where Y is output, A is the level of productivity and K is the installed capital stock.
    a. What is the marginal product of capital?
    b. The firm sells its output at price *P*. Calculate and sketch the firm's revenue and marginal revenue product functions.
    c. The firm can rent each unit of capital from a capital leasing firm. The purchase price is P_k and the rental rate is *r*. Derive and show the firm's total and marginal cost of capital.
    d. Calculate the optimal capital stock of the firm, and show how it is affected by a change in any of the parameters mentioned above.
11. Explain how the existence of credit constraints might affect investment in the Tobin's q model. What factors might lead to financial markets imposing credit constraints?

For further resources, visit
http://www.thomsonlearning.co.uk/chamberlin_yueh

4 Government spending, taxation and debt

Learning objectives

- Understand the nature of government spending and taxation
- Differentiate between government deficits and national debt
- Appreciate the implications of fiscal policy
- Using the Keynesian cross model
- Work through the theory of Ricardian equivalence

4.1 Introduction

There are many possible motivations that justify a role for the government in an economy. These include the correction of market failures, such as the provision of public and merit goods like defence, heath and education. Also, the government may commit resources to redistributing wealth through transfer payments, including pensions and unemployment benefits. Although these motivations are important, the reasons for specific spending and taxes are not so much the concern of macroeconomics. From the macroeconomic perspective, we are interested in the role the government may play in regulating the economy through its central position in the circular flow of income.

Government spending is an injection into the circular flow of income. It represents consumption and investment not undertaken by households and private firms, but rather by the government. The counterpart to spending is taxes, which are a leakage from the circular flow. Taxes on firm profits reduce the internal funds available for investment. Likewise, taxes which reduce real disposable income would be expected to reduce household consumption. Therefore, through its policies, the government may have scope to influence aggregate demand and the level of income.

The Channel Tunnel (or Chunnel) linking Britain and France

Source: Getty Images

This scope, though, is open to debate. Government policies relating to taxes and spending are known as **fiscal policy**. In this chapter, we look at fiscal policy from two perspectives. The first is the Keynesian view, which makes the case that governments can play a major role in determining the level of national income. The alternative is the Ricardian view, which argues that the level of aggregate demand is essentially neutral to government policy. The effectiveness of fiscal policy will therefore depend very much on which view of the world persists.

4.2 Deficits and debts

Government spending is an injection, and taxes are a leakage, into the circular flow of income. The stance of fiscal policy, whether it is expansionary or contractionary, will depend on the difference between the two.

Just like households and firms, a government has a balance sheet, which can be a good indicator of the fiscal position taken by the government. The current government budget balance is the difference between its spending and its receipts.

Simply put:

$$B_t = G_t - T_t \tag{4.1}$$

where B_t is the balance at time t; G_t and T_t are the respective levels of government spending and tax revenue, also at time t.

Figure 4.1 plots the recent history of the UK budget surplus/deficit. What is noticeable is that the current balance largely follows the cyclical path of the economy. The period of strong economic growth at the end of the 1980s, coinciding with the Lawson boom, sees the government running a current budget surplus. This quickly turns into a deficit during the early part of the 1990s, when the UK economic growth collapsed into a recession. This trend is continued into the late 1990s and early part of the new millennium, when stronger economic growth was associated with an improving budget surplus.

The cyclical path of the budget deficit is easily accounted for. When the economy is in a recession, tax revenues fall and government spending on transfer payments, such as unemployment insurance, tends to rise. This moves the government balance towards deficit. Likewise, when the economy is growing strongly, unemployment tends to fall, boosting tax revenues and reducing the need for government spending on income-related benefits. For this reason, the budget deficit can behave as an automatic stabilizer for the economy. When growth is sluggish, taxes (leakages) fall and spending (injections) increases, boosting the circular flow of income. Likewise, in times of strong growth, revenues from taxes on income, spending and profits will rise, along with a fall in spending on transfer payments, both acting to reduce the circular flow of income.

Due to the cyclical nature of the current balance, it is hard to judge the true stance of fiscal policy, that is, whether it is generally expansive or contractionary. For this purpose, the structural or cyclically adjusted balance, which is also plotted in Figure 4.1, may be useful. This takes the cyclical movement of the economy into consideration by simply reflecting what the government's balance would be if the economy were on its trend growth path. In this way, it provides a much clearer indication of the fiscal stance taken by a government.

This can be seen if we compare the current and cyclically adjusted budget balances for the period 1987 to 1996. During this time, the economy moves from a boom to a recession

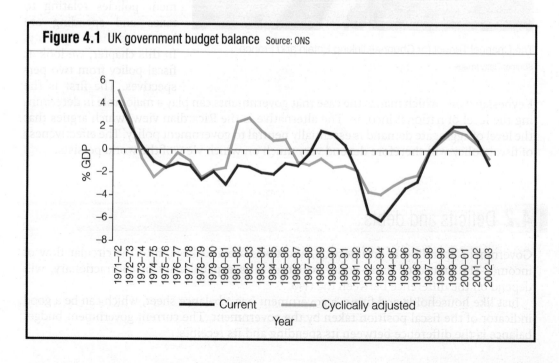

Figure 4.1 UK government budget balance Source: ONS

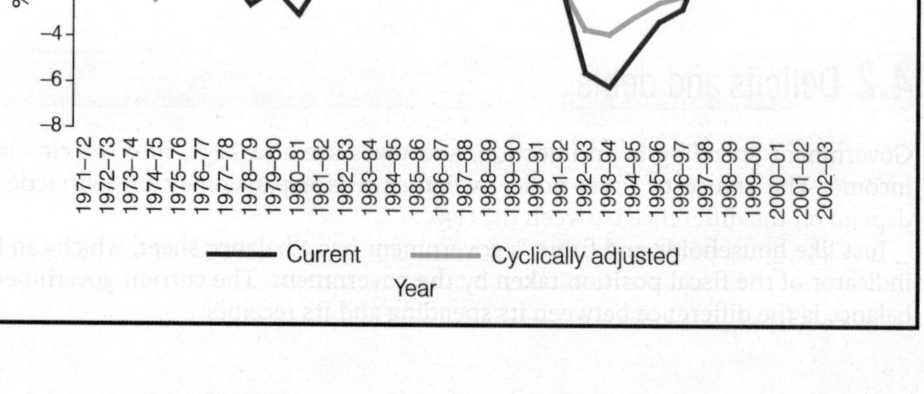

to a recovery, which is indicated in the current deficit. The structural deficit, though, is much more stable reflecting the important role economic fluctuations play. Another interesting period is 1980 to 1986, years which were marked by substantial unemployment. Taking this into consideration, the current deficit would become a surplus once cyclically adjusted.

The government or **national debt/surplus** is the accumulated total of all its deficits and surpluses. However, this is not the complete picture. If the country is running a net debt, it is funded by borrowing on which interest must be paid. Likewise, if the country is running surpluses, it is effectively a net lender and will receive interest payments. Therefore, over time, the dynamics of the national debt (D_t) are not just accumulated deficits and surpluses from the government's budget, but also include the associated interest payments involved in servicing the debt/surplus.

$$D_t = (1 + r)D_{t-1} + B_t \qquad (4.2)$$

The current level of debt is equal to last period's debt level plus all the interest which is accrued and the current budget balance. Therefore, the national debt will evolve as follows:

$$D_t = (1 + r)D_{t-1} + G_t - T_t \qquad (4.3)$$

Figure 4.2 plots the UK national debt from a historical perspective.

What is clear is that the size of the national debt has always been a substantial share of GDP. However, as debts can be rolled over, servicing is not really a problem. In fact, the UK still owes debts incurred from the Napoleonic Wars in the nineenth century.

The most striking features of Figure 4.2 correspond to the large rise in the national debt due to both World Wars. These required large amounts of government spending and very large budget deficits. Another interesting feature, though, of the path of the UK national debt has been its steady decline since the end of the Second World War. In fact, at one point during Mrs. Thatcher's time as Prime Minister in the late 1980s, there was talk of the debt actually being paid off in its entirety. This was premature. The recession of the early 1990s generated relatively large budget deficits, which halted the long and sustained fall in the national debt.

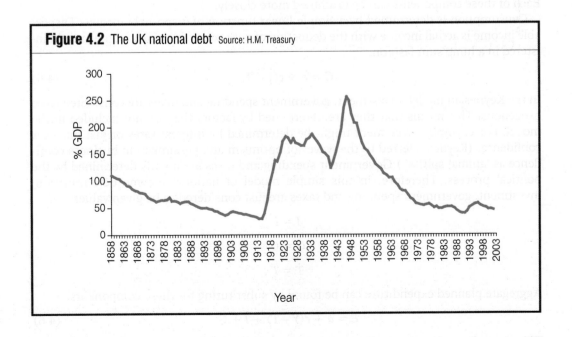

Figure 4.2 The UK national debt Source: H.M. Treasury

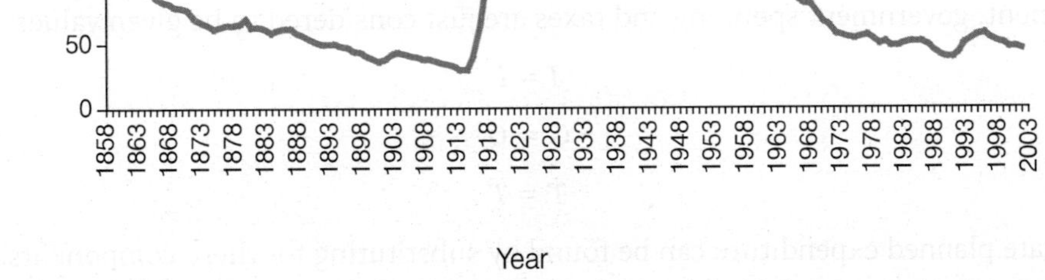

4.3 Fiscal policy and national income

Now we turn to the extent to which fiscal policy can influence aggregate demand and the level of national income. As stated previously, there are two main streams of thought. The Keynesian view is that fiscal policy can play an important role to this end. The government, through spending and tax policies, can play an active role in controlling aggregate demand and the level of national income. Contrary to this is the Ricardian view. This states the opposite case; that fiscal policy has no effect on aggregate demand and thus the level of national income.

The difference between the Keynesian and the Ricardian view of the world comes down to the type of consumption function that is used. In the Keynesian model, unsurprisingly the Keynesian consumption function is prominent. People decide how much to consume on the basis of their current disposable income, which is in turn influenced by fiscal policy. In the Ricardian view, the permanent income hypothesis is central. Consumers are forward-looking and base their decisions on a longer-run view of income. Households will only change consumption plans if they believe their permanent income has changed. If it is accepted that the government must ultimately balance its books, all deficits must be offset by surpluses. In this case, permanent income, consumption, aggregate demand and the level of national income will all be neutral with respect to fiscal policy.

4.4 Keynesian cross model

From the circular flow of income, the economy is clearly in equilibrium when income or output is equal to planned expenditures. In a closed economy (no exports or imports), planned expenditures are just the sum of consumption, investment and government spending:

$$E = C + I + G \tag{4.4}$$

Each of these components can be examined more closely.

Consumption is determined by a simple linear function of disposable income. Disposable income is actual income with the deduction of net taxes, which we assume are administered in a lump sum fashion.

$$C = a + c(Y - T) \tag{4.5}$$

In the Keynesian model, investment, government spending and taxes are considered to be exogenous. This means that they are determined by factors that are not included in the model. For example, investment might be determined by interest rates or just business confidence. (Keynes referred to the waves of optimism and pessimism in business confidence as 'animal spirits'.) Government spending and taxes are mainly determined by the political process. Therefore, in this simple model of national income determination, investment, government spending and taxes are just considered to be given values.

$$I = \bar{I}$$

$$G = \overline{G}$$

$$T = \overline{T}$$

Aggregate planned expenditure can be found by substituting for these components.

$$E = a + c(Y - \overline{T}) + \bar{I} + \overline{G} \tag{4.6}$$

This expenditure function is illustrated in Figure 4.3.

The slope of this expenditure function is given by the marginal propensity to consume (mpc) or c. This is because consumption only depends on income, so changes in income will affect planned expenditures to the extent that consumption changes. This is, in turn, determined by the mpc, which usually takes a value between 0 and 1.

The intercept of the planned expenditure function is: $a - c\overline{T} + \overline{I} + \overline{G}$. This represents all planned expenditures which are undertaken independently of income. These include autonomous consumption ($a - c\overline{T}$), investment ($\overline{I}$) and government spending ($\overline{G}$).

National income/output equilibrium will be where actual income or output is equal to planned expenditures:

$$Y = E$$

This equilibrium line is also shown on Figure 4.3. This is a 45° line so it has a slope equal to unity; every point on it represents a position where actual income or output is equal to planned expenditures.

The equilibrium level of income (Y^*) is determined by where the equilibrium and planned expenditure functions cross.

$$Y^* = a + c(Y^* - \overline{T}) + \overline{I} + \overline{G} \tag{4.7}$$

This can be solved for by Y^* rearranging the above so that:

$$Y^* = \frac{1}{1-c}[a + \overline{I} + \overline{G} - c\overline{T}] \tag{4.8}$$

The equilibrium properties of the model are fairly easy to understand by using Figure 4.3. At income levels below Y^*, planned expenditures exceed income or output. In this case, firms will find that their stocks are being run down as demand exceeds supply. Firms will increase output, and in doing so, hire more labour and income will also rise.

At income levels above Y^*, planned expenditures are clearly below actual output, in which case firms will begin to build up stocks of unsold goods and inventories. As supply

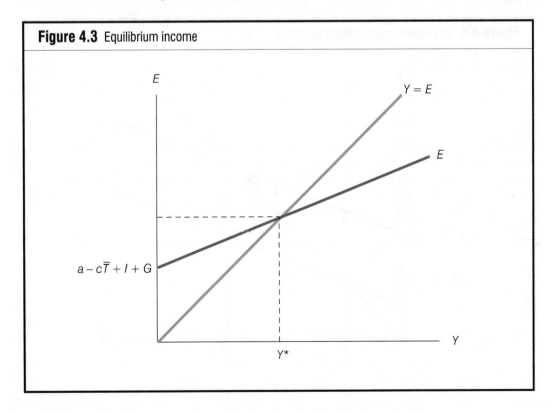

Figure 4.3 Equilibrium income

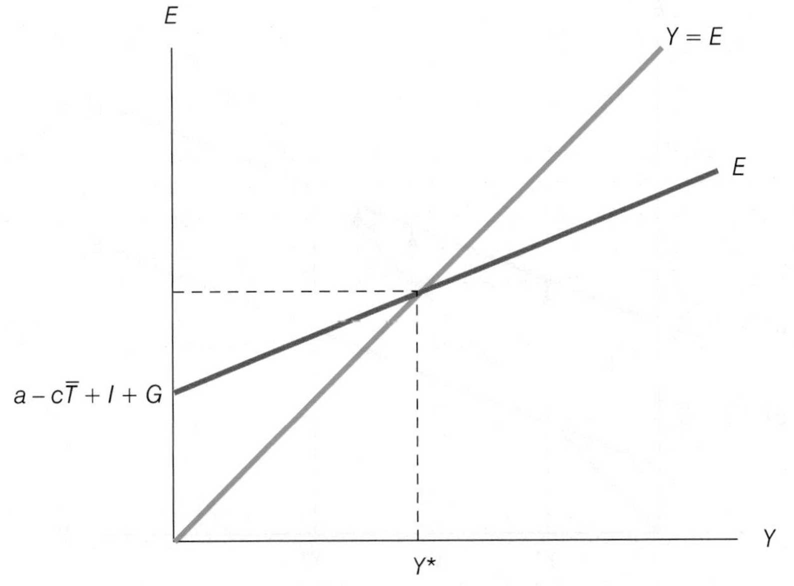

exceeds demand, firms will be encouraged to cut output. Less labour will be hired so income will also fall. It is only at the level of income Y^* where there is no pressure on output to change. This is where demand is equal to supply.

Now that a simple model of national income determination has been established, it can be used to analyse the effects of changes in government spending and taxes.

Government spending

Suppose there was an increase in government spending: $\Delta\overline{G} = \overline{G}_2 - \overline{G}_1$. This means that planned expenditures will now be higher at every level of income, so the planned expenditure function will shift upwards. This is shown in Figure 4.4 as a movement from E_1 to E_2.

What will happen to equilibrium output? Expenditure initially rises by the change in government spending; this is shown as the vertical distance between E_1 and E_2. From the circular flow, income will also rise by this amount. However, the story does not stop there. This initial increase in income will lead to an increase in disposable income and therefore consumption, so aggregate expenditure will rise even further. As expenditure rises, income will also increase further. This process then repeats itself, higher expenditure generating higher income, higher disposable income, higher consumption and so on.

However, because the marginal propensity to consume is less than one, the increase in expenditure gets smaller and smaller each time, so income will eventually converge to a new value rather than keep rising in an unbounded way. This process is shown by the path of arrows in Figure 4.4. The total change in equilibrium income is shown as a movement from Y_1^* to Y_2^*.

This total change in income is a multiple of the initial change in government spending. It is the change in government spending, plus all the subsequent changes in consumption brought about by increasing income. Therefore, the total change in income can be written as:

$$\Delta Y = \Delta\overline{G} + c\Delta\overline{G} + c^2\Delta\overline{G} + c^3\Delta\overline{G} + \ldots$$

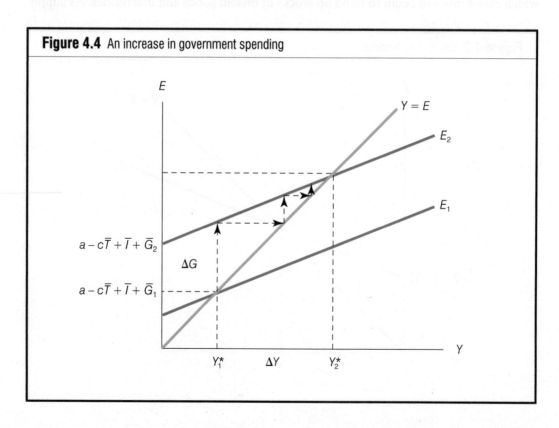

Figure 4.4 An increase in government spending

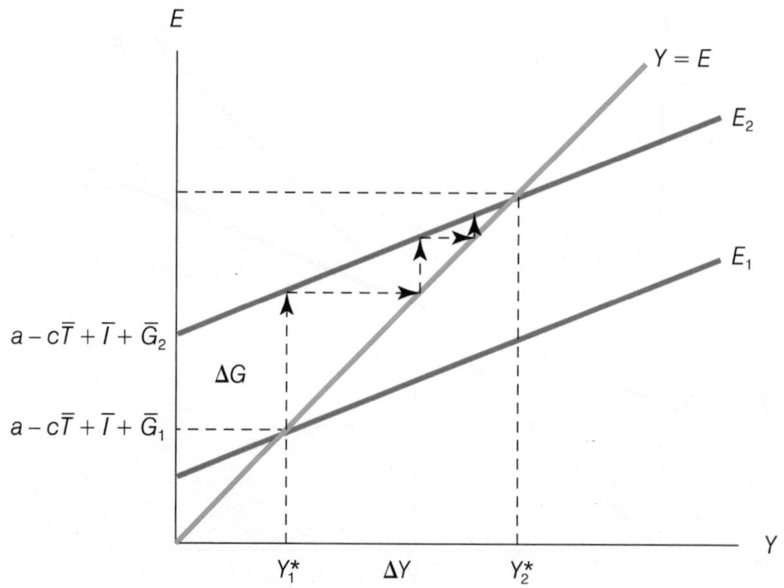

or

$$\Delta Y = k\Delta\bar{G}, \text{ where } k = 1 + c + c^2 + c^3 + \dots \text{ is known as the multiplier.}$$

As $0 < c < 1$, the value of the multiplier can be found by using the sum to infinity:

$$k = \frac{1}{1-c}$$

Therefore, the total change in income resulting from a change in government spending is:

$$\Delta Y = \frac{1}{1-c}\Delta\bar{G} \qquad (4.9)$$

It should be clear intuitively from the above that the size of the multiplier increases as the marginal propensity to consume (mpc) increases. If the mpc is higher, then every increase in income brought about by the initial increase in expenditure will proceed to generate larger further increases in expenditure. As a result, the overall effect on national income will be higher.

So, in conclusion, an increase in government spending will produce a multiplied increase in equilibrium output.

Taxes

Where taxes are levied in a lump sum fashion, an increase in the level of this tax from $\bar{T}_1$ to $\bar{T}_2$ will lead to a downward shift in the expenditure function. The tax rise will lower disposable income resulting in autonomous consumption and thus planned expenditure being lower by an amount equal to $c\Delta T$. This is shown in Figure 4.5 as a movement from E_1 to E_2.

Once again, though, there is more to it. The fall in expenditure will have a multiplied effect on the level of national income. Falling consumption leads to lower income, which in

Figure 4.5 An increase in taxes

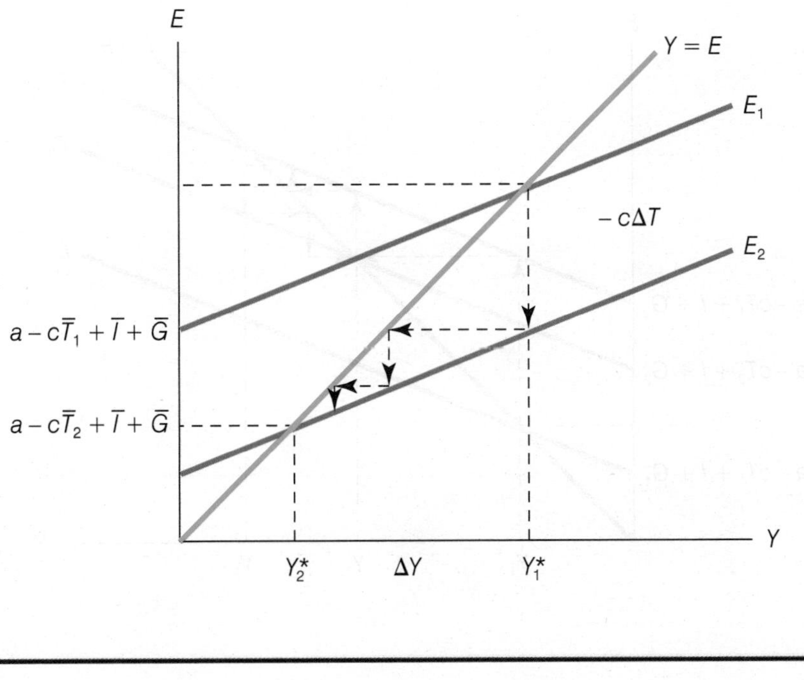

turn leads to lower consumption and so on. The overall effect of the tax rise on national income would be:

$$\Delta Y = \frac{-c}{1-c}\Delta \overline{T} \qquad (4.10)$$

This consists of the initial fall in expenditure ($-c\Delta T$) and the multiplier ($1/1-c$).

A rise in the marginal propensity to consume will have two effects here. First, the initial fall in consumption following the tax cut will be larger, as consumption is more responsive to changes in disposable income. Second, the multiplier will be larger. In both cases, the negative consequences for equilibrium income will be more severe following a tax rise.

The balanced budget multiplier

It is argued that if the government raises government spending and taxes by the same amount, then the effect on income will be zero. The government is adding to the circular flow of income with one hand, while taking an equal amount away from it at the same time with the other. This, though, is not always true. Tax-financed government spending can still have a significant effect on the level of national income. This is a powerful result; the government can use policy to expand the economy without incurring any additional debt.

A tax-financed increase in government spending implies that:

$$\Delta \overline{G} = \Delta \overline{T}$$

The rise in spending as we have seen will lead to an upward shift in the expenditure function and the rise in taxes to a corresponding downward shift. What will be the overall consequence for the equilibrium level of national income?

This question is answered in Figure 4.6. The increase in government spending shifts the expenditure function upwards from E_1 to E_2, whereas the increase in taxes moves it down from E_2 to E_3. From Figure 4.6, it is evident that the equilibrium level of national income

Figure 4.6 A balanced budget increase in government spending

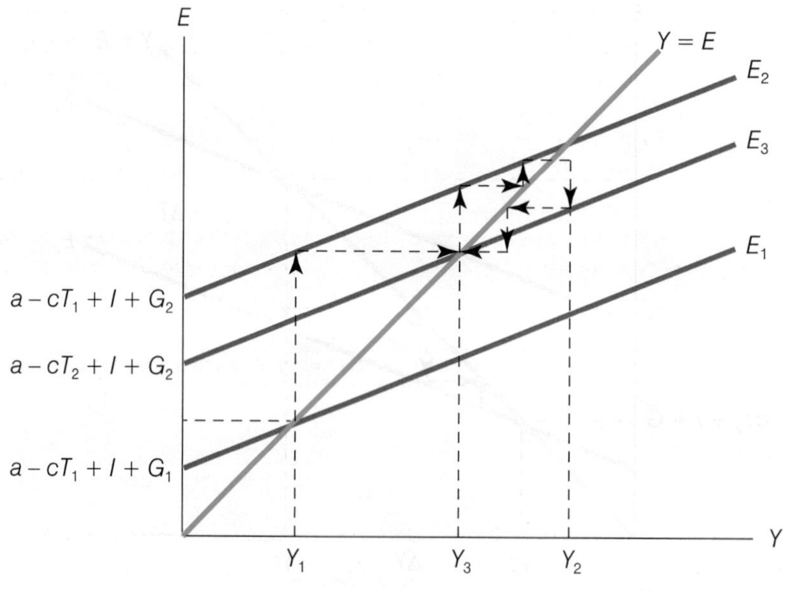

would rise as a result, simply because the upward shift in the expenditure function is greater than the downward shift.

The logic here is fairly simple. Even though $\Delta\overline{G} = \Delta\overline{T}$, the change in expenditure from an increase in government spending, $\Delta E = \Delta\overline{G}$, exceeds the fall in expenditure from the rise in taxes, $\Delta E = c\Delta\overline{T}$. The net change in expenditure is $\Delta E = (1 - c)\Delta\overline{G}$, and this will be positive as long as the mpc is less than one ($c < 1$).

Whenever the marginal propensity to consume is less than one, which is a fairly plausible assumption, aggregate expenditures will rise following a balance budget increase in government spending. This is because some of the disposable income which the government removes in taxes would have been saved in any case. Therefore, the increase in government spending exceeds the fall in consumption. The only situation where this does not hold true is where the marginal propensity to consume is equal to 1. In this case, there is no saving, so any increase in tax-financed government spending will lead to an equal fall in consumption and no change in overall expenditures.

The effect on equilibrium income/output is clearly positive. The economy moves from Y_1 to Y_3 via Y_2. The combined effect of the increases in government spending and taxes is:

$$\Delta Y = \frac{1}{1-c}\Delta\overline{G} - \frac{c}{1-c}\Delta\overline{T} \tag{4.11}$$

Knowing that $\Delta\overline{G} = \Delta\overline{T}$ leaves us with:

$$\Delta Y = \Delta\overline{G} \tag{4.12}$$

The **balanced budget multiplier** is an important concept. It argues that the government's fiscal policy can play a significant role in determining aggregate demand and the level of national income.

4.5 The Ricardian model: fiscal policy with forward-looking consumers

As the basis of the Keynesian cross model is a simple linear consumption function, the model is subject to the same criticisms raised in Chapter 2. Consumption decisions are only based on current disposable income, an action which is at odds with the rational, maximizing household. Such a household could increase welfare by basing their consumption decisions on a notion of permanent rather than current income.

Rational consumers are both forward-looking and consumption smoothers; however, what implication would this behaviour have for government tax and spending policies on national income?

In the simple Keynesian model, changes in government spending or taxes will only affect consumers to the extent that their disposable income changes. On the other hand, forward-looking and rational, utility maximizing consumers must take a much more complicated decision. This is because a government's current tax and spending policies may influence its future tax and spending policies, and therefore have repercussions for a household's future disposable income.

Optimal consumers

Following the two-period model introduced in Chapter 2, a rational consumer will choose consumption to maximize total lifetime utility subject to the constraint:

$$C_1 + \frac{C_2}{(1+r)} \leq Y_1 + \frac{Y_2}{(1+r)} \tag{4.13}$$

This constraint simply implies that the present discounted value of consumption cannot exceed the present discounted value of income.

The solution to the maximization problem is where the indifference curve formed by the consumer's preferences is tangential to the budget constraint. The theory behind this is covered in some depth in Chapter 2, and is shown again in Figure 4.7 below.

The optimal pattern of consumption is given by (C_1^*, C_2^*). This will only change if there are changes in the factors that shift or pivot the budget constraint. Is this something that can be achieved by fiscal policy?

The government debt

Earlier in this chapter, we outlined the evolution of the government debt. The government effectively can borrow large sums for a long period of time, but is it subject to any constraints? Although the government does not have to balance its budget in every period, it is assumed that the government must ultimately balance its books. That is, at the end of time, the government's national debt must be zero.

In the two-period model that we have been using, the end of time is effectively at the end of the second period. Therefore, the evolution of the government's debt must be as follows:

$$0 = (1 + r)(G_1 - T_1) + (G_2 - T_2) \tag{4.14}$$

Dividing both sides by $(1 + r)$ means this can be rewritten as:

$$0 = (G_1 - T_1) + \frac{(G_2 - T_2)}{(1+r)} \tag{4.15}$$

The government's constraint is that the present discounted value of the sum of deficits and surpluses must sum to zero. This constraint simply means that any deficit or surplus would have to be reversed eventually in present value terms. The forward-looking rational consumer will know this. Therefore, when faced with a change in taxes or government spending, their anticipation would be that the policy will eventually be reversed in present

Figure 4.7 Optimal consumption in a two-period model

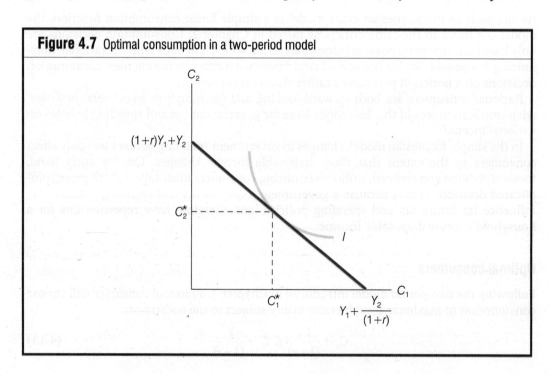

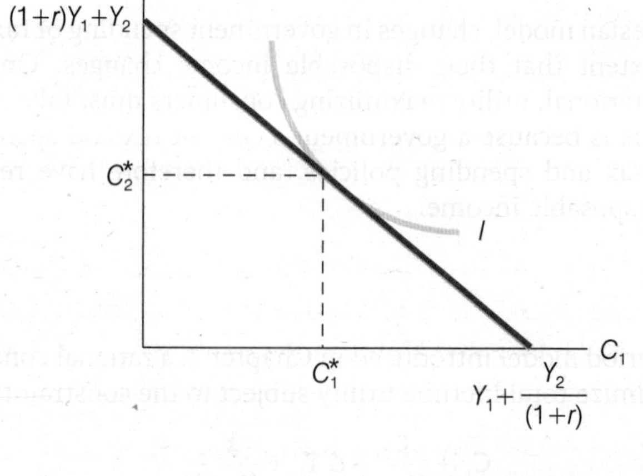

value terms. In that case, they need not view their lifetime resources as being any different, and therefore there is no need to change consumption.

Under these conditions, fiscal policy will have no effect on the economy – a proposition known as **Ricardian equivalence**.

Does the timing of taxes matter for consumption?

The government delivers an immediate tax cut of $\Delta \overline{T}_1$. How should the household respond? According to the predictions of the permanent income hypothesis (PIH), consumption will only change if lifetime resources change. Consumption will be constrained by the following budget constraint:

$$C_1 + \frac{C_2}{1+r} \leq Y_1 - \Delta T_1 + \frac{Y_2 - \Delta T_2}{1+r} \quad (4.16)$$

In this case, the present discounted value of all consumption cannot exceed the present discounted value of all disposable income.

Ignoring government spending and starting from a position of no debt, the tax cut will then create a deficit of ΔT_1. Effectively, this is the amount that the government is giving to each household.

However, the government must have no deficit at the end of period 2, implying:

$$0 = (1 + r)\Delta T_1 + \Delta T_2 \quad (4.17)$$

The government constraint then states that the current tax reduction must be offset in present value terms with a future tax increase:

$$\Delta T_2 = -(1 + r)\Delta T_1 \quad (4.18)$$

Substituting this result into the budget constraint gives:

$$C_1 + \frac{C_2}{1+r} \leq Y_1 - \Delta T_1 + \frac{Y_2 + (1+r)\Delta T_1}{1+r} \quad (4.19)$$

$$C_1 + \frac{C_2}{1+r} \leq Y_1 + \frac{Y_2}{1+r} \quad (4.20)$$

The tax policy does not change the intertemporal budget constraint.

As long as the government runs a balanced budget, the timing of taxes is irrelevant and will have no impact on the intertemporal budget constraint, and therefore consumption. When the government cuts taxes in period 1, a household would experience a rise in their disposable income. Under the auspices of the Keynesian model, consumption would rise. However, the predications of the PIH are all together different. Knowing that future taxes will be higher, households will smooth their consumption by saving the tax cut this period to pay for the higher taxes next period.

The neutrality of government spending

Will an increase in government spending ΔG_1 have any effect on output? The answer is again no. The best way to view this is to assume that government spending is just consumption that the government undertakes on behalf of households. The government is essentially purchasing goods and services and distributing them to households for consumption.

Suppose the government were to increase government spending in period 1 and to finance it by borrowing. In this case, the budget constraint would appear as follows:

$$(C_1 + \Delta G_1) + \frac{C_2}{(1+r)} \leq Y_1 + \frac{Y_2 - \Delta T_2}{(1+r)} \tag{4.21}$$

As before, the government budget constraint implies that future taxes will have to rise by $\Delta T_2 = (1 + r)\Delta G_1$. Substituting in this expression for the change in future taxes, we will once again see that nothing has happened to the intertemporal budget constraint faced by households.

$$(C_1 + G_1) + \frac{C_2}{(1+r)} \leq Y_1 - G_1 + \frac{Y_2}{(1+r)} \tag{4.22}$$

In this case, $C_1 + G_1 = C_1^*$, so $\Delta G_1 = -\Delta C_1$.

An increase in government spending raises household consumption in the first period, but the households know that they will face a higher tax bill in the second period. As a result, the increase in consumption in the first period will be offset by extra saving. All that has happened is that government consumption has replaced private consumption. Instead of households choosing their own consumption, the government is doing it for them.

As government spending crowds out household spending on a one-to-one basis, there will be no change to aggregate demand. Fiscal policy is once again neutral.

Theoretical debates on Ricardian equivalence

In stating the neutrality of fiscal policy, the theory of Ricardian equivalence argues that the government has little role to play in the macroeconomy. This summation, though, is only valid if we can be sure that Ricardian equivalence holds in its entirety. This has led to further debate, and many reasons have subsequently been put forward arguing the case for a more non-Ricardian view on fiscal policy.

Discounting

Future tax increases will only have bearing for the current period if consumers are sufficiently forward-looking. If households do not place much weight on future utility, they will not worry so much about the effects of future tax rises. Consequently, fiscal policy may be successful in influencing the economy as household saving will not change to offset it.

One of the most logical reasons why a household might discount the future is because human mortality means there is a positive probability of death. It is said that 'death and taxes are the only certain things in life', but this is not completely true. Due to the intertemporal nature of the government's budget constraint, current increases in government spending or tax cuts can be funded by borrowing. The tax changes these imply will be levied in the future, by which time death may have occurred. In this case, only death is certain.

However, a famous counter-argument put forward by Robert Barro (1989) is that Ricardian equivalence may still hold even if there is a positive probability of death. The reason is that we care about the utility of our children, and know that even if we will not be around in the future to pay higher taxes, then our children will be. Therefore, following a current tax cut or rise in government spending, we would save more so that we could increase bequests to our offspring.

This is a controversial debate. Although there is ample evidence that bequests are left, for this to maintain the predictions of Ricardian Equivalence it would require each household to be treated as a dynasty. There will also be a large number of possible exceptions to this rule, the most obvious being the households that have no children.

Borrowing constraints

In Chapter 2, we analysed the effects borrowing constraints might have on consumer behaviour. One result was that even if households were permanent income consumers, consumption would tend to be tied to current disposable income. The household would ideally like to increase current consumption, but cannot borrow against future income. Therefore, consumption can only change when current income changes.

In this case, the government can increase current disposable income by cutting taxes, which would lead to a rise in consumption. Alternatively, the government through its spending could purchase goods and services for households, enabling them to increase their consumption towards its desired level. In both cases, fiscal policy will have not neutral but positive consequences for aggregate demand. Effectively, the credit constraints are being circumvented through fiscal policy as the government is just borrowing on behalf on households.

Interest rate effects

Again, in Chapter 2, we argued that most households are likely to be net borrowers. Changes in the interest rate will thus have income effects that work in the same direction. For example, a fall in interest rates would make borrowing cheaper to service, freeing up extra income for consumption.

There is a strong argument that the government may be able to borrow at a lower rate of interest than individual households. This is because the government can always raise taxes to fund its borrowing, so the chances of a default are much less than with an individual household. Therefore, financial institutions may be prepared to lend to the government on more favourable terms.

By funding a cut in taxes or an increase in government spending by borrowing, the government enables households to consume more. This reduces the amount that credit-constrained consumers need to borrow; the government is really just borrowing on their behalf. However, because the rate of interest the government pays is lower, households are effectively swapping high-interest borrowing for low-interest borrowing. This will be expected to generate a positive income effect, increasing current consumption and aggregate demand.

Distortionary taxes

Lump sum taxes are fixed payments and have no consequences on incentives to work. Once your tax liability has been met, 100 per cent of any extra income can be kept as disposable income. This is not true for income taxes, which means that only a proportion of any extra income earned will become disposable income. As the rewards for working are now lower, the incentives to work may be unduly affected.

Therefore, non-lump sum taxes may create distortions which lead to the failure of Ricardian Equivalence. Lower taxes might encourage more work, meaning that income rises. Higher taxes may have the opposite effect. As the budget constraint will shift with changes in income, we can no longer expect consumption to remain unchanged in the face of fiscal policy changes.

4

Global application 4.1

Interest rate subsidies

Figure 1 shows how changes in taxes can have non-Ricardian effects when the government can borrow at a lower interest rate than individual households.

If the household can borrow and save at the interest rate $(1 + r)$, then given a disposable income stream (Y_1, Y_2), the household's optimal consumption choice is the bundle (C_1, C_2). This household is a net borrower to the tune of $C_1 - Y_1$.

If the government faces the same interest rate, then a cut in present taxes will have no effect on the household's lifetime budget constraint. And, if the government's debt must be zero at the end of the second period, then the debt incurred in funding the tax cut would require tax increases of the same present discounted value in the second period.

If the government can borrow at a lower interest rate $(1 + r') < (1 + r)$, then net-borrowing households gain an interest rate subsidy, which produces positive wealth effects. The period 1 tax cut raises current disposable income, which is repaid by higher period 2 taxes. This can be thought of as the government borrowing on behalf of households, which is then paid back at the interest rate the government faces. This enables the household to swap a loan at the rate of $(l + r)$ for one at $(l + r')$, which produces a positive wealth effect.

The lower borrowing cost produces a pivot in the budget constraint shown by the dashed section in Figure 1. The intuition behind the pivot is the more that bank borrowing can be replaced by tax cuts, the larger the implied income effect. The household's optimal consumption bundle will then change to (C_1', C_2'), demonstrating that current consumption is no longer independent of the timing of taxes.

Figure 1 Net borrowers and interest rate subsidies

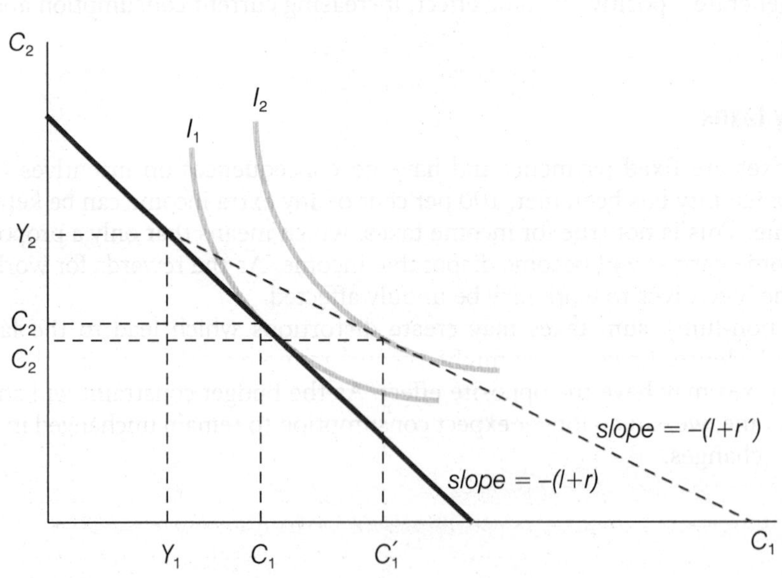

4

Global application 4.2

Taxation and incentives

Changes in the rate of income tax can generate non-Ricardian effects in the economy if it alters incentives to work. Households are assumed to have preferences between work and income such that utility rises with income, but falls with work as this implies less time for leisure.

These preferences can be represented by indifference curves which are upward sloping in work–income ($L - Y$) space. Indifference curves represent the combinations of work and income that generate the same amount of utility. Work is considered to be a 'baddy', because as the amount of it undertaken by the household increases, the only way they can remain at the same level of utility is if they are given a higher income as compensation. In Figure 2, the work–income indifference curve is (I) convex. This reflects the law of diminishing marginal utility to both income and leisure.

The budget constraint reflects the trade-off between work and income (Figure 2). It is assumed that households receive a level of non-work income b, which might reflect benefit payments. As the amount of work becomes positive, the level of non-work income drops to a. The difference $b - a$ reflects the cost of work, which might include forgone benefits and transport costs. However, each unit of labour earns disposable income at the rate of $w(1 - t)$ consisting of a wage rate of w and an income tax rate of t. The budget constraint can then be defined as:

$$Y = b, \text{ if } L = 0$$

$$Y = a + w(1 - t)L, \text{ if } 0 < L \leq \bar{L}$$

where $\bar{L}$ is the maximum possible amount of labour in a given time period.

The optimal amount of work (L^*) is where the indifference curve forms a tangent to the budget constraint. As seen from Figure 2, this implies optimal household income of Y^*. It is not the case, though, that the optimal amount of work is

Figure 2 Optimal work–income trade-off

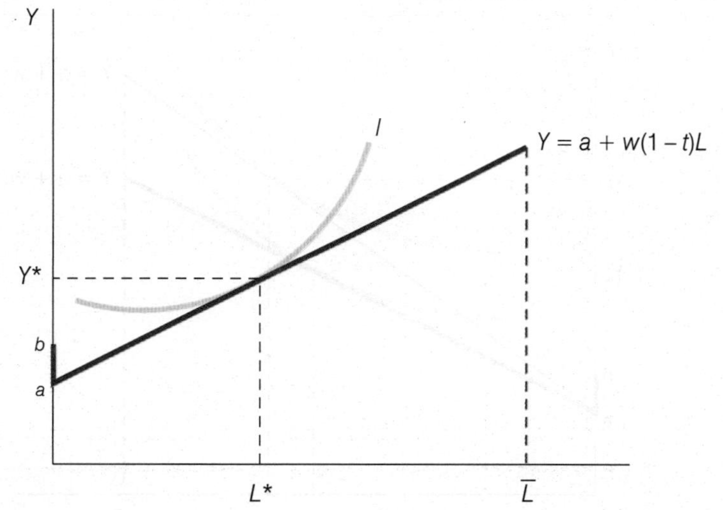

Global application 4.2 (continued)

positive. In Figure 3, the household has relatively high non-work income of b, or large costs of work $b - a$, and the household can move onto a higher indifference curve (I_2) by setting work equal to zero. As the budget constraint is non-linear, it is possible that the solution to the household's utility maximization problem will be at a boundary rather than a tangential point.

Now, what might be the effects on household work and income from a reduction in the rate of income tax ($t_2 < t_1$)? The household budget constraint will pivot upwards for each positive level of work as seen in Figure 4, reflecting the higher take-home pay from each unit of labour.

Faced with the new budget constraint, the household will recalculate the solution to their

Figure 3 Optimal not to work

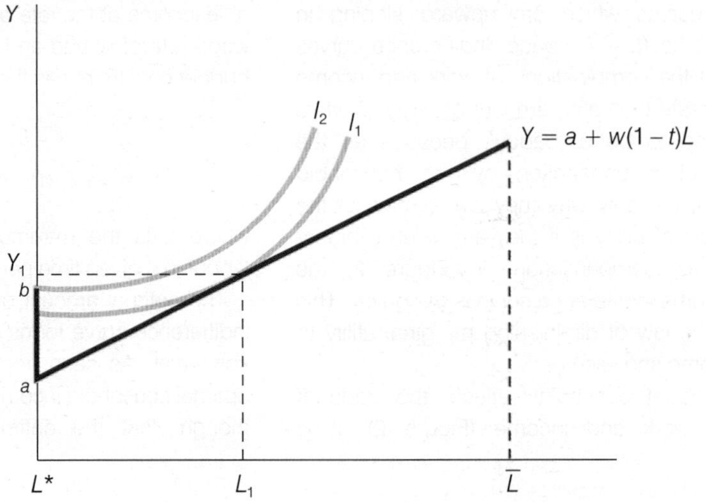

Figure 4 Increase in labour output

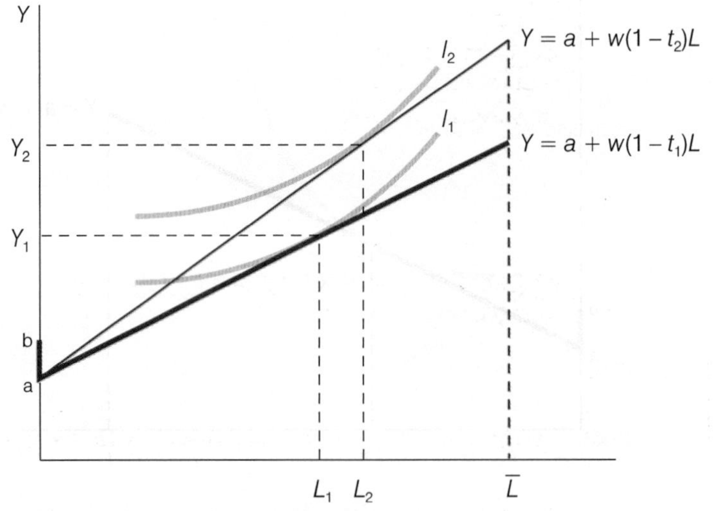

Global application 4.2 (continued)

utility maximization problem. Figure 4 corresponds to the household shown in Figure 1, where the optimal response is to increase labour input from L_1 to L_2. Figure 5 corresponds to the household shown in Figure 3. Here, the cut in taxes is great enough to encourage households to move away from the boundary equilibrium and enter the labour market.

If changes in income tax rates can alter incentives to work, by either encouraging those already in work to work harder or by encouraging those out of work to enter the labour market, then the tax change can have non-Ricardian consequences. For example, if a cut in taxes generates a large increase in work, then labour income in the economy will rise. As tax revenues are just a proportion of income, then it is possible that cutting taxes will actually increase tax revenues. This means that meeting the government's long-run balanced budget constraint will not require the tax cuts to be reversed. The same could happen in reverse where an increase in taxes through greater disincentives to work act to reduce labour incomes and tax revenues.

The relationship between marginal tax rates and incentives to work has been subject to great debate. Several arguments have been made to suggest that the elasticity of labour to tax cuts might be quite low. Workers may have little flexibility to vary their labour input with working hours defined by employers and regulated by labour laws. Therefore, many studies find a limited response in working hours to tax changes in most professions. This argument, though, does not rule out changes in hours through induced changes in labour market participation, which could be significant.

Another argument that tends to suppress the responsiveness of labour input to changes in tax rates are income effects. So far, it has been assumed that the take-home wage represents the opportunity cost of leisure, i.e., the wages that could be earned by swapping leisure for labour. As take-home pay increases, the opportunity cost of leisure rises, encouraging people to substitute leisure time for working time. The income effect, though, works in the opposite direction and could mitigate or be strong enough to offset the substitution effect. If workers set themselves a target income Y_T, a cut in tax rates means that workers can achieve this target income by working fewer hours and therefore enjoying more leisure. Tax reductions therefore prompt a fall in labour input.

Figure 5 Increase in labour participation

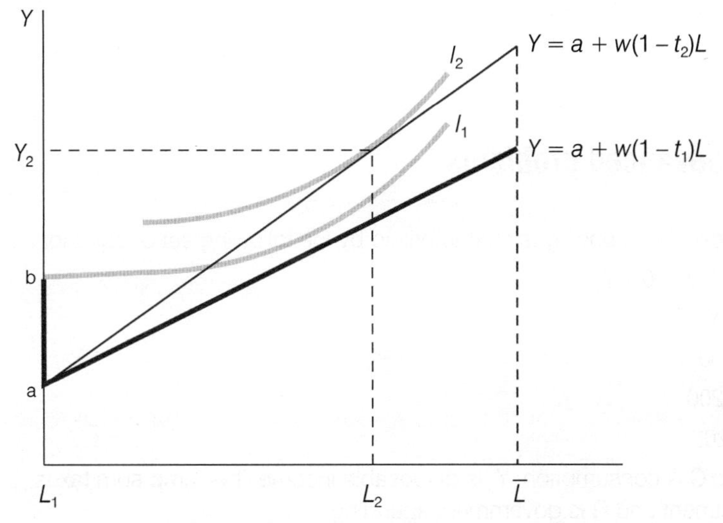

Summary

- In this chapter we have explored the nature of government spending and taxation.
- We analysed the differences between government deficits and national debt.
- Then, we worked through the implications of fiscal policy.
- Using the Keynesian cross model, we analysed planned and actual expenditure functions.
- Finally, we analysed the theory of Ricardian equivalence with forward-looking consumers.

Key terms

Balanced budget multiplier
Fiscal policy
Government spending
National debt/surplus
Ricardian equivalence

Review questions

1. Explain how an increase in government spending and an equal increase in lump sum taxes can generate an increase in equilibrium output. Under what conditions will a balanced budget increase in government spending reduce equilibrium output? Are these conditions realistic?
2. According to the theory of Ricardian equivalence, would there be any discernible differences between the effects of a £1 billion increase in government spending or a £1 billion cut in lump sum taxes?
3. How might a reduction in the tax rate actually lead to an increase in tax revenues? What would be the expected income tax revenues at income tax rates of 0 per cent and 100 per cent? What might the relationship between tax rates and tax revenues look like? Explain your answers.

More advanced problems

4. Suppose the economy is characterized by the following set of equations:

$C = 200 + 0.7\,Y_d$

$Y_d = Y - T$

$I = 100$

$G = 200$

$T = 200,$

where C is consumption, Y_d is disposable income, T is lump sum taxes, Y is GDP, I is investment and G is government spending.

More advanced problems (continued)

a. Calculate the equilibrium level of income in this economy.
b. What is the value of the multiplier?
c. The government decides that income is too low and wishes to expand the economy by cutting lump sum taxes to 100. Calculate the new equilibrium level of income.
d. The government is now concerned about the rising level of government debt so cuts government spending by 100. What happens to the equilibrium level of income? Comment on your findings.

5. Instead of using lump sum taxes the government raises revenue with a proportional income tax:

   $T = tY$, where t is the marginal tax rate.

   a. Derive the new consumption function. Using the Keynesian cross model show how changes in the marginal tax rate affect equilibrium income.
   b. By examining the multiplier, explain why proportional taxes are an automatic stabilizer on output compared to lump sum tax rates.
   c. The government wishes to undertake a programme of public works costing £5 billion but must balance its budget. If the current level of GDP is £100 billion, would the government be correct to raise the tax rate by 5 per cent? Explain your answer.

6. The structure of the economy is fully described by the following equations:

   $Y = C + I + G$

   $Y = 6000$

   $G = 800$

   $T = 800$

   $C = 300 + 0.75\,(Y - T)$

   $I = 1200 - 6000r$

   a. Calculate the equilibrium interest rate, the level of investment, and the government's budget deficit.
   b. Recalculate the items listed in part (a) when the level of government spending rises to 1000. Explain your findings.
   c. Given that the level of GDP is held fixed at 6000, following the increase in government spending in (b) what reasons might account for a policy of raising taxes to 1200?

7. What are the implications for Ricardian equivalence if a proportion τ of the population dies at the end of each period? How would your answer change if it is established that people care about their offspring, and can leave bequests?

8. Explain how borrowing constraints affect the validity of Ricardian equivalence for:
   a. a temporary tax cut
   b. an announced future tax cut.

9. 'The national debt is an irrelevant proposition because it will never be repaid.

   The national debt is irrelevant because we owe it to ourselves.' Discuss.

For further resources, visit
http://www.thomsonlearning.co.uk/chamberlin_yueh

Part III

Money

Having discussed the real side of the macroeconomy, we now turn to the money part. This section covers the money market and financial markets. As the scale and scope of financial markets grow, they have become increasingly important in understanding the functioning of the macroeconomy.

5 The money market

Learning objectives

- Understand the role of money in the economy
- Comprehend of the determinants of the interest rate
- Understand the term structure of interest rates or yield curves
- Assess the impact of different forms of monetary policy

5

5.1 Introduction

Money plays an important role in the economy. It is used to settle the transactions which make up the circular flow of income. Also, the price of holding money is the interest rate, which has a role to play in determining consumption and investment. Therefore, **monetary policy** – the act of controlling the supply or price of money – may exert a powerful influence over the economy.

Like all prices, the interest rate is determined by demand and supply in the money market. The focus of this chapter is to explain how this market works, specifically the factors which influence the demand for money, the supply of money and, therefore, the interest rate. A discussion of the effects of monetary policy on the wider economy will be reserved for later chapters.

5.2 What is money?

Money is defined as anything which performs the following four functions.

Medium of exchange

The most important function of money is in facilitating trade between different parties. For example, a worker can sell his labour to a firm in exchange for money, which can then be used to buy goods and services from other firms. Without money people would have to live in a world of barter, where no trade could take place without a 'double coincidence of wants' and much negotiation. In such a scenario, transactions costs may be so high as to prevent trade from occurring. Money as a medium of exchange therefore plays an essential role in the circular flow of income.

A unit of account

As every good or service is priced in the same units, money provides a numeraire which enables the rate of exchange between goods to be determined.

A store of value

People with a lot of money are regarded as being wealthy. Money is an asset that has purchasing power over goods and services, so it is argued that the more you have the better. However, money gives the holder the opportunity to exercise this purchasing power whenever they like. If wealth were held in perishable commodities, then the choice as to when purchasing power could be exercised would be more limited. By acting as a store of value, money makes future consumption and wealth accumulation possible.

Standard for deferred payments

This simply means that money can be used as the unit of account in debt contracts. For example, if you take out a bank loan, the repayment schedule will be defined in terms of a certain amount of money.

Money is essentially anything that can perform all these functions. The most common type of money, which is currency in the form of notes and coins, is known as *fiat money*. The interesting thing about fiat money is that the intrinsic value of the notes and coins is much less than the value of the goods and services for which they can be exchanged. The face value is upheld by a confidence that these notes and coins will be widely accepted due to government laws (fiat).

5.3 Monetary aggregates

The monetary aggregate is the total quantity of money in an economy. It is much harder to measure than one would have first thought. This is because no one single asset is used to make all transactions. The most obvious medium of exchange is currency in the form of notes and coins. However, demand deposits can also be used for this purpose. These are funds that are held in bank current accounts (also known as sight accounts). If payments are made by personal cheques, debit cards, standing orders, direct debits and so on, then payments are simply made by transferring funds from one account to another. Figure 5.1 plots the ratio of notes and coins to GDP (M0/GDP) for the UK over a number of years. This ratio has tended to fall, implying that other aggregates such as current accounts are being used more actively as a medium of exchange.

A standard definition of the money supply is the total amount of currency and demand deposits. These are aggregates which can be used as a medium of exchange. However, this is regarded as being a narrow definition of the money supply. Once it is accepted that current accounts constitute part of the money supply, it becomes questionable as to where to draw the line. Should savings accounts (also called time accounts) be included? As many current accounts pay interest, it is often difficult to tell the difference between the two.

Also, should financial assets, such as bonds and stocks, be included? Traditionally, these have been very difficult to use as a medium of exchange, but continuing financial innovation has meant that this restriction has fallen over time. For example, it is now possible to save in a mutual fund, where your savings are invested in a portfolio of stocks and shares. However, you can still write personal cheques on the account. So, even though you are saving in stocks and shares, it can still be treated as a medium of exchange.

Therefore, funds invested in saving accounts or mutual funds are thought of as *near money*. Traditionally, these have only performed a role as a store of value, but innovation

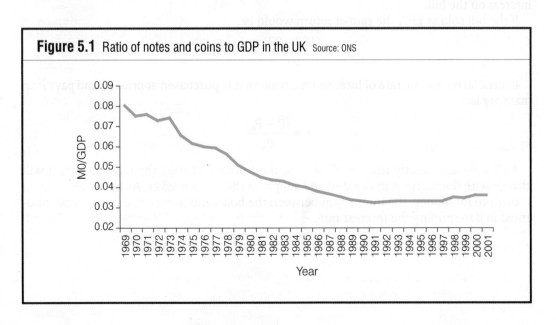

Figure 5.1 Ratio of notes and coins to GDP in the UK Source: ONS

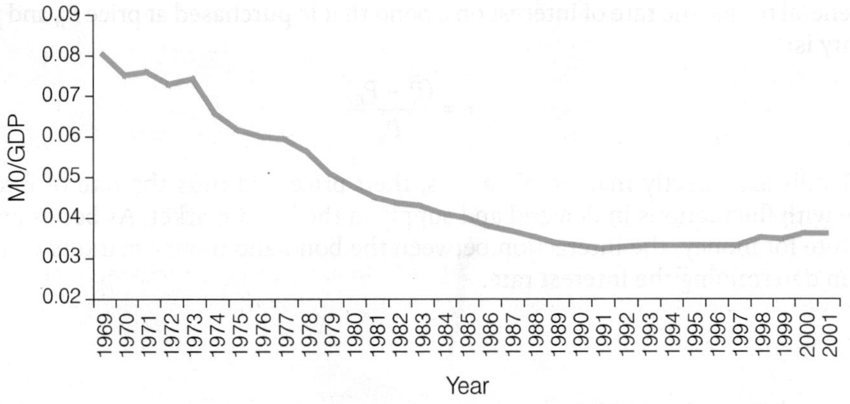

means that they can increasingly be used as a medium of exchange. Therefore, a *broad* definition of the monetary aggregate would not just consist of currency and current accounts, but also these stocks of near money.

Why are we concerned about these different monetary aggregates? Well, at the outset we mentioned that monetary policy is about controlling the price or quantity of money, and this can be used to influence the circular flow of income and the level of income. However, for monetary policy to be used effectively, policy makers must be sure as to what it is they are actually trying to control. By focusing only on the narrow definition of monetary aggregates and ignoring near money, the government may be underestimating the size of the money supply.

5

5.4 The bond market

The opportunity cost of holding money is the rate of interest that could have otherwise been achieved by investing in bonds. It is for this reason that the **interest rate** is referred to as the price of money. In the next chapters, there will be a fuller discussion on bonds and other financial assets. For now, we only need concern ourselves with a simple type of bond known as a Treasury Bill (often referred to as a T-bill).

The Treasury Bill is a means by which the government can borrow to fund its deficits, or, as we see later, to exert some influence in the money markets. They are essentially short-term (usually 90 days in the UK) IOUs, which promise to pay a fixed amount on maturity. For example, the UK government could sell a bill offering to pay £100 in 90 days' time.

The price at which this bill sells is likely to be less than £100, and this is what makes the bill attractive to investors. Suppose the bill is sold for £98. This will offer the investor a return of £2 in 90 days. The rate of return will simply be given by:

$$r = \frac{(100 - 98)}{98} = 2.04\%$$

This is equivalent to an annual interest rate of approximately 8 per cent, because 90 days represents about a quarter of a year. This rate of return can simply be understood as the interest on the bill.

If the bill sold at £97, the rate of return would be:

$$r = \frac{(100 - 97)}{97} = 3.09\%$$

In general terms, the rate of interest on a bond that is purchased at price P_B and pays $\overline{P}$ on maturity is:

$$r = \frac{(\overline{P} - P_B)}{P_B}$$

As T-bills are directly marketable assets, their price and thus the rate of interest will change with fluctuations in demand and supply in the bond market. As bonds are a direct substitute for money, the interaction between the bond and money markets will be influential in determining the interest rate.

5.5 Determining the interest rate

If the interest rate is the price of money then, like all prices, it will be determined by the forces of demand and supply. Once we know what factors are responsible for influencing the demand and supply of money, we will better understand how interest rates are set in the money market.

5.5.1 The demand for money

A simple money demand function could be written as follows:

$$M^d = L(\underset{+}{Y}, \underset{-}{r}, \underset{+}{c})$$

The demand for money will depend on three things: income (Y), interest rates (r) and the cost of liquidating financial assets (c). 5

Income

The main reason for holding money is for the purpose of carrying out transactions. It is fairly intuitive to expect that the number of transactions undertaken will be positively related to income. As income rises, we spend more and therefore require larger money holdings.

Interest rates

This is the opportunity cost of holding money. It represents the rewards from investing in financial assets, such as bonds or saving accounts. As the interest rate rises, these rewards become larger so the demand for money will fall.

Cost of liquidating financial assets

If it were very easy, quick and inexpensive to cash in financial assets, then there would be little reason for holding money. Money could be deposited in bonds, and then when it was needed as a medium of exchange it could be quickly released. However, if it were relatively difficult, then higher cash holding would be required. For this reason, the demand for money will be positively related to the cost of liquidating assets.

Plotting the demand for money against interest rates would lead to a downward-sloping function as shown in Figure 5.2.

Changes in income or in the cost of liquidating assets will lead to shifts in the money demand function. This means that the demand for money is different at each and every level of interest rates. For example, in Figure 5.3 an increase in income ($Y_1 \rightarrow Y_2$) or a rise in liquidation cost ($c_1 \rightarrow c_2$) would lead to an outward shift in the money demand schedule.

Baumol-Tobin model

This is a simple model of the demand for money that incorporates many of the issues discussed above. It is essentially a model of cash management, asking how many times a person should go to the bank during a certain period of time, and therefore what their optimal holdings of money will be. The choice is between making lots of trips to the bank and holding relatively small amounts of money, or making few trips to the bank but holding much larger cash balances.

5

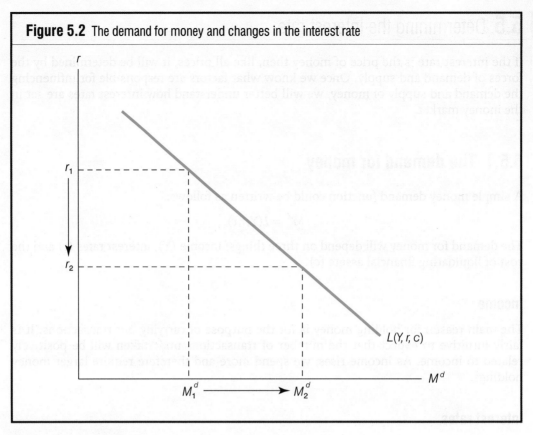

Figure 5.2 The demand for money and changes in the interest rate

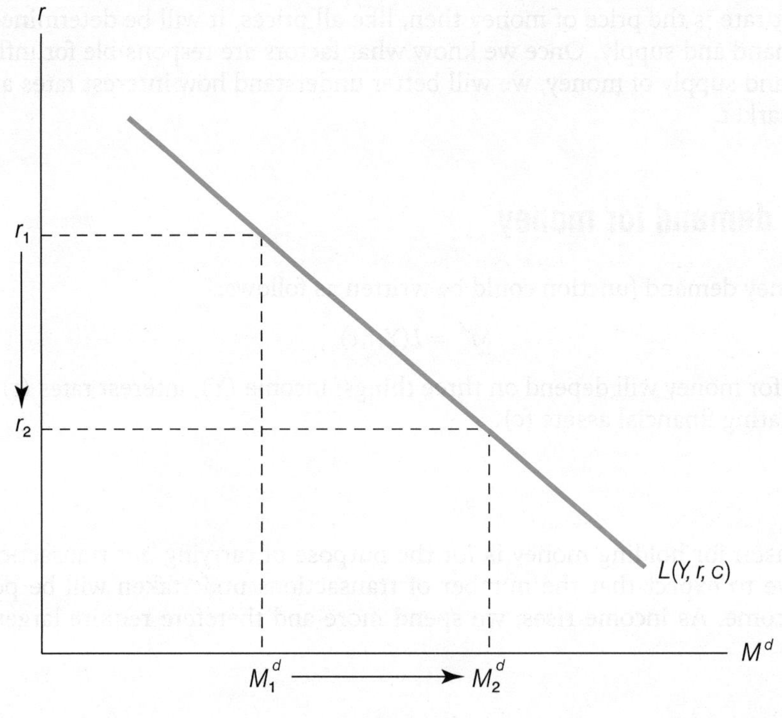

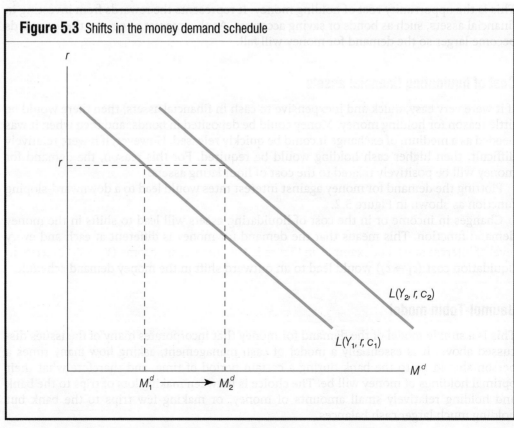

Figure 5.3 Shifts in the money demand schedule

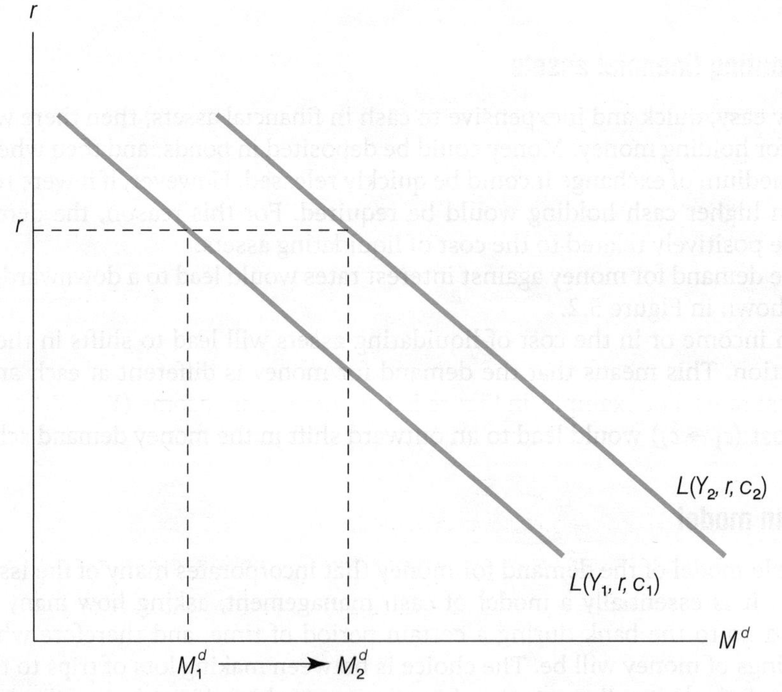

Global application 5.1

Nominal and real interest rates

When we think of the interest rate we are usually thinking of the *nominal interest rate*. The nominal interest rate describes the cost of transferring money across time. It tells us how many pounds we need to pay in the future in exchange for having an extra pound today. The higher the interest rate, the more it costs to transfer money from the future to the present.

However, the value of money in different time periods will also depend on its relative purchasing power. The *real interest rate* refers to the cost of transferring money over time in terms of real goods and services. Nominal and real interest rates will differ when the price of goods and service changes over time. For example, suppose the nominal interest rate was r^{nom} per period, then the monetary value of £X today in the next period is £$(1 + r^{nom})X$. However, the real value of £X today in the next period will depend on what happens to prices over this period.

The change in prices over the period is described by the rate of inflation (π_{t+1}).

$$\pi_{t+1} = \frac{P_{t+1} - P_t}{P_t}$$

If the inflation rate is positive, then goods and services cost more in the future than today, so the purchasing power of a given sum of money falls. Therefore, the real interest rate, r_{real}, is defined as:

$$(1 + r_t^{real}) = \frac{(1 + r_t^{nom})}{(1 + \pi_{t+1})}$$

which implies that the real interest rate at time *t* is approximately equal to the nominal interest minus the inflation rate at time *t*+*1*.

$$r_t^{real} \approx r_t^{nom} - \pi_{t+1}$$

From the other perspective, what would be the cost of transferring money from the future to the present? In money terms, this would just be given by the nominal interest rate. In real terms though, we are also concerned with the relative

Figure 1 Nominal interest rates and inflation in the UK Source: ONS

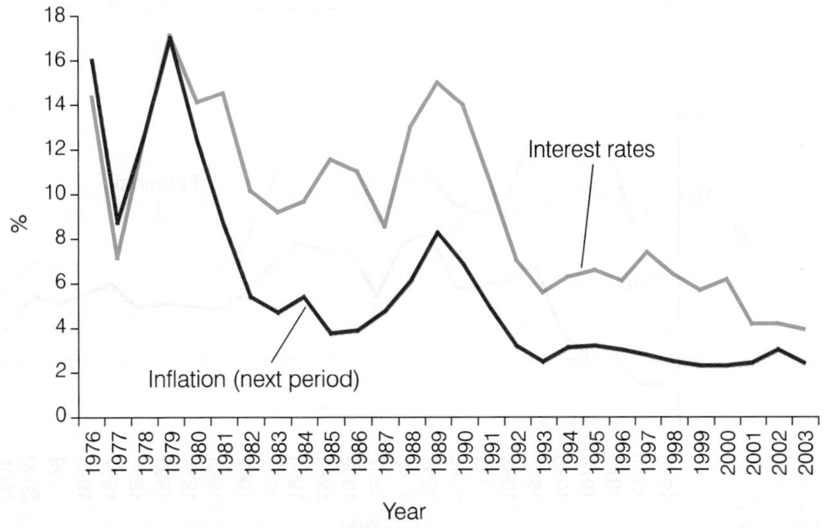

Global application 5.1 (continued)

purchasing power in each period. If inflation is positive then the same goods and services are more expensive in the future than the present. Therefore, fewer future goods and services would need to be sacrificed in order to increase consumption today.

Because inflation is usually positive, it is generally the case that real interest rates are lower than nominal interest rates. Also, because rates of inflation change over time, it is also possible that periods which have similar nominal interest rates will have very different real interest rates.

Figure 1 plots the nominal interest rate and the next period inflation rate in the UK. Using this, the real interest rate is constructed as plotted in Figure 2. On the whole, periods with high nominal rates also have periods of high real interest rates. However, when inflation is as high as it was during the late 1970s, periods of high nominal interest rates will also be periods of low real interest rates.

Because measures of the real interest rate require knowledge of how future prices change, we can only calculate it in retrospect. However, at any point in time, the expected real interest rate will be defined in terms of the expected inflation rate (π^e_{t+1}).

$$E[r_t^{real}] \approx r_t^{nom} - \pi^e_{t+1}$$

Therefore, the real interest rate that prevails at any given time would depend on inflation expectations. If expected inflation is equal to the rate in the prevailing period, then the real interest rate is simply

$$r_t^{real} = r_t^{real} - \pi_t.$$

Real or nominal?

The interest rate plays an important role in the economy. So far, we have seen that it is an important determinant of consumption, investment and government debt. However, should we be more interested in the real or nominal interest rate?

Strictly speaking, it is the real interest rate that should be most important. This is because consumption, investment and the government debt are all real variables, so the real interest rate best describes the cost of transferring resources over time. However, there is strong empirical evidence to suggest that these factors are heavily driven by the nominal interest rate.

One explanation for this is seen in Figure 2. For the most part, movements in the nominal interest rate are reflected in the real rate. In addition, uncertainty over the prevailing rate of inflation may lead households, governments and firms to be more willing to base decisions on the prevailing nominal interest rate.

Figure 2 Nominal interest rates and real interest rates in the UK Source: ONS

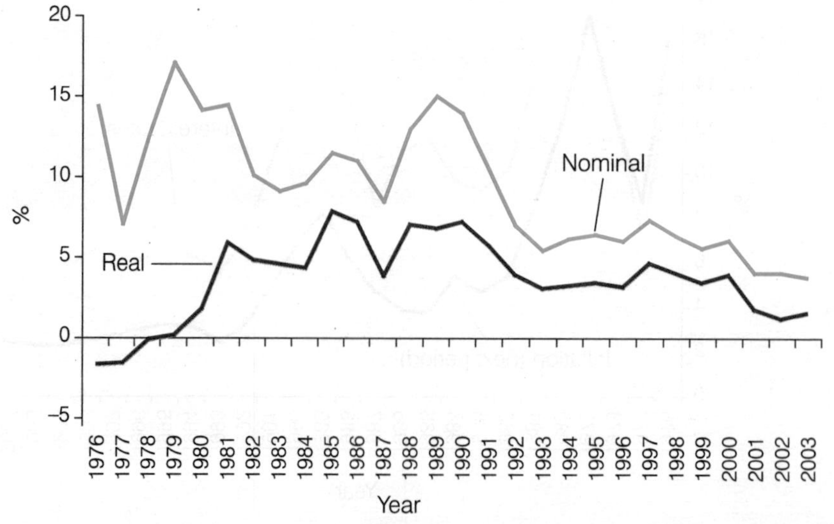

In making this choice, a trade-off is faced. There is a cost of making a trip to the bank; we call this a shoe-leather cost as making cash withdrawals requires walking to the ATM. This shoe-leather cost is essentially the same as the liquidation cost mentioned above. Minimizing these costs would require us to make relatively few trips to the bank and thus hold larger cash balances.

However, the downside to this is that in holding more money, we are giving up the interest that we would otherwise have earned by leaving the money in the bank. If we made more trips so money holdings were lower, more money on average will be left in the bank earning interest. The trade-off between the costs and benefits of holding money is a choice between minimizing liquidation costs or minimizing forgone interest payments.

Assume that in a given time period income Y is earned. If this income is withdrawn straight away in one trip to the bank and spent gradually over this period, then money holdings would be as follows.

The first trip to the bank is made straight away and all the income Y is withdrawn. This means that average money holdings will simply be Y/2. This is shown in Figure 5.4a.

Suppose two trips were made to the bank. Money holdings would follow the pattern in Figure 5.4b.

If two trips are made, half the income Y/2 is withdrawn straight away, with the other half being withdrawn half way through the period. The average money holdings in this case are Y/4.

And, finally, consider the case where three trips were made to the bank.

Each of the three times the bank is visited a total of Y/3 is withdrawn, meaning that average money holdings are Y/6.

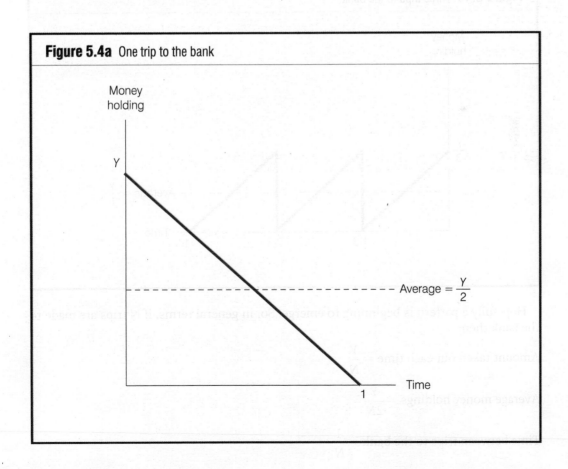

Figure 5.4a One trip to the bank

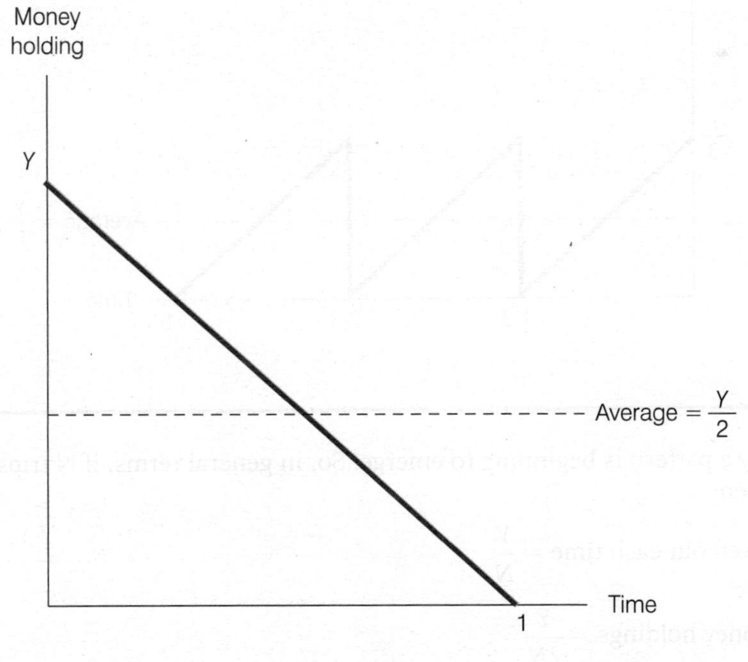

5

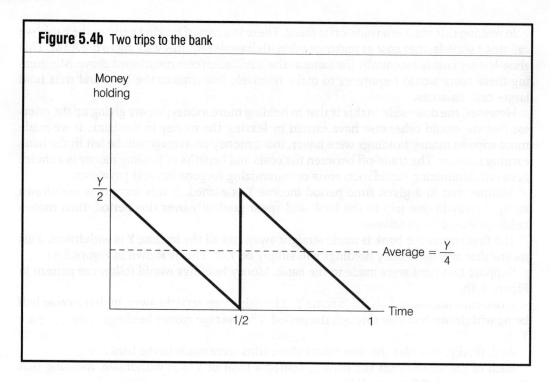

Figure 5.4b Two trips to the bank

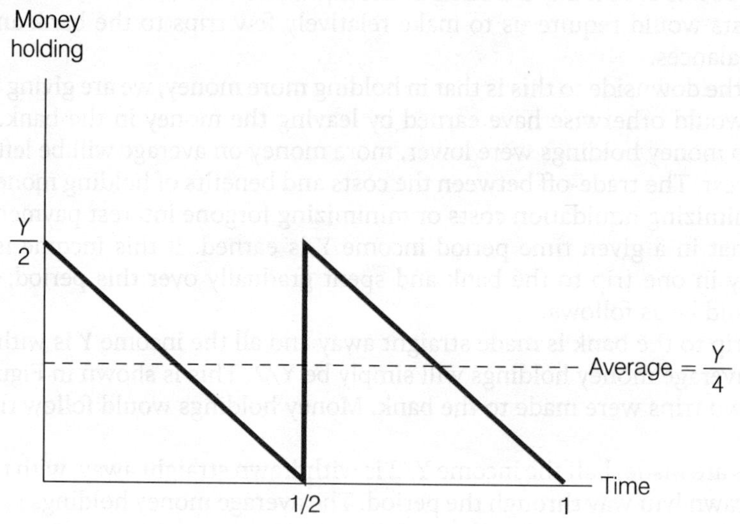

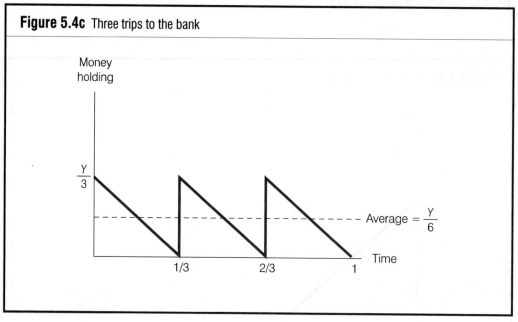

Figure 5.4c Three trips to the bank

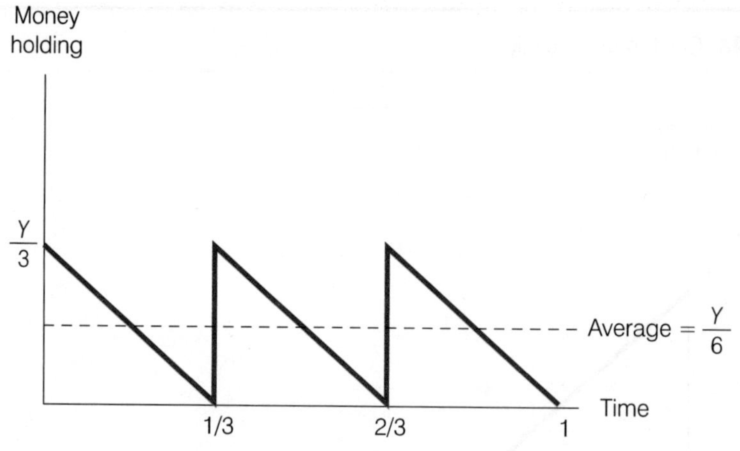

Hopefully a pattern is beginning to emerge. So, in general terms, if N trips are made to the bank then:

$$\text{Amount taken out each time} = \frac{Y}{N}$$

$$\text{Average money holdings} = \frac{Y}{2N}$$

$$\text{Time between trips to the bank} = \frac{1}{N}$$

The household must now decide the optimal number of trips they should make to the bank and therefore the amount of money to hold during this period. If every trip costs *c*, the total shoe-leather cost of making N trips would equal N*c*. In Figure 5.5, total shoe-leather costs will increase as the number of trips to the banks increases.

However, the foregone interest costs must also be considered. If the interest rate is *r*, and the average money holdings are Y/2N, then these costs would amount to *r*Y/2N. The forgone interest costs are also plotted in Figure 5.5. As more trips are made to the bank, average money holdings and therefore these forgone interest rate costs will fall.

Therefore, total costs (TC) associated with N trips to the bank will be given by the sum of the shoe-leather and foregone interest costs:

$$TC = r\frac{Y}{2N} + Nc$$

Effective cash management would aim to choose N so as to minimize these total costs. From Figure 5.5 it can be seen that where these costs are minimized, and therefore the optimal number of trips (N^*) is when the shoe-leather and foregone interest costs are equal.

At points to the left of N^*, foregone interest costs exceed shoe-leather costs. Therefore, making an extra trip to the bank would reduce the foregone interest costs by more than the extra shoe-leather costs involved, so total costs will fall. Alternatively, at points to the right of N^*, shoe-leather costs exceed the foregone interest costs. By reducing the number of trips to the bank by one visit, total costs will fall as the reduction in shoe-leather costs would exceed the increase in foregone interest.

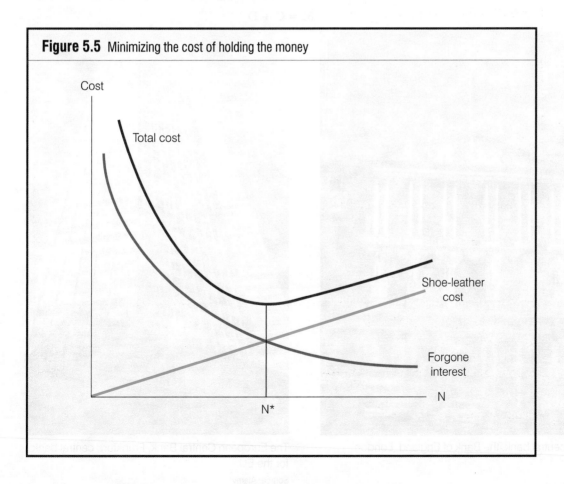

Figure 5.5 Minimizing the cost of holding the money

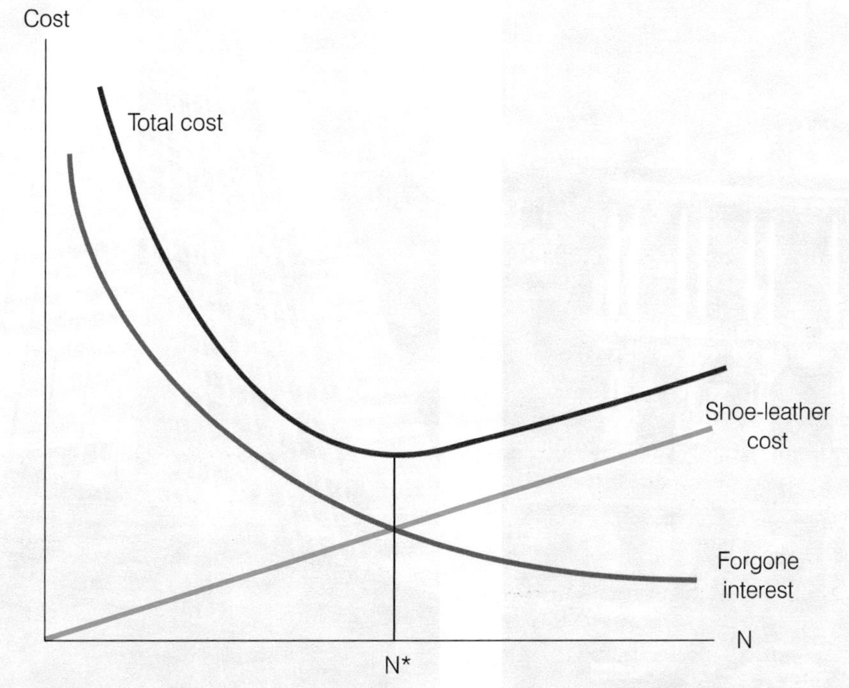

From the parameters of the model (those who like calculus can check for themselves by minimizing TC with respect to N), the optimal number of trips to the bank will be:

$$N^* = \sqrt{\frac{rY}{2c}}$$

From this, we can simply devise the optimal average money holdings as:

$$M^* = \frac{Y}{2N^*} = \sqrt{\frac{Yc}{2r}}$$

We can see that optimal cash holding will increase with income and shoe-leather (liquidation) costs and fall with increases in interest rates. This corresponds to the properties of the money demand function we set out earlier.

5.5.2 Money supply

From previous discussion we established that the supply of money consists of everything that is available as a medium of exchange, which is the total quantity of currency and demand deposits (current accounts). In accepting this (to make the forthcoming analysis much easier), we are disregarding the possible existence of near money.

Money supply = Currency + Demand deposits

M = C + D

The UK's central bank, the Bank of England, London.

Source: PCL

The European Central Bank, Frankfurt: central bank for the EU.

Source: Alamy

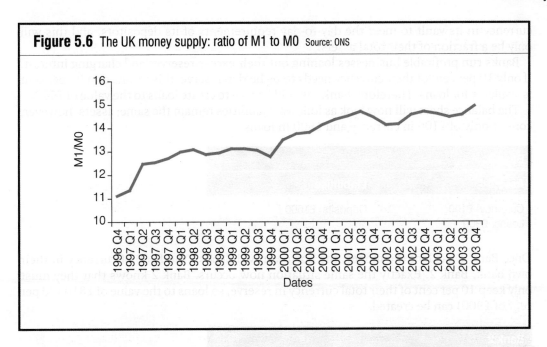

Figure 5.6 The UK money supply: ratio of M1 to M0 Source: ONS

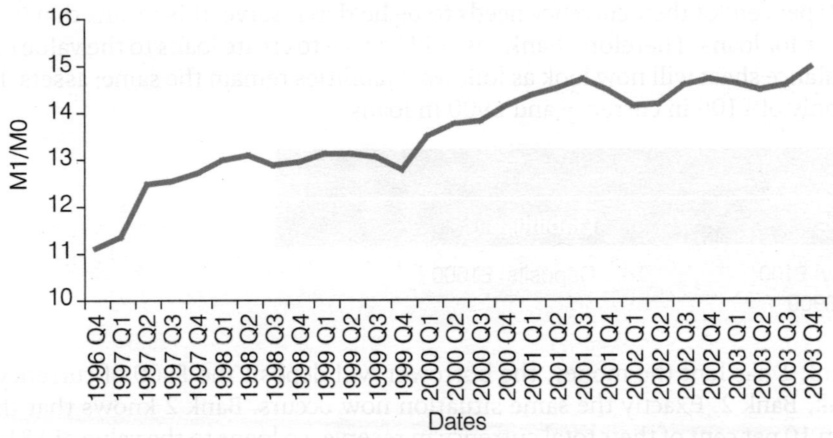

Although the central bank is the monopoly supplier of notes and coins, the actual supply of money is largely determined by the banking system. Figure 5.6 displays some recent evidence for the UK. M0 is the aggregate amount of cash in circulation (C). This is controlled by the central bank, which is the Bank of England in the UK. M1 is the money aggregate which includes M0, as well as current accounts in the banking sector. If we ignore for the moment the problems associated with near money, we might press for a broader definition. M1 effectively represents the money supply. It is everything that can be used as a medium of exchange.

In Figure 5.6 it is clear that M1 is much larger than M0. In fact, throughout recent history, the magnitude has been in the order of around thirteen-fold. As these demand deposits are created by the banking sector, it is clear that they play an important part in determining a nation's supply of money. The process by which these deposits are created will be analysed next.

Money creation

To see how the banking sector can create demand deposits, let us look at a bank's balance sheet.

Bank 1	
Assets	**Liabilities**
Currency: £1000	Deposits: £1000

The bank's (Bank 1) balance sheet is written in double-entry form. Every asset has a corresponding liability. Suppose a depositor invested £1000 of cash in the bank. The bank's assets will consist of this £1000 cash, the liabilities will also be £1000, as this is how much the bank must pay to the depositor on demand.

However, banks know that all their depositors are highly unlikely to turn up and withdraw all their funds at one time. Therefore, the bank is only required to keep enough currency in its vault to meet the day-to-day requirements of its depositors, and this will only be a fraction of their total assets.

Banks run profitable businesses loaning out their excess reserves and charging interest. If only 10 per cent of their currency needs to be held in reserve, this means that 90 per cent is available for loans. Therefore, Bank 1 would be able to create loans to the value of £900.

The balance sheet will now look as follows. Liabilities remain the same; assets, however, consist only of £100 in currency and £900 in loans.

Bank 1	
Assets	**Liabilities**
Currency: £100 Loans: £900	Deposits: £1000

5

Once Bank 1 has lent the money, the borrower will deposit the £900 of currency in their own bank, Bank 2. Exactly the same situation now occurs. Bank 2 knows that they must only keep 10 per cent of their total currency in reserve, so loans to the value of £810 (90 per cent of £900) can be created.

Bank 2	
Assets	**Liabilities**
Currency: £90 Loans: £810	Deposits: £900

This process then continues. The £810 of currency loaned by Bank 2 will find its way into Bank 3, who by keeping 10 per cent in reserve creates loans to the value of £721.

Bank 3	
Assets	**Liabilities**
Currency: £81 Loans: £721	Deposits: £810

Deposit creation will carry on in the same way. What should be clear by now is that the original £1000 in cash has been used to create demand deposits which far exceed this amount.

The total change in deposits is represented by the total change in the assets of the entire banking sector:

Bank 1's assets increase by £1000, Bank 2's by £900 (0.9 × £1000), Bank 3's by £810 (0.9 × £900) and so on. The series representing the change in the banking sector's assets ($\Delta M1$) is:

$$\Delta M1 = £1000 + 0.9(£1000) + 0.9^2(£1000) + 0.9^3(£1000) + \ldots\ldots$$

Summing this process to infinity, we achieve:

$$£1000 \times \frac{1}{1-0.9} = \frac{£1000}{0.1} = £10000$$

Therefore, the original £1000 in cash ($\Delta M0$) increases the money supply ($\Delta M1$) by £10 000, a factor of 10. This implies that:

$$\frac{\Delta M1}{\Delta M0} = 10$$

An alternative, and perhaps easier, way of looking at the same mechanism would be as follows. Bank 1, knowing that total currency reserves do not need to represent more than 10 per cent of total deposits, could just simply increase loans by £9000. This is effectively what would happen anyway if it were the only bank.

Bank 1	
Assets	**Liabilities**
Currency: £1000 Loans: £9000	Deposits: £10 000

The creation of demand deposits is a feature of the fractional reserve banking system, where the banking sector knows that only a limited proportion of total reserves are required to meet daily demands for cash. Because of this, the total money supply will always be a multiple of the amount of currency. For this reason, the total amount of currency is known as the *monetary base* or the stock of *high powered money*.

The money multiplier

The stock of high powered money is given by C and the reserve asset ratio is given by rr.

Therefore,

$$M = C + (1 - rr)C + (1 - rr)^2 C + (1 - rr)^3 C + \ldots\ldots$$

Using the sum to infinity, we achieve:

$$M = \frac{1}{1-(1-rr)} C$$

$$M = \frac{1}{rr} C$$

$$M = mC, \text{ where } m = \frac{1}{rr}$$

The **money multiplier** is 1 over the reserve ratio. In the example we gave above, C = £1000, m = 1/0.1 = 10, so M = £10 000.

Extensions to the multiplier theory

There are two further considerations which may affect the size of the money multiplier.

Leakages Not all currency necessarily finds its way into, or stays in, the banking system. The banking sector can only create deposits on its reserves. If households decide to hold some of their deposits in currency, this reduces the reserves of the banking sector and the ability to create money.

The currency deposit ratio (cr = C/D) represents the proportion of deposits households hold as cash. If this exceeds zero, then there is a leakage from the banking system, which will reduce the size of the money multiplier.

The money supply again consists of total currency and demand deposits.

$$M = C + D$$

The stock of high powered money, H, or in other words, the monetary base, is

$$H = C + R$$

This consist of currency held by households (C) and the reserves of the banking sector (R). The money multiplier is simply the ratio of the total money supply to the money base:

$$\frac{M}{H} = \frac{C+D}{C+R}$$

If we divide the top and bottom parts of the ratio by D, we can rewrite the above in the following way:

$$\frac{M}{H} = \frac{C/D+1}{C/D+R/D}$$

$$\frac{M}{H} = \frac{cr+1}{cr+rr}$$

where rr = (R/D), the reserve deposit ratio.

$$M = m'H, \text{ where } m' = \frac{cr+1}{cr+rr}$$

As long as $cr > 0$, it will be true that $m' < m$.

Therefore, changes in the currency-deposit ratio of households would change the value of the money multiplier.

Banking behaviour There is no reason to argue that banks always maintain their balance sheets at the minimum permitted reserve asset requirement. In fact, this would also be arguing that banks can always find customers for any loans they wish to create. There are many reasons why the bank may hold higher reserves than the minimum permitted reserve-deposit ratio.

First, banks may not wish to advance loans if they consider lending to be too risky. In a recession when bankruptcies tend to rise, the risk of default on any loan also tends to rise, which may discourage bank lending. In Figure 5.6, the slight upward trend in the multiplier is probably reflective of the strong performance of the economy over this period. Second, a bank may decide to keep some reserves for future business. For example, if future interest rates were predicted to rise, the bank may withhold current lending with the aim of lending in the future at the higher rate.

These two factors both suggest that calculating the actual money multiplier may be more complicated than finding the inverse of the minimum permitted reserve-deposit ratio of the banking sector.

Changing the money supply

The stock of money is independent of the interest rate, so the money supply function will be vertical. Changes in the money supply will lead to shifts in the function, an increase to the right and a decrease to the left. This can be seen in Figure 5.7.

There are effectively two ways in which the government can control the money supply. It can either act to control the stock of high powered money, or the size of the money multiplier.

Open market operations

By buying and selling bonds to the general public, the government can attempt to control the size of the monetary base, and therefore the money supply. When the government sells bonds, the private sector purchases them with cash, drawn from the reserves of the banking sector. The money supply would then be expected to fall by an amount equal to the product of these reserves and the money multiplier. Likewise, if the government wished to

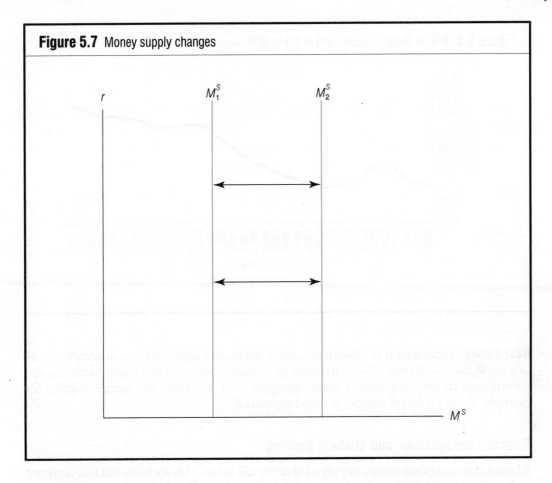

Figure 5.7 Money supply changes

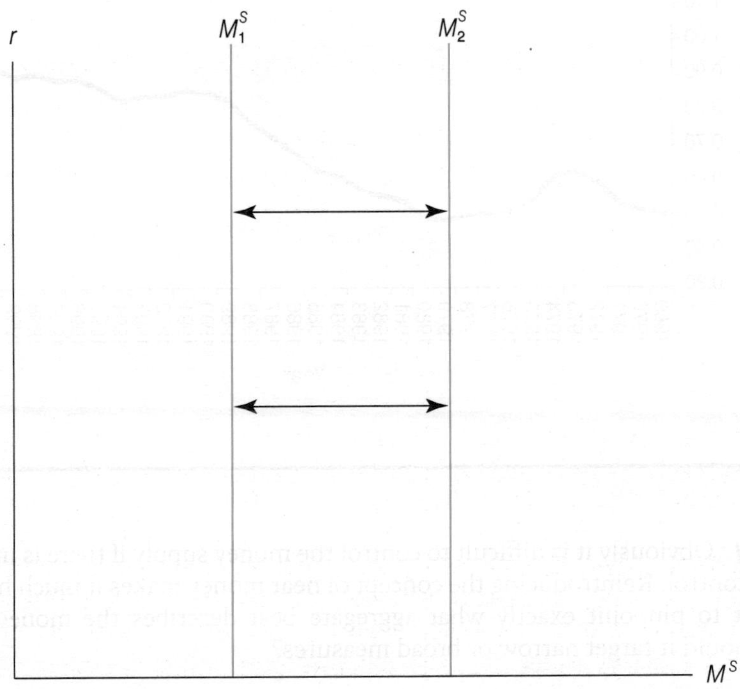

increase the money supply, then it would simply purchase bonds from the private sector. Cash would then be deposited in the banks and lead to a multiplied increase in the money supply.

Reserve asset requirements

Simply by controlling the size of the reserve asset requirement (rr), the government can control the size of the entire money stock. A higher reserve asset ratio will reduce the size of the multiplier, and therefore the extent to which the money supply can be expanded from the stock of high powered money. A lower reserve asset ratio will, of course, have the opposite effect, and generate an increase in the money supply.

Problems in controlling the money supply

Although the government, through its central bank, has a monopoly in the supply of currency, there may still be large operational problems in controlling the money supply.

Estimating the size of the multiplier The government has control over the monetary base, but the money supply is largely determined by the size of the multiplier. As this will depend on the behaviour of households and banks (see above), calculating the actual value of the multiplier might be quite difficult.

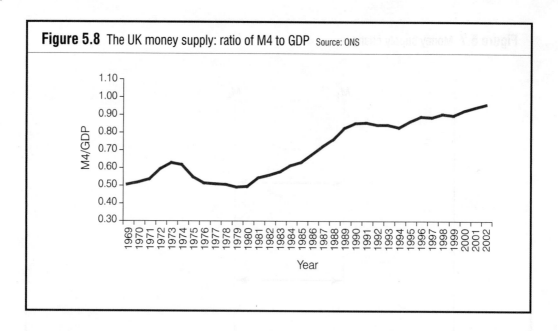

Figure 5.8 The UK money supply: ratio of M4 to GDP Source: ONS

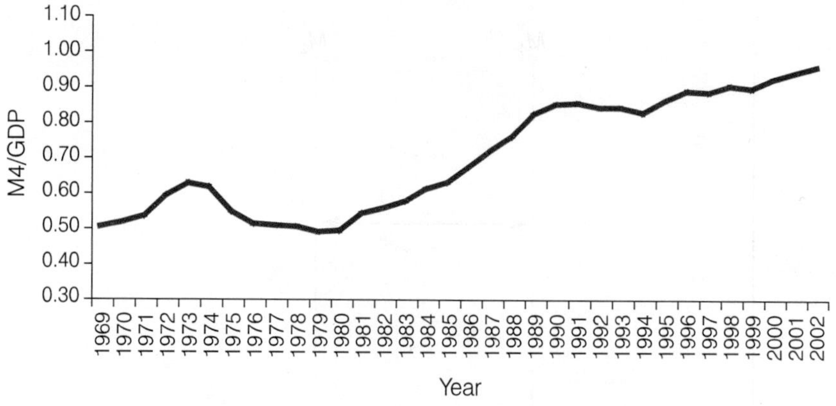

Near money Obviously it is difficult to control the money supply if there is uncertainty as to what to control. Reintroducing the concept of near money makes it much harder for the government to pinpoint exactly what aggregate best describes the money supply; for example, should it target narrow or broad measures?

Financial deregulation and offshore banking

A broad measure of the money supply used in the UK is M4. This includes not just currency and current accounts, but also longer-term saving accounts which may constitute near money. Figure 5.8 plots the ratio of M4 to GDP over recent decades. A striking feature of Figure 5.8 is the persistent rise in this ratio between 1979 and 1988. This represented a period of sustained financial market deregulation.

In 1979, exchange controls were lifted. Previously there were strict limits on the amount of foreign exchange transactions that a household or firm could undertake. Removing these restrictions effectively opened up the possibility of borrowing from overseas. This means that the domestic money supply will include demand deposits generated by institutions from other countries. The government therefore loses some control on the money supply, as it can only control the process of domestic credit creation.

In 1986, a wave of reforms was introduced to deregulate financial markets. The motivation was to encourage greater competition whereby credit would become more widely available and cheaper. However, in ceding its regulatory powers, the government faced a trade-off in losing some of its ability to directly intervene in the credit creation process.

Therefore, the combination of an increasingly international and liberalized credit market means that policy makers will find it much harder to control the money supply.

5.5.3 Equilibrium in the money market

Equilibrium in the money market is simply determined by the intersection of money demand and money supply. This is shown in Figure 5.9. Because bonds are the substitute to holding money, a description of how the interest rate is determined lies in how the money and bond markets interact with each other.

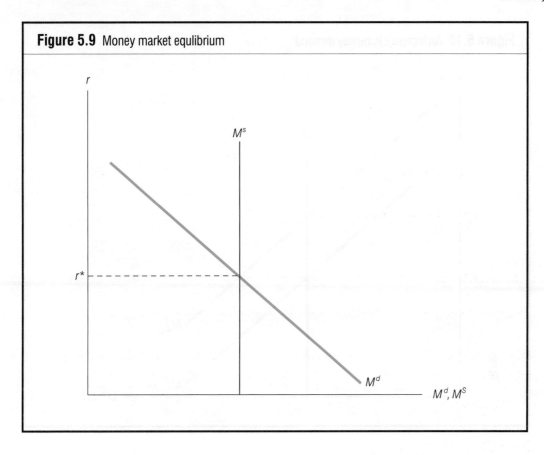

Figure 5.9 Money market equlibrium

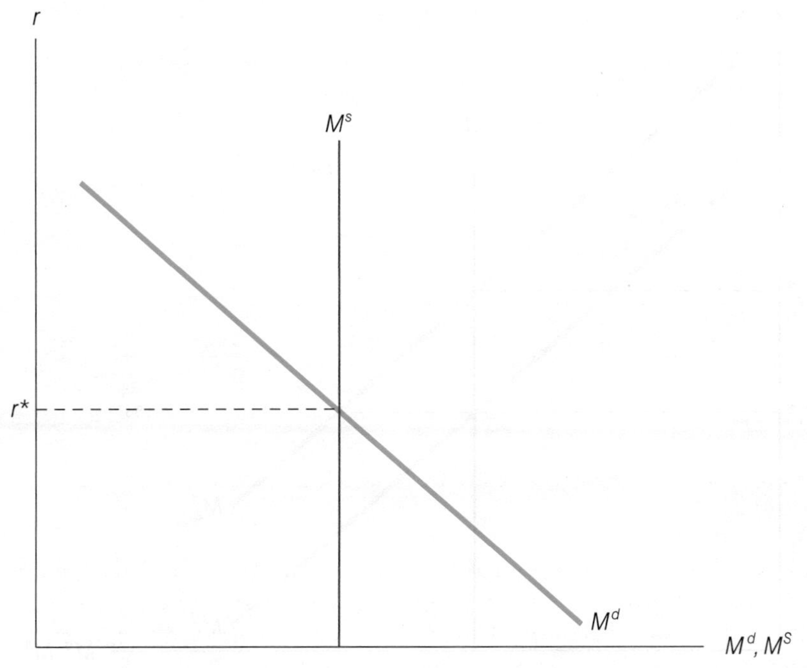

The equilibrium interest rate is given by r^*. Suppose the interest rate was above this level ($r > r^*$). As a result, the demand for money would be less than the supply of money ($M^s > M^d$), so households are holding more currency than they wish to. The logical response is to invest the excess holdings in bonds so that interest can be earned. However, as bonds are purchased, their price rises which leads to a fall in the interest rate back to r^*.

Alternatively, suppose the interest rate was below the equilibrium level ($r < r^*$). In this case, there is excess demand for money ($M^s < M^d$). Households wish to hold more currency than there is supply. In order to raise this cash, households will attempt to sell any bonds they own, but this act of selling would force bond prices down and the rate of interest upwards. Therefore, the level of interest r^* is synonymous with equilibrium in both the bond and money markets.

Anything that acts to shift the demand or supply of money would be expected to change the equilibrium interest rate.

Changes in money demand

Previously, we noted that changes in income or the cost of liquidating financial assets will lead to shifts in the demand for money. An increase in the demand for money would be expected to put upward pressure on the interest rate (Figure 5.10).

Starting at an equilibrium interest rate of r_1^*, an increase in income leads to an outward shift in the money demand curve ($M_1^d \rightarrow M_2^d$). At this initial interest rate, there is an excess demand for money. Households will attempt to cash in bonds, which will reduce their price and lead to an increase in interest rates to r_2^*. Actions that reduce the demand for money would naturally have the opposite effect, putting downward pressure on the equilibrium interest rate.

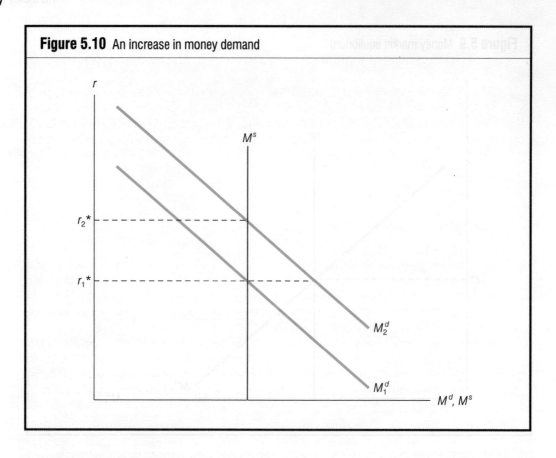

Figure 5.10 An increase in money demand

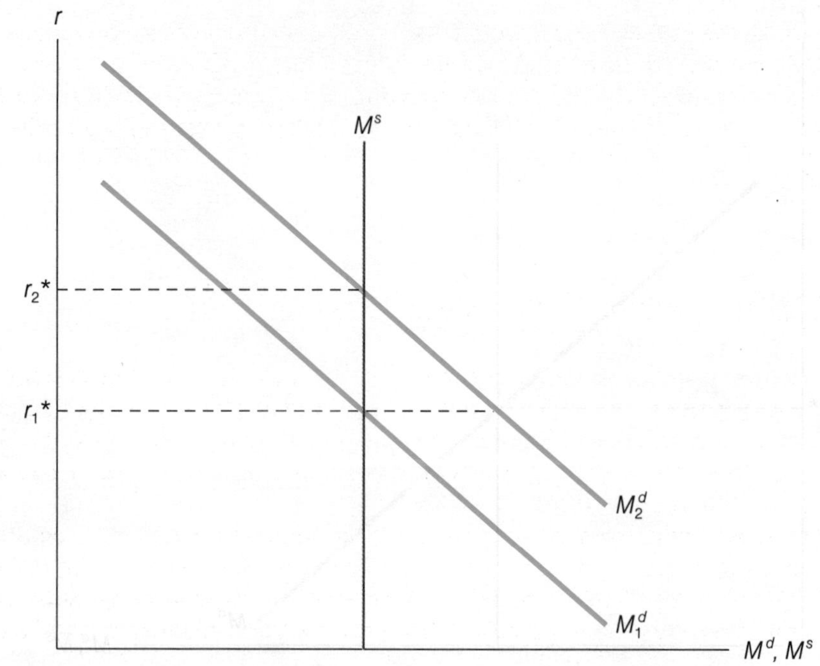

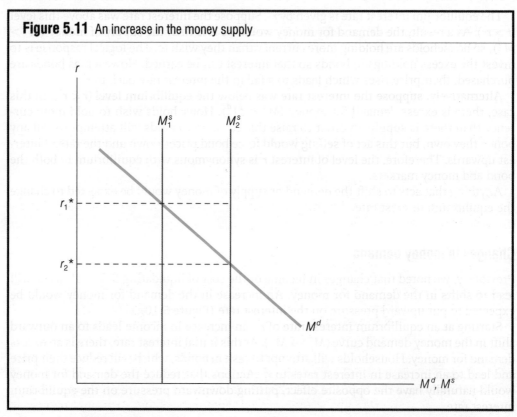

Figure 5.11 An increase in the money supply

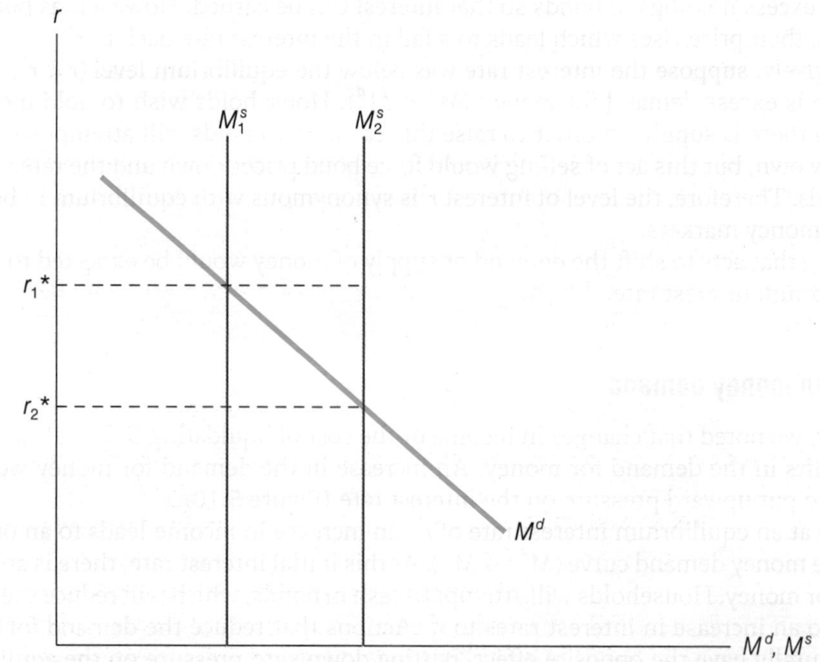

Changes in the money supply

Changes in the money supply will lead to simple shifts in the money supply schedule (Figure 5.11).

An increase in the money supply would lead to an outward shift in the money supply schedule ($M_1^s \rightarrow M_2^s$). At the initial equilibrium interest rate, r_1^*, there will now be an excess supply of money. Households will attempt to reduce this by using their excess cash holdings to buy bonds. This will push the bond price upwards and reduce the equilibrium interest rate to r_2^*.

5.6 The term structure of interest rates: yield curves

5

The maturity of a bond is the length of time over which the bond makes payments. The yield on a bond describes the per period return until its maturity and can be thought of as the average return each period. The yields on bonds with maturities of a year or less are known as short-run interest rates, while the yields on bonds of longer maturities are described as long-run interest rates.

There is no reason why the short-run and long-run interest rates need to be the same. This is because the demand and supply of money and therefore the equilibrium interest rate can change over time. For example, if it is expected that future income or prices will be higher with no offsetting changes in supply, then the money demand curve will shift outwards and future interest rates will be higher than present.

The term structure of interest rates describes the yields on bonds of different maturities. The yield curve is a graphical representation of this concept, which plots yields against maturity. If the yield curve is upward-sloping, then it suggests that future interest rates are expected to be above current rates. Likewise, if the yield curve is downward-sloping, then it suggests that short-term rates exceed long-term rates.

The yield at each maturity is calculated by finding the geometric average of all the per period interest rates.

$$\text{One-period yield} = (1 + r_1)$$

$$\text{Two-period yield: } \sqrt{(1+r_1)(1+r_2)}$$

Therefore, if the interest rate is 2 per cent this period, and 5 per cent in period two, then the two-period yield is:

$$= \sqrt{(1+0.02)(1+0.05)} = \sqrt{1.02 \times 1.05} = 1.035 \text{ or } 3.5\%$$

The two-period yield is above the one-period yield simply because the second-period interest rate exceeds that in the first.

In general,

$$\text{N-period yield: } = \sqrt[n]{(1+r_1)(1+r_2)\ldots\ldots..(1+r_n)}$$

This can be approximated by taking the arithmetic mean of all the interest rates.

$$\text{N-period yield} \approx \frac{(1+r_1)+(1+r_2)+\ldots\ldots+(1+r_n)}{n}$$

The shape of the yield curve can be informative (Figure 5.12). It is a useful description of the expectations that financial markets have concerning the future state of the economy. Normally, an upward-sloping yield curve implies that growth and/or inflation will increase in the future, so long-term interest rates exceed those in the short term. Alternatively, a

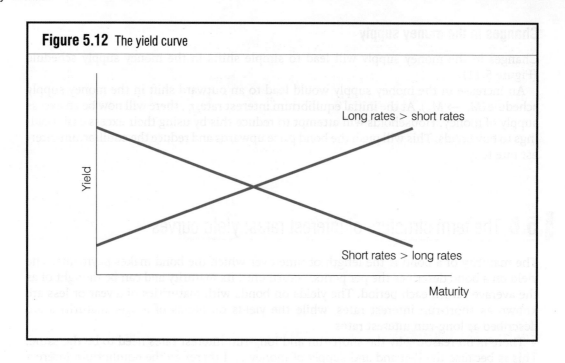

Figure 5.12 The yield curve

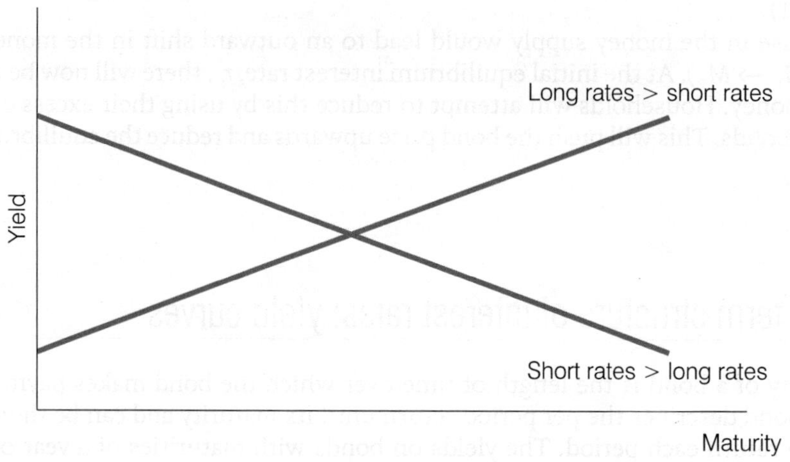

downward-sloping yield curve is an indicator that growth and/or inflation will be lower in the future, implying a downward trend in interest rates over time.

5.7 Monetary policy: money supply or interest rate?

The government, through its central bank, is the monopoly supplier of currency. It is a standard result that monopolies cannot control both the price and quantity of their output. They can either set the price and let output be determined by demand; or alternatively, they can set the supply and let the price be determined by demand and supply. Exactly the same result must apply to the operation of monetary policy. The government cannot target both the money supply and the interest rate.

We have already covered in detail how the money supply will be set. However, because the operation of monetary policy in most countries is concerned with setting interest rates, this deserves some further discussion.

The general mechanism that central banks use to set the interest rate is known as discounting. If the bank wishes to change the interest rate, it could sell excess bonds to the private sector, which will purchase these using reserves from its bank accounts. This will make the banking sector short of cash, which would force it to borrow reserves from the central bank in order to maintain sufficient reserves to meet daily demand for cash. The rate of interest at which the central bank makes these loans is called the *discount rate*. By changing the discount rate, the government can effectively change the rate of interest set by the entire banking sector.

The Bank of England uses this principle in setting UK interest rates. The way the Bank of England lends to the banking sector is through repurchase agreements, also known as *repos*. When the banking sector receives loans in the form of cash from the central bank, they must deposit eligible assets, such as Treasury Bills, to the value of the loan in special accounts at the Bank of England. At a later date, these will be repurchased at a set lower price, which in turn determines the interest rate on the loan. This interest rate is known as the *repo rate*. Once again, changes in this rate will effectively determine the interest rate set by the entire banking sector.

In a later chapter, we will discuss the formation of monetary policy along these principles and touch on the current vogue in policy making, the notion of central bank independence.

Summary

- In this chapter, we have analysed what constitutes money and its role in the economy.
- We examined the determinants of the interest rate, including money demand, supply and equilibrium in the money market.
- We also analysed the term structure of interest rates or yield curves.
- Finally, we concluded with an assessment of different forms of monetary policy.

Key terms

Interest rate
Monetary policy
Money
Money multiplier

Review questions

1. A bond promises to pay £250 in one year's time.
   a. What will the interest rate on the bond at current market prices £185, £200 and £230, respectively?
   b. What is the price of the bond at interest rates of 5 per cent, 7.5 per cent and 10 per cent?
   c. What is the relationship between bond prices and interest rates?
2. Compute the money multiplier when the required reserve assets ratio is 3 per cent and the public decides to hold 15 per cent of its money in cash. What actions could the central bank undertake to raise the money supply by £100 million?
3. Explain how the following will affect the equilibrium level of interest rates.
   a. a large increase in the cost of using ATMs
   b. a requirement for all banks to deposit a proportion of their reserves in a non-interest bearing account at the central bank
   c. the government runs a substantial budget surplus and repurchases bonds from the private sector
   d. a fall in consumer confidence.

More advanced problems

4. The demand for money is given by:
   $M_d = 0.5Y - 2000r$.
   a. If the income level is $Y = 1000$, and the interest rate is $r = 10\%$, what is the demand for money?
   b. What is the equilibrium level of interest rates when the supply of money is equal to 200?
   c. What happens to the equilibrium rate of interest following:
   - an increase in the money supply to 400?
   - an increase in income to 1500?
5. An individual has take-home pay of £15 000 per year and spends all of it at a uniform rate over the course of a year. He pays for everything in cash and earns 10 per cent interest on his bank account. However, long queues at the cash machine mean that each visit to the machine costs £10 in lost wages.
   a. How many times does the individual go to the bank and how much is withdrawn at each visit?
   b. How would the answers to part (a) change if:
   - a new cash machine opens which reduces queueing times, meaning the cost of each withdrawal falls to £5?
   - to encourage saving, the bank increases its interest rate to 15 per cent per annum?
   - a strengthening economy sees the individual's take-home pay rise to £20 000?
6. The real interest rate rises from 3 per cent to 5 per cent, while the nominal interest remains unchanged at 7 per cent. Explain how this scenario arose and what the implications are for the demand for money.
7. Why might the slope of the yield curve be a good predictor of future GDP? How might the term structure of interest rates be important for investment and the servicing of government debt?

For further resources, visit
http://www.thomsonlearning.co.uk/chamberlin_yueh

6 Financial markets

Learning objectives

- Understand the nature of financial markets and why they are an important determinant of consumption and investment.
- Analyse the expected dividends model and the process of arbitrage.
- Introduce the capital asset pricing model (CAPM), a consumption-based model which implies that assets with higher returns offer less opportunity to hedge against income risks.
- Discuss the Tobin model of portfolio selection, which describes how investors choose the optimal combination of risk and return in their portfolios.
- Investigate the efficient markets hypothesis (EMH) that financial asset prices should reflect all available information and that asset prices follow a random walk process.
- Evaluate the empirical tests which tend to reject the EMH because the volatility of asset prices is greater than the volatility of news regarding fundamentals.
- Define and learn about bubbles in financial markets, such as the dotcom bubble in the late 1990s.
- Learn about crashes, which refer to a large and sudden drop in market values, and the role of traders.

6.1 Introduction

In the previous chapter we introduced the main features of the money market. In doing so, we only considered two types of assets, money itself and interest-bearing bonds. This chapter extends the analysis to look at financial markets – by which we predominately mean the stock market. The stock market is where equities, such as stocks and shares, are traded and prices are determined.

We have seen that stock market valuations play a very important role in the economy. Movements in share prices have consequences for the value of investments, and therefore would be expected to have implications for wealth and consumption. Although there is some evidence to suggest that consumption is rather insensitive to movements in the stock market, the evidence probably plays down the true impact. This is because the major investors in stocks and shares are pensions and life insurance companies, which are effectively saving on behalf of households. Falling share prices would reduce pension wealth, implying that households must increase saving (reduce consumption) in order to fund adequate pensions. Chapter 4 introduced Tobin's q as a model explaining investment. This is heavily related to stock market valuations of firms, so it is clear that stock markets play an important role in allocating investment funds.

Financial markets are therefore at the centre of the circular flow of income and play an important allocative role by intermediating between savers and borrowers. Financial markets are said to be efficient if asset prices reflect all of the available and relevant information. In this scenario, savings will be directed to where they achieve the highest returns, which also implies that only the best yielding investment opportunities are undertaken.

In performing this allocative role, it is not just the level of return that matters but also the risks that are attached. Bonds are largely considered to be riskless assets; this is because they are usually issued by governments that have tax-raising powers so default risk is minimal. This cannot be said of private sector companies. Different investments may offer different expected rates of returns, but the variance or level of uncertainty can also differ. Therefore, efficient pricing of shares requires a consideration of both risk and return. This is another avenue in which financial markets play an important allocative role in the economy. If they are efficient at pricing risks and uncertainties, then they offer investors an opportunity to manage risks effectively.

However, this does not preclude the notion that financial markets can be inefficient, and actually be a hindrance to the functioning of the economy. If asset prices become detached from fundamental values, then it can disrupt the choices between saving and consumption, and also the assets among which saving is allocated. Because of the potential misallocations that can result, the study of where financial markets go wrong is of great interest to economists.

The focus of this chapter will include the study of both efficient and inefficient financial markets.

6.2 Efficient markets: asset pricing models

If financial markets are efficient, then the price of a financial asset should reflect all available information concerning the fundamentals of risk and return. In these circumstances, it would be expected that assets which offer relatively high and certain returns would be highly priced accordingly.

In this section, we introduce two models of asset price determination. The first is what has been termed the **expected dividend model**. This relates the price of an asset to the stream of expected future dividends that the asset pays. The **Gordon model** is a commonly used variant of this model. By assuming that the stream of future dividends are described by a constant growth rule, it enables the expected dividend model to be written down in a simple way. These models, though, only concentrate on expected returns and do not take account of risks.

The second model we consider is widely used in corporate finance. The **capital asset pricing model**, or **CAPM**, argues that the value of an asset is strongly related to its ability to diversify risks. This is a consumption-based model in which assets that offer high returns in states of the world when income is low are relatively highly priced. This is because individuals can use them to maintain income levels in situations when they would otherwise be poor. In the opposite vein, assets that offer high returns in high income states would offer limited ability to diversify wealth and be priced lower.

6.2.1 Expected dividend model

Dividends and expected discounted values

A firm listed on the stock market has been split into a number of shares, with each share representing ownership of a certain proportion of the company. These shares are marketable so their value is determined by demand and supply. The total value of the company (V_t) is found by simply calculating its market value, that is, the number of shares (N_t) multiplied by the price of each share (P_t).

$$V_t = N_t \times P_t$$

There are two elements that make up the returns from holding shares. The first is the entitlement to a share of the firm's earnings, which are usually paid as dividends. The second arises from the gains or losses that accrue from the resale value of the share. If the share price rises (or falls) in the period of ownership, then a capital gain (or loss) is made. These returns, though, are uncertain. The motive for buying or holding a certain share must therefore come from its expected future returns given the information available at the time.

Assume that:

P_t is the price of the financial asset at time t.

I_t is the information set available at time t.

The expected dividend paid, given this information, is $E(D_{t+1}|I_t)$, and also conditional on the information available, the expected asset price next period is $E(P_{t+1}|I_t)$. These values, though, will only be obtained in the next period at time $t+1$. In order to present them in present (time t) values, they need to be discounted by the interest rate $(1 + r)$. The reason for applying this discount factor has been explained in many of the previous chapters and readers are recommended to refer to Global application 2.1, if necessary.

The efficient price of the financial asset will therefore be set equal to the expected discounted value of the future dividend payment and resale price.

$$P_t = [E(D_{t+1}|I_t) + E(P_{t+1}|I_t)]/(1+r) \quad (6.1)$$

If the asset price were to deviate from this, then there would be opportunities for traders to make profits. If the asset price were above its efficient value, then those who hold the asset would be best advised to sell the asset. This is because the proceeds could then be invested at the safe interest rate $(1 + r)$ and higher returns would be achieved than from the dividend and the resale price. This pressure to sell would be sufficient to push the overvalued assets back toward their efficient price.

The opposite would be true if the current asset price were below this efficient price. Buying the asset would lead to an expected return in excess of the basic interest rate $(1 + r)$, so any investor would make money by borrowing from the bank or cashing in bonds and buying the asset. This buying pressure would push the asset price up towards its efficient values.

The process that drives asset prices to their efficient values is known as *arbitrage*. When people think of financial markets, they often think of traders who are buying and selling assets in order to achieve trading profits. These traders can be thought of as *arbitrageurs*. Their whole basis for trading is to try and profit from mis-pricings and they can trade aggressively to do so, but the outcome will be to drive asset prices toward fundamental values.

If a trader believes the asset to be underpriced, then they will take a *long position* in the asset. This means that they have a positive holding in their portfolio under the expectation that the asset will rise in value and they can sell for a profit. The act of buying the asset, though, will bid its price upwards. If, instead, the trader believes the asset to be overvalued then they can take a *short position*. This involves borrowing the asset from another trader and selling it on the open market. The borrowed asset must be eventually returned by repurchasing it on the open market, but if in the meantime its price has fallen then a profit is made. Once again though, the act of selling the asset would force the asset price downwards. An important factor here is that a trader does not need to own an asset to effectively sell it.

By combining long and short positions, it is possible for a trader to hold a portfolio that does not cost anything. For example, its long positions in certain assets are funded by short positions in others. For this reason, arbitrage can be a strong phenomenon as traders can take positions in order to profit from expected movements in asset prices.

The **expected dividend model** implies that the efficient price of an asset can be written in terms of the stream of future expected discounted dividend payments the asset generates. This is because equation (6.1) can be written solely in terms of future dividend payments.

From (6.1) the expected price of the asset at time $(t+1)$ will be determined in exactly the same fashion as it was in time t:

$$E(P_{t+1}|I_t) = [E(D_{t+2}|I_t) + E(P_{t+2}|I_t)]/(1+r) \tag{6.2}$$

Equation (6.2) states that, if priced efficiently, the expected price of the asset at time $t+1$ will equal the sum of the expected discounted dividend payment and asset price at time $t+2$.

If (6.2) is substituted into (6.1), then a new equation for the asset price at time t can be derived:

$$P_t = [E(D_{t+1}|I_t) + [E(D_{t+2}|I_t) + E(P_{t+2}|I_t)]/(1+r)]/(1+r) \tag{6.3}$$

Alternatively, this can be written as:

$$P_t = \frac{E(D_{t+1}|I_t)}{(1+r)} + \frac{E(D_{t+2}|I_t)}{(1+r)^2} + \frac{E(P_{t+2}|I_t)}{(1+r)^2} \tag{6.4}$$

Therefore, the current price of the asset is equal to the expected discounted dividend payments over the next two years and the expected discounted resale price in two periods' time. Note that the payments which accrue two periods in the future are discounted twice.

Hopefully, you can now see a pattern beginning to emerge. The expected asset price in two periods' time would be equal to the sum of the expected discounted dividend payment and asset price in time $t+3$.

$$E(P_{t+2}|I_t) = [E(D_{t+3}|I_t) + E(P_{t+3}|I_t)]/(1+r) \tag{6.5}$$

Substituting (6.5) into (6.3) gives the current asset price as a function of dividends over the next three periods and the asset price at time $t+3$.

$$P_t = \left[E(D_{t+1}|I_t)\left[E(D_{t+2}|I_t) + \left[E(D_{t+3}|I_t) + E(P_{t+3}|I_t)\right]/(1+r)\right]/(1+r)\right]/(1+r) \quad (6.6)$$

This can be seen more clearly by rearranging the above:

$$P_t = \frac{E(D_{t+1}|I_t)}{(1+r)} + \frac{E(D_{t+2}|I_t)}{(1+r)^2} + \frac{E(D_{t+3}|I_t)}{(1+r)^3} + \frac{E(P_{t+3}|I_t)}{(1+r)^3} \quad (6.7)$$

Once again, note that the values which accrue in three periods' time are discounted three times.

By continuing this repeated substitution to infinity, we can derive a very simple formula for the fundamental value of an asset solely in terms of its dividend stream.

$$P_t = \frac{E(D_{t+1}|I_t)}{(1+r)} + \frac{E(D_{t+2}|I_t)}{(1+r)^2} + \frac{E(D_{t+3}|I_t)}{(1+r)^3} + \ldots\ldots\ldots + \frac{E(P_{t+\infty}|I_t)}{(1+r)^\infty} \quad (6.8)$$

Payments that arise a substantial time in the future are discounted more heavily, so in present value terms their value will head to zero. Therefore, we would expect that as time goes to infinity that the expected discounted asset price will head towards zero:

$$\frac{E(P_{t+\infty}|I_t)}{(1+r)^\infty} \to 0$$

This leaves the current asset price as being determined only by the stream of expected future discounted dividend payments:

$$P_t = \sum_{i=1}^{\infty} E(D_{t+i}|I_t)/(1+r)^i \quad (6.9)$$

Exchange dealer in the Euro Dollar Pit at the Chicago Mercantile Exchange.

Source: © John Gregg/Reuters/Corbis

Equation (6.9) is the essentially the same as (6.1). The expected dividends model is fairly intuitive in that it links asset values according to the returns that the asset produces. If all assets are priced at their efficient levels, then investors will obtain the same rate of return regardless of which asset they buy. This will be the rate of interest $(1 + r)$, so the investor will also be indifferent between holding any asset and bonds. It is easy to understand why. Any asset that offers higher expected dividend will be correspondingly priced. The only way to make a return in excess of $(1 + r)$ would be to try to profit from any mis-pricings.

6

Global application 6.1

Market makers and spreads

Generally, when buying or selling a financial asset the price at which the transaction occurs is different from the actual market price. The *bid price* is the price at which an asset is sold, and is usually lower than the market price. The *ask price* is the price at which an asset is bought and is generally higher than the market price. The difference between the bid price and the ask price is known as the *bid–ask spread* or just simply the *spread*. No doubt most of us are aware of spreads when we come to make foreign exchange transactions. If we go to a bank or a bureau de change, it is rare to be able to buy and sell currency at the official market rate.

When buying or selling a financial asset, whether it is a share, currency, commodity, etc., it is unlikely that we have to wait for a trader to come along who wishes to make the opposite trade. For example, if we wish to buy dollars we do not need to search for somebody wishing to sell them, we just go to the bureau de change. Likewise, when trading assets we simply lodge a buy or sell order with a recognized brokerage firm or stock exchange. These are all examples of market makers, whose function is to facilitate trade between buyers and sellers in financial markets.

The bid–ask spread represents the payment the market maker receives for providing intermediary services. Without these traders, we would be forced to barter, which would result in high search and negotiation costs. As buyers and sellers do not arrive at the market in a synchronized fashion, the market maker faces risks; i.e., while waiting for a buy or sell order, asset prices may move against them leaving them with capital losses.

The size of spreads reflects many factors. The more regularly an asset is traded the lower the spread, as market makers do not have to hold open positions for long periods of time while waiting for a buy or sell order. The justification for the spread here is market failure. If the market maker was not compensated for providing intermediary services, then the market maker would exit and the market for the asset will collapse. Also, spreads tend to be lower when competition among market makers is greater. This relates spreads to market power, reflecting the profit motive for providing intermediary services.

This model is quite simple, but it can be used to analyse the causes of stock market changes. These broadly fall into two categories. The first is any factor that is likely to affect the flow of future dividend payments, which are in turn derived from the firm's earnings. This could be almost anything – a technological breakthrough, changes in the management structure, specific government regulations, the state of the economy and consumer demand, the condition of the firm's competitors, and so on. The second is the interest rate, which represents the opportunity cost of holding equities, as any investor could always invest in bonds instead. It is easily seen from (6.9) that higher interest rates imply future dividend payments are more heavily discounted, so share prices would be expected to fall.

Gordon growth model

A simple variant of the expected dividend model is the **Gordon model**. This uses exactly the same framework as above, but specifies a rule that describes how dividends grow over time. This model reaches broadly the same conclusions, but is widely used due to its simplicity.

The most important assumption is that dividends grow at the rate of g each period. Therefore:

$$D_{t+1} = (1+g)D_t$$

$$D_{t+2} = (1+g)D_{t+1} = (1+g)^2 D_t$$

$$D_{t+3} = (1+g)D_{t+2} = (1+g)^3 D_t$$

And so on.

If we substitute this dividend stream into (6.8), then the current asset price can be written as follows:

$$P_t = \frac{D_t(1+g)}{(1+r)} + \frac{D_t(1+g)^2}{(1+r)^2} + \frac{D_t(1+g)^3}{(1+r)^3} + \ldots\ldots \tag{6.10}$$

The expression in (6.10) can be simplified further to produce a very simple rule for asset prices.

The first step is to factorize (6.10) by collecting the common term D_t on the right-hand side:

$$P = D_t\left[\left(\frac{1+g}{1+r}\right) + \left(\frac{1+g}{1+r}\right)^2 + \left(\frac{1+g}{1+r}\right)^3 + \ldots\ldots\right] \tag{6.11}$$

Next, we need to make an assumption that the growth rate is less than the interest rate $(g < r)$. In doing so, it is then the case that $\left(\frac{1+g}{1+r}\right) < 1$.

This assumption is convenient because it makes the mathematics easier to solve, but there is also a strong economic reason for doing it this way.

Imagine what will happen to the present discounted value of future dividend payments if dividends grow at a faster rate than the interest rate. As we progress further and further into the future, the actual value of dividend payments will become very large and the discounted value will also increase over time. Holding the asset will then guarantee you an explosive growth in dividend payments. The sum of discounted dividend payments as shown in (6.11) will therefore go to infinity.

This situation will be avoided by imposing the rule that dividends grow at a lower rate than the rate of interest. In this scenario, future dividend payments will be increasingly discounted so their present discounted value will trend to zero. This means that the asset price described in (6.11) will converge to a non-infinite number. This seems to make sense both intuitively and empirically.

However, as mentioned above it also makes the mathematics easier. In (6.11), the terms in the square brackets can be simplified by using the rule for finding a sum to infinity.

$$S_\infty = \frac{a}{1-rr}$$

a is the initial starting value and rr is the ratio between successive components.

In the case of (6.11):

$$a = \left(\frac{1+g}{1+r}\right) \quad rr = \left(\frac{1+g}{1+r}\right)$$

So, substituting these into the above rule gives:

$$P_t = D_t \left[\frac{\left(\frac{1+g}{1+r}\right)}{1-\left(\frac{1+g}{1+r}\right)} \right] \tag{6.12}$$

Which, in turn, can be simplified to:

$$P_t = D_t \left[\frac{1+g}{r-g} \right]$$

And, because $D_1 = (1+g)D_0$, we can reach our bottom line of:

$$P_t = \frac{D_{t+1}}{r-g} \tag{6.13}$$

Equation (6.14) is the **Gordon model** and we can see that again there are two factors which determine the price of a financial asset. The first is the interest rate – as this rises, the efficient asset price falls. The second is the growth rate of dividend payments. The implication here is that firms which experience higher earnings growth will be valued more. If we wished to, we could reinsert the notion of uncertainty by arguing that it was expected rather than actual growth which mattered. This means that asset prices will be determined by many factors, such as those listed above.

6

The discounted dividend and Gordon models are essentially the same and relate asset prices to company earnings. However, as mentioned in the introduction, these basic models do not consider the impact of different risks and uncertainties on asset prices, and it is to this issue that we turn to next.

6.2.2 Uncertainty and the capital asset pricing model

The expected discounted dividend model is widely used, but lacks one important ingredient. Assets are valued in accordance with their income streams, so assets with a command over higher future dividends will have a greater price. However, there is one important ingredient that is missing in valuing assets this way – risk. In this section, we will introduce the **capital asset pricing model (CAPM)** in which assets are valued in terms of their ability to diversify risks.

This is a consumption-based model. Asset pricing models of these types are driven by the law of diminishing marginal utility of consumption. This states that as consumption increases, total utility increases but at a declining rate. In Chapter 2, we saw that this had important implications for the pattern of consumption over time. One of the main features of the permanent income hypothesis is that smoothing consumption over time is consistent with utility maximizing behaviour.

The typical way of representing uncertainty in economics is to define several possible states of the world and attach a probability to each occurring. This is the same type of uncertainty when faced with tossing a coin or rolling a dice, and can be thought of as being made to undertake a gamble. When presented with a choice of accepting a sure amount of £X, and a gamble that offers the same expected value, £X + 1000 and £X – 1000 each with an equal probability, the tendency is to opt for the sure thing. The reason: fair bets in money terms are not a fair bets in terms of utility. Because marginal utility falls with consumption, increases in wealth are less valuable than falls in terms of utility.

Under the permanent income hypothesis, consumption can be smoothed over time by using saving and borrowing to offset transitory movements in consumption. It is less obvious how an individual can smooth consumption over different states of the world, although it would be logical to do so from the standpoint of maximizing expected utility. This is where financial markets have a role to play. Different assets will generate different returns in different states of the world, so giving investors an opportunity to manage risks and uncertainty. This idea of using financial assets to diversify wealth or income uncertainties is the guiding principal behind consumption-based models, which argue that assets should be priced in accordance to their abilities to do this.

CAPM argues that assets should be valued according to their degree of income diversification. The law of diminishing marginal utility of consumption implies that as consumption increases ($C\uparrow$), the marginal utility of an extra unit of consumption falls ($MU(C)\downarrow$). In terms of pricing assets, this implies that dividend payments paid in periods of high income, and therefore high consumption, should be weighted less than dividends paid in periods of low income. This is because although they might have similar money values, they have very different values in terms of utility. Incorporating this feature into the asset pricing model in (6.9) yields the following:

$$P_t = \sum_{i=1}^{\infty} \frac{MU(E(C_{t+i}|I_t))}{MU(C_t)} \frac{E(D_{t+i}|I_t)}{(1+r)^i} \tag{6.15}$$

The expected dividend model is extended so that the expected discounted dividends in the future are weighted according to the marginal utility of expected consumption in each period. As mentioned earlier, this means that expected dividend payments in times when expected consumption is expected to be high will be weighted less than the same dividend payment in a time where the level of expected consumption is low.

This relationship underlies the CAPM model. The higher the covariance of an asset's returns with the marginal utility of consumption, the lower is the value of the asset. An asset where returns are negatively correlated with the marginal propensity to consume will be worth more because it enables the holders to hedge against low consumption.

The CAPM pricing rule can be derived in the following fashion:

$E[R_i]$ is the expected return on an certain asset i.

If R_{rf} is the expected return on a risk-free asset, then it is possible to write the following identity:

$$E[R_i] = R_{rf} + E[R_i - R_{rf}] \tag{6.16}$$

$E[r_m]$ is the expected return from holding the market portfolio. The market portfolio is where the same amount of each asset is held. So, if there were 50 assets traded on the market, the market portfolio will consist of holdings of $\frac{1}{50}$th of each asset.

The CAPM relationship can now be written in the following way:

$$E[R_i] - R_{rf} = \beta_i\ (E[R_m] - R_{rf} \tag{6.17}$$

For each asset, the excess return over the risk-free rate is related to the excess return of the market portfolio over the risk-free rate of return by the coefficient, β_i. This is the central element of the CAPM model. Each beta gives an indication as to how an asset can be used to diversify risks.

If $\beta_i = 1$, then the returns of asset i move directly in line with the market portfolio. In fact, asset i is the market portfolio. As the market portfolio is expected to move in line with the economy as a whole, this asset would not be expected to diversify income.

If $\beta_i < 1$, then the returns of asset i move less than the market portfolio. This offers individuals the ability to diversify income shocks. For example, if $0 < \beta_i < 1$, then following a fall in the overall stock market, the fall in the returns of asset i would be correspondingly less. It is even better in terms of diversification if $\beta_i < 0$, as the asset returns are negatively correlated with movements in the market portfolio, which offers a more complete opportunity to diversify income risks.

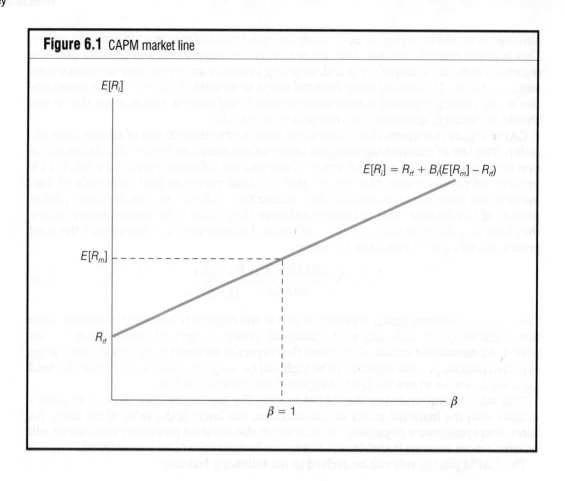

Figure 6.1 CAPM market line

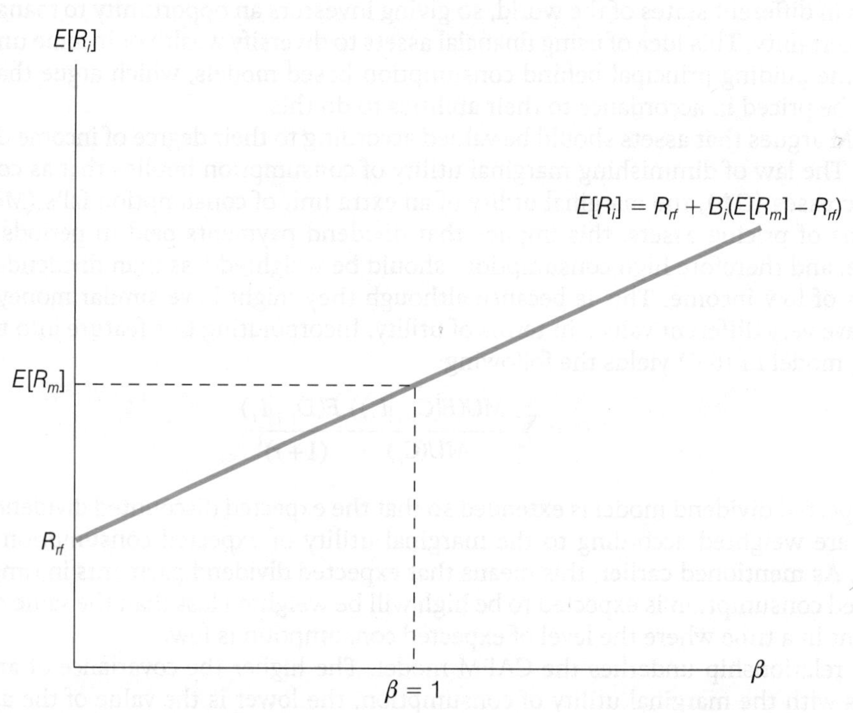

If $\beta_i > 1$, then the returns on asset *i* would be more volatile than movement in the market as a whole.

The CAPM relationship in (6.17) is known as the *market line* and is plotted in Figure 6.1. Assets that offer higher expected returns have higher betas, whereas the assets that offer lower returns have lower betas. The market line reflects a trade-off between risk and return from holding different portfolios of assets. Those which offer high expected returns are more risky, as they offer limited ability to diversify income. On the other hand, assets with low expected returns offer the compensation of a low beta, and so are better able to hedge against low income.

6.3 Portfolio selection: Tobin model

CAPM argues that assets with high returns have low betas. Therefore, there is an inherent risk-return trade-off: assets with high returns have low ability to diversify against income uncertainty. In this case, the higher return is a *risk premium* which compensates for the greater risk of holding the asset.

In the CAPM model, the riskiness of an asset is defined in terms of its ability to hedge against risks and uncertainties. However, when thinking about the riskiness of an asset, it is common to think of the uncertainty regarding its returns. A risky asset is one where expected returns are highly uncertain or volatile. These would be expected to offer higher

Global application 6.2

Estimating CAPM betas

The CAPM market line relates the expected returns of an asset to its ability to diversify risk.

$$E[R_i] - R_{rf} = \beta_i(E[R_m] - R_{rf})$$

This is just a repeat of (6.17) in the main text. For each asset i, it is possible to estimate the CAPM beta (β) by running a regression of this equation.

Ordinary least squares (OLS) regression will calculate the beta for each asset in the following way:

$$\beta_i = \frac{\text{cov}(R_i, R_m)}{\text{var}(R_m)}$$

Therefore, the higher the covariance between the expected returns of the asset and the market portfolio, the higher the measured beta. Table 1 records estimations of betas for the shares of different industries in the US.

Each of these betas describes how share prices move in relation to the market portfolio. Airlines have the highest beta. For every \$1 increase in the market, shares in firms in this industry rise by \$1.80. The same scale of movements would apply if the market portfolio moved downwards.

The expected return on this asset would be relatively high as, on the whole, markets move upwards over time. However, when the market falls due to a recession perhaps, the shares in airline firms will fall by a considerable amount relative to the general market. Therefore, the ability to protect consumption levels in periods of low income and depressed markets is low.

At the other end of the scale, gold has a very low beta showing that its price moves very little in relation to the market portfolio. This means that its expected returns will be low, as when the market moves upwards its value will move by a relatively small amount. However, in a downturn, gold will largely preserve its value and so can be used to protect against low consumption. It is a general trait that gold is treated as a safe haven because it is a precious metal with limited supply. In times of great economic and political uncertainty, it is common for investors to substitute out of equities and into gold.

Table 1 Industry asset betas (Mullins 1982)

Industry	Beta	Industry	Beta
Airlines	1.80	Agriculture	1.00
Electronics	1.60	Food	1.00
Consumer durables	1.45	Liquor	0.90
Producer goods	1.30	Banks	0.85
Chemicals	1.25	International oils	0.85
Shipping	1.20	Tobacco	0.80
Steel	1.05	Telephone utilities	0.75
Containers	1.05	Energy utilities	0.60
Non-ferrous metals	1.00	Gold	0.35

returns to compensate for the risk. Risk-free assets, which offer certain return such as government bonds, would have a lower risk premium and therefore offer lower rates of returns.

The relationship between risk and return, and the optimal amount of each asset that an investor desires to hold, is explained in the **Tobin model of portfolio selection**. A portfolio represents the combination of different assets that an investor holds. The overall risk and return of the portfolio will reflect the composition of the assets in the portfolio.

Assume for simplicity there are two types of assets. The first is a risk-free asset which offers a guaranteed rate of return R_{rf} with zero variance, $\sigma_{rf}^2 = 0$. The second is a risky asset which offers a higher rate of return, but these returns are uncertain and have a positive variance of σ_r^2. A portfolio can be constructed by choosing a combination of these two assets, with a proportion w of the risky asset and $(1 - w)$ of the risk-free asset.

The expected return from the portfolio, $E(R_p)$, is derived as follows:

$$E(R_p) = w * E(R_r) + (1 - w)*R_{rf} \quad (6.18a)$$

As the proportion of the risky asset in the portfolio increases, the expected return also increases. Equation (6.18a) can be rearranged,

$$E(R_p) = R_{rf} + w * [E(R_r) - R_{rf}] \quad (6.18b)$$

The riskiness of the portfolio, though, depends on the relative variances of the two assets. As the risk-free asset delivers certain returns, its variance is zero, $\sigma_{rf}^2 = 0$, whereas the variance of the risky asset is $\sigma_r^2 = 1$. The variance of the portfolio is then:

$$\sigma_p^2 = w^2 * \sigma_r^2 + (1 - w)^2 * \sigma_{rf}^2 \quad (6.19)$$

$$\sigma_p^2 = w^2 * \sigma_r^2$$

This can be rearranged so that the weight w can be expressed as the ratio of the standard deviation of the portfolio to the risky asset:

$$\sigma_p = \sqrt{w^2 * \sigma_r^2} = w * \sigma_r \quad (6.20)$$

$$w = \frac{\sigma_p}{\sigma_r}$$

Substituting this ratio into (6.18) gives us an equation which describes the risk–return trade-off that the investor faces.

$$E(R_p) = R_{rf} + \frac{\sigma_p}{\sigma_r} * [E(R_r) - R_{rf}] \quad (6.21)$$

Equation (6.21) fully describes the risk–return trade-off an investor faces. The excess expected return of the portfolio over the risk-free asset increases as the proportion of the risky asset in the portfolio increases. However, the variance of the returns will increase as a result. From (6.21), if the portfolio consists of just the risk-free asset so that $w = 0$, then $\sigma_p / \sigma_r = 0$ and $E(R_p) = R_{rf}$. If the portfolio consists only of the risky asset, then $w = 1$, $\sigma_p / \sigma_r = 1$, and $E(R_p) = E[R_r]$.

Plotting (6.21) on a set of axis in Figure 6.2 graphically shows the risk–return trade-off, which has a very similar form to the market line derived in the CAPM.

Figures 6.1 and 6.2 are broadly similar, showing a risk–return trade-off. The only difference is how risk is measured. In the CAPM model in Figure 6.1, risk is determined in terms of the beta – with a higher beta indicating that the portfolio has less ability to hedge against income uncertainties. In Figure 6.2, the risk of a portfolio is defined in terms of the variance or uncertainty of asset returns.

The assumption of there being only two assets is just a simplifying assumption. If there were many assets, the same trade-off between risk and return would exist, but would reflect the minimum variance of each portfolio for every level of expected returns. It would still be the case that as the portfolio becomes more risky, the expected returns would increase to reflect a risk premium.

Figure 6.2 Risk–return trade-off

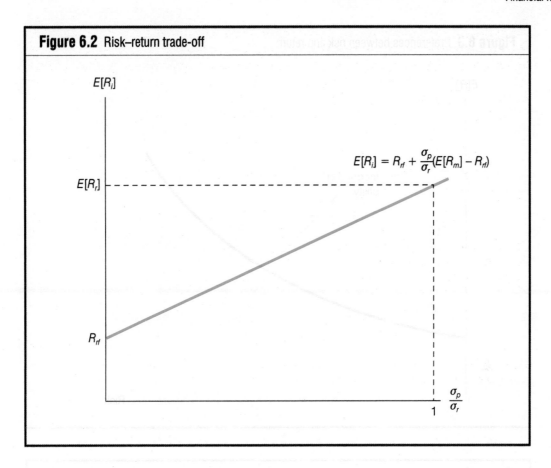

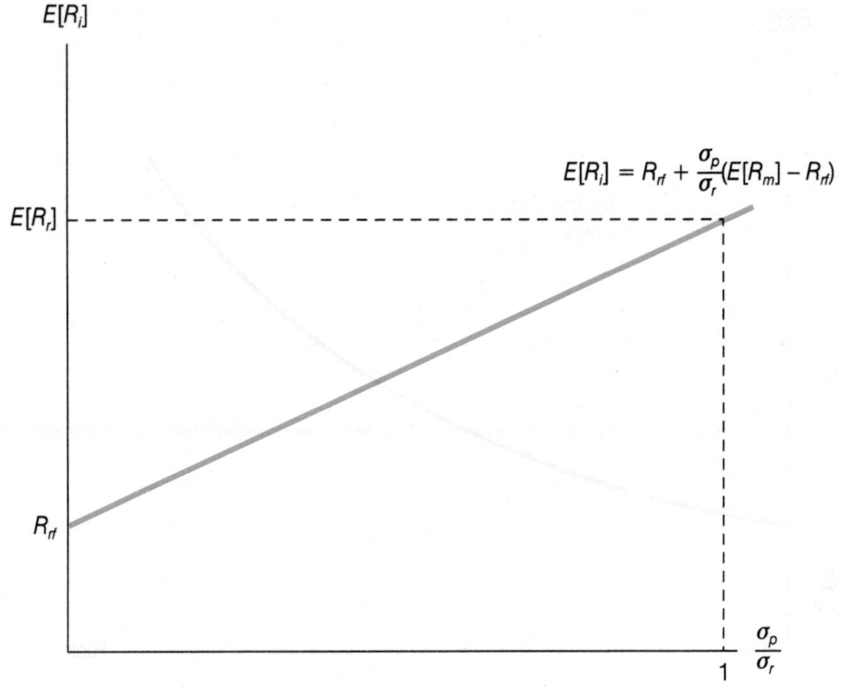

The Tobin Model describes how investors choose the risk and return composition of their portfolio. It is assumed that each trader has preferences over risk and return which can be represented in a utility function.

$$U = U(R,\sigma) \tag{6.22}$$

This utility function generates a suite of indifferences curves, which shows the combinations of risk and return that provide the investor with a given level of utility. These indifference curves are upward-sloping because investors see returns as a good thing, but risk as a bad thing. Therefore, as the investor is forced to hold a portfolio with greater risk, they require higher returns in order to keep their utility at the same level (see Figure 6.3). The slope of the indifference return reflects the rate at which the investor is prepared to trade-off risk for return. The more willing the investor is to do this, the flatter the indifference curve becomes, as it implies she needs lower extra returns in order to be encouraged to hold a riskier portfolio. As the investor becomes increasingly risk averse, the indifference curve becomes more convex.

The trader can be made better off in terms of utility if she can move to a higher indifference curve, offering higher expected returns or lower risk.

The utility maximizing decision of the risk and return structure of the portfolio is found by moving on to the highest possible indifference curve, subject to the market line which determines the feasible risk–return combinations available. This is presented in Figure 6.4, where given the preferences of the investor, the optimal risk–return trade-off is found at $(E[R^*],\sigma^*)$.

The choice of portfolio will be determined predominately by the preferences of the investor. Those who are less risk averse will likely have an optimal portfolio offering higher

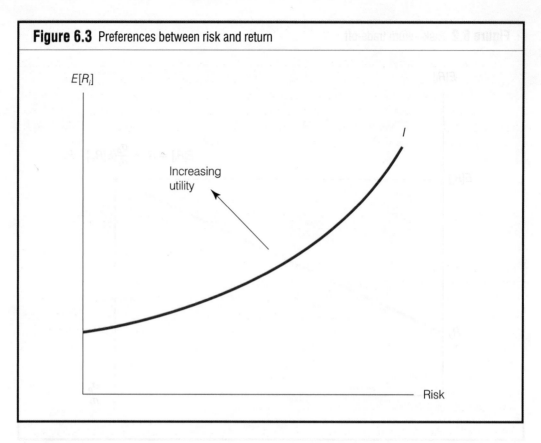

Figure 6.3 Preferences between risk and return

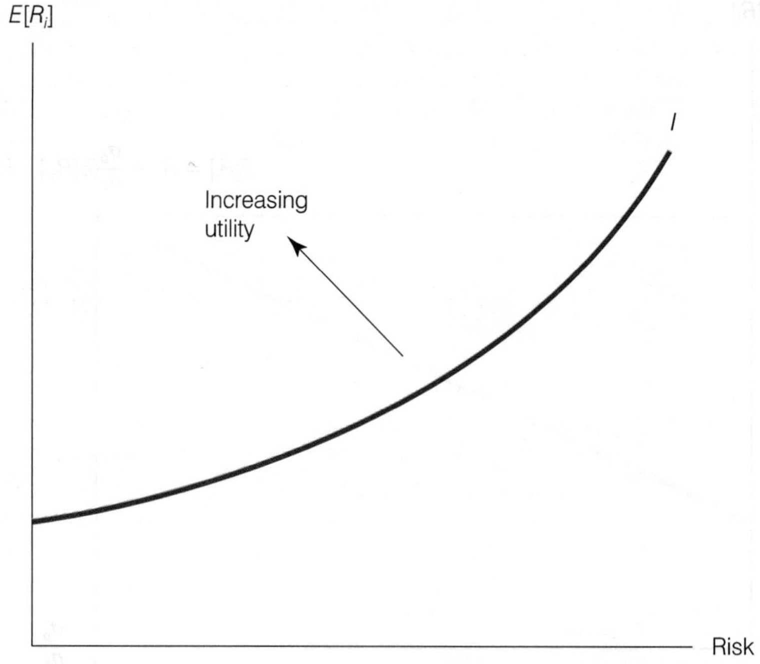

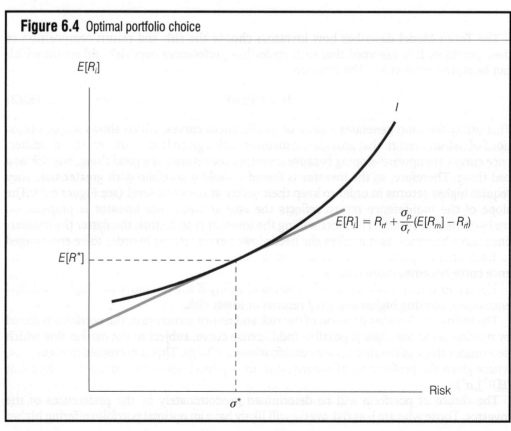

Figure 6.4 Optimal portfolio choice

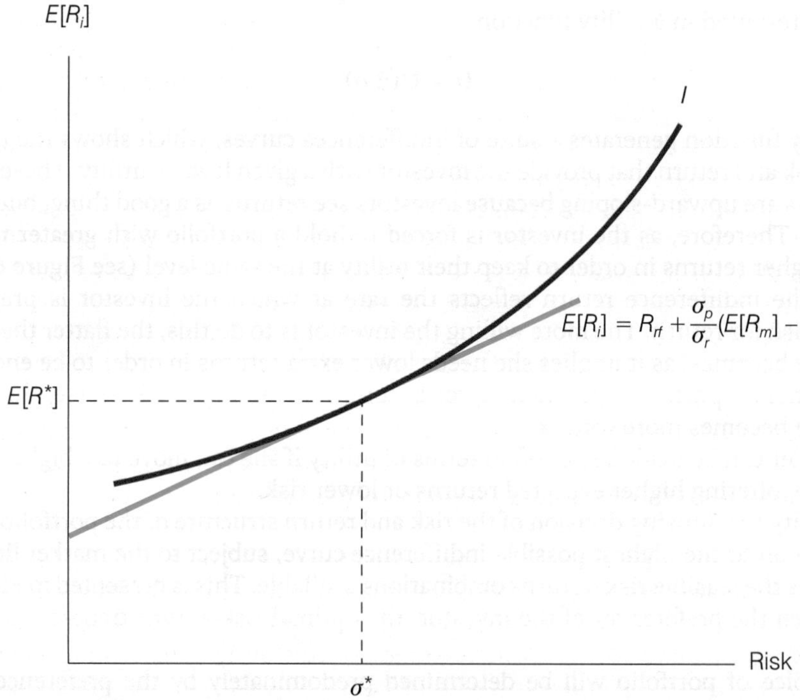

risks but also higher expected returns. The opposite would apply to more risk-averse investors.

The CAPM and Tobin models both introduce the element of risk into asset pricing. The Expected dividend model implies that assets which offer higher returns should be valued more highly. However, if these greater risks simply reflect the existence of a risk premium, then it is not necessarily the case that investors will choose to hold assets with higher expected returns. If investors are sufficiently risk averse, their optimal portfolio might consist of lower return but safer assets.

6.4 Financial market volatility: efficient and inefficient markets

The **efficient markets hypothesis (EMH)** has been the central proposition in finance theory since Fama first presented the idea in 1970. In its most basic form, it implies that prices in financial markets fully reflect the available information as in the expected dividend model in (6.9). The strong implication is that any investor cannot hope to consistently beat the market because arbitrage is strong enough to correct any mis-pricings. Spending vast resources on trying to gain an informational advantage would be wasted as all information will be incorporated correctly and quickly into asset prices; it would simply be better to passively hold the market portfolio.

The theoretical foundations of the EMH: arbitrage

There are several foundations to the EMH. First, investors are assumed to be rational, so financial assets are valued according to the expected discounted value of future dividends as explained in (6.9). The price of an asset is equal to the discounted value of all future dividends that the asset is expected to yield based on all current information. This can be thought of as the fundamental value of the asset. As soon as investors receive new information concerning the path of future dividends, prices must change accordingly. In this way, if investors are rational, financial asset prices will reflect all available and relevant information, and market efficiency will prevail as assets are priced according to their fundamental values. To the extent that some traders are irrational, then their trades are assumed to be random and therefore will cancel each other out. Hence, asset prices will continue to trade at prices close to fundamental values.

However, it is the force of arbitrage that acts as the ultimate defensive line for the EMH, driving asset prices towards their fundamental values. A textbook definition defines arbitrage as the simultaneous purchase and sale of some essentially similar security in two different markets at advantageously different prices. Suppose some stock becomes overvalued in a market relative to its fundamental value. This security now represents a bad buy, because its price exceeds the properly risk-adjusted net present value of its cash flows or dividends. Noting this overpricing, smart investors or arbitrageurs would sell or even sell short this expensive security and simultaneously purchase other essentially similar securities. If these substitute securities are available and arbitrageurs can trade them, they can earn a profit. As they are 'short' in the expensive securities and 'long' in similar (so therefore no added risk is involved) but cheaper securities, an eventual risk-free capital gain will be made.

The effect of this selling by arbitrage is to bring the price of the overpriced security down towards its fundamental value. In fact, if arbitrage is quick and effective because enough possible substitute assets exist and the arbitrageurs are competing with each other to earn profits, then the price of a security can never move too far away from its fundamental value; therefore, arbitrageurs are unable to earn much of an abnormal return. Arbitrage is continually acting to bring security prices in line with their fundamental values.

Arbitrage has a further implication. To the extent that the securities which irrational and uninformed traders are purchasing are overpriced, or selling are underpriced, this means that these investors earn lower profits than their contemporaries. Therefore, irrational investors lose money, but as Friedman pointed out in 1953, they cannot continue to lose money forever. Eventually they will become less wealthy and disappear from the market. So, even if arbitrage cannot eliminate their effects on asset prices, market forces will eventually act to eliminate them from the market. Therefore, even if arbitrage is limited, competitive selection means that market efficiency will prevail.

The econometrics of the EMH

The EMH implies that the prices of financial assets include all the available information regarding the expected future earnings of that asset. Therefore, any change in asset prices reflects new market information about these expected future earnings. Under rational expectations, these are incorporated immediately into the asset price. The only reason for asset prices to change between time t–1 and t is because new information is available at time t which was unavailable at time t–1. Because this new information is unpredictable, financial assets are said to follow a *random walk* process.

$$P_t = P_{t-1} + \varepsilon_t \tag{6.23}$$

where ε_t is a stochastic term which represents new innovations. The change in asset prices solely reflects the arrival of fresh news.

$$\Delta P_t = \varepsilon_t \tag{6.24}$$

As new information is always arriving in the market, we would expect prices to be continuously changing. Therefore, volatility in financial asset prices should not necessarily be unexpected or regarded as unfavourable: the quick and continuous reaction of asset prices is part of the efficient pricing process. Volatility in financial asset prices is not at in conflict with the predictions of the EMH.

Figure 6.5 Daily FTSE100 prices during the financial year 2003–04

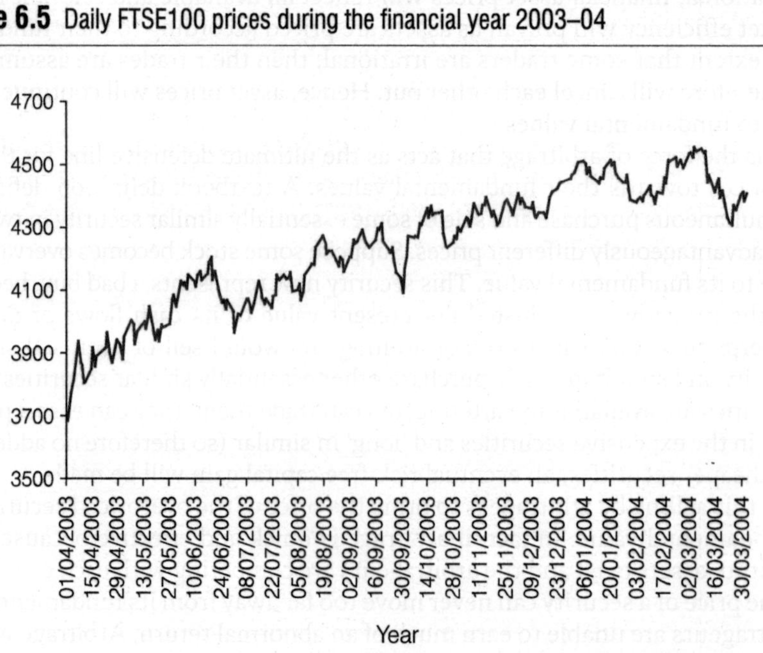

This prognosis is concurred by the evidence in Figure 6.5, which shows daily changes in asset prices in the London-based Financial Times Stock Exchange (FTSE). It is clear that daily changes in prices are indeed volatile. We see that stock market prices, although volatile on a daily basis, tend to trend upward over time. This reflects the fact that economies grow over time and this growth is reflected in the fundamental values of assets. Because of this, a better description of the process driving asset prices is a *random walk with drift*.

$$\Delta P_t = \mu + \varepsilon_t \tag{6.25}$$

This states that the change in asset prices is equal to a constant and an innovative factor. A random walk with drift process will be a series that is volatile, but fluctuates around a trend line, so will grow over time.

Efficient markets hypothesis: a critique

In the first decade after its inception, the EMH was an enormous empirical and theoretical success. However, over the course of the following 20 years, there have been a growing number of challenges to the theoretical foundation of the EMH and the evidence supporting it. The key forces by which markets are supposed to attain efficiency, such as arbitrage, are likely to be less powerful than efficient markets theorists first believed. With new theory and evidence, behavioural finance has emerged to provide an alternative view of financial markets. Systematic and significant deviations from efficient prices can therefore be expected to persist for long periods of time.

6

A simple empirical/econometric test for the EMH is simply to test asset prices for the presence of a random walk. From the above, it must be true that if the EMH holds, then the variance of stock market changes, $\mathrm{var}(\Delta P_t)$, should equal the variance of the innovations, $\mathrm{var}(\varepsilon_t)$, that underlie them. This presents an intuitive way to test the ramifications of the EMH: can changes in asset prices be related to changes in news about fundamentals?

An early and historically important challenge to the EMH was Shiller's (1981) work on stock market volatility, which showed that stock market prices are far more volatile than can be justified by a simple model in which prices are equal to the expected net present value of future dividends. This suggests that financial markets may react to non-information. The most salient piece of evidence concerning this is the 1987 stock market crash. On Monday 19 October, the Dow Jones Industrial Average in the US fell by 22.6%; the largest one-day drop in its history. The surprising feature of this crash is that no news or announcements could be identified as the source of this crash. In fact, many sharp movements in asset prices seem not to appear to accompany significant news. Cutler *et al.* (1991) examine the 50 largest one-day percentage drops in the US stock market since the Second World War, and find that many of them arose on days where there were no significant announcements. As it appears to be the case that $\mathrm{var}(\Delta P_t) > \mathrm{var}(\varepsilon_t)$, it is concluded that more than news is responsible for moving stock prices.

An interesting and similar conclusion was reached by Roll (1984) after examining news about the weather and effects on the price of orange juice futures. Roll argues that because the production of oranges for juice in the US is very geographically concentrated and tastes for orange juice are very stable, it should be news about the weather that accounts for most of the volatility in futures prices. He finds, though, that weather news appears to account for a very small proportion of these movements.

Roll (1988) extends this idea to individual stocks. He calculates the share variation in the returns of large stocks explained by aggregate economic influences, the contemporary returns on other stocks in the same industry, and public firm-specific news events. He finds that only 35 per cent of the total volatility in share prices can be accounted for by this information on monthly data, and only 20 per cent on daily data. This again implies that movements in stock prices are largely unaccounted for by public news.

According to the EMH, changes in asset prices should be unpredictable from past data. This is simply because past information will already have been incorporated into asset prices if traders are rational and markets are efficient. In this case:

$$\Delta P_t = \beta \Delta P_{t-1} + \varepsilon_t \tag{6.26}$$

For the EMH to describe asset prices, it is required that $\beta = 0$, i.e., no past changes in prices are significant determinants of current price changes.

Work by DeBondt and Thaler (1985) finds against the notion that past information cannot be used to predict future asset prices, implying that $\beta \neq 0$. They compare the performance of two groups of companies: extreme losers and extreme winners. For each year since 1933, they form portfolios of the best and the worst performing stocks over the previous three years. They then compute the returns of these portfolios over the following five years and find that the extreme loser portfolio does significantly better than the extreme winner portfolio. The explanation is that stock prices overreact; extreme losers become too cheap and bounce backwards, whereas the extreme winners become too expensive and must subsequently fall. This explanation fits in well with psychology: the extreme losers are typically companies with several years of poor news, which investors are likely to extrapolate into the future thereby undervaluing these firms. Likewise, extreme winners induce overvaluation.

The upshot is that there is substantial empirical evidence which points towards a rejection of the EMH. Volatility analysis (event studies) implies that financial asset prices appear to have larger variance than the fundamentals they claim to be built upon. Also, changes in asset prices may not be totally unpredictable, with past price changes being an indicator of current and future movements.

Theoretical challenges to the EMH

The lacklustre empirical performance of the EMH suggests that financial market prices appear to be more volatile than fundamentals would suggest. The fact that asset prices seem to deviate away from efficiency has prompted a new questioning of the theoretical precepts that support the EMH.

First, do financial market participants always behave in a rational way, and value assets according to fundamental values? There are several arguments that call into question the rationality of decision making. Many investors are seen to react to irrelevant information, following the advice of gurus or simple maxims. A favourite technique in predicting uncertain outcomes is to take a short history of recent data and extrapolate it to the future. Modelling in this way (chartist), though, does not pay enough attention to the possibility that recent history is generated by chance rather than the model they are constructing. This is not always a stupid policy; identifying patterns in the data can be useful heuristically. However, it can also lead investors astray. For example, extrapolating short histories of rapid earnings growth too far into the future may overprice glamorous companies, with the consequence that such overreaction will lower future growth rates.

However, the second line of defence implies that to the extent that traders are irrational, their trades are random and will cancel each other out. This though appears not to be the case. Financial market operatives tend to deviate in the same direction, so instead of cancelling each other out they tend to reinforce each other. That traders tend to concentrate their behaviour in the same direction is often referred to as *herding*.

The simple idea is that the actions of one person may subsequently influence the actions of another in the same direction. This notion of recruitment and herding is nicely summarized in a paper by Kirman (1993) that looks at the behaviour of ants. Given the choice of identical food sources, all ants will head toward the same one so that a very polarized distribution of ants at each of the food sources occurs. This arises because ants either lay a chemical trail or secrete hormones that attract fellow ants in the same direction.

The same ideas can then be used to explain trends observed in economics or finance. This idea of recruitment or herding can easily be viewed from an economics perspective if we argue that recruitment takes the following forms:

1. An agent may persuade another of the superiority of his choice because of better information or superior understanding as to how the market works.
2. There is an externality that leads from one agent concurring to the choice made by the other.

The first refers to the fact that investors may believe that others have better information than they do (this may not actually be true but just a perception) and will therefore adjust their own behaviour accordingly.

Second, it is true that through the effect on market prices, the trades made by one trader will affect others. For example, suppose one trader had private information concerning the fundamentals of a particular asset that was pessimistic. In this case, it would be rational to sell the asset if it is overvalued. However, if you are aware that other traders are generally optimistic about the fundamentals, then their trades will lead to an increase in price. Therefore, even if you were sure that your prognosis was correct, you would be reluctant to sell the asset, knowing that the future price may be upwards. In addition, the fact that you are not submitting sell orders removes the downward pressure on the asset price, making the rising price more likely.

Keynes famously referred to this externality argument as a beauty contest. In the British tabloid press in the 1930s, there was a competition where readers had to select the best-looking lady from a choice of several. However, the best-looking lady was not decided by a panel of judges; it would be the one who received the most votes from the readers. In order to win the competition, it was necessary not to pick the lady you personally thought was best-looking, but to choose the lady you thought average opinion would consider the most beautiful. However, this would also be the strategy adopted by everybody else taking part in the competition.

Keynes argued that success was therefore down to predicting what average opinion expected average opinion to be. This was paralleled to financial markets, where Keynes argued that successful trading required not so much knowledge of fundamentals, but knowledge of the actions of other traders. These externalities therefore provide a powerful coordinating incentive leading to traders conjugating on one side of the market.

There are countless examples of where contagion, mimicking or herding may be important in financial markets. It can also offer an intuitive explanation as to why financial asset prices may be excessively volatile. It is now no longer the case that financial market participants just react to news about fundamentals; they must also react to the reactions of other financial agents. The upshot is asset prices may subsequently over- or underreact to new information and become mis-priced according to fundamental values.

Ultimately though, the theoretical case for efficient markets depends upon the effectiveness of arbitrage. Even if irrational traders lead asset prices away from fundamental values, arbitrageurs will seek to profit from the mis-pricings and in so doing reinforce efficient pricing. However, a central concept of behavioural finance is that arbitrage is risky, and therefore limited. The effectiveness of arbitrage relies crucially on the presence of close substitutes. However, many securities do not have obvious substitutes, and if they become mis-priced there is no riskless hedge for the arbitrageur to undertake. The finite risk-bearing capacity of arbitrageurs reduces their ability to bring prices fully into line.

For example, suppose an arbitrageur is convinced that the shares of Ford are expensive relative to General Motors and Chrysler. If Ford shares are sold short and a long position is taken in a combination of General Motors and Chrysler shares, then the arbitrageur may be able to diversify some of the general risks of the automobile industry, but will still be exposed to the possibility that Ford does surprisingly well or that Chrysler or General Motors do surprisingly badly leading to arbitrage losses.

An important source of risk for the arbitrageur comes from the unpredictability of the future resale price, or put differently, that the mis-pricing may become worse before it eventually disappears. If an overpriced asset become more overpriced in the short run, or an underpriced asset becomes more underpriced, even if they will both converge to their fundamental values, there are possible short-term losses for the arbitrageur. If they can maintain their position throughout such losses, they can still count on a positive return. But, in situations where their position cannot be maintained, arbitrage may be limited. 'Noise traders' are those that trade on non-fundamental information, i.e., the irrational traders we described above. Their presence in the market and effect on prices create what is called 'noise trader risk'. This refers to the fact that for the arbitrageur, prices may get worse before they get better, implying that arbitrage is risky.

Noise trader risk in financial markets and the EMH

6

Arbitrage is an important feature of financial markets, as its effect is to bring prices towards fundamental levels and keep markets efficient. The most common explanation for incomplete arbitrage is the presence of transaction costs or imperfect substitutes. The type of risk we are concerned with here is mis-pricing that can worsen in the short run. These types of movements are very important for short horizon investors engaged in arbitrage against noise traders: this is the risk that noise traders' beliefs become more extreme before reverting to the mean.

If noise traders are pessimistic about an asset and have driven its price downwards, an arbitrageur who buys this asset must accept the possibility that in the near future noise traders may become even more pessimistic and drive the price down further. If the arbitrageur is forced to liquidate their asset holding before the price recovers, then they face a loss. Fear of this loss may limit the original arbitrage position. It is the risk of further movements in noise traders' beliefs away from the mean (this is what noise trader risk is defined by) that must limit the willingness to bet against noise traders.

The short-term outlook of arbitrageurs plays an important role in limiting the effectiveness of arbitrage. This can be justified in several ways, predominantly because most arbitrageurs just act as agents for investors, who make evaluations at relatively short intervals. Moreover, many arbitrageurs borrow short-term funds to finance their position, on which they have to pay interest and face liquidation if the price moves against them, reducing their collateral.

The result of limited arbitrage is that substitute assets may end up selling at two different prices, an outright contradiction of the EMH. Mis-pricing can lead to enormous inefficiencies that, in the absence of arbitrage behaviour, can be sustained. As a result, large deviations of prices from fundamental values may arise from risky arbitrage that takes some time to correct.

Example: US stocks An example may help to illuminate the idea of risky and limited arbitrage. Consider the case of American stocks in the late 1990s. At the end of 1998, large US corporations were trading at some of their historically highest market values relative to most measures of their profitability. For example, the ratio of market value of the S&P 500 relative to the aggregate earnings of the underlying companies stood at 32, compared to the post-war average of 15. Many economists, and US Federal Reserve Chairman Alan Greenspan himself, called attention to these possible overvaluations as early as 1996, but their warnings were contradicted by several financial gurus who argued that US companies were now operating in a world of higher growth and lower risks, and therefore rationally required higher valuations. This has close bearings to the comments of Irving Fisher in 1929, just before the famous crash.

Figure 6.6 S&P 500 stock prices, 1990–2004

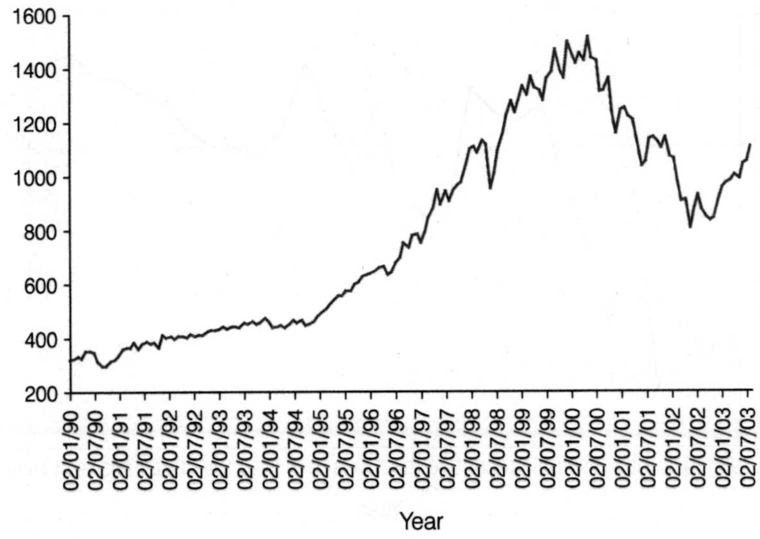

Well, if God himself – Alan Greenspan – suggests that financial market prices are overvalued, what should an arbitrageur do? If, in 1998, he sold the S&P 500 short at the beginning of the year when the price-to-earnings ratio was 24, he would have suffered a 28.6% loss by the end of that year. If he had sold short in 1997, he would have lost 33.4% and then 28.6% the year later. There are not many good substitutes for the whole S&P 500 market and market prices moved substantially out of line, so we can see that arbitrage is extremely risky. In fact, any arbitrageur that tried to exploit this apparent mis-pricing would probably have gone out of business.

Example: Royal Dutch Shell Economists have a strong intuition that fundamentally identical assets must trade at identical prices; this is just the workings of arbitrage. However, this is not always the case, and the presence of noise trader risk appears to be an explanation of price divergences between two fundamentally identical securities.

Royal Dutch and Shell are independently incorporated in the Netherlands and England, respectively. The structure has grown out of a 1907 alliance between Royal Dutch and Shell Transport in which the two companies agreed to merge their interests on a 60:40 basis, while remaining separate and distinct entities. All sets of cash flows are effectively split in these proportions. The only real difference between the two firms is that Royal Dutch trades in Holland and on the US S&P 500, while Shell trades predominately in the UK on the FTSE. In sum, if the market values of the securities were equal to the net present values of future cash flows, the value of Royal Dutch equity should be 1.5 times the value of Shell equity.

Figure 6.7 presents the percentage deviation from the 60:40 ratio in market values between September 1980 and September 1995. It shows a tremendous amount of deviation, from an underpricing of 35 per cent to an overpricing of 10 per cent of Royal Dutch relative to Shell.

There are no real structural explanations for these differences. We would not expect these deviations to arise and persist in a market where arbitrageurs are present and face a long-time horizon. This evidence thus poses a deep challenge to the EMH. The difference

Figure 6.7 Stock price of Royal Dutch relative to Shell (% deviation from 60:40 values)

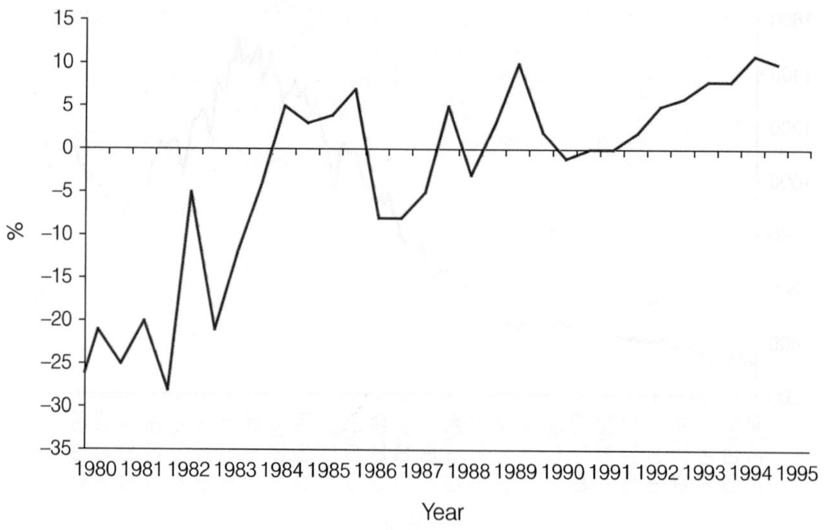

6

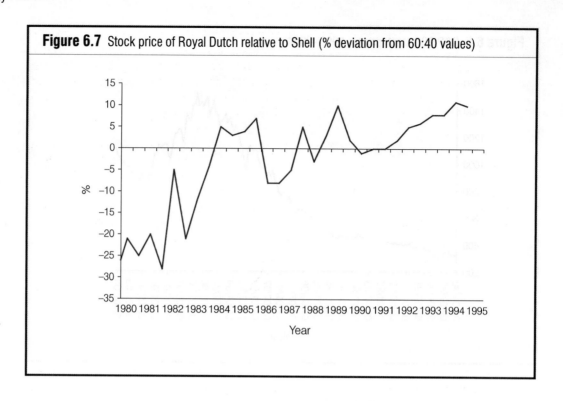

in returns cannot be attributed to compensation for risk; in effect, two identical assets are selling at different prices.

Analysing Figure 6.7 points to a crucial cost of arbitrage in Royal Dutch and Shell; notably, the risk of mis-pricing can become more extreme. An arbitrageur who bought the relatively cheap Royal Dutch shares and sold a corresponding number of the relatively expensive Shell shares in mid-1983 when the discount was 10 per cent would have experienced a severe deterioration in their position as the discount factor widened to nearly 25 per cent six months later. If this investor had leveraged, or had to explain their losses to investors, they may have failed to survive these losses and might have been forced to liquidate. For this trader, noise trader risk is very important.

It takes about four years for the 30 per cent mis-pricing of Royal Dutch and Shell that was prevalent in September 1980 to eventually disappear. In return for bearing this risk, the arbitrageur earns about 7 per cent per year. For reasons such as the costs of leveraging, and the presence of possible liquidation should further mis-pricing occur, arbitrageurs may have found it unattractive to arbitrage in September 1980, even with a 30 per cent mis-pricing of two identical securities. Therefore, mis-pricing can be seen to take a while to correct, and so enormous inefficiencies can be maintained without aggressive arbitrage activity coming in to correct them. From the point of view of the EMH, this is crucial as it suggests that even with identical securities noise trader risk may be large enough to cause large and sustained price deviations from fundamental values.

Professional arbitrage

So far we have considered arbitrageurs who use their own wealth to trade, and therefore are limited by their own risk aversion. In reality, arbitrage is conducted by relatively few professional, highly specialized investors who combine their knowledge with the resources of outside investors to take large positions. In this respect, traders and financers are separated by an agency relationship.

The fact that arbitrage requires capital is very important in the agency context. When the arbitrageur is managing other people's money, and his or her investors do not fully understand what he or she is doing, they can only observe him or her losing money if prices happen to move further out of line from fundamental values. These losses may lead them to infer that the arbitrageur is not as competent as they previously thought, and therefore refuse to provide him or her with more capital, and although the expected return has now increased they may withdraw some of his or her existing capital.

The responsiveness of funds under management to past returns is referred to as *performance-based arbitrage* (PBA). Investors may rationally allocate funds based on the past returns of arbitrageurs, and withdraw funds after poor performance. Poor performance thus limits the equity base and borrowing capacity of an arbitrageur, regardless of the attractiveness of the opportunities they face. As a consequence, when arbitrage requires debt or equity capital, arbitrageurs can become most constrained precisely when they have the best opportunities. Consequently, arbitrageurs become less aggressive in betting against mis-pricing. Performance-based arbitrage is extremely ineffective in extreme circumstances when prices are substantially out of line and arbitrageurs are fully invested. In such panics, arbitrageurs may bail out of the market, voluntarily or not, exactly at the point of time where their participation is most needed.

Discussion of PBA

Are the consequences of PBA really this bad? Even if funds under management are withdrawn, it may only be with a lag, by which time the price could have started to recover. Also, if arbitrageurs are diversified, then not all their holdings will lose money at the same time. Finally, arbitrageurs with long and successful track records may be able to avoid equity withdrawals from investors.

Each of these objections has merit, yet the case for the importance of PBA remains strong. First, the lag on fund withdrawals is typically very short. In most arbitrage funds, investors have the right to withdraw some of their funds exceptionally rapidly if performance is poor. Contractual relationships which prevent some withdrawal and force investors to be stuck with a bad fund manager for some time are relatively uncommon. The majority of hedge funds allow investors to withdraw funds with only a couple of week's notice.

Furthermore, a factor that shortens the lags is voluntary liquidation. If prices move against a risk-averse arbitrageur, they may choose to liquidate rather than wait for a situation which is then forced upon them for fear that further adverse price movements will spark an outflow of funds and liquidation at even worse prices. In this respect, the fear of future withdrawals will have an effect as bad as an actual withdrawal.

The biggest reason why poor performance may lend itself to quick asset sales is liquidation by the creditors themselves. Creditors usually demand immediate repayment, or else liquidate the collateral when the value of this approaches the debt level. Creditors have every incentive to get their money back ahead of equity investors, and this is a cause of significant instability. This is made more precarious as arbitrageurs must come up with funds at a time when they are fully invested. If arbitrageurs cannot come up with the cash, their portfolios are liquidated, often in fire sales at extremely low prices, with the result that markets become even more inefficient. Moreover, such liquidations spread across markets as funds attempt to liquidate their positions in other markets to meet lender's calls for funds and avoid further liquidations.

There are several other problems associated with liquidations by creditors. If creditors can liquidate themselves, but the amount owed to them is less than the actual value of the collateral, they do not care at which price they liquidate, as the difference belongs to the borrower.

Suppose that a hedge fund borrows $80 million from a bank, collateralized by $100 million of securities, for which the fund must put up 20 per cent or $20 million of its own equity. Suppose the market value of the securities falls to $90 million, the bank is only willing to lend 80 per cent or $72 million and demands repayment of $8 million. If the fund does not have the cash, then the bank has the right to sell the securities, but has no incentive to sell them for greater than $80 million because the difference belongs to the fund. Although the bank must solicit multiple bids, it may well sell the securities at lower rather than higher prices. This may push the value of the securities down to $80 million, causing the fund to lose all its equity in those securities.

There is a further moral hazard problem here, which comes from the part of the creditors, and is known as *front running*. If the bank in question knows what some of the holdings of the fund are, and knows in advance that the fund may be liquidating these involuntarily, it has an incentive to sell short these securities and buy them back later at lower prices when the fund is liquidating. This puts downward pressure on prices and speeds up liquidation.

In conclusion, the performance of PBA leads to potential instability of financial markets. This arises from both voluntary and involuntary liquidations of money losing positions by arbitrageurs and their creditors, even when these positions have longer-term positive expected returns. This instability manifests itself in substantial deviations of security prices from fundamental values in times of crisis. Also, liquidations in one market may turn into liquidations in other markets, particularly if shocks are very large. This points to the possibility of financial contagion without any fundamental reason as to why different markets should move together.

6.5 Bubbles and crashes in financial markets

So far we have investigated how financial assets may become mis-priced relative to fundamentals. The EMH states vehemently that prices will always converge towards fundamental values, as mis-pricings present profitable opportunities to traders. Acting on this is known as arbitrage, and has the consequence of restoring efficient pricing. However, arbitrage may be much weaker than many EMH proponents first realized. Noise trader risk essentially refers to the fact that mis-pricings may become worse before they become better. As a result, although arbitrage offers long-term gains, the arbitrageur may be subject to short-term losses.

An inability to absorb short-term losses will limit the initial arbitrage position. Therefore, the pressure returning prices towards fundamental levels would be significantly weaker. The short-term horizons of arbitrageurs are easily reconciled when it is acknowledged that most arbitrageurs fund their positions on borrowed capital, of which it is fairly common for lenders to demand quick repayment. Therefore, short-term losses may lead to liquidation or a withdrawal of arbitrage funds through performance-based arbitrage (PBA). Arbitrageurs become more constrained exactly at the point where mis-pricing is at the greatest.

Much volatility in financial markets thus results because herding behaviour or irrational investors are allowed to influence market prices, as their actions will not be corrected by arbitrage. This means that trading on noise rather than fundamentals may come to drive market prices. We now turn to look at two important cases of financial market volatility – bubbles and crashes.

A bubble sees long sustained rises in prices away from fundamental values. Bubbles are characterized by their self-fulfilling nature. Even if investors know that prices are

Global application 6.3

Tulipmania

Tulip bulbs came to Western Europe in the sixteenth century. As knowledge and appreciation of the flower spread, increasing prestige was attached to the possession and the growth of the flower. The demand for rarer bulbs increased dramatically, and this led to substantial price rises.

The rush to invest infected the entire Dutch population and tulip bulb prices rose to extraordinary levels. By 1636, a bulb of no real distinction or previous worth could be exchanged for a new carriage, two grey horses and a complete harness. As speculation increased, turnover became faster and faster at ever-increasing prices.

Confidence always remained high that ever-increasing wealth could be achieved from the acquisition of tulip bulbs and that prices would rise in perpetuity. People of all classes converted their property into cash, often at very low prices and invested the proceeds in tulip bulbs. With each upsurge in prices, more speculators were encouraged to participate. This justified the hopes of those already participating paving the way for yet further speculation.

The end came in 1637. Certain investors left the market – the reason why has never been accounted for. And others seeing them go led to a rush to the exit. As panic ensued, prices fell dramatically. Those who bought, often using property as collateral for loans, were left bankrupt. Those who had contracted to purchase at the inflated prices defaulted en masse and the angry sellers were left unsupported by unsympathetic courts that saw the whole practice as a gambling operation.

Banks and savings and loans associations went bankrupt and the Dutch economy entered a sizeable depression. The effects on the Dutch economy can still be seen to this day. The period of Tulipmania led to the large cultivation of tulip bulbs and wide markets eventually developed for bulbs and flowers, for which the Netherlands is now well known.

overvalued, the anticipation that prices will rise further makes further acquisition of the asset profitable. Therefore, prices can rise in a marked fashion for a considerable period of time.

Crashes refer to sudden and sharp drops in market prices. This need not be at odds with market rationality. It could be the case that a crash results from the arrival of very bad news. Also, a crash may manifest itself in a collapsing bubble, which should just be seen as a correction in market prices. However, there are also examples of sharp asset price drops that cannot be related to either of these explanations; therefore, there may be something inherently irrational about them in that prices are driven down to unjustifiably low levels. The October 1987 stock market crash is a recent example which will form the basis of some brief analysis.

Bubbles in asset prices: the tech boom

A bubble describes the situation where asset prices have grown in excess of their intrinsic fundamental values due to speculative mania. A famous historical example is the period of Tulipmania which is described in Global application 6.3. During this period, people were literally willing to sell everything they had in order to invest in tulip bulbs under the strong belief that rapidly increasing prices would yield them a fortune. This is just one example of many bubbles that have occurred through time. The hallmark of a bubble is that even if

Figure 6.8 Share prices, NASDAQ composite and S&P 500

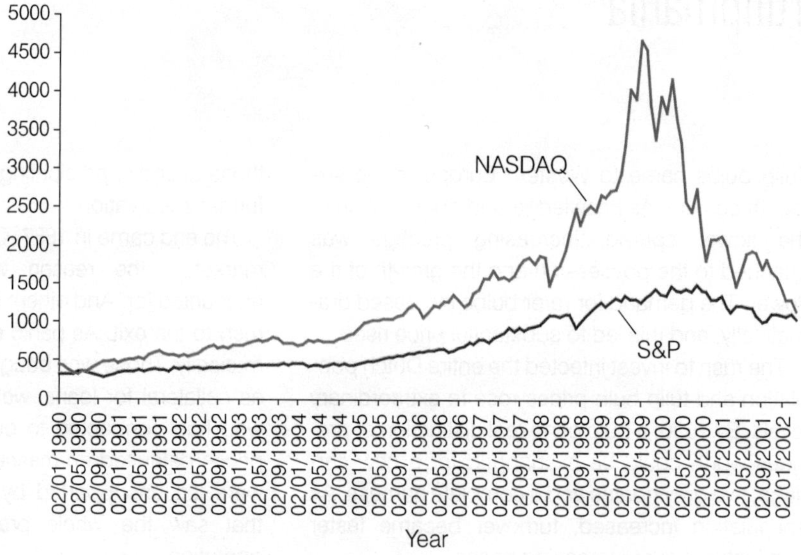

traders know that stocks are overpriced, they will continue to buy them or at the very least refuse to sell them as they are expecting prices to go even higher. So price rises take on a self-fulfilling nature.

Figure 6.8 plots the recent history of the NASDAQ and the S&P 500 stock market indices since 1990. There is clear evidence of a dramatic rise in US share prices during the period 1995-2000, followed by a large collapse over the following two years, a pattern which is highly indicative of a bubble and its bursting.

Between 1995 and 2000 it is possible to see that the S&P 500 doubled in value, but this trend is hard to observe when it is pitted against the almost tenfold increase in the NASDAQ. The NASDAQ is the index on which the new technology shares are traded. Because the dramatic rise in the stock market was driven by IT companies, and especially those involved in Internet technologies, this period has been widely christened as dotcom mania. Global application 6.4 tells some well-known stories of the extraordinary events and valuations that were symbolic of this period.

When stock prices start to increase quickly, further price rises are fuelled by others who jump on the bandwagon through fear of missing out on easy profits. However, for this process to begin, there has to be something that justifies an initial strong rise in prices. These reasons will also provide comfort for those who continue to buy at higher and higher prices, who can be convinced that stock markets offer a one-way bet.

Two of the arguments put forward justifying the strong rise in share prices were as follows. First, over the period 1995–2000, the US economy grew at unprecedented rates. This was based on an improvement in the trend rate of productivity growth, which in turn was attributed to the increasing adoption of information and communication technologies (ICT). As growth was based on these new technologies, the whole episode was dubbed as the 'new economy'. This galvanized the strong belief that the US was at the outset of a new golden economic era and asset prices should rise to reflect this.

The second relates to the idea that it takes time for new technology to be represented in asset prices. This is because the firms listed on the major stock markets, such as the

Global application 6.4

Tales of dotcom mania

The large and sustained increases in US stock markets during the late 1990s was particularly evident in IT and Internet companies. Here we present a few simple examples where the stock market valuation of these firms appears to have been extraordinary and the actions of traders was irrational, giving rise to the term dotcom mania.

Initial Public Offerings (IPO)

An IPO refers to the new listing of a company on a stock exchange and marks the first time that the company's shares can be bought and sold by the public. In corporate finance, one of the best-known facts is the underpricing of IPOs. So, it is normal for a new firm to see its share price rise on the first day of trading. However, the apparent underpricing of Internet firms appears extreme. Ofek and Richardson (2002) calculate the mean and median first-day return on Internet IPOs as 95.5 per cent and 63.1 per cent, respectively.

On 7 December 1999, Andover.net completed an IPO at a public offering of $18. This IPO was fairly unique, as prior to the IPO some shares were sold in a sealed bid auction over the Internet where the market clearing price was $24. The decision to IPO at $18 implies a 25 per cent underpricing. However, during the first day of trading, Andover.net's price jumped to $63.38, which represented a 252 per cent one-day return and a 164 per cent premium over the auction clearing price. What information arrived to justify this massive increase in prices is uncertain. It also hard to account for why investors chose not to participate in the Internet auction, even though it was highly publicized and would have enabled stock to be purchased at a bargain $24 per share.

Name changes

Zapata was an oil and gas company founded in 1953 by the former president of the USA, George Bush Senior. By early 1998, the focus of the company had changed to specializing in meat casings and fish oil. In April 1998, the company's management announced that it was going to form a new company that acquired and consolidated Internet and e-commerce businesses. In the following May, it bid for the major Internet search company Excite but its bid was firmly rejected due to a lack of synergies.

In July, Zapata announced that it was starting an Internet portal and had set about accumulating 30 websites. Following a slowdown in the market for Internet stocks in the summer and autumn of 1998, the firm changed direction and claimed to be no longer interested in purchasing the websites. However, this proclamation did not last long and by December of that year, Zapata announced its aim of establishing a subsidiary known as Zap.com. On this news, its shares rose by 98 per cent on the NYSE composite.

Internet subsidiary mis-pricing

On 13 September 1999, 3 com announced its intention to take one of its subsidiaries, Palm Computing, public. Palm was principally a manufacturer of pocket computers and electronic organizers, and on 2 March 2000 it was floated on the NASDAQ. Initially, 3 Com sold 6 per cent of the company at $38 a share, which was much higher than its IPO range of $14–$16. The remaining 94 per cent was to be divested to 3 Com shareholders within six months.

On the first day of trading, Palm opened at $145 and reached a high of $165 before finally closing at $95.06. At this price, Palm was valued at $53.4 billion which stood in stark contrast to 3 Com's value of $28.5 billion. This meant that 3 Com's 94 per cent stake in Palm had a market value of $50 billion. So, despite owning assets of $50 billion, 3 Com itself was only valued at $28.5 billion. This implies that either 3 Com's assets must have a very large negative value, or that it was massively underpriced. As both of these are unlikely, the only other alternative is that Palm was massively over-valued.

Global application 6.5

The IT revolution and the stock market

This Global application outlines a simple model by Lucas (1978) which can be used to describe the impact of new technology on the stock market.

The model assumes that a tree yields one unit of output every year forever, which goes to the owner of the tree as a dividend. Dividends paid in the future are discounted at the rate β each period. Therefore, if the price of the tree reflects the expected discounted value of dividends, its price at time zero is:

$$P_0 = \sum_{t=0}^{\infty} \beta^t = 1 + \beta + \beta^2 + \ldots\ldots = \frac{1}{1-\beta}$$

It is then announced at this time ($t = 0$) that at a future time (*time* $= T$), these trees will die and be replaced by better trees which produce output/dividends of $1 + z$ per period. These more productive/higher yielding trees would be expected to live forever.

As a result the output (y_t) of the trees will be:

$$y_t = 1 \text{ for } t < T$$

$$y_t = 1 + z \text{ for } t \geq T$$

What will happen to the stock market price of old trees? Given that they will now die at time T rather than live forever, their value will converge towards zero at time T. The initial price of the asset will still reflect the expected discounted sum of its dividends, but these dividends will only accrue until time T so its value will fall.

Therefore:

$$P_0 = \sum_{t=0}^{T} \beta^t = 1 + \beta + \ldots + \beta^T = \frac{1-\beta^T}{1-\beta}$$

At time T, though, the new stock arrives and because it then pays a dividend of $(1 + z)$ forever, its price will reflect the expected discounted value of its future dividends:

$$P_T = \sum_{t=T}^{\infty} \beta^{t-T}(1+z) = (1+z) + \beta(1+z) + \beta^2(1+z) + \ldots\ldots = \frac{(1+z)}{1-\beta}$$

Therefore, overall the path of the stock market is now summarized as follows and plotted in Figure 1:

Figure 1 Tree prices following the announcement of better trees arriving at time T

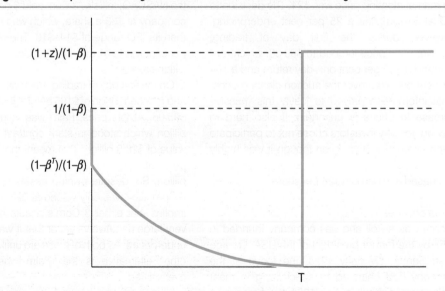

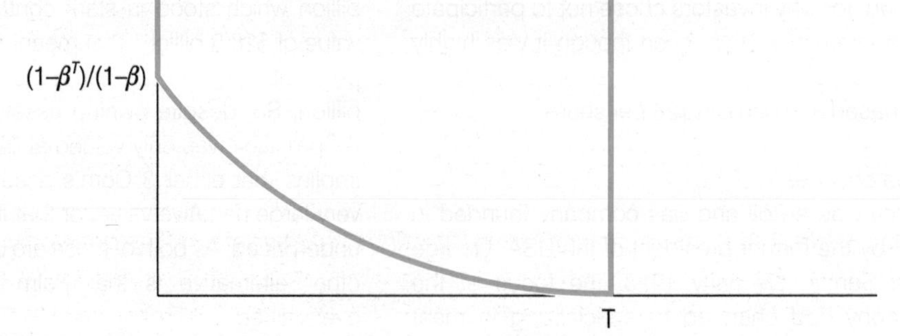

Global application 6.5 (continued)

$$P_t = \frac{1-\beta^{T-t}}{1-\beta} \text{ for } t \le T$$

$$P_t = \frac{(1+z)}{1-\beta} \text{ for } t \ge T$$

This simple model explains what effect the arrival of new technology might have on stock markets. The use of IT started to become more widespread during the 1960s with the development of mainframe computers, but despite the existence of the technology there would be a delay before it emerged onto stock market listings. This is because it would take time before the power and the cost of IT equipment encouraged wide-scale adoption, and also for IT firms to reach a position where they are large enough to warrant a stock market listing.

However, the expectation of the future emergence of IT firms and technology would lead to an expectation that old technology firms will eventually be supplanted, both in terms of the market and in terms of stock market listings. As a result, the stock market would fall as the value of old technology firms fell, but then rise sharply when they are replaced in the index by higher earning, new technology firms. This is the path predicted by the model used to construct Figure 1, but does bear some resemblance to actual stock market movements.

Figure 2 plots the real value (inflation adjusted) of the Dow Jones Industrial Average from 1950 to 2000. It is clear that the movements in this series conform to the story told in Figure 1. However, it must also be noted that the jump in stock prices during the 1990s was exceptionally large, which would tend to imply that IT has had a massive effect on productivity and dividends (i.e., the value of z is large). If this is indeed the case, then the large increase in stock prices can be justified.

Figure 2 Dow Jones Industrial Average/US price index, 1950–2000

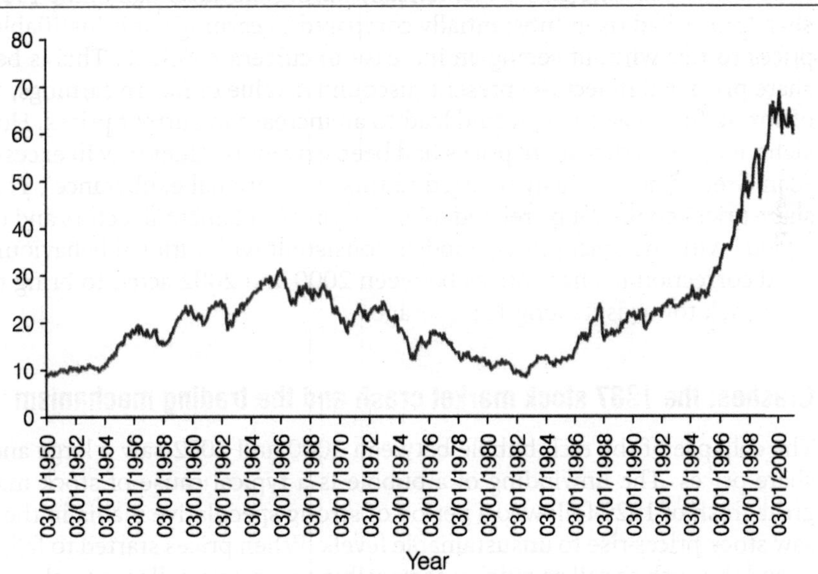

NASDAQ and the S&P 500, are older and well-established enterprises. The development of new technologies often occurs in small firms, and it will take many years for these to reach a position where they are large enough to be listed on stock markets. Information technology began to emerge in the 1960s; the sharp rise in asset prices during the 1990s simply reflects the new economy firms replacing the old economy firms in the stock market listings. This argument is set out in more detail in Global application 6.5.

6

Figure 6.9 A history of the price-earnings ratio on the S&P 500

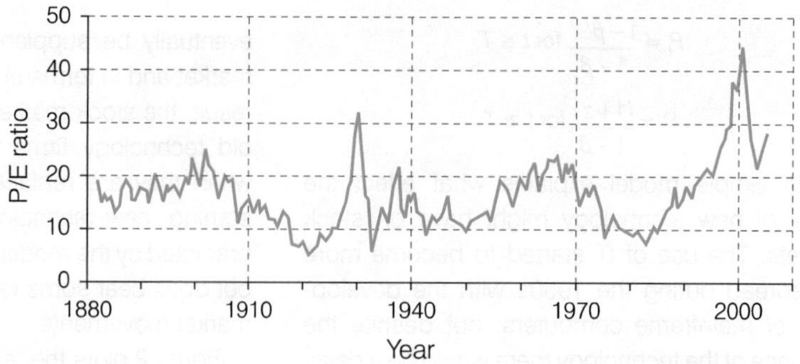

6

The emergence of ICT and the new economy may certainly have provided some grounds for an increase in stock market prices. However, was the scale of this rise justified when compared to fundamentals such as earnings? The price–earnings ratio is the price of a share divided by the level of corporate earnings per share. According to simple models of asset pricing such as the expected dividends model, this would relate the price of a firm's equity to a fundamental factor, such as its expected profits, sales, market share and so on.

Figure 6.9 plots the price–earnings ratio for the S&P 500 index over a 120-year period. It is clear that this ratio grows dramatically during the latter half of the 1990s, indicating that share prices had risen substantially compared to earnings. It is justifiable for current share prices to rise without seeing an increase in current earnings. This is because the current share price will reflect the present discounted value of future earnings, so the expectation of strong future earnings would lead to an increase in current prices. However, with hindsight, it appears that share prices had been driven to values way in excess of fundamentals. Alan Greenspan famously referred to this as 'irrational exuberance'. The large increase in share prices could not be related to underlying fundamental factors and therefore had to be at odds with the asset pricing models consistent with rational behaviour. The large downward correction in share prices between 2000 and 2002 acted to bring the price–earnings ratio back towards its long-run average.

Crashes: the 1987 stock market crash and the trading mechanism

The collapse of the tech bubble between 2000 and 2002 saw a large and sustained fall in share prices. The unwinding of a bubble is a typical cause of stock market crashes. The great crash of 1929 followed a period of strong speculative mania in the late 1920s, which saw stock prices rise to unsustainable levels. When prices started to fall, outright panic set in and the rush to sell as quickly as possible saw prices collapse to almost zero in two days of trading. Crashes refer to sudden and sharp falls in asset valuations. The unwinding of the tech boom occurred over a two-year period. Although it marked a large fall in prices, it was not characterized by the panic selling and a drop in prices that occurred in days or hours.

While financial markets are intrinsically volatile, some of the sharper movements are harder to explain in terms of existing models. The crash on 19 October 1987 led to losses of around $700 billion, amounting to about 20 per cent of the total pre-crash stock value of $3.5 trillion. This dramatic fall, though, was brought on by a much smaller amount of selling in comparative terms. Although trading on this day was three times the average,

Figure 6.10 S&P 500 during October 1987

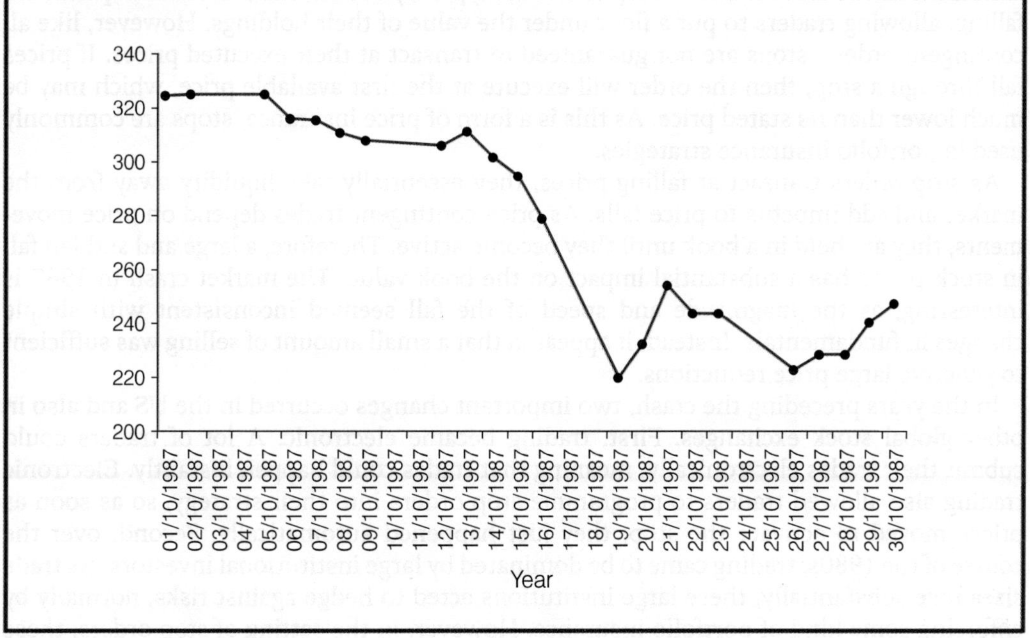

only $6 billion (0.2% of total equity value) worth of trades were responsible for this huge collapse in prices. The curiosity was how such a small amount of selling could explain such a large decline in stock prices (see Figure 6.10).

Fundamentals vs. the market mechanism

According to the predictions of the EMH, the large decline in asset values should be associated with announcements of bad news concerning the fundamental values of equities. Preceding the crash, there were the following pieces of bad economic news:

- press speculation concerning the Federal Reserve raising the discount rate
- Federal Reserve announced decision to depreciate the $ against the DM
- US bombing of an Iranian oil platform in the Gulf
- trade deficit was worse than expected by about $1.5 billion.

However, none of these could be deemed significant enough to match the huge fall in asset prices.

In financial markets a wide variety of order types can be found. Although most trading does happen at the prevailing price, there are other types of trades that are contingent on a variety of conditions. For example, a 'market at close' order allows traders to specify the exact time at which their order is executed. Orders, such as 'Fill or Kill', or 'Immediate or Cancel' orders, allow traders to control the quantity or execution of their trades. However, by far and away, the most common are *price-contingent orders*.

Orders contingent on prices can take many forms. The most common are *limit orders,* which specify a price and a quantity at which trades transact. As a limit trade at current prices is just a market order, a limit order must specify a price outside of the existing quote. If a limit order executes, the trader receives a better price than from submitting a market order. However, obviously execution is not always guaranteed as market prices may not move so as to enact the limit order.

A similar type of order is a *stop order*, this specifies a price and a quantity where the price is worse than the current quote. Stop orders are typically used to sell stocks when prices are falling, allowing traders to put a floor under the value of their holdings. However, like all contingent orders, stops are not guaranteed to transact at their executed prices. If prices fall through a stop, then the order will execute at the first available price, which may be much lower than its stated price. As this is a form of price insurance, stops are commonly used in portfolio insurance strategies.

As stop orders transact at falling prices, they essentially take liquidity away from the market and add impetus to price falls. As price-contingent trades depend on price movements, they are held in a book until they become active. Therefore, a large and sudden fall in stock prices has a substantial impact on the book value. The market crash in 1987 is interesting, as the magnitude and speed of the fall seemed inconsistent with simple changes in fundamentals. Instead, it appeared that a small amount of selling was sufficient to generate large price reductions.

In the years preceding the crash, two important changes occurred in the US and also in other global stock exchanges. First, trading became electronic. A lot of traders could submit their trades electronically, meaning that trades could happen instantly. Electronic trading also allowed traders to programme stop orders into their strategy, so as soon as prices moved to activate the stop, they just happened automatically. Second, over the course of the 1980s, trading came to be dominated by large institutional investors. As trade sizes rose substantially, these large institutions acted to hedge against risks, normally by enforcing some kind of portfolio insurance. However, in the setting of stop orders, these institutions did not take account of the effect that the stop orders of other institutional investors would have on market prices. Specifically, the execution of one stop order could create a cascade of similar executions.

Summary

- Financial markets are where financial assets are traded. The value of financial assets is an important determinant of consumption and investment.
- The expected dividends model implies that the value of an asset is equal to the expected present discounted value of its earnings (such as dividends). This can be thought of as the fundamental value of an asset. The Gordon model is a simplified version of the expected dividends model, which relates asset valuations to the growth in dividend payments. The process of arbitrage – where traders act to profit from the over- or underpricing of financial assets – acts to drive asset prices towards fundamental values.
- Assets with higher returns might be riskier and, therefore, asset pricing models ought to value both risk and return. The capital asset pricing model (CAPM) is a consumption-based model which implies that assets with higher returns offer less opportunity to hedge against income risks. The CAPM beta reflects the covariance between an asset's returns and those of the market portfolio. The higher the beta, the lower the ability to hedge.
- The Tobin Model of portfolio selection describes how investors choose the optimal combination of risk and return in their portfolios.
- The efficient markets hypothesis (EMH) states that financial asset prices should reflect all available information. As a result, whenever new information arrives at the market asset prices will change quickly to reflect it. This implies that asset prices follow a random walk process.

- Empirical tests tend to reject the EMH as the volatility of asset prices is greater than the volatility of news regarding fundamentals. One of the explanations for this is the presence of noise trader risks. Because asset prices might become more mis-priced before moving to fundamental values, the power of arbitrage is less than the EMH suggests. Therefore, financial market mis-pricings (inefficiencies) can be sustained for long periods of time.
- A bubble refers to the self-fulfilling process where asset prices are driven upwards by the expectation of further increases in prices. As a result, asset prices can rise to levels far in excess of fundamentals. The strong rise in US stock markets (particularly the NASDAQ) during the second half of the 1990s is an example relating to the boom in the share prices of new technology firms.
- A crash refers to a large and sudden drop in market values. These can result from a sudden deterioration in fundamentals, but also through the sharp unwinding of a bubble. The October 1987 crash demonstrates the roles that the market mechanism and the strategies of traders can play in precipitating a sudden collapse in prices.

Key terms

Capital asset pricing model (CAPM)
Efficient markets hypothesis (EMH)
Expected dividend model
Gordon model
Tobin model of portfolio selection

Review questions

1. Using the models developed in Chapters 2 and 3, explain how changes in financial asset prices affect consumption and investment.
2. What effect on stock markets might the following have? Explain your answers:
   a. a substantial rise in oil prices
   b. a cut in interest rates
   c. a major company announces large profits, but these are slightly lower than anticipated
   d. an accountancy scandal where a firm has overstated its profits
   e. the release of government figures showing strong retail sales growth
   f. a report by the central bank showing lower projections of government borrowing
   g. a new era of low and stable inflation.
3. Is financial market volatility a sign of efficient or inefficient markets?

More advanced problems

4. Why might a firm's share price rise even though it has decided not to distribute profits as dividends to shareholders?
5. What policies could a government implement to reduce the likelihood of:
   a. bubbles
   b. crashes.

For further resources, visit
http://www.thomsonlearning.co.uk/chamberlin_yueh

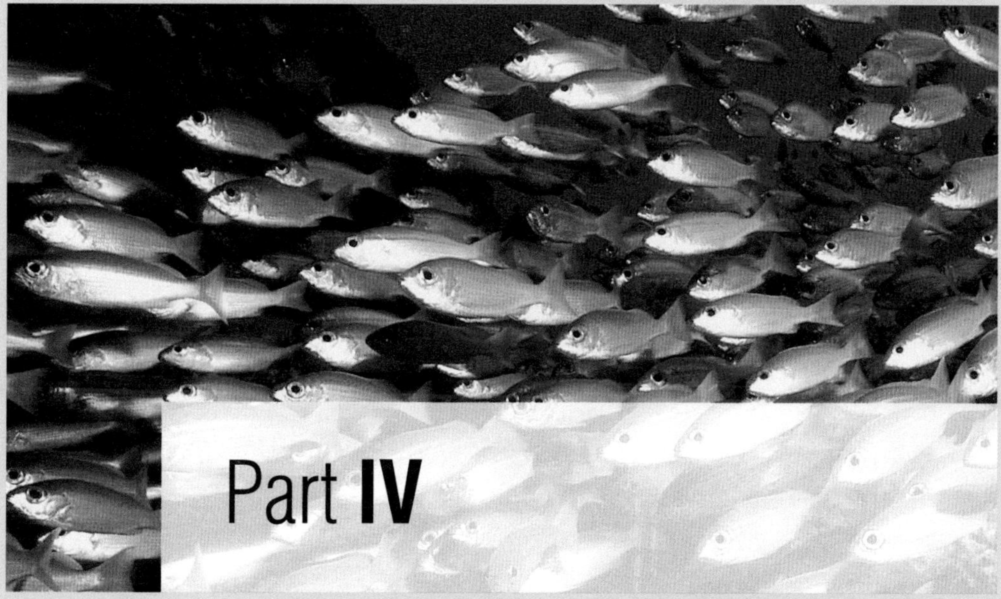

Part IV

Models of the economy

The previous sections developed the major components of the macroeconomy. This section brings together these factors in two general equilibrium models of the economy. The IS-LM and AD-AS models are presented in their closed economy forms. Later on, the open economy versions will be introduced.

7 The IS-LM model

Learning objectives

- Understand the importance of macroeconomic models for analysing the economy
- Derive the IS curve as the equilibrium in the goods market
- Derive the LM curve as the equilibrium in the money market
- Construct the IS-LM model as a general equilibrium model of the economy
- Use the IS-LM model to analyse the effects of monetary and fiscal policies on the economy
- Extend the IS-LM model to explain changes in prices

7.1 Introduction

In the previous chapters we have explained and accounted for the decisions made by individual sectors of the economy. These have included the household decision to consume; the firm decision to invest; government levels of spending and taxes; and also the actions of the banking and financial sectors. As macroeconomists, we know that the path the economy takes will be determined by how these sectors interact with each other. For example, the firm decision to invest might depend on expected future sales. However, these sales will depend on households' expected future income, which is in turn linked to their employment prospects and thus firm investment. It is clear that the working of the economy is more complex than a series of individual relationships.

To this end models are an extremely useful tool in economic analysis. They summarize all these relationships and enable us to analyse the economy as a whole. The **IS-LM model** is one particular type that has been widely used by economists and policy makers. For many decades, it has been valuable in explaining trends in the economy and for making predictions and forecasts, particularly with regard to the potential effects of monetary and fiscal policies.

The IS-LM model consists of two parts.

7

- The IS (investment-saving) curve represents equilibrium in the *goods market*. This is where the demand and supply are equal and output is determined.
- The LM (liquidity-money) curve represents equilibrium in the *money market*. The demand for money is known as the demand for liquidity, and equilibrium persists when this is equal to the money supply. The money market determines the interest rate in the economy.

The IS-LM model is a *general equilibrium model,* which determines the combinations of income (Y) and interest rates (r) where both the goods (real side of the economy) and money markets (nominal side of the economy) are in equilibrium.

The IS-LM model as we present it in this chapter does have some weaknesses, which are largely a result of its historical perspective. First, prices are not explicitly included in the model, so the IS-LM model cannot offer insights into what factors might be responsible for determining inflation. Second, the basic IS-LM model is a closed-economy model, meaning that there is no international trade in goods and services and there are no international financial markets. When the model was first derived, economies tended to be fairly closed and persistent inflation was not a problem. However, these features will be covered in later chapters and the model as it stands is still a useful one which is widely used in policy circles.

When thinking about the IS-LM model, it is worth remembering that it is always the case that output is determined in the goods market, and the interest rate is determined in the money market. In this way, the IS-LM model is firmly built on the analysis of Chapters 4 and 5.

7.2 The IS curve: equilibrium in the goods market

The IS curve describes how the equilibrium level of income varies with the interest rate. Following the analysis of Chapter 4, the equilibrium level of income is found where *planned expenditures* are equal to the actual level of income. This is equivalent to saying that the goods market is in equilibrium. If the demand and supply of goods and services are equal, then firms have no unplanned changes to their inventories and no incentive to change output.

When planned expenditures are equal to actual income, the following equality holds:

$$Y = C + I + G \tag{7.1}$$

where

Y = Output/income

C = Consumption

I = Investment

G = Government spending

Much effort was spent during Part II of this book in explaining the factors that account for each of the components of planned expenditures. Therefore, these will only be presented briefly here and in a manner that helps us to build and understand the model.

Consumption

This is determined by the simple Keynesian consumption function outlined in Chapter 2. Consumption is written as a linear function of disposable income.

$$C = a + c(Y - T) \tag{7.2}$$

where

a = autonomous consumption

c = marginal propensity to consume

$Y - T$ = disposable income, where Y is actual income and T is the level of lump sum taxes levied by the government.

The IS-LM model very much hails from a Keynesian background, so it is predictable that this form of consumption function is used. However, the analysis of Chapter 2 suggests that the determinants of consumption may be much broader than this simple function suggests. Looking at the optimal consumption model, we can see that factors such as expectations about future income, wealth and interest rates may also be very important. However, as these do not have any effect on current disposable income, it is hard to see how they might be incorporated into this model as determinants of current consumption. Without doubt, if the model is to be considered plausible and have useful applications, it should have some ability to incorporate these features.

A convenient way of doing this is to consider them as determinants of autonomous consumption – these are factors other than the level of current income which will lead to a change in consumption. When the level of autonomous consumption changes, it will lead to an entire shift in the consumption function. For example, if wealth was to rise, or households had more optimistic expectations concerning future income, then current consumption would rise even though there had not been any change in current disposable income. Autonomous consumption would increase from a to a' and the consumption function would shift upwards (see Figure 7.1). The level of current consumption is now higher at every level of income.

Naturally, the opposite would happen if there were a fall in autonomous consumption. If households hold a pessimistic outlook about the future, or there is a negative wealth shock such as a collapse in asset prices, then we would expect autonomous consumption to fall and the consumption function to shift downwards.

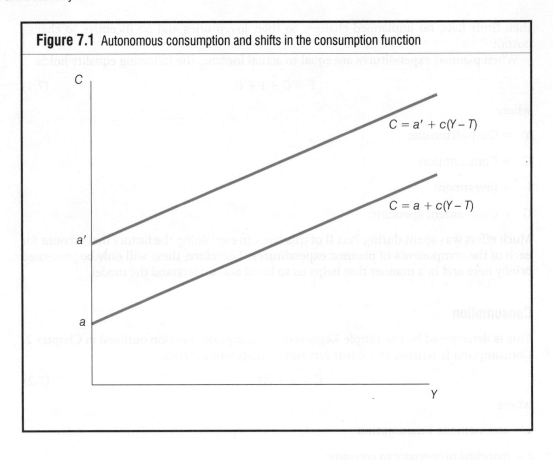

Figure 7.1 Autonomous consumption and shifts in the consumption function

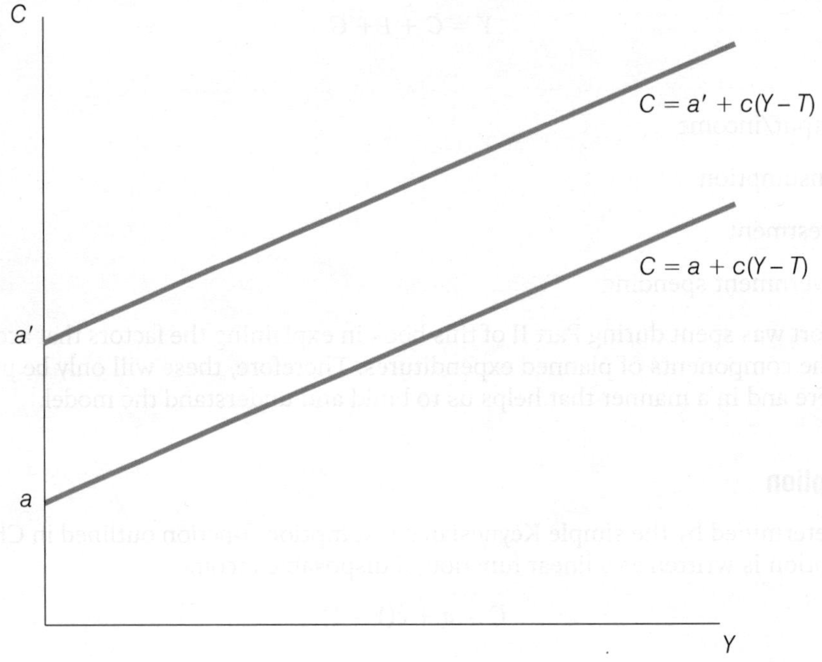

7

Investment

The analysis of Chapter 3 discusses a multitude of factors which may be important in determining investment. Prominent in all models is the rate of interest. This is considered to be the opportunity cost of undertaking investment projects, as it represents the rate of return that could otherwise have been achieved by investing in a safe asset, such as government bonds. In this respect, the interest rate is very much taken to be the price of investment.

In the IS-LM model the level of investment is derived from a simple investment demand curve.

$$I = I(r,\Theta), \quad \frac{\Delta I}{\Delta r} < 0 \qquad (7.3)$$

It consists of the interest rate (r) and a set of other factors represented by Θ.

The **investment demand schedule** will be like any other demand curve – downward-sloping with respect to price – and the price of investment is the interest rate. This is shown in Figure 7.2, where a fall in interest rates from r_1 to r_2 leads to an increase in investment from I_1 to I_2.

The parameter Θ represents the determinants of investment other than interest rates, which might include the following:

- investment taxes and subsidies
- productivity shocks
- investor confidence (Keynes referred to the waves of optimism and pessimism in investor confidence as 'animal spirits').

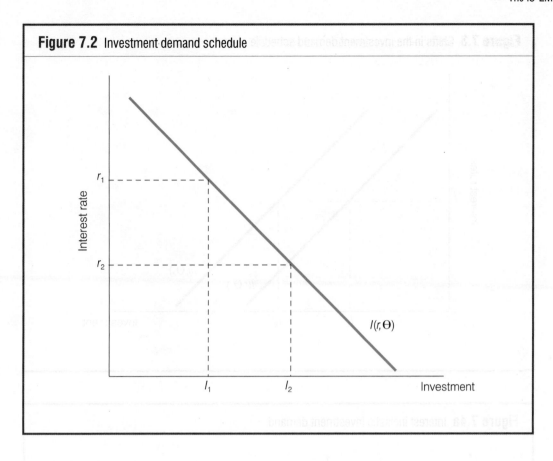

Figure 7.2 Investment demand schedule

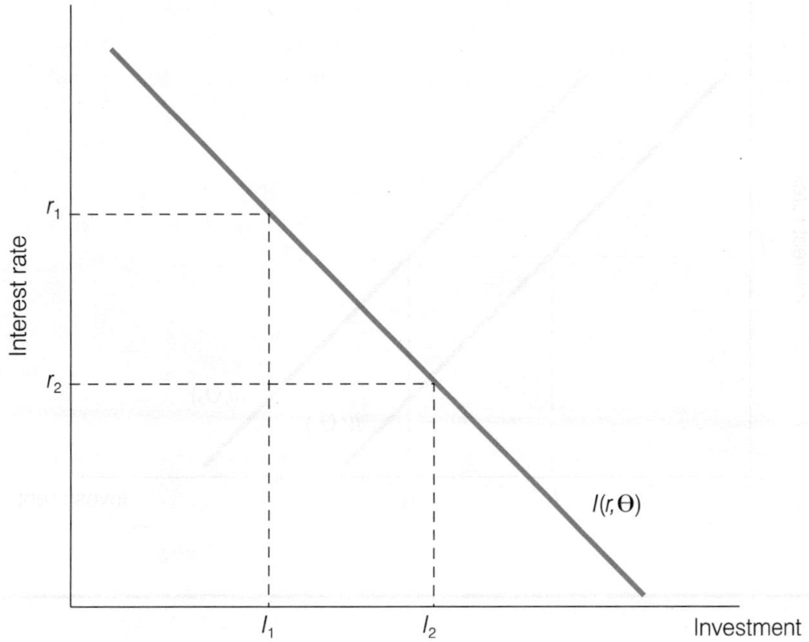

These are discussed in some length in Chapter 3. If any of these changes, then the investment demand schedule will shift, meaning that a different level of investment would prevail at the same interest rate. If there were a technological breakthrough or very rosy expectations concerning the future ($\Theta_1 \rightarrow \Theta_2$), then firms will be willing to undertake more investment and the entire investment demand curve would shift to the right.

It will be seen that the relationship between interest rates and investment plays a pivotal role in the workings of the IS-LM Model. This relationship is summed up by the slope of the investment demand function, which tells us how sensitive investment is to changes in interest rates. This sensitivity can be measured by the *interest elasticity of investment,* ${}^r\varepsilon_I$.

$$
{}^r\varepsilon_I = \frac{\%\Delta I}{\%\Delta r}
$$

The interest elasticity of investment is simply the ratio of the percentage change in investment and the percentage change in interest rate. As investment is expected to fall when the interest rate rises, the elasticity should be negative. However, just how negative it will be is important, as it tells us how much investment would be expected to fall if interest rates were to rise.

If $0 > {}^r\varepsilon_I > -1$, then changes in interest rate will have a less than proportional effect on investment. In this case, investment is said to be *interest inelastic*. The investment demand curve will be relatively steep implying that changes in interest rates will only have small effects on investment.

If ${}^r\varepsilon_I < -1$, then changes in interest rate will have a more than proportional effect on investment. In this case, investment is *interest elastic*. The investment demand curve will be relatively flat, implying that changes in interest rates will have larger effects on investment.

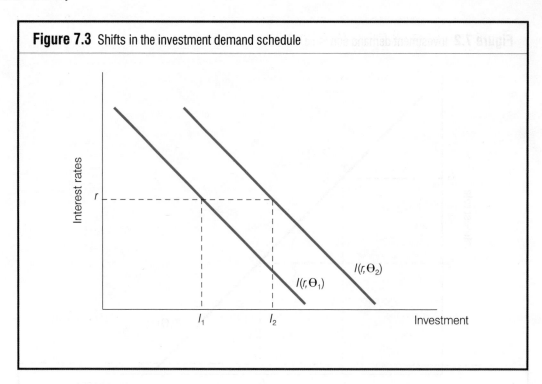

Figure 7.3 Shifts in the investment demand schedule

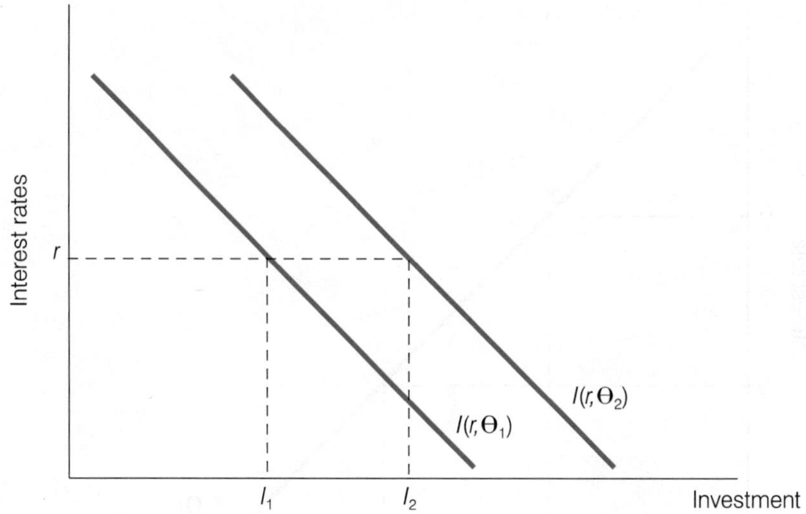

7

Figure 7.4a Interest inelastic investment demand

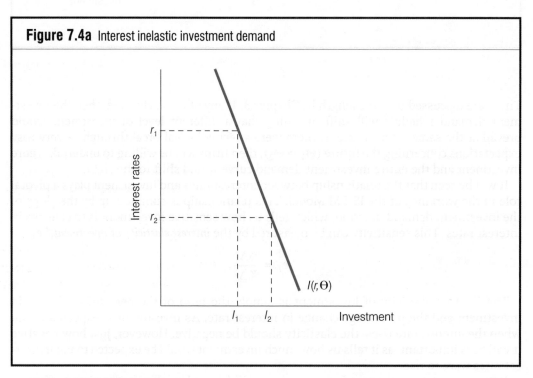

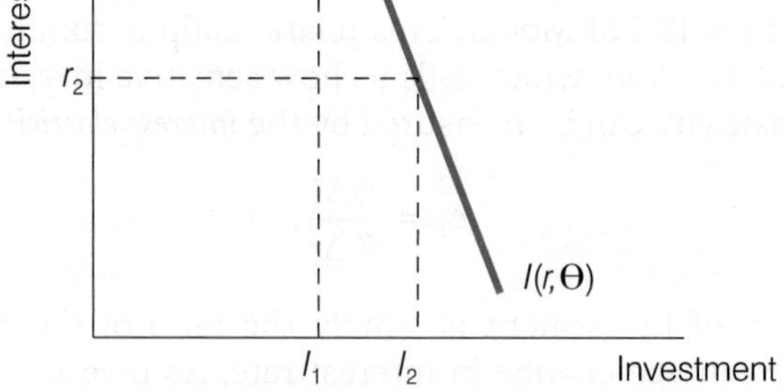

The importance of elasticities is clearly demonstrated in Figure 7.4. In both Figure 7.4(a) and 7.4(b), the same change in interest rates generates a very different response in investment depending on the elasticity of investment demand. As the interest rate falls from r_1 to r_2, investment will increase from I_1 to I_2. The change in investment will be very much larger when investment demand is more interest elastic.

Figure 7.4b Interest elastic investment demand

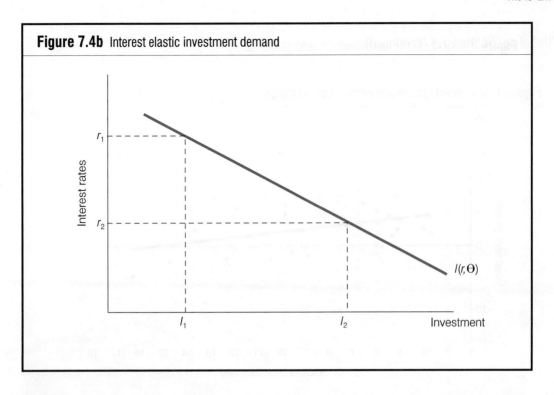

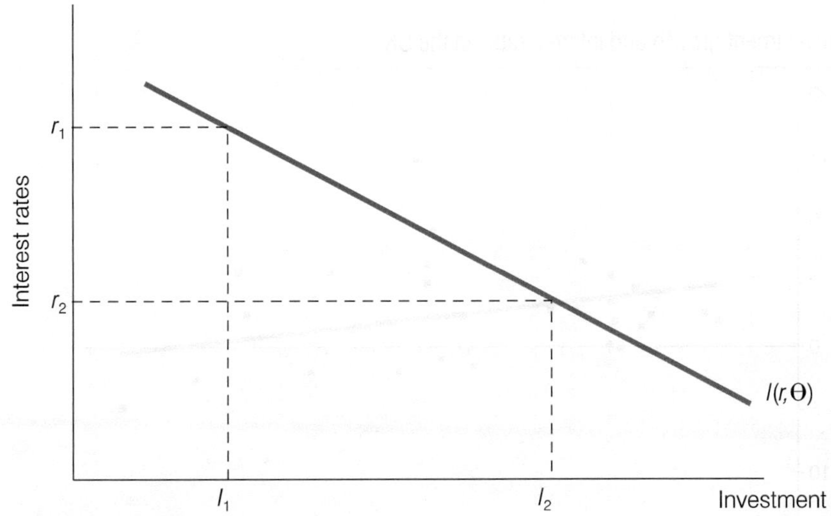

Global application 7.1

How sensitive to interest rates is investment?

The interest elasticity of investment is a key factor behind the slope of the IS curve. The more interest elastic the IS curve, the flatter the schedule. Some evidence on the relationship between investment and interest rates is presented in Figure 1. This is a scatter plot between the commercial bank interest rate and the rate of growth in investment.

The line of best fit suggests a negative relationship between investment growth and the interest rate, justifying a downward-sloping IS curve. However, there is a reasonably large degree of variability around the best fit line, suggesting that the correlation is less than perfect.

This is evidence that investment is negatively related to the level of interest rates, but that other factors are also likely to be important determinants of investment. These might include productivity, uncertainty over demand, the availability of finance and taxes and subsidies on investment. This would tend to suggest that the investment demand curve is interest inelastic and relatively steep.

Global application 7.1 (continued)

Figure 1 Investment growth and interest rates in the UK

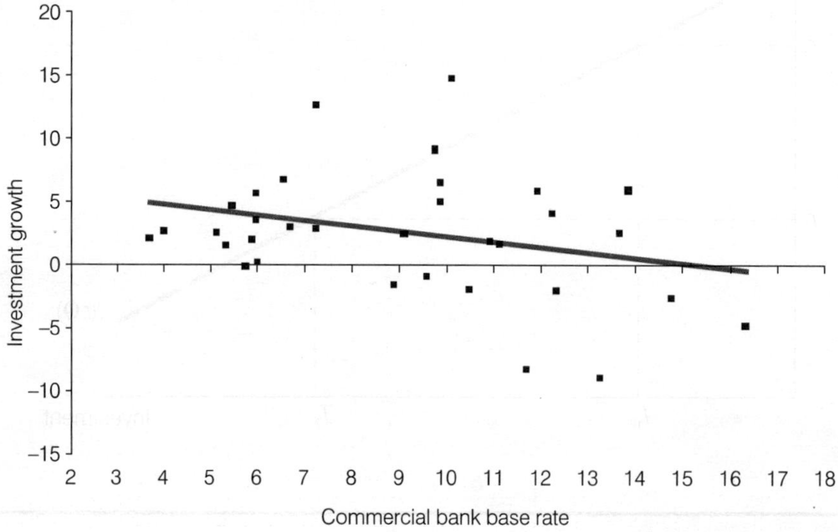

7

Government spending and taxes

The levels of government spending and taxation are really the outcome of choices made by politicians. Therefore, they are just treated as exogenously given values.

$$G = \overline{G}$$

$$T = \overline{T}$$

Equilibrium: the Keynesian cross

Having defined the components of planned expenditures, equilibrium in the goods market is where planned expenditures (E) equal actual output/income (Y). Following the analysis in Chapter 4, we can use the Keynesian cross to represent equilibrium graphically.

Planned expenditures are given by:

$$E = a + c(Y - \overline{T}) + I(r,\Theta) + \overline{G} \qquad (7.4)$$

and equilibrium in the goods market is where

$$Y = E \qquad (7.5)$$

These two equations are plotted in Figure 7.5.

Equilibrium in the goods market is where the two relationships intersect, which is at Y^*. Any position away from Y^* would imply that demand does not equal supply in the goods market. If output were below the equilibrium level ($Y < Y^*$), then planned expenditures would exceed output ($E > Y$). In this case, firms would see their stocks of inventories being run down and will increase production to satisfy the excess demand. The opposite would be true if output were above the equilibrium level ($Y > Y^*$). There would now be excess

Figure 7.5 Equilibrium in the goods market and the Keynesian cross

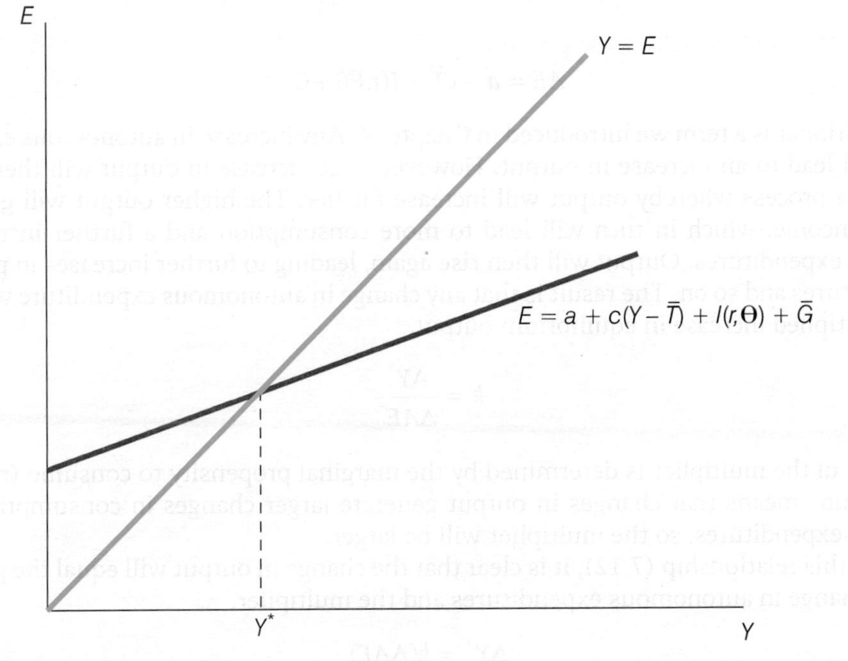

supply in the goods market ($Y > E$). Firms would then see stocks of unsold inventories begin to pile up and will subsequently cut production. Only at Y^* will firms not face the need to change output levels.

The equilibrium level of output (Y^*) can be derived algebraically as follows:

If $Y = E$, we can first just substitute in our equation for planned expenditures (7.4).

$$Y = a + c(Y - \overline{T}) + I(r,\Theta) + \overline{G} \tag{7.6}$$

The next step is to move all the income terms over to the left-hand side of the equation and to simplify.

$$Y - cY = a - c\overline{T} + I(r,\Theta) + \overline{G} \tag{7.7}$$

$$Y(1 - c) = a - c\overline{T} + I(r,\Theta) + \overline{G} \tag{7.8}$$

Now, all we need to do is divide both sides by $(1 - c)$ and we are left with the equilibrium level of output.

$$\begin{aligned} Y^* &= \frac{a - c\overline{T} + I(r,\Theta) + \overline{G}}{1 - c} \\ &= k(a - c\overline{T} + I(r,\Theta) + \overline{G}) \end{aligned} \tag{7.9}$$

where $k = \dfrac{1}{1-c}$ is known as the multiplier.

This is an interesting equation. It argues that the equilibrium level of output is the product of the multiplier and the total amount of *autonomous expenditure* (AE). Autonomous expenditure is, of course, any expenditure that is taken independently of the level of income.

Therefore,

$$Y^* = k\,(AE) \tag{7.10}$$

where

$$AE = a - c\overline{T} + I(r,\Theta) + \overline{G} \tag{7.11}$$

The multiplier is a term we introduced in Chapter 4. Any increase in autonomous expenditure will lead to an increase in output. However, that increase in output will then set in motion a process whereby output will increase further. The higher output will generate higher income, which in turn will lead to more consumption and a further increase in planned expenditures. Output will then rise again, leading to further increases in planned expenditures and so on. The result is that any change in autonomous expenditure will lead to a multiplied increase in equilibrium output.

$$k = \frac{\Delta Y^*}{\Delta AE^*} \tag{7.12}$$

The size of the multiplier is determined by the marginal propensity to consume (mpc). A higher mpc means that changes in output generate larger changes in consumption and planned expenditures, so the multiplier will be larger.

7

From this relationship (7.12), it is clear that the change in output will equal the product of the change in autonomous expenditures and the multiplier.

$$\Delta Y^* = k(\Delta AE) \tag{7.13}$$

Figure 7.6 A fall in the interest rate and an increase in output

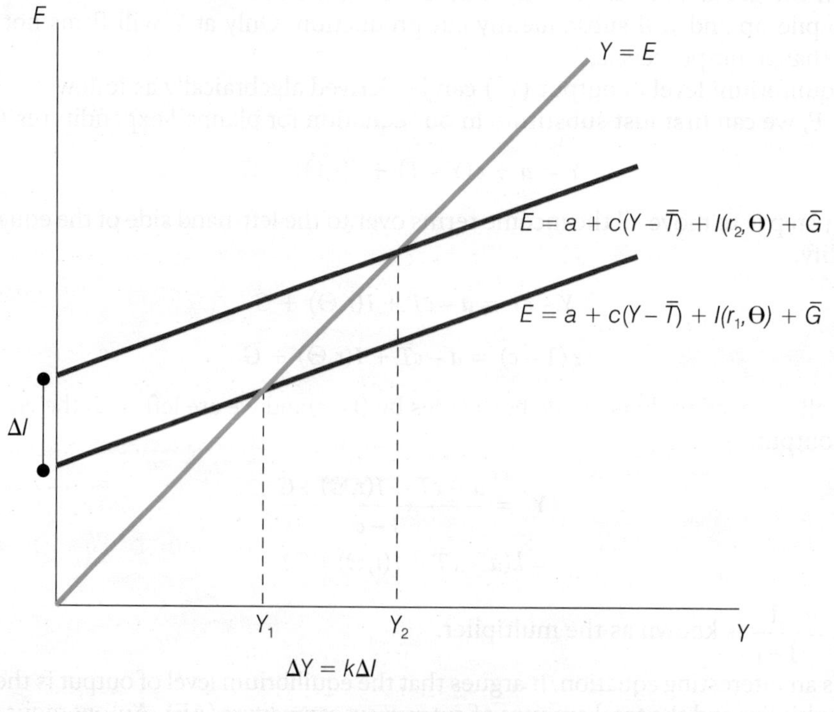

What happens if the interest rate falls?

Using the simple Keynesian cross, it is easy to show how changes in interest rates will affect the equilibrium level of output.

Looking at the investment schedule in Figure 7.2, a fall in the interest rate will lead to an increase in investment. It is worth bearing in mind that the magnitude of this will be decided by the interest elasticity of investment. Moreover, this change in investment constitutes a change in planned expenditures which will lead to a multiplied increase in output. This is shown in Figure 7.6.

Here the change in autonomous expenditures is the change in investment.

$$\Delta AE = \Delta I = I_2 - I_1$$

The change in income is $\Delta Y^* = Y_2 - Y_1$, such that $\Delta Y^* = k\Delta I$.

Therefore, it is seen that a fall in interest rates r leads to an increase in Y^*.

Deriving the IS curve

The IS curve plots the combinations of output (Y) and interest rates (r), where the real side of the economy is in equilibrium. From the above, it should be intuitive that the IS curve is a downward-sloping function in Y-r space – as r falls, Y rises. In effect, the IS curve simply tells us what the equilibrium level of output is at each level of interest rate. This derivation is shown in Figure 7.7.

7

From Figure 7.7:

1. In panel (a), the interest rate falls $r_1 \rightarrow r_2$ and investment increases $I_1 \rightarrow I_2$.
2. Panel (b) shows a 45-degree line, which just reflects investment from the horizontal to the vertical axis.
3. In panel (c), the rise in investment leads to an increase in planned expenditures $E_1 \rightarrow E_2$ and a multiplied increase in output $Y_1 \rightarrow Y_2$.
4. In panel (d), the relationship between interest rates and equilibrium income/output is plotted. This inverse relationship is the IS curve.

The slope of the IS curve tells us what effect a given change in interest rates has on the equilibrium level of output. As $\Delta Y^* = k\Delta I$, then the slope will depend on two things. The first is the change in investment induced by the interest rate change, which is summed up by the interest elasticity of investment demand. The second is the multiplier.

1. The interest elasticity of investment, ${}^{r}\varepsilon_{I}$: as investment becomes more interest elastic, a given change in interest rates will generate a larger increase in investment and hence equilibrium output. In this case, the IS curve becomes flatter. This situation is portrayed in Figure 7.8, where the IS curve, IS', generated from the more elastic investment demand schedule (I') is clearly flatter. When investment is interest inelastic, the IS curve will be steeper. Reductions in the interest rate produce smaller increases in investment and so output increases by a smaller amount.
2. The multiplier, k: as the size of the multiplier increases (k gets larger), the increase in investment following a fall in the interest rate will generate a larger effect on equilibrium output, hence the IS curve also becomes flatter. This is shown in Figure 7.9, where in panel (c) the dashed expenditure functions are steeper due to a higher multiplier. The corresponding IS curve (IS') is seen to be flatter. A smaller multiplier would be consistent with a steeper IS schedule.

Two important IS curves are shown in Figure 7.10. When the investment demand curve is *perfectly inelastic* (${}^{r}\varepsilon_{I} = 0$), changes in the interest rate fail to alter investment, hence the IS curve is vertical. Likewise, when investment is *perfectly elastic* (${}^{r}\varepsilon_{I} = \infty$) with respect to the interest rate, small changes in the interest rate generate very large responses in investment, so the IS curve becomes horizontal.

Figure 7.7 Deriving the IS curve

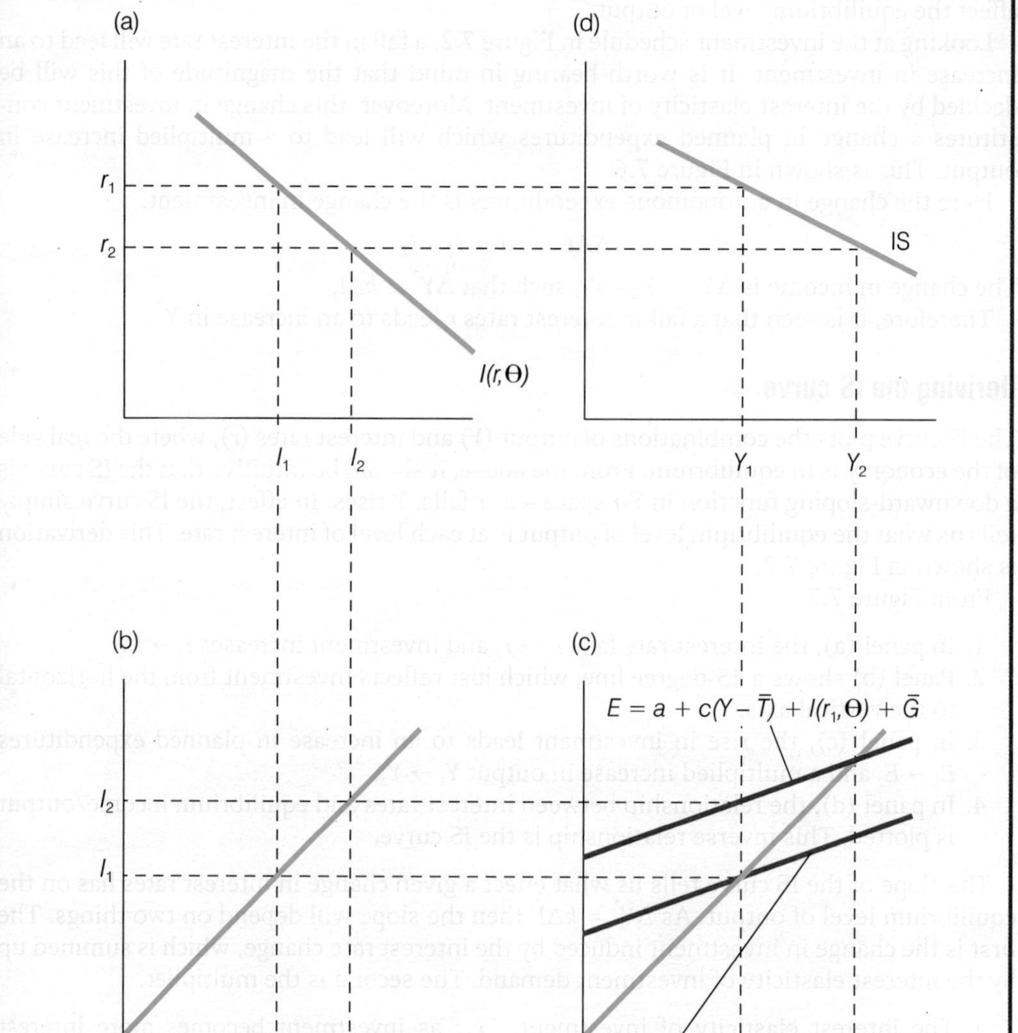

Figure 7.8 The interest elasticity of investment and the slope of the IS curve

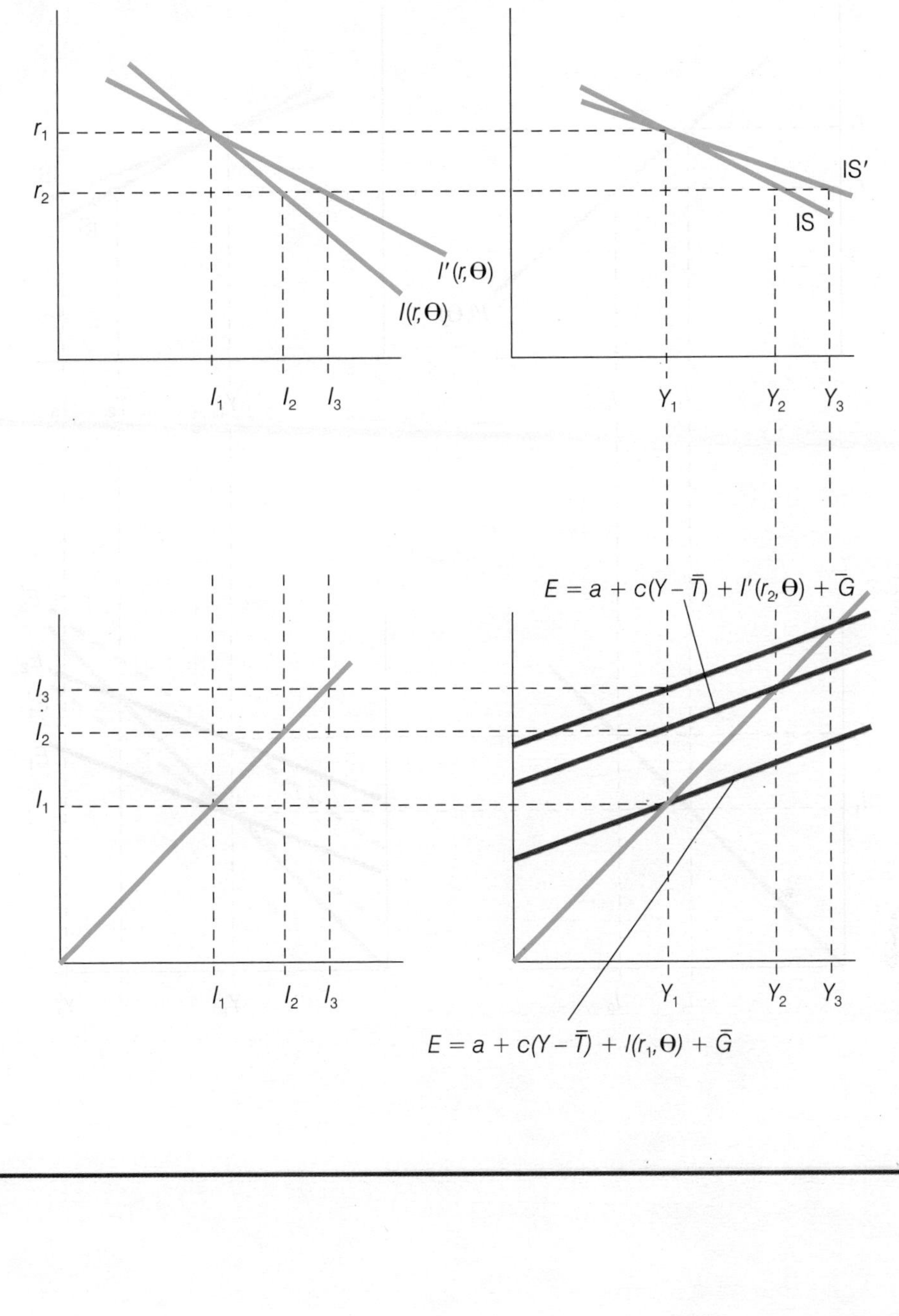

Figure 7.9 The multiplier and the slope of the IS curve

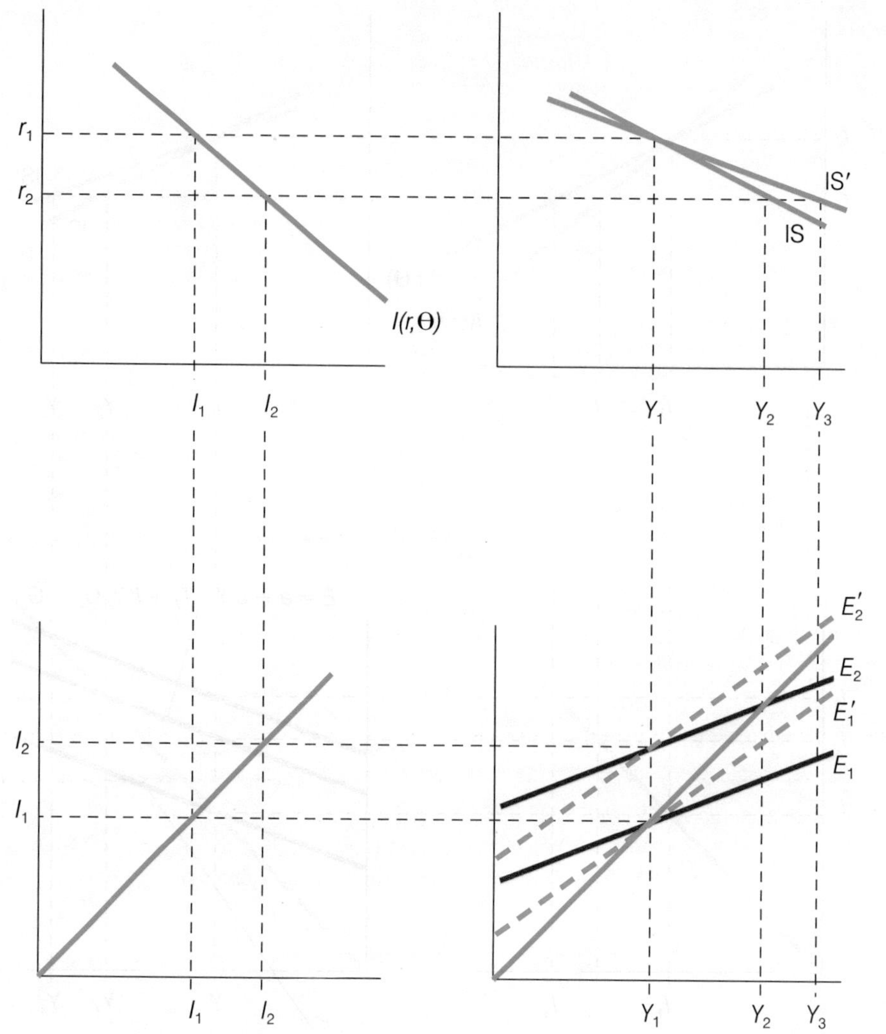

Figure 7.10a IS curve where investment is perfectly interest inelastic

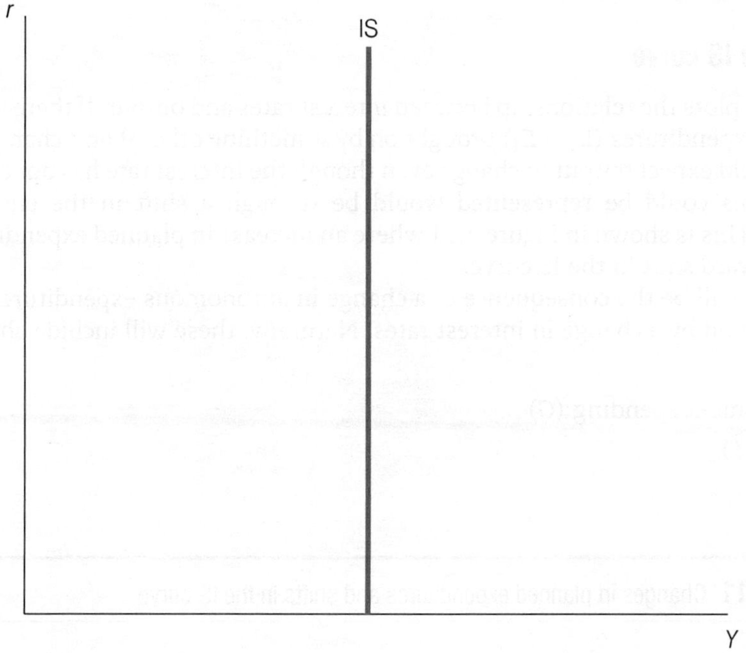

Figure 7.10b IS curve where investment is perfectly interest elastic

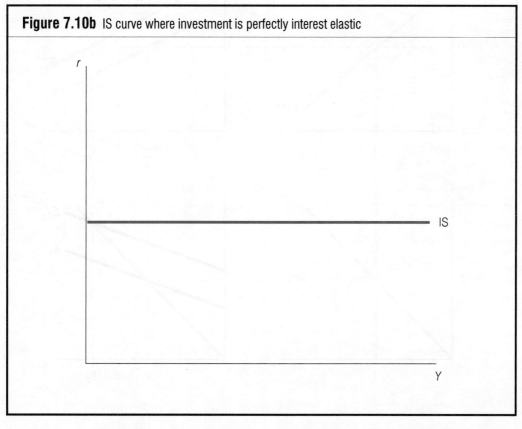

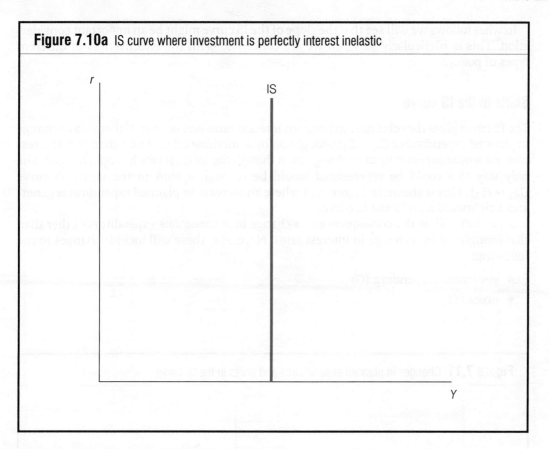

In what follows we will see that the slope of the IS curve might be an important consideration. This is particularly so when we are concerned with the effectiveness of different types of policy.

Shifts in the IS curve

The IS curve plots the relationship between interest rates and output. If there was a change in planned expenditures ($E_1 \rightarrow E_2$) brought on by something other than a change in interest rate, we would expect output to change even though the interest rate has not changed. The only way this could be represented would be through a shift in the entire IS curve ($IS_1 \rightarrow IS_2$). This is shown in Figure 7.11 where an increase in planned expenditures generates a rightward shift in the IS curve.

So, a shift will be the consequence of a change in autonomous expenditures other than that brought on by a change in interest rates. Naturally, these will include changes in the following:

- government spending (G)
- taxes (T)

Figure 7.11 Changes in planned expenditures and shifts in the IS curve

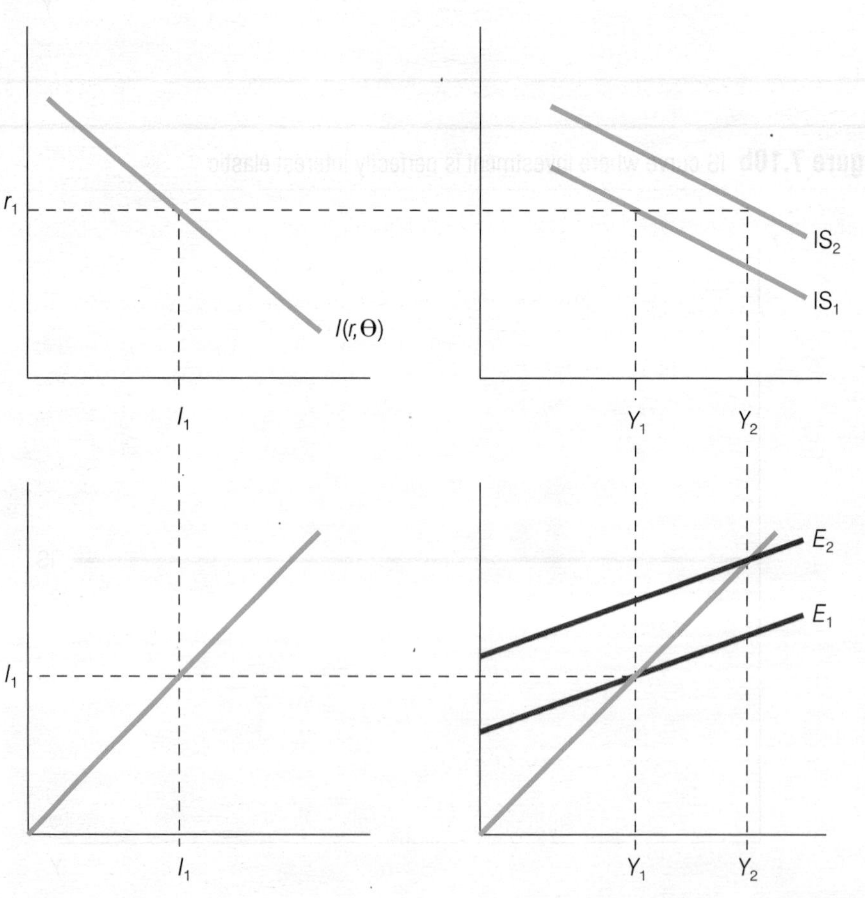

- autonomous consumption (a)
- investment other than interest-induced (Θ).

Any change in these types of autonomous expenditures will lead to a horizontal shift in the schedule. Remembering the rule, $\Delta Y^* = k(\Delta AE)$, the size of this shift will, of course, depend on the size of the multiplier and the size of the change in expenditure.

We have now fully determined the IS curve – we know what it represents, what determines its slope, and why and how it may shift. We now turn our attention to answering the same set of questions for the LM curve.

Global application 7.2

Consumption and interest rates

In the construction of the IS curve, consumption is determined by the Keynesian consumption function. This makes no explicit link between consumption and interest rates, leading the slope of the IS curve to be driven predominately by the interest elasticity of investment demand. The empirical evidence (see Global application 7.1) points to this elasticity being fairly low – with investment being driven by other factors, so the IS curve is steep.

In Chapter 2, we saw that as most households are net borrowers because of mortgage debt, interest rates will be an important determinant of consumption. This view is confirmed in Figure 2, which plots the level of building society mortgage rates and the degree of consumer confidence in the UK economy.

Figure 2 reports a relatively strong negative relationship between consumer confidence and mortgage rates. If the IS curve were extended to incorporate the sensitivity of consumption to interest rates, it would justify a much flatter schedule as interest rates changes will generate large changes in planned expenditures.

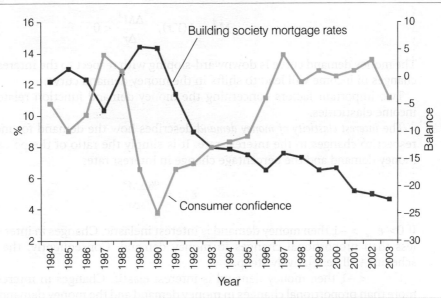

Figure 2 Mortgage rates and consumer confidence in the UK

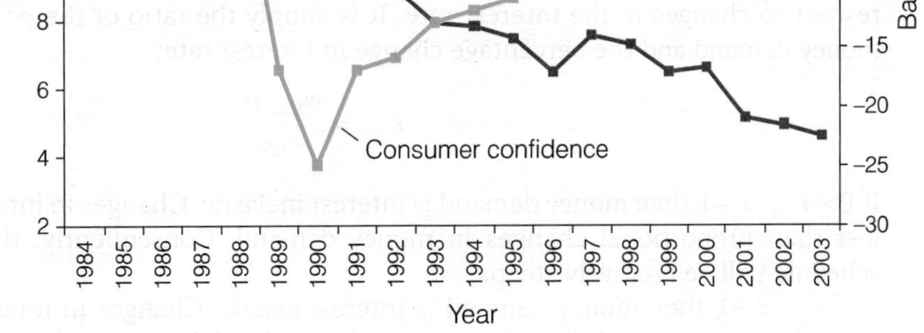

7.3 The LM curve: equilibrium in the money market

The LM curve represents the combinations of income and interest rates where the money market is in equilibrium – or where the demand and supply of money are equal to each other.

$$M^s = M^d \qquad (7.14)$$

A fairly complete description of the money market in given in Chapter 5, but a brief description will be given here for the purpose of constructing and understanding the model.

The money supply is simply determined by the value of the real money stock.

$$M^s = \frac{M}{P} \qquad (7.15)$$

An increase in the money supply can come from either an increase in the money stock or through a fall in the price level. Both of these would have the same effect. For example, if there was 10 per cent more money in circulation, then 10 per cent more could be purchased. If, instead, there was no change in the money in circulation, but all prices were 10 per cent cheaper, then it is obvious that the same amount of money would be capable of buying 10 per cent more. The money supply is therefore determined not just by the physical amount of money, but also the value of that money.

The demand for money is described by the theory of liquidity preference. In Chapter 5 this is discussed in some detail, but to simplify the analysis let us just assume that there are two factors which determine the demand for money.

1. Income (Y): consumer expenditure tends to rise with income as more money is demanded for transaction purposes.
2. Interest rate (r): this represents the opportunity cost of holding money. Instead of holding money in the form of notes and coins, the alternative is buying a bond which pays a positive rate of interest. As the interest rate rises, it encourages people to substitute away from money towards bonds.

The money demand curve takes the following form and is shown in Figure 7.12:

$$M^d = L(Y,r), \quad \frac{\Delta M^d}{\Delta r} < 0 \qquad (7.15)$$

The money demand curve is downward-sloping with respect to the interest rate. However, changes in income will lead to shifts in the money demand curve.

Two important factors concerning the money demand function relate to interest and income elasticities.

The *interest elasticity of money demand* describes how the demand for money varies with respect to changes in the interest rate. It is simply the ratio of the percentage change in money demand and the percentage change in interest rates.

$$^{r}\varepsilon_{M^d} = \frac{\%\Delta M^d}{\%\Delta r}$$

If $0 > {}^{r}\varepsilon_{M^d} > -1$, then money demand is interest inelastic. Changes in interest rates generate less than proportional changes in money demand. Consequently, the money demand schedule will be relatively steep.

If $\varepsilon_{M^d} < -1$, then money demand is interest elastic. Changes in interest rates generate more than proportional changes in money demand and the money demand schedule will be relatively flat.

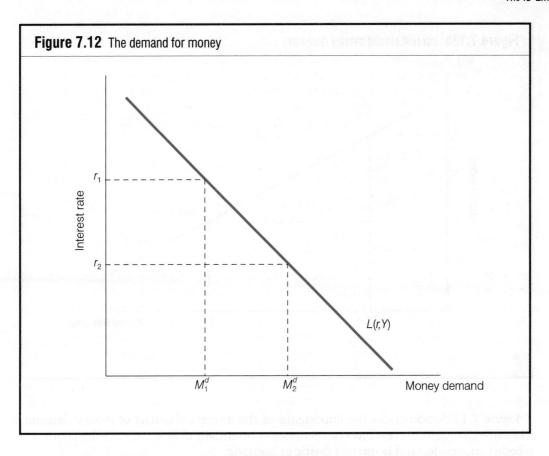

Figure 7.12 The demand for money

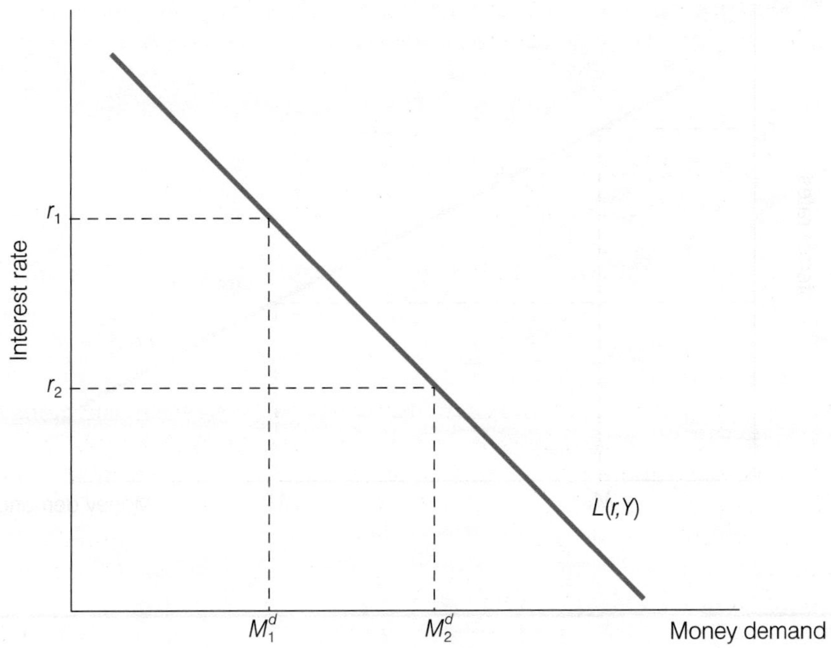

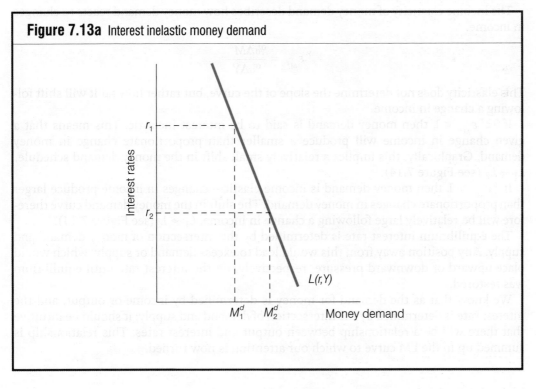

Figure 7.13a Interest inelastic money demand

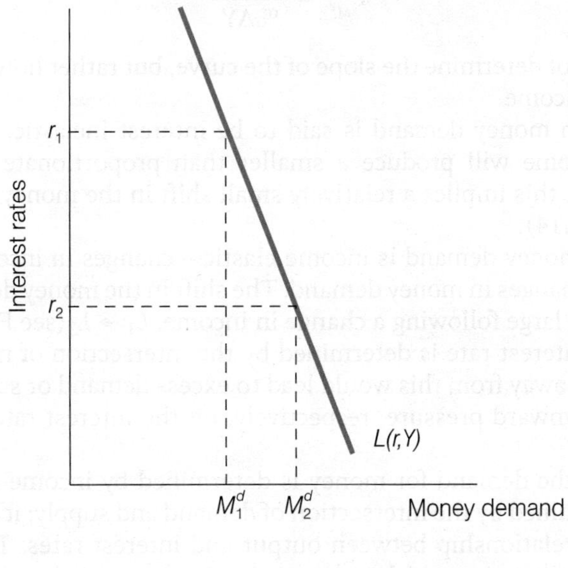

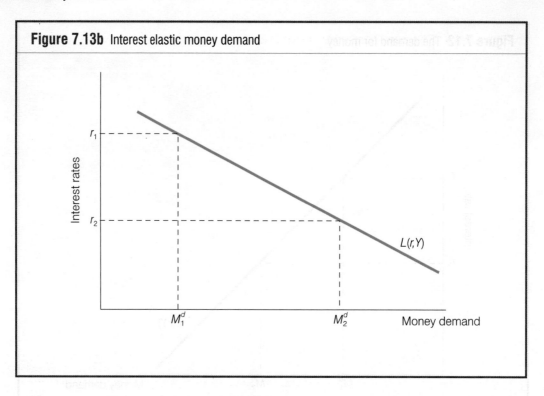

Figure 7.13b Interest elastic money demand

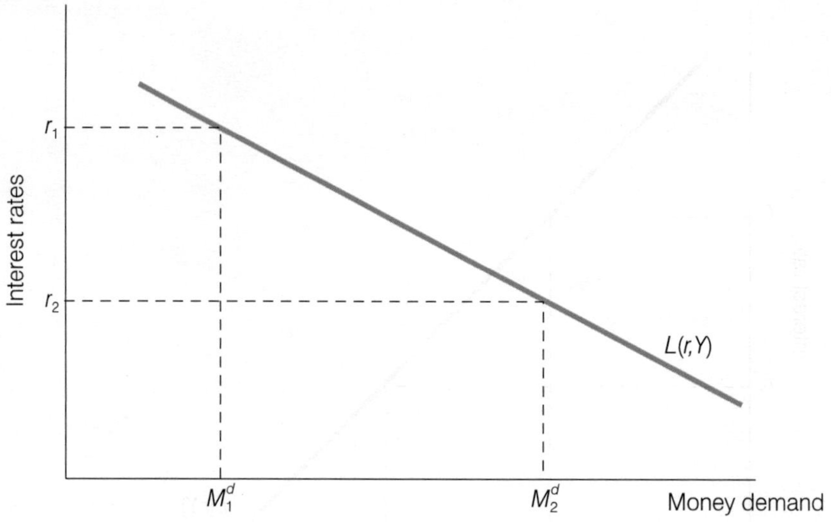

7

Figure 7.13 demonstrates the importance of the interest elasticity of money demand. The same change in interest rates can generate substantially different results depending on whether money demand is interest elastic or inelastic.

The income elasticity of money demand describes how money demand reacts to changes in income.

$$^{Y}\varepsilon_{M^d} = \frac{\%\Delta M^d}{\%\Delta Y}$$

This elasticity does not determine the slope of the curve, but rather how far it will shift following a change in income.

If $0 < {}^{Y}\varepsilon_{M^d} < 1$, then money demand is said to be interest inelastic. This means that a given change in income will produce a smaller than proportionate change in money demand. Graphically, this implies a relatively small shift in the money demand schedule, $L_1 \rightarrow L_2$ (see Figure 7.14).

If ${}^{Y}\varepsilon_{M^d} > 1$, then money demand is income elastic – changes in income produce larger than proportionate changes in money demand. The shift in the money demand curve therefore will be relatively large following a change in income, $L_1 \rightarrow L_3$ (see Figure 7.14).

The equilibrium interest rate is determined by the intersection of money demand and supply. Any position away from this would lead to excess demand or supply, which would place upward or downward pressure, respectively, on the interest rate until equilibrium was restored.

We know that as the demand for money is determined by income or output, and the interest rate is determined by the intersection of demand and supply; it should be intuitive that there will be a relationship between output and interest rates. This relationship is summed up in the LM curve to which our attention is now turned.

Figure 7.14 The income elasticity of money demand

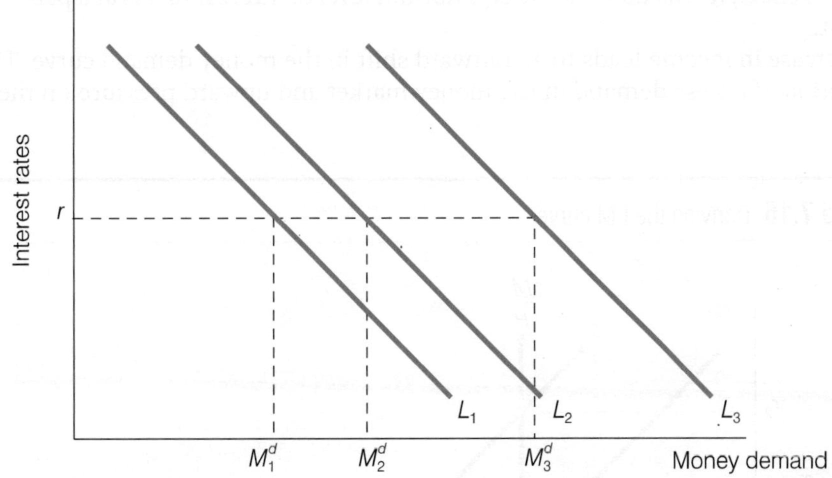

Figure 7.15 Equilibrium in the money market and the determination of the interest rate

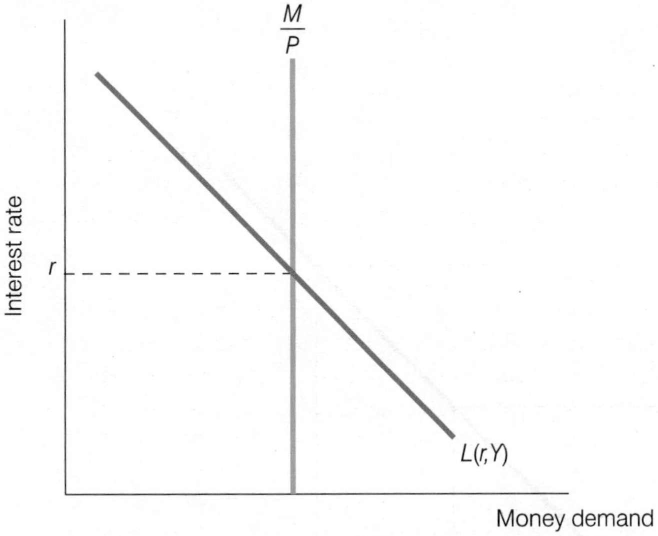

7

Deriving the LM curve

In the IS-LM model, the interest rate is determined in the money market. The LM curve plots the combinations of output *Y* and interest rates *r* where the money market is in equilibrium. In effect, it tells us what the equilibrium level of interest rate is at a particular level of output.

An increase in income leads to an outward shift in the money demand curve. This leads to a position of excess demand in the money market and upward pressure on the interest

Figure 7.16 Deriving the LM curve

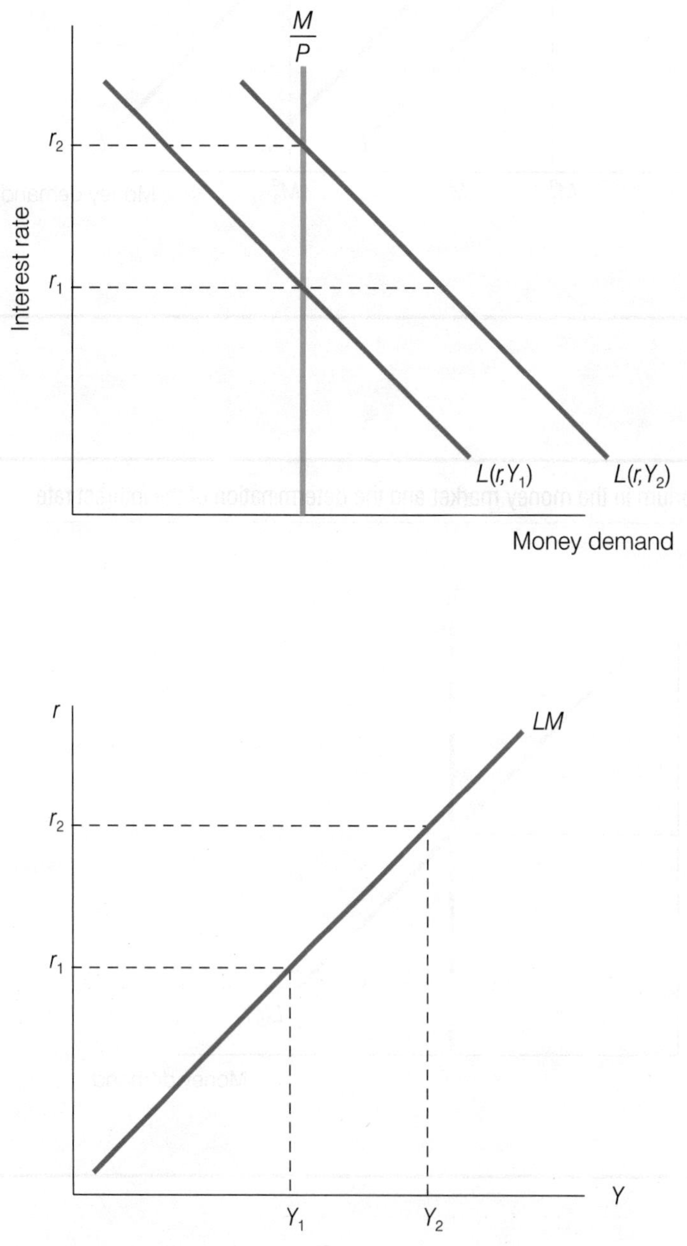

rate. For money demand to once again equal money supply at this higher level of income, interest rates must rise. In Chapter 5, we described how changes in bond prices would bring this about and, if necessary, the reader is recommended to refer back to this chapter.

So, as Figure 7.16 shows, the position of excess demand in the money market following an increase in output can only be offset if the interest rate also increases. The LM curve is therefore an upward-sloping function.

It will be seen that the slope of the LM curve is potentially very important and is determined by the two elasticities we have mentioned above.

Figure 7.17 The income elasticity of the demand for money and the slope of the LM curve

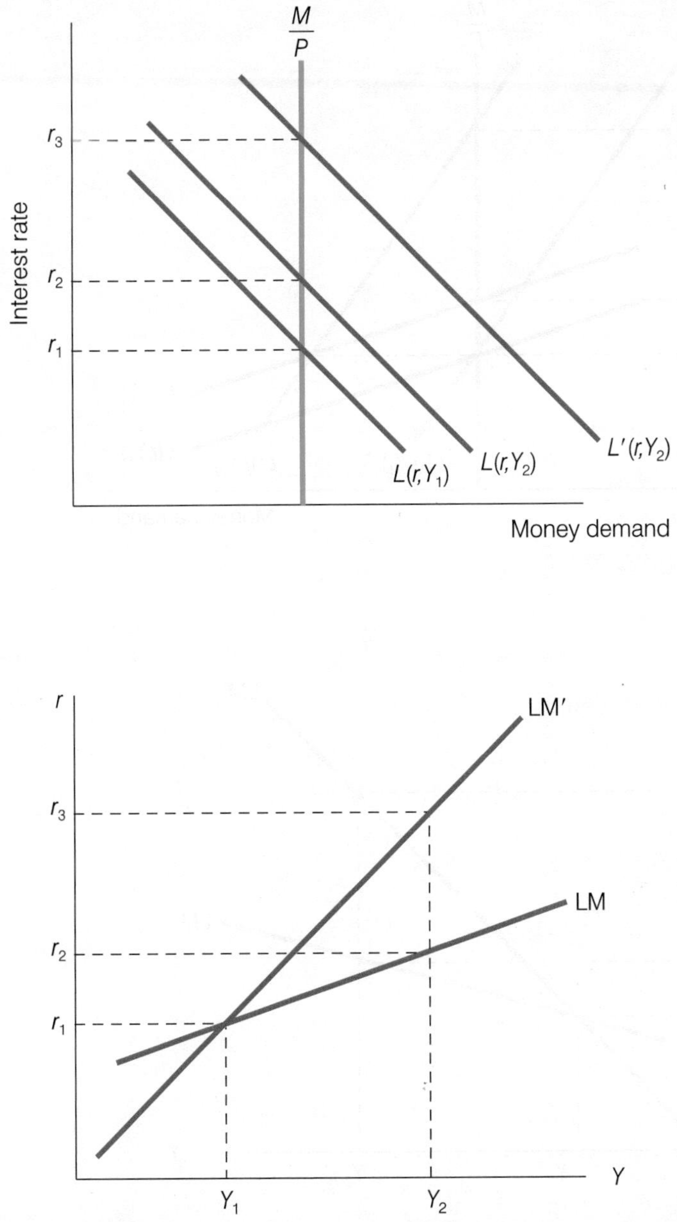

1. ${}^{Y}\varepsilon_{M^d}$: the income elasticity describes the change in money demand following a change in income. From the derivation of the LM schedule, we know that once income increases, interest rates must also rise to prevent the demand for money changing. The extent to which interest rates must rise, though, will be determined by how much money demand changes with income in the first place. This is clearly shown in Figure 7.17.

When money demand is income elastic, an increase in income from Y_1 to Y_2 will generate a relatively substantial shift in the money demand curve. To re-equilibrate

7

Figure 7.18 The interest elasticity of the demand for money and the slope of the LM curve

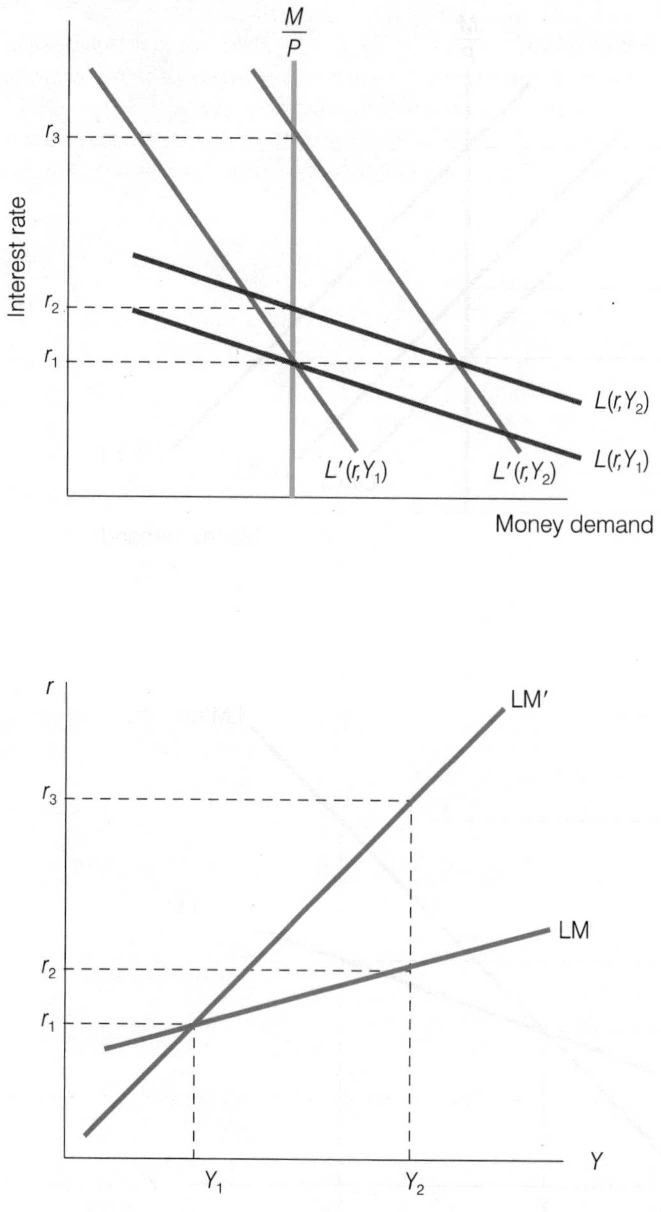

the money market, a large rise in interest rates ($r_1 \rightarrow r_3$) would be required. The slope of the LM curve would thus appear to be steeper.

If money demand was income inelastic, the same increase in income would produce a smaller shift in money demand and the required rise in interest ($r_1 \rightarrow r_2$) rates would be correspondingly smaller. Consequently, the LM curve is flatter.

2. ${}^r\varepsilon_{M^d}$: the interest elasticity of money demand is very important for determining the slope of the LM curve. When income rises and the money demand curve shifts to the right, what size increase in interest rates is required in order to re-equilibrate the money market? If money demand is interest elastic, then only a relatively small increase in interest rates ($r_1 \rightarrow r_2$) would be required. As can be seen from Figure 7.18, money demand is very sensitive to interest rates and the LM curve would be fairly flat. However, if money demand were interest inelastic, a much larger rise in interest rates ($r_1 \rightarrow r_3$) would be required and the LM curve would be steeper.

There are two special cases concerning the LM curve that are worth noting. First, if the demand for money is perfectly interest elastic (${}^r\varepsilon_{M^d} = \infty$), the LM curve will be horizontal as only a miniscule increase in interest rates would be required to restore money market equilibrium following an increase in income. Alternatively, if (${}^r\varepsilon_{M^d} = 0$), the demand for money is perfectly inelastic, the LM curve would be vertical. Given that money demand is insensitive to interest rate changes, an infinite increase would be needed. These two cases are displayed in Figure 7.19.

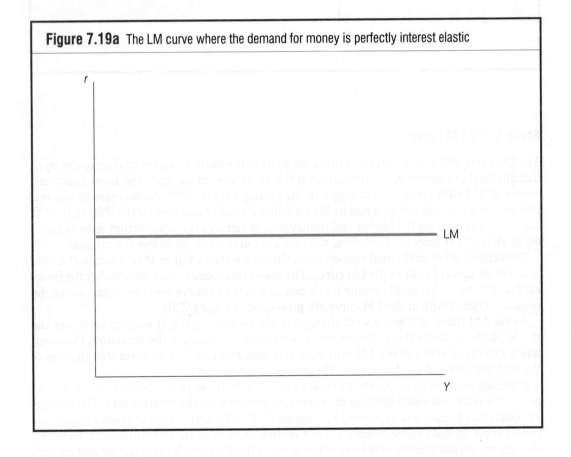

Figure 7.19a The LM curve where the demand for money is perfectly interest elastic

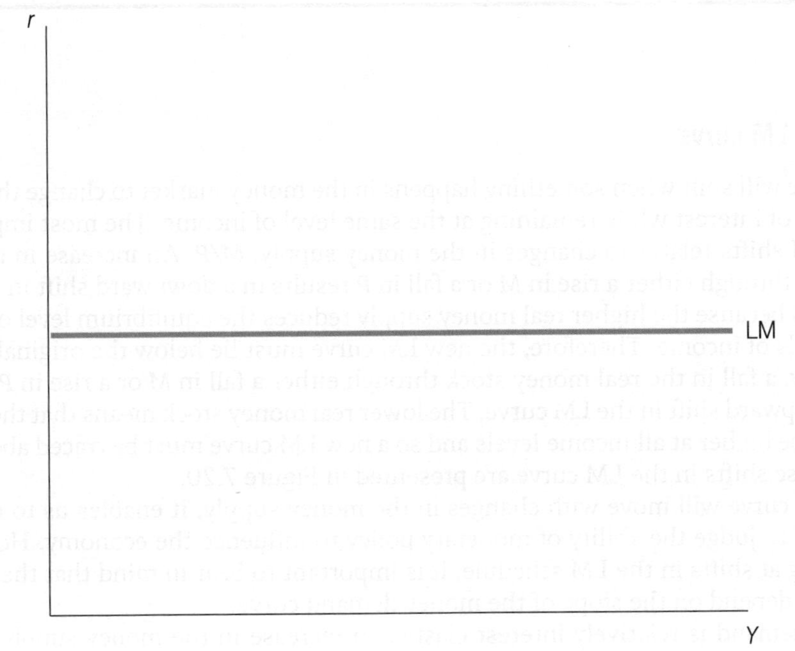

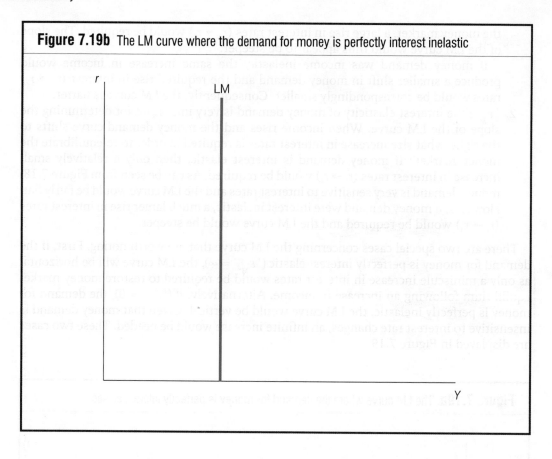

Figure 7.19b The LM curve where the demand for money is perfectly interest inelastic

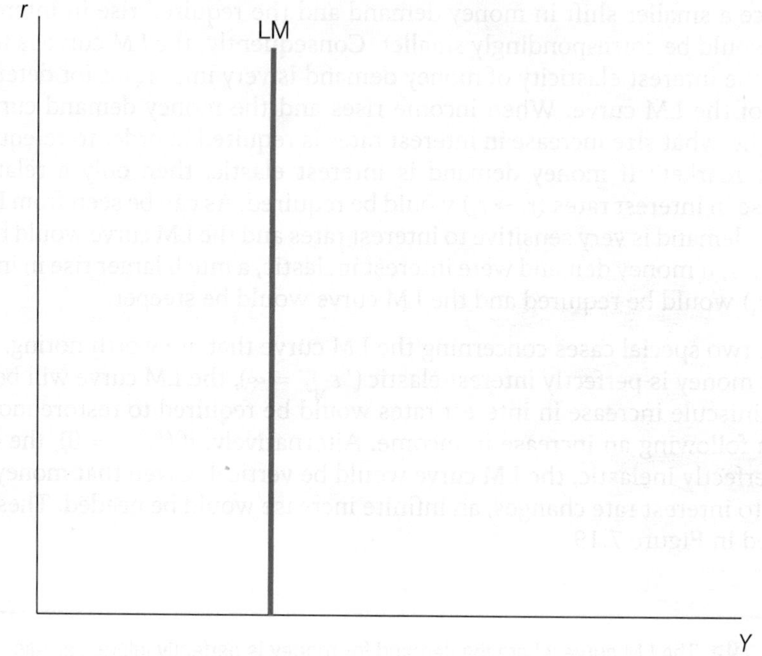

Shifts in the LM curve

The LM curve will shift when something happens in the money market to change the equilibrium level of interest while remaining at the same level of income. The most important source of LM shifts relates to changes in the money supply, *M/P*. An increase in the real money stock through either a rise in *M* or a fall in *P* results in a downward shift in the LM curve. This is because the higher real money supply reduces the equilibrium level of interest at all levels of income. Therefore, the new LM curve must lie below the original.

Conversely, a fall in the real money stock through either a fall in *M* or a rise in *P* would result in an upward shift in the LM curve. The lower real money stock means that the interest rate will be higher at all income levels and so a new LM curve must be traced above the original. These shifts in the LM curve are presented in Figure 7.20.

As the LM curve will move with changes in the money supply, it enables us to use the IS-LM model to judge the ability of monetary policy to influence the economy. However, when looking at shifts in the LM schedule, it is important to bear in mind that the size of the shift will depend on the slope of the money demand curve.

If money demand is relatively interest elastic, an increase in the money supply would only put a relatively small amount of downward pressure on the interest rate. The process by which this happens is explained in Chapter 5. Briefly, with a higher money supply we need people to hold more money for the money market to be in equilibrium. How far, though, would the interest rate have to fall to make holding bonds unattractive and encourage people to switch to money? If the demand for money is highly sensitive to interest rates, then the answer is not by much and the shift in the LM curve would be relatively small.

Figure 7.20 Changes in the money supply and shifts in the LM curve

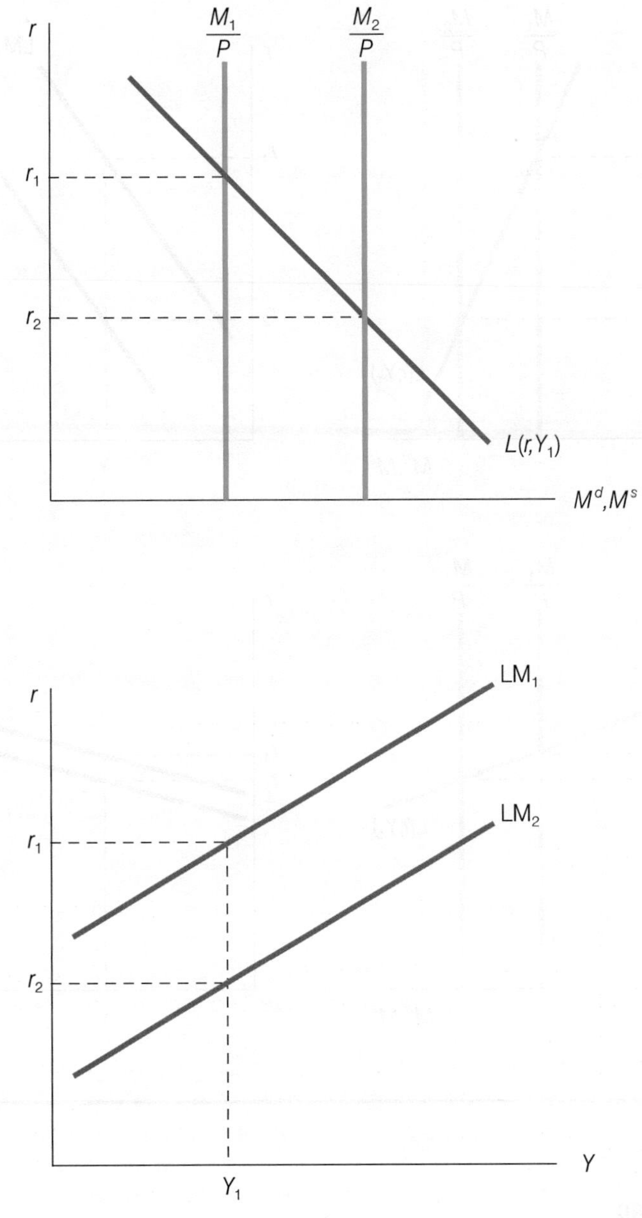

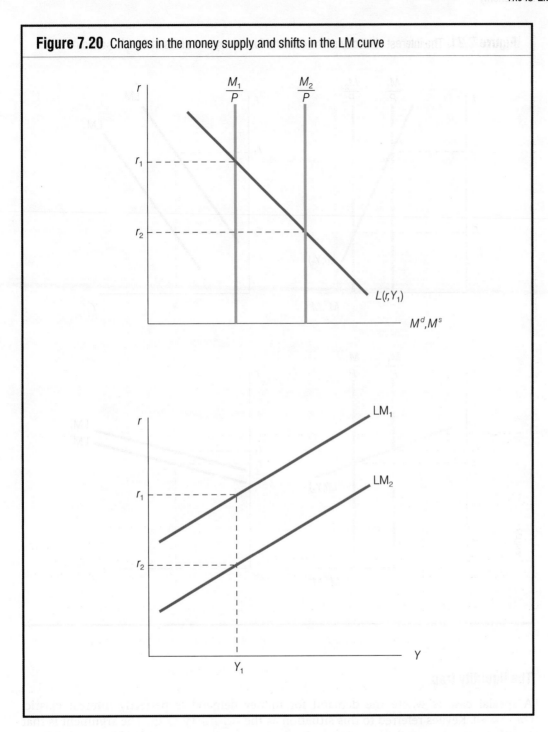

When the demand for money curve is interest inelastic, changes in the money supply instigate relatively large movements in the interest rate. As money demand is not sensitive to interest rates, a large fall would be required to encourage people to hold the higher money balances. The vertical shift in the LM schedule therefore would be expected to be much larger. These cases are shown in Figure 7.21.

Figure 7.21 The interest elasticity of the demand for money and shifts in the LM schedule

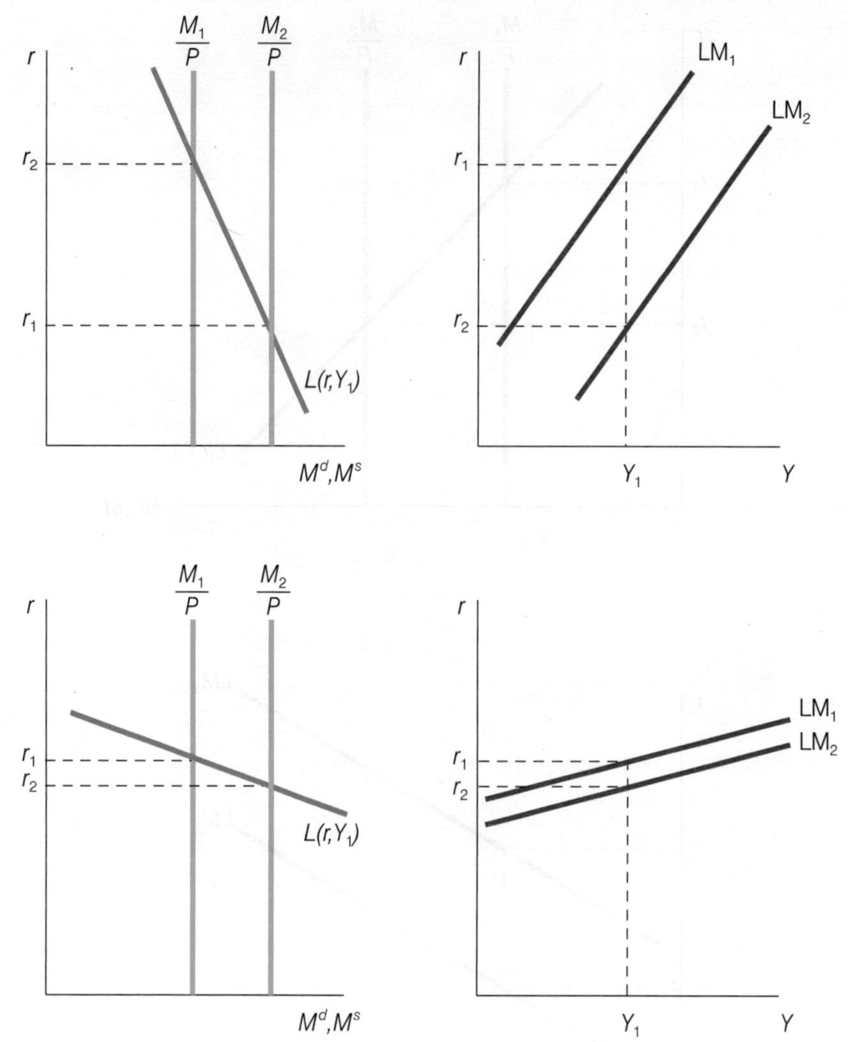

7

The liquidity trap

A special case is where the demand for money demand is perfectly interest elastic, (${}^{r}\varepsilon_{M^d} = \infty$). Keynes referred to this situation as the **liquidity trap**. The argument is that once interest rates reach a certain low level, the opportunity cost of holding cash falls to zero and bonds become unattractive. This does not have to be at a zero interest rate, but just at a rate (r_{LT}) where the opportunity cost of holding money is below the value of liquidity. This is why it is called the liquidity trap – the interest rate is so low that people are unwilling to forgo the benefits of holding money by investing in bonds.

In this case, the demand for money schedule is completely horizontal (see Figure 7.22). So, when the interest rate has fallen to a sufficiently low level, changes in the real money supply will not change the equilibrium interest rate. The LM curve becomes horizontal and invariant to changes in the money supply. This is when the liquidity trap is reached.

The concept of a liquidity trap is important to policy makers. If this scenario were to arise, then policy makers would find that the effectiveness of using monetary policy to control the interest rate to be severely limited. Any attempts to use monetary policy to control the economy would be futile.

Figure 7.22 The liquidity trap

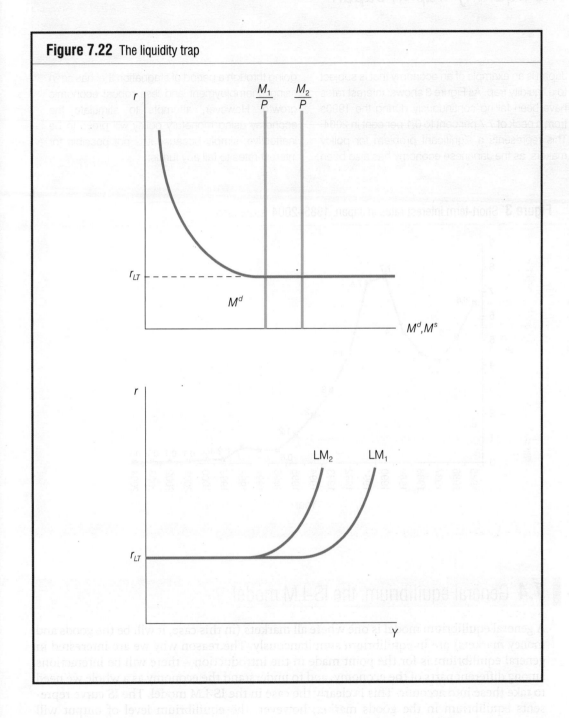

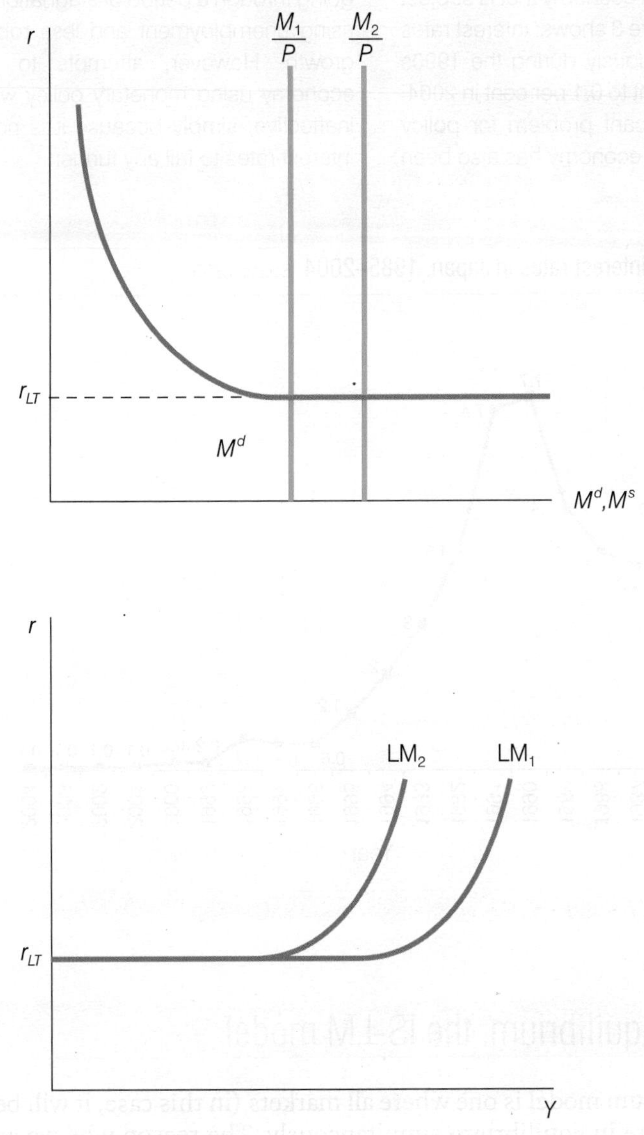

Global application 7.3

The liquidity trap in Japan

Japan is an example of an economy that is subject to a liquidity trap. As Figure 3 shows, interest rates have been falling continuously during the 1990s from a peak of 7.7 per cent to 0.1 per cent in 2004. This represents a significant problem for policy makers, as the Japanese economy has also been going through a period of stagnation that has seen rising unemployment and less robust economic growth. However, attempts to stimulate the economy using monetary policy will prove to be ineffective, simply because it is not possible for interest rates to fall any further.

Figure 3 Short-term interest rates in Japan, 1985–2004 Source: OECD

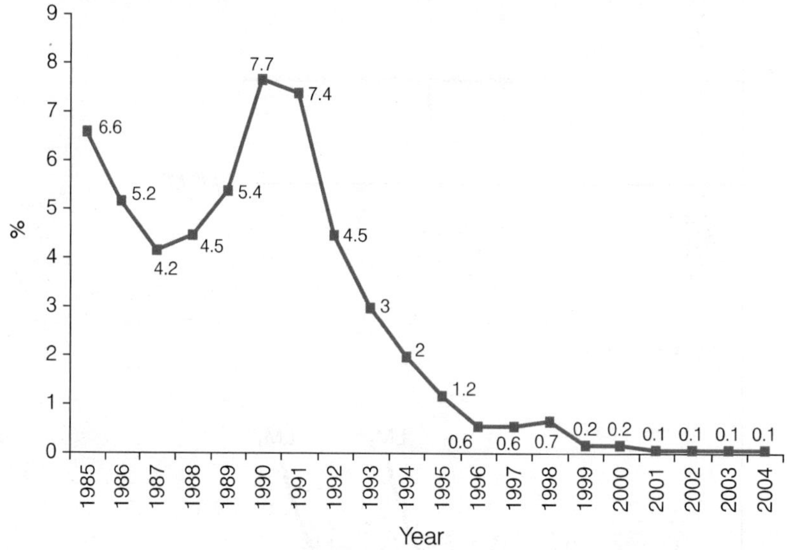

7

7.4 General equilibrium: the IS-LM model

A general equilibrium model is one where all markets (in this case, it will be the goods and money markets) are in equilibrium simultaneously. The reason why we are interested in general equilibrium is for the point made in the introduction – there will be interactions among different parts of the economy, and to understand the economy as a whole we need to take these into account. This is clearly the case in the IS-LM model. The IS curve represents equilibrium in the goods market; however, the equilibrium level of output will depend on the interest rate which is determined in the money market. Likewise, although interest rates are determined in the money market, the level of output determined in the goods market will be a powerful force driving the demand for money. By recognizing this, we are better able to understand the path the economy may take.

Figure 7.23 Equilibrium in the IS-LM Model

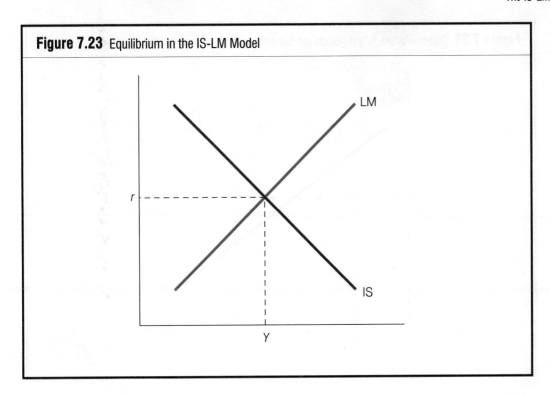

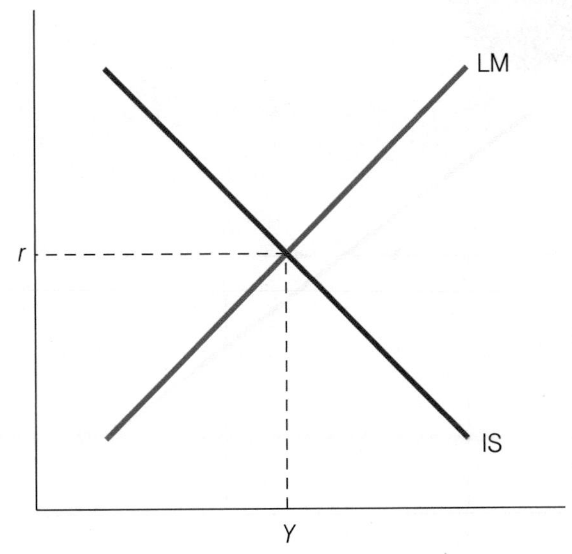

The equilibrium level of output and interest rate for an economy is found at the intersection of the IS and LM schedules (Figure 7.23).

If the economy were in any position away from this equilibrium point, it is easy to show that the economy will fall onto a path that brings it back towards equilibrium. The intuition behind this is relatively easy to understand – it just assumes that markets will clear, so any position that infers excess demand or supply is not sustainable.

Suppose we were in a position that was off the IS curve. From Figure 7.24, at an interest rate of r, the equilibrium level of output would be Y_{IS}, which would equal the level of planned expenditures. A position to the left of this, say at output level Y_1, would imply that planned expenditures exceed the level of output ($Y_{IS} > Y_1$), given the interest rate. The goods market will be in excess demand, and firms seeing their inventory stocks being run down would be pressed into action. It would be expected that output would then increase towards Y_{IS}.

A position to the right of equilibrium would invoke the opposite movement in output. If output were at a level equal to Y_2, then it is the case that planned expenditures are below the current level of output ($Y_{IS} < Y_2$). Firms will find themselves accumulating stocks of unsold goods and will naturally cut back output in response towards a level of Y_{IS}.

Therefore, if we are ever in a position off the IS curve, this would correspond to excess demand or supply in the goods market, and output would move towards its equilibrium value. Market clearing in the goods market will always move us back to a position on the IS curve.

A similar analysis holds with the LM schedule. Looking at Figure 7.25, at a given level of income Y, there is an interest rate r_{LM} where the demand and supply of money are equal to each other. This corresponds to a position on the LM curve, so any position off the LM curve must point to some disequilibrium in the money market.

Suppose we are in a position below the LM curve where the interest rate is equal to r_1. Here, at an output level of Y, there would be excess demand for money. To satisfy the demand for liquidity, people would sell bonds, forcing bond prices downwards and the

Figure 7.24 Disequilibrium in the goods market and adjustment back to the IS curve

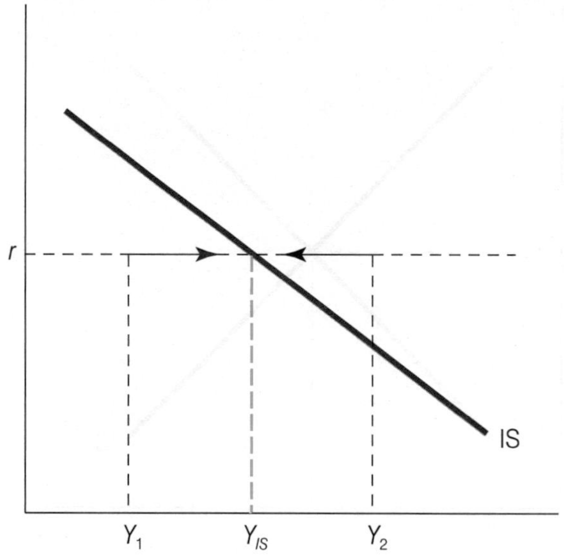

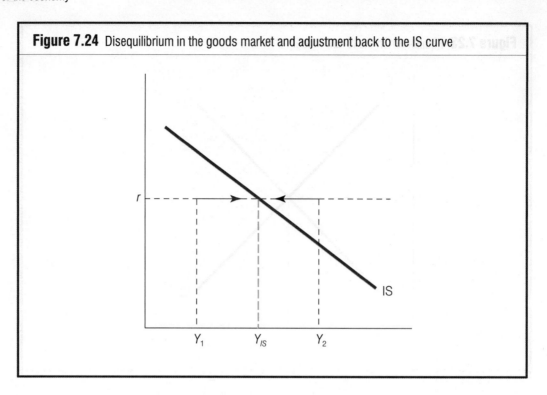

Figure 7.25 Disequilibrium in the money market and adjustment towards the LM curve

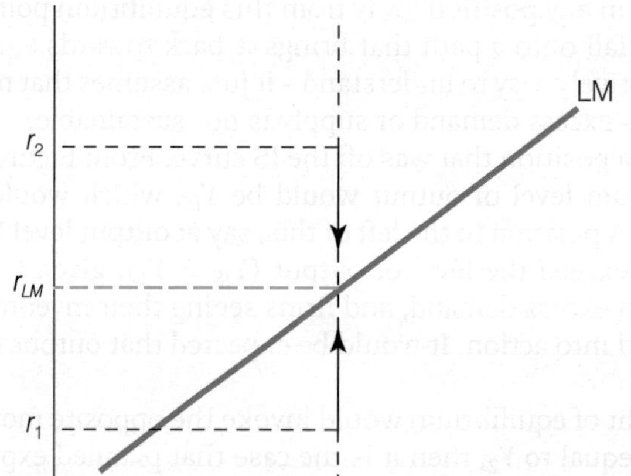

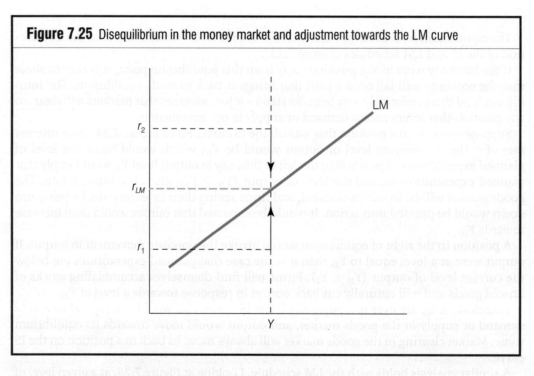

interest rate would rise back to its equilibrium level. At a position above the LM curve, say with an interest rate of r_2, there would be excess supply in the money market. In order to reduce their holdings of cash, people would buy bonds, which of course will force bond prices upwards and the interest rate would fall towards r_{LM}. It is clear that the workings of the money market will ensure that we always move back to a position on the LM schedule.

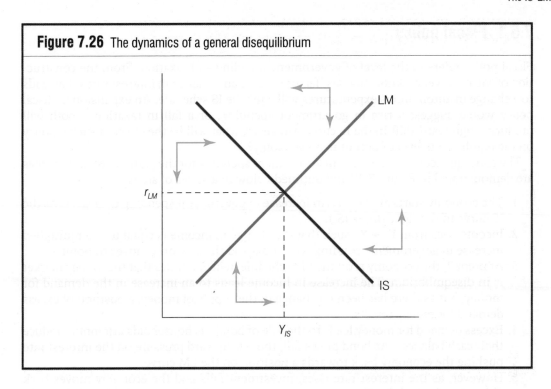

Figure 7.26 The dynamics of a general disequilibrium

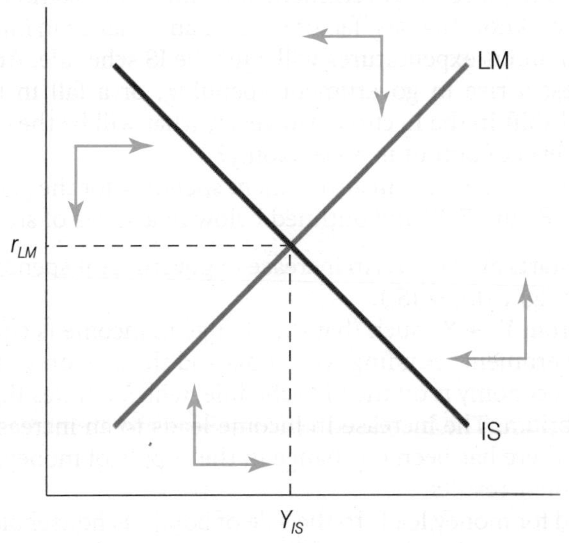

Putting all of this together, we find that if we are at any position away from equilibrium in the IS-LM model there will be movements in the goods and/or money markets to restore the economy's general equilibrium. Taking a look at Figure 7.26, which combines the analysis of Figures 7.24 and 7.25, will confirm this. If we start at any point on the diagram, there will be a movement in output or interest rates which pushes us onto the IS and LM schedules. Only at an interest rate of r_{LM} and at output level of Y_{IS} will there be no excess demand or supply in either market and no further movement in output or interest rate. This position is, of course, marked by the intersection of the IS and LM curves.

7.5 Comparative statics

Now that the IS-LM model has been fully derived and the equilibrium established, we can use the model to analyse a range of different economic scenarios. Most notably, the model is very useful for investigating the effects of monetary and fiscal policies in the economy. The term *comparative statics* refers to the idea of comparing different equilibria. In analysing the consequences of a particular policy or shock on the economy, all we have to do is compare the equilibrium before and afterward.

In this section, we will focus on assessing the effectiveness of expansionary monetary and fiscal policies on the level of equilibrium output. Fiscal policy will imply IS curve shifts, whereas monetary policy will shift the LM schedule. We know and accept that there may be other factors which cause either of these curves to shift, but the reader will understand that to treat each of these individually would be very repetitive. For example, once we know the issues involved in shifting the IS curve due to an increase in government spending, then the same analysis will apply if we want to know what would happen following a shift in the IS induced by other changes in autonomous expenditures (e.g., autonomous consumption, investment, taxes, etc.).

7.5.1 Fiscal policy

Fiscal policy refers to the level of government spending and taxation. From the construction of the IS curve, we know that any factor other than a change in interest rates that leads to a change in autonomous expenditures will shift the IS schedule. An expansionary fiscal policy would suggest a rise in government spending, or a fall in taxation – both will produce a rightward shift in the IS curve. However, what will be the effect of such a policy on the equilibrium level of output in an economy?

The consequences of an increase in government spending for the path the economy takes are demonstrated in Figure 7.27 and outlined below in a series of steps.

1. The economy starts at point 1. An increase in government spending $G_1 \rightarrow G_2$ shifts the IS curve to the right ($IS_1 \rightarrow IS_2$).
2. Income rises from $Y_1 \rightarrow Y_2$, such that the change in income is equal to the multiplied increase in government spending $\Delta Y = k\Delta G$ and the economy moves to point 2.
3. At point 2, the economy is off the LM schedule, which implies that the money market is in disequilibrium. The increase in income leads to an increase in the demand for money, but as there has been no change in the supply of money, a position of excess demand for money results.
4. Excess demand for money leads to the sale of bonds as households attempt to reduce their cash balances. As bond prices fall, there is upward pressure on the interest rate pushing the economy back towards a position on the LM curve.
5. However, as the interest rate rises, investment falls and the economy moves back along the IS schedule. The economy forms a new equilibrium position at point 3. At the new equilibrium, income (Y_3) and interest rates (r_2) are both higher.

An expansionary fiscal policy in the form of an increase in government spending acts to increase output Y. The final outcome, though, differs from the analysis of Chapter 4. In that case, output would settle at Y_2 and success will depend only on the size of the multiplier.

Figure 7.27 An expansionary fiscal policy

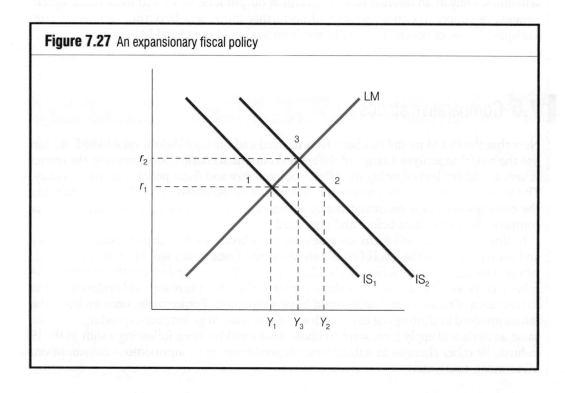

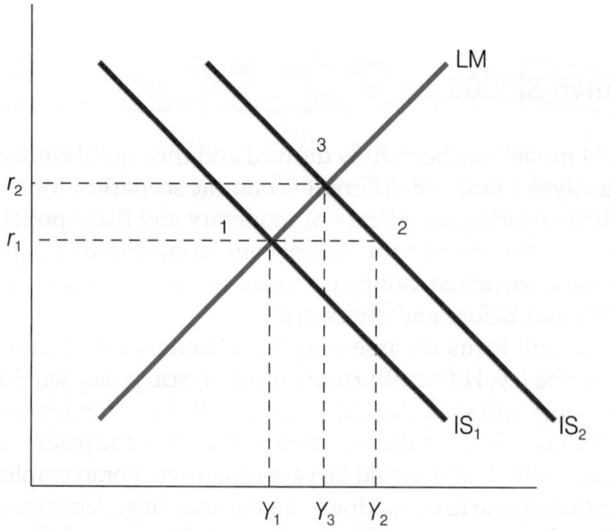

However, the IS-LM model also considers the impact of rising output on the interest rate, which is determined in the money market.

As output rises, the demand for money puts upward pressure on the interest rate. From Figure 7.27, we can see that this will reduce investment expenditures and lower output, so ultimately the equilibrium is at a level of output Y_3, which is below Y_2.

This fall in output ($Y_2 - Y_3$) is known as the **crowding out** effect. Naturally, the size of this will significantly affect the success of using fiscal policy to increase output.

To best show the importance of, and understand the conditions which determine the size of the crowding out effect, we shall consider the two extreme cases. This is where there is either 0 per cent or 100 per cent crowding out from fiscal policy.

Nought per cent crowding out

There are two scenarios where there will be no crowding out effect of fiscal policy. In this case, output will rise and stay at a level Y_2.

If the IS curve is vertical, then an increase in government spending will shift the IS curve to the right. The horizontal difference between the two IS curves is given by $k\Delta G$. We can see from Figure 7.28 that the economy moves to a new equilibrium where output rises and stays at Y_2. It is also true that the equilibrium interest rate rises from $r_1 \rightarrow r_2$, but this fails to produce any crowding out.

Remembering our work from earlier in the chapter, we know that when the IS curve is vertical, it implies that investment is completely interest inelastic (${}^r\varepsilon_I = 0$). This means that changes in the interest rate have no effect whatsoever on investment – even though the interest rate rises, it will not crowd out investment and reduce output.

The second scenario where there is no crowding out is when the LM curve is horizontal. This arises when the demand for money is perfectly interest elastic (${}^r\varepsilon_{M^d} = \infty$). Looking at Figure 7.29, an increase in government spending will not generate any increases in interest rates. So, even if investment were interest elastic, there will be no crowding out effect.

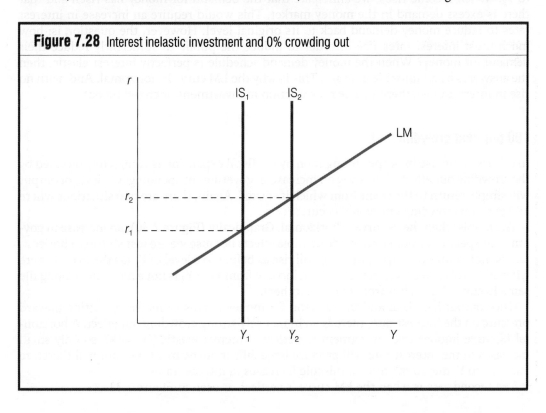

Figure 7.28 Interest inelastic investment and 0% crowding out

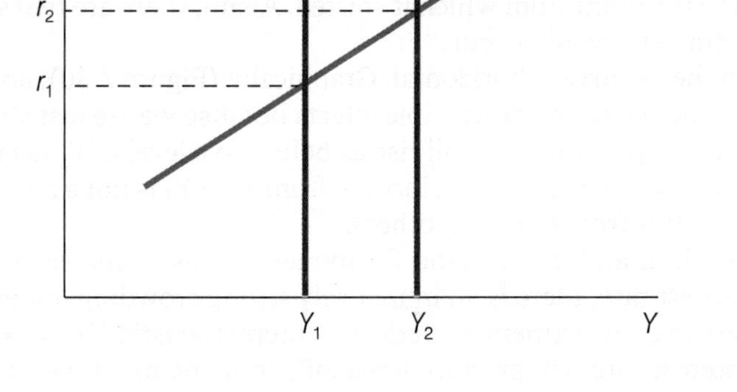

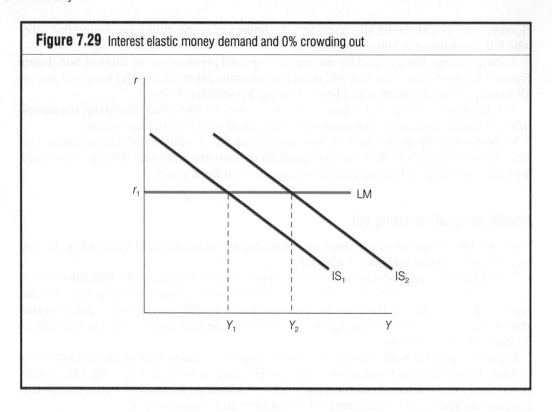

Figure 7.29 Interest elastic money demand and 0% crowding out

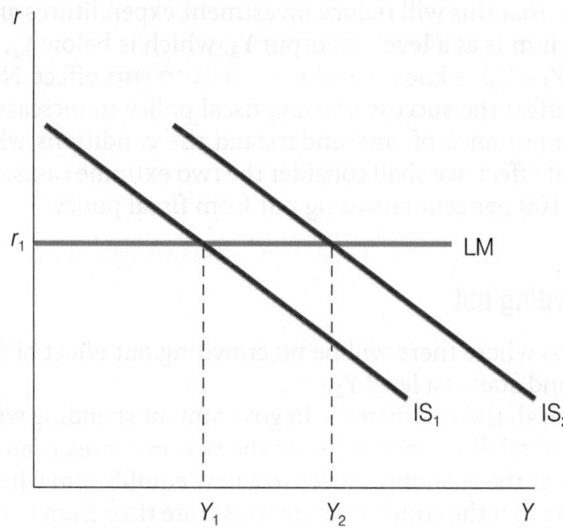

Why is there no upward pressure on interest rates, even though output has risen from Y_1 to Y_2? When income rises, we anticipate that the demand for money has risen and that there is excess demand in the money market. This would require an increase in interest rates to reduce money demand back to its original level. However, the question is: how much must interest rates rise in order to induce the public to sufficiently reduce their demand for money? When the money demand schedule is perfectly interest elastic, then the answer is by a miniscule amount. This is why the LM curve is horizontal. And, with no rise in interest rates, there will be no reduction in investment or crowding out.

100 per cent crowding out

In this case, the rise in output brought on by the fiscal expansion is completely reversed by the crowding out effect. Following an increase in government spending, the level of output will simply return to the point from which it started. Again, there are two situations where 100 per cent crowding out would occur.

The first is when the IS curve is horizontal. Graphically (Figure 7.30), an increase in government spending would have no discernible effects because we are just shifting a horizontal line horizontally. Output, though, will rise as before to a level of Y_2 (as the IS curves are lying on top of each other, the increase in income from $Y_1 \rightarrow Y_2$ is not a movement along the same IS curve, but a shift from one to another).

Once output has risen and the demand for money begins to increase, putting upward pressure on the interest rate, there is an immensely strong crowding out effect. A horizontal IS curve implies that investment is perfectly interest elastic (${}^r\varepsilon_I = \infty$), so only small increases in the interest rate will produce large falls in investment. Output will therefore fall back to Y_1 due to the most miniscule increases in interest rates.

The second case is when the LM curve is vertical, as seen in Figure 7.31.

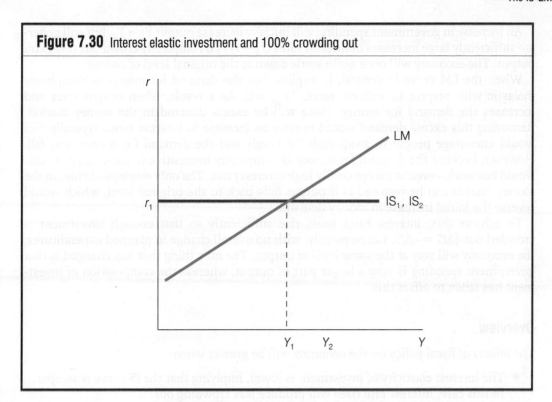

Figure 7.30 Interest elastic investment and 100% crowding out

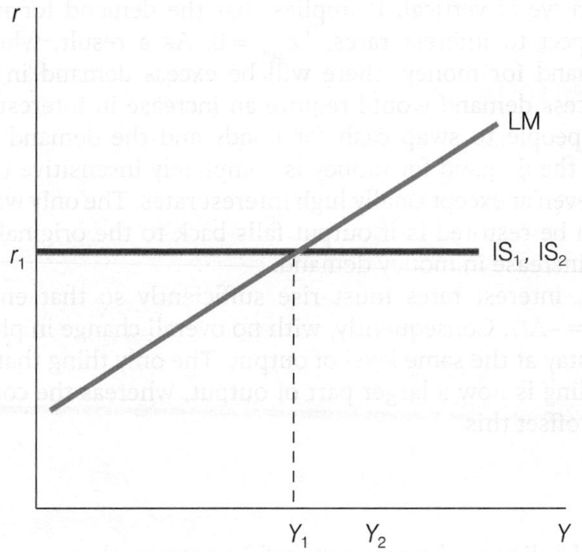

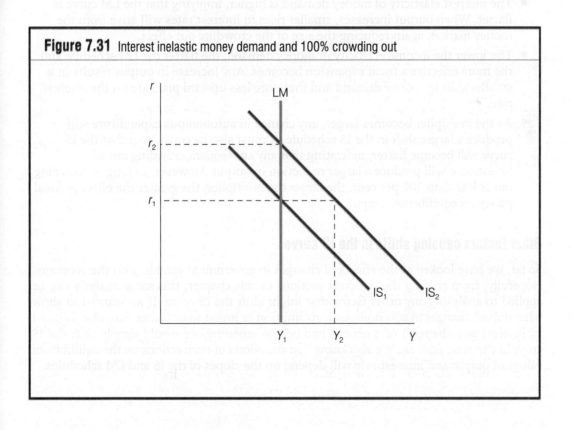

Figure 7.31 Interest inelastic money demand and 100% crowding out

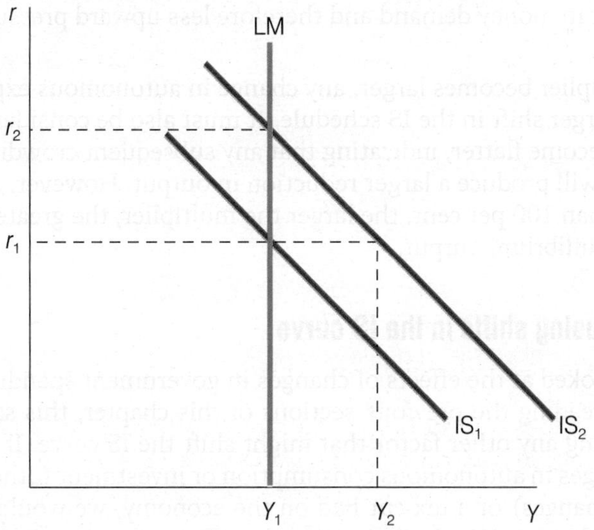

An increase in government spending will initially increase output $Y_1 \rightarrow Y_2$, but will generate sufficiently large increases in interest rates ($r_1 \rightarrow r_2$) t o completely crowd out this extra output. The economy will once again settle down at the original level of output.

When the LM curve is vertical, it implies that the demand for money is completely inelastic with respect to interest rates, ${}^{r}\varepsilon_{M^d} = 0$. As a result, when output rises and increases the demand for money, there will be excess demand in the money market. Removing this excess demand would require an increase in interest rates, typically this would encourage people to swap cash for bonds and the demand for money will fall. However, because the demand for money is completely insensitive to interest rates, this would not work – even at exceptionally high interest rates. The only way equilibrium in the money market can be restored is if output falls back to the original level, which would reverse the initial increase in money demand.

To achieve this, interest rates must rise sufficiently so that enough investment is crowded out ($\Delta G = -\Delta I$). Consequently, with no overall change in planned expenditures, the economy will stay at the same level of output. The only thing that has changed is that government spending is now a larger part of output, whereas the composition of investment has fallen to offset this.

Overview

The effects of fiscal policy on the economy will be greater when:

- The interest elasticity of investment is lower, implying that the IS curve is steeper. In this case, interest rate rises will produce less crowding out.
- The interest elasticity of money demand is higher, implying that the LM curve is flatter. When output increases, smaller rises in interest rates will arise from the money market, again reducing the size of the crowding out effect.
- The lower the income elasticity of money demand, the flatter the LM schedule and the more effective a fiscal expansion becomes. Any increase in output results in a smaller shift in money demand and therefore less upward pressure on the interest rate.
- As the multiplier becomes larger, any change in autonomous expenditure will produce a larger shift in the IS schedule. It must also be considered that the IS curve will become flatter, indicating that any subsequent crowding out of investment will produce a larger reduction in output. However, as long as crowding out is less than 100 per cent, the larger the multiplier, the greater the effect of fiscal policy on equilibrium output.

Other factors causing shifts in the IS curve

So far, we have looked at the effects of changes in government spending on the economy. Hopefully, from reading the previous sections of this chapter, this same analysis can be applied to analysing any other factor that might shift the IS curve. If we wanted to show what impact changes in autonomous consumption or investment (other than that induced by interest rate changes) or a tax cut had on the economy, we would simply shift the IS curve in the same fashion. We also know that the effects of such actions on the equilibrium values of output and interest rate will depend on the slopes of the IS and LM schedules.

Global application 7.4

Ricardian equivalence revisited

Using the IS-LM model, an expansionary fiscal policy (an increase in government spending or a cut in taxes) shifts the IS curve to the right. This is shown in Figure 4 as a shift from IS_1 to IS_2, leading to an increase in income from Y_1 to Y_2. However, because income has risen, the demand for money will rise, pushing up interest rates which will crowd out investment. Depending on the degree of crowding out, the equilibrium level of output will fall to Y_3. Providing that crowding out is less than 100 per cent, it will be the case that an expansionary fiscal policy will increase equilibrium output in the economy.

In Chapter 4, it was noted that if consumers are forward-looking and rational in seeking to maximize their lifetime utility, then fiscal expansions will have no effect on the equilibrium level of income in the economy. This result is known as Ricardian equivalence. If the government ultimately balances its books, all deficits will need to be offset by equivalent surpluses in present value terms. Therefore, consumers would realize that the current fiscal expansion will be reversed in the future by an equal amount in present value terms.

Faced with higher taxes in the long run or lower services/income provided by the government, consumers will respond by increasing current levels of saving. The fiscal expansion will thus be offset immediately by a fall in autonomous consumption, such that $\Delta G = -\Delta a$. As a result, $\Delta G + \Delta a = 0$, so there will be no change in autonomous expenditures and no shift in the IS curve. Therefore, Ricardian equivalence suggests fiscal policy is immediately crowded out 100 per cent and the IS curve remains stationary.

Figure 4 A fiscal expansion in the IS-LM model

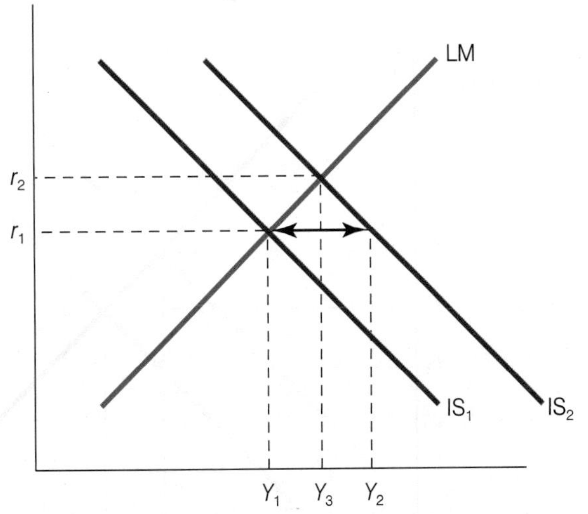

7

7.5.2 Monetary policy

Having completed a fairly exhaustive look at shifts in the IS curve, and relating them to fiscal policy, let us now turn our attention to the other side of the model. The LM curve will shift with changes in the money supply. Monetary policy refers to changes in either the quantity (the money stock) or the price (interest rate) of money. By controlling one of these, the government can hope to exert some control over the economy.

An expansionary monetary policy could consist of an increase in the money supply. We have seen that this would lead to a downward shift in the LM schedule. The effects on the economy are shown in Figure 7.32 and are traced out below.

1. An increase in the money supply $M_1 \rightarrow M_2$ leads to a downward shift in the LM schedule ($LM_1 \rightarrow LM_2$).
2. Interest rates fall from $r_1 \rightarrow r_2$ and the economy moves from point 1 to point 2.
3. At point 2, we are at a position to the left of the IS curve. Lower interest rates stimulate investment, as there is now excess demand in the goods market and output Y begins to rise.
4. As output rises, higher money demand puts upward pressure on the interest rate, so the interest rate begins to increase.
5. The new equilibrium at point 3 sees a lower interest rate, r_3, and higher income, Y_2.

7

Monetary expansion reduces the interest rate which in turn stimulates investment. For the policy to work in producing higher output, both these two processes must be working. The success of this policy will obviously depend on how changes in the money supply change the interest rate – and then on how investment responds to a change in the interest rate. Considering these two elements, we can see that the success of monetary policy is inherently linked to the slopes of the IS and LM curves.

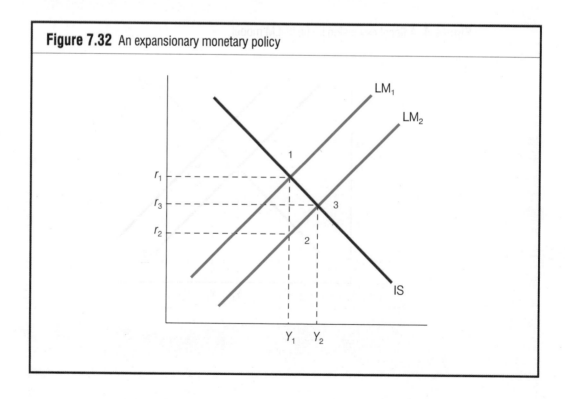

Figure 7.32 An expansionary monetary policy

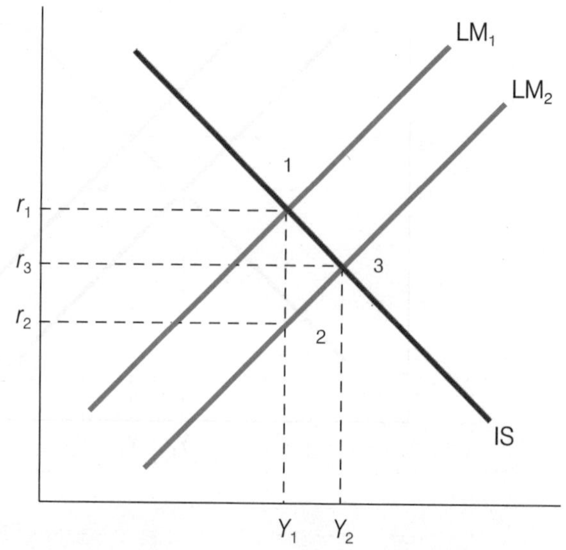

Effective monetary policy

There are two cases where monetary policy is extremely effective in raising the level of output.

When the demand for money is perfectly inelastic (${}^{r}\varepsilon_{M^d} = 0$) with respect to the interest rate, the LM curve will be vertical. Following an increase in the money supply, the economy will move from point 1 to point 2 in Figure 7.33 with a large increase in output.

An explanation as to why monetary policy is highly effective in this case is as follows. An increase in the money supply would lead to a position of excess supply in the money market. For equilibrium to be restored, money demand must increase. The conventional way to do this is to reduce the interest rate – this encourages households to substitute out of bonds and into cash. It also stimulates investment, which raises income and leads to an increase in money demand for transaction purposes. When the demand for money is interest inelastic, a large fall in the interest rate will not produce any substitution effect. Therefore, the only way to eliminate excess supply is through the output increase. Output must increase by a more substantial amount because the fall in interest rate is ineffective in raising money demand.

The second case is where investment is perfectly interest elastic (${}^{r}\varepsilon_{I} = \infty$), which describes the situation where the IS curve is horizontal (Figure 7.34). A small reduction in interest rates is all that is required to generate a very large increase in investment and therefore output.

7

Ineffective monetary policy

The cases where monetary policy fails to increase output are the opposite of those stated above.

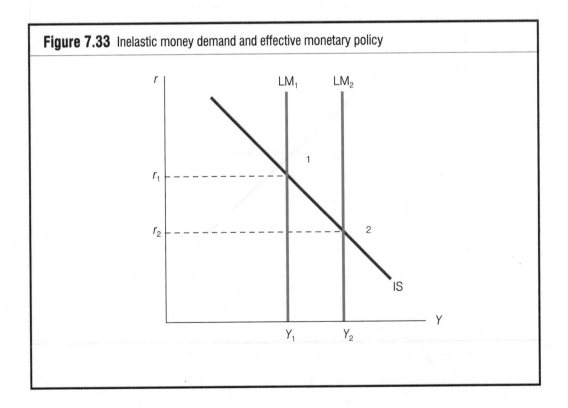

Figure 7.33 Inelastic money demand and effective monetary policy

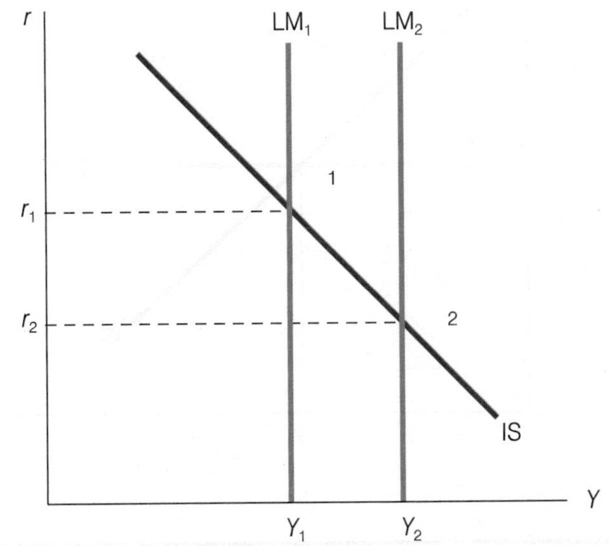

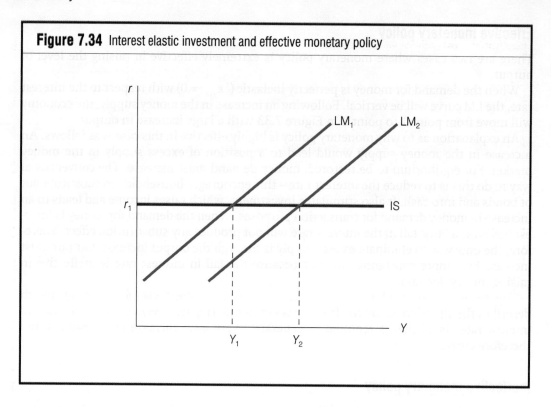

Figure 7.34 Interest elastic investment and effective monetary policy

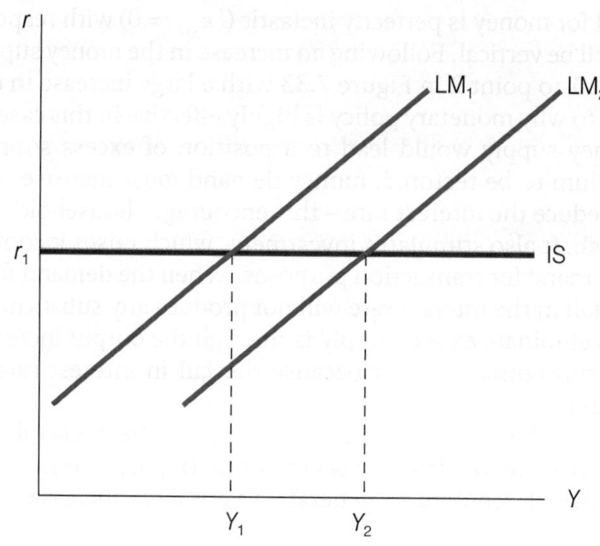

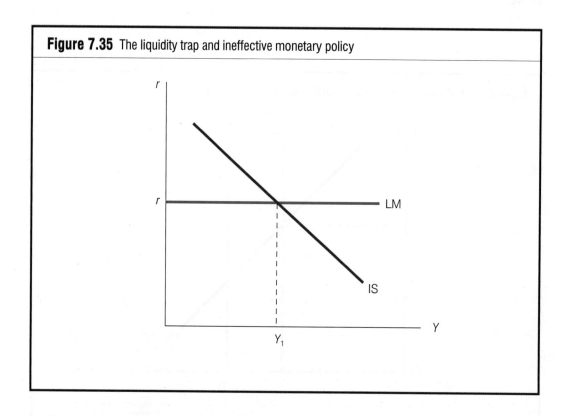

Figure 7.35 The liquidity trap and ineffective monetary policy

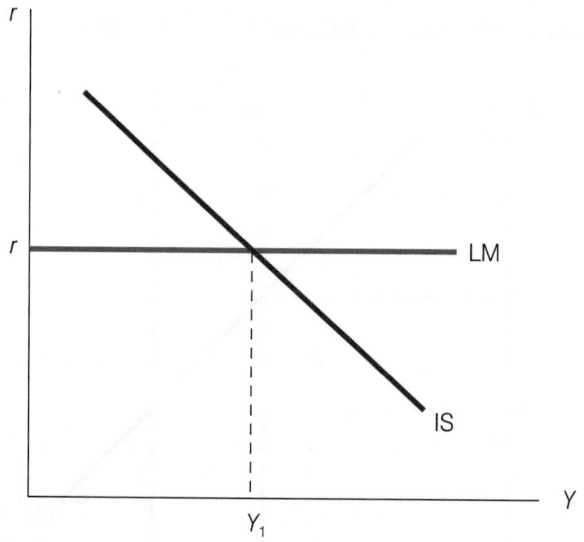

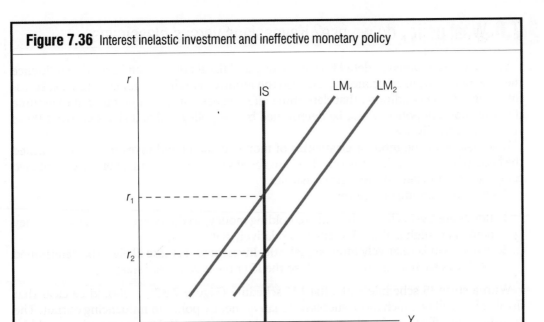

Figure 7.36 Interest inelastic investment and ineffective monetary policy

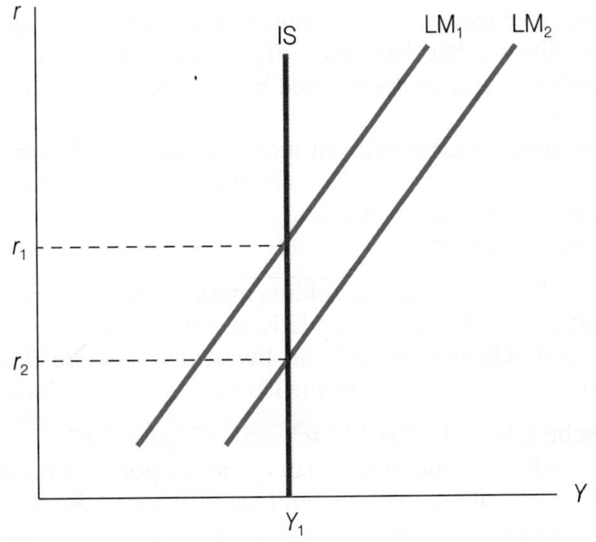

First, when the LM curve is horizontal, we know that this refers to the situation of a liquidity trap. The demand for money is perfectly interest elastic (${}^{r}\varepsilon_{M^d} = \infty$), so any increase in the money supply would fail to put downward pressure on the interest rate. Households will simply just hold the extra money balances in cash, probably because interest rates are sufficiently low to make investing in bonds unattractive. If no reduction in interest rate is achieved, then there is nothing on which investment can bite and the level of output will remain unchanged (Figure 7.35).

Second, even if an increase in the money supply is successful in reducing the interest rate, it will only lead to an increase in output if extra investment is then forthcoming. When investment is interest inelastic (${}^{r}\varepsilon_{I} = 0$), the IS curve will be vertical. An increase in the money supply may be successful in reducing the interest rate ($r_1 \rightarrow r_2$), but because investment is completely unresponsive to this, output will again remain unchanged (Figure 7.36).

Overview

From what we have just investigated, we can conclude that monetary policy is more successful when:

- Investment is interest elastic: the IS curve is flatter because any change in interest rates generates a proportionally greater change in investment.
- The demand for money is interest inelastic. This means that the LM curve is steeper. Here, any change in the money supply has greater effects on the equilibrium interest rates, i.e., a change in the money supply generates a larger vertical shift in the LM schedule.
- The higher the multiplier, the flatter the IS curve. This implies that the response of output to any change in investment induced by a change in interest rates will be greater.

7.6 What policy do we use? Keynesians versus classicists

We have now studied in detail how monetary and fiscal policies can be used to influence the level of output in an economy, and also the required conditions for each to be successful. As it is these conditions that determine effectiveness, it would be rational to assume that the choice of policy would be determined by the policy maker's views on what these conditions actually are.

Discussions of the interest elasticities of money demand and investment have formed the basis of a long-standing historical debate about which policy is most effective. The two camps are the Keynesians and the classicists.

Keynesian economists believe:

1. Bonds are a very close substitute to holding money, so the interest elasticity of money demand is high and the LM curve is relatively flat.
2. Investment is relatively interest inelastic. Investment is more likely to be determined by things such as 'animal spirits', so the IS curve is relatively steep.

With a steep IS schedule and a flat LM schedule (Figure 7.37), it should be clear that fiscal policy will be much more successful than monetary policy in influencing output. The crowding out effect of a fiscal expansion would be fairly small. Monetary policy would be relatively ineffective as an increase in the money supply would only exert a small amount of downward pressure on interest rates, and investment is insensitive to interest rate changes.

Classical economists believe:

1. Money demand is interest inelastic, as the main reason for holding money is for transactions purposes, so the LM curve is fairly steep.
2. Investment is interest sensitive, hence the IS curve is relatively flat.

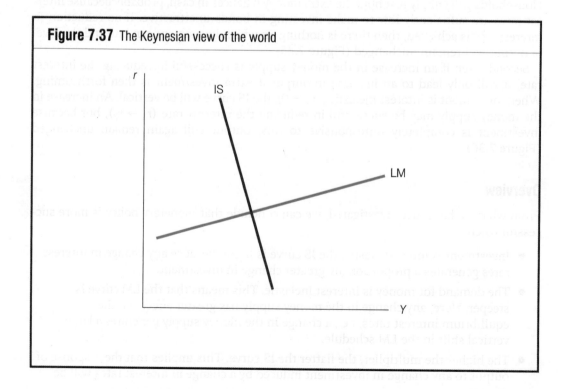

Figure 7.37 The Keynesian view of the world

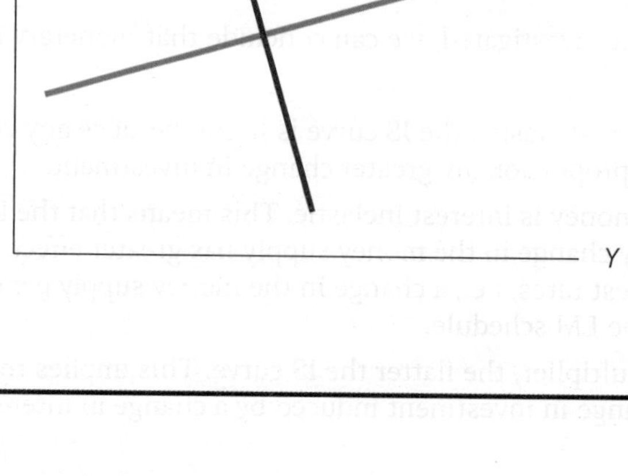

Global application 7.5

The monetary and fiscal policy mix

The IS-LM model is a useful framework for analysing the effects of monetary and fiscal policy on the economy. In Figure 5, it is clear that a target level of income $\tilde{Y}$ can be achieved by a number of policy mixes. Figure 5 shows two.

The first is given by tight fiscal policy (G_1) but loose monetary policy (M_1). In this case, the composition of output consists of a low level of government spending, but because the equilibrium interest rate (r_1) is low, the investment composition is relatively high.

When fiscal policy is loose (G_2), government spending represents a higher proportion of output. However, tighter monetary policy (M_2) implies a higher equilibrium level of interest rate (r_2) and a lower proportion of investment in output.

Therefore, changing the mix of monetary and fiscal policies is likely to have an impact on the composition of output via the equilibrium level of interest rates. If $\tilde{Y}$ is deemed to be a sustainable level of output, then the policy mix has an important bearing on the composition of this output. The actual policy mix then reflects the relative importance that policy makers attach to each component of total output. For example:

1. Personal consumption: the government may wish to increase the share of consumption because this directly enhances the current welfare of households. This can be achieved by cutting taxes, but also by reducing the share of investment through tightening monetary policy.
2. Government expenditure: increasing the composition of this might reflect the desire to improve public services through spending on infrastructure, education and health, or also through income redistribution in funding welfare payments. Again, increasing the composition of government spending would involve tighter monetary policy and reducing the share of private investment.
3. Investment: this is considered to be an important driver of long-run economic growth and job creation. Promoting investment would require loosening monetary policy to lower the equilibrium interest rate. This would then require tighter fiscal policy through lower government spending or higher personal taxes.

Figure 5 Achieving a target level of output

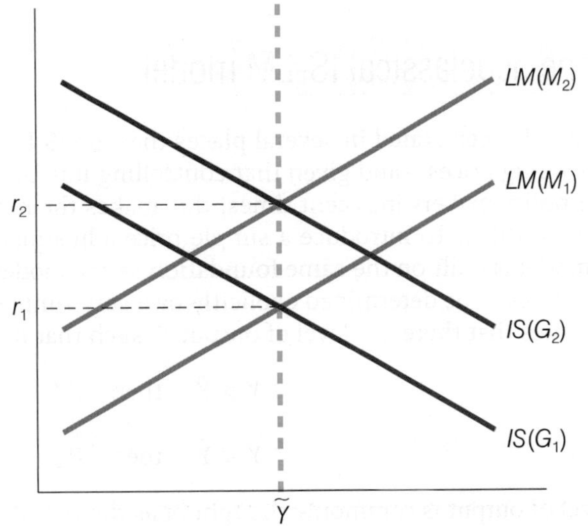

7

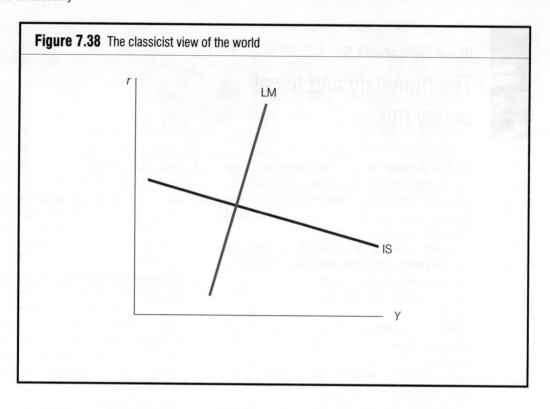

Figure 7.38 The classicist view of the world

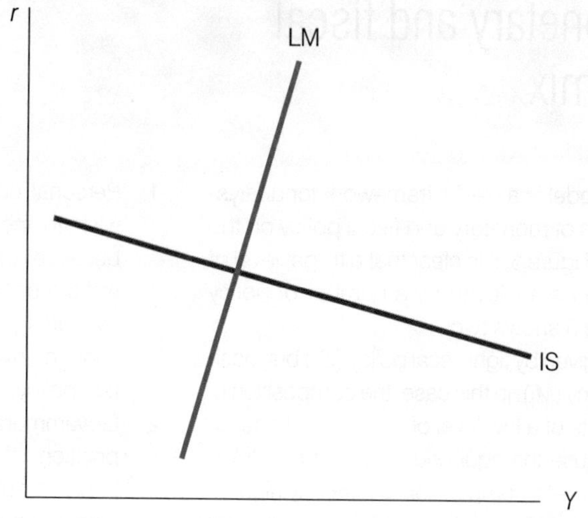

Given this view of the world (Figure 7.38), it is now the case that monetary policy is preferable. A monetary expansion would exert strong downward pressure on interest rates and this will be successful in stimulating extra investment, which is highly sensitive to interest rates. Fiscal policy, on the other hand, would be very limited due to significant crowding out effects.

When using the IS-LM model, it is always a good rule to think about how the slopes of the curves might be important. The outcome of a policy change, or a shock that leads to a shift in either of the IS and LM curves, will depend on the relative slopes of each. We have seen here that this may have an important bearing on what type of policy it is best to use.

7.7 The neoclassical IS-LM model

It has already been stated in several places that the IS-LM model suffers from the flaw of not explaining prices – and given that controlling inflation has been one of the main concerns of policy makers in recent times, this makes the model less applicable. One simple way around this is to introduce a simple price adjustment mechanism. The neoclassical IS-LM model is built on the same foundation as the model we have outlined so far. It just enables prices to be determined explicitly by a very simple rule.

It assumes that there is a level of output $\hat{Y}$, such that if:

$$Y > \hat{Y} \quad \text{then} \quad P\uparrow$$

$$Y < \hat{Y} \quad \text{then} \quad P\downarrow$$

This level of output is commonly thought of as the **full employment level of output**. Prices will rise if output exceeds this level. In this situation, workers will find themselves

Figure 7.39 The neoclassical IS-LM model

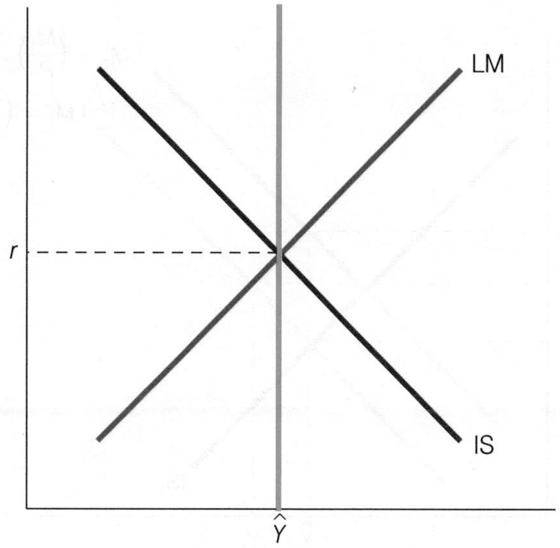

7

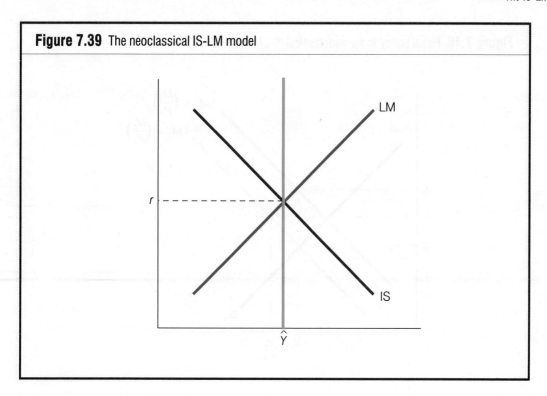

in a very strong position; there is a glut of vacancies so wages are bid upwards. This pushes up costs and therefore prices.

By turning the story around, we can explain why prices might fall when output falls below its full employment level. As unemployed workers may be prepared to accept lower wages in order to price themselves into jobs, wages might be expected to fall. This then lowers the costs of production and prices fall. The full employment level of output is historically important. Governments are aware that unemployment has significant social and economic costs, so minimizing unemployment minimizes the burden of these costs. Full employment has therefore always been a major goal of policy making.

As prices will change depending on whether or not output is above or below its full employment level, equilibrium now requires three conditions. We need the goods market to be in equilibrium, which is the IS curve; the money market will be in equilibrium in any position on the LM curve; and finally, prices will be stable when output is at the full employment level, $Y = \hat{Y}$. Putting these three relationships together in Figure 7.39 gives us the neoclassical IS-LM model.

We can now turn to a discussion of the effects of monetary and fiscal policies in this version of the model.

Fiscal policy

The economy starts off in a position where the IS and LM schedules intersect at the full employment level of output. An expansionary fiscal policy then takes place in the form of an increase in government spending. The path the economy takes is shown in Figure 7.40.

1. Starting from a position of equilibrium $Y = \hat{Y}$, an expansionary fiscal policy $IS_1 \rightarrow IS_2$ raises output to $Y_1 > \hat{Y}$. The economy has moved from point 1 to point 2.

Figure 7.40 Fiscal policy in the neoclassical IS-LM model

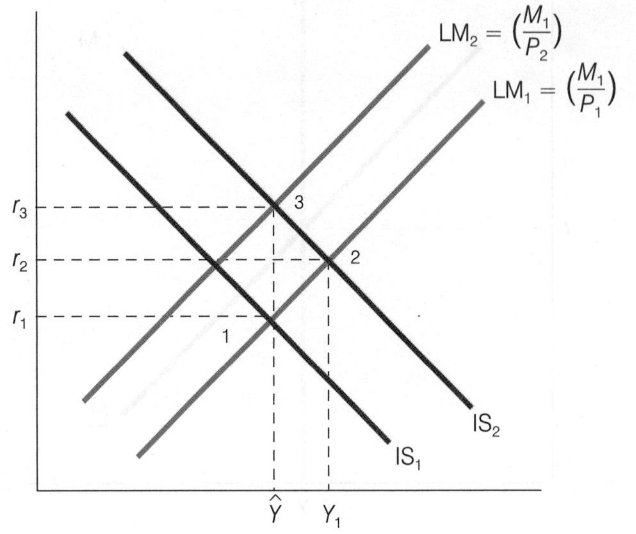

2. As output has moved above its full employment value, prices will begin to rise. This acts to reduce the real value of the money stock, so it has the same consequences as a fall in the money supply. The LM schedule will begin to shift upwards.
3. As the interest rate rises, there is crowding out of investment and a movement along the IS curve.
4. The economy eventually returns to $Y = \hat{Y}$ with higher equilibrium interest rates and higher prices, $P_1 \rightarrow P_2$. The economy is now at point 3.

There are two things to note here. First, expansionary fiscal policy only manages to raise output successfully in the short run. In the long run, once prices adjust, output will return to its full employment value. The second point to note here is that fiscal policy cannot ultimately change the level of output, but it will change the composition. The increase in government spending via a rise in prices, a contraction in the real money stock and a rise in interest rates will crowd out investment. The outcome is that the economy stays at its full employment level, but now has more expenditure from the public sector and less from private investment.

Monetary policy

The effects of an increase in the money supply in the neoclassical IS-LM model are shown in Figure 7.41.

1. An expansion in the money supply $M_1 \rightarrow M_2$ leads to a downward shift in the LM curve.
2. As the interest rate has fallen, extra investment is induced and the economy moves along the IS curve from point 1 to point 2.
3. Output rises to $Y_1 > \hat{Y}$. However, as this is above the full employment level, there is upward pressure on prices.

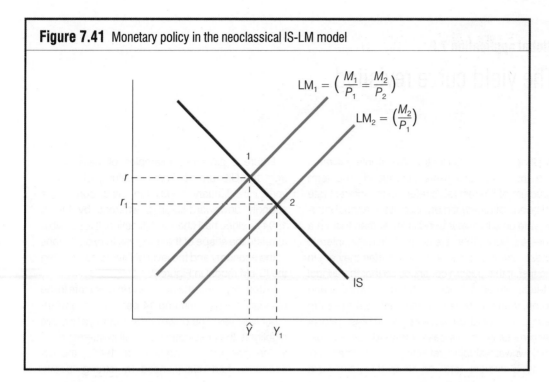

Figure 7.41 Monetary policy in the neoclassical IS-LM model

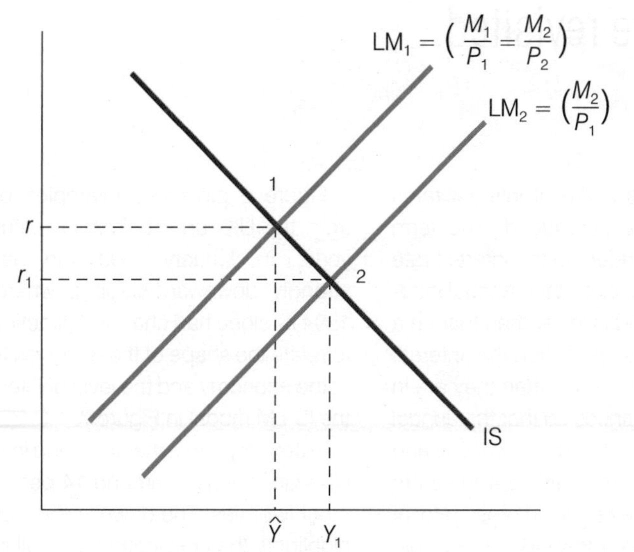

4. As prices increase $P_1 \rightarrow P_2$, the real money stock falls. This places upward pressure on the interest rate and the LM curve moves back towards its initial position.
5. The economy again returns to the full employment level of output. Although the money stock is higher, the price level has risen in the same proportion leaving the real money stock unaltered.

Again there are two things to note from this example. The first is a repetition – that the monetary expansion only appears to have a transitory effect on the level of output in the economy. In the long run, there is no escaping the full employment level as this is the only position where prices are stable. The second is that the only effect of an increase in the money stock is an increase in prices, which leaves the real money stock unchanged.

These two features are regarded as the **neutrality of money**. This states that money is incapable of altering the real parts of the economy; its only impact will be on the nominal factors, such as prices. The neutrality of money has powerful influence in policy circles. The monetarist doctrine, espoused by economists such as Milton Friedman, has argued that tight control must be exercised over the use of monetary policy since it has no long-run effects on output in order to maintain price stability.

Keynes vs the classicists once again

We have already delved into one debate between these two branches of economic ideology. This has to do with the question: What policy would be more effective for controlling the level of output in the economy? By introducing price adjustment, the neoclassical IS-LM model asks a much more profound question: Can the government control the level of output? The two views on this question are as follows.

Classicists We have seen in the neoclassical IS-LM model that attempting to use monetary or fiscal policies to control the economy is futile. The classical economists believe that

Global application 7.6

The yield curve revisited

In Chapter 5, the term structure of interest rates and the yield curve were introduced. The term structure of interest rates refers to the interest rate on bonds of different maturities. If the annual interest rate on a two-year bond is lower than that on a one-year bond, then it is an indication that interest rates in the second year are lower than they are in the first. If this pattern continues so that the annual interest rate on a three-year bond is lower still and so on, then it implies that future interest rates are falling. The yield curve plots the interest rate at each maturity. In this case, the yield curve would be downward-sloping, reflecting the anticipation of a falling interest rate. An upward-sloping yield curve would reflect the opposite situation in the term structure of interest rates.

As the shape of yield curves is an indicator of the future path of interest rates, which are themselves determined by the equilibrium of the economy, the shape of the yield curve may contain valuable information about the expected movements in the economy.

Figure 6 plots two examples of yield curves from the UK ranging from a maturity of 1 to 21 years. In January 1990, the yield curve was strongly downward-sloping, whereas by March 1994 its slope had changed direction. It is possible to relate the shape of these curves to expectations of the economy and the level of interest rates using the IS-LM model in Figure 7.

In January 1990, the prevailing interest rate in the UK was very high, around 14 per cent on government liabilities. The downward-sloping yield curve highlights the anticipation of a fall in interest rates in the long run. During the late 1980s, the UK economy had experienced a strong boom, induced by a strong housing market, financial deregulation and credit expansion, falling unemployment, and reductions in income taxes.

If the economy starts off at point *a* in Figure 7, the increase in aggregate demand produces a shift in the IS curve, $IS_1 \rightarrow IS_2$. The economy then moves to point *b* and income increases, $\hat{Y} \rightarrow Y_1$. Output has now risen above the full employment level, leading

Figure 6 UK government liability yield curve (nominal rates)

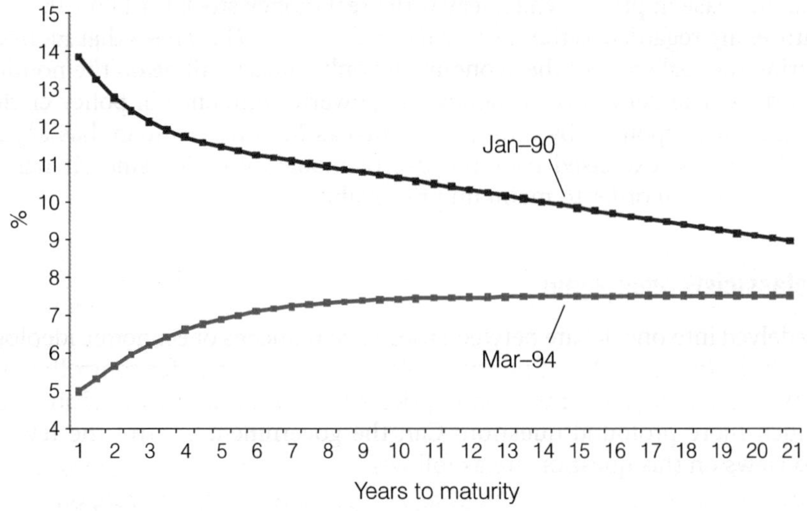

Global application 7.6 (continued)

Figure 7 The IS-LM model movements in long-run interest rates

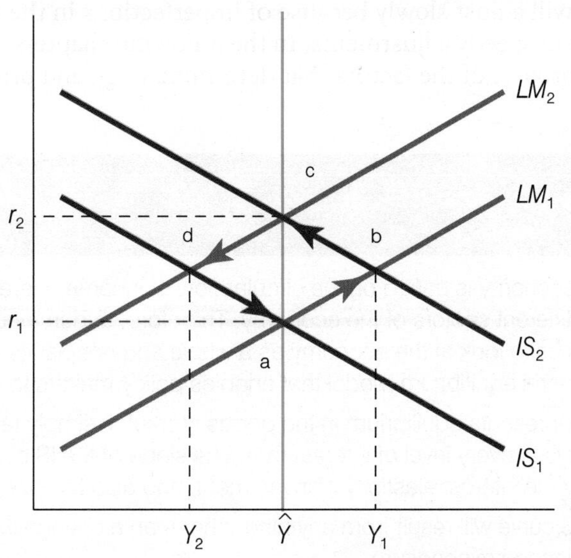

to an increase in inflation and a rise in interest rates, moving the economy to point *c*, generating high equilibrium interest rates of r_2. This represents the position of the economy around January 1990.

The anticipation of a reversal in aggregate demand would see the IS curve shift backwards, pushing the level of output below its full employment level to *d*. As the economy enters recession with falling prices, the long-run expectation is for interest rates to fall back towards r_1. Therefore, the downward-sloping yield curve is an indication of the expected slowdown in growth and inflation leading to lower long-run equilibrium interest rates.

In a similar vein, the upward-sloping yield curve in March 1994 reflects the anticipation of stronger growth and higher equilibrium interest rates in the long run. Following the recession in the early 1990s, the UK economy may have found itself back to point *a* in Figure 7. Growing aggregate demand would then see the IS curve shift rightwards, leading to the anticipation of higher equilibrium income and interest rates, justifying the upward-sloping yield curve.

markets clear quickly; therefore, if there is any position of excess demand or supply, it will be the case that wages and prices adjust quickly. The use of these policies will only be effective in the very short run. The only long-run consequence of the policy will be to increase the price level. The government's best course of action is not to interfere in the economy, as it will only have very limited effects on output and will just be inflationary.

Keynesians The Keynesian viewpoint is the opposite of this. The reason comes down to the question how long is the long run. Keynesians accept that in the long run, output will return to its full employment level. But, if this adjustment is slow, then the short run may be a significant period of time. The government will then look at active monetary and fiscal policy as being useful. The famous quote which sums up the position well is: 'in the long run we are all dead' – emphasizing the importance of the short run.

For the short run effectively to be a considerable amount of time, it must be the case that wages and prices adjust very slowly. As it is adjustments in these variables that move us back to the full employment level of output, it is conceivable that if they work very slowly we can be away from the full employment level of output for some time. Keynes believed that prices will adjust slowly because of imperfections in the labour and product markets, which prevent speedy adjustments. In the following chapters we will focus in greater detail on the importance of the factors that determine wage and price flexibility.

Summary

- As the macroeconomy is based on the circular flow of income, there will be interactions between the different sectors of the economy. Therefore, understanding the path an economy takes requires us to look at the economy as a whole and not just its individual parts. The IS-LM model is a general equilibrium model that enables policy makers to do just this.
- The IS curve represents equilibrium in the goods market. It simply tells us what the equilibrium level of output is at every level of interest rate. The slope of the IS curve is important – and is determined by the interest elasticity of investment, and also the size of the multiplier.
- A shift in the IS curve will result from anything other than a change in interest rates that leads to a change in planned expenditure.
- The LM curve represents equilibrium in the money market and plots the equilibrium rate of interest against different output levels. The slope of the LM curve is determined by the income and interest elasticities of money demand.
- Anything that leads to a change in the real money stock will result in a shift in the LM curve.
- Where the IS and LM curves intersect represents the general equilibrium in the economy, i.e., where both the goods and money markets are in equilibrium at the same time. The IS-LM model therefore determines the equilibrium rate of interest and level of output. The IS-LM model is self-equilibrating because any position away from equilibrium will imply a disequilibrium in either the goods or money market. As a result, output and interest rates will adjust to move the economy back to its equilibrium position.
- A comparative static exercise involves the comparison of the economy's equilibrium before and after a shock or a policy change. The IS-LM model enables us to analyse what impact shocks or policies may have on the equilibrium rate of interest and level of output.
- Fiscal policy changes result in shifts in the IS curve. The effectiveness of fiscal policy in influencing output will depend upon the subsequent level of crowding out. Fiscal policy will be more successful when investment is interest inelastic (so the IS curve is steep) or when the demand for money is interest elastic (so the LM curve is flat).
- Shifts in the LM curve are the outcome of monetary policy changes. Monetary policy will be more effective in influencing output when the LM curve is steep (implying a low interest elasticity of money demand) or when the IS curve is horizontal (implying that investment is interest elastic).
- A policy maker's decision as to whether to use monetary or fiscal policy is likely to be determined by the view of the world they take, which is summed up in the relative slopes of the IS and LM curves. The classicist view favours the use of monetary policy, whereas the Keynesians believe fiscal policy to be more effective.

- The neoclassical IS-LM model is an extension of the basic model that incorporates a very simple price adjustment mechanism. In this model, prices will always adjust to restore full employment in the long run, so monetary and fiscal policies can only affect output in the short run. This raises another issue between classical and Keynesian economists regarding the duration of the short run and hence the effectiveness of active government policy – monetary or fiscal. The classical belief is that prices adjust quickly so the economy always moves towards its full employment level. Keynesians, though, argue that wage and price flexibility is low, giving room for active policy to exert an important role in the economy.

Key terms

Crowding out
Full employment level of output
Investment demand schedule
IS-LM model
Liquidity trap
Neutrality of money

Review questions

1. How is the IS curve derived and what factors determine its slope? What happens to the slope of the IS curve if consumption is interest elastic?
2. How is the LM curve derived and what factors determine its slope? What happens to the LM curve if there is an increase in the cost of liquidating financial assets?
3. Using the IS-LM model, explain how the equilibrium rate of interest and level of output will respond to the following:
   a. expectations of a future increase in unemployment
   b. financial deregulation leading to the abolition of reserve-asset ratios
   c. a fall in corporate profits
   d. a house price boom
   e. a programme of investment in new ATMs
4. How is the effectiveness of monetary and fiscal policy affected by:
   a. the slopes of the IS and LM curves
   b. a positive relationship between prices and the deviation of output from its full employment level?

More advanced problems

5. Consider the following:

$C = 400 + 0.4Y_d$

$Y_d = Y - T$

$T = 100$

$I = 400 - 1000r$

$G = 100$

$(M/P)_d = 3Y - 10000r$

$M = 1000$

$P = 1$

where C is consumption, Y_d is disposable income, Y is income, T is the level of lump sum taxes, I is investment, r is the interest rate, G is government spending, $(M/P)_d$ is real money demand, M is the money supply and P is the price level.

a. Calculate the IS and LM curves and find the equilibrium level of interest rates and income. What is the level of investment in equilibrium?

b. Concerned that the current level of income is too low, the government announces an expansionary fiscal policy and increases government spending by 200. Find the new equilibrium values of output and interest rates. By how much has investment been crowded out?

c. The level of income calculated in (b) is the full employment level. What might be expected to happen if the government does not increase spending by 200 as in (b)?

6. Suppose the government changes the tax system from lump sum taxes to a proportional income tax. Tax revenue is now equal to *tY,* where *t* is the marginal tax rate.

a. Write down the new consumption function and derive the IS curve.

b. Use the IS-LM diagram to show how changes in the marginal tax rate will affect the equilibrium level of output.

7. The economy is characterized by the following set of relations:

$C = 100 + 0.8Y_d$

$Y_d = Y - tY$

$t = 1/6$

$I = 100 - 1000r$

$G = 100$

$M_d = 2Y - 9000r$

$M = 300$

where C is consumption, Y_d is disposable income, Y is income, t is the tax rate, I is investment, r is the interest rate, G is government spending, M_d is money demand and M is money supply.

a. Derive the IS and LM schedules.

b. Calculate the equilibrium level of income (Y) and interest rate (r) in the economy.

c. At the equilibrium in (a), the economy is below its full employment level of output, $Y^* = 750$. By how much does the government have to increase its expenditure in order to reach this level of income? What is the budget deficit/surplus at this point? What is the new equilibrium rate of interest and how much is investment crowded out?

More advanced problems (continued)

d. Suppose the government decides against a fiscal expansion and decides to implement a monetary expansion. What increase in the money supply would be required to reach the target, $Y^* = 750$. What is the government deficit/surplus at that point?

e. The government's fiscal rules imply that it must run a balanced budget. What combination of fiscal policy (increasing G) and monetary policy (increasing M) would enable it to reach the full employment level of output while maintaining the balanced budget?

8. What policies could the government use to keep income at its previous level following:
   a. an increase in reported credit card fraud
   b. a rise in the marginal propensity to save?
9. Using the IS-LM model, suggest a suitable policy mix to achieve the following:
   a. an increase in income while keeping r constant
   b. a decrease in the fiscal deficit while keeping Y constant
   c. an increase in the share of investment in GDP.
10. It is argued that the following equation is an accurate description of investment behaviour.

$$I = \bar{I} + \beta Y$$

Investment is equal to a fixed quantity $\bar{I}$ and positively related to income, Y.

a. What factors might justify this form of investment function?
b. Using this new investment equation, construct an IS curve. What happens to the size of the multiplier?
c. Using the new IS curve, examine the effects of fiscal policy on equilibrium output.

For further resources, visit
http://www.thomsonlearning.co.uk/chamberlin_yueh

8 The AD-AS model

Learning objectives

- Understand the relationship between prices and aggregate demand
- Determine the non-accelerating inflation rate of unemployment (NAIRU) and the long-run aggregate supply for an economy
- Identify the factors that lead to shifts in the long-run aggregate supply curve
- Acknowledge that, in the short run, output can deviate from its long-run equilibrium level by moving along a short-run aggregate supply curve
- Understand the difference between adaptive and rational expectations formation
- Construct the AD-AS model and use it in comparative statics exercises

8.1 Introduction

In the previous chapter, we outlined the IS-LM model which, over the years, has proved to be an important model in economic analysis. However, we also made note of the model's shortcomings. The failure to give a convincing account as to how prices are determined is a significant weakness. Given that much of economic policy making over the last three decades has been directed at maintaining price stability, the usefulness of the IS-LM model is therefore compromised.

The **aggregate demand** and **aggregate supply (AD-AS) model** answers this problem by simultaneously determining output and prices. Its foundation and workings are very similar to the conventional demand and supply theory that determines quantities and prices for individual goods and services. This model simply aggregates across all goods and services; in which case, we are determining the average price level and the total level of output in the economy.

The model is useful to policy makers who, in recent decades, have become increasingly concerned with how prices are determined, as well as with output. In this chapter, we will outline how the model is constructed, and then show how it can be used to analyse the effects of certain shocks, policy or otherwise, on output and prices. The AD-AS model shares many common features with the IS-LM model, particularly the neoclassical version, and to some extent the two can be used interchangeably. However, it is fair to say that in the AD-AS model, the supply side and price determination are both treated much more rigorously.

8.2 The aggregate demand schedule

The AD schedule plots the relationship between the price level and aggregate demand. Its construction comes directly from the IS-LM model – all we have to do is think about what happens to planned expenditures when prices fall. When the IS-LM model is in equilibrium, planned expenditures are equal to actual output, so all we need to do is identify the effect of falling prices on the equilibrium level of output.

Changes in the price level have repercussions for the level of the real money stock. A fall in the price level would increase the real value of the outstanding money stock; hence, the LM curve would be expected to shift downwards. Providing the liquidity trap is not relevant and that investment is sufficiently interest sensitive, this will produce a fall in the interest rate, stimulate investment and result in an increase in output. This is pictured in Figure 8.1. As the average price level falls from P_1 to P_3, output expands from Y_1 to Y_3. It is clear that there is an inverse relationship between prices and output. The combinations of prices and output can be plotted to form the downward sloping aggregate demand (AD) schedule.

An increase in the price level would, of course, have the opposite effect. The real money stock would decline, the LM curve would shift upwards and aggregate demand would fall. Looking at Figure 8.1, this would be shown by a movement in prices from P_3 to P_1 and a corresponding fall in output from Y_3 to Y_1.

The AD curve just tells us what the level of aggregate demand, or planned expenditure, is at each price level. Changes in the price level will relate to movements along the curve. However, if aggregate demand were to change due to a factor other than prices, the AD curve would shift.

Shifts in the AD curve (see Figure 8.2) result from anything that shifts the IS or LM curve, other than a change in the price level. In the previous chapter, these were discussed in some detail and include all the elements of planned expenditure (government spending, taxes, consumption and investment) and also the money supply. An outward shift in the IS or the LM curve will lead to an outward shift in the AD schedule ($AD_2 \rightarrow AD_3$), as at every price level, output is higher. Likewise, an inward shift in the IS or LM curve will lead to an inward shift in the AD schedule $AD_2 \rightarrow AD_1$, as at every price level output will be lower.

Figure 8.1 Deriving the aggregate demand curve

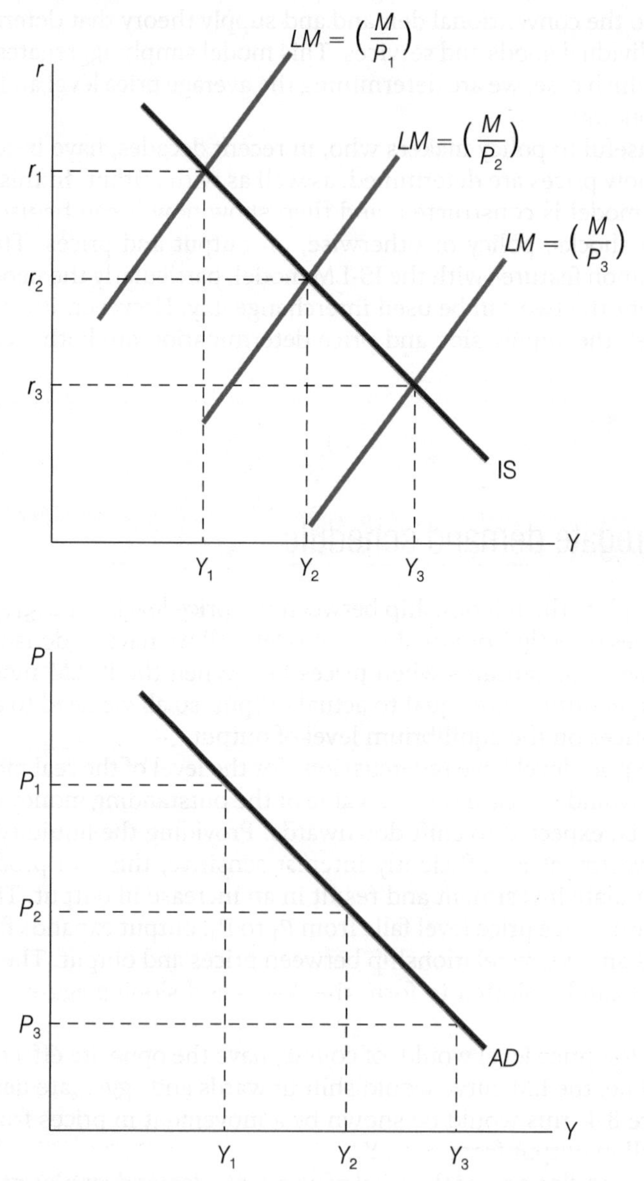

Figure 8.2 Shifts in the AD curve

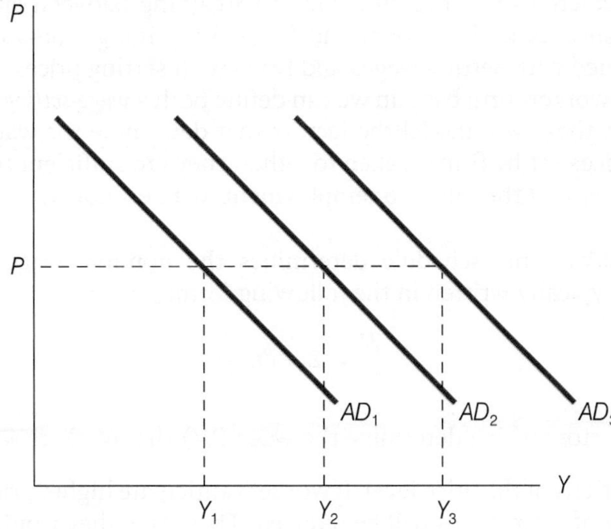

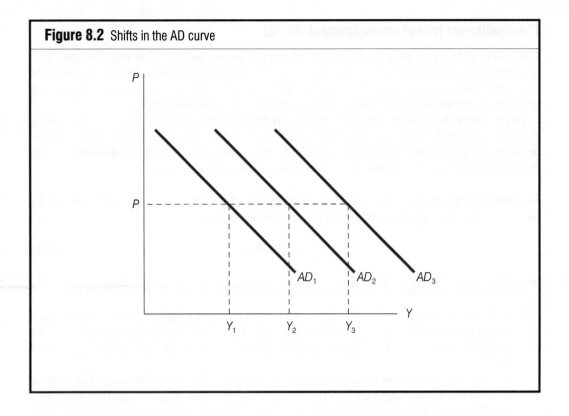

8.3 The aggregate supply schedule

The **aggregate supply (AS) schedule** plots the relationship between the output of an economy and the price level. In essence, it sums all the output decisions by productive agents in the domestic economy. An important distinction, though, exists between aggregate supply in the short and the long run. We will see that output in the short run can deviate from its long-run level if markets are in disequilibrium for a period of time because wages and prices adjust slowly towards equilibrium values.

8.3.1 Long-run aggregate supply

In the long run, the supply decisions of firms are independent of prices. Prices are considered to be a *nominal* factor, whereas production decisions will be based on *real* concerns. In the proceeding paragraphs, we will see that these might include productivity, labour force participation, product market conditions, or factors determining the bargaining power of labour. **Long-run aggregate supply** is fixed at the long-run equilibrium level of output, which in turn corresponds to the level of output consistent with equilibrium in the labour market. This level of output is often referred to as the *natural level of output*.

Establishing the equilibrium level of output therefore requires us to investigate the equilibrium in the labour market. More specifically, we will be concerned with the equilibrium rate of unemployment, which is often referred to as the **non-accelerating inflation rate of unemployment** or the **NAIRU**. At this rate, there is no pressure on wages to change. And, as prices are simply a mark-up on wage costs, it must also be the case that there is no pressure on prices to change either.

The equilibrium rate of unemployment/NAIRU

This refers to the rate of unemployment where the labour market is in equilibrium. This equilibrium is considered to be the outcome of bargaining between labour (sometimes organized bodies, such as trade unions) and firms. Bargaining works by assuming that workers are concerned with setting wages and firms with setting prices.

To represent the worker–firm bargain we can define both a *wage-setting* and a *price-setting* curve. Respectively, these will model the factors that determine the wages demanded by workers and the prices set by firms. Taken together, they are sufficient to determine both the level of real wages and the rate of unemployment in an economy.

The wage-setting curve This schedule determines the nominal wage (W) desired by labour, and can be typically written in the following form:

$$\frac{W}{P^e} = Z - \beta u \qquad (8.1)$$

There are three factors which determine the wage (W) that workers will push for.

1. P^e are expectations of the price level. If workers anticipate higher prices, then the purchasing power of their wages will be reduced. Therefore, they would push for higher nominal wages so as to maintain the value of their real wages (purchasing power of wages).
2. u is the unemployment rate and exerts a negative force on wage demands. The reserve army of the unemployed are taken to be the surplus labour that is available to employers. The larger this pool becomes, the more moderate wage demands will be. Workers know that if they push for wages that are too much higher they may be substituted for cheaper unemployed labour. Also, when unemployment is high, workers anticipate that finding new employment when unemployed will be much trickier. This forms a powerful incentive to avoid becoming unemployed in the first place by moderating wage demands. The converse is also true. At low levels of unemployment, workers would be more confident in pushing for higher wages.
3. Z is really a catch-all variable which consists of a number of items that may influence wage demands. These fall into two camps.
   - The first are those factors which influence the bargaining power of workers. Trade unions bargaining collectively or employment laws giving rights to workers would be examples. These would be expected to increase workers' ability to push for higher wages if their demands were backed by industrial action or legislation.
   - The second consists of items which raise the *opportunity cost* of working. For example, if unemployment benefits were relatively generous, then the costs of unemployment would be correspondingly lower which would lead to more ambitious wage demands.

For simplicity, it is assumed that workers form correct expectations concerning the price level, then $P^e = P$. In this case, the wage-setting relationship can be expressed in terms of the real wage (ω), which is plotted in Figure 8.3.

$$w = \frac{W}{P} = Z - \beta u \qquad (8.2)$$

The wage-setting relationship implies that the bargained real wage falls as unemployment rises. Changes in Z (the set of catch-all variables) would lead to shifts in the entire function, meaning that at each level of unemployment workers would target a different real wage.

8

Figure 8.3 The wage-setting schedule

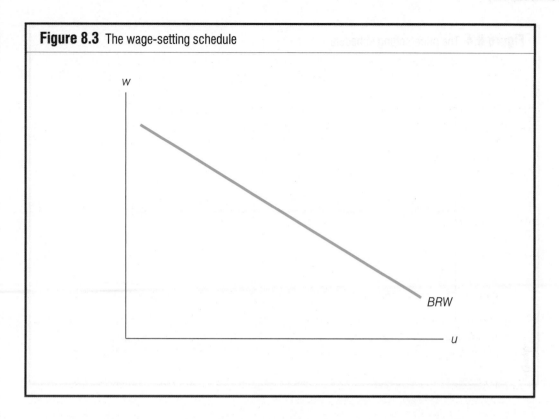

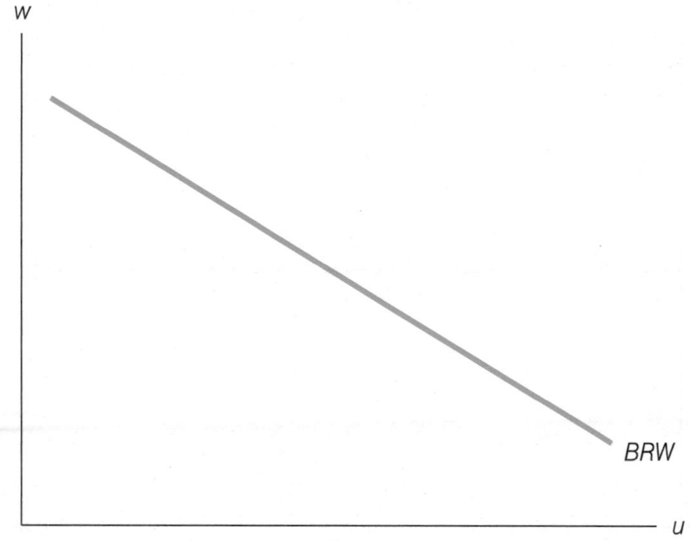

8

The wage-setting relationship is also known as the bargained real wage (BRW), as it is the real wage that unions demand in their bargaining with employers (firms).

Price-setting relationship Firms are simply assumed to set prices as a mark-up on wage costs. Although in the real world, firms will face other costs such as rents and interest payments on capital, these can be ignored in this simple model.

$$P = (1 + \mu)\frac{W}{LP} \tag{8.3}$$

where μ is the mark-up and LP is labour productivity.

Costs are given by the ratio of wages (W) to labour productivity (LP). Firm costs will rise if either wages rise, or labour productivity falls. If both move in the same proportion, then costs will remain unchanged.

For example, if wages and labour productivity both increase by 10 per cent, then wage costs will remain unchanged. Although labour is now 10 per cent more expensive, we can produce the same output with 10 per cent less of it due to the increase in productivity. Therefore, as the two effects are completely offsetting, it is the case that total cost remains unchanged.

The mark-up μ is largely determined by product market conditions, which primarily refer to the degree of competition in the market. Where markets are relatively competitive, the mark-up would be expected to be low, and under perfectly competitive conditions it would be expected to be zero (which means that firms set prices equal to marginal costs and only make normal profits). When firms can exert significant market power, the mark-up would rise, of course, and firms would take more of a profit margin on their sales. One factor which might be crucial in determining the size of the mark-up could be the level of competition policy in existence and how strongly it is enforced. When markets are

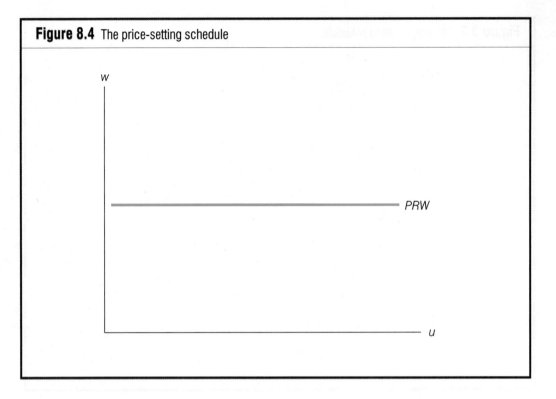

Figure 8.4 The price-setting schedule

8

generally more competitive, which could be the consequence of anti-trust legislation, the mark-up would generally be expected to be lower.

The price-setting relationship above (8.3) can be rearranged so it is also expressed in terms of the real wage.

$$w = \frac{W}{P} = \frac{LP}{(1+\mu)} \tag{8.4}$$

The price-setting function is plotted in Figure 8.4. It has been drawn as a horizontal line indicating that price-setting is independent of the level of unemployment. This makes the model easier to use, but is in itself is a debatable proposition. Some discussion justifying this assumption is presented in Global application 8.1.

The price-setting relationship is also known as the feasible or price-determined real wage (PRW), as it states the real wage that firms can afford to pay workers given the productivity of labour and product market conditions (which affect the mark-up). Naturally, if there is movement in either of these two fields, then the feasible real wage will change and the price-setting schedule will shift.

An increase in labour productivity would increase the feasible real wage and hence the price-setting schedule will shift upwards. If every employed worker now produces more, firms would be able to fund higher compensation in terms of real wages.

An increase in the mark-up would lower the price-setting schedule. This is simply because higher mark-ups imply higher goods prices and therefore a lower real wage. The mark-up is essentially transferring rents from consumers or workers towards producers.

Equilibrium The equilibrium rate of unemployment or the NAIRU ($\hat{u}$) is where the price-setting and wage-setting curves intersect. This is simply where the bargained and feasible real wages are consistent with one another as shown in Figure 8.5.

Global application 8.1

Should the price-setting curve be horizontal?

It is usually assumed that there are diminishing returns to scale in the production process. That is, as we keep adding inputs of a factor of production, output will rise but at a declining rate. In this case, we are suggesting that the marginal product of labour falls as employment rises.

Several explanations have been offered as a justification for a falling marginal product. The first is that labour inputs are not homogenous; some are better endowed with skills and productivity than others. When hiring labour, firms are more likely to hire the better quality labour first, so as employment expands the marginal product of labour should fall simply because poorer and poorer quality labour is hired. Likewise, when making redundancies, it would be rational for the firm to lay off the least productive workers first.

Another possible justification is that firms have a relatively fixed (especially in the short run) level of capital stock for labour to work with. As employment gets larger and larger, this capital stock becomes more thinly spread over more workers. Each therefore uses less capital, becomes less productive, and their marginal product falls.

Therefore, if labour productivity falls with employment, surely it should actually rise with unemployment. (If the labour force stays constant and employment rises, then unemployment falls.) So, if labour productivity increases with unemployment, then shouldn't the price-setting wage derived above actually be upward-sloping?

Accepting this line of reasoning begs the question how we can justify a horizontal price-setting relationship? The reason is linked to empirical evidence, which tends to suggest that labour productivity is relatively constant with respect to the level of unemployment. There does not appear to be an overwhelming case for drawing

Figure 1 The marginal product of labour

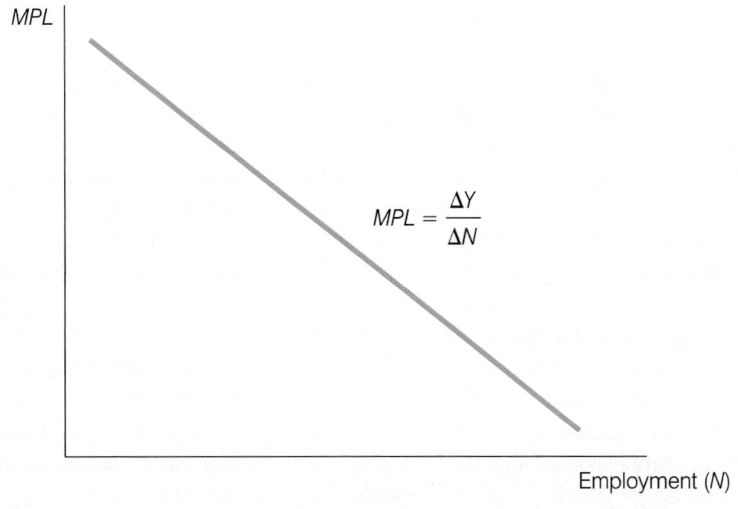

Global application 8.1 (continued)

Figure 2 An upward-sloping price-setting schedule

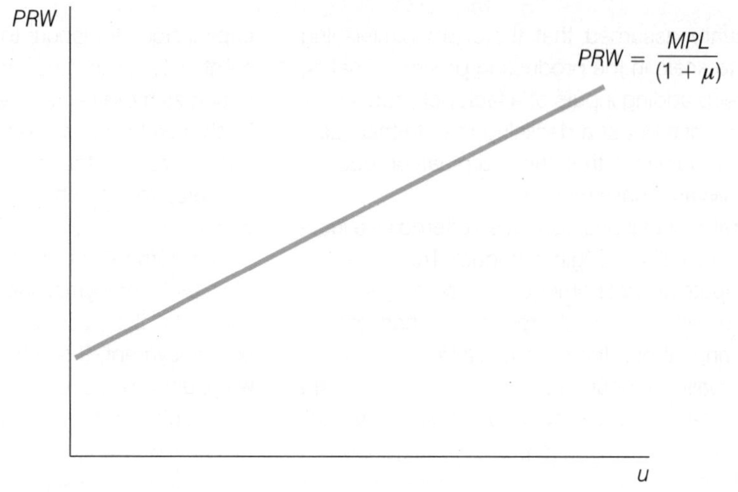

an upward-sloping price-setting relationship. Therefore, accepting a constant level of labour productivity is not at odds with real world experience.

Even if we find it difficult to forgo the idea of a declining marginal product of labour, there is still a feasible route to a horizontal price-setting relationship.

Remember that the price-setting relationship sets the real wage equal to the ratio of labour productivity and the mark-up. For this ratio to stay constant, all we need is for these two components to move in the same direction. If, as unemployment rises, labour productivity rises, the feasible real wage will remain unchanged if the mark-up increases in roughly the same proportion. The remaining question, though, is why would the mark-up increase as unemployment rises?

Again, there are several possible explanations. The first argues that mark-ups are counter-cyclical because of competition effects. When unemployment is low, aggregate demand in the economy is high, so more businesses are viable. If high demand supports more firms, then competition will be greater and, therefore, mark-ups lower. The opposite is true when unemployment is high. This corresponds to weak aggregate demand: few firms are sustainable and product market competition is weaker. This gives firms an opportunity to raise their margins.

An alternative explanation is that firms have implicit contracts with their customers. This is perfectly sensible if customers are repeat purchasers, as there is an opportunity to build up long-term relationships. One way a firm may cultivate this relationship is to limit the number of price changes it makes. It can do this by once again changing its margins to absorb the effects of productivity changes. In this way, the firm is offering a form of price insurance to its customers.

Finally, firms may engage in an activity known as *pricing to market*. This is where the determination of prices is somewhat removed from cost considerations and set at a level which may reflect a degree of strategic behaviour. For example, a luxury car manufacturer may resist reducing the prices of their cars if they fear that consumers will consider lower prices to be a sign of poorer quality. Alternatively, a firm may resist raising prices if they think it will lead to a loss of market

Global application 8.1 (continued)

Figure 3 The counter-cyclical mark-up and the horizontal price-setting curve

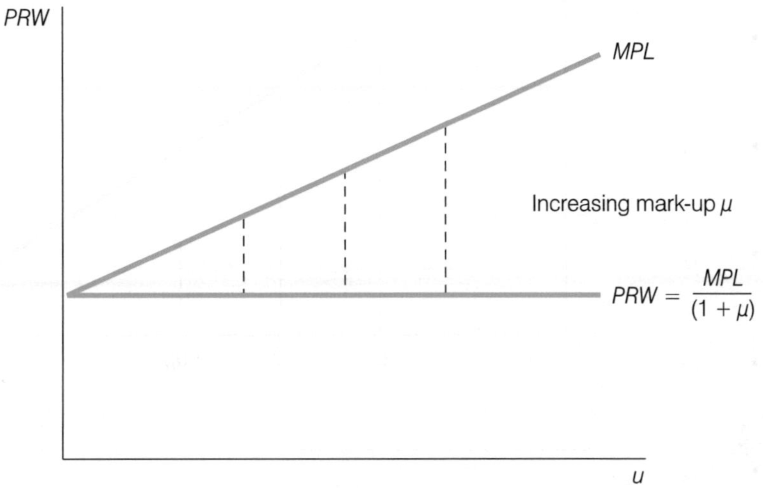

share which would be difficult to recapture in the future. In these types of circumstances, firms would be prepared to absorb cost fluctuations into margins in order to maintain a certain price.

Either way, although it is perfectly rational to draw an upward-sloping price-setting curve, we will follow common practice and draw it as horizontal. This also, it has to be said, makes the proceeding analysis much easier without compromising on the theory.

8

The dynamics of this model will always move toward the equilibrium level of unemployment. Any level of unemployment away from this would induce changes in either or both wages and prices, so that the real wage and unemployment are restored to their equilibrium values.

If unemployment was low so that $u_L < \hat{u}$, then it is the case that the wage-setting schedule lies above the price-setting schedule, $PS < WS$. This implies that the real wage demanded by unions is greater than that which firms can afford, given the current level of labour productivity and product market conditions. Consequently, two things will happen to reduce the value of the real wage and restore unemployment back to its original level where $u = \hat{u}$ and $PS = WS$.

The first is that firms, unable to pay the high wages demanded by workers, will cut back on employment. As unemployment begins to rise, workers will begin to moderate their wage demands, so nominal wages (W) will fall. Second, if firms face high wage costs, they will attempt to cover these by raising prices. However, as prices rise, aggregate demand in the economy will fall, which will reduce employment and push up the unemployment rate. Therefore, a combination of changing wages and prices will restore the equilibrium level of unemployment.

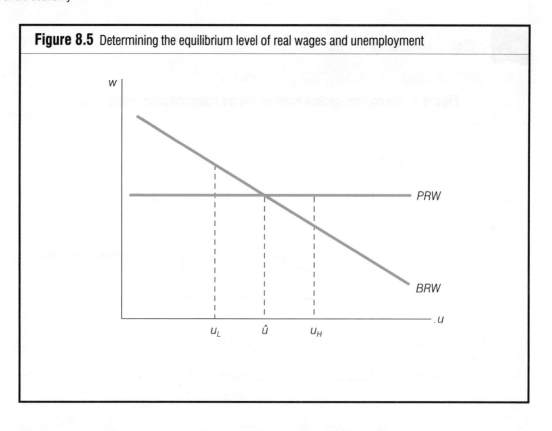

Figure 8.5 Determining the equilibrium level of real wages and unemployment

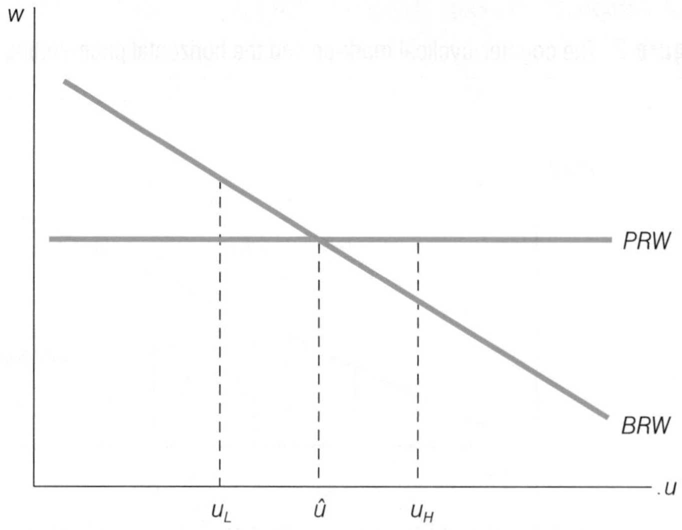

If unemployment is above the equilibrium level, then the reverse will happen. At a rate of unemployment $u_H > \hat{u}$, it is the case that $PS > WS$. The real wage that firms think feasible exceeds that demanded by unions. Again, changes in wages and prices will act to restore equilibrium. As labour is seen as relatively cheap, employment expands, unemployment will thus fall until $u = \hat{u}$ and $PS = WS$. As unemployment falls, workers push for higher nominal wages (W) and the real wage increases. Alternatively, if wages are low, then firms facing lower costs will cut prices. This will increase aggregate demand and again reduce unemployment.

It is evident that changes in prices and nominal wages will act to restore the equilibrium value of real wages and the rate of unemployment. A point that is worth thinking about now, as it will be the basis of a lot of discussion in this and proceeding chapters, is how quickly wages and prices adjust in this model. If adjustment is slow, then it is possible that unemployment may deviate from its equilibrium level for sustained periods of time.

Deriving the long-run aggregate supply curve

The relationship between output and employment (*N*) is given by a production function.

$$Y = F(N) \tag{8.5}$$

This simply defines the aggregate level of output for each level of employment, but can also be written in terms of the unemployment rate. The total labour force (*L*) consists of employed (*N*) and unemployed workers (*U*).

$$L = N + U$$

The unemployment rate is the proportion of the labour force that is unemployed.

$$u = U/L$$

Therefore, the proportion of the labour force that is employed and unemployed should just add up to one.

$$1 = N/L + U/L$$

$$1 = N/L + u$$

This can be rearranged to give employment as a function of the unemployment rate.

$$N/L = 1 - u$$

$$N = L(1 - u) \qquad (8.6)$$

Equation (8.6) reports that the level of employment is equal to the proportion of the labour force (L) that is not unemployed. If the unemployment rate is u, then this proportion will be equal to $1 - u$.

Finally, to find the equilibrium level of output, all we need to do is substitute this relationship between employment and unemployment (8.6) back into the production function (8.5).

$$\hat{Y} = F(L(1 - \hat{u})) \qquad (8.7)$$

These steps for deriving the long-run aggregate supply curve are shown graphically in Figure 8.6.

In panel (a), the equilibrium rate of unemployment is determined by the intersection of the wage- and price-setting schedules.

In panel (b), the relationship between unemployment and employment is plotted. Corresponding to the equilibrium level of unemployment ($\hat{u}$), there is an equilibrium level of employment ($\hat{N}$).

8

Figure 8.6 Deriving the long-run aggregate supply curve

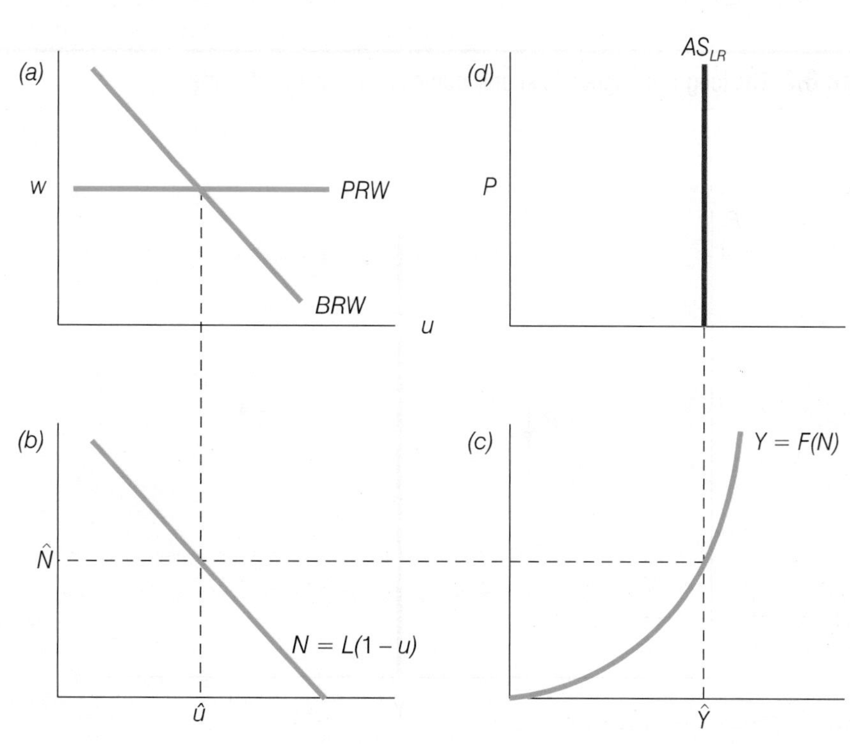

In panel (c), the production function is shown, relating employment to output.

Finally, panel (d) plots the long run aggregate supply function (AS_{LR}). It is vertical at the equilibrium level of output.

If output were above the equilibrium level, there would be upward pressure on prices. This is clearly understandable from the analysis above. Output above the equilibrium level corresponds to unemployment below the equilibrium rate, at which point there are high wage demands and upward pressure on prices (see Figure 8.7). Correspondingly, at levels of output below the equilibrium level, there will be rates of unemployment higher than the equilibrium rate. Therefore, wage demands will be lower, and prices will fall.

This makes it clear why the equilibrium level of unemployment is referred to as the NAIRU. It is the rate of unemployment where there is no pressure on prices to change. The equilibrium level of output, which then defines the position of the long-run aggregate supply curve, is just the level of output at the NAIRU.

However, it should be obvious that shifts in the long-run aggregate supply schedule will result from anything that acts to alter the equilibrium level of output. In Figure 8.8, if the equilibrium level of output were to increase, then the long-run aggregate supply curve would shift to the right ($AS_{LR} \rightarrow AS'_{LR}$), implying that prices would be constant at a higher level of output/lower rate of unemployment. A shift to the left ($AS_{LR} \rightarrow AS''_{LR}$) represents a fall in the equilibrium level of output.

These shifts in long-run aggregate supply (AS) can come from four sources:

1. *LP*: As labour productivity improves, the equilibrium rate of unemployment falls and equilibrium employment and output both rise. As a result, the long-run AS schedule will shift to the right. This is shown in Figure 8.9. As a consequence of higher productivity, the price-setting schedule shifts upwards such that $PRW \rightarrow PRW'$. Working through the rest of Figure 8.9, we can see that, subsequently, the equilibrium rate of unemployment falls $\hat{u} \rightarrow \hat{u}'$, the equilibrium level of output rises $\hat{Y} \rightarrow \hat{Y}'$, and the long-run aggregate supply curve shifts to the right, $AS_{LR} \rightarrow AS'_{LR}$.

8

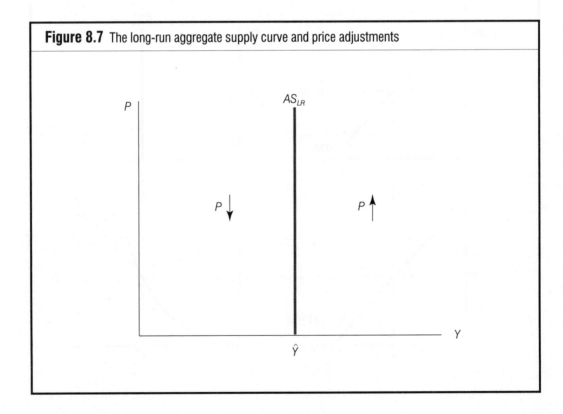

Figure 8.7 The long-run aggregate supply curve and price adjustments

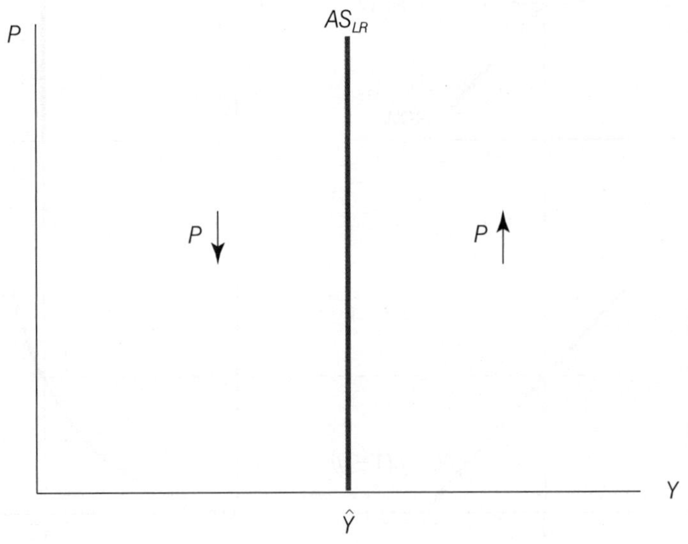

Figure 8.8 Shifts in the long-run aggregate supply schedule

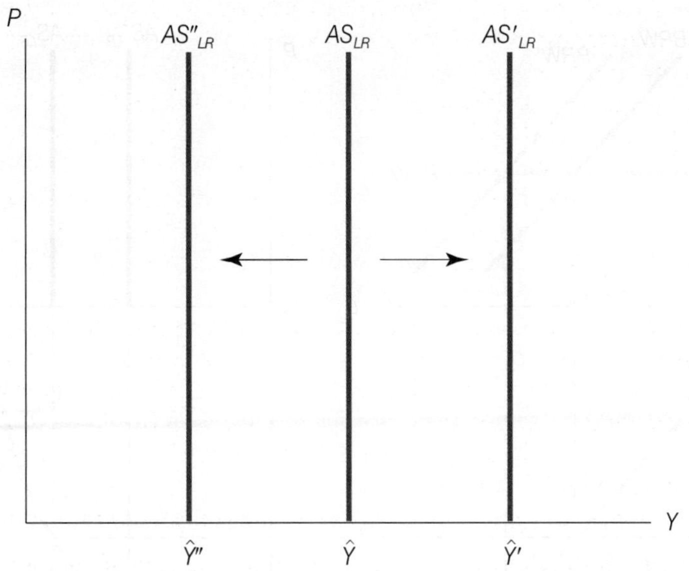

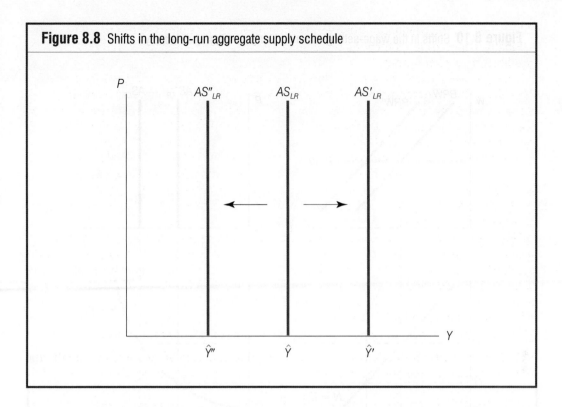

Figure 8.9 Shifts in the price-setting schedule and changes in long-run aggregate supply

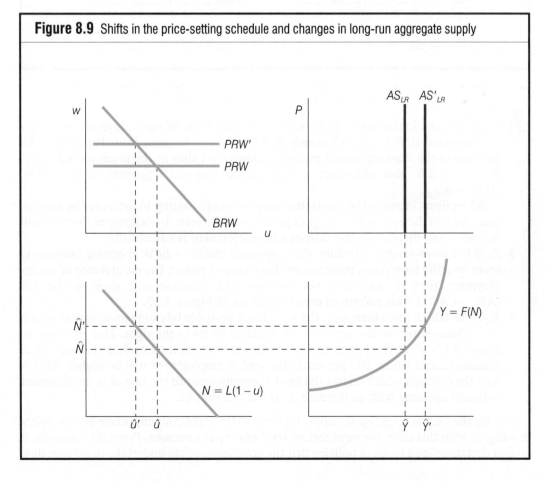

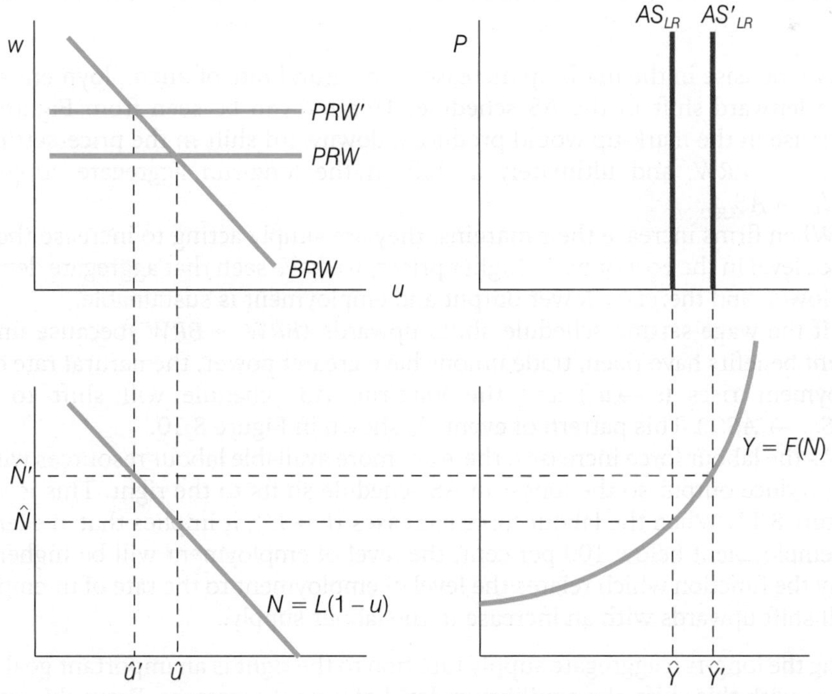

Figure 8.10 Shifts in the wage-setting curve and long-run aggregate supply

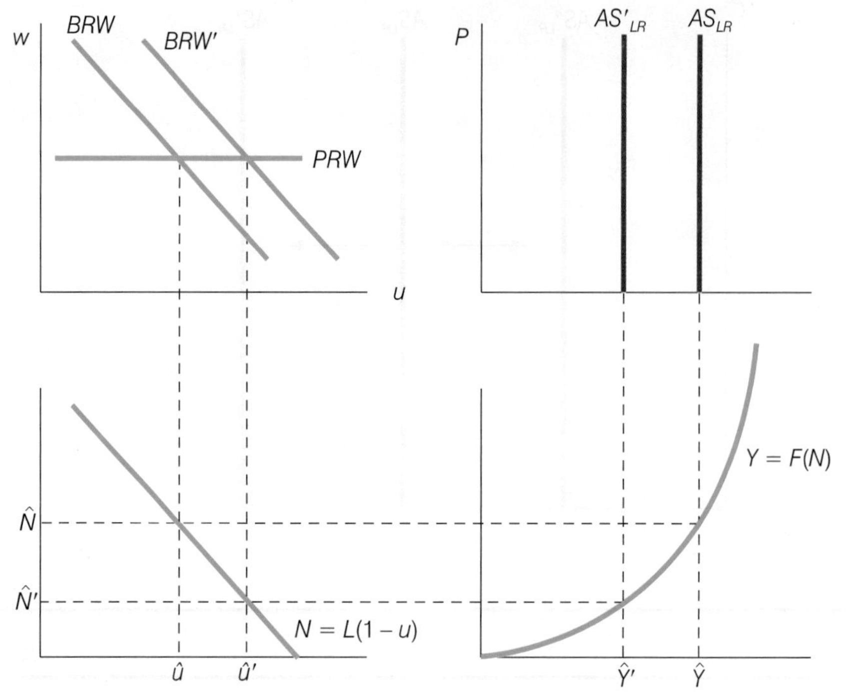

8

2. μ: An increase in the mark-up increases the natural rate of unemployment and leads to a leftward shift in the AS schedule. This too can be seen from Figure 8.9. An increase in the mark-up would produce a downward shift in the price-setting curve, $PRW' \rightarrow PRW$, and ultimately a shift in the long-run aggregate supply curve, $AS'_{LR} \rightarrow AS_{LR}$.

   When firms increase their margins, they are simply acting to increase the average price level in the economy. At higher prices, we have seen that aggregate demand will be lower, and therefore lower output and employment is sustainable.
3. Z: If the wage-setting schedule shifts upwards ($BRW \rightarrow BRW'$)because unemployment benefits have risen, trade unions have greater power, the natural rate of unemployment rises ($\hat{u} \rightarrow \hat{u}'$) and the long-run AS schedule will shift to the left ($AS_{LR} \rightarrow AS'_{LR}$). This pattern of events is shown in Figure 8.10.
4. L: As the labour force increases, there are more available labour resources with which to produce output so the long-run AS schedule shifts to the right. This is shown in Figure 8.11. When the labour force increases ($L \rightarrow L'$), it implies that at every rate of unemployment below 100 per cent, the level of employment will be higher. This is why the function which relates the level of employment to the rate of unemployment will shift upwards with an increase in the labour supply.

Shifting the long-run aggregate supply function to the right is an important goal in policy making, as with this shift, the equilibrium level of output increases. From this analysis, it is clear that there are a range of policies that the government may undertake to achieve this.

Figure 8.11 Changes in labour force participation and long-run aggregate supply

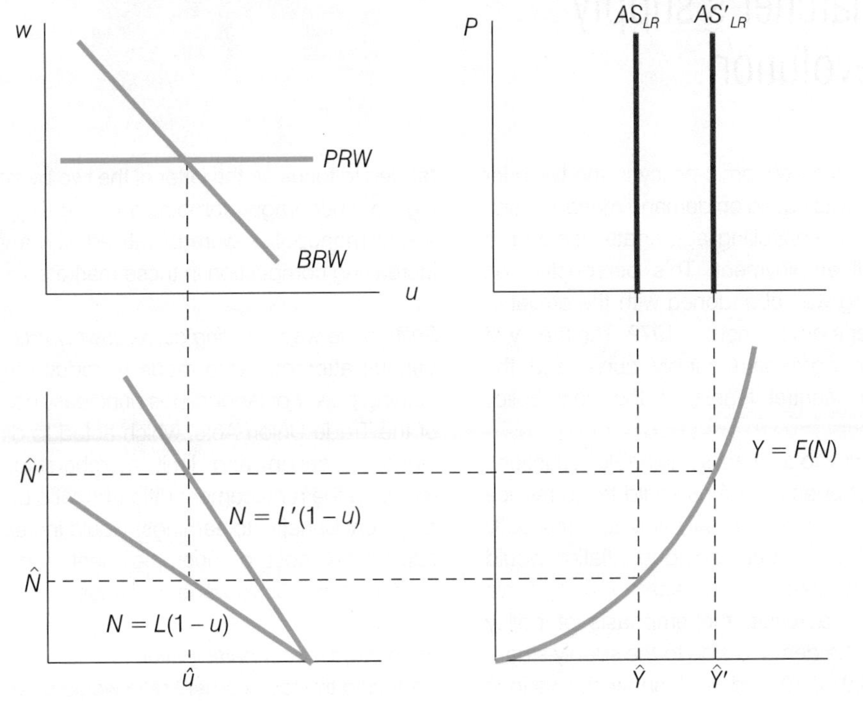

- Policies to improve productivity (higher LP).
- Policies to improve labour market flexibility/competition (lower Z).
- Policies to induce higher labour market participation (higher L).
- Policies to improve product market competition (lower mark-up, μ).

Taken collectively, attempts to shift the long-run aggregate supply curve are known as *supply side policies*.

8.3.2 Short-run aggregate supply

In the long run, the willingness of firms to produce does not depend on the price level, and therefore the aggregate supply function is vertical. Aggregate supply in the short run, though, is different. In this case, it is argued that the schedule is upward-sloping, so supply rises with prices. This is how we would expect a conventional supply curve to look.

To accept an aggregate supply function which slopes upwards with prices means that we must justify why output can or might deviate from its equilibrium level. Also, as output is always expected to return eventually to its equilibrium level, we have to explain why these deviations are only temporary.

From the deviation of the equilibrium level of output, we know that a disequilibrium will be corrected by movements in wages and prices. If wages and prices move slowly, then output will be away from the equilibrium level for some time. Therefore, accepting and

8

Global application 8.2

Mrs Thatcher's supply side revolution

Traditional macroeconomic policy in the UK prior to the 1980s was based on demand management, which involved controlling aggregate demand to maintain full employment. This perspective on policy making was abandoned with the arrival of Mrs Thatcher's government in 1979. The theory of the long-run aggregate supply curve and the NAIRU were central tenets of the new policy regime.

The only way to achieve sustainable reductions in the rate of unemployment would be to reduce the NAIRU. Likewise, the only way to continually increase output without leading to inflation would be to shift the long-run aggregate supply curve outwards. As a result, the emphasis of policy shifted from the demand side to the supply side.

Figures 8.9, 8.10 and 8.11 show the various ways in which a reduction in the NAIRU or a shift in the long-run aggregate supply curve can be achieved. Supply side policies introduced in the 1980s fit well into this framework.

Shifting the price-setting curve upwards

This can be achieved either by increasing productivity or reducing the mark-up. Policy in the 1980s tended to focus on the latter of the two by attempting to encourage competition. The big public sector monopolies were privatized with a view to increasing competition in these markets.

Shifting the wage-setting curve downwards

Various attempts were made to reduce the bargaining power of labour. This principally consisted of the Trade Union Acts, which acted to diminish industrial action and limit membership. Also, reducing the replacement ratio (the ratio of unemployment benefits to earnings) would increase the opportunity cost of unemployment and act to moderate excessive wage demands.

Encourage labour participation

Reducing the replacement ratio would be one way of encouraging people to substitute voluntary unemployment for employment. This could be achieved in two ways. Either the value of unemployment benefits could be reduced or the value of wages increased. The latter of the two was achieved by cutting income tax rates in order to increase the take-home pay from working.

Union members vote on a ballot in an industrial dispute in the UK

Source: Getty Images

accounting for wage and price rigidities, which prevent output always instantly veering to the equilibrium level, is important.

Also important is the role that is played by expectations. When deriving the long-run equilibrium level of output, we assumed that price expectations were made correctly, so that $P^e = P$ is always the case. In the short run, though, we break this assumption and actual prices can deviate from expected prices. This too accounts for why aggregate supply may differ in the short and long run. We will also observe that the way expectations are formed will play a critical role in the dynamics that link the short and long run.

The short-run aggregate supply function

One of the key features of the short-run aggregate supply function is that output and prices are positively related. As output increases, then prices will also rise. To understand what factors might be responsible for this relationship, we need to consider how prices are actually determined – a process which we have already argued is summarized by the price-setting behaviour of firms.

From the price-setting relationship, prices are just a mark-up on wage costs.

$$P = (1 + \mu)\frac{W}{LP}$$

The level of wages, on the other hand, is derived from the wage-setting relationship.

$$W = P^e(Z - \beta u)$$

If we substitute the wage-setting equation into the price-setting equation, we end up with an equation which tells us how prices are determined in the economy.

$$P = (1 + \mu)\frac{P^e(Z - \beta u)}{LP} \qquad (8.8)$$

Now the price-setting equation consists of a number of variables. These factors can, in turn, be split into long-run and short-run determinants of the price level. We have already seen that changes in labour productivity (LP), labour supply factors (Z) and the mark-up (μ) will lead to shifts in the long-run aggregate supply curve. For this reason, we can ignore these as determining prices in the short run because any change in these variables will lead to a change in the equilibrium level of output.

The two remaining variables are the level of unemployment (which is linked strongly to output) and the level of price expectations. Therefore, it seems logical that an explanation for an upward-sloping aggregate supply curve lies in the relationship between prices and these two factors.

Unemployment/output

From the above price-setting equation, we can see that prices are negatively related to unemployment. This follows readily from the bargaining model we outlined earlier in the chapter.

At rates of unemployment below the equilibrium level ($u < \hat{u}$), the bargained real wage should lie above the feasible real wage. For unemployment to rise back to the equilibrium level, two things must happen. First, there needs to be an increase in the nominal wage – by making labour more expensive, labour will start to price itself out of jobs. The second movement requires an increase in prices. If wages are rising, then firms should see their costs rising and wish to raise prices. At higher prices, aggregate demand will be lower and therefore higher unemployment is sustainable.

It should not require much convincing to accept that unemployment and output are inversely related, so a rise in output must be associated with a fall in unemployment. This inverse relationship is known as Okun's Law. This can be shown easily by using Figure 8.6 backwards. If we start in panel (d) and output levels rise above the equilibrium level ($Y > \hat{Y}$), then from panel (c) it is also clear that more employment is needed in order to produce the higher level of output ($N > \hat{N}$). Panel (b) relates this to unemployment – given a fixed labour force, a higher level of employment relates to a lower level of unemployment ($u < \hat{u}$). So, output levels above the equilibrium level of output are commensurate with lower than equilibrium rates of unemployment.

Finally, panel (a) links this to the expected changes in wages and prices through the interaction of the wage- and price-setting curves outlined above. The lower rate of unemployment would be expected to generate a rise in wages and prices. Therefore, the relationship between output and prices can be summed up in the following way:

$$Y\uparrow \rightarrow u\downarrow \rightarrow W\uparrow \rightarrow P\uparrow$$

This mechanism explains why prices will rise with output, but it does not explain why output may deviate from its equilibrium level. Up to now, we have assumed that markets clear quite quickly, so movements in wages and prices will restore quickly to equilibrium values of output and unemployment. This would account for a vertical aggregate supply curve.

Suppose we were to start off at the equilibrium rate of output, and the price level is correctly anticipated at $P^e = P_0$. If output were then to rise so that $Y_2 > \hat{Y}$, then following the mechanism above, there would be upward pressure on wages and prices. If these moved rapidly so that markets cleared instantaneously, then the deviation of output from its equilibrium level would disappear in the blink of an eye – the economy would move very rapidly from point **A** to **B**. However, market clearing then imposes higher equilibrium prices at P_2. This is shown in Figure 8.12.

8

However, suppose markets did not clear. Suppose that when output rises to a level $Y_2 > \hat{Y}$, there was no upward pressure on prices so that $P = P_0$ remains. Because there is no

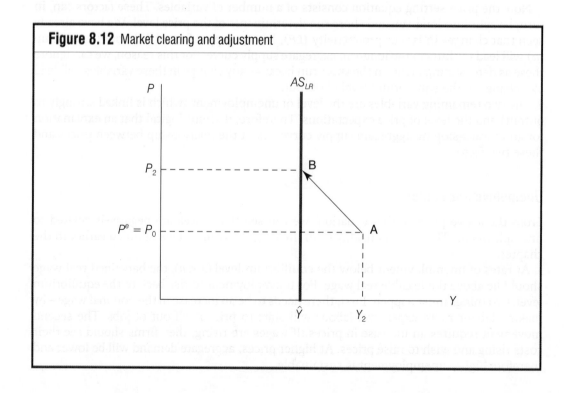

Figure 8.12 Market clearing and adjustment

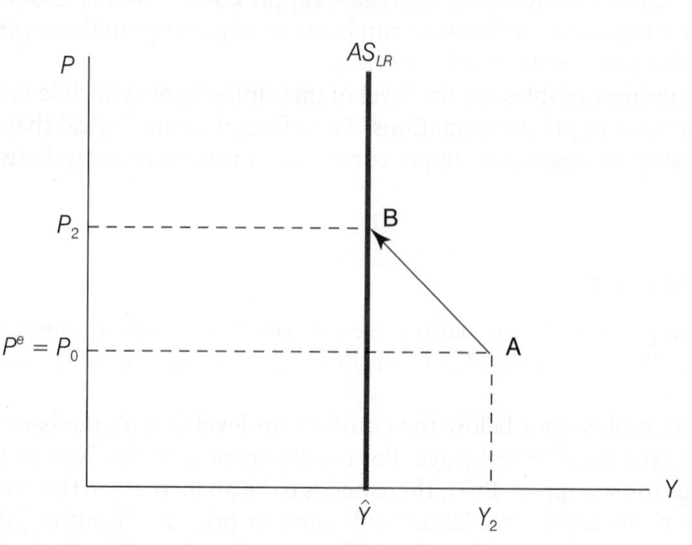

change in either wages or prices, there is no mechanism that returns output to the equilibrium level. The economy now gets stuck in a position off the long-run aggregate supply curve at point **A**.

We have presented two polar cases here. The first is where markets clear instantly so wages and prices adjust immediately to move the economy onto the long-run aggregate supply curve. The second is where there is no market clearing whatsoever, in which case no movements in wages and prices enable disequilibrium levels of output to persist and we move away from the long-run aggregate supply curve. In reality, actual experience is likely to lie somewhere between the two extremes.

The conventional wisdom is that, in the long-run, markets will clear (so the long-run aggregate supply is vertical) but, in the short run, wages and prices will only adjust gradually (so in the short run we can justify a position off the long-run aggregate supply curve). In the short run, an increase in output above the equilibrium level would only be corrected partially by movements in wages and prices. Therefore, prices will be expected to increase to, say, an intermediate level P_1, such that ($P_2 > P_1 > P_0$). Because prices partially adjust, output will remain above the equilibrium level, but would be lower than Y_2 where there was no movement in prices. Therefore, output too will stay at an intermediate level Y_1, such that ($Y_2 > Y_1 > \hat{Y}$). This output–price (Y_1,P_1) combination would then be expected to lie on a short-run aggregate supply curve, which is plotted in Figure 8.13.

So far the story behind the short-run aggregate supply curve is palatable, but you have probably noticed that two questions remain unanswered.

The first is why markets do not immediately clear to correct any disequilibrium position in output or unemployment? The short-run aggregate supply curve therefore requires us to rationalize rigidities in wages and prices. If the reader spends some moments in thought, they may be able to think of several reasons why wages and prices are not totally flexible. These might include the presence of contracts which prevent immediate changes. Also, there may be costs to changing prices which limit the number of price changes firms wish to make. 8

There could also be more sophisticated explanations behind the rigidities. In models of imperfect competition, firms may be reluctant to change prices without first seeing what

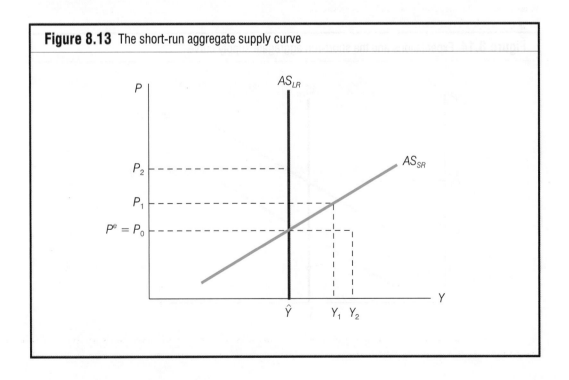

Figure 8.13 The short-run aggregate supply curve

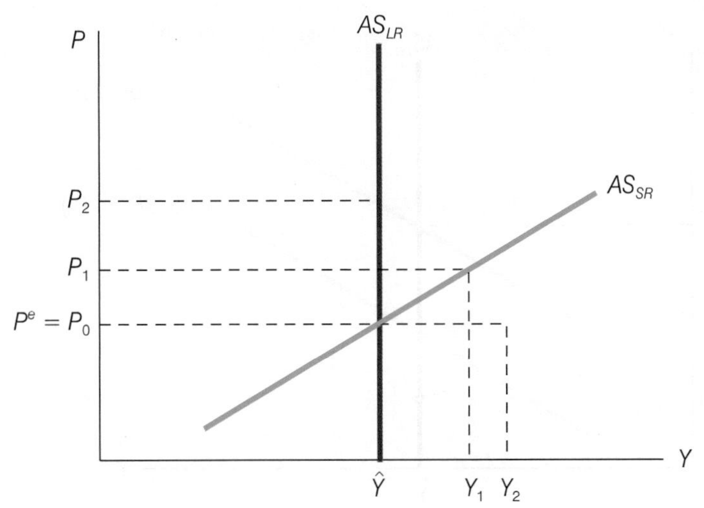

action their competitors take. Also, firms may offer wages away from the market clearing level for a variety of reasons, such as rewarding good performance and attracting and keeping good quality workers. In this case, the wage is set for reasons other than that determined by demand and supply, and could account for a general unwillingness for it to change with market conditions. The many factors which account for wage and price rigidities will be covered in some depth in the following chapter.

The second remaining question relates to expectations. We can see above that we started off from the initial expectation that $P^e = P_0$. However, if the price level was to rise to either P_1 or P_2, then it is clear that actual prices exceed expected prices. It is only if prices do not change at all that actual and expected prices continue to coincide. In this case, it is entirely by chance that wages and prices are completely inflexible. Therefore, a position on the short-run aggregate supply curve away from the equilibrium level of output implies that actual prices must differ from expected prices.

Changes in price expectations

The price-setting relationship above shows that prices will respond positively with respect to the level of price expectations. This is easily understood from the nature of the wage-bargaining process.

Workers are concerned typically with the real value of their wages. However, they can only set its nominal value and only form an expectation as to what actual prices will be. If they expect prices in the future to be higher, then in order to preserve the real value of wages, they will push for higher nominal wages. These in turn represent a cost to firms, who will respond by increasing prices. Therefore, there is a clear relationship between expected and actual prices.

$$P^e\uparrow \rightarrow W\uparrow \rightarrow P\uparrow$$

An increase in price expectations will lead to an upward shift in the short-run aggregate supply curve. This is because higher expectations lead to higher prices regardless of the level of output.

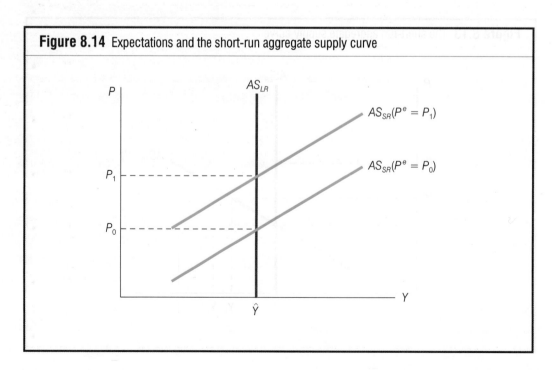

Figure 8.14 Expectations and the short-run aggregate supply curve

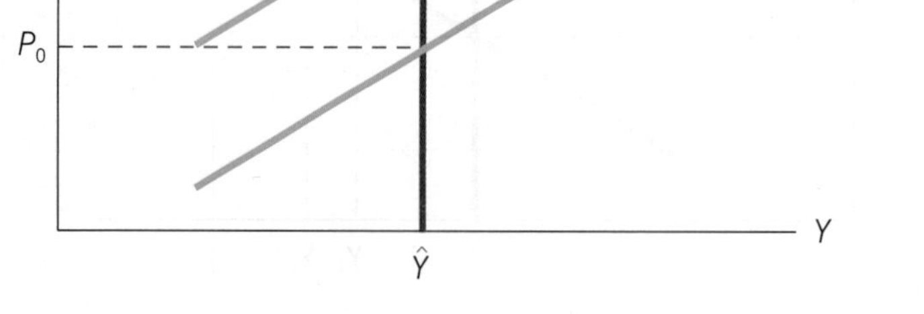

How are price expectations formed?

It is generally accepted that there are two ways in which expectations are formed. This is either adaptively or rationally.

Adaptive expectations In forming expectations adaptively, it is stated that current expectations are derived from past observations or experiences. In this way, price expectations are formed by a backward looking rule such as:

$$P_t^e = \lambda P_{t-1}^e + (1-\lambda)P_{t-1}, \text{ where } 0 < \lambda < 1 \quad (8.9)$$

In each period, the expected price is a weighted average of the actual and expected prices from the previous period. If actual prices exceeded expectations, then the next period's expectation will be revised upwards. Each time expectations are adjusted, the short-run aggregate supply curve will shift. It is only when actual and expected prices are equal that no further changes to expectations will be required.

For example, suppose at time, $t = 0$, the expected price is $P_0^e = P_0$, but the new actual and equilibrium price level is higher at $\widetilde{P}$. Given that actual prices exceed expected prices, then how will expectations be adjusted upwards so that eventually, $P^e = \widetilde{P}$? The process of adjustment will, of course, come through expectations being continually updated according to the adaptive rule.

So, at time $t = 1$,

$$P_1^e = \lambda P_0^e + (1-\lambda)\widetilde{P}$$

$$P_1^e = \lambda P_0 + (1-\lambda)\widetilde{P}$$

such that

$$P_0 < P_1^e < \widetilde{P}$$

However, because actual prices continue to exceed expected prices, a further revision would be required at time, $t = 2$.

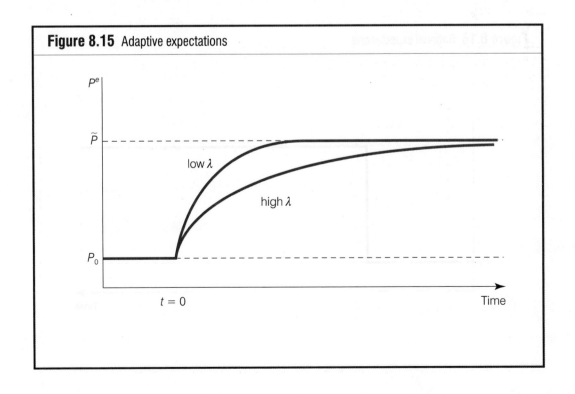

Figure 8.15 Adaptive expectations

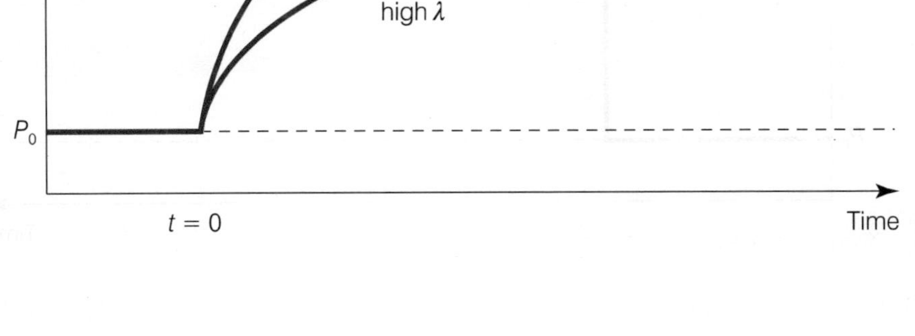

$$P_2^e = \lambda P_1^e + (1-\lambda)\widetilde{P}$$

$$P_2^e = \lambda(\lambda P_0 + (1-\lambda)\widetilde{P}) + (1-\lambda)\widetilde{P}$$

but, once again, it is the case that $P_2^e < \widetilde{P}$.

Price expectations will then be updated again and again until it is the case that $P^e = \widetilde{P}$. At this point, actual and expected prices coincide and no further revisions to price expectations are required.

Therefore, over time, expectations will eventually converge to the correct price level. The speed at which expectations are updated is given by the parameter λ. As this tends towards zero, a higher weight is placed on the previous actual rather than expected prices and so convergence is faster.

Rational expectations These are expectations that are formed using all available information.

$$P_t^e = E[P_t|I_t] \quad (8.10)$$

where I_t is the set of information available at time t.

As new information comes to light, expectations will adjust immediately to incorporate it. Therefore, instead of seeing the gradual adjustment under adaptive expectations, there would be a single immediate adjustment following new information about higher prices. In the above example, once it is deemed that the new price level is $\widetilde{P}$, expected prices will immediately jump to this level, as seen in Figure 8.16.

8

Rational versus adaptive expectations

There is some debate over which form of expectations formation is the most realistic/conclusive. Rational expectations are considered by many to be the most plausible. The main criticism with the adaptive framework is that expectations are simply backward-looking

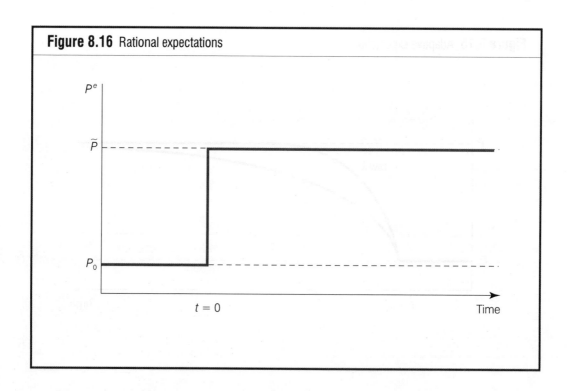

Figure 8.16 Rational expectations

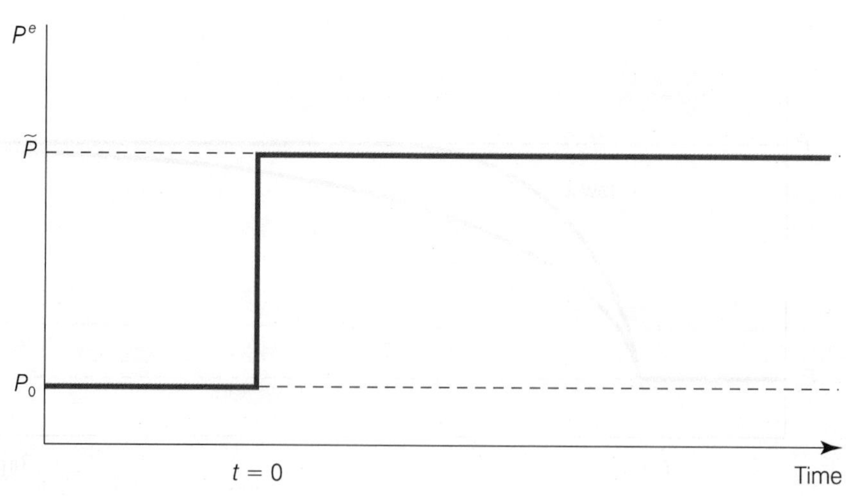

and therefore would ignore important and relevant information which should be incorporated. Therefore, past mistakes would continue to be made even though individuals have the information to correct them.

This is very apparent in the previous examples. If expectations were formed rationally, the correct expected price would be derived much faster. It is clear from this example that adaptive and rational expectations would coincide if $\lambda = 0$. So, what justification could there be for setting this parameter in the range $0 < \lambda < 1$and having adaptive expectations?

The case for adaptive expectations becomes stronger when people have less than full and perfect information. In the above example, we are comparing the two mechanisms when it is announced that the new price level is $\widetilde{P}$. In this case, there is little uncertainty as to what expectations should be and therefore rational expectations appears to be far more efficient.

However, would the nature of expectations formation change if changes in equilibrium prices were much harder to ascertain? If price changes are fairly volatile, then forming expectations about the future becomes much harder. In which case, it might become optimal to make smaller adjustments to expectations. In the above example, we might observe a current price level of $\widetilde{P}$. But, if we weren't armed with the relevant information, how could we be sure that this is the actual equilibrium price and that prices will not change again in the future? Therefore, λ would take on a higher value as expectations are adjusted more cautiously. When we start moving away from a world of complete and perfect information, adaptive expectations may become a more plausible model.

It is for this reason that increased attention is now being played to adaptive rules. This is because economic theory is now turning more and more towards learning behaviour. Accepting that individuals can only hold imperfect or incomplete information about the world, then it is easy to hypothesize that they will attempt to learn over time in order to improve their decision making. Therefore, the adaptive rule can be thought of as some kind of learning mechanism. We accept that we do not have perfect knowledge about the workings of the economy or the significance of certain events, so the optimal course of action would be a gradual adjustment in expectations over time as more and more information is observed.

8

8.4 Equilibrium in the AD-AS model

The long-run equilibrium in the AD-AS model is simply where the aggregate demand and both the long-run and short-run aggregate supply curves all intersect. This means that output is at its equilibrium level ($Y = \hat{Y}$) and also that actual and expected prices are equal at the market-clearing level, ($P^e = \hat{P}$).

However, in the short run the economy can deviate from the equilibrium level of output by moving to a position along the short-run aggregate supply curve. This would imply a disequilibrium in either the goods or the labour market and a gap between actual and expected prices. Such a position can be sustained as long as these two conditions continue to hold.

In the long run, though, a disequilibrium in the labour or goods market would be expected to lead to adjustments in wages and prices, and price expectations would be updated. Both of these movements act to reassert the long-run equilibrium position. However, because markets tend not to clear instantaneously and expectations may be updated adaptively, it may take some time for the economy to move back to the long-run aggregate supply curve. This implies that the short run actually may be a significant period of time.

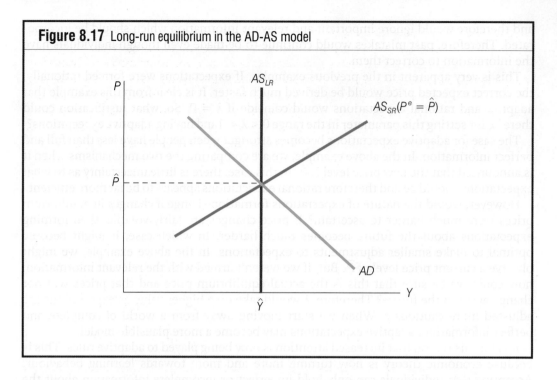

Figure 8.17 Long-run equilibrium in the AD-AS model

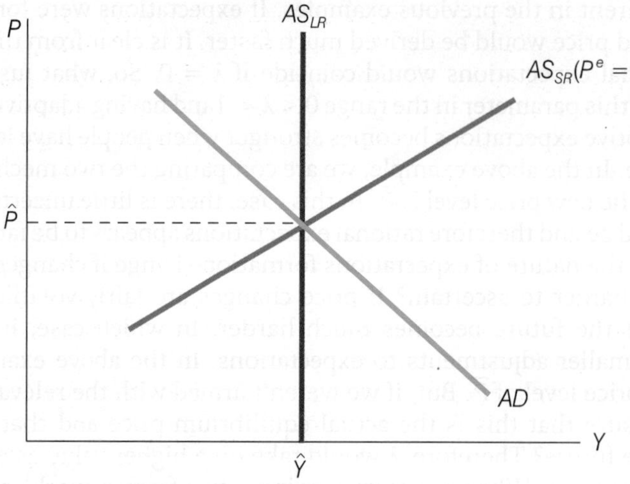

8

8.5 Comparative statics

We turn our attention to analysing the comparative statics of demand and supply changes in the economy. A comparative static tends to compare the economy's equilibrium before and after a shock. However, in understanding the path the economy takes over time, there is much to be gained in also considering the dynamics that link the short and long runs. We will see, with the use of several examples, that considering the dynamics enables us to explain output and price trends recently experienced in several countries.

Having fully established the AD-AS model, it can now be used to perform a number of comparative statics exercises. There are two types of exercise that we will be interested in.

Shifts in the aggregate demand curve result from anything that would shift the IS or the LM curve other than a change in prices. An outward shift in the AD curve could result from one or more of the following:

- an increase in government spending
- a cut in taxes
- a fall in interest rates or an increase in the money supply
- more optimistic expectations of the future leading to higher consumption and/or investment
- added wealth effects on consumption.

Shifts in the long-run aggregate supply curve result from changes in the equilibrium level of output, of which there appear to be two main causes.

- productivity shocks
- supply side policies.

When analysing the effects of demand and supply shocks using the AD-AS model, it is common practice to assume some price rigidities and adaptive expectations. It is reasonable to argue that markets do not clear instantaneously, and in the next chapter several plausible reasons will be given to account for wage and price rigidities.

Accepting adaptive expectations is sensible as households and firms only have imperfect information. Following a shock, it is unlikely that they will be able to work out quickly and correctly what the new equilibrium price level will be and then simply change their expectations accordingly. So, it is likely that expectations will tend to follow actual prices.

The one type of demand shock where rational expectations may be more significant is in shocks to the money supply. This is because it is considered to be easier to predict the effects that nominal shocks will have on prices.

Figure 8.18 An expansion in aggregate demand

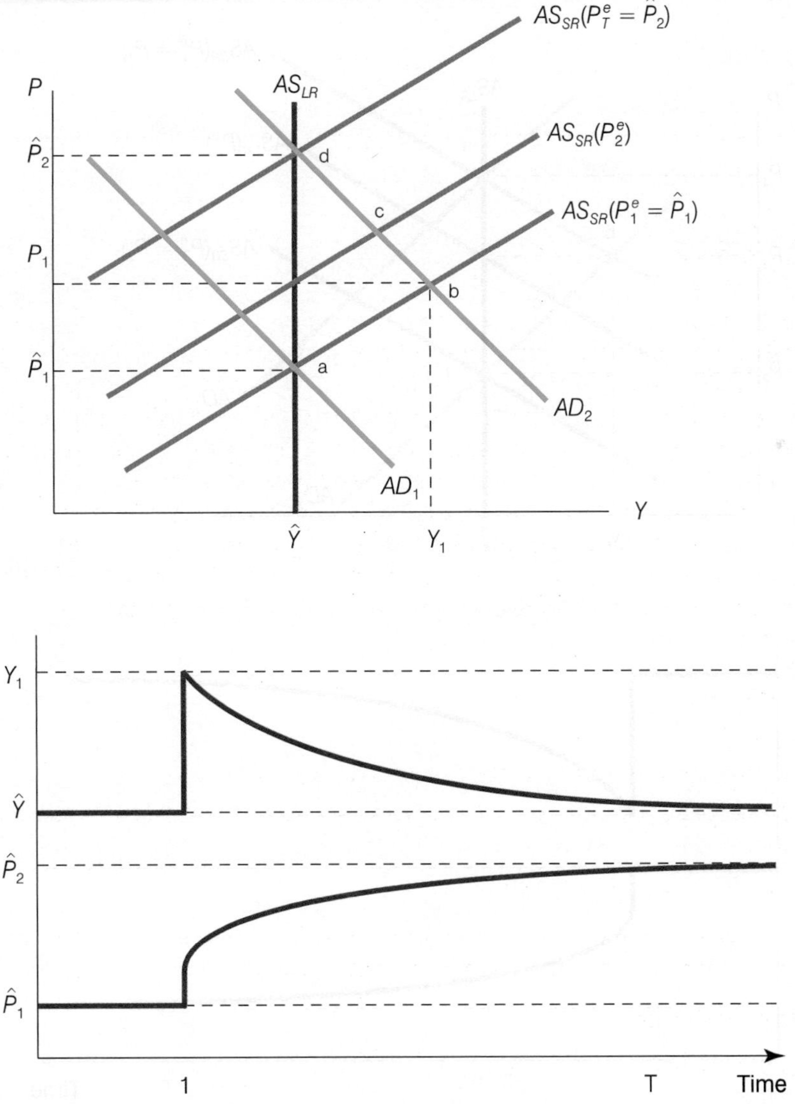

8.5.1 Aggregate demand shocks

The effect of an expansion in aggregate demand is shown in Figure 8.18 and outlined below.

1. The economy is initially in equilibrium where $Y = \hat{Y}$, $\hat{P}_1 = P_1^e$, and AD = AS_{SR} = AS_{LR}. This is point *a* in Figure 8.18.
2. An expansion in aggregate demand shifts the AD curve to the right, $AD_1 \rightarrow AD_2$. As a result, output rises to $Y_1 > \hat{Y}$ and prices from $\hat{P}_1 \rightarrow P_1$. The economy has now moved to point *b*.
3. It is now apparent that actual prices exceed expected prices, at which point expectations will be revised upwards, $P_2^e = \lambda P_1^e + (1-\lambda)P_1$, and the short-run aggregate

Figure 8.19 A contraction in aggregate demand

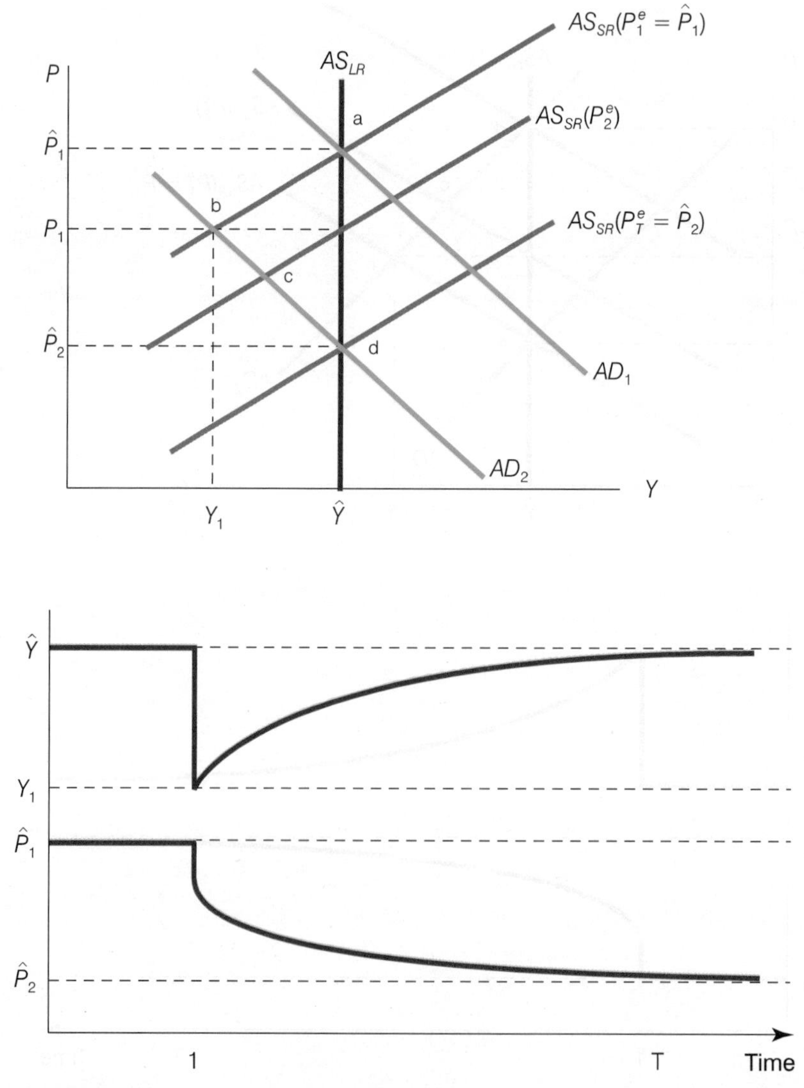

supply curve will shift upwards in light of the higher expectation. This puts upward pressure on prices and the economy moves to point *c*.

4. At point *c*, output continues to be above the equilibrium level, so there would be further upward pressure on prices. Also, prices will rise as expectations are adjusted upwards.
5. This process of increasing prices continues until output returns to the equilibrium level and actual and expected prices coincide. After a total of T periods, the economy will settle down at point *d*. The only long-run effect is a higher price level of $\hat{P}_2$.

The transition from the short to the long run sees prices rise for as long as the economy operates above the equilibrium level of output. The length of time it takes the economy to move from point *b* to point *c* will depend on how quickly expectations are updated, and on how flexible wages and prices are.

The effects of a contraction in aggregate demand are shown in Figure 8.19.

The path the economy takes is the opposite of that described above. Output will fall below the equilibrium level, but will eventually be restored over time by falling prices. The economy follows a path marked *a* → *b* → *c* → *d*, and the only long-run effect is a lower price level.

Global application 8.3

Boom and bust in the UK economy: aggregate demand shocks, output and inflation

Figures 8.18 and 8.19 describe the movements in output and prices following an expansion and a contraction in aggregate demand. This can be used to explain the path the UK economy took in the late 1980s and early 1990s, a period which has come to be known as 'boom and bust'.

Table 1 displays the annual rates of economic growth and inflation in the UK between 1983 and 1993.

The late 1980s boom refers to the high rates of economic growth experienced between 1986 and 1988. An annual growth rate of over 4 per cent was well above the historical average. However, linked to this was rapidly increasing prices, with inflation taking off towards the end of the decade. This pattern in output and inflation readily corresponds to the expansion in aggregate demand shown in Figure 8.18.

The boom is the economy was largely attributed to the economic policies of the Chancellor of the Exchequer, Nigel Lawson. First, income tax rates were cut in both 1987 and 1988. Second, interest rates were kept at a low level. Finally, financial markets were deregulated in 1986, which led to a large proliferation in the availability of credit. This in turn helped to produce rapidly rising house prices, increasing the personal wealth of homeowners. All these factors led to a large increase in aggregate demand.

However, it is now clear that the economy had expanded beyond its capacity, which would explain the large increases in inflation towards the end of the decade. In effect, by the time 1990 was reached, the economy was at point *d* in Figure 8.18.

The period 1990–1992 represented a severe recession in the UK economy, with growth being negative in both 1991 and 1992. At the same time, the rate of inflation fell. These output and price movements would correspond to the path plotted in Figure 8.19, showing a contraction in aggregate demand. In the UK economy, the collapse in aggregate demand was initiated by hikes in interest rates designed to combat inflation. This had a powerful effect on the economy by prompting a collapse in house prices, leaving many house owners with negative equity.

Global application 8.3 (continued)

Table 1 Annual rates of economic growth and inflation in the UK, 1983–1994

Year	Economic growth %	Inflation %
1983	3.43	4.6
1984	2.24	5.0
1985	3.74	6.1
1986	3.71	3.4
1987	4.37	4.2
1988	4.75	4.9
1989	2.22	7.8
1990	1.05	9.5
1991	–0.91	5.9
1992	–0.56	3.7
1993	2.37	1.6
1994	4.51	2.5

Global application 8.4

Rational expectations and the neutrality of money

Rational expectations are more likely to come into play when it is easier to predict what will happen to equilibrium prices following a certain shock. This is true in the case of monetary shocks.

The conventional wisdom states that monetary shocks can have no long-run effects on output. Nominal policies can only influence nominal variables; in this case, prices. This is a prediction of the famous *quantity theory of money*.

$$Mv = PY$$

where M is the money stock, v is the velocity of circulation, P is the price level, and Y is the level of output.

The velocity of circulation is assumed to be a constant, and output will equal its equilibrium level. Therefore, a change in the money supply can mean only one thing – a change in the price level. Therefore, the prediction of the quantity theory of money is that changes in the money supply will generate proportional changes in the price level. A 10 per cent increase in the money supply would be expected to produce a 10 per cent change in prices.

If expectations are formed rationally, then changes in the money supply should lead to immediate changes in price expectations in line with the quantity theory of money. The effects this will have on the economy are shown in Figure 4.

Global application 8.4 (continued)

Figure 4 A monetary expansion under rational expectations

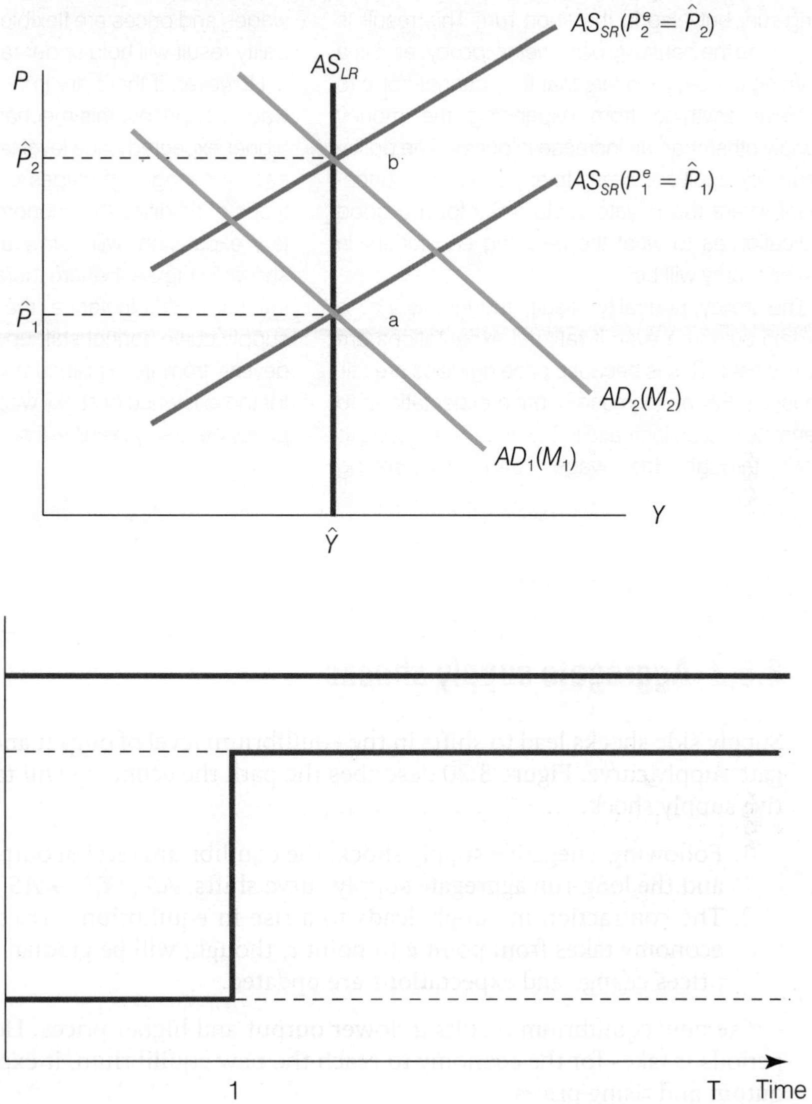

1. The economy is initially in equilibrium at point a where $Y = \hat{Y}$ and $P_1^e = \hat{P}_1$.
2. A publicly announced monetary expansion $M_1 \rightarrow M_2$ shifts the AD curve to the right, $AD_1(M_1) \rightarrow AD_2(M_2)$.
3. Under rational expectations, households will have a good estimate of what will happen to equilibrium prices so $P_2^e = E[P_2|M_2]$, and the expected price level will adjust immediately to take account of the new higher money stock.
4. The short-run aggregate supply curve will immediately shift upwards, $AS_{SR}(P^e = \hat{P}_1) \rightarrow AS_{SR}(P^e = \hat{P}_2)$. Output will not deviate from the natural rate and the only consequence of the monetary expansion is to raise prices, $\hat{P}_1 \rightarrow \hat{P}_2$.

Global application 3.1 (continued)

Policy implications

This is a strong result – implying that monetary policy is unable to influence output not just in the long run, but also in the short run. This result is known as the *neutrality of monetary policy*, as it is a warning to policy makers that they cannot hope to achieve anything from expanding the money supply other than an increase in prices. The policy neutrality result will extend to any policy announcement where the private sector may form a good indication as to what the resulting equilibrium in the economy will be.

The policy neutrality result, though, is not a certain outcome even if rational expectations are widely held. This is because price rigidities are still an issue. For an increase in price expectations to translate into an increase in the price level, it has to work through the wage- and price-setting schedules outlined earlier. Higher price expectations lead to the setting of higher wages. Higher wages are then transferred into higher prices. If wages and prices are flexible, then the policy neutrality result will hold under rational expectations.

However, if there are impediments to changing wages or prices, this mechanism breaks down. A higher expected price level fails to lead to the necessary changes in wages or prices. Under these types of rigidities the economy, following a monetary expansion, will follow a path similar to that shown in Figure 4 where there are adaptive expectations. In this instance, the short-run aggregate supply curve cannot shift upwards and output will deviate from its equilibrium value. Once we allow for the existence of sticky wages and/or prices, the policy neutrality result will not hold.

8.5.2 Aggregate supply shocks

Supply side shocks lead to shifts in the equilibrium level of output and the long-run aggregate supply curve. Figure 8.20 describes the path the economy will take following a negative supply shock.

1. Following a negative supply shock, the equilibrium level of output falls from $\hat{Y}_1 \rightarrow \hat{Y}_2$ and the long-run aggregate supply curve shifts, $AS_{LR}(\hat{Y}_1) \rightarrow AS_{LR}(\hat{Y}_2)$.
2. The contraction in supply leads to a rise in equilibrium prices to $\hat{P}_2$. The path the economy takes from point *a* to point *c*, though, will be gradual – changing slowly as prices change and expectations are updated.

The new equilibrium results in lower output and higher prices. However, during the T periods it takes for the economy to reach the new equilibrium, it experiences both falling output and rising prices.

A positive productivity shock would have entirely the opposite consequences. This is shown in Figure 8.21. A higher established level of equilibrium income produces a rightward shift in the long-run aggregate supply curve. The economy will then experience a process of falling prices and rising output.

Under demand shocks, it is expected that output and prices will move in the same direction. Under a supply shock, they move in the opposite direction to each other. Supply side shocks may arise from productivity shocks. In Chapter 3, Global applications 3.1 and 3.2 described two important productivity shocks. The first referred to the oil price shocks during the 1970s and the second to the emergence of the new economy in the second half of the 1990s.

A negative productivity shock, by shifting the long-run aggregate supply curve inwards, would see a period of falling output and rising prices. Table 8.1 compares the average rate

Figure 8.20 A negative productivity shock and stagflation

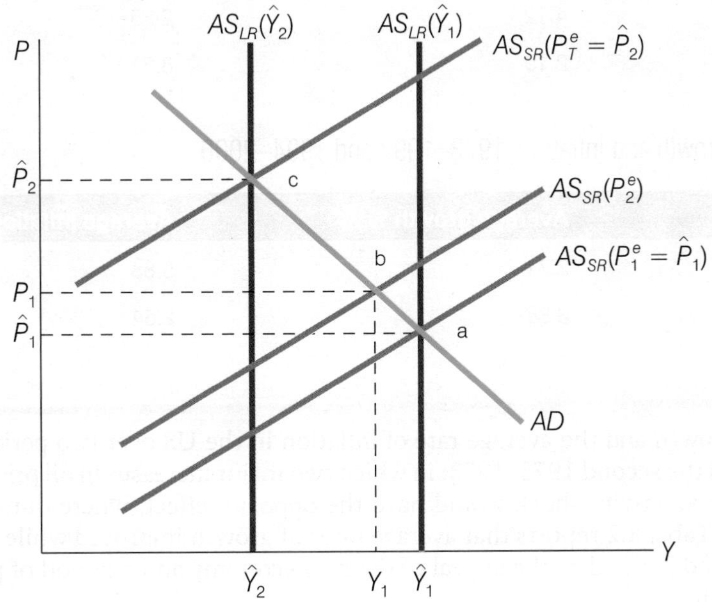

Figure 8.21 A positive productivity shock

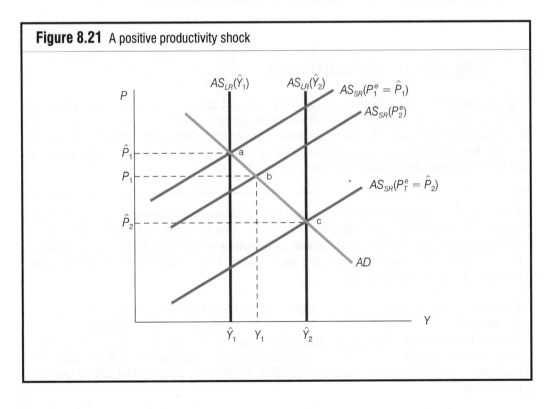

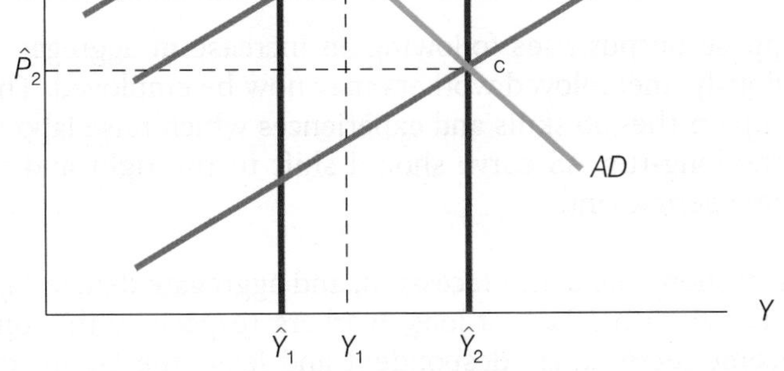

8

Table 8.1 US average growth and inflation, 1950–1972 and 1973–83

Years	Average growth %	Average inflation %
1950–1972	4.12	2.55
1973–1983	2.19	8.24

Table 8.2 US average growth and inflation, 1973–1993 and 1994–2000

Years	Average growth %	Average inflation %
1973–1993	2.71	5.88
1994–2000	3.86	2.54

of economic growth and the average rate of inflation in the US over two periods, the first 1950–1972 and the second 1973–1983, in which two major increases in oil price occurred.

A positive productivity shock would have the opposite effect, where output increases and prices fall. Table 8.2 reports that average rates of growth improved while inflation fell during the period marked as the arrival of the new economy and a period of positive productivity growth.

8

In addition, because the only way to increase output in the long-run is to shift the long run aggregate supply curve outwards, policy makers have a strong incentive to try to increase the equilibrium level of output through supply side policies.

8.5 Hysteresis and the medium run

So far it has been established that aggregate demand shocks have temporary effects on output, whereas aggregate supply shocks have permanent effects. **Hysteresis** describes a situation where demand shocks may leave permanent effects on output. This works because the initial change in output induced by a change in aggregate demand may then lead to a change in the equilibrium level of output.

Example 1: Suppose output rises following an increase in aggregate demand. This means that previously unemployed workers may now be employed. This could result in them picking up on-the-job skills and experiences which raise labour productivity, in which case, the long-run AS curve should shift to the right and the increase in output will become permanent.

Example 2: The economy falls into recession, and aggregate demand falls and unemployment rises. Faced with a lack of jobs, workers (especially the long-term unemployed) may become increasingly despondent and leave the labour force. Workers' skills become obsolete and they lose human capital. Therefore, L will fall and the long-run aggregate supply schedule will shift to the left, making the fall in output permanent.

These are just two simple examples of hysteresis. In fact, there is quite a large economic literature offering various explanations for hysteresis which we will cover in a later chapter (this is because its main application is in accounting for the persistence of unemployment rather than output movements).

Summary

- The aggregate demand and aggregate supply model can be used to explain how the levels of output and prices are determined in an economy.
- The aggregate demand curve identifies the total amount of planned expenditure at each price level. It is a downward-sloping function, as at higher prices the real money stock is lower, interest rates are higher and, therefore, planned expenditures will be lower.
- Aggregate supply in the long run is fixed at the equilibrium level of output. This represents the level of output where there is no pressure on prices to change. At output levels above the equilibrium level, prices will rise, and at output levels below the equilibrium level, prices will fall.
- The equilibrium level of output is derived from the equilibrium rate of unemployment, also called the non-accelerating rate of inflation unemployment (NAIRU). This is established from a labour–firm bargaining model, where firms set prices and workers set wages. The equilibrium level of real wages and the NAIRU is determined where the wage- and price-setting curves intersect.
- Anything that causes either the wage- or price-setting curves to shift will establish a new NAIRU level of equilibrium unemployment and, therefore, long-run aggregate supply curve. Relevant factors might include the level of productivity, the labour supply and the degree of competition in the goods market.
- In the short run, aggregate supply can deviate from the equilibrium level of output if markets do not clear and a gap emerges between actual and expected prices. Therefore, in the short run it is possible to justify an upward-sloping aggregate supply curve. However, any deviation of output from the equilibrium level can only be temporary. In the long run, prices will adjust to clear markets and expectations will be updated.
- The long-run equilibrium of the economy is established at the equilibrium level of output, and at a price level where actual and expected prices coincide.
- The AD-AS model can be used to analyse the effects of aggregate demand and aggregate supply shocks on the level of output and prices in an economy.
- Conventionally, aggregate demand shocks only have temporary effects on output. This is because markets clear slowly and expectations are adjusted adaptively. The more rigidity in wages and prices, and the more adaptively expectations are formed, the longer it takes for output to return to the equilibrium level.
- Aggregate supply shocks have permanent effects on both output and prices. As an improvement in aggregate supply generates both permanently higher output and lower prices, governments take seriously the use of supply side policies.
- Hysteresis is a powerful concept which explains why aggregate demand shocks can have very long-lasting effects on the economy. The hysteresis mechanism works by relating temporary changes in output to changes in the equilibrium level of output. Therefore, aggregate demand shocks may produce reaffirming shifts in long-run aggregate supply.

Key terms

AD-AS model
Aggregate demand (AD) schedule
Aggregate supply (AS) schedule
Hysteresis
Long-run aggregate supply
Non-accelerating inflation rate of unemployment (NAIRU)
Short-run aggregate supply

Review questions

1. Using the IS-LM model, show what effect the following have on the shape of the aggregate demand curve:
   a. a high interest elasticity of investment
   b. a low interest elasticity of money demand
   c. a small marginal propensity to consume.
2. Explain how the following will influence the non-accelerating inflation rate of unemployment (NAIRU) and the long-run aggregate supply curve:
   a. a subsidy on new capital goods
   b. a tax on childcare workers in private households
   c. an increase in the national minimum wage
   d. an increase in value-added sales taxes
   e. a fall in the rate of tax on corporate profits
   f. a cut in mandatory redundancy payments.
3. What factors account for an upward-sloping short-run aggregate supply curve?
4. At time t the expected price level $P_t^e = 1$, whereas the actual price level is $P_t = 2$. If expectations are updated according to the rule $P_{t+1}^e = \lambda P_t + (1 - \lambda)P_t^e$:
   a. find the level of price expectations at times, $t+1$, $t+2$, $t+3$, $t+5$ and $t+10$, when $\lambda = 0.3$ and $\lambda = 0.8$.
   b. what is the relationship between λ and the speed at which expectations are updated? What factors are likely to determine the size of λ?
5. The government is concerned about the current level of unemployment. It decides that an immediate reduction in interest rates is required to boost aggregate demand. What factors will determine the success of this policy?

8

More advanced problems

6. Is fiscal policy neutral in the short run? Is fiscal policy neutral in the long run?
7. There are two governments: one cares about keeping output stable and the other cares about keeping prices stable. What would be their reactions to:
   a. an increase in consumer confidence
   b. an increase in the price of oil?
8. How would the following affect the level of output in the short run and the long run?
   a. an increase in the proportion of skilled labour in the work force
   b. globalization
   c. increased immigration.

For further resources, visit
http://www.thomsonlearning.co.uk/chamberlin_yueh

Part V

Short-run fluctuations and stabilization

Economies undergo cyclical fluctuations and are not always in equilibrium. This part discusses business cycles and associated stabilization policy. It then moves on to the major topics of unemployment, inflation and monetary policy.

9 Business cycles and stabilization policy

Learning objectives

- Recognize the existence of business cycles
- Understand the two main theories of business cycles: real business cycles and new Keynesian economics
- Analyse new Keynesian theories of short-run fluctuations in output
- Identify sources of wage and price rigidities in the Keynesian frameworks
- Consider the welfare effects of short-run fluctuations
- Evaluate stabilization policies

9.1 Introduction

If we look at the path taken by a country's GDP over time, it is hard not to notice the presence of cycles. Although output tends to rise over time, this upward march is not smooth but punctuated by alternating periods of high and low (including negative) growth. We often attach labels such as booms and recessions to describe these output movements. This chapter aims to explain why economies are marked by short-run fluctuations in economic growth, which is known as the **business cycle**.

The economics literature has thrown up two main approaches to understanding these cycles. The first is termed as **real business cycle (RBC) theory**. This suggests that output movements are driven by productivity shocks, which hit an economy and lead to shifts in its production function. Although these shocks are considered to be both quick and temporary, they can lead to persistent movements in output.

The second is dubbed as the **new Keynesian theories of fluctuations**. Cyclical output movements here are predominately the result of demand shocks which have a long-lasting although temporary effect on output. In this way, booms and recessions are seen as periods of excess demand or supply. However, to generate cycles in output, it has to be the case that these disequilibria are not quickly corrected by movements in wages or prices. Therefore, persistent output movements are explained by slow market clearing. New Keynesian theory is, then, all about accounting for why wages and prices move only sluggishly – meaning that in the short run, demand shocks will have significant effects on output.

Another relevant question is why we might care about the business cycle, particularly because trend output is upwards, so any period of low or negative growth is only going to be temporary. An answer will require us to analyse the welfare effects of fluctuating output.

9

Whether or not we feel we should be worried about business cycles, it is certainly true that governments and policy makers over the years have made substantial efforts to control them. The government can use monetary and fiscal policies in order to offset the cycle; this is known as **stabilization policy**. Traditionally, it has also been referred to as demand management. The reason for this is because fluctuations were deemed to be caused by changes in aggregate demand. Therefore, any policy which cancels out these movements in aggregate demand will be successful in controlling output.

However, the use of stabilization policy is not uniformly welcomed. Those against the use of active policy have proposed a two-pronged attack. The first questions the need for stabilization policy, arguing that economies will self-correct. This is really a *market clearing* issue, booms and recessions are just the outcome of excess demand or supply in an economy, so changes in prices will ultimately correct the disequilibrium. The second forms the *policy inadequacy* debate. Although the case for active stabilization policy is recognized, in essence it is very difficult to implement the correct policies. Therefore, it is argued that active policy, if inappropriate, may do more harm than good and is best not implemented.

So, the focus of this chapter is on explaining the causes of short-run economic growth and offering an analysis on the advantages and disadvantages of stabilization policy. Economic growth in the long run is discussed in detail later on in the book.

9.2 Economic cycles

A simple way of looking at the path of output is to divide it up into a trend and cycle component.

$$\text{Output} = \text{Trend} + \text{Cycle}$$

The trend component represents the long-run rate of economic growth for an economy. However, the actual path the economy takes fluctuates considerably around this trend. These cyclical components are short-run, temporary fluctuations in output, described as the business cycle.

Figures 9.1 and 9.2 plot the levels of actual and trend real GDP since the Second World War in the US and the UK.

Figure 9.1 Actual and trend GDP in the US

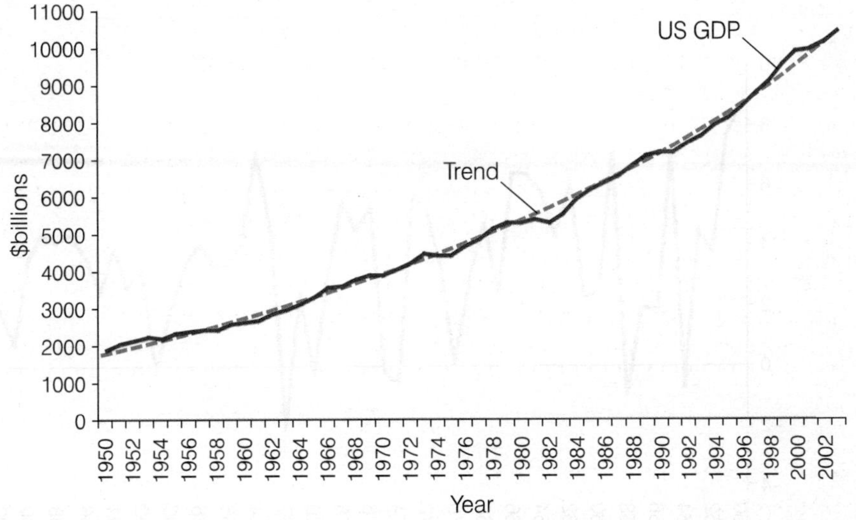

Figure 9.2 Actual and trend output in the UK

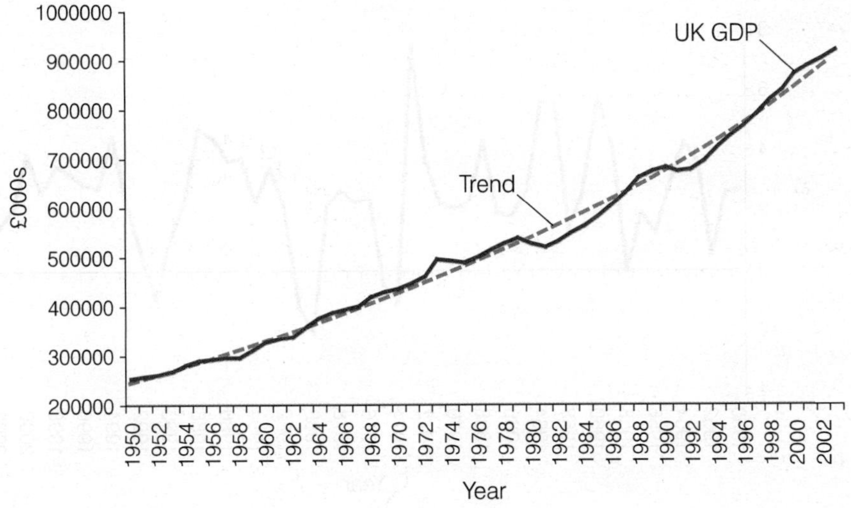

The cycle is driven by short-term fluctuations in the rate of economic growth. The annual growth rates for the US and the UK are plotted in Figures 9.3 and 9.4, and it is clear that growth rates are variable over time. The goal of business cycle theory is to account for these persistent fluctuations in growth.

The next section presents the two main theories which account for business cycles. The first is known as real business cycle theory, which argues that output fluctuations are the result of productivity shocks. The second is known as the New Keynesian approach. This suggests that cycles are the result of price and wage rigidities, which prevent markets from

Figure 9.3 US economic growth

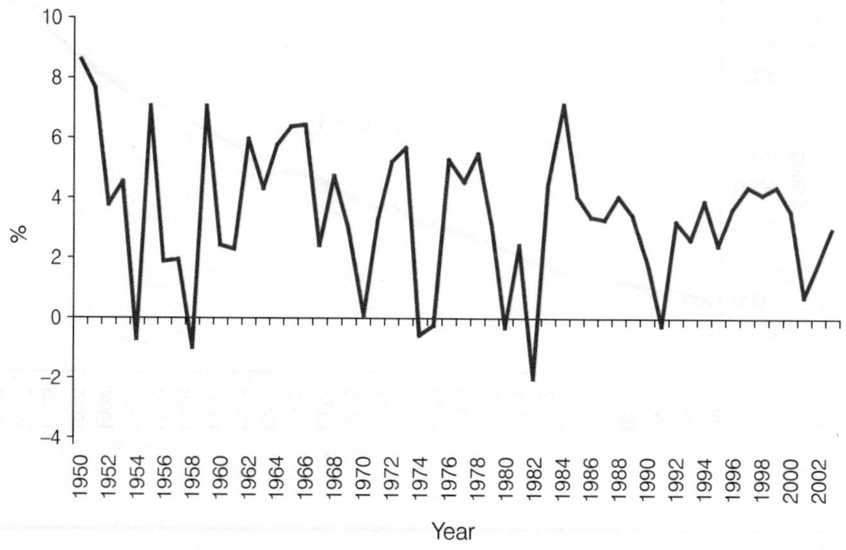

Figure 9.4 UK economic growth

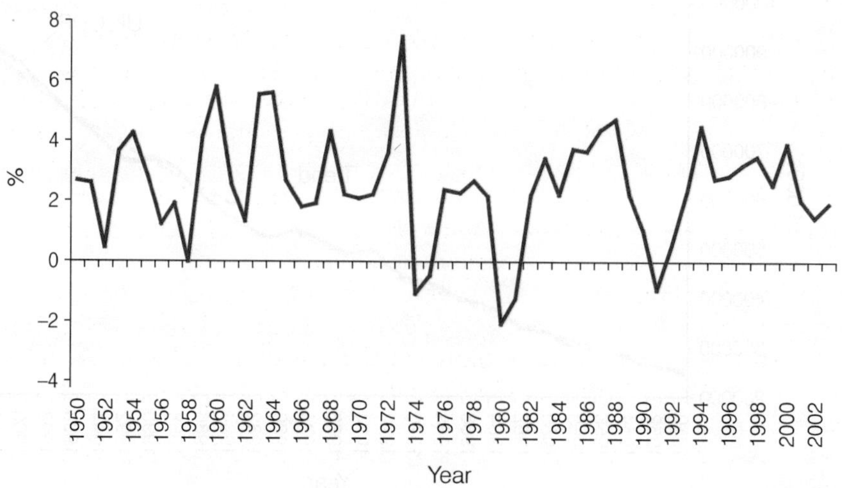

clearing. Once we acknowledge that output can persistently deviate from its equilibrium level (let's think of this as the trend level of GDP), we then have a basis for explaining cycles.

9.3 Real business cycles

Real business cycle theory (RBC) emphasizes the importance of 'real' factors in determining cycles. This is simply because RBC theorists have a strong belief that markets clear and that information is close to perfect. In this case, the source of output fluctuations will come from 'real' factors which alter an economy's production function – these are predominately technology or productivity shocks. As seen in Chapter 8, nominal factors, which include price and money shocks, have no impact on the real economy when information is complete and prices are flexible. They are not considered to play an important role in generating cycles.

A key part of explaining cycles is to account for how a given shock can then generate a sustained movement in output. If we look at the cycle dynamics in Figures 9.1 to 9.4, we are certainly made aware that cycles have a duration of at least several quarters, and typically several years. Therefore, a key part of the theory must be to explain how very short and temporary shocks generate these sustained movements in output. The response of RBC theory is to consider cycles as being generated by the combination of two elements: impulse and propagation.

- The **impulse** is the initial productivity or technological shock. This is a sudden and very short-lived innovation.
- The **propagation mechanism** then describes how the shock generates a persistent movement in output.

Without the propagation mechanism, there would be no real explanation of the business cycle. A temporary productivity shock would lead to a change in the equilibrium level of output and a shift in the long-run aggregate supply curve, but once the shock disappeared or was reversed, the economy would jump back to where it started. As productivity shocks are largely seen as very short-lived innovations, it would be hard to see how they can account for cycles of several years in duration.

The propagation mechanism is therefore central to the understanding of real business cycles. One approach, following the seminal models of Ramsey (1928) and Diamond (1965), argues that the persistence in output movements results from a sustained increase in capital investment following a productivity shock. The propagation mechanism at work here is consumption smoothing. A positive productivity shock would increase current income, but if households are permanent income consumers, they will rationally attempt to spread this gain over time so as to maximize their lifetime utility. The way this can be achieved is by investing some of the present income gain in capital, which will then lead to higher income being generated in subsequent periods.

The main features of this model can be outlined using a conventional two-period optimal consumption model; the type of which is covered in some detail in Chapter 2. It is recommended that the reader refers back to this chapter if any of the following is unclear.

The two-period optimal consumption model aims to account for the pattern of consumption undertaken by a household. Basically, a household wants to choose consumption in both periods so as to maximize their total lifetime utility. This is described by a utility function:

$$U = U(C_1, C_2) \tag{9.1}$$

9

The utility function just measures the total utility a household will achieve from a given pattern of consumption over the two periods. From this, an indifference curve can be constructed, which gives the combinations of consumption (C_1,C_2) that yield a certain amount of utility. Accepting the law of diminishing marginal utility of consumption, these indifference curves will be convex in shape.

Naturally, the household consumption decision is constrained by lifetime resources, which is defined by household income in each period (Y_1,Y_2). The two-period budget constraint ties the present discounted value of lifetime consumption to be no greater than the present discounted value of lifetime resources.

$$C_1 + \frac{C_2}{(1+r)} \leq Y_1 + \frac{Y_2}{(1+r)} \tag{9.2}$$

The optimal consumption decision (C_1^*,C_2^*)sees the household choosing consumption so that they can reach the highest level of utility given their lifetime resources. This is where the indifference curve (I_2) forms a tangent to the budget constraint and is shown in Figure 9.5.

A key feature of this model is that optimal consumption decisions imply consumption-smoothing behaviour. Faced with fluctuations in income, households are generally better off if they can use saving and borrowing in order to smooth consumption. This is shown quite clearly in Figure 9.5. Ironing out fluctuations in income enables the household to move on to a higher indifference curve ($I_1 \rightarrow I_2$) which represents the achievement of a higher level of lifetime utility, while still being consistent with their lifetime budget constraint. This result is due to the convexity of the indifference curves, which in turn is a consequence of the law of diminishing marginal utility. This always leads to a preference of averages over extremes.

9

So far, this follows the basic model in Chapter 2. Where we now depart is to elaborate more on the process that describes how income is determined.

First, due to the circular flow of income, total household income should equal aggregate output. Output in turn is determined by two things, the level of productivity and the level of capital stock. This can be represented using a simple production function.

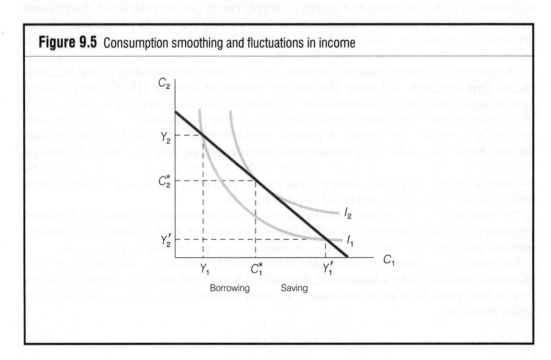

Figure 9.5 Consumption smoothing and fluctuations in income

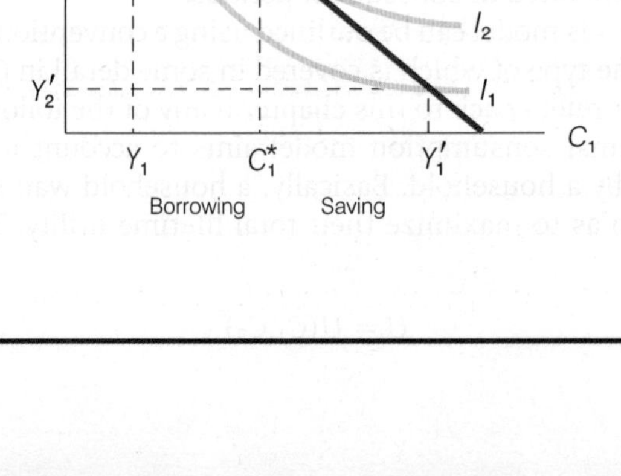

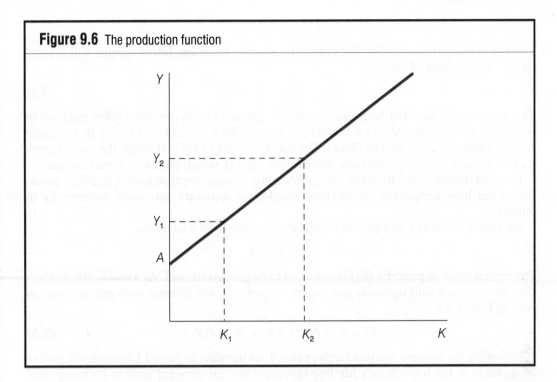

Figure 9.6 The production function

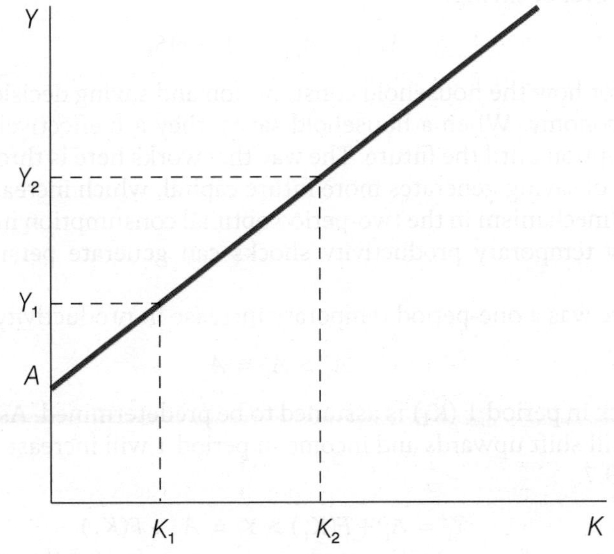

$$Y_t = A_t + (1 + r)K_t \tag{9.3}$$

The production function describes the level of output an economy can produce at each level of capital stock, as seen from Figure 9.6. First, a higher level of capital stock enables a higher level of output to be produced. The production function is linear because there are constant returns to scale with respect to the capital stock. Second, a change in the current level of productivity (A) would lead to a shift in the production function, implying that the same level of capital can then produce a different level of output. No attempt is made in this model to account for the current level of productivity; it can just be thought of as 'manna from heaven'.

By writing the production function in this form – with additive productivity and constant returns in production – the marginal product of capital will always be constant regardless of the current level of productivity or the size of the capital stock. In Chapter 3, we saw that in the optimal capital stock model, investment is largely driven by changes in the marginal product of capital. This form of production function is a simplifying assumption but allows us to emphasize the role that consumption smoothing may play as a propagation mechanism.

The capital stock is determined by the level of saving undertaken by households. Any income that is not used for consumption is saved. However, this will be deposited in financial institutions, which will recycle the funds by lending to firms who will invest. Therefore, the link between saving and capital can be established via a number of identities.

First, all income is either consumed or saved.

$$C_t + S_t = Y_t$$

From the circular flow of income, income and output must be equal to expenditure.

$$C_t + I_t = Y_t$$

Therefore, it can be instantly seen that:

$$S_t = I_t$$

Current investment will then generate the size of the capital stock in the following period.

$$K_{t+1} = I_t$$

Therefore, using these relationships in the production function, future income will depend on the current level of saving.

$$Y_{t+1} = A_{t+1} + (1 + r)S_t \qquad (9.4)$$

This accounts for how the household consumption and saving decisions affect the level of output in an economy. When a household saves, they are effectively trying to postpone current consumption until the future. The way that works here is through the capital stock – a higher level of saving generates more future capital, which increases future income.

By using this mechanism in the two-period optimal consumption model, it is then possible to see how temporary productivity shocks can generate persistent movements in output.

Suppose there was a one-period temporary increase in productivity,

$$A_1' > A_1 = A_2$$

The capital stock in period 1 (K_1) is assumed to be predetermined. As a result, the production function will shift upwards and income in period 1 will increase with productivity, as seen in Figure 9.7.

$$Y_1' = A_1' + F(K_1) > Y_1 = A_1 + F(K_1) \qquad (9.5)$$

Following the unexpected productivity shock, an increase in period 1 income will lead to an increase in the household's lifetime resources and an outward shift in its two-period budget constraint.

$$C_1 + \frac{C_2}{(1+r)} \leq Y_1' + \frac{Y_2}{(1+r)} \qquad (9.6)$$

However, utility maximizing behaviour would require the household to smooth their consumption, so although period 1 income has risen, the household would optimally

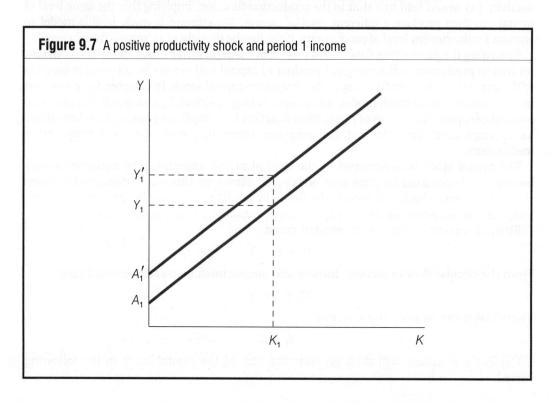

Figure 9.7 A positive productivity shock and period 1 income

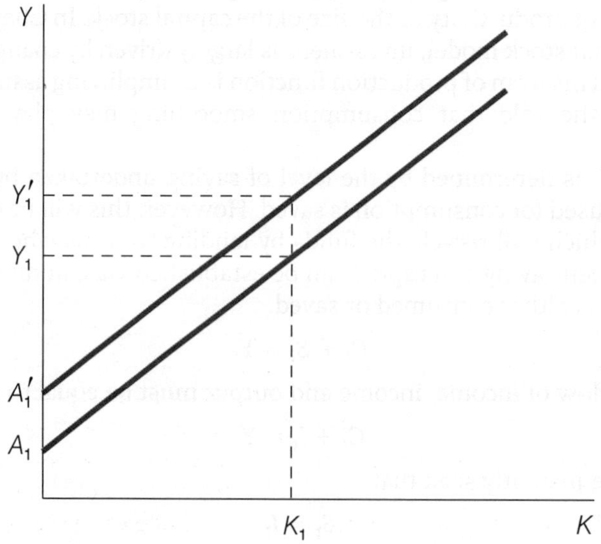

Figure 9.8 An increase in period 1 income and consumption smoothing

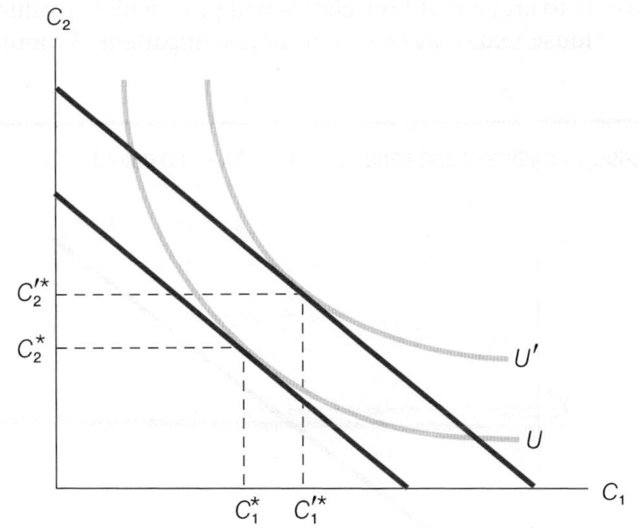

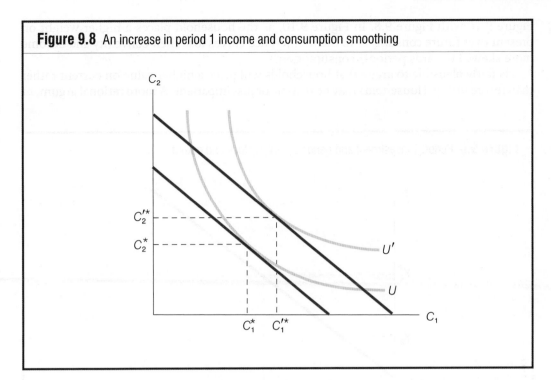

prefer to save more and enjoy higher period 2 consumption as well. In Figure 9.8, the new optimal consumption decision sees higher consumption in both periods.

Postponing consumption requires the household to save some of the current rise in their income for future use. This is achieved through investment. By increasing the period 2 capital stock ($K_2 \rightarrow K'_2$), they can increase future income ($Y_2 \rightarrow Y_2'$), which funds higher future consumption, as seen in Figure 9.9.

This consumption-smoothing behaviour acts as the propagation mechanism which can turn temporary productivity shocks into fairly persistent changes in output. For simplicity, we have just used a two-period model, but the results can be easily generalized to n periods. In this case, consumption-smoothing behaviour would try to increase consumption in all n periods following an initial positive productivity shock. Therefore, the initial increase in income would lead to a higher level of saving, capital stock and output in all of the proceeding periods.

Output persistence and the degree of consumption smoothing

The persistence of output movements depends entirely upon the strength of the propagation mechanism, which in this case is the consumption-smoothing behaviour of households.

The desire to smooth consumption results from the convexity of the indifference curve. The more convex, the more willing households are to smooth consumption. As a result, an initial shock can be propagated over a long period of time. In fact, if there was pure consumption smoothing, then output would rise by the same amount in all periods.

The household indifference curve, however, will lose its convexity the more that future utility is discounted. Effectively, the household's preferences are more weighted towards current consumption, which will be reflected in the shape of the indifference curves. An increase in current income therefore will not generate large increases in saving, and hence the propagation mechanism would be fairly weak. This can be identified by comparing

Figure 9.10 with Figure 9.8. In Figure 9.10, as the household places a higher weight on present over future consumption, the indifference curves lose their convexity and become more skewed towards period 1 consumption.

It is fairly plausible to argue that households will place a higher value on current rather than future utility. Households may be myopic or just impatient. A more rational argument

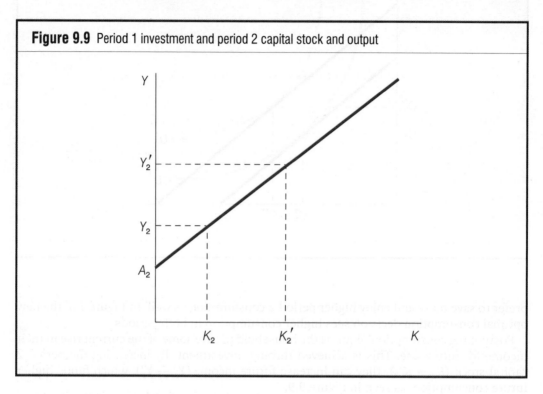

Figure 9.9 Period 1 investment and period 2 capital stock and output

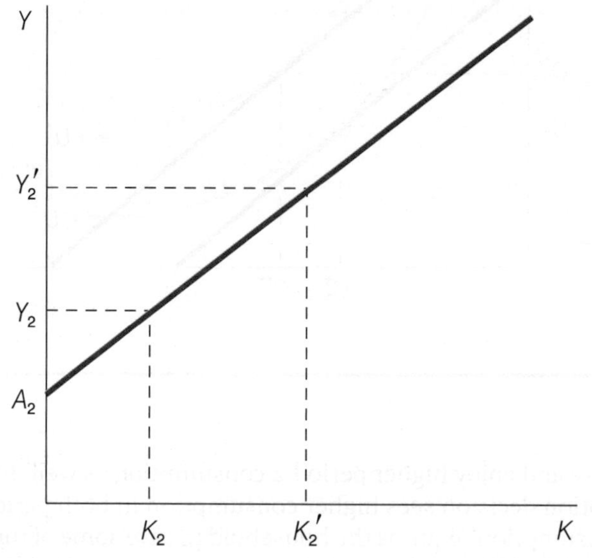

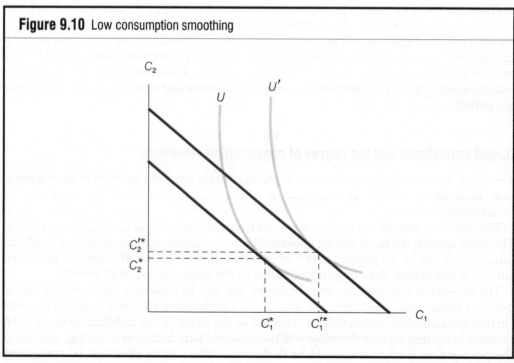

Figure 9.10 Low consumption smoothing

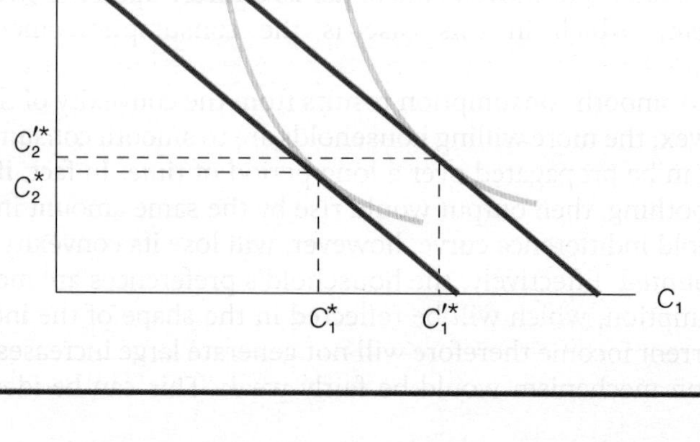

Figure 9.11 Output persistence and discounting

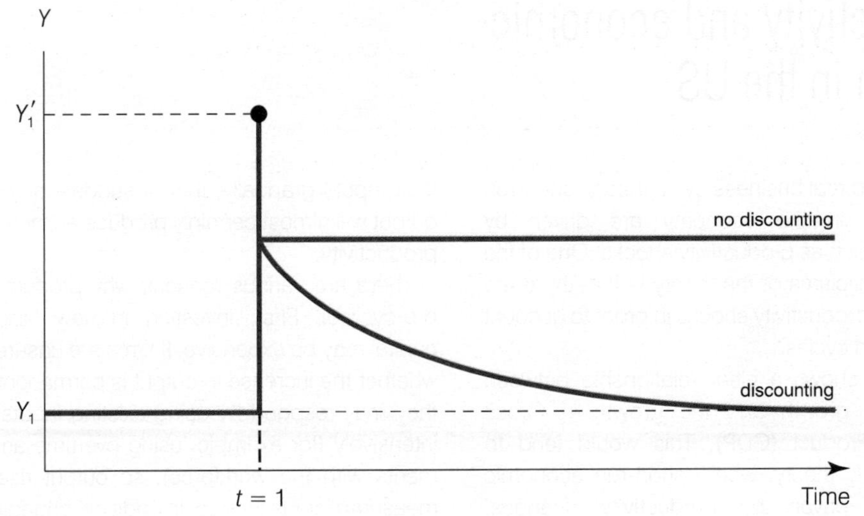

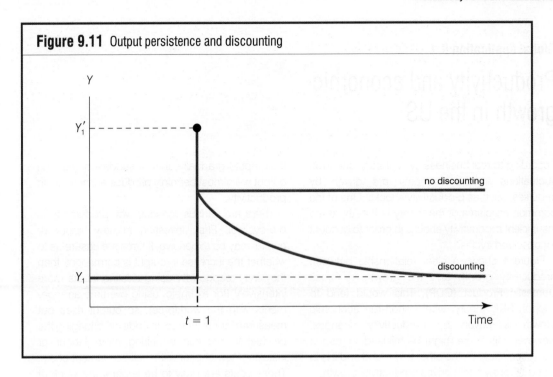

for discounting the future would be a reflection of human mortality – there is less point in making provision for the future when there is a probability that death will occur before it is reached.

Once the future is increasingly discounted, we begin to move away from perfect consumption smoothing. In this case, a current period productivity shock will lead to less persistence in output, as saving and investment taper off over time. This is shown in Figure 9.11, where a positive productivity shock occurs at time $t = 1$, which leads to a one-period increase in income. The extent to which this is propagated forward over time depends on how highly future consumption is discounted.

Evaluating real business cycle models

Theoretically, real business cycles can take some of the intellectual high ground. They produce an explanation of business cycle movements that is fully consistent with households maximizing utility and with market clearing.

Real business cycles are just the combination of impulses and propagation. Therefore, an evaluation of the theory can centre on each of these two parts. In terms of impulses, it could be asked if there are enough of them, and whether are they sufficiently large in order to create the type of cycles that have been experienced in developed economies? In addition, are the propagation mechanisms strong enough to produce the necessary persistence in output movements? These issues are discussed more fully in Global applications 9.1 and 9.2.

Global application 9.1

Productivity and economic growth in the US

According to real business cycle theory, short-run fluctuations in the economy are driven by impulses, such as productivity shocks. One of the common criticisms of the theory is that there are insufficient productivity shocks in order to account for observed cycles.

Figure 1 shows a clear relationship between productivity growth and the growth in Gross Domestic Product (GDP). This would tend to support RBC theory, where short-run economic growth is driven by productivity changes. However, this figure might be misleading, as the causation could be the other way round and it is in fact GDP growth that drives productivity growth.

Productivity is usually defined as the ratio of output to inputs. An increase in productivity refers to the situation where the same amount of input produces greater output. If firms can only adjust their inputs gradually, then a sudden increase in output will almost certainly produce an increase in productivity.

There are various reasons why productivity is pro-cyclical. First, investing in new labour or capital may be expensive. If firms are unsure as to whether the increase in output is permanent, then they may respond by using existing inputs more intensively (for example, using overtime arrangements with the workforce), so output rises but measured inputs less so. In addition, changing the production process by hiring more labour or installing new capital will entail adjustment costs. These costs are likely to be larger if the stock of inputs is changed more rapidly, so gradual adjustments are optimal. This too would account for the pro-cyclicality of productivity.

9

Figure 1 Productivity and GDP growth in the US

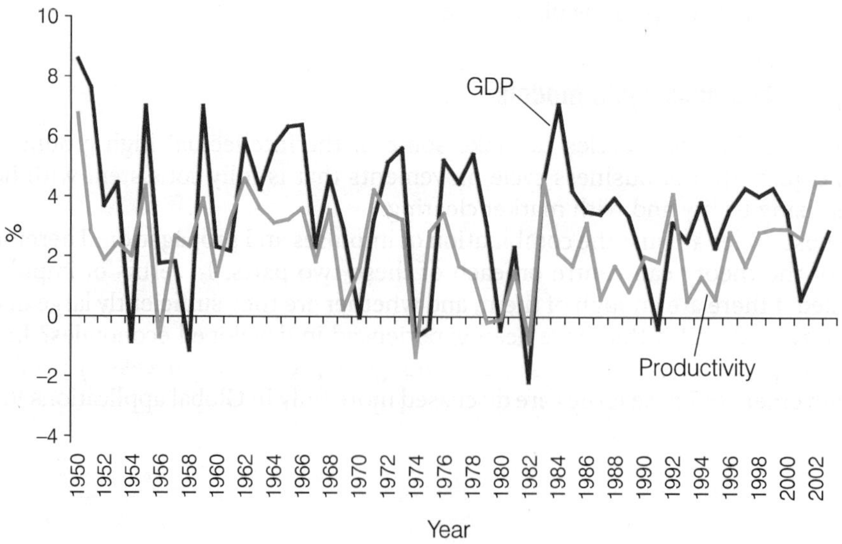

Global application 9.2

Output and employment fluctuations

An important feature of business cycles is there is a large co-movement between employment and output. Hours worked typically account for a large proportion of the change in output. Additionally, the real wage tends to be pro-cyclical, so higher employment is associated with higher real wages. Therefore, if RBC models are to be a credible explanation of cycles, they need to account for these trends.

Intertemporal substitution of work

One explanation for these large pro-cyclical movements in employment was offered by Lucas and Rapping (1969). They suggest that the decision to work and take leisure is part of the household's choice framework, and the decisions made will be consistent with utility maximizing behaviour.

In each time period the household faces a trade-off. Hours spent at work create disutility. Work requires effort and it is time which otherwise could have been spent at leisure. However, by working, households earn income which provides them with the means to consume – an act which generates positive utility. In a single period, the household's hours of work will be determined by its relative preference between consumption and leisure. When this decision becomes a multi-period one, the analysis becomes more complex.

Lucas and Rapping consider a two-period model, where the household utility function will be a function of consumption and work in each period.

$$U = U(C_1, C_2, N_1, N_2)$$

where consumption (C) provides positive utility and work (N) disutility. In making its choice of working hours and consumption level, however, the household will be constrained by an intertemporal budget constraint:

$$C_1 + \frac{C_2}{(1+r)} \leq w_1N_1 + \frac{w_2N_2}{(1+r)}$$

where w is the real wage.

Figure 2a Output and employment growth in the US

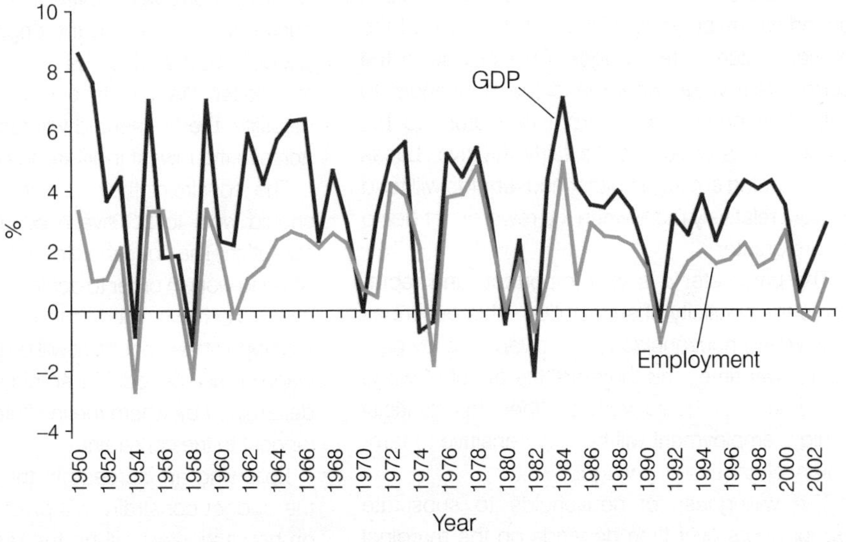

Global application 9.2 (continued)

Figure 2b Output and employment growth in the UK

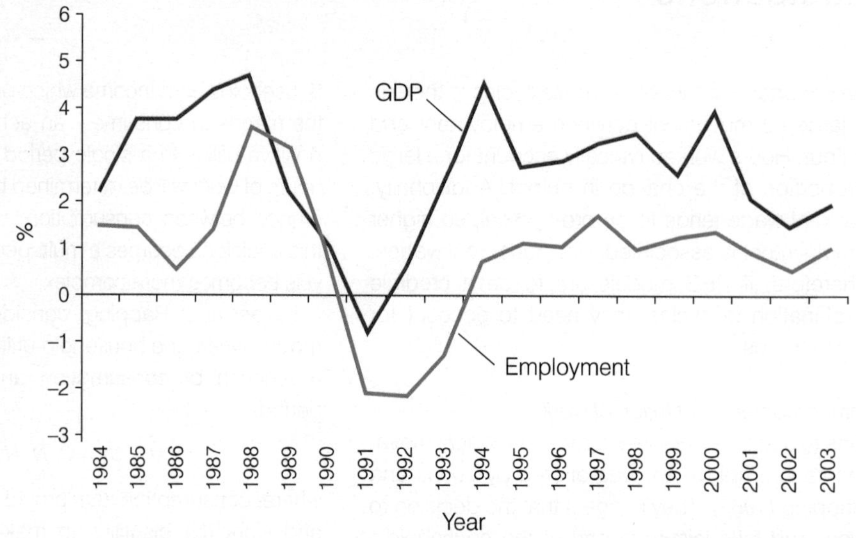

The solution to this maximization problem forms the main conclusion from Lucas and Rapping's work. They derive the following relationship between the number of hours worked in each period and the wage on offer.

$$\frac{N_2}{N_1} = \left(\frac{w_2/(1+r)}{w_1}\right)^{\sigma}$$

The ratio of the number of hours worked in each period will respond positively with the ratio of the present value of real wages. An increase in the current real wage would lead the household to substitute hours worked from the future to the present. This conclusion is fairly intuitive. Lucas and Rapping are arguing that households will tend to work relatively more when the rewards for doing so are greater.

The parameter σ is very important, and represents the elasticity of substitution. This describes how willing households are to swap employment hours over time, and therefore the effect of wage movements on hours worked. When this elasticity is high, employment will be very sensitive to temporary changes in the wage.

The willingness of households to substitute labour hours over time depends on the marginal disutility of work. If working a few extra hours generates a large amount of disutility, then workers will be unprepared to increase their labour hours, even if they are offered higher wages in compensation. When the marginal disutility of work is low, the substitution of hours worked will be that much greater.

This can be understood by considering Figure 3. Here, a household is trying to minimize their disutility from work over time. The indifference curves are concave to the origin as work in either period is bad, and for the household the less done the better. As this is a question of minimizing disutility, the household will rationally be trying to achieve the lowest indifference curve possible.

The constraint they face represents hours they should work to achieve a certain amount of consumption. The household decision is then to choose when to work in order to achieve sufficient resources so as to achieve a certain level of consumption, and the slope of the constraint will be given by the relative wage in each period. The employment choice is then determined by where the indifference curve forms a tangent to the constraint.

Following an increase in the first period wage, the budget constraint will pivot. The overall effect on hours worked will be the result of substitution

Global application 9.2 (continued)

Figure 3 The elasticity of substitution and hours worked

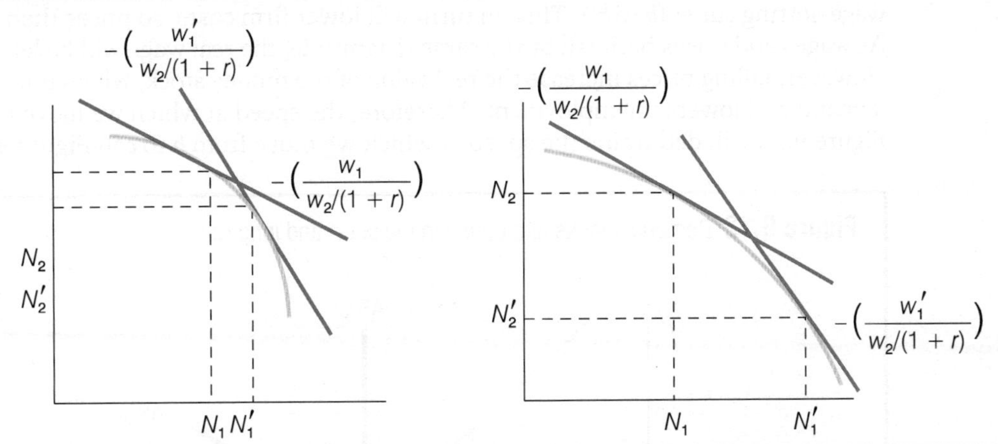

and income effects. An income effect would be expected to reduce the number of hours worked in each period, as now wages are higher so the same level of consumption is achievable with fewer overall hours being worked. Lucas and Rapping argue though that income effects will be small when considering short-run and temporary changes in wages. They argue that the substitution effect will be more significant.

It is clear from Figure 3 that the substitution effect is much greater where the concavity of the indifference curve is lower. This represents a higher elasticity of substitution.

Temporary versus permanent changes in the real wage

If the change in wages were permanent, then there would be no need to substitute hours of work across periods. In this case, there would be no change in the ratio of wages and no change in the ratio of hours worked. The only impact is an income effect which leads either to changes in leisure or consumption.

Therefore, generating a strong co-movement between output (productivity shocks) and employment requires an elastic response to temporary changes in the real wage.

9

9.4 New Keynesian theories of fluctuations

In the previous chapter, we dedicated a significant amount of time to deriving and using the aggregate demand and supply (AD-AS) model. What is clear is that, in the long run, the economy cannot deviate from the equilibrium level of output. However, this is not the case for the short run. Therefore, following a demand shock, the economy can settle at a different level of output in both the short and the long run.

In Figure 9.12, it can be seen that following a negative demand shock, output will fall below the equilibrium level of output in the short run. Over time, wages and prices will fall and the economy will move to its new long-run equilibrium, but this may only happen gradually, in which case the demand shock has a persistent effect on output. This type of slow adjustment is required to account for cycles of a reasonable duration.

When output falls below its equilibrium level, it implies that unemployment has risen above the non-accelerating inflation rate of unemployment (NAIRU). The process by which unemployment returns to the NAIRU and output to the equilibrium level is seen in the bargaining model introduced in the previous chapter.

Once unemployment is above the natural rate, two things must happen for it to return to the natural rate. The first is that nominal wages must fall, so that we move back onto the wage-setting curve (*b* to *b'*). This, in turn, will lower firm costs, so prices then fall (*b'* to *c*). As wages and prices both fall by the same magnitude, the real wage will be left unchanged. However, falling prices increase the real value of the money stock, which boosts aggregate demand and lowers unemployment. Therefore, the speed at which we move from *b* to *c* in Figure 9.13 will determine the speed at which we move from *b* to *c* in Figure 9.12.

Figure 9.12 Demand shocks and output in the short and long run

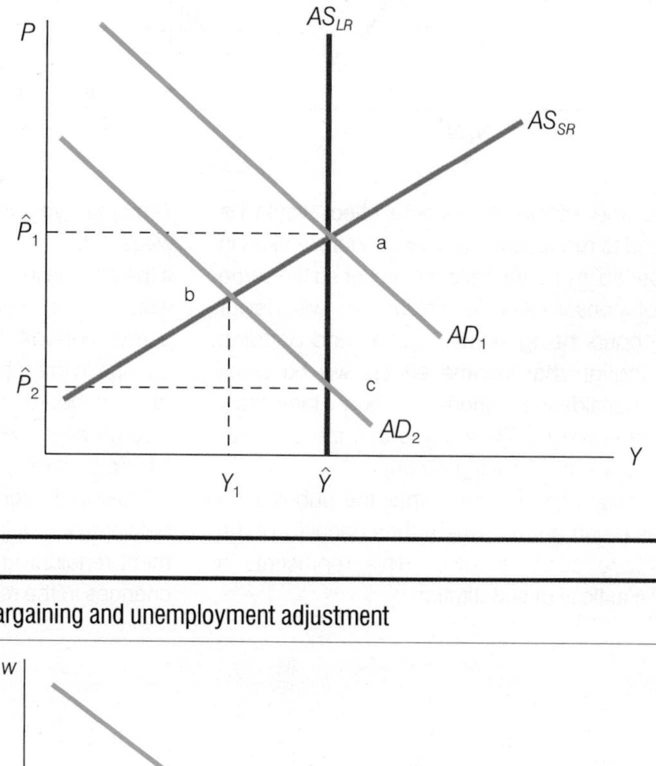

Figure 9.13 Bargaining and unemployment adjustment

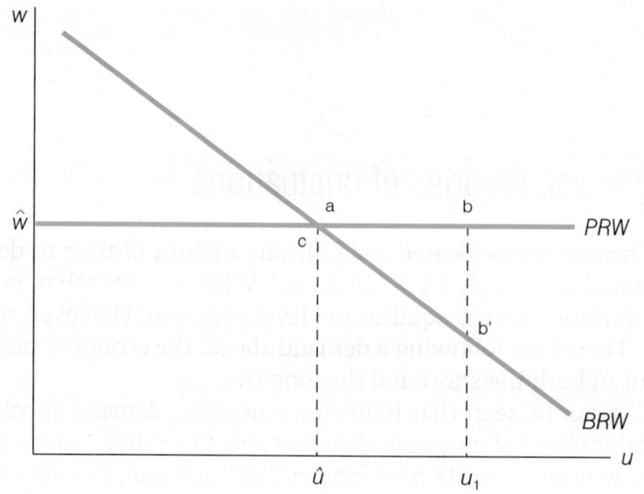

Once it is accepted that wages and prices might adjust slowly, it is then apparent why output can deviate from the equilibrium level for sustained periods. The new Keynesian approach to business cycles argues that this is the case – demand shocks will generate persistent movements in output because wages and prices respond very sluggishly. The new Keynesian contribution to the study of business cycles is to account for rigidities in wages and prices.

9.4.1 Wage rigidities

There are several factors which may account for slow wage adjustments when the labour market is in a position of excess demand or supply. These fall into three camps. The first simply looks at contracting, suggesting that there is only a limited ability to change wages at a given moment in time. The second considers the category of efficiency wages. This argues that wages may actually be set by firms, and at levels which take into consideration a much larger array of factors than just current unemployment. Therefore, there is less reason for wages to change because of a disequilibrium in the labour market. Finally we look at the bargaining and institutional structures which make up the labour market, and what effect they might have on wage flexibility.

Wage bargaining on pay day is usually unproductive…

Source: Getty Images

Contracts

As wage negotiations tend to be done annually, it follows that at any other point in time there may be a very limited scope to adjust wages. Therefore, it is not surprising that wages may only adjust slowly and with lags to shocks. However, is this sufficient to explain cycles that may last for several years?

In addition, contracts may be designed so as to provide workers with a type of wage insurance. We have seen in Chapter 2, and also earlier in this chapter, that it might be an optimal course of action for households to try to smooth consumption in the face of fluctuating income. However, households may be constrained in their access

9

to credit markets, which prevents the effective smoothing of fluctuating income over the cycle. Firms, though, have better access to capital markets and can maintain income insurance with their workers.

Although a plausible-sounding argument, wage insurance must be viewed with a degree of caution. After all, why would workers choose wage insurance over job insurance? Global application 9.3 discusses some of the issues.

Global application 9.3

Wage insurance or job insurance?

A simple type of bargaining model between a firm and a labour union is known as the *right to manage*. The union chooses the wage and once this has been decided, the firm then chooses employment. Therefore, what wage should the union press for?

In deciding the wage, the union will take into account the employment actions of the firm. The amount of labour the firm will hire given the wage will be determined by a downward-sloping labour demand curve. If the union has preferences over employment and wages, they will choose the combination that enables them to achieve the highest possible indifference curve subject to the constraint of the firm's labour demand curve.

The union's utility maximizing choice of employment and wage is given by (W_1,N_1).

If the demand for labour were to fall, would it be optimal for the union to continue to push for a wage of W_1? In Figure 5, labour demand falls, $N_1^d \rightarrow N_2^d$. The union would clearly be better off by choosing the combination (W_2,N_2) over (W_1,N_3).

Therefore, as long as the union has a preference for employment as well as wages, it is hard to see why they will contract on fixed wages. In fact, as the preference for maintaining employment becomes stronger, workers will be more prepared to compromise on wages in order to maintain employment levels.

9

Figure 4 Union choice of wages and employment

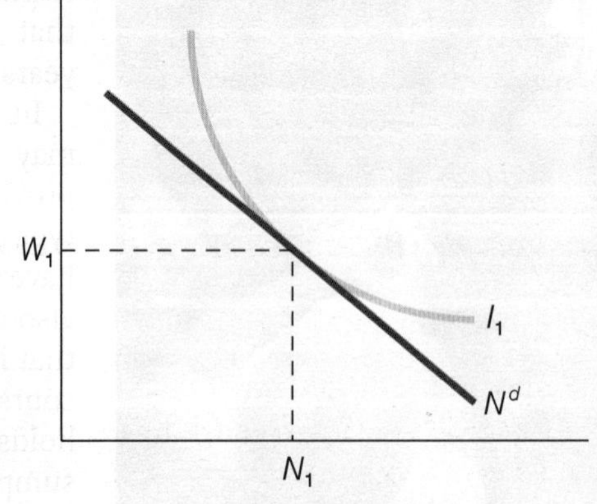

Global application 9.3 (continued)

Figure 5 A fall in labour demand and the wage–employment bargain

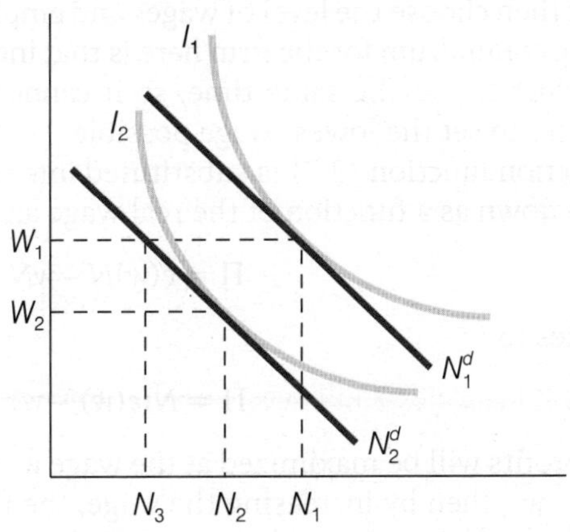

Efficiency wages

Typically, wages are seen as a cost to firms and therefore the lower they are the better. The general concept of an efficiency wage, though, is that wage cuts may actually be counter-productive to a firm's performance. Although it would enable the firm to cut costs, a lower wage may actually act to reduce the firm's output or quality of its goods or services.

Efficiency wage theories start from the premise that worker effort or quality may increase with the level of the wage offered. Therefore, increasing wages may increase wage costs, but at the same time by raising productivity, they also act to effectively reduce costs. This explains why wages might be rigid, especially in a downward fashion. Firms are concerned that cutting wages will damage productivity.

A basic model of efficiency wages Following Solow (1979), output does not just depend upon the amount of labour employed, but also on the effort which is exerted.

$$Y = e(w)N \tag{9.7}$$

where e is effort, w the real wage and N is employment. In this case, $e(w)N$ can be thought of as the effective labour input, i.e., the number of workers multiplied by the effort exerted by each.

The effort level exerted by workers is deemed to increase with the wage offered.

$$\frac{\Delta e(w)}{\Delta w} > 0$$

The demand for labour is derived from the demand for output. Once the firm knows what the demand for its product is, it then hires sufficient labour in order to produce that level of output.

$$N^d = \frac{Y}{e(w)} \tag{9.8}$$

9

The labour demand curve therefore will be downward sloping with respect to the wage. As the wage falls, each worker that the firm hires will exert less effort. Therefore, to produce each level of output the firm must hire more workers.

The firm's profits are determined by revenues minus costs:

$$\Pi = Y - wN \tag{9.9}$$

The firm must then choose the level of wages and employment in order to maximize profit. The interesting conundrum for the firm here is that increasing wages both increases labour costs and productivity at the same time, so it cannot be taken for granted that the firm would simply try to set the lowest wage possible.

If the production function (9.7) is substituted into the profit function (9.9), then profits can be written down as a function of the real wage and employment.

$$\Pi = e(w)N - wN \tag{9.10}$$

which simplifies to

$$\Pi = N(e(w) - w) \tag{9.11}$$

Therefore, profits will be maximized at the wage w^* where the value of $(e(w^*) - w^*)$ is the greatest. If $w < w^*$, then by increasing the wage, the firm can increase profits because the marginal product of labour exceeds its marginal cost. A wage increase will lead to more effort and the value of the extra output produced will exceed the extra cost of the labour, so profits will rise. When $w > w^*$, reducing the wage will increase profits because the wage costs saved would exceed the value of output lost through lower effort. The firm will maximize profits by setting wages $w = w^*$. At this wage level, employment is simply given by:

$$N^d = \frac{Y}{e(w^*)} \tag{9.12}$$

9

Changes in demand will have no impact on the wage, only on the level of employment.

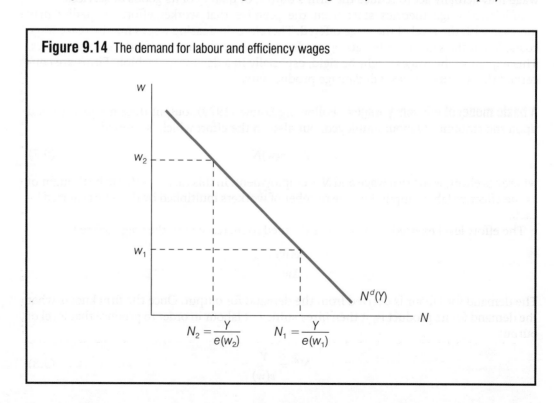

Figure 9.14 The demand for labour and efficiency wages

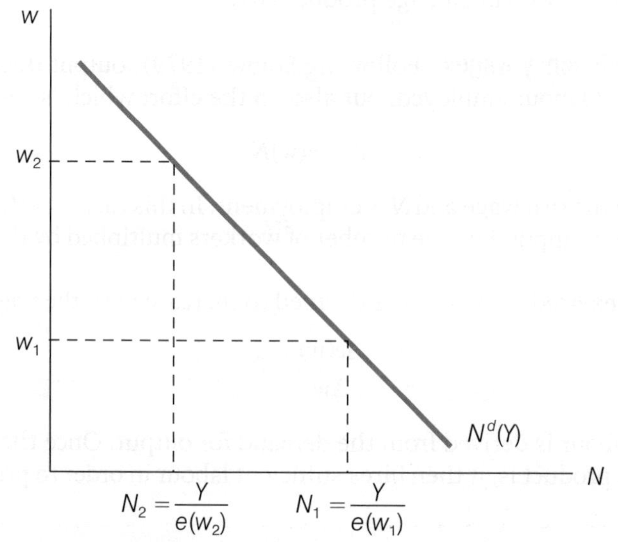

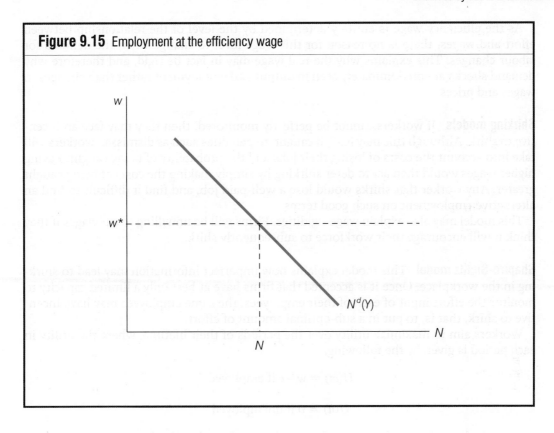

Figure 9.15 Employment at the efficiency wage

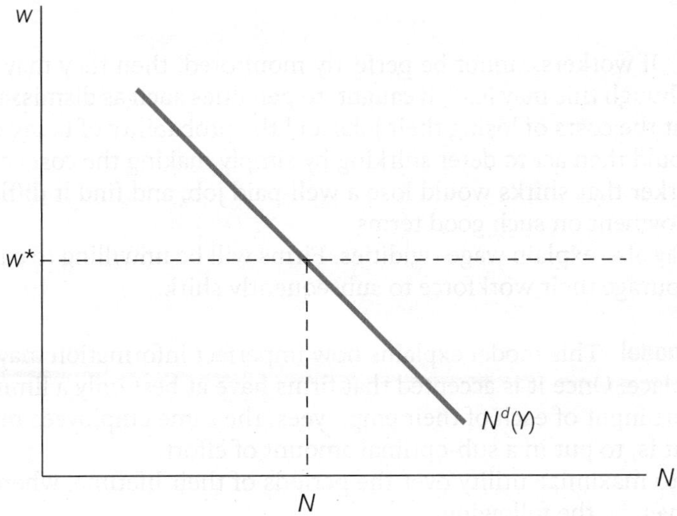

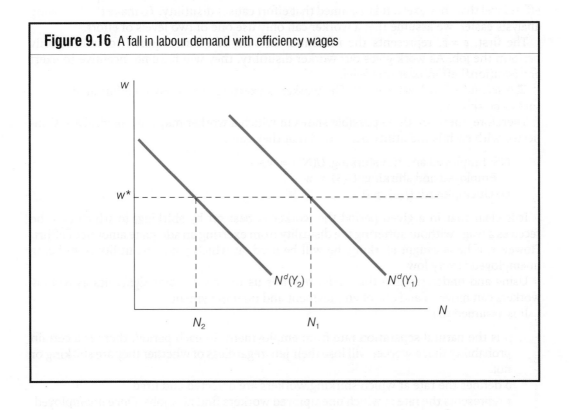

Figure 9.16 A fall in labour demand with efficiency wages

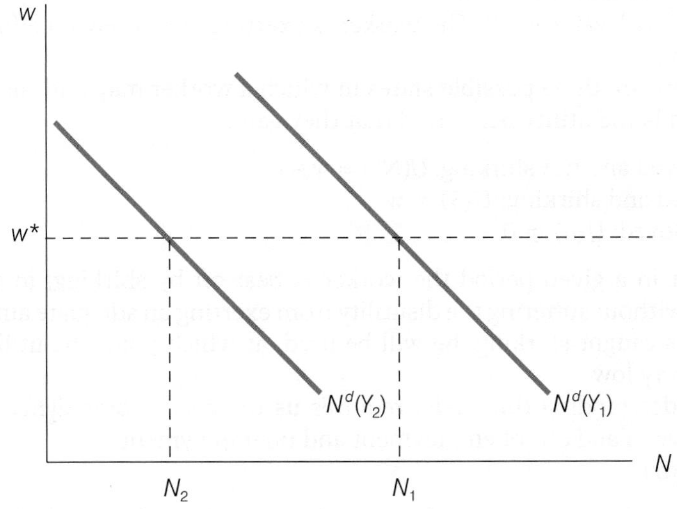

As the efficiency wage is entirely determined by the level of the relationship between effort and wages, there is no reason for this wage level to change when the demand for labour changes. This explains why the real wage may in fact be rigid, and therefore why demand shocks are predominately seen in output and employment rather than changes in wages and prices.

Shirking models If workers cannot be perfectly monitored, then they may face an incentive to shirk. Although this may lead, if caught, to penalties such as dismissal, workers will take into account the costs of losing their jobs and the probability of being caught. Paying higher wages would then act to deter shirking by simply making the costs of being caught greater. Any worker that shirks would lose a well-paid job, and find it difficult to find an alternative employment on such good terms.

This model may also explain wage rigidities. Firms will be unwilling to cut wages if they think it will encourage their workforce to subsequently shirk.

Shapiro-Siglitz model This model explains how imperfect information may lead to shirking in the workplace. Once it is accepted that firms have at best only a limited capacity to monitor the effort input of each of their employees, the same employees may have incentive to shirk, that is, to put in a sub-optimal amount of effort.

Workers aim to maximize utility over the periods of their lifetime, where the utility in each period is given by the following:

$$U(N) = w - e \text{ if employed}$$

$$U(u) = 0 \text{ if unemployed}$$

where w is the real wage that an employee will earn if employed, whereas e represents the effort level that they exert. It is assumed that effort causes disutility. To make the following analysis easier, we assume that a worker can only use one of two levels of effort.

9

The first, $e = \bar{e}$, represents the minimum amount of effort required to satisfactorily perform the job. As work gives our worker disutility, they will have no incentive to exert any additional effort over this level.

The second effort level is $e = 0$. The worker is exerting absolutely no effort at all and is said to be shirking.

Therefore, there are three possible states in which a worker may find themselves. Connected with each is the utility per period that they gain.

NS: Employed and not shirking: $U(NS) = w - \bar{e}$
S: Employed and shirking: $U(S) = w$
U: Unemployed: $U(u) = 0$

It is clear that in a given period the worker is best off by shirking, in which case he receives a wage without suffering the disutility from exerting an adequate amount of effort. However, if he is caught shirking, he will be fired, at which point the utility from being unemployed is very low.

Using and understanding the model requires us to specify some dynamics as to how workers can move in and out of employment and unemployment.

It is assumed that:

ρ is the natural separation rate from employment. In each period, there is a certain probability that a worker will lose their job, regardless of whether they are shirking or not.

δ defines the rate at which shirking workers are detected and fired.

τ represents the rate at which unemployed workers find new jobs. Once unemployed, workers may be rehired by other firms.

Figure 9.17 The no shirking condition (NSC)

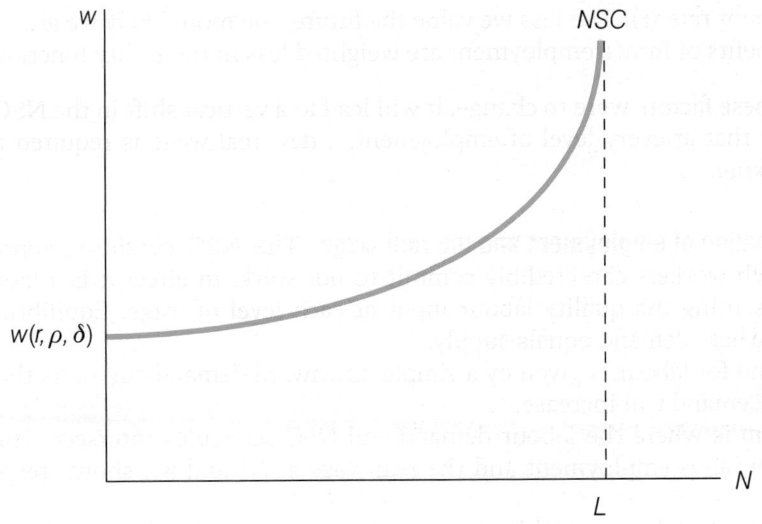

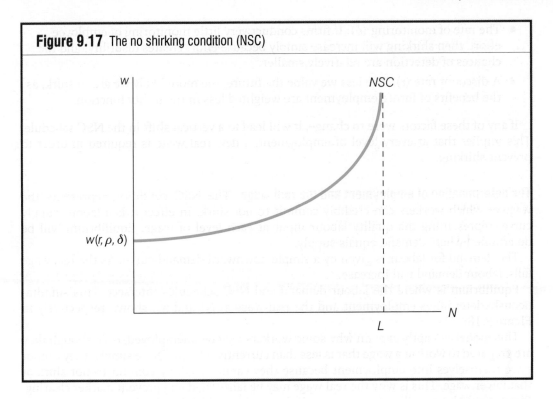

This is all we need to know in order to derive the no shirking condition (NSC). This is defined as the level of wage at which the worker will decide it is optimal not to shirk. Simply put, it is the level of wages where the benefits of working and exerting effort outweigh the benefits of shirking.

The no shirking condition (NSC) is a function of employment; it tells us the wage at each level of employment the firm must offer to prevent its workforce from shirking. An example of such a rule is shown in Figure 9.17.

There are two important things to note about the NSC curve. It is upward-sloping with respect to the level of employment and becomes asymptotic when approaching the full employment level.

The reason for this is fairly intuitive. As we reach full employment, the probability of finding another job if made unemployed (τ) approaches 1. Therefore, there is no incentive not to shirk, as even if you are detected and fired, then the chances of immediately being rehired are very good. Unemployment can serve as a worker disciplining device, but if the labour market is very buoyant there is little disciplining effect. The only recourse open to the firm to prevent shirking is to offer a high wage which would encourage workers to value their existing employment. However, because other firms will find themselves in a similar position, the alternative wage prospects will also be very high, so the wage would have to rise fairly quickly to prevent shirking as the full employment level is reached.

The second important consideration concerning the NSC is where the curve intersects the wage axis. This tells us the level of wages required so that the first employee will not shirk. It will depend upon:

- The natural separation rate (ρ): As this increases workers are more likely to shirk. This is because the incentives not to shirk arise from the ability to draw a good future wage. If there is a high separation rate, then a higher initial wage must be paid to induce the required effort level.

- The rate of monitoring (δ): If firms conduct very little monitoring of employee effort, then shirking will increase simply because effort creates disutility, and the chances of detection are relatively smaller.
- A discount rate (r): The less we value the future, the more likely we are to shirk, as the benefits of future employment are weighted less in the utility function.

If any of these factors were to change, it will lead to a vertical shift in the NSC schedule. This implies that at every level of employment, a new real wage is required in order to prevent shirking.

The determination of employment and the real wage The NSC condition represents the wage at which workers can credibly commit to not shirk. In effect it is a labour supply curve, representing the quality labour input at each level of wage. Equilibrium will be determined where demand equals supply.

The demand for labour is given by a simple downward demand curve. As the real wage falls, labour demand will increase.

Equilibrium is where the labour demand and NSC schedules intersect. This simultaneously determines employment and the real wage at N^* and w^*, shown respectively in Figure 9.18.

This model can aptly explain why some workers may be unemployed, even though they are prepared to work at a wage that is less than currently offered. Quite simply, they cannot price themselves into employment because they cannot credibly commit to not shirk at that lower wage. This is why the real wage may be fairly rigid and prevent market clearing. Firms would be unwilling to cut wages if they feel it will lead to a substantial decrease in effort.

Therefore, following a fall in labour demand, it is plausible that the equilibrium wage will only fall to a limited extent, and much of the fall in demand will translate itself into a fall in employment (see Figure 9.19).

Figure 9.18 Equilibrium wages and employment

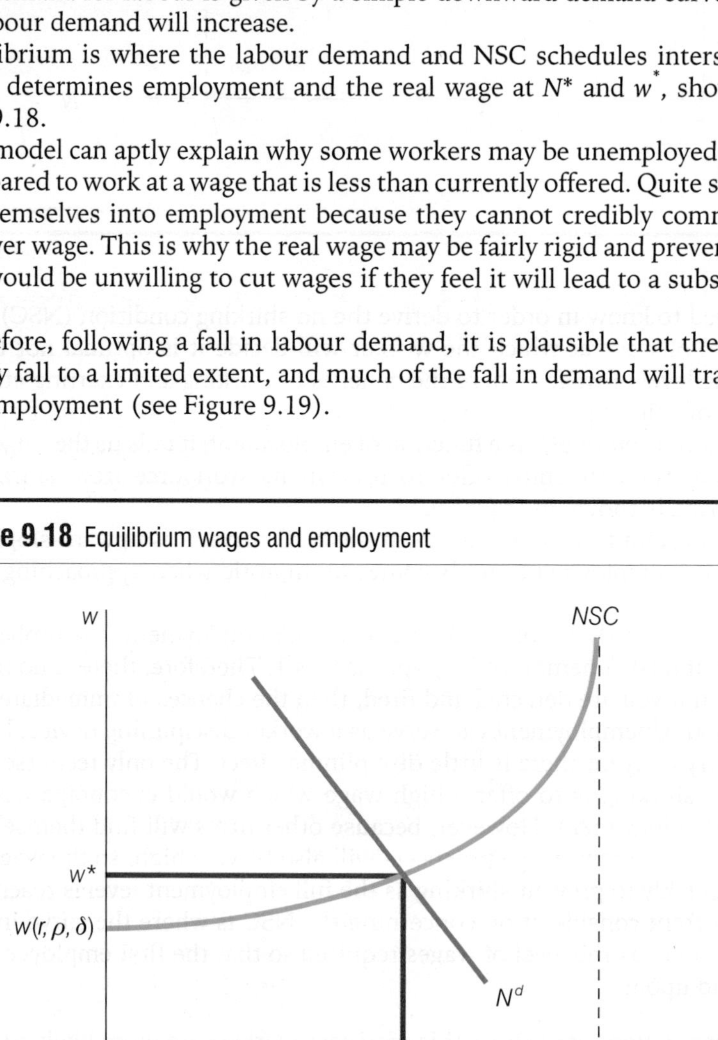

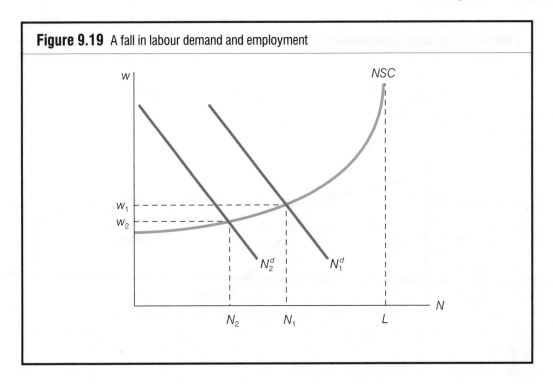

Figure 9.19 A fall in labour demand and employment

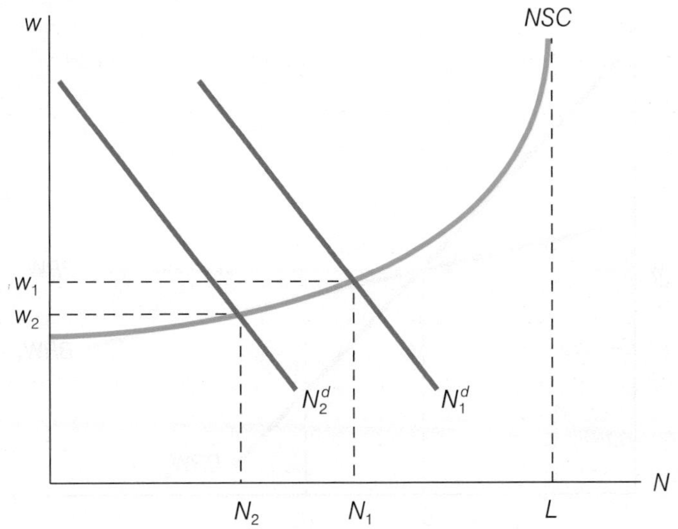

This Shapiro-Stiglitz model offers an explanation as to why firms are happier to lay-off workers rather than reduce wages or come up with work-sharing agreements. Shocks to aggregate demand therefore will be felt more heavily in changes in employment rather than wages.

All models of efficiency wages share the idea that wages are set at an optimal level, usually to maximize the productivity of labour. Therefore, following an increase in unemployment, firms are reluctant to let wages drop and are more content to allow for adjustments to bear on employment.

Labour market institutions

The wage-setting curve outlined in the previous section identifies the wage that workers will push for at every level of unemployment.

$$\frac{W}{P} = Z - \beta u \tag{9.13}$$

A key feature of this relationship is the parameter β. This describes the responsiveness of wage claims to the level of unemployment, and therefore plays an important role in defining how quickly wages will adjust when the labour market is in excess demand or supply.

The larger the value of β, the more responsive wage demands are to unemployment and the steeper is the wage-setting curve. If we look at Figure 9.20, we will see that when β is lower, the wage-setting curve is flatter (BRW_1). A rise in unemployment to u_1 will only generate a small reduction in the bargained real wage, so wage adjustment would be smaller. This would then feed into smaller price adjustments and higher unemployment becomes more persistent.

When β is larger, the wage-setting schedule is steeper (BRW_2), so the bargained real wage responds much faster to unemployment. If this then feeds through into prices, adjustment back to $\hat{u}$ will be more rapid, so the increase in unemployment is less persistent.

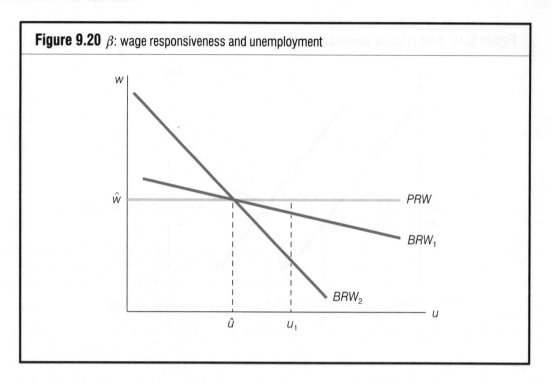

Figure 9.20 β: wage responsiveness and unemployment

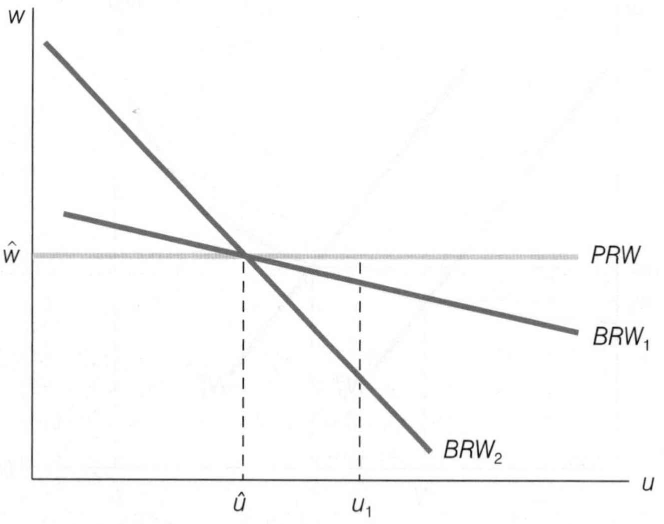

In explaining adjustments, the size of β then takes on an added importance, but what is it that determines the size of this parameter? One line of reasoning is that it is largely accounted for by the institutional structure of the labour market. If unemployment were to rise, then downward pressure on wages and then prices would be sufficient to restore unemployment to the equilibrium rate. However, under what types of market structure are wages most likely to fall?

Competitive labour markets A competitive labour market is characterized by a high degree of mobility. This means that a large number of workers can quickly fill any position.

Therefore, in competitive labour markets, the reserve army effect of unemployed workers would be expected to be very strong. Any worker would know and anticipate that unemployed workers could successfully price themselves into work by offering to work at lower wages. In the presence of unemployment, it would then be expected that wages would be very flexible.

Imperfect labour markets Under imperfect competition, there is some degree of control over the labour supply, perhaps due to union power. Workers have more power because they cannot be replaced quickly by unemployed workers. The outcome of wage bargaining then might generate rigidities in wages.

In imperfect labour markets, a fall in labour demand creating unemployment would create a conundrum for a union. If all unions were to push for lower wages, then lower prices would result and unemployment will begin to correct. However, a typical labour union would work in the best interests of its members, and this may create incentives to not cut wages.

For example, if all the other unions were to cut their wages, then the price level in the economy would be expected to fall sufficiently to restore aggregate demand. However, if one union were to resist cutting wages, its members would continue to enjoy higher wages, and at the same time, because they only represent a small subset of the labour market, they have not prevented the aggregate price level from falling sufficiently.

Figure 9.21 The prisoner's dilemma game and wage bargaining

		Union 2	
		Cut	Fix
Union 1	Cut	5,5	–5,10
	Fix	10,–5	0,0

Also, suppose no other union were to cut its wages. Would it be optimal for this union to press a wage reduction on its members? The answer is obviously no. As all the other unions have failed to cut wages, one union acting on its own is unlikely to lower the price level to restore aggregate demand, but in doing so would lower the compensation of their members.

Therefore, regardless of the actions of other unions, each union always faces a fairly powerful incentive to avoid making wage cuts. This can lead the economy to become stuck in a high wage, high unemployment equilibrium. This scenario is an application of the well-known prisoner's dilemma game. An example of this game is represented in Figure 9.21.

There are two unions who each attempt to achieve the highest pay-off possible. Each union has the choice of cutting the wage or fixing it at its current level. If neither cuts wages, then each receives a pay-off of zero. However, if they both cut their wages, then it would lower firm costs and lead to an improvement in aggregate demand and employment.

When one union cuts its wage, it is optimal for the other to keep its fixed. This way the union benefits from the other unions cutting their wages, but at the same time keeps high wages for its own members. The solution of this game is for both unions to fix their wage. This is because no matter what one union does, it is always optimal for the other to keep their wages fixed. However, the fix-fix equilibrium is purely sub-optimal, as all unions would be better if they could move to the cut-cut equilibrium.

Fixed wages arise due to a failure in coordination among unions. One union will only benefit from cutting wages if the action is reciprocated by the others. But, as other unions cut wages, the benefits of fixing the wage become larger.

Corporatism One solution to the prisoner's dilemma game outlined above would be to try to get unions to coordinate their actions. If this were possible, then they would recognize that by working together and cutting wages in the face of unemployment a mutually agreeable outcome would arise. The problem though now becomes, how can we get unions to coordinate their actions?

A natural solution is corporatism. This refers to the very centralized system of bargaining primarily used in Scandinavian countries up to the 1990s. Under a corporatist labour market, bargaining is conducted at a highly centralized level, where all unions and employer groups meet to determine labour contracts. Making it much easier for unions to coordinate their actions in order to restore employment.

Therefore, it appears to be the case that wage rigidities may be linked to the degree of centralization in the wage bargaining process. At low and high levels of centralization respectively (the competitive and corporatist structures) wages tend to be more flexible and unemployment is more short-lived. However, in markets characterized by imperfect competition, evidence suggests that wage rigidities may lead to longer-lasting unemployment.

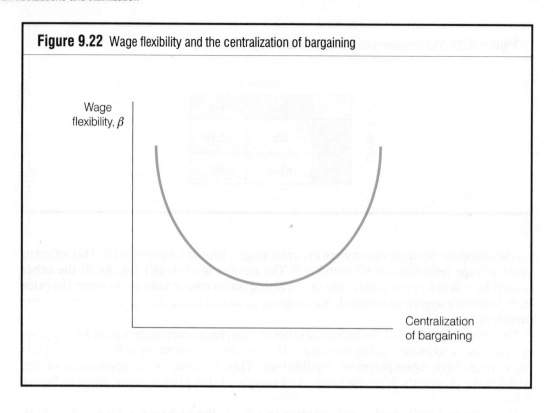

Figure 9.22 Wage flexibility and the centralization of bargaining

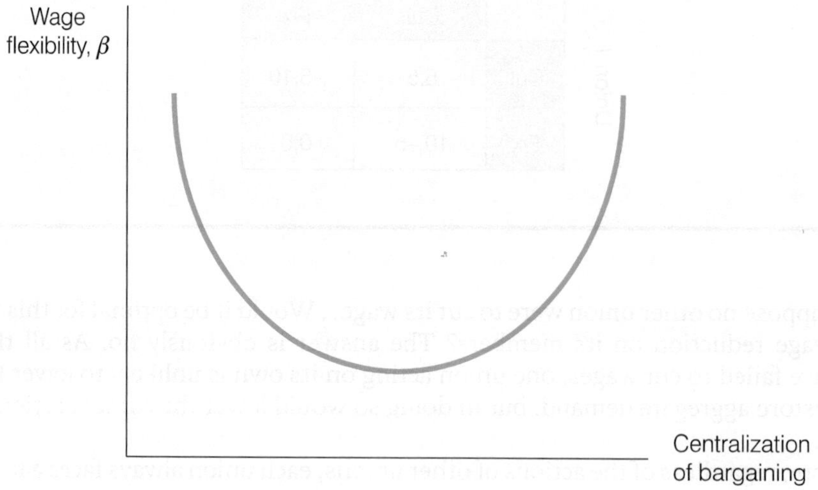

9.4.2 Price rigidities

Menu costs

These are the real resources that are used up in changing prices; for example, if a restaurant had to reprint its menus. It is often argued that these play a limited role in creating price rigidities. Menu costs are not considered to be important, and a typical firm will usually change prices when the costs of not doing so exceed the menu cost.

However, if combined with other factors, the small rigidities implied by menu costs actually may be much more significant. If firms face little incentive to change prices in the first place, then the additional menu costs of doing so may be very significant at the margin.

From the price-setting curve, we can see that prices are set as a mark-up on labour costs. If there are wage rigidities, then fluctuations in unemployment will generate small increases in wage demands and therefore a small incentive for the firm to change prices. The imposition of small menu costs can then act to reinforce price rigidities.

Kinked demand curve

The kinked demand curve is a concept of oligopolistic markets. An oligopoly is a form of imperfect competition where the market consists of a few large firms. The kink in the demand curve arises because the price elasticity of demand is different depending on whether the firm is raising or cutting prices.

When a firm cuts prices, other firms will respond in a similar fashion in order to preserve their market share. Therefore, demand is price inelastic and a cut in prices will reduce revenues. If, however, a firm were to increase prices, the other firms would not follow and

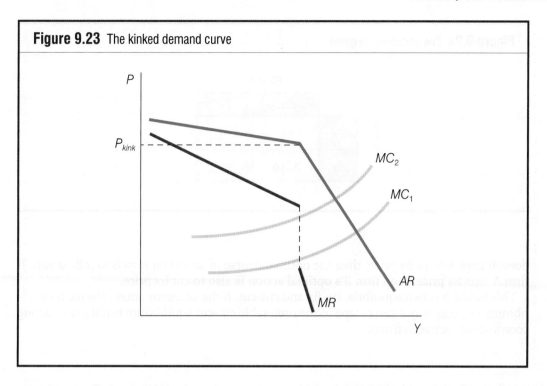

Figure 9.23 The kinked demand curve

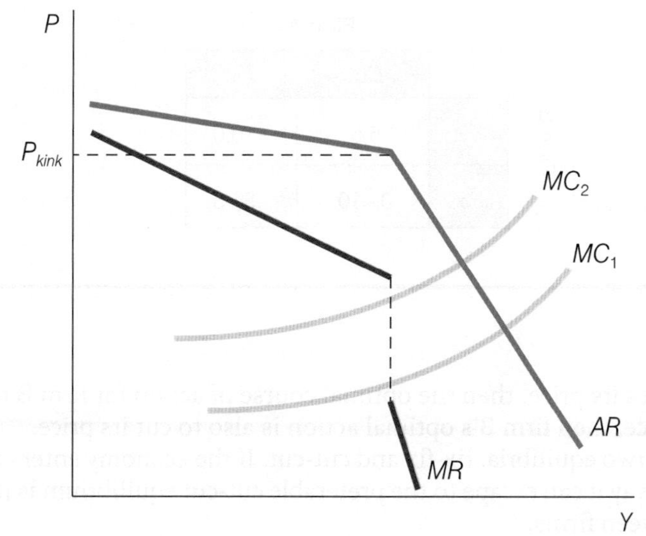

instead would be happy to snap up an increased market share. Demand is now price elastic, so raising the price will also lead to a fall in revenues (see Figure 9.23).

Prices are set to maximize profits, which is where marginal revenue is equal to marginal cost. With a kink in the demand curve, there will be a discontinuity in the corresponding marginal revenue curve. As a result, there are several different levels of marginal cost that all have the same level of profit maximizing prices. In this case, prices will be rigid.

One possible justification for the kinked demand curve is proposed by Stiglitz. If consumers search across many firms for the lowest prices and all prices start off being equal, then a kinked demand curve can result. If firms were to lower prices, it will attract few additional customers, simply because searching is expensive. However, if it were to raise prices, it will lose customers who may feel that they can achieve a better price else where.

Recessions as the result of coordination failure

An important issue in price setting is an externality relationship among firms. If one firm were to reduce prices, it should have a small effect on the overall price level, which then subsequently affects the demand for the products made by other firms. Blanchard and Kiyotaki (1987) refer to this as an aggregate demand externality. Its presence is potentially very important in explaining why prices are rigid. An individual firm will not take these externalities into consideration when setting prices, but in the aggregate they are very important. Price rigidities result. A lack of coordination among firms leads to only very gradual or staggered changes in prices, where firms wait and see what others have done before setting prices.

The coordination problem can best be viewed by using a common game known as the coordination game (see Figure 9.24).

There are two firms which can each decide whether or not to cut prices. For the economy to recover from the recession, both need to cut prices. This is an example of a coordination game because the optimal course of action is for each firm to do exactly what the other

Figure 9.24 The coordination game

Firm B \ Firm A	Cut	Fix
Cut	5,5	−10,0
Fix	0,−10	−5,−5

does. If firm A fixes its price, then the optimal course of action for firm B to follow suit. If firm A cuts its price, then firm B's optimal action is also to cut its price.

This model has two equilibria: fix-fix and cut-cut. If the economy enters the fix-fix equilibrium, the only way it can escape to the preferable cut-cut equilibrium is if there is strong coordination between firms.

9.5 Stabilization policies

There are two main reasons why policy makers might wish to intervene and iron out the business cycle. First, there are welfare losses associated with fluctuating income. If households are permanent income consumers, they are made better off in terms of lifetime utility if they can smooth income. Second, short-run cycles may actually lower the trend rate of growth. Volatility could impede investment which drives long-run growth, and hysteresis mechanisms imply that short-run movements in output and unemployment can be very persistent.

Despite this, there are several grounds against using an active policy response to smooth the economic cycle. If markets clear quickly, then active policy will be unnecessary, as prices will adjust and quickly reverse the cycle. In addition, policy intervention may be harmful as it can interfere with this automatic adjustment process. Second, policy makers may find it difficult to implement the correct policies for two reasons.

Lags

Recognition lags relate to the fact that before the government can implement corrective policy, it must first recognize the problem that needs to be tackled. *Implementation lags* refer to the issue that policy cannot be altered straight away. Fiscal policy can be changed once a year, and monetary policy once a month perhaps.

There are also *effectiveness lags*. Once a policy change has been undertaken, its effects on the economy may come with a delay. This is particularly true for monetary policy, with some estimates suggesting that it may take upwards of two years for monetary policy changes to entirely feed through the economy.

The presence of lags makes the timing of policy difficult. Instead of correcting the economic cycle, the policy maker may actually make it worse.

Coefficient sizes and the multiplier

To prescribe the right corrective policy, the government must have complete knowledge of the structure of the economy, including the interest sensitivity of investment, the marginal propensity to consume, the size of the multiplier, and so on. Without all of this accurate information, prescribing the right policy action becomes exceedingly difficult.

In addition, the Lucas critique argues that these coefficients will not stay constant following a change in policy. For example, if a new low income tax regime is introduced, there is no guarantee that the marginal propensity to consume out of disposable income (*c*) will remain the same. It might rise because of increasing consumer confidence following a tax cut. The general idea is that predicting the effects of policy changes on the equilibrium level of income/output is very difficult because major economic relationships are unstable over different policy regimes.

Figure 9.25 Correcting or enhancing the cycle

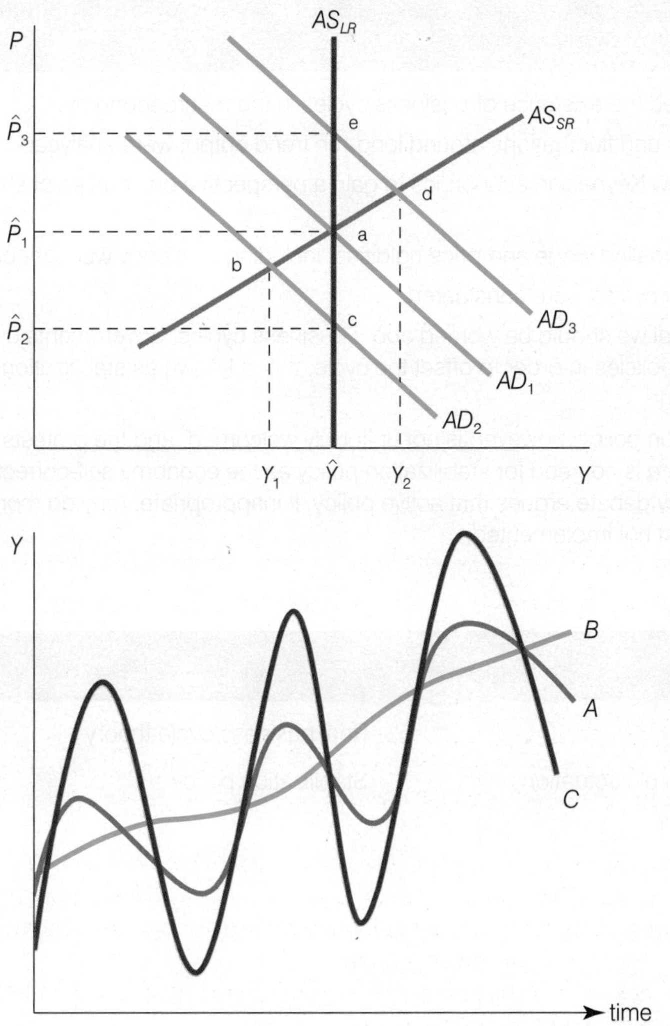

9

The issues involved in using stabilisation policies are summed up in Figure 9.25.

Following a fall in aggregate demand ($AD_1 \rightarrow AD_2$), the economy will move from point *a* to point *b* and output will fall below the equilibrium level. Eventually prices will fall and output will be restored at the equilibrium level. In the long run, the economy will move back to point *c*.

If policy makers believe that the economy will only make this adjustment over a long period of time, they may choose to use active policy to restore output. This would simply act to shift the aggregate demand curve back to whence it came. However, those against active policy would make the two arguments above, and suggest that active policy will enhance rather than neutralize the cycle.

If the policy maker cannot calculate the exact policy requirement, then there is a risk that policy may be overactive and move the economy from $AD_1 \rightarrow AD_3$. Output will now rise too far and require further policy in order to control prices (to d and e). If the economy follows path *A* in Figure 9.23, then the aim of stabilization policy is to move it onto a path *B*. However, incorrectly administered policy could move it on to a different path, such as *C*.

Summary

- This chapter evaluated the existence of business cycles in the macroeconomy.
- Real business cycles and fluctuations around long-run trend output were analysed.
- We then turned to new Keynesian economics to gain a perspective on sources of short-run fluctuations.
- We identified and modelled wage and price rigidities, including efficiency wage theories.
- The welfare effects of cycles were considered.
- Whether or not we feel we should be worried about business cycles, governments use monetary and fiscal policies in order to offset the cycle: this is known as stabilization policy or demand management.
- The use of stabilization policy, however, is not uniformly welcomed, and the protests fall into two camps. First, there is no need for stabilization policy as the economy self-corrects. Second, the policy inadequacy debate argues that active policy, if inappropriate, may do more harm than good and is best not implemented.

Key terms

Business cycle

New Keynesian theories of fluctuations

Real business cycle theory

Stabilization policy

Review questions

1. Using the AD-AS model, show that if markets clear and agents have rational expectations, then temporary productivity shocks cannot have persistent effects on output.
2. How does real business cycle theory explain fluctuations in output and employment?
3. Using the AD-AS model, explain how the presence of wage and/or price rigidities can lead to persistent movements in output following demand shocks.
4. Explain how more accurate economic forecasting can make it easier for policy makers to stabilize the economy. What other problems might policy makers face in operating stabilization policy?

More advanced problems

5. If monetary shocks are correlated with output movements, does this suggest that real business cycle theory is irrelevant?

For further resources, visit
http://www.thomsonlearning.co.uk/chamberlin_yueh

10 Unemployment, inflation and monetary policy

Learning objectives

- Understand the theory of the Phillips curve, which shows that there is a trade-off between unemployment and inflation
- Recognize that the trade-off is different in the short run and the long run, and the transition between short and long run is governed by the way expectations are formed and the degree of flexibility in wages and prices

- Analyse the policy choices while considering the costs of unemployment and inflation
- Explain how monetary policy can be used to control the rate of inflation, and how the Phillips curve framework is used to formulate monetary policy
- Recognize how the importance of monetary policy has grown as policy makers place an increasing emphasis on the control of inflation
- Investigate the reasons behind the recent trend for making central banks independent and analyse the time inconsistency problem
- Cover the concepts of seignorage and hyper-inflation

10.1 Introduction

The control of unemployment and inflation has been a long-standing preoccupation of macroeconomists. This takes on an added degree of fascination, as the theory of the Phillips curve argues that there is a trade-off between the two. Therefore, policy makers are faced with a conundrum: if either unemployment or inflation can only be controlled at the expense of the other, then which combination is the best choice? The aim of this chapter is to focus on this debate which has raged at the centre of macroeconomics for over 60 years.

To shed some light on this question, two sets of issues need to be discussed. First, what are the relative costs of unemployment and inflation? Second, what is the nature of the trade-off between the two? The nature of the trade-off is where economic theory has a lot to contribute. There is ample evidence to suggest that the trade-off is different in the short run and the long run, and the transition between short and long run is governed by the way expectations are formed and the degree of flexibility in wages and prices. We will see that the theory of the Phillips curve is very similar to that behind the aggregate demand and supply (AD-AS) model which was presented in Chapter 8.

Monetary policy refers to the control of either the quantity or the price of money. The importance of monetary policy has grown as policy makers place a growing emphasis on the control of inflation. The traditional goal of full employment has been supplanted by the target of economic stability and, as a result, the tools the government uses to control the economy have shifted away from fiscal (demand management) to monetary policy. Global application 10.1 gives a brief account of how the control of inflation came to the forefront in macroeconomic policy making.

The theory of the Phillips curve is very useful here, as it can explain how monetary policy could be used to control the rate of inflation. More than this, it is the framework that is generally used to formulate monetary policy. For example, the reasons behind the recent trend for making central banks independent can be described using the Phillips curve theory.

10.2 The Phillips curve: the unemployment–inflation trade-off

The level of inflation π refers to the rate at which prices are changing.

$$\pi = \frac{\Delta P}{P}$$

Global application 10.1

The long history of prices and inflation

Figure 1 plots the price level in the UK since 1800. The striking feature of this diagram is the relative stability of the price level right up to the end of the Second World War. Here, the price level began a gradual increase, but during the mid-1970s, the growth in the price level really took off.

Figure 2 accounts for the large increase in the price level during the last three decades of the last

Figure 1 The UK price level (Jan 1974 = 100), 1800–2003

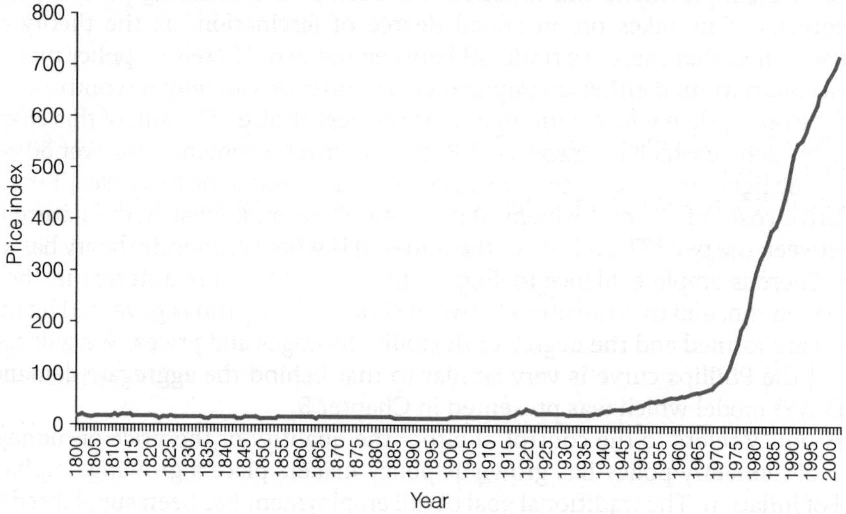

Figure 2 UK inflation rate, 1800–2003

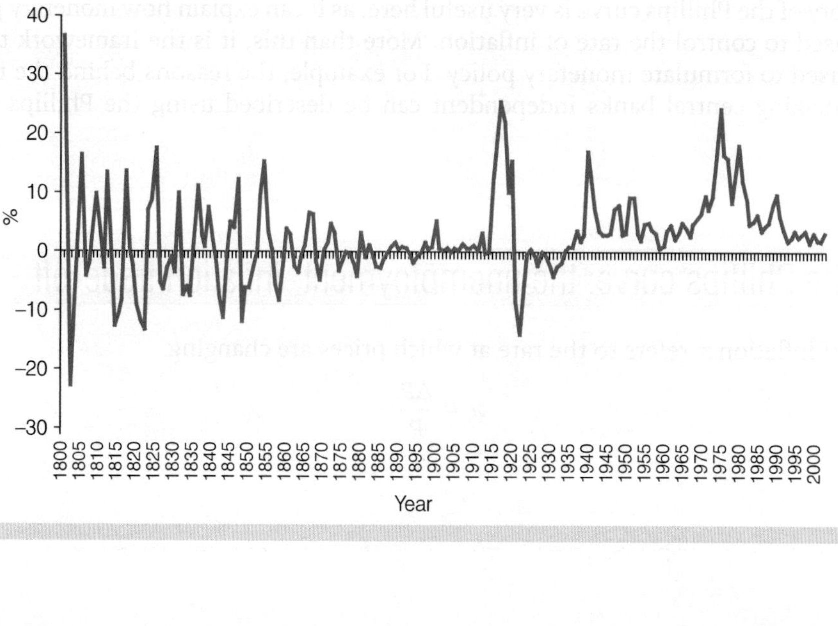

Global application 10.1 (continued)

millennium. Inflation refers to the rise in the general price level and has always been a feature of the economy. In fact, throughout history, there have been periods of fairly strong inflation with the price level frequently rising by over 20 per cent a year. However, the overall price level has tended to remain stable because periods of strong inflation are then offset by periods of strong deflation, or a fall in the general price level.

During the 1970s, though, there appeared to be a regime change in the inflation process. Inflation rates were persistently positive, so over time, the price level rose substantially. This is clearly seen in Figure 2. The change in inflation regime ushered in a new era of policy orientation.

The traditional aim of macroeconomic policy making had been the target of full employment. However, the emergence of persistent inflation introduced a new goal of inflation or price stability. The government's role changed from trying to manage aggregate demand to maintaining economic stability.

The definition of unemployment varies, but the accepted International Labour Organization (ILO) measure describes it as those who are without a job, and are both looking and are available for work.

A proposed link between unemployment and inflation is described by the Phillips curve.

The **Phillips curve** has been at the centre of economic policy making for over 40 years. It originated from a simple empirical relationship discovered by A.W.H. Phillips (who was actually an engineer and also invented the Phillips machine highlighted in Chapter 1), which showed an inverse relationship between unemployment and inflation. As unemployment falls, inflation would be expected to rise, and vice versa. Figure 10.1 shows the relationship between unemployment and inflation in the US during the 1960s.

Following the empirical evidence, economists developed the theory behind the trade-off relationship. The basic rationale accounting for the Phillips curve is taken to be a disequilibrium relationship in the labour market.

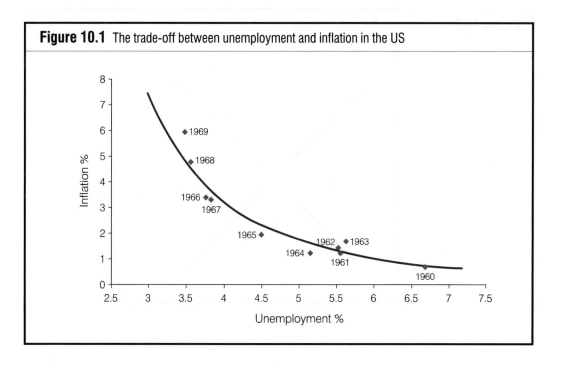

Figure 10.1 The trade-off between unemployment and inflation in the US

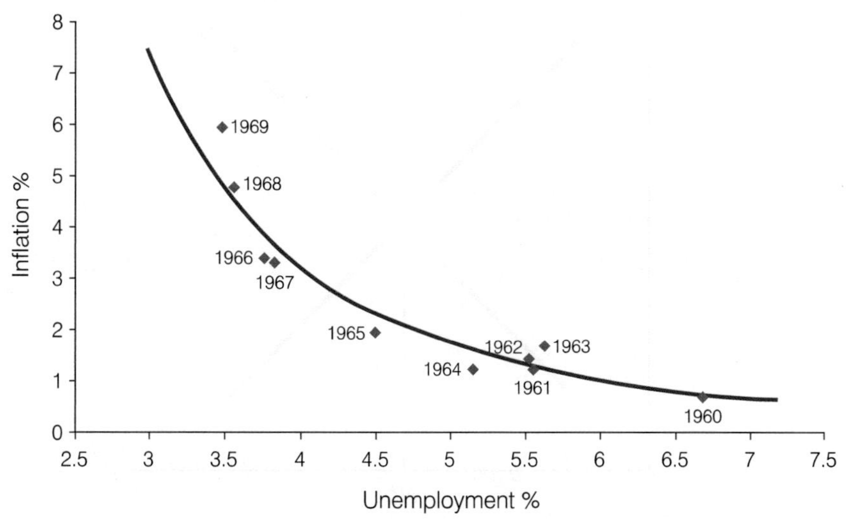

10.3 Theories of unemployment

There are two important concepts of labour market equilibrium, but both share similar foundations, that is wages will move in the same direction as the difference between demand and supply pressures in the labour market.

The **natural rate of unemployment** is essentially the level of unemployment that results when the labour market is in equilibrium. Under competitive conditions, the labour market is in equilibrium when the demand and supply of labour are equal to each other. Such a position is shown in Figure 10.2.

The price of labour is the wage. The demand for labour is downward-sloping, meaning that as the wage falls, firms demand more labour. The supply of labour is upward-sloping – as the wage increases, more workers are prepared to swap leisure for work, so supply increases. If there are L people in the labour market, then this will consist of employed (N) and unemployed (U) workers, so $L = N + U$. If N^* is the level of employment in a labour market in equilibrium, then the corresponding equilibrium level of unemployment is $U^* = L - N^*$. The natural rate of unemployment (u_{nr}) can then be defined as $u_{nr} = U^*/L$.

If the labour market behaves like a standard competitive market, then the wage will respond to any imbalance between demand and supply. If the wage is below its market clearing level, there will be excess demand for labour (see Figure 10.3a) and firms will bid up wages in order to attract labour. Likewise, if the wage is above its full employment level, then the labour market will be in a position of excess supply (see Figure 10.3b). This would put downward pressure on wages.

The nature of the labour market suggests that the change in wages is related to the size of the disequilibrium in the labour market. When there is a large degree of excess demand, the rate of wage increase will be much higher than at levels of low excess demand. Likewise, the downward rate of wage inflation (wage deflation) will be greater when there is higher excess supply.

10

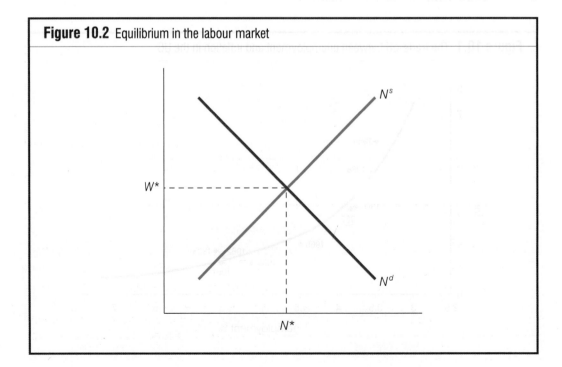

Figure 10.2 Equilibrium in the labour market

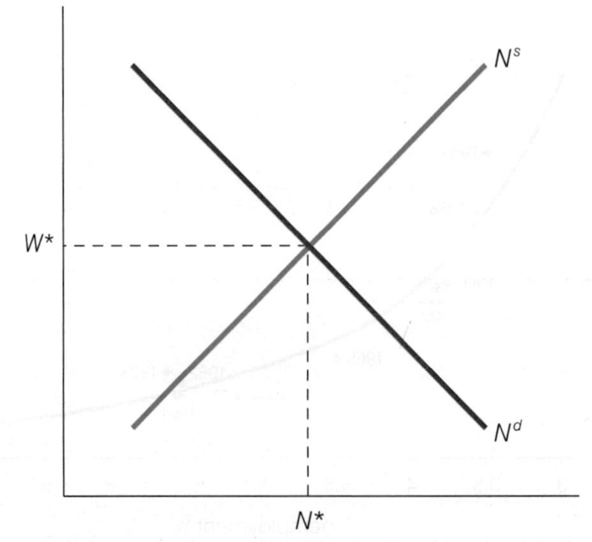

Figure 10.3a Excess demand in the labour market

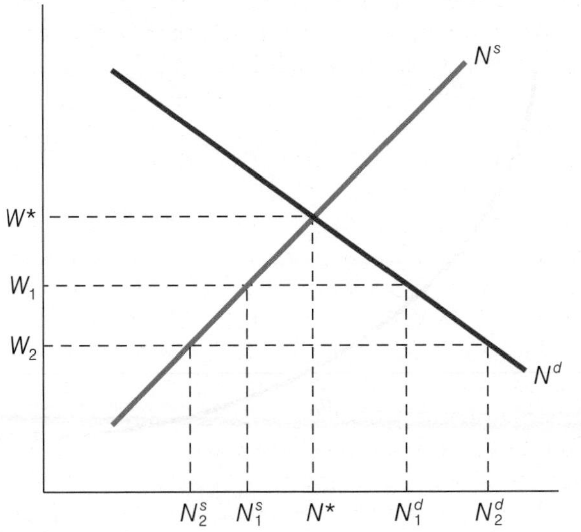

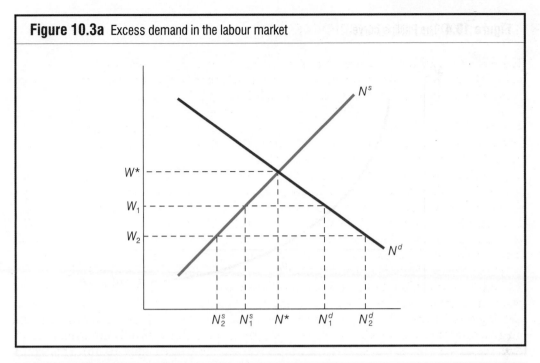

Figure 10.3b Excess supply in the labour market

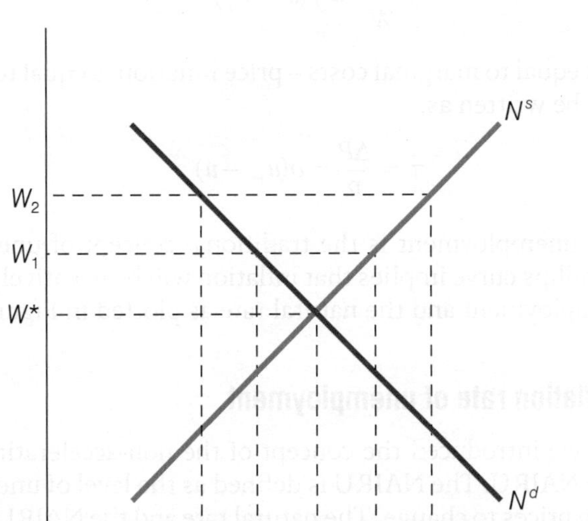

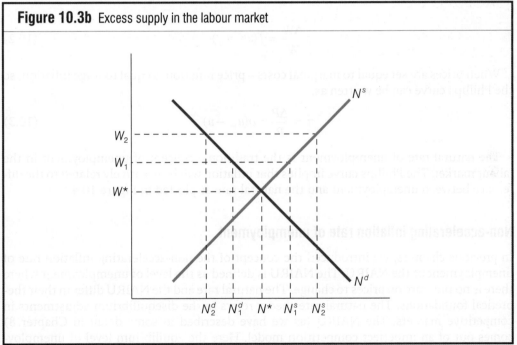

$$\frac{\Delta W}{W} = \lambda(N^d - N^S) \tag{10.1}$$

Therefore, the change in wages can be written as a negative function of the level of unemployment. More specifically, the relationship between demand and supply in the labour market will be related to the difference between the actual and equilibrium level of unemployment, $N^d - N^S = \gamma(U^* - U)$, so the change in wages is a function of the difference between unemployment and its equilibrium level.

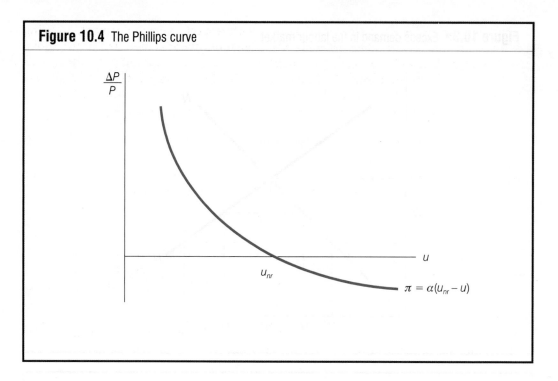

Figure 10.4 The Phillips curve

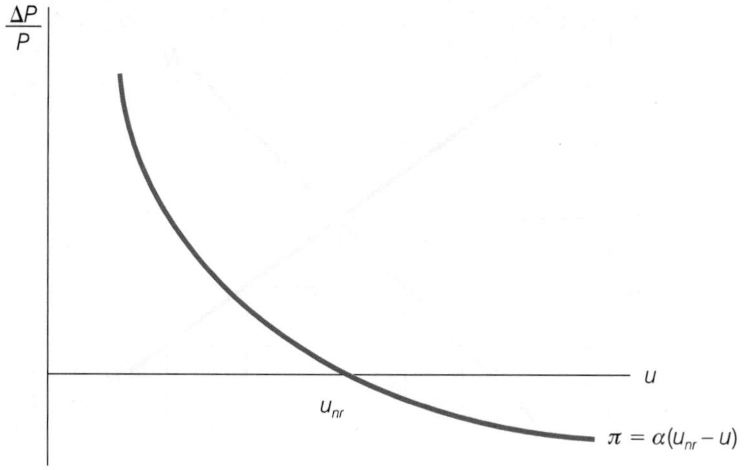

$$\frac{\Delta W}{W} = f(u - u_{nr}) \tag{10.2}$$

When prices are set equal to marginal costs – price inflation is equal to wage inflation, so the Phillips curve can be written as:

$$\pi = \frac{\Delta P}{P} = \alpha(u_{nr} - u) \tag{10.3}$$

The natural rate of unemployment is the traditional concept of unemployment in the labour market. The Phillips curve implies that inflation will be negatively related to the difference between unemployment and the natural rate as plotted in Figure 10.4.

Non-accelerating inflation rate of unemployment

In previous chapters, we introduced the concept of the non-accelerating inflation rate of unemployment or the NAIRU. The NAIRU is defined as the level of unemployment where there is no pressure on prices to change. The natural rate and the NAIRU differ in their theoretical foundations. The natural rate theory refers to the disequilibrium adjustments in competitive markets. The NAIRU (as we have described in some detail in Chapter 8) comes out of an imperfect competition model. Here the equilibrium level of unemployment and wages are the result of bargaining between firms and labour (unions). Both the unions and firms have some power to determine wages and prices, so the price level is not competitively determined.

In this set up, unions set wages and firms set prices. The wage-setting relationship, described as the bargained real wage (BRW), implies these nominal wage demands are positively related to expected prices, negatively related to unemployment, and are also determined by a set of factors Z, which accounts for things such as trade union power and the replacement ratio of unemployment benefits to wages, and so on.

$$W = P^e(Z - \beta u) \tag{10.4}$$

The bargained real wage is downward-sloping with respect to unemployment, implying that unions will moderate wage demands when unemployment is high, but in times of a tight labour market, will be more ambitious about what can be achieved.

The price-setting relationship, also known as the feasible or price-determined real wage (PRW), describes the way that firms set prices. Essentially, these are just a mark-up over costs, which are in turn defined by the ratio of wages to labour productivity (LP).

$$P = (1 + \mu)\frac{W}{LP} \tag{10.5}$$

In terms of the real wage, the FRW is unrelated to the level of unemployment (see Global application 8.1) and is just determined by product market conditions (mark-up) and productivity.

The NAIRU (u_n) is found at the intersection of the price-setting (PRW) and wage-setting (BRW) schedules (Figure 10.5). Once again, prices will change as a result of disequilibrium. If unemployment is below the NAIRU, then the BRW is above the PRW. Consequently, high wage demands by workers will lead to higher prices. Correspondingly, when unemployment is above the NAIRU, moderating wage demands will put downward pressure on prices. Again, the rate at which prices change is assumed to be proportionally related to the size of the disequilibrium.

As the change in nominal wages reflects the difference between unemployment and the NAIRU, then we can once again generate a Phillips curve-type relationship.

$$\frac{\Delta W}{W} = g(u_n - u) \tag{10.6}$$

$$\pi = \alpha(u_n - u) \tag{10.7}$$

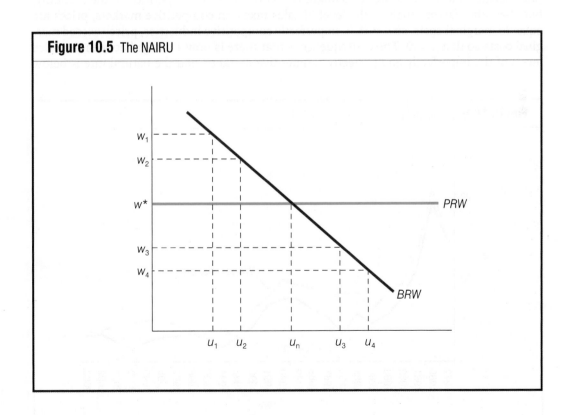

Figure 10.5 The NAIRU

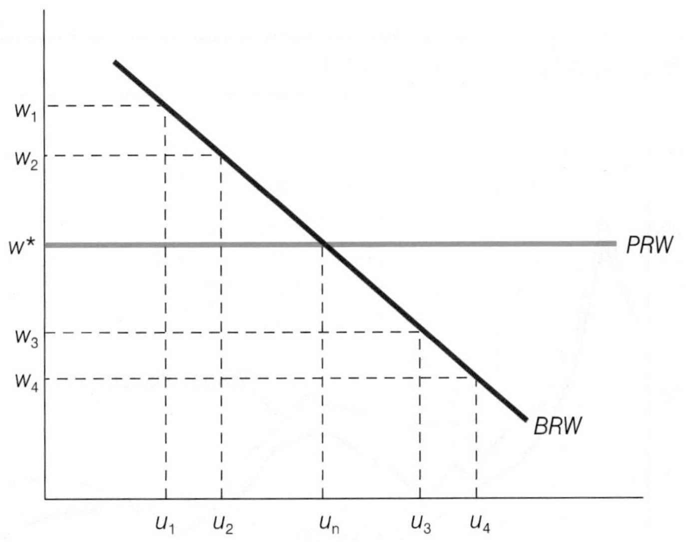

10

Natural rate or NAIRU?

Both the natural rate of unemployment (u_{nr}) and the NAIRU (u_n) reflect an equilibrium position in the labour market. Any movement of actual unemployment away from this position generates a change in wages proportional to the disequilibrium. Because prices are just a mark-up on wages, wage inflation feeds directly into price inflation.

$$\pi = \frac{\Delta P}{P} = \frac{\Delta W}{W}$$

Figure 10.6 shows some empirical evidence on the relationship between wage and price inflation. In general, wage inflation lies above price inflation, although both clearly follow similar trends. The difference is mainly accounted for by a positive growth in productivity, which allows the real wage to grow over time in line with living standards.

Many economists use the concepts of the natural rate and the NAIRU interchangeably. Although the two measures are similar – strictly speaking, they are not the same. The main difference concerns the existence of involuntary unemployment. In the natural rate definition, there is no involuntary unemployment. As it purports to an equilibrium position in the labour market, then the unemployed simply must be unwilling to work at the prevailing wage. The unemployed workers represent the portion of the labour supply curve that lies above the equilibrium wage and are termed as voluntary unemployed. By definition, the involuntary unemployed are those that are prepared to work at the prevailing wage rate, but are unable to find employment because the level of aggregate demand is too low to sustain that level of employment. If involuntary unemployment is positive, then the NAIRU will exceed the natural rate.

The difference can then largely be summed up by the size of the mark-up μ in the price-setting (FRW) schedule. This might reflect the level of competition in the economy, but also other factors such as the level of sales taxes. In competitive markets, prices are equal to marginal costs, so $\mu = 0$. In imperfectly competitive industries, prices exceed marginal costs so that $\mu > 0$. The consequence is that there is now a wedge between the price levels of the imperfectly and perfectly competitive markets, and the natural rate is below

10

Figure 10.6 Wage and price inflation in the UK

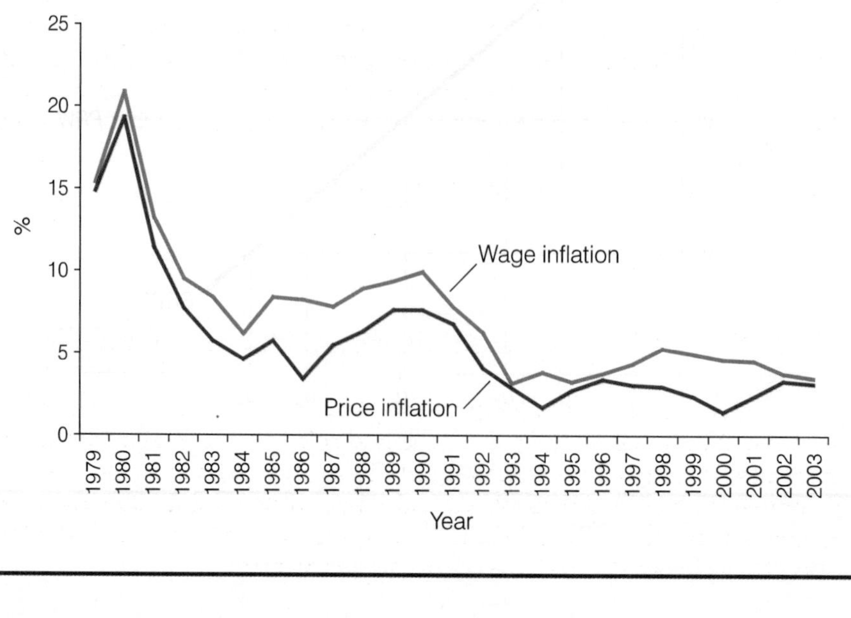

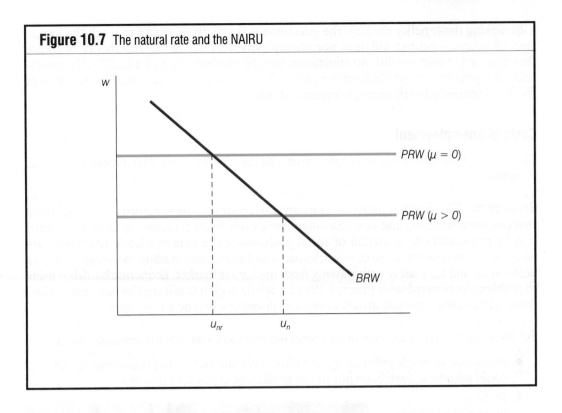

Figure 10.7 The natural rate and the NAIRU

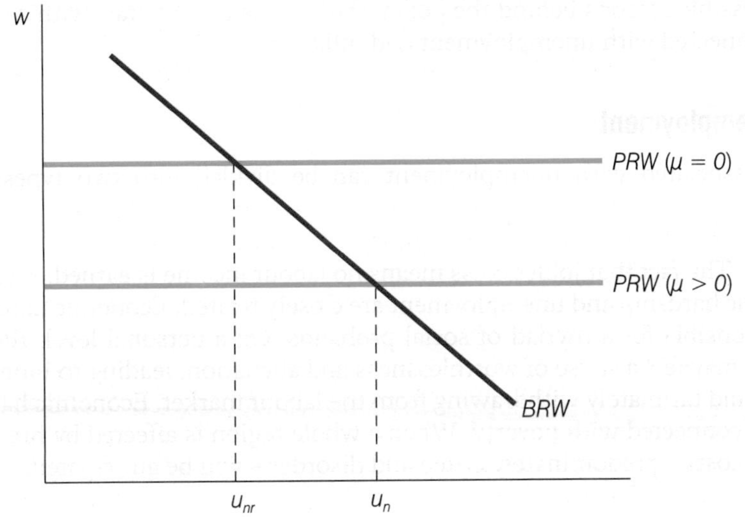

the NAIRU. This is easily seen from the imperfect competition model where the NAIRU falls with a declining mark-up (Figure 10.7).

Unemployment rises with the size of μ because increasing prices reduce aggregate demand. As the NAIRU lies above the natural rate of unemployment, inflation will be higher at every level of unemployment, so the presence of market imperfections will create an inflation wedge.

This the main difference between the natural rate and the NAIRU. In the analysis of this chapter, we will concentrate on the NAIRU, as most policy makers throughout the world do. The reason is not just because of some empirical justification, but also because the imperfect competition model provides a useful model for analysing structural factors in the labour market. These structural factors can be analysed just as well in the natural rate model. For example, an improvement in labour productivity would shift the feasible real wage, but also would shift the labour demand curve. A reduction in trade union power would shift the BRW schedule, but also the labour supply curve. However, it is clear that in the imperfect competition model, these factors are treated much more explicitly, which makes it a good model for investigating their effects.

10.4 The costs and benefits of unemployment and inflation

Although the trade-off between unemployment and inflation started out as an empirical observation, the Phillips curve has played a central role in policy making for more than 30 years. The Phillips curve was seen as a trade-off frontier for policy makers. It represents the different combinations of unemployment and inflation that are feasible for an economy. Lower unemployment can be bought with higher inflation and vice versa. The role of economic policy is to choose the preferred point on this frontier.

In making these policy choices, the government is effectively trying to reach the lowest level of misery – neither inflation nor unemployment is desirable. The theory of choice therefore is not about utility maximization but the minimization of disutility. To understand the possible reasons behind the policy choice, it is best to start with a discussion of the costs connected with unemployment and inflation.

Costs of unemployment

The costs associated with unemployment can be divided into two types: social and economic.

Social costs The fact that joblessness means no labour income is earned; it is no surprise that economic hardship and unemployment are closely related. Economic hardship in turn may be responsible for a myriad of social problems. On a personal level, those who are unemployed may feel a sense of worthlessness and alienation, leading to illnesses such as depression, and ultimately withdrawing from the labour market. Economic hardship leads to problems connected with poverty. When a whole region is affected by high unemployment, social costs – predominately crime and disorder – will be anticipated.

Economic costs There are two main economic costs associated with unemployment.

- Efficiency: unemployed workers are effectively idle factors of production, which could otherwise have been put to use producing goods and services.
- Budgetary: unemployed labour pays no taxes, and receives unemployment benefits. Therefore, fiscally, it can be very expensive for the government. The evidence in Chapter 4 shows a clear relationship between the current budget surplus/deficit and the level of unemployment. These fiscal costs, of course, have an opportunity cost – in either lower taxes or higher government spending. The government is committing real resources to pay for idle factors of production.

Thousands of job-seekers flock to a job fair in Hebei province, China, 19 February 2005.
Source: Getty Images

Is zero unemployment a sensible policy?

Recognizing that unemployment is costly, governments might optimally pursue a policy of zero unemployment. In fact, it has been stated throughout this book that full employment was the goal of policy makers for many decades. However, are full employment and zero unemployment the same thing? Would it be possible for an optimal choice to have a positive amount of unemployment?

At any one point in time, there will be some people who are between jobs; this is known as frictional unemployment. The presence of this could be optimal, as the process of job matching is not an immediate occurrence. It takes time both for employers to find the best person for a vacancy, and likewise for an individual to find the best possible job. If both were to jump at the first person or opportunity that came along, then inefficient matches might result. Therefore, some positive level of unemployment might be optimal. However, this does not discount the usefulness of policies that reduce frictional unemployment by increasing the speed of efficient job matching.

Costs of inflation

The costs associated with rising prices can be split, depending on whether inflation is anticipated or unanticipated.

Anticipated: *menu and shoe leather costs* Changing prices may exert real physical costs on firms and individuals. Menu costs are the real resources that are incurred when changing prices (they refer to the costs of having to reprint menus). Shoe leather costs refer to the costs involved in having to handle larger money holdings on account of higher prices. The term shoe leather costs suggests this will involve making more trips to the bank.

Unanticipated: *redistribution* Inflation has the effect of redistributing wealth. Those on fixed incomes are usually made worse off by rising prices. Inflation also erodes the real value of debts, so borrowers are made better off relative to savers or creditors. As the government is usually a major debtor, inflation may play an important role in dealing with the public finances: these are known as seignorage revenues (which will be discussed further later in this chapter). The government will also benefit financially from a process of *fiscal drag*. If wages adjust for inflation, but income tax bands do not, then some people, despite not having seen an increase in their real wage, will end up in a higher tax band.

These are all costs associated with unanticipated inflation. A simple solution to this would be to index all payments which may be affected by inflation. If incomes, benefits and interest payments were automatically adjusted for inflation, then these problems would be mitigated.

Unanticipated: *instability* Arguably, the main reason for maintaining low and stable inflation is that it creates conditions which are amenable for long-term investment. This in itself is an important determinant of long-term economic growth and employment. In Chapter 3, the determinants of investment were discussed in some detail. The decision to undertake an investment project requires the evaluation of expected future cash flows, which becomes much harder if prices are unstable. If firms face more uncertainty, then they are less likely to undertake investment projects. Low and stable inflation is therefore required for encouraging investment. As Table 10.1 shows, high inflation is closely linked to unstable inflation.

Table 10.1 Inflation levels and variance in the UK

Year	Average inflation %	Inflation variance %
1950–1972	4.40	6.06
1973–1982	14.19	24.74
1983–1992	5.79	4.12
1993–2003	2.48	0.55

Benefits of inflation

If there are costs to inflation, should policy makers aim to achieve zero inflation? In fact, should we go further and actually target a negative rate of inflation? This would imply falling prices known as deflation. After all, if there are costs associated with inflation, the converse would suggest that there are benefits with deflation.

The answers to these questions are that policy makers tend to prefer a low positive rate of inflation rather than zero inflation, and deflation is regarded as being just as bad, if not worse, than high inflation.

There might be some benefits to having a low and stable rate of inflation. Several reasons account for this view. First, if nominal wages are very resistant to downward movements, firms can still reduce the real wage by simply allowing prices to rise at a faster rate than wages.

Deflation, however, is potentially disastrous. An expectation of falling prices would lead to consumers postponing purchases until later, but the current fall in demand would further exasperate the deflation. In addition, once a country enters a deflationary cycle, it can be extremely hard to get out of it. The recent experiences of deflation in Japan are outlined in Global application 10.2.

10

10.5 Policy choices: preferences between unemployment and inflation

We have now discussed the costs connected with unemployment and inflation. If the Phillips curve acts as a constraint on policy making, then it is just left to policy makers to choose their most preferred combination on this frontier. The rational choice would be that which maximizes utility, or in this case minimizes disutility.

The policy choice will depend on the preferences of the policy maker, which are represented in a utility function.

$$U = U(\pi, u) \qquad (10.9)$$

An indifference curve plots the combinations of inflation and unemployment that give the same level of (dis)utility. Each level of (dis)utility will be synonymous with a different indifference curve. As both inflation and unemployment are 'baddies', the lower the indifference curve, the better. This is shown in Figure 10.8, where the policy maker is made better off as they move from $I_1 \rightarrow I_2 \rightarrow I_3$.

A further point to make about the indifference curves regards their shape. These are concave to the origin, which implies that policy makers prefer averages to extremes. This suggests that if unemployment is high, the policy maker would be more likely to trade-off a higher increase in inflation to reduce unemployment than would be the case if unemployment were low. The same would apply to inflation. At high rates of inflation, the policy

Global application 10.2

Deflation in Japan: What went wrong?

Figure 3 gives an accurate description of the current state of the Japanese economy. Growth in the economy has been faltering generating an increase in unemployment. The rate of inflation has fallen and Japan has experienced deflation for several years. The economy therefore appears to be stuck in a deflationary position, where falling prices and stagnant growth reinforce each other.

One of the visible problems with deflation is that Japan has entered a liquidity trap. As Figure 4 shows, Japanese interest rates have been pushed down to almost zero. Monetary policy is

Figure 3 Japan's unemployment and inflation

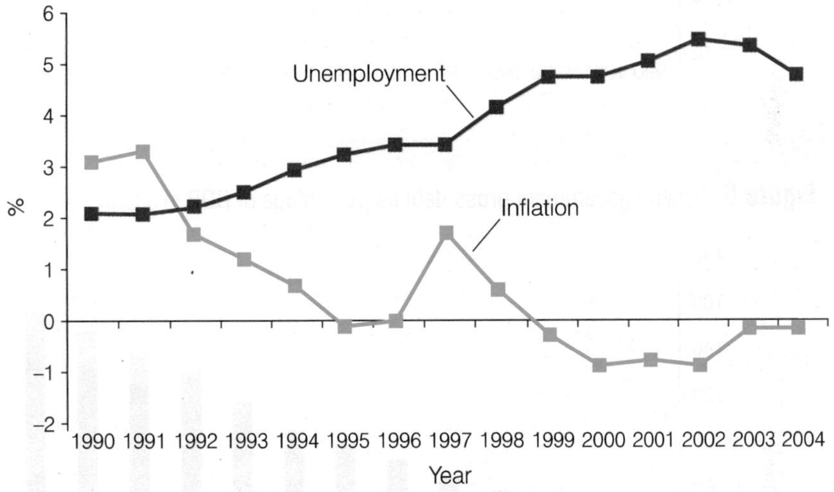

Figure 4 Japan's domestic interest rates

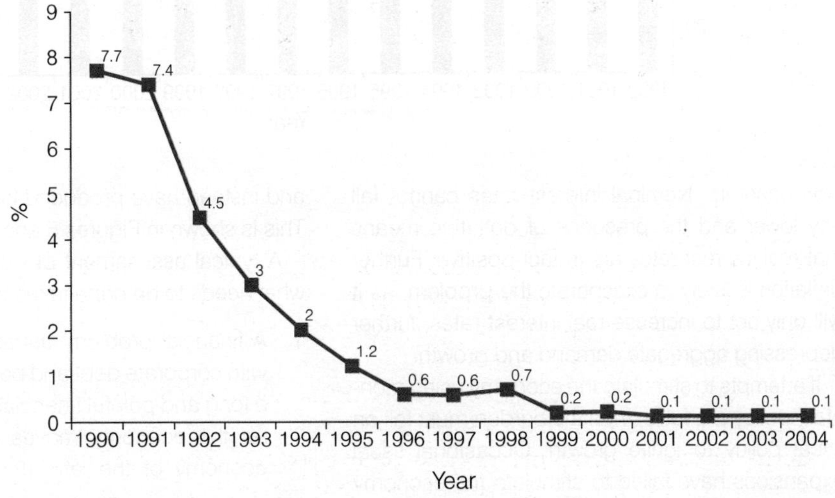

Global application 10.2 (continued)

Figure 5 General government budget as percentage of GDP in Japan

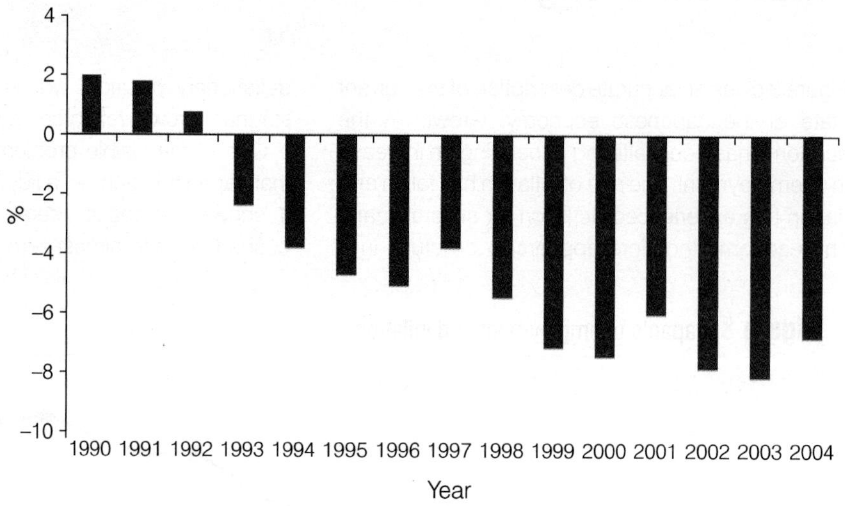

Figure 6 General government gross debt as percentage of GDP in Japan

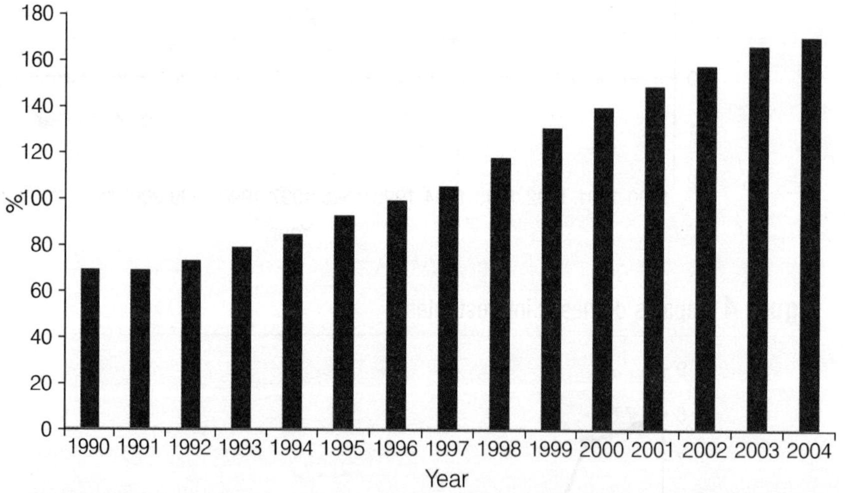

now anaemic. Nominal interest rates cannot fall any lower and the presence of deflation means that real interest rates are in fact positive. Further deflation is likely to exasperate the problem, as it will only act to increase real interest rates, further depressing aggregate demand and growth.

If attempts to stimulate the economy using monetary policy are futile, then the burden must fall on fiscal policy to ignite growth. Occasional fiscal expansions have failed to stimulate the economy and instead have produced higher levels of debt. This is shown in Figures 5 and 6.

A typical assessment of what went wrong and what needs to be done takes the following form:

1. A financial problem. Japan is over-burdened with corporate debt and bad loans, so it needs a long and painful financial house clean.
2. As the economy moves out of the bubble economy of the late 1980s, the depressed

Global application 10.2 (continued)

economy has led to continually depressed expectations. As a result, all Japan needs is a large jolt to jump start its economy.

Problem 1 is somewhat discounted. If Japan's problems lie on the demand side, then financial problems may result in low borrowing, but investment as a proportion of GDP is high compared to most advanced economies.

Problem 2 is problematic as fiscal expansions do not seem to work. The criticism is that fiscal expansions have not been large or sustained enough to provide a sufficient jolt to the economy.

An alternative third explanation is a combination of ideology and demography. Japan's ageing society, due to low birth rates and immigration, means that it faces a falling working age population. Preparing for the future has led to higher saving, but investment opportunities are limited, so there will be a glut of saving even at a zero interest rate. Permanent recession ensues due to S > I (think about the circular flow of income).

The solution is to promise Japan inflation in the future. This would reduce the real effective rate on borrowing to below zero – borrowers will pay back less in real terms than the value of their loans and will be prepared to spend more. The promise of future inflation is what Japan needs. Therefore, inflation is the key to growth in Japan.

maker is more likely to accept higher unemployment in order to reduce inflation than if inflation were low.

Given the map of indifference curves in Figure 10.8, the policy maker will act to minimize the total amount of disutility that is suffered. The Phillips curve in this case represents the menu of inflation–unemployment outcomes from which the policy maker can choose. The rational choice is the lowest indifference curve that is consistent with a position on the Phillips curve. This is where the two curves are tangential to each other. In Figure 10.9, this gives the optimal unemployment–inflation combination (π^*, u^*).

10

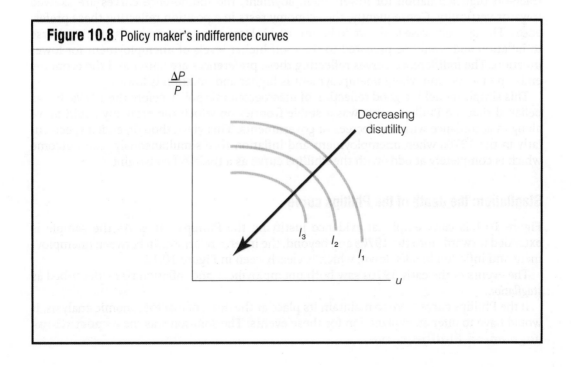

Figure 10.8 Policy maker's indifference curves

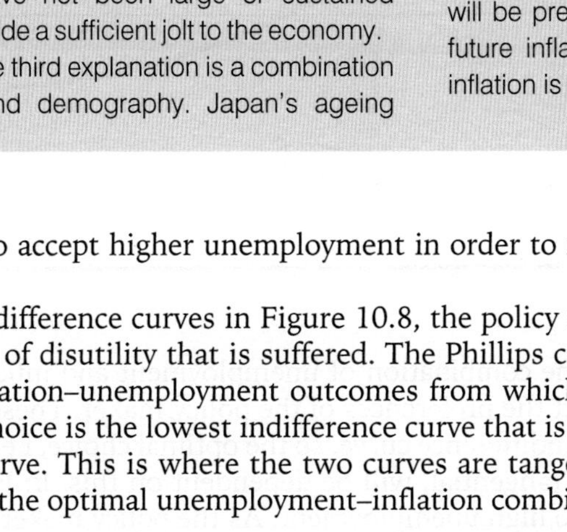

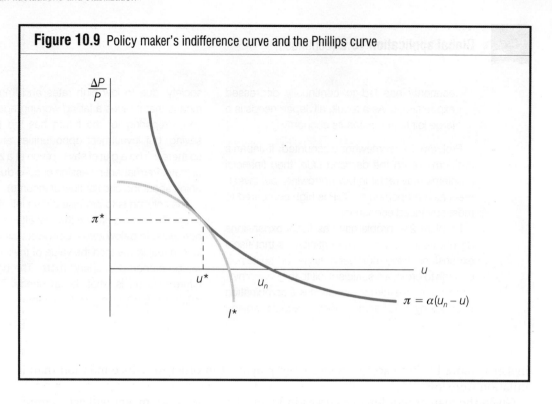

Figure 10.9 Policy maker's indifference curve and the Phillips curve

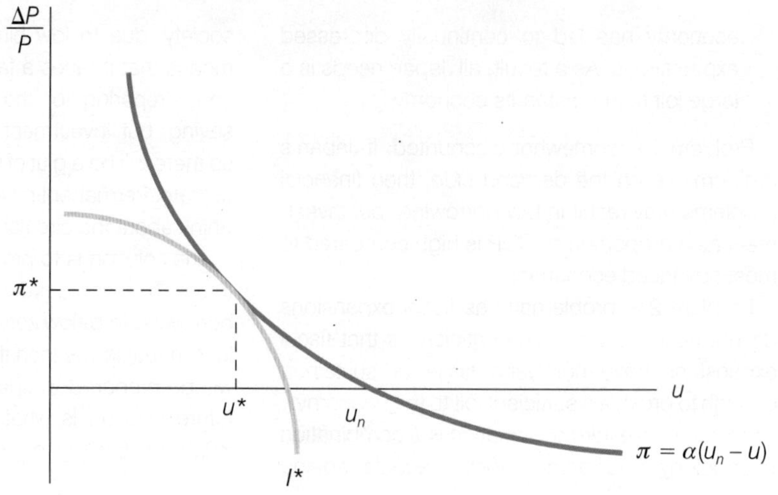

In this framework, the combination of unemployment and inflation that the economy ends up with will reflect the preferences of the policy maker. These preferences are manifest in the shape of the indifference curve, so the optimal choice, i.e. where the Phillips and indifference curves are tangential, will be dependent on this. In Figure 10.10, the policy maker is very adverse to high unemployment. As the policy maker is now more willing to trade-off higher inflation for lower unemployment, the indifference curves are skewed towards verticality. Consequently, the economy rests in a position reflecting these preferences. The opposite case is shown in Figure 10.11. Here, the policy maker is highly adverse to inflation and would be prepared to trade-off higher levels of unemployment for lower inflation. The indifference curves reflecting these preferences are flatter and the economy ends up in a position where unemployment is higher and inflation is lower.

This simple model is a good reflection of macroeconomic policy before the 1970s. It was believed that the Phillips curve was a stable frontier on which the economy could move along in accordance with the decrees of governments. This view, though, ended spectacularly in the 1970s when unemployment and inflation rose simultaneously – an outcome which is completely at odds with the Phillips curve as a trade-off constraint.

Stagflation: the death of the Phillips curve

Figure 10.1 is early empirical evidence justifying the Phillips curve. As the sample is extended forwards into the 1970s and beyond, the inverse relationship between unemployment and inflation breaks down, which is clearly seen in Figure 10.12.

The events of the early 1970s saw both unemployment and inflation rise – described as *stagflation*.

If the Phillips curve were to maintain its place at the heart of macroeconomic analysis, it would have to offer an explanation for these events. The solution was the **expectations augmented Phillips curve**.

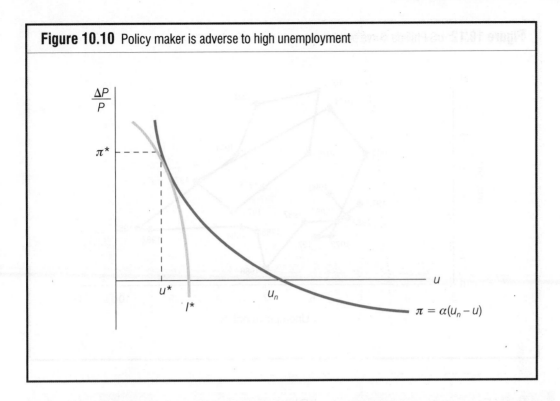

Figure 10.10 Policy maker is adverse to high unemployment

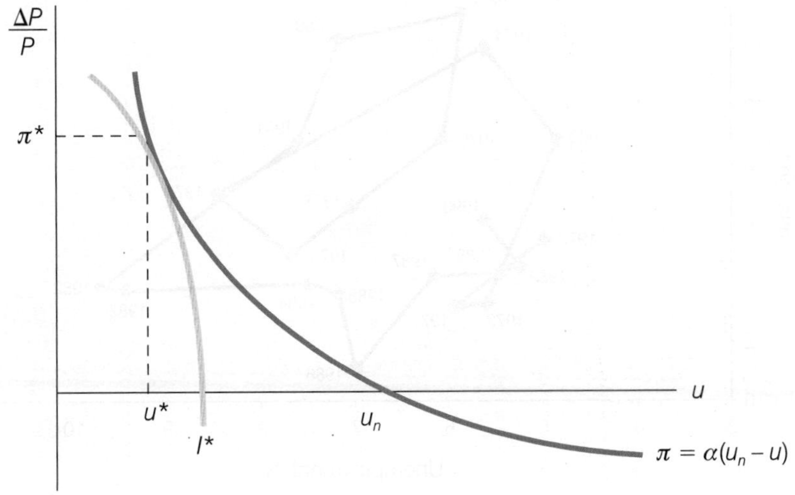

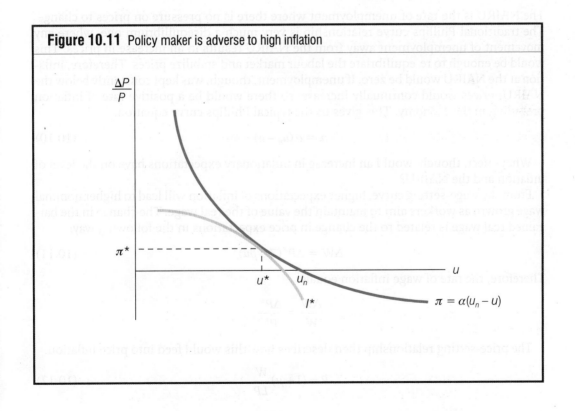

Figure 10.11 Policy maker is adverse to high inflation

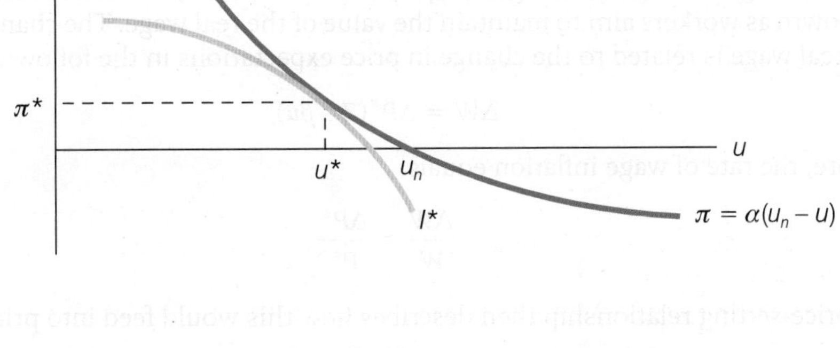

Figure 10.12 US Phillips curve breaks down

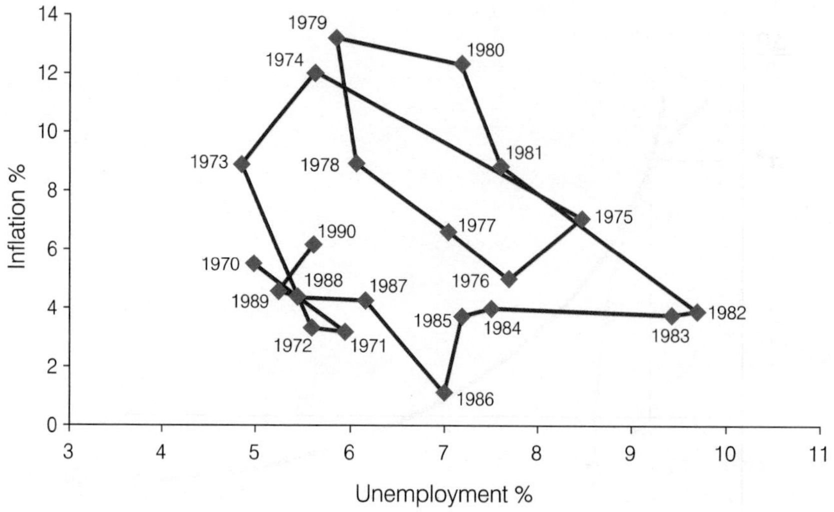

10.6 Expectations augmented Phillips curve

The NAIRU is the rate of unemployment where there is no pressure on prices to change. The traditional Phillips curve relationship is very much a disequilibrium one, where any movement of unemployment away from the NAIRU results in an increase in prices. This would be enough to re-equilibriate the labour market and stabilize prices. Therefore, inflation at the NAIRU would be zero. If unemployment, though, was kept constantly below the NAIRU, prices would continually increase, so there would be a positive rate of inflation prevailing in the economy. This gives us the typical Phillips curve equation.

$$\pi = \alpha(u_n - u) \tag{10.10}$$

What effect, though, would an increase in inflationary expectations have on the level of inflation and the NAIRU?

From the wage-setting curve, higher expectations of inflation will lead to higher nominal wage growth as workers aim to maintain the value of the real wage. The change in the bargained real wage is related to the change in price expectations in the following way:

$$\Delta W = \Delta P^e(Z - \beta u) \tag{10.11}$$

Therefore, the rate of wage inflation equals:

$$\frac{\Delta W}{W} = \frac{\Delta P^e}{P^e}$$

The price-setting relationship then describes how this would feed into price inflation.

$$P = (1+\mu)\frac{W}{LP} \tag{10.12}$$

$$\Delta P = \frac{\Delta W}{LP} \tag{10.13}$$

10

$$\frac{\Delta P}{P} = \frac{\Delta W}{W}$$

Therefore,

$$\frac{\Delta P^e}{P^e} = \frac{\Delta W}{W} = \frac{\Delta P}{P}$$

A persistent increase in the rate of expected inflation will lead to a persistent increase in the actual level of inflation, but what would be the impact on the NAIRU?

The answer is nothing. As the rate of wage and price inflation is the same, the real wage will remain constant. A 10 per cent increase in the wage level will have no effect on the real wage if the price level also increases by 10 per cent. As a result, a change in inflation expectations produces a change in the inflation rate in the economy, but does not affect the NAIRU.

This means that different rates of inflation are possible at the same rate of unemployment depending on prevailing inflation expectations. This gives rise to the expectations augmented Phillips curve.

$$\pi = \alpha(u_n - u) + \pi^e \qquad (10.14)$$

The actual rate of inflation is now the product of the disequilibrium in the labour market, and also the expected level of inflation. Therefore, the Phillips curve will shift vertically with changes in the expected level of inflation; this is shown in Figure 10.13.

10.6.1 Long-run Phillips curve

The expectations augmented Phillips curve posits that inflation is the product of two factors. The first is the disequilibrium between the rate of unemployment and the NAIRU, and the second is the degree of inflation expectations. The disequilibrium story gives rise to the traditional Phillips curve. This is known as the *short-run Phillips curve,* as disequilibria

Figure 10.13 Long-run Phillips curve

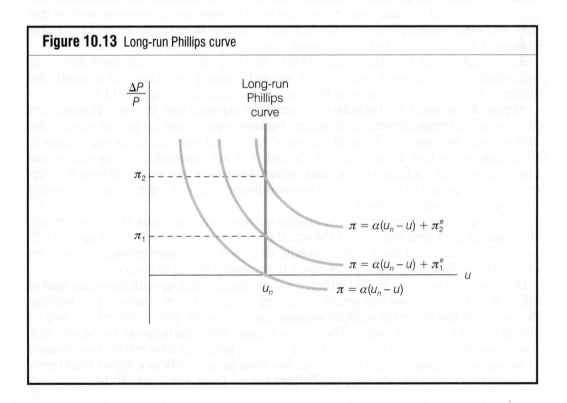

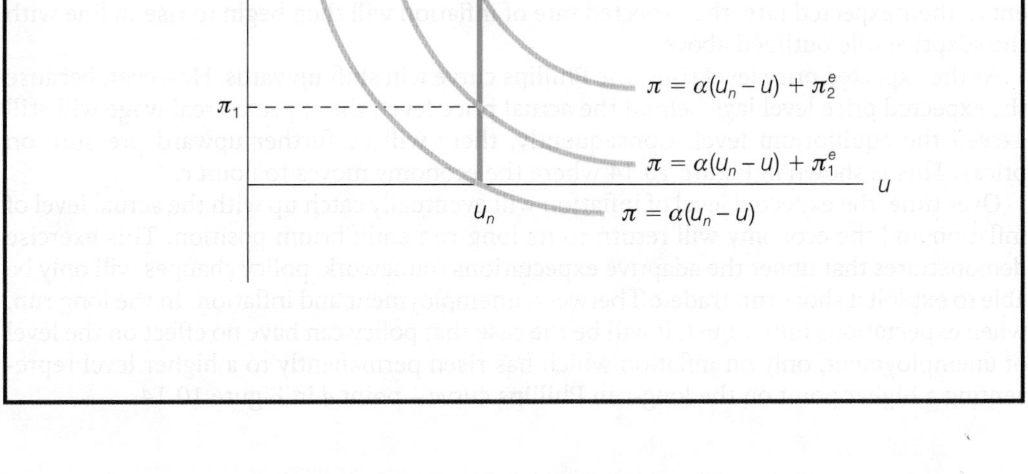

are not expected to persist in the long run. Also, the change in prices is expected to push the economy back to the NAIRU.

In the long run, the economy will rest at its NAIRU, but there are many different rates of inflation that are consistent with this depending on the rate of inflation expectations. This gives rise to a **long-run Phillips curve**, which is vertical at the NAIRU.

One question worth asking is why the Phillips curve had remained so stable until the stagflation of the 1970s? The answer, Milton Friedman stated, was that up until this time, there had not been any significant inflation in the major developed economies. Therefore, inflation expectations had effectively been set at zero, $\pi^e = 0$. Only with the advent of very high inflation, did the private sector begin to anticipate a positive rate of inflation. The sharp jolt the global economy took from rising oil prices in the 1970s introduced a significant amount of inflation into the economy.

10.6.2 Processes of expectations formation

We have seen in previous chapters the importance of expectations and how they are formed. The two most common approaches of expectations formation are adaptive and rational expectations.

Adaptive expectations

Under adaptive expectations, inflation expectations are a weighted average of last period's actual and expected rates of inflation.

$$\pi_t^e = \alpha\pi_{t-1}^e + (1-\alpha)\pi_{t-1} \qquad (10.15)$$

This backward-looking approach has clear implications for how the economy will react to shocks and policies. Suppose the economy starts of with unemployment at the NAIRU, and actual and expected inflation equal to one another. The government, however, decides that the current rate of unemployment is too high and unleashes an expansionary policy (fiscal or monetary) with the aim of reducing unemployment to its target level ($u_T < u_n$).

10

As unemployment falls below the NAIRU, the bargained real wage rises above the price-determined real wage and there is upward pressure on prices. As a result, the economy moves along the short-run Phillips curve to position *b* (Figure 10.14).

At point *b*, the actual level of inflation exceeds the expected level ($\pi > \pi^e$). This explains how the fall in unemployment materializes, because expectations lag behind actual inflation, so wage increases will lag price increases and the real wage falls. Although agents in the private sector have been caught on the hop, it is not expected that they will remain oblivious to the new inflation rate forever. When they realize that actual inflation is different to their expected rate, the expected rate of inflation will then begin to rise in line with the adaptive rule outlined above.

As the expected price level rises, the Phillips curve will shift upwards. However, because the expected price level lags behind the actual price level, the expected real wage will still exceed the equilibrium level. Consequently, there will be further upward pressure on prices. This is shown in Figure 10.14 where the economy moves to point *c*.

Over time, the expected level of inflation will eventually catch up with the actual level of inflation and the economy will return to its long-run equilibrium position. This exercise demonstrates that under the adaptive expectations framework, policy changes will only be able to exploit a short-run trade-off between unemployment and inflation. In the long run, when expectations fully adjust, it will be the case that policy can have no effect on the level of unemployment, only on inflation which has risen permanently to a higher level representing a higher point on the long-run Phillips curve – point *d* in Figure 10.14.

Figure 10.14 Expansionary fiscal/monetary policy in the Phillips curve framework

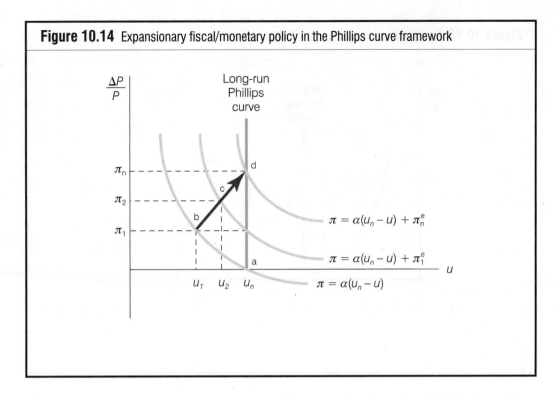

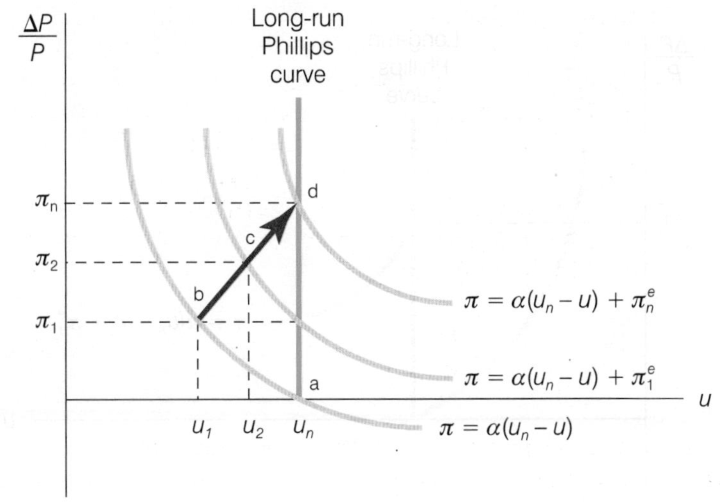

Rational expectations

The major criticism levelled at adaptive expectations is that it only makes use of past information. Forming expectations using only a subset of the information available is deemed to be sub-optimal and irrational behaviour. Expectations which are formed rationally use all available information:

$$\pi_t^e = E(\pi | I_t) \tag{10.16}$$

where I_t represents the set of information available to the private sector at time t.

Rational expectations was a revolutionary concept, arguing that the short-run trade-off between unemployment and inflation no longer existed.

When expectations are formed rationally, changes in policy will not influence the level of unemployment at all, not even in the short run. Agents in the private sector are fully aware of the consequences of the policy action and will immediately adjust their expectations of inflation. Consequently, wages will stay in tune with prices. If the real wage does not change, the rate of unemployment will not deviate from the NAIRU. This is shown in Figure 10.15 as a movement up the long-run Phillips curve.

In Chapter 9, we argue that the concept of rational expectations is most easily applicable in situations where the effects of policy changes on prices are fairly easy to discern. The point made in Chapter 9 was that this was most likely to be the case with monetary policy changes, as agents can anticipate that there will be no long-term real effects. Fiscal policy, on the other hand, is much harder to judge. Here, issues connected to the multiplier and the crowding out of investment (Ricardian Equivalence, see Chapter 4) make the longer-term consequences of fiscal policy much harder to predict. It is also the case that even if fiscal policy ultimately does nothing to the level of GDP, it can still have substantial consequences for its composition.

The issue of rational expectations and the vertical long-run Phillips curve is therefore a very important issue in monetary policy. The second half of this chapter will be devoted to

10

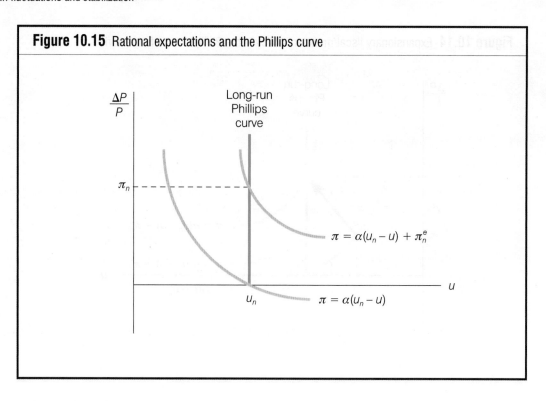

Figure 10.15 Rational expectations and the Phillips curve

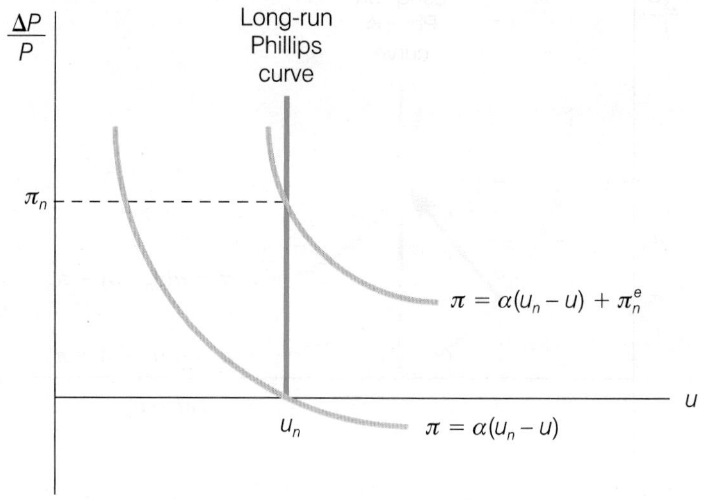

exploring these issues further. It will be seen that the theory of the Phillips curve outlined here has played a central role in determining and forming different types of monetary policy over the years in a number of countries. Global application 10.3 gives the evidence for an accelerationist, expectations augmented Phillips curve.

In the previous chapter, we described how economic cycles can result from adaptive expectations of either wage or price rigidities. In either scenario, there will be incomplete nominal adjustment to shocks or policies creating movements in real variables, such as output, employment, etc. Over time, full adjustment will restore equilibrium to the economy, but the economy can be subject to transitory short-run movements. The analysis of the Phillips curve in the short and the long run is not too different from the analysis of aggregate demand and supply covered earlier in the book.

10.6.3 Supply shocks

The expectations augmented Phillips curve goes a long way to explaining the breakdown of the Phillips curve. This implies that a different level of inflation can result at the same level of unemployment, leading to a departure from the inverse trade-off that is the traditional Phillips curve. This also led to the establishment of the long-run Phillips curve, which is vertical at the NAIRU. Although the economy can depart from the NAIRU in the short run by moving along the short-run Phillips curve, this is only possible due to nominal inertia or a separation of actual and expected inflation. Eventually, the economy will return to the NAIRU.

Thus, a long-run change in the unemployment rate can only result from a change in the NAIRU itself. Supply side shocks can lead to a change in the equilibrium level of unemployment. These have been explained in the previous two chapters and principally fall into two categories. First, there are factors which impact upon labour productivity, which leads to shifts in the price-setting or feasible real wage schedule. Also, anything which affects the

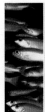

Global application 10.3

Accelerationist Phillips curve

The stagflation of the 1970s saw inflation and unemployment rise simultaneously, leading to a breakdown in the Phillips curve. The new inflation paradigm was explained by the role of inflation expectations, leading to the expectations augmented Phillips curve.

It appears now that there is a new inverse relationship between the rate of increase in inflation and the rate of unemployment. Allowing for the expectations augmented Phillips curve means that unemployment will eventually return to the NAIRU. If unemployment is to be maintained at a position away from the NAIRU, then it will require a persistent change in the rate of inflation. This is shown in Figure 7 for the US economy for 1970–1990 and is representative of the accelerationist Phillips curve model.

Figure 7 The rate of change in inflation and the level of unemployment in the US, 1970–1990

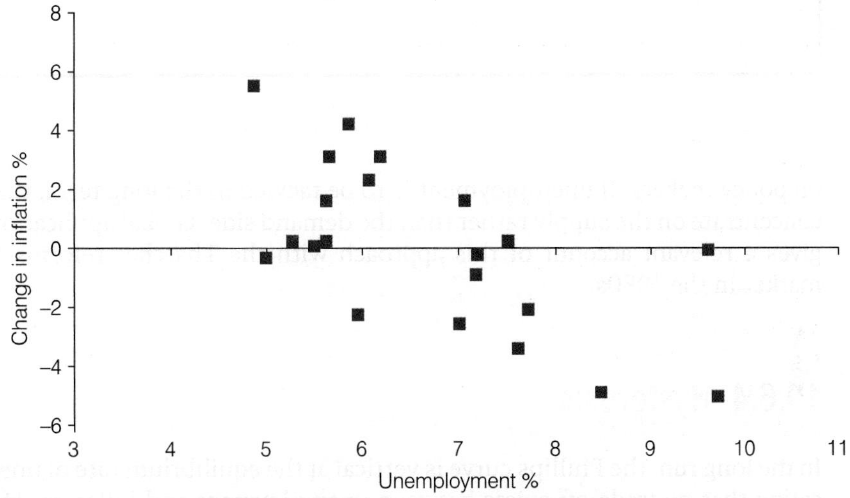

bargaining power of labour will also influence the equilibrium level of unemployment via movements in the wage-setting or bargained real wage schedule. These might include labour market legislation, trade union power, and the replacement ratio, amongst others. These possibilities are shown in Figure 10.16.

As movements in the long-run Phillips curve are caused by the same factors, and have similar consequences as shifts in the long-run aggregate supply curve, readers are advised to turn to the examples in Chapter 8. These include the effects of the oil price increases in the 1970s, the new economy effects of information and communication technologies (ICT) in the 1990s, and various supply side policies.

The important implication of the NAIRU concept is that, in the long run, the unemployment rate can only change as a result of a change in the NAIRU. This has a strong bearing

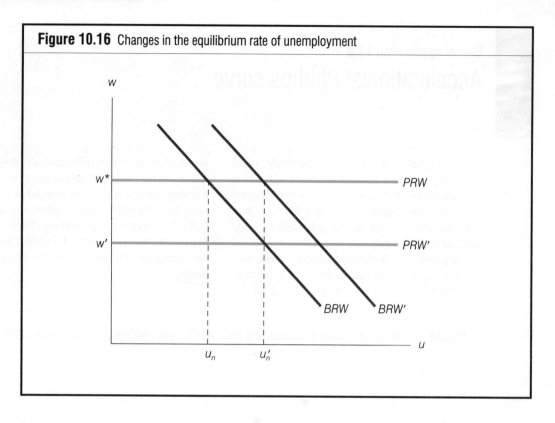

Figure 10.16 Changes in the equilibrium rate of unemployment

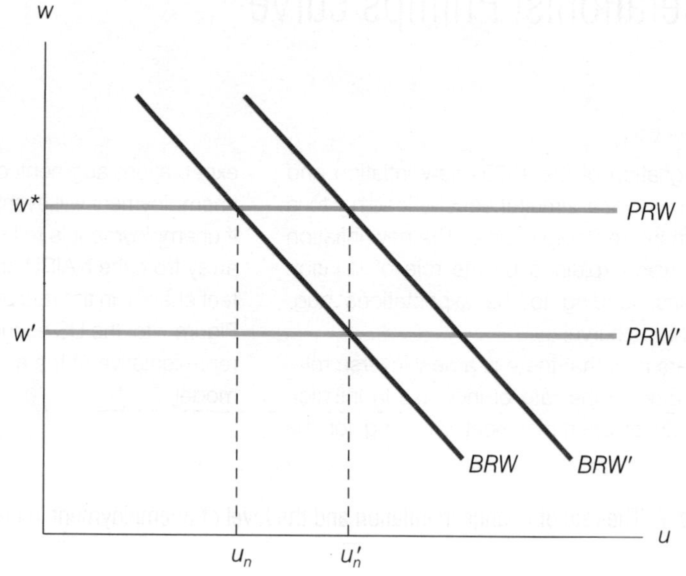

on policy makers. If unemployment is to be tackled in the long term, then policies should concentrate on the supply rather than the demand side. Global application 8.2 in Chapter 8 gives a relevant account of this approach with the Thatcher reforms to the UK labour market in the 1980s.

10

10.6.4 Hysteresis

In the long run, the Phillips curve is vertical at the equilibrium rate of unemployment, indicating that no trade-off exists between unemployment and inflation. However, this does not rule out the possibility that the equilibrium rate of unemployment itself is open to change. The NAIRU has been found to have changed over time and the evidence suggests that there is a close relationship between the NAIRU and the actual rate of unemployment. Hysteresis refers to the notion that short-run changes in unemployment can influence the NAIRU. In this case, short-run changes in unemployment can become remarkably persistent.

This is shown in Figure 10.17. The economy starts off at the NAIRU and the inflation rate π_1. If unemployment were to rise to u_1 due to a negative shock, then the normal Phillips curve story would proceed as follows. At higher levels of unemployment, workers will moderate wage demands, and wage and price inflation will fall. As inflation expectations decline, the short-run Phillips curve will shift downwards and the economy will return to the NAIRU but at a lower rate of inflation.

However, suppose that when unemployment increased to u_1, the NAIRU also increased to this level. In this case, the long-run Phillips curve will shift outwards to this level and the economy will settle down at this new long-run equilibrium. The short-run increase in unemployment is now a permanent result.

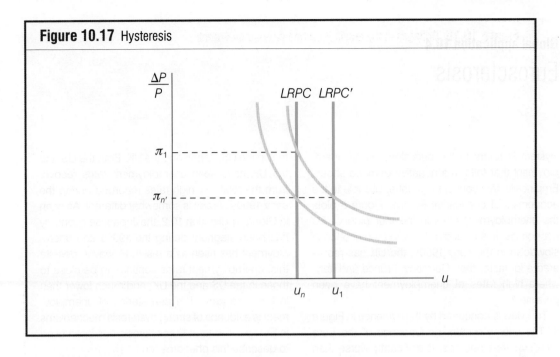

Figure 10.17 Hysteresis

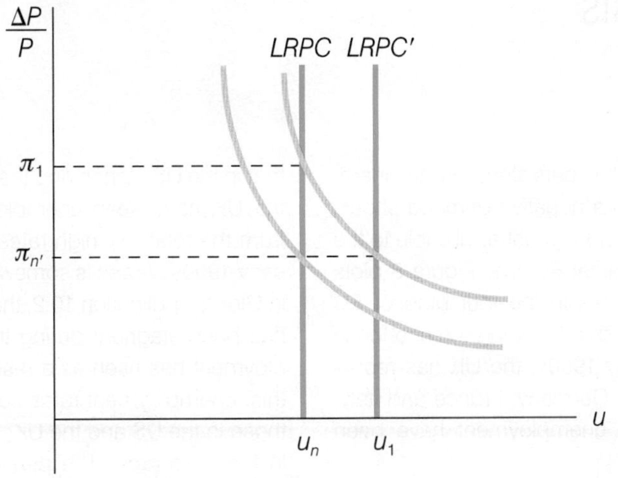

The concept of hysteresis is of growing importance in economics. This is due to a new interest in what is defined as the *medium run*. As the short run can effectively be a considerable period of time, the medium run is used to describe situations where there are fairly persistent, but not necessarily permanent, movements in a series such as unemployment. This might be one reason why estimates of the NAIRU tend to track the actual rate of unemployment. One important example of hysteresis is the rise in unemployment in Europe. This has come to be known as Eurosclerosis and empirical evidence is offered in Global application 10.4.

Hysteresis mechanisms

How do short-run movements in the unemployment rate become permanent? Several different types of hysteresis mechanisms have been proposed.

Insider-outsider mechanisms There are two types of workers. Insiders are those who have firm-specific skills which give them a degree of exclusivity. Outsiders, by contrast, do not offer the firm any input which could not be substituted easily by other members of the workforce. This gives insiders a powerful position when bargaining over wages with the firm. They will be able to push for higher wages without outsiders acting as a moderating force. Outsiders without work would rationally try to price themselves into work, but because they lack the exclusive skills of insiders, they are not as valuable to the firm.

The optimal bargaining strategy for insiders is to push for the highest wages while remaining in employment. Figure 10.18 represents the preferences of insider workers. If the original level of employment was at point N_0, then the insider workers are only made better off by achieving higher wage settlements. For this reason, the indifference curves are horizontal and emanate from the original employment level. No benefit is obtained from the employment of more workers. At the same wage rate, an insider is indifferent between an employment level N_1 or N_0.

Figure 10.19 shows what might happen to the level of employment when there are shifts in the demand for labour. At the initial employment level N_0, labour demand is $N_0^d(w)$ and

10

Global application 10.4

Eurosclerosis

Hysteresis refers to the persistent rise in unemployment that follows a negative demand shock. Empirically, this concept is most applicable to the economies of continental Europe. Figure 8 plots the unemployment rates in the four biggest EU economies. It is clear that following the economic slowdown in the early 1990s, the UK has recovered a lot faster than Germany, France and Italy, where high rates of unemployment have been persistent.

This view is concurred by the evidence in Figure 9. The unemployment performance of the Euro area countries has been significantly worse than that in the US, Japan and the UK. Both the US and the UK have seen unemployment rates recover from the relatively high rates recorded during the early 1990s. Japan is somewhat different. As seen in Global application 10.2, the Japanese economy has been stagnant during the 1990s and unemployment has risen as a result. However, despite this, unemployment rates continue to be close to those in the US and the UK, and much lower than in the Euro area. The persistence of unemployment is evidence of strong hysteresis mechanisms in Europe. The term Eurosclerosis has been used to describe this phenomenon.

Figure 8 Unemployment in the EU

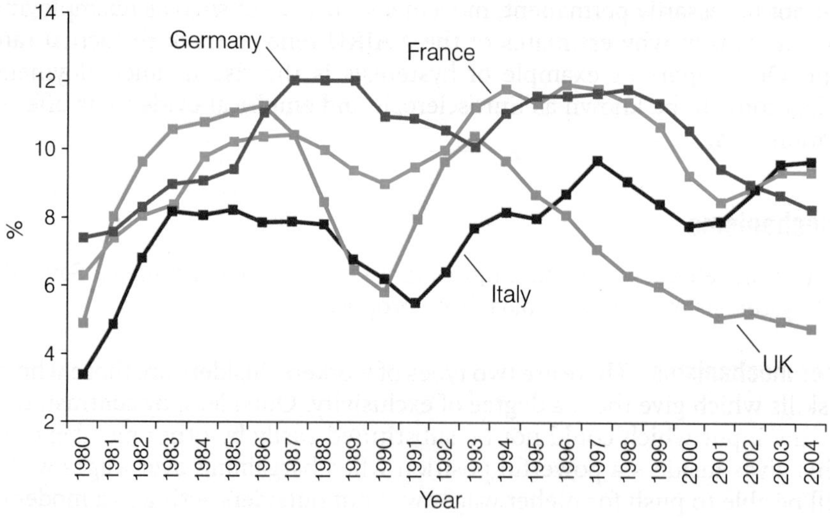

Global application 10.4 (continued)

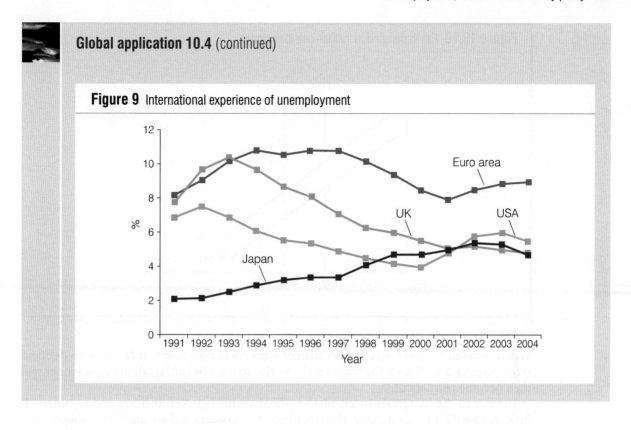

Figure 9 International experience of unemployment

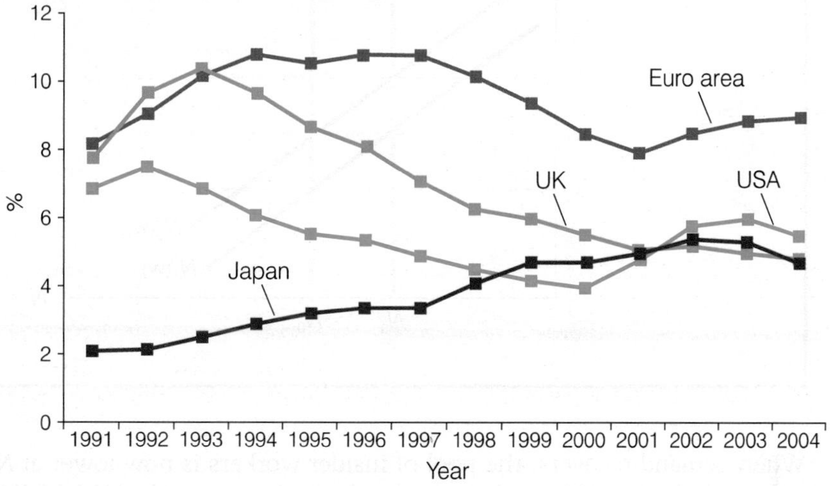

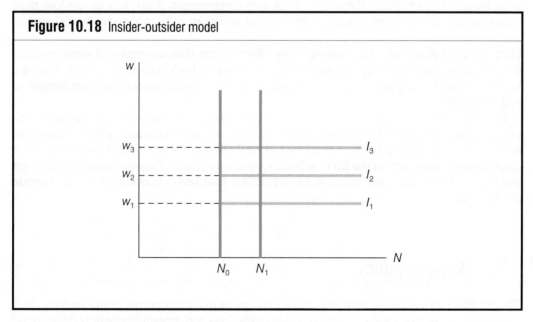

Figure 10.18 Insider-outsider model

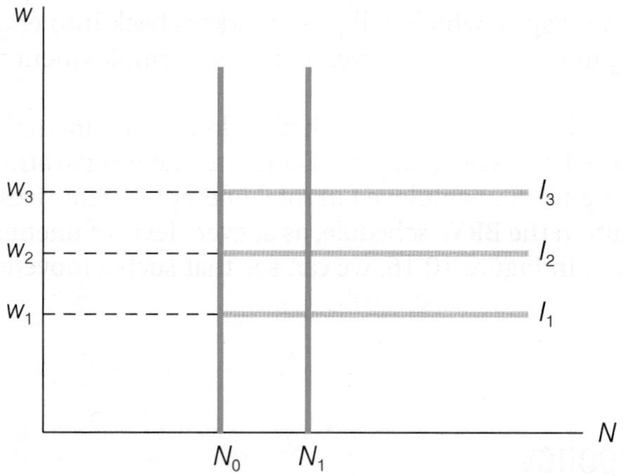

the wage level is w_1. If there was a fall in demand to $N_1^d(w)$, then the insiders would choose the highest wage level subject to them remaining in employment. The wage would drop to w_2 and the employment level will be maintained at N_0.

Things get interesting when the demand shock is unanticipated. In this case, a number of insiders demanding a wage of w_1 will be displaced and employment will fall to N_1. The displaced workers will then lose their insider status and firm-specific skills will be eroded.

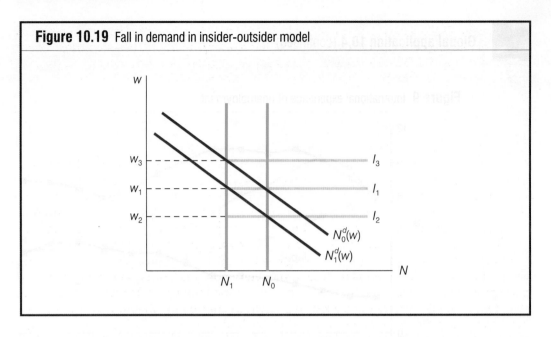

Figure 10.19 Fall in demand in insider-outsider model

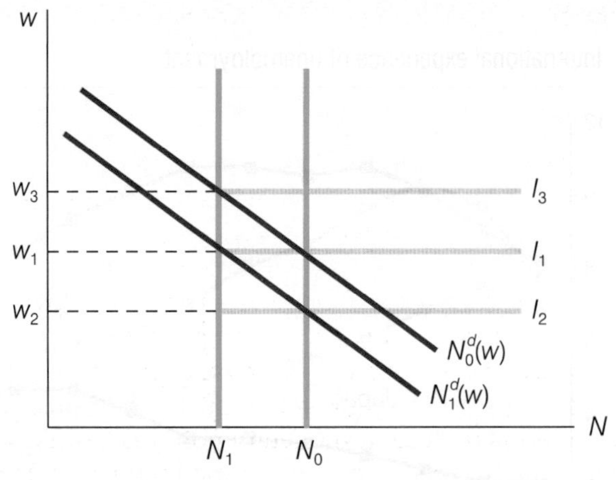

When demand recovers, the pool of insider workers is now lower at N_1, so with demand recovering back to $N_0^d(w)$, the wage level will rise to w_3. The initial fall in employment will then become permanent.

The key to the hysteresis mechanism is the dynamic between insiders and outsiders. If insiders lose their status quickly, then they become outsiders and are unable to influence the wage bargain so as to bring themselves back into employment. If insiders do not lose their firm-specific capabilities so quickly, then they can still exert influence on the wage bargain.

Long-run unemployment The reserve army effect means that unemployed workers exert downward pressures on wages, which will price workers back into employment. This is a key feature of the bargained real wage curve, where as unemployment rises, the bargained real wage falls.

10

There have been several studies suggesting that the long-term unemployed may lose motivation and are less active in searching for jobs. Therefore, the reserve army effect is weakened as the proportion of long-term unemployed in total unemployment rises. This will manifest itself in an outward shift in the BRW schedule, as at every level of unemployment, the target real wage will be higher. In Figure 10.16, we can see that such a movement acts to increase the NAIRU.

10.7 Monetary policy

The NAIRU has become a very important concept in macroeconomic policy making. It is significant in two main ways. The first is that in the long run, unemployment is determined by structural factors; therefore, the only way to reduce unemployment is to reduce the NAIRU. Hysteresis adds another dimension to this and explains how unemployment movements that originate in the short run can become very persistent.

The second area where the NAIRU is undoubtedly important is in the operation of monetary policy. Inflation arises as unemployment deviates from the NAIRU, so any attempt at controlling inflation would involve running the economy close to its NAIRU level. Inflation expectations are also important since this will determine the economy's position on the long-run Phillips curve. As the control of inflation has become the increasing preoccupation of macroeconomic policy, the NAIRU has gained importance by association. There is now a strong link between monetary policy and the NAIRU, which will be investigated further in the final section of this chapter.

10.7.1 Monetary policy and inflation

Controlling inflation has been the predominant aim of government policy in recent times. This possibly reflects the changing emphasis of economic policy – away from direct intervention and maintaining full employment, and towards creating a stable economic environment in which private sector firms can prosper. As inflation is considered to be a root cause of economic instability, monetary policy has become increasingly important for maintaining price stability as much as an influence on aggregate demand and output.

So far, this chapter has examined the link between unemployment and inflation. It has been established that in terms of output, monetary policy is neutral in the long run, and perhaps also in the short run if expectations are formed rationally. Therefore, controlling the money supply appears to be a key ingredient in controlling inflation. In addition, we have seen that inflation expectations feed through directly into inflation, so the management of expectations is also important. These are among the main factors that have guided the formulation of monetary policy in developed economies.

Controlling the money supply

Recall that the quantity theory of money suggests the following relationship between the level of nominal output and the amount of money in circulation.

$$Mv = PY$$

M is the money stock
v is the velocity of circulation
P is the price level
Y is the level of real output

The main prediction of the quantity theory of money is that changes in the money supply will generate proportional effects in prices, and no effect at all on output. This is because the velocity of circulation is assumed to be fixed, and output is at the equilibrium level determined by the NAIRU.

As v and Y are fixed, then the quantity theory equation can be rearranged so that:

$$P = (v/Y)M$$

and

$$\Delta P = (v/Y)\Delta M$$

So:

$$\frac{\Delta P}{P} = \frac{\Delta M}{M}$$

The predictions of the quantity theory of money are the same as the expectations augmented Phillips curve model under the assumptions of rational expectations. Any increase in the rate of growth of the money supply will lead to an immediate increase in prices of the same proportion.

The policy prescription suggested by the quantity theory is that controlling the growth of the money supply is key to controlling inflation. Inflation is a result of an excessive growth

10

in the money supply. Over time, the equilibrium level of output is likely to increase with productivity growth, but if the money stock is allowed to increase at a faster rate, the result will be higher prices as the excess money balance chases a relatively smaller number of goods and services.

Chapter 5 discusses various approaches to controlling the money supply, such as open market operations, special deposits and reserve asset ratios. These have typically been the traditional tools for controlling inflation by exerting influence over the money supply.

Monetary targeting

The expectations augmented Phillips curve highlights the important role that expectations of inflation play in establishing the actual rate of inflation in an economy.

If the government considered the current level of inflation to be too high, it could simply reduce the money supply. When expectations are formed adaptively, the level of unemployment will rise above the natural rate and there will be downward pressure on prices. Eventually, as expectations catch up with the actual rate of inflation, the economy will settle at the equilibrium rate of unemployment, but also at a lower actual and expected rate of inflation. This is shown in Figure 10.20, where the inflation is gradually reduced from π_1 to π_2. However, in the interim period, unemployment will rise above the NAIRU, so controlling inflation requires policy to generate a recession.

However, under rational expectations, the use of monetary policy is far more successful, in that higher unemployment does not need to be created in order to reduce the rate of inflation. In fact, not even a contraction in the money supply is required – only a credible announcement of such. Once the government or other monetary policy authority has made public their intentions to reduce the money supply, then rational inflation expectations will be immediately revised downwards. These lower expectations will then feed through the economy through wage bargains and the lower actual rate of inflation will arise. In Figure 10.20, the inflation rate will simply move down the long-run Phillips curve from π_1 to π_2.

10

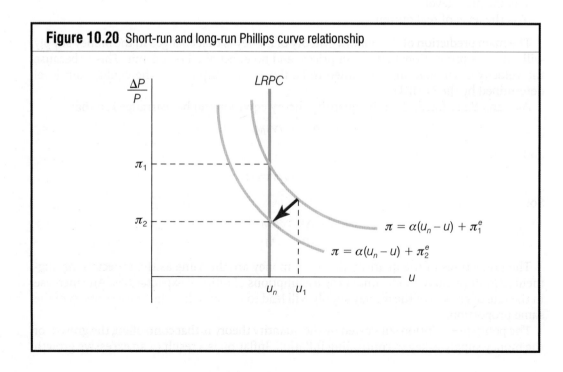

Figure 10.20 Short-run and long-run Phillips curve relationship

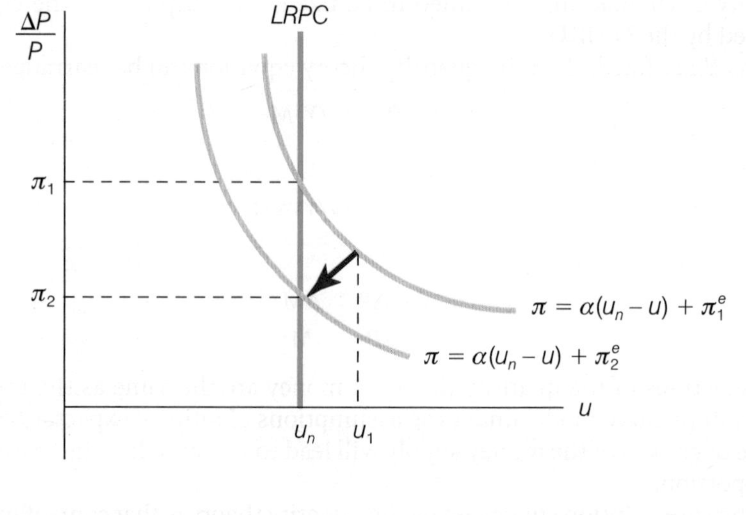

This represents a painless disinflation in the sense that there will be no interim increase in unemployment. Inflation can be controlled by just anchoring expectations through policy announcement, no actual money contraction or increase in unemployment is necessary. A policy of monetary targeting sets out to do exactly this. The government pre-announces the growth of the money supply as a way of influencing private sector expectations.

Global application 10.5 gives an example of the policy of monetary targeting in the UK during the early 1980s and highlights the difficulties of controlling inflation through direct control and pre-announcements of the growth in the money supply.

Global application 10.5

The medium term financial strategy (MTFS)

The MTFS was the cornerstone of monetary policy in the UK during the early 1980s. The aim was to pre-announce increases in the money supply, which in turn would anchor inflation expectations and wage demands. This approach reflects the theory of the expectations augmented Phillips curve, where the key to controlling inflation is to control expectations of inflation.

The MTFS was outlined in the March 1980 budget. The central tenet of the policy was to pre-announce progressive reductions in the broad monetary aggregate £M3, with the initial target ranges of:

1980–1981:	7–11 per cent
1983–1984:	4–8 per cent

These targets were not achieved and in 1985 the £M3 target was abandoned by the Chancellor. It was reinstated in the 11–15 per cent range in the March 1986 budget, but was abandoned when the actual growth of the money supply came in at 20 per cent. What factors might account for the failure of monetary targeting in this period?

Financial deregulation

The growth of the broad money aggregate £M3 had been linked historically to the growth in public sector borrowing. However, this aggregate was also strongly influenced by the growth in bank lending. The difficulty of controlling the money supply occurred against a backdrop of financial deregulation. The outcome of this was to increase the power of financial institutions to create credit; hence, the government had limited ability to control the money supply.

Financial liberalization commenced in October 1979 with the abolition of exchange controls. In the 1960s, Britons travelling abroad were limited to £50 spending money. Domestic firms wishing to invest overseas had to do so through a separate investment currency market which charged a premium over the market exchange rate. These controls were implemented due to the vulnerability of the UK balance of payments and exchange rate at the time.

The need for exchange controls in order to support the exchange rate and the balance of payments was alleviated by the emergence of North Sea oil. Oil exports moved the trade balance into surplus, and petro currency status strengthened the value of sterling. The lifting of exchange controls had direct effects on domestic monetary policy. At the time, the Bank of England operated a special supplementary deposit scheme known as the corset. By forcing banks to keep a proportion of their deposits in non-interest-bearing special deposits at the Bank of England, the stock of high powered money on which credit could be created was reduced. In addition, the reserve asset ratio had required banks to hold 12.5 per cent of their sterling liabilities in reserve assets. This would act to limit the size of the money multiplier and the overall money supply. However, in an open

Global application 10.5 (continued)

financial market, any bank could bypass these regulations by lending to British consumers from overseas subsidiaries.

Following the abolition of exchange controls, the minimum reserve asset ratio and the corset became increasingly irrelevant and were abolished in June 1980 and in August 1981, respectively. The deregulation of domestic credit markets also reflected the pro-competition ideology of the government.

At the time the UK mortgage market was effectively a cartel run by the Building Societies Association which fixed interest rates. The demand for loans exceeded the supply so mortgage credit was rationed. Waiting lists for mortgages existed, and priority was given to those who had a history of saving with the institution. A two-year waiting list for mortgage credit was not uncommon.

Banks were keen to crack the mortgage market, especially given that the failure of emerging markets in the 1970s and 1980s had encouraged them to look for safer domestic investments. In response to new competition from banks, the Building Societies Association announced that borrowing and lending rates would simply be advised rates and, in 1986, even stopped recommending rates altogether. As a result, rates became market determined and rationing was less important, so the availability of mortgage credit expanded.

Deregulation worked both ways. From 1983 onwards, building societies were given access to money markets for wholesale funds, which enabled them to extend their lending activities to areas traditionally served by banks. Increased competition led to an expansion in the availability of credit cards, hire purchase agreements and personal loans.

Financial liberalization had the effect of boosting bank lending, making £M3 difficult to interpret, and its control almost impossible. Therefore, an inconsistency existed in the government's monetary policy. On the one hand, it was trying to exert control over the growth of the money supply but, on the other, was reducing its ability to exert control by promoting competition through deregulation. In effect, the MTFS was control without controls.

Credibility

The idea behind the MTFS was that pre-announcements of the money supply would anchor inflation expectations. If trade unions pushed for wage increases in excess of the announced growth in the money supply, then the result would be increasing interest rates and unemployment. This would constrain trade unions to moderating wage demands to the government's target.

Trade unions, though, did not feel constrained. Each attempted to achieve the best possible deal for their members. If prices rose in excess of the money supply, then any resulting unemployment would be the government's problem. In fact, they believed that if faced with the choice between accommodating price increases with adequate money growth or generating unemployment, the government would opt for the former.

The pre-announcements therefore lacked credibility and failed to anchor inflation expectations.

These two failings of the MTFS were to have a significant effect on the future operation of monetary policy. First, with financial deregulation, it became apparent that the government could only achieve limited success at controlling the money supply. The focus of monetary policy therefore shifted towards controlling the price of money: the interest rate. The policy of inflation targeting replaced monetary targeting, and simply involved setting interest rates to control the level of inflation in the economy.

Second, monetary policy lacked credibility because when it came down to it, the government would be politically inclined to trade-off higher inflation for lower unemployment. Credibility, though, could be achieved if monetary policy was delegated to an agency that did not share the same trade-off. This is typically an independent central bank, because its mandate simply involves achieving a certain inflation target and so its announcements would carry greater credibility.

Inflation targeting

Global application 10.5 highlights the problems of controlling the money supply in the current era. Continued financial deregulation means that monetary authorities are unlikely to exert complete control over the domestic money supply. This was described as 'trying to control without controls'. The policy of targeting the money supply is aimed at achieving a target inflation rate. The solution to the problem might be to target the inflation rate directly.

Inflation is likely to arise when the economy deviates from the NAIRU. Therefore, maintaining an inflation target requires the economy to be maintained at this level. Although controlling the quantity of money is difficult in liberalized financial markets, monetary authorities still have the power to control its price. As the interest rate is likely to control domestic activity, it can be used to keep the economy at its NAIRU.

The credibility of inflation targets

For monetary or inflation targeting to work, any announcement has to be seen as credible. That is, the private sector really must believe that the monetary policy authority will be prepared to make the contraction in the money policy it has announced – even if it may create unemployment. A reason why targeting may fail could well be because these policy announcements just aren't viewed as being credible. If it came down to it, would the government really risk its own popularity and its re-election chances by tightening the money supply and creating unemployment?

Once the private sector has doubts over the government's resolve to carry out the means necessary to reduce inflation, it will no longer rationally reduce inflation expectations downwards on announcement. Credibility in the setting of monetary policy has become a major issue recently, and is the subject we turn to next.

10.7.2 The time inconsistency problem and central bank independence

If agents have rational expectations, then inflation targeting should prove to be remarkably successful. Whenever a new target is announced, inflation expectations will automatically adjust to the new level. No policy needs to be activated, the private sector is simply aware that if inflation differs from the target then policy would be forthcoming. Therefore, changing expectations will simply pre-empt any need for policy implementation.

However, when a target is announced should the government be believed? Looking at the Phillips curve relationship, it is clear that in the long run there is no trade-off between unemployment and inflation. Accepting this, the government would probably have a preferred level of inflation towards the bottom of the vertical line. All that is required is for the government to choose their favoured position on the long-run Phillips curve and announce it as their inflation target.

The problem, though, for the government is in making its announcements credible. Credibility becomes an issue because of the presence of the short-run Phillips curve. This is more intriguing when we consider that the position of this curve depends on inflation expectations.

If the government were to announce a low inflation target which is adopted into private sector expectations, the government may then face an incentive to expand the economy. This is shown in Figure 10.21, where the policy maker wishes to target an inflation rate of π_1. If the public believes this announcement and sets expectations equal to the target inflation rate, then the short-run Phillips curve with this expectation $\pi = \alpha(u_n - u) + \pi_1^e$ forms the policy frontier faced by the government.

Figure 10.21 Time inconsistency problem

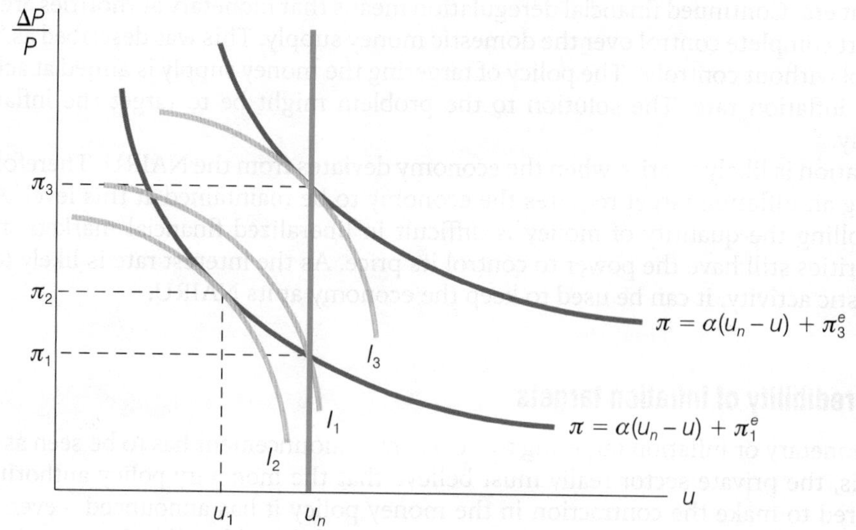

This original inflation announcement is now incredible. It is clearly the case that the government can move on to a lower indifference curve ($I_1 \rightarrow I_2$) by trading off higher inflation ($\pi_2 > \pi_1$) for lower unemployment. The public is aware of the government's preferences and can therefore establish that the government would not be able to credibly commit to this inflation announcement, so it should not be believed. This inflation announcement is *time inconsistent*. If the public were to believe it, the government would then have the incentive to renege on the target.

In fact, the lowest level of inflation where time inconsistency does not occur is π_3. If this is the public's inflation expectation then the government cannot move to a lower indifference curve by launching an inflation 'surprise'. At any inflation announcement below this level, the incentive to cheat would be restored. The public would therefore not believe any inflation announcement below π_3.

This problem with credibility is known as the time inconsistency of low inflation monetary policy. Low inflation announcements cannot be believed because once they are acted upon, the government has the incentive to change their target level of inflation. The private sector is fully aware of these incentives and will not allow themselves to be duped. Therefore, their anticipated level of inflation would be somewhat higher.

The presence of the opportunity to exploit a short-run gain can actually make the government worse off in the long run. This is an important feature of time inconsistency in policy making. Even if a government is sincere in its proclamations, it will find it hard to enforce its best outcome.

Solving the time inconsistency problem in monetary policy

Delegating policy to conservative central bankers The time inconsistency problem arises because in the government's utility function there will be an incentive to trade-off inflation for unemployment. These preferences are known to the private sector, which will

Figure 10.22 Solving the time consistency problem with a central banker

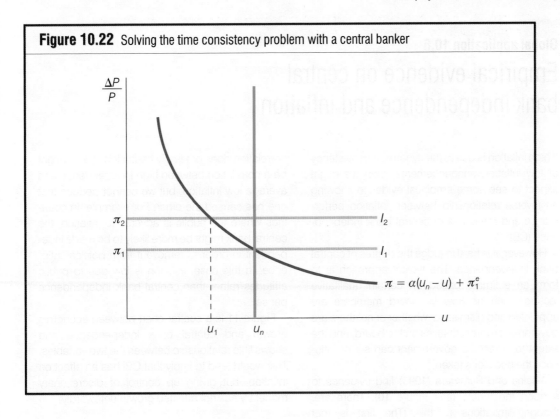

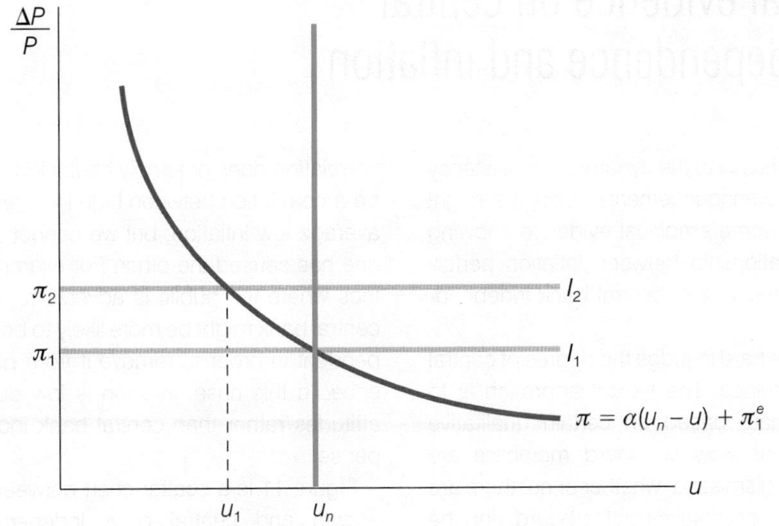

rationally choose to reject low inflation announcements. One possible solution would be to delegate monetary policy making to an agent or an institution that does not share the same incentives over unemployment and inflation: this is Rogoff's famous conservative central banker. If the public is aware of these preferences, then low inflation announcements are seen to be much more credible.

In Figure 10.22, monetary policy is set by an independent central bank which is only interested in achieving the target rate of inflation. As its objective is independent of the rate of unemployment, its indifference curves are horizontal. Inflation announcements are now highly credible.

This is the logic behind the move to make central banks independent. Governments must be popular to achieve re-election, so their commitment to inflation targets when there is an opportunity to lower unemployment might be questionable. The same is not true for an independent central bank that is free from the need to pursue politically motivated policies.

Optimal contracts Delegation does not necessarily need to be made to a central banker with very conservative attitudes towards inflation. All that is required is that the central bankers are given the incentives to act in such a way. These incentives can be formalized through performance contracts; these are known as Walsh contracts, after Carl Walsh who proposed the idea.

Reputation Looking at the time inconsistency problem, it is clear that the government is made worse off in the long run. Given that this is universally known, the government should be able to find a credible way of maintaining a low inflation announcement. This simply requires the government to care about the future. If the government has a sufficiently long horizon, then they may have an incentive to try to build a reputation on being tough on inflation.

Global application 10.6

Empirical evidence on central bank independence and inflation

If high inflation is due to the dynamic inconsistency of low inflation announcements, then we might expect to see some empirical evidence showing an inverse relationship between inflation performance and measures of central bank independence (CBI).

However, it is hard to judge the degree of central bank independence. The typical approach is to form an estimate based on certain qualitative factors, such as how its board members are appointed and dismissed, whether or not there are government representatives on the board, and the extent to which the government can set or influence the decisions taken.

Alesina and Summers (1993) find evidence to support the theory (see Figure 10). There are, though, limitations to this. The first is that correlation does not imply causation. There might be a correlation between high independence and average low inflation, but we cannot deduce that one has caused the other. For example, in countries where the public is adverse to inflation, the central bank might be more likely to be made independent in order to remove it from political influence. In this case, inflation is low due to public attitudes rather than central bank independence per se.

Figure 11 is a scatter chart between economic growth and central bank independence and shows little relationship between the two variables. This would tend to imply that CBI has an effect on inflation, but giving up control of discretionary monetary has not affected growth untowardly.

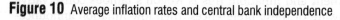

Figure 10 Average inflation rates and central bank independence

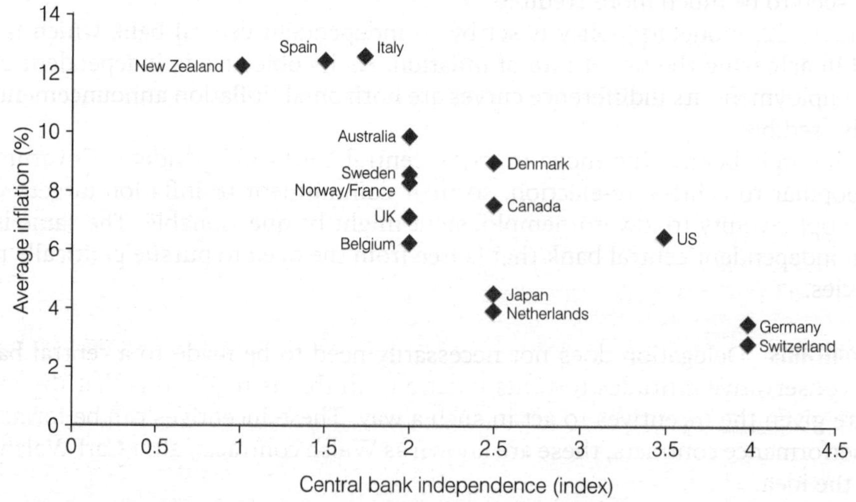

10

Global application 10.6 (continued)

Figure 11 CBI and average GNP growth rates

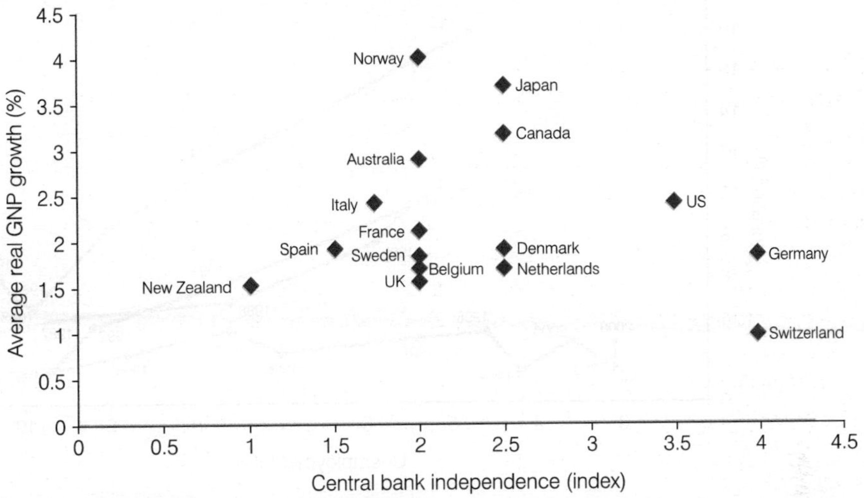

Global application 10.7

The end of the trade-off in the UK

Recent plots of the Phillips curve in the UK produce a startling result (Figure 12). Evidence from 1980 to the first half of the 1990s clearly shows an inverse relationship between unemployment and inflation. Although this relationship has shifted over time – the pattern of the Phillips curve is distinct. Data on unemployment and inflation from 1994 onwards, though, shows a clear lack of a Phillips curve relationship. Unemployment has fallen constantly to historically low levels without any impact on inflation, which also has stabilized at low levels. Based on past relationships, the current level of unemployment would be synonymous with double-digit inflation rates.

It is reported that the Phillips curve is now dead. But what factors might be responsible for these recent trends?

Inflation targeting

Since the UK's exit from the exchange rate mechanism in 1992, monetary policy has been conducted by setting a target for the rate of inflation with the implicit assumption that interest rates would be used to keep inflation near its target. This policy was cemented in 1997 when the Bank of England was given operational independence. Although politicians continue to set the inflation target, the power to set interest rates in view of this target has been transferred to the Bank of England.

According to economic theory, this ought to remove the time-inconsistency element from inflation announcements and hence the inflation bias that is the result of discretionary policy making. In these circumstances, low inflation announcements gain credibility because the public realizes that the

Global application 10.7 (continued)

Figure 12 Unemployment and inflation in the UK

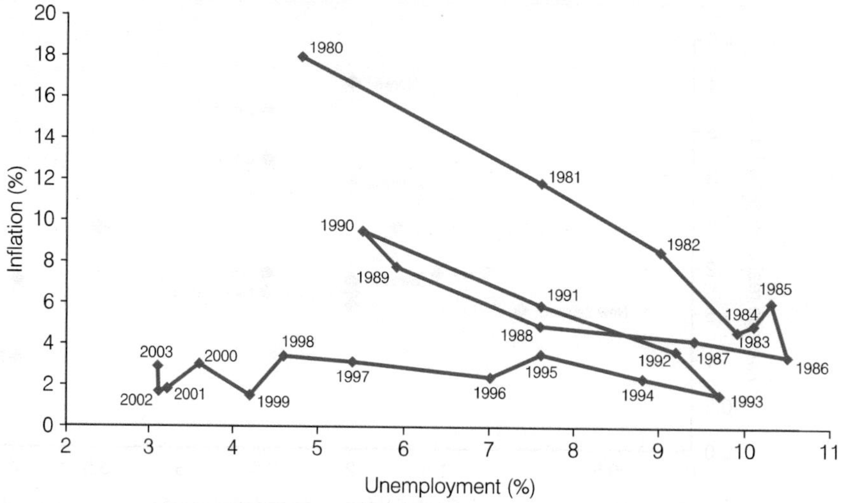

Bank of England faces no political costs to raising interest rates, if necessary. Therefore, despite low levels of unemployment, inflation expectations are sufficiently anchored at low levels.

A fall in the NAIRU

A combination of low inflation and low unemployment is evidence that there might have been a substantial fall in the NAIRU (non-accelerating inflation rate of unemployment). This reflects an improvement in the supply side of the economy, which enables lower rates of unemployment to exist without generating inflation. A number of factors accounting for this have been proposed.

Supply side reforms in the 1980s

During the 1980s a number of reforms were made to labour market laws and regulations, along with further policies designed to improve competition. Believing these policies to have had a significant effect on the supply side of the economy, the expansion in aggregate demand during the late 1980s was allowed to proceed unchecked, but ultimately generated high levels of inflation.

One view is that these supply side reforms simply took time to become effective, so a fall in the NAIRU during the 1990s reflects a delayed reaction to policies implemented in the 1980s. This is not unreasonable – as changes to the way prices are set or how wages are bargained might not respond immediately to the new environment.

New economy

The advances in new information technology could be expected to lower the NAIRU in two ways. First, new technology might improve productivity by enabling firms to manage and produce more efficiently, as well as increasing the range of goods and services that can feasibly be produced. Second, by making it easier for consumers to find and compare prices, the Internet has undoubtedly increased competition in some sectors of the economy. The effects of increased competition would put pressure on margins and lower prices.

Globalization

Low inflation has been a global phenomenon, which implies that it might be driven by factors that are not specific to certain countries. During the 1990s, the growth in world trade has continued to outstrip that of GDP, implying that economies are becoming increasingly open. Like the Internet, this would also be expected to produce lower prices due to more intensive competition in product markets. It could also be the case that the emergence of China as a major exporter of low-priced manufactured goods could be driving global prices downwards. These open economy effects on the NAIRU will be expanded on in later chapters.

The problem with reputation-building is that government terms are finite and relatively short. As the electoral cycle is usually no more than five years, there may be inadequate time available to build a reputation for low inflation. And, even if successful – there is a chance that the government will not be re-elected and therefore cannot benefit from their enhanced reputation in the future.

It is undoubtedly true that the current vogue in monetary policy is for independence of the central bank. This is the case in most of the economically advanced countries throughout the world. In recent years, the world has managed to achieve consistently low levels of inflation, so it looks like the argument is working.

However, there is still an intellectual debate on the importance of independent central banks. It is a feature of history that economic paradigms are treated as best practice right up to the moment that they fail. Global applications 10.8 and 10.9 give some wider consideration on central bank independence.

10.7.3 Seignorage and hyper-inflation

There are two ways in which a government can finance a deficit other than restricting fiscal policy. The first and conventional way is to borrow by issuing bonds. The second is that the government, usually with the cooperation of the central bank, can finance its deficit by printing money. The value of the real resources (real goods and services) that the government obtains by simply running the printing presses is known as *seignorage* revenue.

If the change in the money stock is ΔM, and the price level in the economy is P, then seignorage revenue S is given as follows:

$$S = \frac{\Delta M}{P} \qquad (10.17)$$

Alternatively, if both sides of this equation are multiplied and divided by M, then:

$$S = \frac{\Delta M}{M} \times \frac{M}{P}, \text{ or } S = g_M \times \frac{M}{P}$$

Seignorage is equal to the growth in the money supply (g_M) multiplied by the current real money stock (M/P).

If the government wished to fund its budget deficit (B) from seignorage revenues (so $S = B$), then the required growth in the money stock can be found from rearranging (10.17):

$$g_M = B\Big/\left(\frac{M}{P}\right) \qquad (10.18)$$

Judging from (10.18), if the current budget deficit represents x percent of the money stock, then this is the required growth rate of the money stock – or so we would think! The reason why the relationship is not as clear cut as this is because the current money stock might be influenced by the growth in the money supply.

In Chapter 5, the amount of money balances that the public are willing to hold is given by liquidity preference theory.

$$\frac{M}{P} = L(Y,r)$$

where the demand for money balances is positively related to income (Y) and negatively related to the level of interest rates (r). The nominal interest rate represents the

10

Global application 10.8

Coordinating monetary and fiscal policy

Central bank independence is a popular policy. Since the stagflation of the 1970s, almost all OECD nations have made the target of low and steady inflation the cornerstone of economic policy. Monetary independence is an easily understood and intuitive policy with this aim. However, separation of policy control may lead to a lack of coordination, resulting in an inferior policy mix, skewed to loose fiscal policy and tight monetary policy.

Nordhaus (1994) presents this argument from the standpoint of the Clinton administration's attempt to reduce the US budget deficit. A fiscal contraction, unless offset by an immediate monetary expansion, would result in a recession. Self-interested politicians may then consider the high deficit equilibrium to be the lesser evil. The coordination problem arises as the monetary authorities may be sluggish or cautious in reaction to fiscal policies. Therefore, the five-year plan proposed to cut the US budget deficit by $143 billion is a gamble, as there is a strong reliance on the fact that monetary policy will be sufficiently loose to stimulate offsetting investment and consumption.

Figure 13 identifies the problem in graphical form. The economy can be considered to be at point 1, where the government's fiscal position is S_1 and the interest rate set by the Federal Bank is r_1. If the government wishes to reduce the fiscal deficit to S_2, it will need to either cut spending or raise taxes, either of which will lead to a fall in aggregate demand, shifting the IS curve inwards.

The impact on real GDP, though, could be offset by an immediate reduction in interest rates. However, the US Federal bank is unlikely to pre-emptively cut interest rates unless inflation has fallen below target. Therefore, the economy will end up at point 2 rather than move to point 3.

If the fiscal authority is aware of this, it creates a disincentive to deal with the fiscal policy position in the first place. Therefore, the equilibrium of such a game is for the economy to get stuck in a high interest rate, high deficit equilibrium. A lower deficit outcome with lower interest rates might be more preferable and would have no impact on GDP, apart from redistribution by reducing government spending and increasing investment and household consumption. This is coordination failure.

Figure 13 The coordination problem

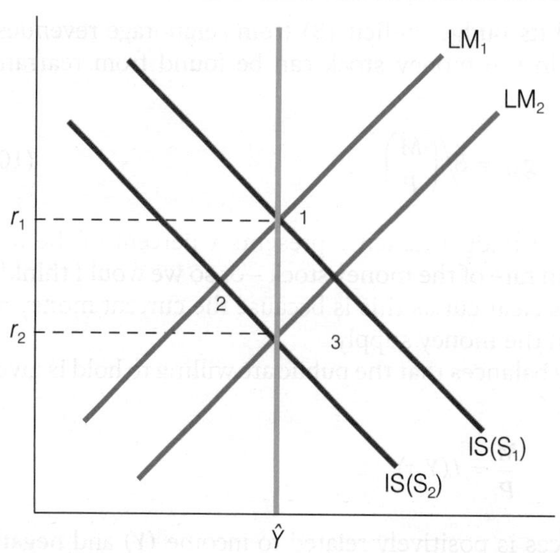

Global application 10.9

What is left for discretionary fiscal policy?

Before the inflation of the 1970s, discretionary macroeconomic policy played an important role in stabilizing the economy. Since then, monetary policy has become increasingly prominent, and the role of fiscal policy has appeared to be relegated to a subservient role.

Following Taylor (2000), the workings of the economy can be described by three simple relationships.

- First, the central bank sets interest rates in order to hit a target inflation rate.
- Second, there is an inverse relationship between aggregate demand and the interest rate, which can be summed up by the IS curve.
- The third relationship is an expectations augmented Phillips curve relationship, where inflation responds positively to a deviation of actual output from potential GDP.

The monetary policy framework implies that aggregate demand (AD) is inversely related to inflation. If the current level of inflation exceeds the target rate, the central bank will increase interest rates. This will then reduce aggregate demand below the potential level of GDP and push inflation down towards its target rate. Alternatively, if inflation is below its target rate, the central bank will reduce interest rates, aggregate demand will expand above potential GDP and inflation will rise towards its target level.

Figure 14 plots the aggregate demand curve. The goal of monetary policy is to set interest rates so that aggregate demand is kept as close as possible to potential GDP at the target inflation rate.

The two dashed lines in Figure 14 show two different aggregate demand curves: one that has shifted to the right (AD_2) and the other that has shifted to the left (AD_1).

The task of countercyclical monetary policy is to offset these AD shocks in order to move the economy back to the original AD schedule. This would prevent GDP from deviating from its potential level and generating inflation or disinflation, respectively.

10

Figure 14 The Goldilocks economy

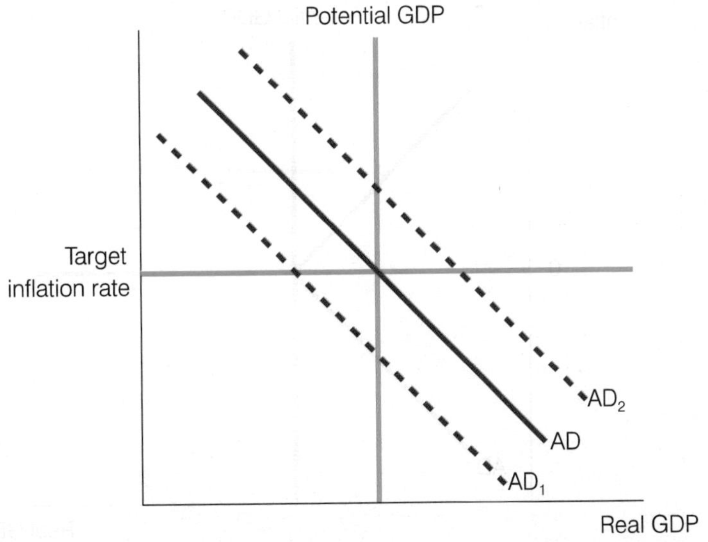

Global application 10.9 (continued)

This model describes what has come to be known as the 'Goldilocks economy', where policy is set so that the economy is 'not too hot' or 'not too cold.' Monetary policy plays the central role, but where does this leave fiscal policy?

Fiscal policy also has the ability to shift the AD curve through changes in government spending or taxation. Discretionary changes are those that are undertaken by legislation or executive decisions of government, whereas automatic stabilizers are the automatic reactions of spending and taxation over the business cycle. Both affect aggregate demand, but the impact of automatic stabilizers is quicker and more predictable.

Discretionary fiscal policy could be used to offset aggregate demand shocks in Figure 14 in the same way as monetary policy. However, for the purposes of stabilizing the economy, monetary policy has a large comparative advantage over fiscal policy. As implementation lags for monetary policy are much shorter, it can react faster to offset shocks, so it is better for governments to just let the central bank do the job.

What is left for discretionary policy?

As macroeconomic policy shifts towards the Goldilocks economy and inflation targeting (monetary policy), it is argued that there is no longer any role for discretionary fiscal policy. In fact, by generating shifts in the AD schedule, discretionary fiscal policy may even harm the ability of monetary policy to stabilize the economy. Therefore, fiscal policy should be restricted so that it cannot get in the way of monetary policy.

These restrictions have taken the form of fiscal policy rules. In the Euro area, monetary policy is set by the independent European Central Bank (ECB) and fiscal policy is constrained by the Stability and Growth Pact (SGP), which places restrictions on the level of current budget deficits and debt. In the UK, monetary policy is operated by the independent Bank of England, but fiscal policy is also constrained by rules on the level of the structural budget deficit. In each of these instances, the aim of the fiscal rule is to clear the path for monetary policy to stabilize the economy.

However, discretionary fiscal policy may still have a role to play in stabilizing the economy in some situations. The most obvious is when the economy experiences deflation. As there is a zero bound on the nominal interest rate, monetary policy becomes highly impotent when the economy experiences deflation and enters the liquidity trap.

10

Figure 15 Deflation, real interest rates and aggregate demand

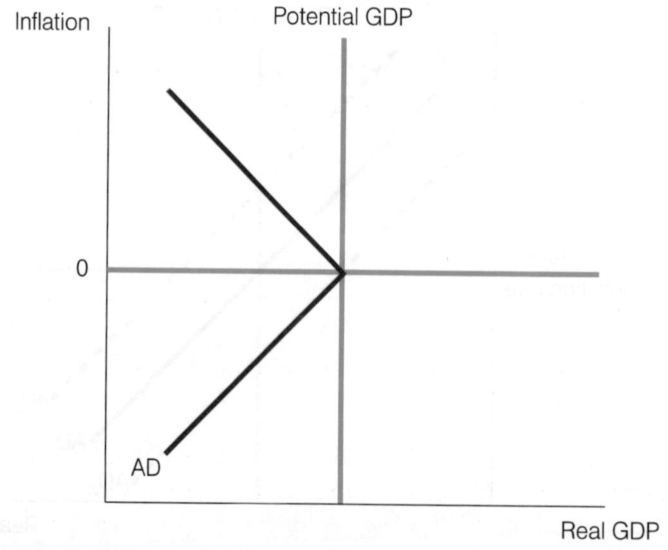

Global application 10.9 (continued)

This is shown in Figure 15 where the aggregate demand schedule develops a kink when the inflation rate is zero.

When the nominal interest rate approaches zero, deflation will put upward pressure on the real interest rate. This would drive the level of aggregate demand further below the potential GDP level, generating more deflation and higher real interest rates. Therefore, once the economy enters a deflationary spiral, there is little monetary policy can do. However, fiscal policy would still have the ability to generate shifts in the aggregate demand schedule, and can therefore be used to escape from a liquidity trap and deflationary spirals.

opportunity cost of money. It consists of two parts, the real interest rate and the expected level of inflation.

$$r = r_{nominal} = r_{real} + \pi^e$$

The growth in the money supply, through the quantity theory of money, will lead to an increase in the rate of inflation. As inflation increases, the value of the domestic money stock falls. Given the reduction in purchasing power, people move out of money into either financial assets or real goods and services.

The current money stock will be determined by the expected rate of inflation, and hence the expected rate of money growth. Therefore, equation (10.18) can be rewritten:

$$S = g_M\, L(Y, r_{real} + \pi^e)$$

$$S = g_M\, L(Y, r_{real} + g_M)$$

The growth in the money supply has two effects on seignorage revenues. Higher g_M will increase seignorage revenues gained from the existing money stock, but it will also have the effect of reducing the money stock held by the public on which seignorage revenues can be obtained. As the growth in the money stock rises, seignorage revenues will at first rise, but eventually the second order effect where money demand falls will dominate. Therefore, the revenue from seignorage will be ∩- shaped with respect to the growth in the money supply (see Figure 10.23). The government will maximize seignorage revenue (S^*) obtained at g_M^*.

Seignorage can be thought of as an inflation tax, if $g_M = \pi$. Essentially, the government generates inflation by increasing the money supply and this devalues the existing stock of monetary balances. The real value of money balances held by the public is devalued and transferred to the government.

10

Hyper-inflation

In the short run, an increase in the growth rate of the money supply may lead to little change in real money balances. However, over time as prices adjust, the government will find the same rate of money growth yields lower seignorage revenue. Therefore, in order to fund persistent deficits, it will have to continuously increase the growth of its money supply.

If there was no lag between money growth and the updating of inflation expectations, then the demand for money would fall immediately when the money growth rate was increased. Therefore, hyper-inflation requires the acceleration in the growth of money to stay one step ahead of the updating of expectations. Ever-increasing growth in the money stock will generate further seignorage revenues.

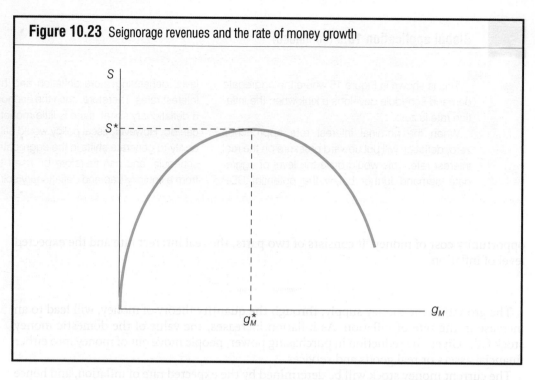

Figure 10.23 Seignorage revenues and the rate of money growth

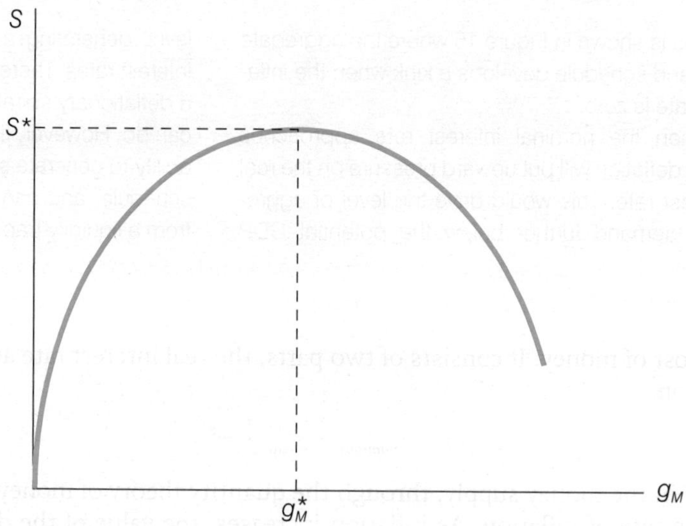

Hyper-inflation usually starts when a government faces a large budget deficit that requires painful policy measures to offset. Seignorage is then seen as an easy way out. A famous example relates to Germany in 1922–1923 where the payment of reparations to the Allies after the First World War generated large deficits and set in process a period of very high and accelerating inflation. Table 10.2 shows the incredible spiralling of prices between January 1922 and October 1923.

This rise in prices is incredible. In October 1923 prices were rising at 29,720 per cent a month, prices were 191,891,890 times greater than in January 1922. Hyper-inflations arise because once prices start to rise quickly, expectations of further price increases lead to the ever spiralling of prices in a self-fulfilling cycle.

Table 10.2 German hyper-inflation

Date	Currency (Jan 1922 =1)	Prices (Jan 1922 =1)	Inflation (% per month)
January 1922	1	1	1
January 1923	16	75	189
March 1923	45	132	–12
May 1923	70	221	157
July 1923	354	2 021	386
August 1923	5 394	25 515	1 262
September 1923	227 777	645 946	2 532
October 1923	20 201 256	191 891 890	29 720

Source: Holtfrerich 1986

Hyper-inflations do not blow themselves out; inflation will continue to accelerate and can only be stopped by intervention, such as:

- a credible commitment to reducing the budget deficit through tax increases or reductions in government spending.
- a credible commitment from the monetary authorities to stop printing money for the purposes of paying the debt.

For example, the end of the period of German hyper-inflation in 1922–1923 came from a reduction in reparations and replacing the central bank with a new institution that was much more independent.

Achieving the necessary level of credibility, though, can be painful and involve considerable welfare losses. This could be ironic as the reason for printing money in the first place could be to avoid implementing such policies.

Summary

- The control of unemployment and inflation has been a long-standing preoccupation of macroeconomists. This chapter covered the theory of the Phillips curve, which shows that there is a trade-off between the two.
- There is ample evidence to suggest that the trade-off is different in the short run and the long run, and the transition between short and long run is governed by the way expectations are formed and the degree of flexibility in wages and prices.
- Policy makers face a dilemma in trading-off unemployment and inflation. They use policy to make the trade-off based on their preferences between unemployment and inflation.
- The theory of the Phillips curve is very useful here, as it can be used to explain how monetary policy can be used to control the rate of inflation. More than this, it is the framework that is generally used to formulate monetary policy.
- The importance of monetary policy has grown as policy makers place an increasing emphasis on the control of inflation. Also, the traditional goal of full employment has been supplanted by the target of economic stability and as a result, the tools the government uses to control the economy have shifted away from fiscal (demand management) to monetary policy.
- The reasons behind the recent trend for making central banks independent can be described using the Phillips curve theory. In particular, the time inconsistency problem can be understood.
- Solving the time inconsistency problem involves delegation of monetary policy and the creation of an independent central bank.
- Finally, seignorage and hyper-inflation were covered as interesting episodes.

Key terms

Expectations augmented Phillips curve
Inflation
Long-run Phillips curve
Monetary policy
NAIRU
Natural rate of unemployment
Phillips curve

Review questions

1. How can one account for a short-run trade-off between inflation and unemployment? What is the difference between the natural rate of unemployment and the NAIRU?
2. The Phillips curve is written as:

$$\pi_t = \pi_{t-1} + 0.8(0.05 - u)$$

   a. What is the natural rate of unemployment?
   b. Graph the relationship between inflation and unemployment; graph the relationship between the acceleration in inflation and unemployment.
   c. What level of unemployment is required to reduce inflation by 3 per cent?
   d. What policies can the government use to achieve a 3 per cent fall in inflation?
3. Suppose a government overestimates the NAIRU, and attempts to prevent inflation from rising by contracting aggregate demand. Show the likely outcome of this policy in the short run, and the long run.
4. Under what circumstances is it possible to reduce inflation without increasing unemployment?
5. What would be the effects on inflation and unemployment of:
   a. a substantial rise in oil prices
   b. a major improvement in productivity
   c. a reform of labour market institutions.

More advanced problems

6. The government can do nothing about the NAIRU, so should it just target inflation and let unemployment settle at the lowest rate possible?
7. Explain how a recession might raise the NAIRU.
8. What are the costs of inflation? Does the control of inflation deserve its pre-eminent position in policy circles?
9. 'Policymakers would better attain their macroeconomic objectives if they had their discretion taken away from them.' Discuss.
10. Would a decrease in the central bank's inflation target affect the level of unemployment?
11. During the Second World War, both Germany and Britain printed large amounts of the other's currency. Why might dropping this on an enemy city cause more damage than high explosives?

10

For further resources, visit
http://www.thomsonlearning.co.uk/chamberlin_yueh

Part VI

The open economy

This section presents the external element of the macroeconomy and the open economy versions of the general equilibrium models covered earlier. Balance of payments rounds out the external accounts of the real macroeconomy, while the exchange rate introduces another element in determining the macroeconomy. The open economy version of the IS-LM model is presented, which is the IS-LM-BP model. The aggregate demand and aggregate supply (AD–AS) model is also extended to the open economy.

11 The balance of payments and exchange rates

Learning objectives

- Introduce the important features of the open economy
- Construct the balance of payments
- Define and describe exchange rates
- Introduce the two main theories of exchange rate determination: purchasing power parity (PPP) and uncovered interest parity (UIP)
- Examine the Dornbusch model of exchange rate overshooting
- Analyse important interactions between the exchange rate and the balance of payments

11.1 Introduction

In this chapter, we introduce and analyse the two main features of an open economy. The first is the balance of payments, which records one nation's trade with the rest of the world. This trade is not just limited to the imports and exports of goods and services, but also in capital goods and increasingly so in financial assets. Successive waves of liberalization have led to increasing integration between financial markets in different countries and trade in financial assets has grown phenomenally. In fact, the value of financial assets-based trades is a large multiple of conventional trade in goods and services. Global application 11.1 provides some evidence on how the global economy is becoming more open.

The second main feature of an open economy is the exchange rate. This defines the rate at which one currency can be converted into another. The exchange rate is important when analysed in conjunction with the balance of payments. This chapter will demonstrate that the exchange rate affects both the competitiveness of exports and imports, and also the returns on different financial assets. Also, the demand for different currencies and hence the exchange rate is determined by international trade flows. Therefore, the exchange rate is a fundamental driver of the balance of payments and vice-versa.

As international trade feeds into the circular flow of income, it would be a folly to analyse the economy in isolation of the rest of the world. Exports and imports feed directly into the circular flow as injections and leakages, respectively. Capital goods are important for the productive capacity of the economy. Trade in financial assets will have a large bearing on the price and availability of finance in the domestic economy, which will then have implications for domestic consumption and investment. Policy makers must be aware of this as developments in the rest of the world can be transmitted into the domestic economy. Also, the effectiveness of domestic policy will depend on the actions and reactions of other economies. This is recognized in the following chapters where the traditional macroeconomic models are extended to include these international linkages.

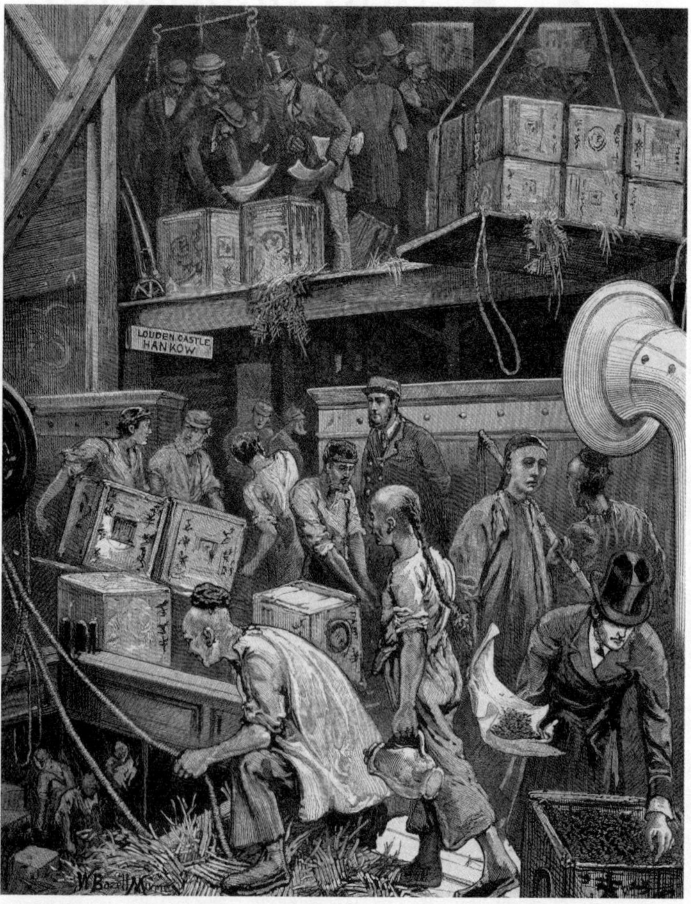

Breaking bulk on board a tea ship in the London docks
Source: Getty Images

11

Global application 11.1

Trends in market openness

The term 'global economy' arises because individual countries are becoming increasingly integrated. This is happening in two ways, first through trade and second through financial markets. As Table 1 shows, both trade and external finance have grown as a proportion of GDP over the last two decades.

The trade figures relate to the change in the ratio of the sum of exports and imports to GDP, and the external finance figures to the change in the ratio of the sum of external assets and liabilities of foreign direct investment and portfolio investment to GDP. It is clear that both these ratios have increased over the sample period for industrial and developing countries.

The largest increase was in the external finance figures for industrial countries. These figures, if anything, actually underestimate the extent of the growth in the trade of financial assets as they do not include the very volatile series, such as bank debts and short-term hot money flows, which are very sizeable. The explosion in the international trading of financial assets has grown through deregulation and increased competition among different financial centres throughout the world.

Trends in trade

As Figure 1 demonstrates for the G7 countries, exports and imports as a proportion of GDP have been rising in industrial countries for many decades. Tables 2 and 3 show that, in the advanced countries, domestic economies are increasingly subject to foreign competition.

Table 1 Trade and financial integration

	Change in the ratio to GDP from 1981–85 to 1997–2001	
	Trade	External finance
Industrial countries	3.9	77.3
Developing countries	15.4	19.9

Source: IMF, World Economic Outlook

Table 2 Import penetration rates for manufacturing industries (%)

	1970	1975	1980	1985	1990	1995
US	5.3	6.7	8.9	12.3	14.5	17.9
Japan	4.0	4.2	5.5	5.4	6.8	7.7
EU	7.2	8.9	10.3	11.3	10.7	12.7
Canada	25.2	28.1	30.6	35.7	37.3	49.7
Australia	16.2	17.9	21.5	26.4	24.2	31.9

Notes: EU figures are net of intra-EU trade and exclude Austria, Belgium, Ireland and Luxembourg.
Import penetration = ratio of manufacturing imports to the total domestic consumption of manufactured goods.

Global application 11.1 (continued)

Table 3 Exposure to foreign competition for manufacturing industries (%)

	1970	1975	1980	1985	1990	1995
US	10.6	14.2	17.5	18.9	24.2	29.2
Japan	12.1	15.1	16.7	19.0	18.0	19.4
EU	15.9	20.2	22.0	24.6	20.9	26.6
Canada	45.1	44.7	51.4	58.4	59.8	74.9
Australia	25.9	29.0	34.2	37.2	24.8	45.5

Notes: Exposure to foreign competition (E) is given by: $E = X/Y + (1-X/Y)*M/D$, where Y is total output, M is total imports, X is total exports and D is total domestic demand.
Sources: OECD STAN database; Coppel and Durand (1999)

There are several explanations for why world trade has persistently grown faster than world output. Between 1980 and 2002, world trade has more than tripled while world output has only doubled. This trend is common across most countries and regions, although the relative growth has varied. The obvious reasons for this are the reductions in trade barriers and in transport costs. Bank of England and IMF statistics estimate that between 1970 and 2002, transport, insurance and freight costs as a share of total import costs has fallen from 8 per cent to 3 per cent.

An alternative explanation lies in the structure of world trade. Most trade takes place between nations of a similar economic development, 80 per cent of OECD trade takes place with other OECD

Figure 1 Exports and imports as a percentage of GDP

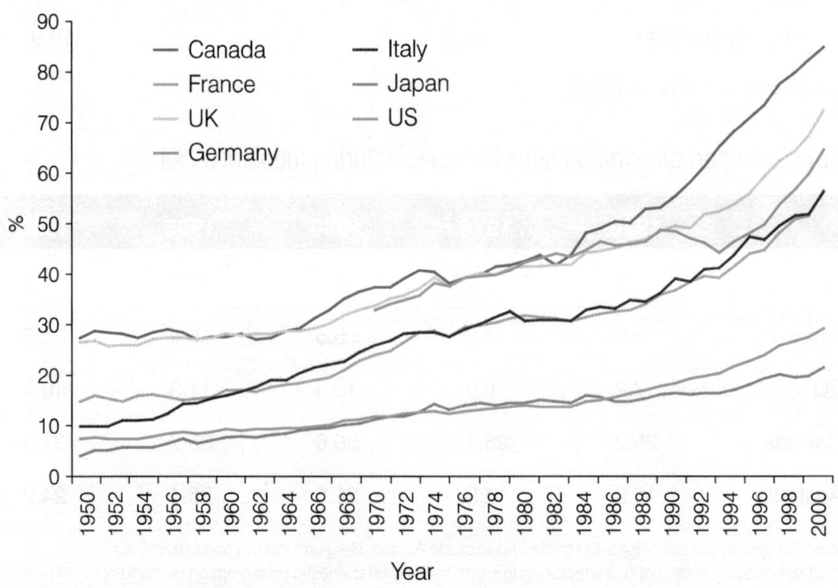

Global application 11.1 (continued)

countries. As per capita incomes have increased, there is a shift away from basics to manufactures, which also allows more scope for product differentiation and trade. Therefore, increasing intra-industry trade (that is, countries both importing and exporting the same type of good with each other – for example, the UK might export Rolls Royces to Japan while at the same time importing Mazdas) might account for the strong growth in trade. As Table 4 shows, intra-industry trade is a high and growing proportion of the total trade in manufacturing.

Trends in international financial market integration
Deregulation of financial markets and the removal of exchange controls (which limited the ability to exchange one currency for another) mean that savers and lenders are no longer restricted to the domestic financial market. A consequence of this is that financial markets throughout the world have become increasingly competitive, as investors try to achieve the best possible returns with no attention paid to national borders.

Standard economic theory teaches us that as markets become more competitive, individual prices will converge to the competitive limit. The same should be true for financial markets. As financial markets become more competitive, the prices of similar financial assets in different markets should converge. Figure 2 offers some evidence that shows this has happened in long-term real interest rates and stock prices in the G10 group of nations.

The trends indicate that the correlation between asset price movements in the G10 financial markets has generally increased over the last two and a half decades during a period that has seen substantial deregulation. The 'global financial market' picks up on this. Although each nation may have its own financial centre, each is strongly influenced by developments in others, and so cannot be treated in isolation. This rise in integration has been driven predominately by competition induced by the larger and freer movement of capital around the world.

Table 4 Share of intra-industry trade in total manufacturing

	1988–1991	1992–1995	1996–2000
Belgium/Luxembourg	77.6	77.7	71.4
Canada	73.5	74.7	76.2
France	75.9	77.6	77.5
Germany	67.1	72.0	72.0
Italy	61.6	64.0	64.7
Japan	37.6	40.8	47.6
Netherlands	69.2	70.4	68.9
Sweden	64.2	64.6	66.6
UK	70.1	73.1	73.7
US	63.5	65.3	68.5
Average	66.0	68.0	68.7

Source: OECD Economic Outlook no. 71.

Global application 11.1 (continued)

Figure 2 Correlation of long-term real interest rates and stock prices across the G10

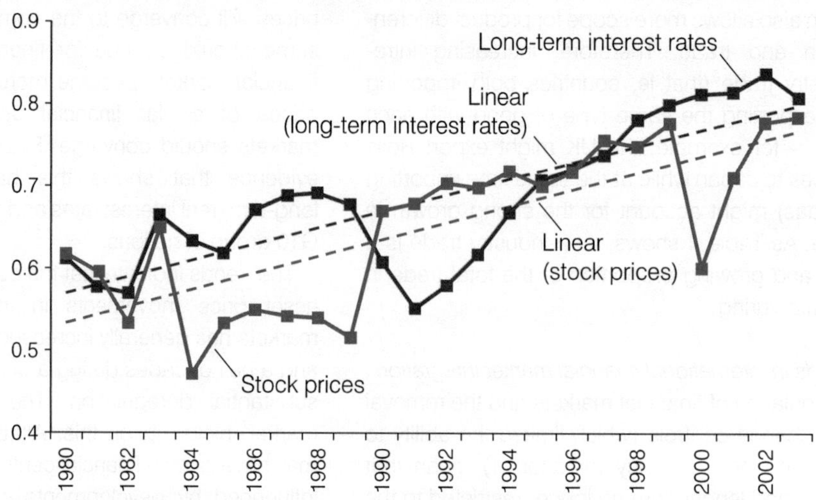

11.2 The balance of payments

The **balance of payments** is simply one nation's accounts with the rest of the world. Like any form of accounting, it describes and sums all the transactions the residents of one country make with residents from other countries. Sales of goods, services, physical capital and financial assets from domestic to overseas residents are credits on the balance of payments. The reverse, purchases by domestic residents from those overseas, are recorded as debits.

The overall position of the balance of payments is simply the netting out of these credits and debits. However, the balance of payments is constructed so that it always adds to zero: a position of no overall surplus or deficit. This is because of the role of *official financing*, which is described in more detail below.

The balance of payments is presented in terms of the different types of transactions that are made between domestic and international parties. Table 11.1 is a simplified version of the UK balance of payments in 2000. There are four main parts: the current account, the capital account, the balancing item and official financing.

Current account

This is the balance on the trade in goods and services with transfer payments. The trade position is simply the difference between exports and imports, and is often referred to as the *trade gap* or the *balance of trade*. Transfer payments represent the net income flows (foreign aid, budget contributions to the EU, net factor incomes such as interest, profits, dividends, etc.) among countries. A surplus (deficit) on the current account simply means that a nation's foreign income exceeds (is less than) foreign expenditures.

Table 11.1 The UK balance of payments, 2000

	£ billions
Current account	
Net trade in goods	–30.4
Net trade in services	+14.7
Net income	+6.1
Net transfers	–8.8
Current account balance	–18.4
Captial account	
Foreign investment in the UK	+534.6
UK investment abroad	–502.2
Capital account balance	32.4
Balancing item	–10.0
Official financing	
Decrease in official UK reserves	–4.0

Source: UK balance of payments, The Pink Book 2001, ONS

Capital account

The capital account records international purchases and sales of financial assets. These assets can either be portfolio (stocks and shares, government bonds, foreign bank accounts) or direct (machinery, technology, property, firm overseas investment). From Table 11.1, it is clear that the volume of these flows far exceeds those that make up the current account.

Balancing item

This is a statistical adjustment which accounts for the fact that many of the above items may be incorrectly measured and also accounts for transactions that have been omitted from official records.

Official financing

Adding the three previous items gives the balance of payments position. This shows the net inflow of money into the country (the circular flow) from foreign transactions. A surplus results when income from abroad exceeds expenditures, and a deficit is vice-versa. However, the balance of payments must be in overall balance; this remaining balance is therefore countered by official financing.

Nations have a stock of foreign currency reserves. If foreign expenditures exceed income, then the difference will be matched by a change in the nation's foreign reserves, which will be run down accordingly to fund the gap. Likewise, surpluses will be balanced by a net inflow that increases foreign reserves. This represents the required financing of the difference between the current and capital accounts. In practice, this official financing should be included as part of the financial flow that constitutes the capital account. Therefore, the balance of payments will always equate to zero.

The official financing of the balance of payments can be an important issue. The UK generally has little problem achieving this, but for some developing and transitional

Global application 11.2

The world current account balance

Given that one nation's exports constitute the imports of others, it seems logical that current account balances over the world should sum to zero. However, the reality is somewhat different. Over the last three decades, the world economy has been running a current account deficit with itself. Since 1999, this has become fairly significant at an amount bordering 2 per cent of total global imports.

Because the world economy as a whole is clearly a closed economy, the existence of this discrepancy is a puzzle. One possible explanation is that measurement errors are to blame. Due to transportation lags, exports are officially recorded before imports. If this lag spans separate accountancy periods, then at any particular point in time exports or imports will not offset each other in published figures. These types of delays could also arise if there are lags or delays in the collection and processing of data. A further measurement error results because much of the world's shipping fleet is registered in countries that do not report freight earnings to the IMF. These unrecorded earnings could conceivably make up a large part of the missing surplus.

Another important reason is that foreign investment income tends to be underreported, as it is not declared to the respective authorities in the recipient's home country. Often, interest payments are simply credited to a foreign bank account and do not even cross borders. On the whole, there is a tendency to observe a persistent deficit on interest flows, which is made even more significant by the rise in offshore banking centres.

Table 5 Measured world current account balance: 1994–2003 ($US billions)

1993	1994	1995	1996	1997	1998	1999	2000	2001	2002	2003
–65.2	–62.8	–53.6	–49.8	–4.6	–81.3	–126.8	–163.8	–163.4	–132.2	–97.7

Source: IMF, World Economic Outlook (September 2004)

economies, it could be hugely problematic. If reserves are exhausted, then painful policies may be required to correct the deficit. A typical response might be to try to attract foreign inflows by offering high interest rates, but as we have seen this might be damaging to economic growth. Alternatively, the government may be forced to use contractionary policies to curb spending on imports. These problems are addressed in some detail when looking at the onset of currency crises in Chapter 15.

11.3 Exchange rates

Different nations have their own currencies; the exchange rate is simply the rate at which one currency can be converted into another. There are, though, many different definitions of the exchange rate which are used in economics.

Nominal exchange rate

This is the simple exchange rate between two currencies. It is expressed as a ratio indicating how much of one currency can be traded for a unit of another. Care must be taken though as to which way up this ratio is defined. Take the £–$ exchange rate, the financial press will express the exchange rate (E) as:

$$E = \$/£$$

This basically tells us how many $s can be bought with each £. If the pound were to strengthen against the dollar – known as a pound *appreciation* – then the same £ will be able to purchase more $s, so the exchange rate E will rise. Likewise, a fall in the pound against the dollar – known as a *depreciation* – implies that E will fall, as £1 will purchase fewer $s.

However, the economics literature actually defines the exchange rate the other way up and it will be vitally important to remember this fact in this and the following chapters.

$$E = £/\$$$

This implies that the exchange rate is defined by the number of £s required to purchase $1. In this case, an appreciation in the pound means that fewer £s are required to buy $1, so E falls. A depreciation of the £ implies that more of them are now required, so that E rises. It seems paradoxical that a rise in the value of a currency or an appreciation is defined by a fall in E. But, once again, this is a relationship that is important not to forget. It is especially hard to do this given that the media present exchange rates in the reverse way.

Real exchange rate

If we are interested in the choice of buying either domestic or foreign goods, the nominal exchange rate only provides part of the required information. The nominal exchange rate only tells us about the movements in the relative price of two currencies. However, in trading goods, we want to know not just how many dollars we can get for one pound, but

Figure 11.1 The nominal £–$ exchange rate, 1980–2004

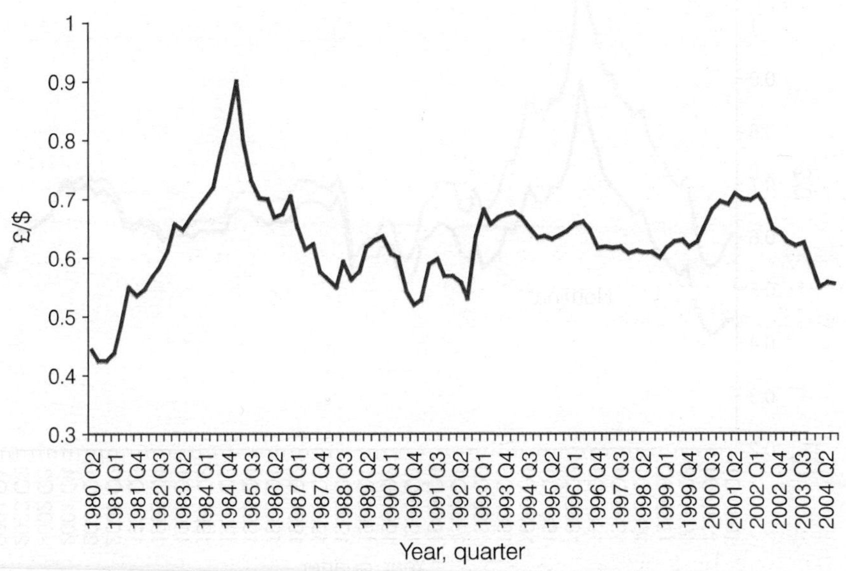

11

how many US goods we can get for a pound. The real exchange rate does this by comparing the price of foreign goods and services to domestic goods and services. For example, the real £–$ exchange rate (R) compares the price of US goods relative to UK goods.

$$R = (£/\$) * (P_{US}/P_{UK})$$

where P_{US} and P_{UK} are the respective price levels in the US and the UK. This is just the nominal exchange multiplied by the ratio of prices.

From Figure 11.2, it is clear that the real exchange rate tends to follow the same trends as the nominal exchange rate. This implies that the nominal exchange rate is the main factor in determining the difference in prices between goods and services in different countries, and that fluctuation in exchange rates is much larger than that in relative prices.

Effective exchange rate

So far, we have considered what are known as bilateral exchange rates; this is just the rate of exchange between two different currencies. However, there are a very large number of currencies, so each currency will have a potentially large number of exchange rates. At any one time, a particular currency might be appreciating against some while depreciating against others. So, what conclusions can we make about the overall strength of the currency?

The effective exchange rate (also known as the multilateral exchange rate) is the exchange rate against a basket of various currencies. This is like a weighted average of bilateral exchange rates and provides a more realistic idea of a currency's strength. The weights attached to each bilateral exchange rate are usually taken from trade shares, as this will weight the bilateral exchange rate according to its importance to the economy.

Figure 11.2 The real and nominal £–$ exchange rate, 1980–2004

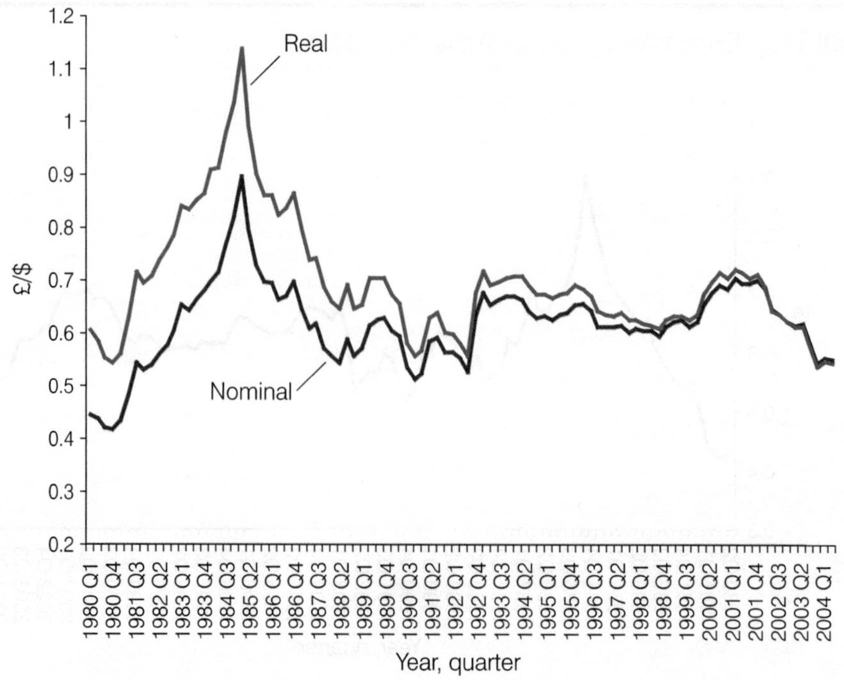

Global application 11.3

Real exchange rates in the Euro area

In 1999, the 11 countries listed in Table 6 adopted the euro as a single currency. Obviously with a common currency, the nominal exchange rate is unity: one euro can be exchanged for one euro. The real exchange rate, though, refers to the amount of goods and services that can be purchased with a unit of currency. Even with a fixed nominal exchange rate of unity, the real exchange rates among the members of the euro area can still vary depending on the relative inflation rates.

Table 6 shows the average annual inflation rates in the EU-11, and performance has been diverse. Inflation in Ireland is around 4.1 per cent, compared to about 1.3 per cent in Germany. As the prices of goods and services in Ireland are rising faster than in Germany, the rate at which German goods can be converted into Irish goods is falling. Therefore, the Irish real exchange rate is appreciating against Germany.

On a similar note, despite a single currency, the effective exchange rate of the EU-11 member countries can also differ. This is because each country will have different trade patterns with countries outside the EU, so each effective exchange rate will be calculated using different weights. For example, Ireland has much higher trade content with the UK than other countries. Movements in sterling will then have a much larger impact on the Irish effective exchange rate than on the other countries in the single currency.

Table 6 Average annual inflation rates in the euro area

	Inflation rate %
Germany (DEU)	1.271
Austria (AUT)	1.554
France (FRA)	1.656
Belgium (BEL)	1.859
Finland (FIN)	2.048
Italy (ITA)	2.399
Spain (ESP)	2.878
Netherlands (NLD)	3.119
Greece (GRE)	3.233
Portugal (PRT)	3.287
Ireland (IRE)	4.095

Source: IMF World Economic Outlook

Spot and forward exchange rates

The exchanges rates defined above are spot rates – quite literally because these are the rates that would apply to foreign exchange transactions taken relatively immediately or 'on the spot'. However, many international transactions are not taken on the spot and hence the current spot exchange rate may not be appropriate for defining the price at which these trades actually take place.

For example, if a domestic firm were to place an order with a foreign firm, they will be invoiced in foreign currency. The price in domestic currency is then sensitive to exchange rate movements. If the ordering and delivering process is not instantaneous and takes a while, then a significant amount of time may elapse between placing an order and settling the final invoice after delivery. Meanwhile, any movement in the exchange rate in this interim period could lead to substantial changes in the actual price the firm must pay.

The uncertainty over the future exchange rate may then act as an impediment to otherwise valuable trade. The firm in question could be relieved of this uncertainty if it could be guaranteed a given exchange rate for the purpose of undertaking a future transaction. A *forward* rate does just this. It specifies the rate of exchange between two currencies that will apply to foreign exchange transactions at some specified point in the future. This might be 30 days, 90 days, 180 days or even several years in the future.

A forward exchange rate is typically offered by a market-maker, such as a bank or other financial institution. As these are large organizations, the exchange rate risk specific to one firm will only represent a miniscule risk on their balance sheets, so they are better able to deal with the uncertainty posed by exchange rate volatility. In providing the forward rate, the market-maker will usually seek some profit by either imposing a spread or a transactions charge on the transaction (see Chapter 6 for a description on how market-makers operate).

Figure 11.3 The £–$ effective exchange rate, 1980–2004

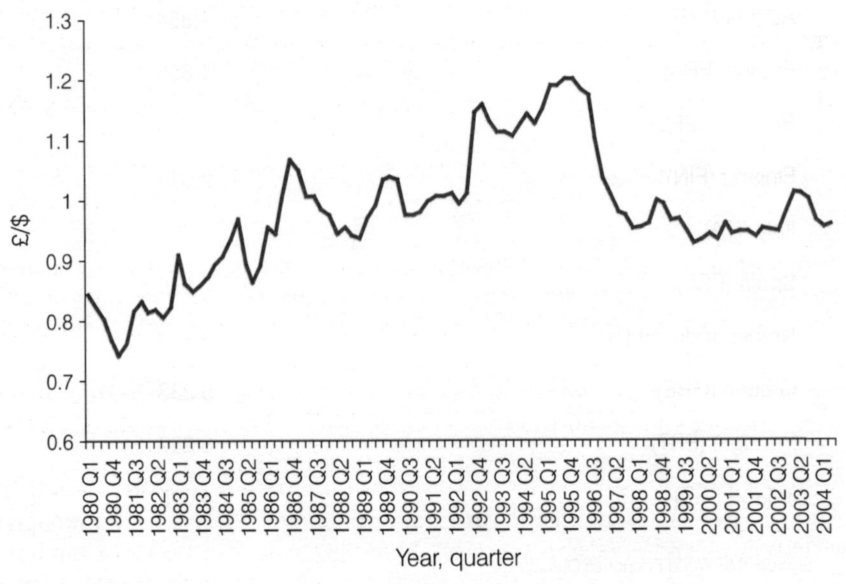

11

Figure 11.4 The £–$ 12 month forward exchange rate, 1980–2004

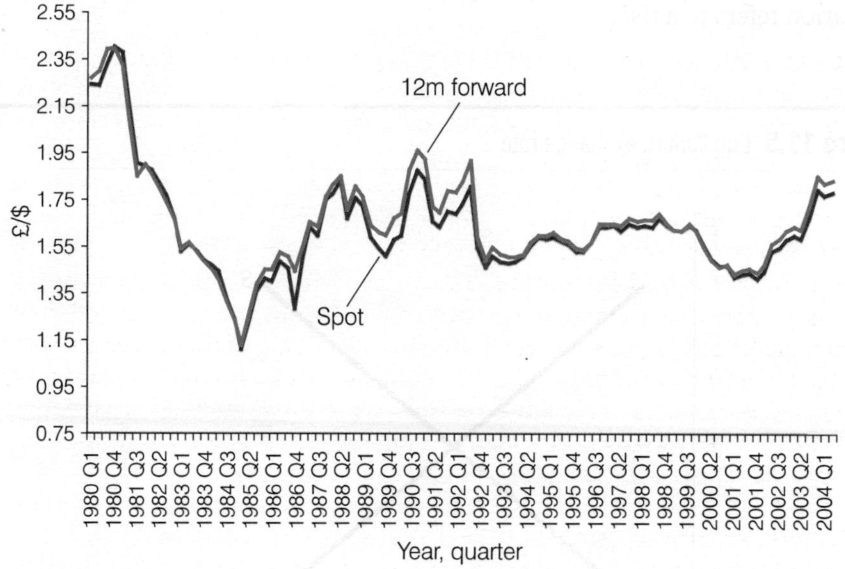

11.4 Theories of exchange rate determination

The exchange rate is simply the price of one currency in terms of another. Therefore, like all prices, the rate will be determined by the relative demands and supplies of each currency. When demand for a currency rises relative to its supply, that currency's value relative to others will rise – this is known as an appreciation in the currency. Likewise, when demand falls relative to supply for a particular currency, its value will fall – this is known as a currency depreciation.

The demand for a currency is a form of derived demand. This means that foreign exchange is not held for its own sake, but in order to carry out transactions. The supply of currency is the counterpart to this. When buying foreign currency, the domestic currency is offered in exchange, which determines the supply of domestic currency to the currency markets.

The demand and supply of currency are both taken to depend on the exchange rate. An appreciation in the domestic currency leads to an increase in demand for foreign currency. This is because the appreciation makes goods denominated in foreign currency cheaper. In a corresponding fashion, a depreciation in the exchange rate means that goods denoted in foreign currencies become more expensive in domestic currency terms; therefore, the demand for foreign goods and thus currency will fall. The demand for foreign currencies will be downward-sloping with respect to the exchange rate.

The supply of foreign currency will also be conventional – an upward-sloping function of the exchange rate. As the domestic currency depreciates relative to the foreign currency, domestically produced goods and services become cheaper in terms of foreign currency. Foreign residents then attempt to purchase these, but in order to purchase the necessary currency, the foreign currency must be supplied to the currency markets. An appreciation of the domestic currency will, of course, have the opposite effect and reduce the supply of foreign currency to the markets.

The exchange rate, then, is determined by the intersection of demand and supply. This is shown in Figure 11.5. The exchange rate E is defined as the amount of domestic currency required to purchase a unit of foreign currency, so appreciation refers to a fall in E and depreciation refers to a rise.

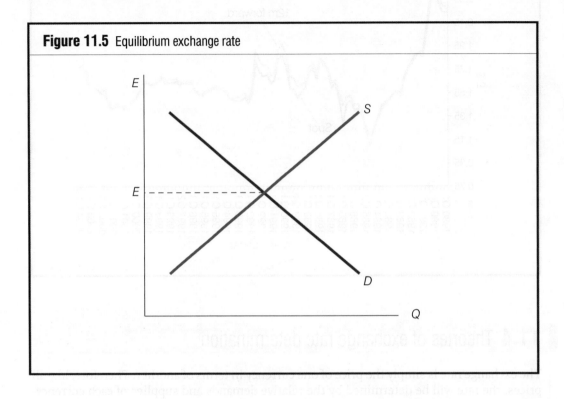

Figure 11.5 Equilibrium exchange rate

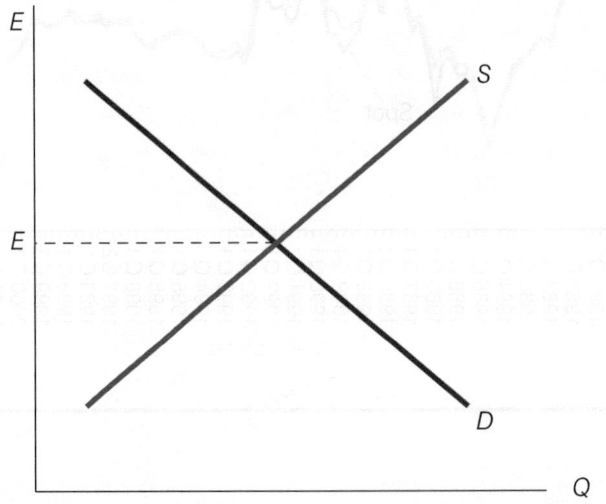

Figure 11.6 A fall in demand for domestic goods and the exchange rate

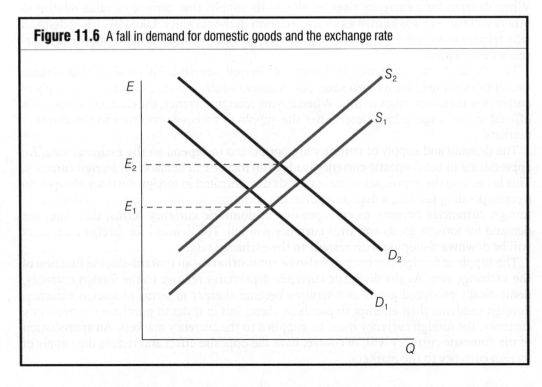

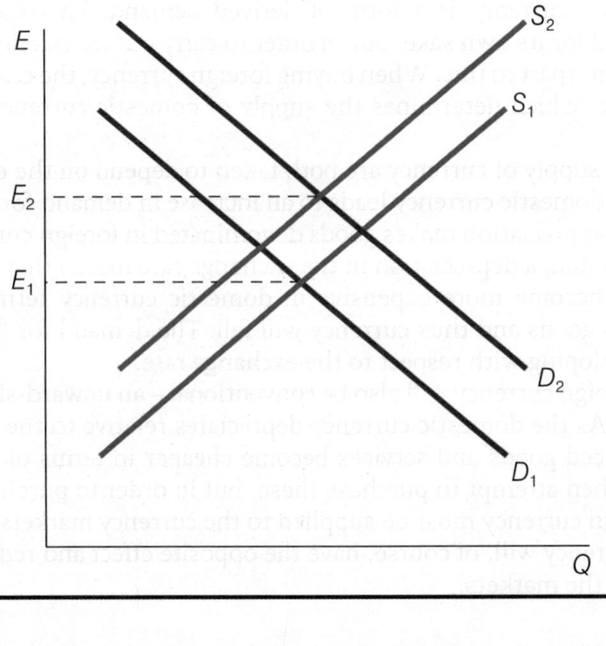

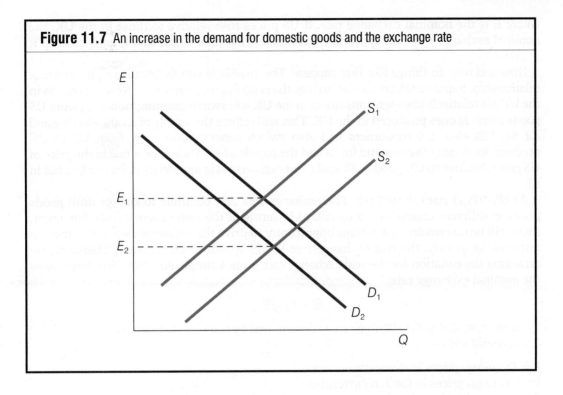

Figure 11.7 An increase in the demand for domestic goods and the exchange rate

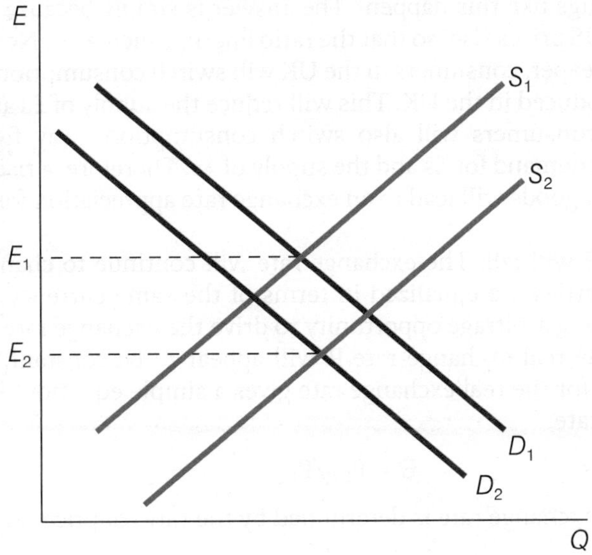

It is now easy to see why the exchange rate is determined by trade flows. For example, if there is now a preference for foreign-produced goods, then two things will happen. The first is that domestic residents will switch their consumption from domestic to foreign goods, so the demand for foreign currency will rise. This is shown in Figure 11.6 with the shift in the demand schedule from D_1 to D_2. In addition, foreign residents will switch their consumption towards the goods produced in their own country, so the supply of foreign currency will fall – shifting the supply curve of foreign currency from S_1 to S_2. Taking both these movements together, the domestic exchange rate will depreciate from E_1 to E_2. The weakness in the domestic currency reflects the fall in demand for domestically produced goods.

Figure 11.7 shows the opposite case, where the demand shift is towards domestically produced goods. In this case, the demand for foreign currency will fall and the supply of foreign currency will rise. This changing pattern of trade, where there is an increasing preference for domestic goods, will lead to an appreciation in the exchange rate from E_1 to E_2.

The relative demands and supplies of currencies, and therefore the exchange rates, are trade determined. With this in mind, there are two main theories of exchange rate determination. **Purchasing power parity** (PPP) refers to trade in goods and services, and **uncovered interest parity** (UIP) refers to the trade in financial assets.

11.4.1 PPP: purchasing power parity

This theory argues that the exchange rate will change so that the price of a particular good or service will be the same regardless of where you buy it. For this reason, the theory of PPP is often known as the *law of one price*. The theory of PPP therefore argues that the nominal exchange rate will change to offset price differences and the real exchange rate should remain constant. If we recall, the £–$ real exchange rate was defined as:

$$R = (£/\$) * (P_{US}/P_{UK}) = E * (P_{US}/P_{UK})$$

11

where E is the nominal exchange rate. If US prices rose relative to those in the UK, the nominal exchange rate will appreciate (remember that this means that E falls) to keep R constant.

How and why do things like this happen? The answer is simply because of an arbitrage relationship. Suppose US prices rise, so that the ratio P_{US}/P_{UK} increases. Now that goods in the UK are relatively cheaper, consumers in the UK will switch consumption away from US goods towards ones produced in the UK. This will reduce the supply of £s and the demand for $s. Likewise, US consumers will also switch consumption away from US to UK produce, increasing the demand for £s and the supply of $s. Therefore, a rise in the price of US goods relative to UK goods will lead to an exchange rate appreciation for the £ (a fall in E).

As (P_{US}/P_{UK}) rises, E will fall. The exchange rate will continue to change until goods prices in different countries are equalized in terms of the same currency. At this point, there will be no remaining arbitrage opportunity to drive the exchange rate. If this mechanism works quickly, the real exchange rate R will appear to be constant. Therefore, rearranging the equation for the real exchange rate gives a simple equation that determines the nominal exchange rate:

$$E = P_{UK}/P_{US}$$

So, the nominal £–$ exchange rate is determined by the ratio of price levels.

In general terms:

P = Domestic prices in domestic currency
P^* = Foreign prices in foreign currencies
E = Nominal exchange rate between domestic and foreign currencies
EP^* = Foreign prices in domestic currency

Therefore, arbitrage requires that domestic and foreign goods prices are equalized in terms of domestic currency:

$$P = EP^*$$

which can be rearranged to give:

$$E = P/P^*$$

11

A rise (fall) in domestic relative to foreign prices will induce a nominal exchange rate depreciation (appreciation). This relationship is shown in Figure 11.8 below. A rise in domestic prices from P_1 to P_2 leads to a depreciation in the exchange rate from E_1 to E_2.

The PPP equation is a levels equation, where the exchange rate is simply the ratio of domestic and foreign prices. A commonly used variant expresses this equation in terms of differences, relating the change in the nominal exchange rate to the change in relative prices. This is known as *relative PPP*.

$$\%\Delta E = \%\Delta P - \%\Delta P^*$$

If the overseas price level is taken to be constant, $\%\Delta P^* = 0$, then the relative PPP equation can be simplified to:

$$\%\Delta E = \%\Delta P$$

The change in the nominal exchange rate is directly proportional to the change in the price level.

Figure 11.8 Purchasing power parity

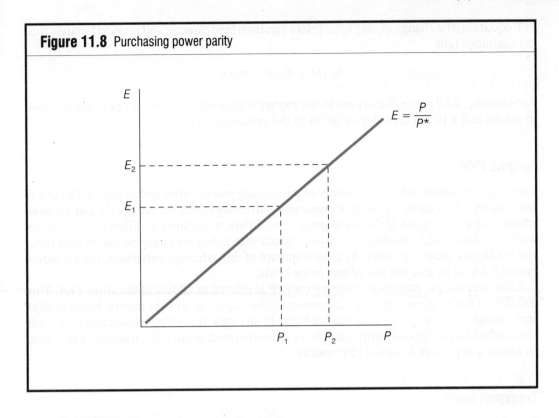

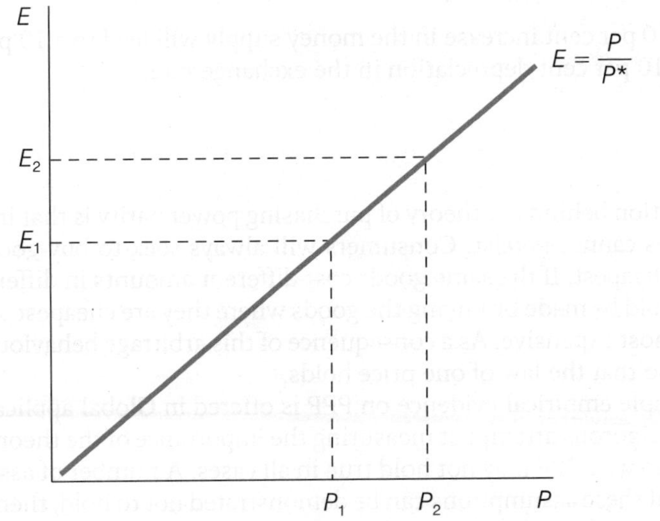

The monetary theory of the exchange rate

PPP suggests that the nominal exchange rate is determined mainly by factors that influence the domestic price level. In previous chapters, we have argued that the money supply might be an important determinant of the price level, and therefore could be an indirect factor in influencing the exchange rate. The monetary theory of the exchange rate is really an open economy extension to the simple quantity theory of money. In this way, the exchange rate is determined by the actions of the domestic monetary authority.

The well-known quantity theory of money equation is:

$$Mv = PY$$

where

M = Money stock
v = Velocity of circulation
P = Price level
Y = Full employment output

As v and Y are constants, this can be rearranged to give:

$$P = 1/v\ (M/Y)$$

Therefore, $\%\Delta M = \%\Delta P$, so changes in the money supply have a directly proportional impact on the price level. If the money stock rises without a corresponding increase in output, the additional money supply will simply bid up prices. The price level is everywhere a monetary phenomenon, with inflation just a product of excessive money supply growth.

If relative prices are determined by different monetary regimes, then it is easy to make the additional step to see how the nominal exchange rate is determined. Using the relative

PPP equation, the change in domestic prices can then feed directly and proportionately into the exchange rate.

$$\%\Delta M = \%\Delta P = \%\Delta E$$

For example, a 10 per cent increase in the money supply will lead to a 10 per cent increase in prices, and a 10 per cent depreciation in the exchange rate.

Judging PPP

The simple intuition behind the theory of purchasing power parity is that international differences in prices cannot persist. Consumers will always seek to buy goods and services where they are cheapest. If the same goods cost different amounts in different parts of the world, profits could be made by buying the goods where they are cheapest and selling them where they are most expensive. As a consequence of this arbitrage behaviour, the exchange rate will adjust so that the law of one price holds.

Some very simple empirical evidence on PPP is offered in Global application 11.4. This certainly is not a rigorous attempt at measuring the importance of the theory, but may offer some insight as to why PPP may not hold true in all cases. A number of assumptions must be satisfied, but if these assumptions can be demonstrated not to hold, then there is reason to expect a departure from the PPP results.

Transport costs

For arbitrage always to reinstate the law of one price it must be able to operate without any costs or friction. The arbitrage mechanism will be strongest when it can work in a quick and cheap fashion. When it comes to international trade, this is clearly not the case, as physical goods cannot be transported costlessly or instantaneously around the world. Transport costs can therefore refer to both the costs of moving goods around the world or any costs that arise due to the delay in their deliveries.

Adding transport costs to the price of foreign goods changes the PPP relationship in the following way:

11

$$P = EP^* + TC$$

where TC are transport costs which drive a wedge between the effective actual and listed prices of foreign goods.

If foreign goods are cheaper than domestic goods so that $P > EP^*$, then trade will only result if the price differential is greater than the transport costs involved, i.e., $P - EP^* > TC$. The inclusion of transport costs certainly implies that PPP may not hold in its level form. However, the relative version of PPP would continue to hold.

Search costs

On a similar note, for arbitrage to work effectively, consumers must have a large amount of information available to them. More specifically, they must have knowledge of all goods and prices produced throughout the world. They can then act on any price differences, which then lead to the assertion of the law of one price.

If information though is bounded, there is no reason why arbitrage should be strong enough to do this. In fact, it is perhaps one of the reasons why PPP is regarded as a long-run theory of the exchange rate. It simply takes time for people to gather the required information in order to act upon international price differences.

Global application 11.4

The Big Mac index

Every year, *The Economist* magazine publishes its Big Mac index (Table 7).

This is an interesting application of PPP. The first column shows the Big Mac price in each country in terms of US dollars. These are calculated by using the official nominal exchange rate. We can see that there is a range here, from $1.33 in Malaysia to $4.90 in Switzerland. The second column then gives the implied PPP exchange rate of the US dollar. This is the exchange rate (i.e., the number

Table 7 Big Mac index

	Big Mac price in dollars	Implied PPP of the dollar	% under (–) or over (+) valuation against the dollar
US	2.90	–	–
Argentina	1.48	1.50	–49
Australia	2.27	1.12	–22
Brazil	1.70	1.86	–41
Britain	3.37	1.54	+16
Canada	2.33	1.10	–20
Chile	2.18	483	–25
China	1.26	3.59	–57
Czech Republic	2.13	19.5	–27
Denmark	4.46	9.57	+54
Egypt	1.62	3.45	–44
Euro area	3.28	1.06	+13
Honk Kong	1.54	4.14	–47
Hungary	2.52	183	–47
Indonesia	1.77	5552	–39
Japan	2.33	90.3	–20
Malaysia	1.33	1.74	–54
Mexico	2.08	8.28	–28
New Zealand	2.65	1.50	–8
Peru	2.57	3.10	–11
Philippines	1.23	23.8	–57
Poland	1.63	2.17	–44
Russia	1.45	14.5	–50
Singapore	1.92	1.14	–34
South Africa	1.86	4.28	–36
South Korea	2.72	1103	–6
Sweden	3.94	10.3	+36
Switzerland	4.90	2.17	+69
Taiwan	2.24	25.9	–23
Thailand	1.45	20.3	–50
Turkey	2.58	1362069	–11
Venezuela	1.48	1517	–49

Source: *The Economist*, 27 May 2004

11

Global application 11.4 (continued)

of units of a foreign currency that can be exchanged for $US 1), which would equalize the US dollar price of a Big Mac. The final column then shows how this PPP exchange rate compares to the official nominal exchange rate.

The Big Mac is chosen as the basis of comparison because it is a uniform good throughout the world. Figure 3 shows a scatter plot between an index of the US dollar price of a Big Mac and the calculated PPP domestic price level, also shown in terms of the $US during 2000 taken from the Penn World Tables. It is clear that, although stylised, the Big Mac, index is not a bad proxy measure of PPP rates.

Table 7 is evidence that PPP does not hold explicitly. For example, the official nominal exchange rate shows the Swiss Franc to be 69 per cent overvalued against the US dollar and the Malaysian Ringgit to be undervalued by 54 per cent compared to the PPP rates. There are many reasons that might account for this. In general terms, PPP may fail to hold due to trade restrictions, transport costs, domestic taxes on consumption goods, pricing to market effects, and the Balassa-Samuelson effect.

Figure 3 PPP from the Penn World Tables and the Big Mac index (2000)

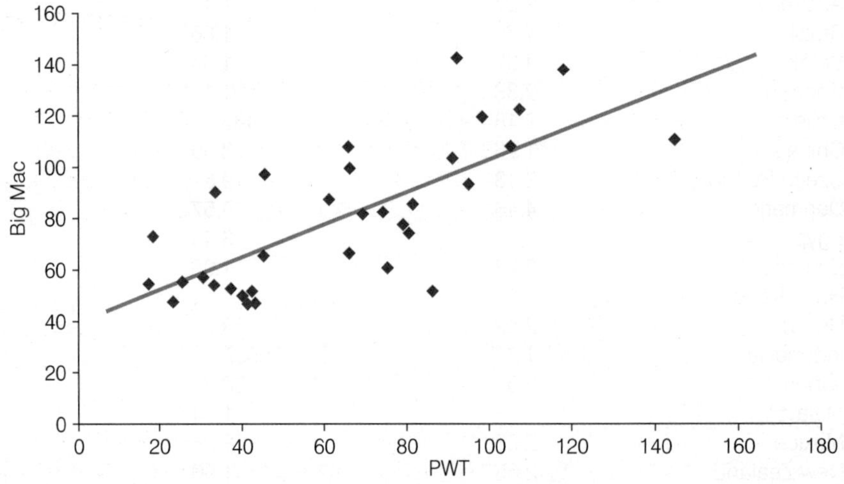

Imperfect competition

The law of one price is grounded in the world of perfect competition where all goods are homogeneous and each firm is a price-taker. Moving away from these assumptions leads us into the world of imperfect competition, where goods are differentiated and producers have some power to set prices away from marginal costs.

When firms produce differentiated goods, then consumers no longer purchase on the basis of price but also in terms of specifications and quality. Therefore, price differences between the outputs of different nations might be expected to persist.

Second, the fact that goods are differentiated means that the demand curve is no longer horizontal but downward-sloping. This gives firms the ability to set prices away from marginal costs. One of the consequences of price-setting is that price discrimination is possible. Different prices can be charged in different markets.

The size of these mark-ups is likely to be determined by the elasticity of demand for the product in each country. Where elasticities differ, different prices may be charged. However, a fundamental consideration is that the different markets can be segregated in order to prevent resale in markets where the good is cheaper. The process by which firms charge different prices in different markets is known as *pricing to market*.

Non-traded goods

Arbitrage in international goods prices can only be expected in goods that are traded. This will only apply to a certain proportion of all the goods produced and sold in an economy. Therefore, we would not expect PPP to hold outside of the traded goods sector and for the economy as a whole.

This is most apparent in developing nations, where the price levels are much lower than in the developed world. However, this has not been associated with a rapid appreciation in their currency. Average price levels are low, but there is no pressure on the exchange rate to adjust accordingly. One explanation of why this happens is known as the *Balassa-Samuelson effect*. This describes how there will be price equalization in the traded goods sector and yet different prices can emerge in the non-traded goods sector.

In developing nations, the productivity of firms is lower than that in more developed nations. This might be a consequence of lower stocks of human and physical capital. Therefore, if international markets are competitive and all traded goods output is sold at the same price, then low productivity means low wages.

If the domestic labour market is competitive, then these low wages are carried over into the non-traded sector – and if prices are just a mark-up on these labour costs, then the general price level will also be very low. Therefore, price levels can be systematically lower in developing countries than in developed ones, when prices are measured in a common currency. In short, international differences in productivity lie at the heart of the Balassa-Samuelson effect.

All in all there appears to be evidence – both empirical and theoretical – to justify a departure from strict PPP theory. The conventional wisdom is that as a theory, PPP is most useful and realistic in the longer term. This point is partially made in Figure 11.9, which plots quarterly percentage changes in nominal exchange rates and relative prices.

In the short run, the nominal exchange rate is much more volatile than the theory of PPP would imply. This can be taken as an indication that there may be other factors which drive the nominal exchange rate. The theory of purchasing power parity predominately relates to the trade in physical goods and services, but looking at Table 11.1, it is obvious that these current account trades only make up a small part of the overall balance of payments. Capital account transactions are very important and much larger in terms of relative magnitude, so they might have an important bearing on the exchange rate. Given that much of the capital account constitutes short-term financial flows, it may also account for the observed volatility in short-term exchange rates. The theory of uncovered interest parity (UIP) looks at the exchange rate being determined in the market for internationally traded financial assets and it is to this that we turn to next.

Figure 11.9 Quarterly volatility of the nominal £–$ exchange rate and UK and US relative prices

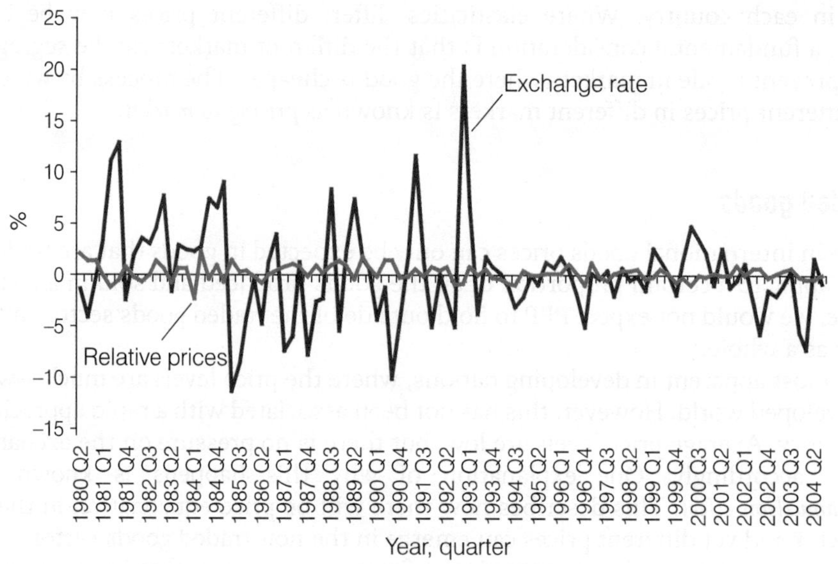

11.4.2 UIP: uncovered interest parity

Whereas PPP determines the exchange rate to arbitrage prices in the goods market, **uncovered interest parity** (UIP) does a similar thing in the financial assets market. Since the 1980s, liberalization in the world's financial markets means that currency transactions related to the trade in financial assets outweigh those in goods and services by as much as 100:1 in value terms. Much of this is very liquid and can move around the world at great speeds in search of the best returns. UIP models the exchange rate through relative asset returns.

The two key assumptions in this model are that assets are perfectly substitutable, and there is perfect international capital mobility. As a result, arbitrage means that the exchange rate will change so that the returns on all financial assets should be equalized.

When you purchase a foreign asset, there are two things that determine the returns that are derived from it:

1. the overseas interest rate (defined by r^*)
2. exchange rate movements (ΔE).

The first of these is obvious. If the interest rate on foreign assets rises above that on domestic assets, then international investors would be expected to substitute out of domestic and into foreign assets. The respective currency transactions would lead to a depreciation in the domestic currency.

The second, though, requires a little clarification. Having purchased a foreign asset, the returns are only realized once they have been converted back into domestic currency. If, however, the exchange rate changes, the rate at which this conversion takes place will also change. If the domestic currency depreciates, then additional gains will be made as the foreign currency can be converted back at a higher rate. If the exchange rate were to appreciate, then foreign returns can only be converted back into domestic currency at a lower rate, which will reduce their value in domestic currency terms.

Global application 11.5

Evidence of the international Ballassa-Samuelson effect

Figure 4 is a scatter plot of GDP per capita in $US and the domestic price level, which is also expressed in $US and is calculated using PPP exchange rates. The prediction of the Ballassa-Samuelson model is that these two variables should be positively correlated. Countries with low income will also have a low price level. It is clear that the evidence presented in Figure 4 supports this hypothesis.

More specifically, the Ballassa-Samuelson model alludes to price differences in the non-traded sector arising from differences in productivity. This will mean that labour costs and therefore prices will be lower in nations with lower income per head. Such a relationship is identified in Figure 5, which plots the average net hourly wage against the price of a Big Mac. This gives clear evidence of a strong positive relationship between hourly wages and the price of a Big Mac. As both these variables are expressed in terms of US dollars and calculated using implied PPP exchange rates, Figure 5 gives a good indication that the Ballassa-Samuelson effect is important in explaining international differences in prices and deviations from the theory of PPP.

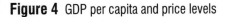

Figure 4 GDP per capita and price levels

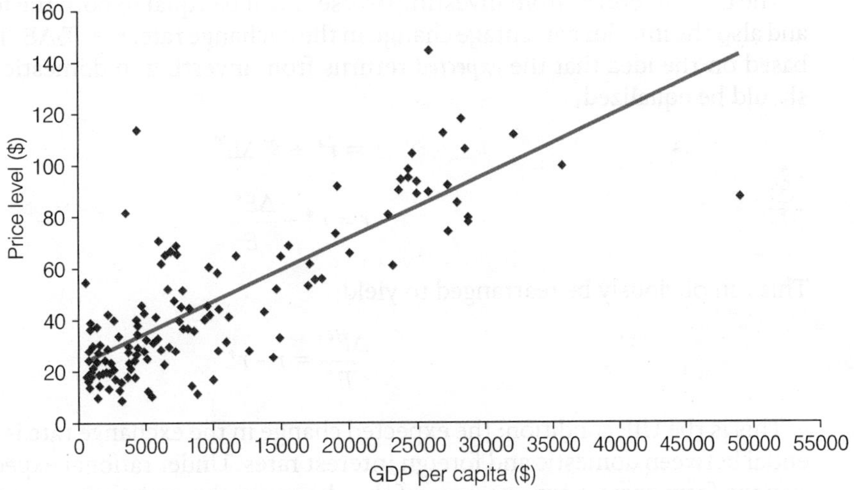

Source: Penn World Table 2000

Global application 11.5 (continued)

Figure 5 Hourly wage and Big Mac prices

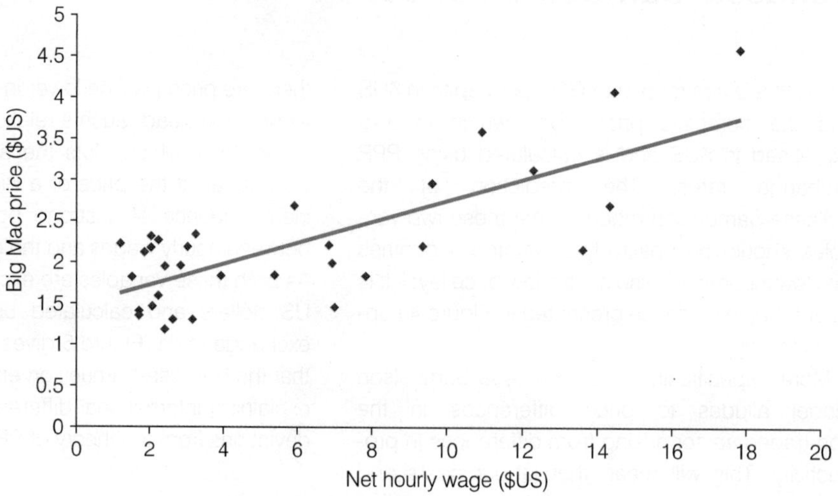

The overall returns from investing overseas will be equal to both the foreign interest rate and also the interim percentage change in the exchange rate: $r^* + \%\Delta E$. The theory of UIP is based on the idea that the *expected* returns from investing in domestic and foreign assets should be equalized.

$$r = r^* + \%\Delta E^e$$

$$r = r^* + \frac{\Delta E^e}{E}$$

This can obviously be rearranged to yield:

$$\frac{\Delta E^e}{E} = r - r^*$$

This is the UIP condition: the expected change in the exchange rate is equal to the differential between domestic and foreign interest rates. Under rational expectations, people on average form correct expectations of the change in the exchange rate so:

$$\frac{\Delta E^e}{E} = \frac{\Delta E}{E}$$

$$\frac{\Delta E}{E} = r - r^*$$

If the domestic interest rate rises above (falls below) the foreign rate, then there will be an expectation of a depreciation (an appreciation) in the exchange rate. This relationship is shown in Figure 11.10.

The best approach to explaining how UIP works is through a very simple example. Suppose that initially the domestic and foreign interest rates were equal. In this case,

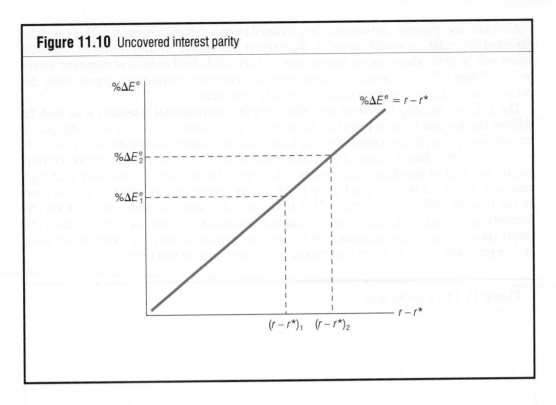

Figure 11.10 Uncovered interest parity

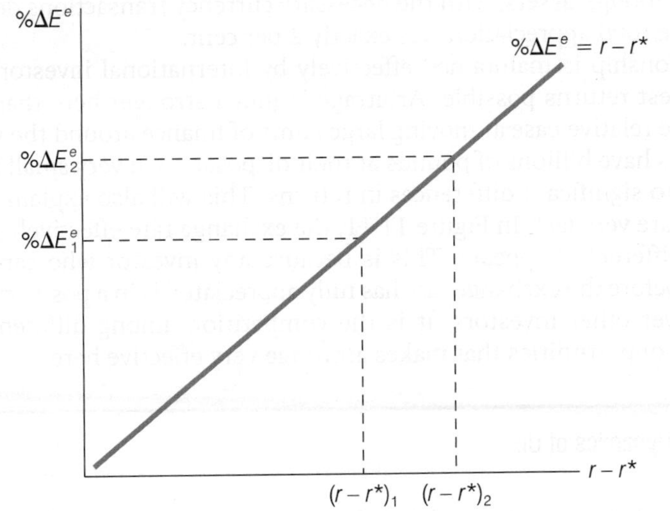

international investors are indifferent between choosing domestic and foreign assets, and there is no expected change in the exchange rate.

However, the domestic interest rate then rises by 2 per cent for one period, after which it returns to its original level. The effect on the exchange rate can be viewed in Figure 11.7. Now that domestic assets offer higher returns, the demand for foreign currency will fall as domestic investors substitute out of foreign and into domestic assets. The supply of foreign currency will also increase as foreign investors do the same. Consequently, the domestic exchange will appreciate from E_1 to E_2.

However, once that interest differential disappears, what should happen to the exchange rate? As domestic assets are no longer offering higher returns than on foreign assets, there is no reason for the demand and supply curves to stay at D_2 and S_2, respectively. Both will return to their initial levels and the exchange rate will return to E_1. The initial appreciation in the exchange rate will only last as long as the interest differential is expected to persist.

However, by how much will the domestic exchange rate appreciate (E_1 to E_2 in Figure 11.7)? Well, according to the UIP condition, this will be by 2 per cent. We know that once the interest rate falls back to its initial value, the exchange rate must return to its initial value. Therefore, this immediate appreciation must be stimulating expectations of a depreciation, and from UIP, this expected depreciation will be 2 per cent. So, in order to depreciate 2 per cent back to its initial value, the exchange rate must first of all appreciate by the same – exactly 2 per cent. This is shown in Figure 11.11.

The movements in the exchange rate act to equalize the returns on domestic and foreign assets, just as UIP predicts. Although domestic assets offer 2 per cent more than those abroad, this is countered by the expected 2 per cent depreciation in the currency.

What if the exchange rate were to initially appreciate by less than 2 per cent? In this case, the interest differential would be 2 per cent, but the expected depreciation would be less than 2 per cent. Domestic assets would offer higher returns than those overseas, so encouraging further purchases of domestic assets would then appreciate the exchange rate further until the appreciation had reached 2 per cent.

11

Alternatively, suppose the currency appreciated by more than 2 per cent. In this case, the expected depreciation would outweigh the interest differential so the returns on domestic assets will be lower than that on foreign assets. This would lead to sales of domestic assets and purchases of foreign assets, with the necessary currency transactions depreciating the currency until the total appreciation was exactly 2 per cent.

The UIP relationship is maintained effectively by international investors who seek to achieve the highest returns possible. Arbitrage is much stronger here than in the goods market due to the relative ease at moving large sums of finance around the world. If international investors have billions of pounds at their disposal, then very small interest differentials will lead to significant differences in returns. This will also explain why exchange rate movements are very fast. In Figure 11.11, the exchange rate effectively jumps as soon as the interest differential appears. This is because any investor who can purchase the domestic assets before the exchange rate has fully appreciated is in a position to make additional returns over other investors. It is the competition among different investors to realize profitable opportunities that makes arbitrage very effective here.

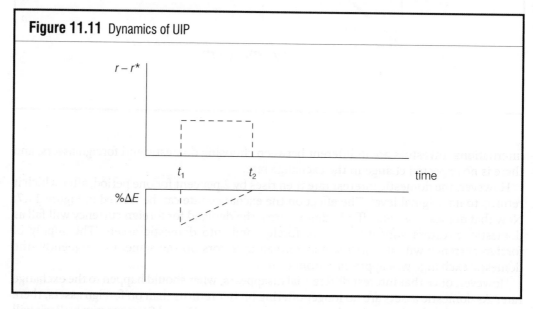

Figure 11.11 Dynamics of UIP

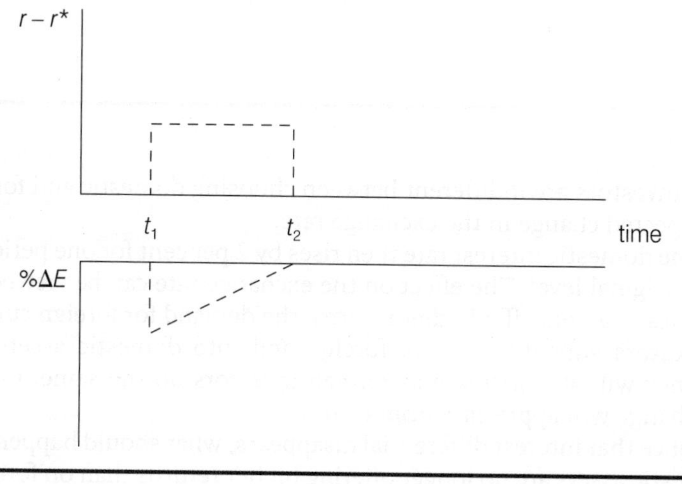

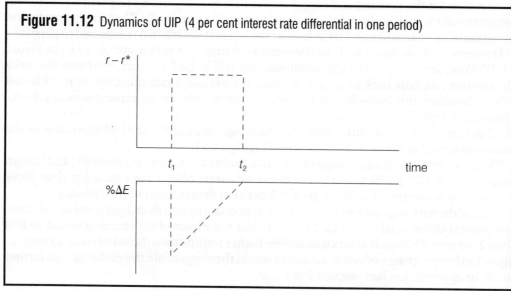

Figure 11.12 Dynamics of UIP (4 per cent interest rate differential in one period)

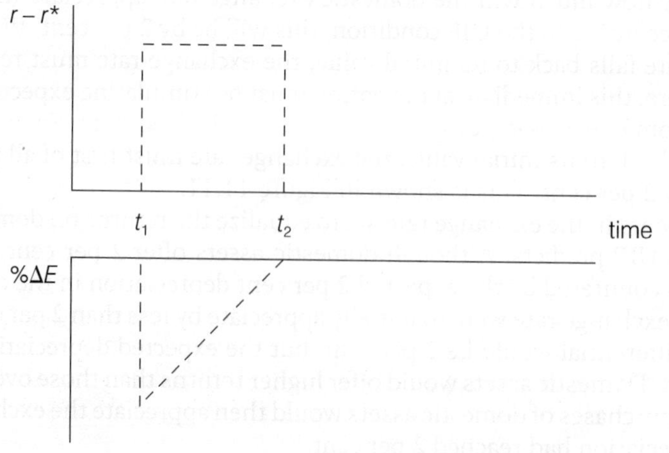

The size of exchange rate changes following interest rate movements depends on both the size and the persistence of interest rate differentials. In Figure 11.12, the one period interest differential is 4 per cent. This would then generate an initial appreciation of the same amount with, of course, an expected depreciation of also 4 per cent over the period.

If the interest differential were 2 per cent but was maintained for two periods, then the initial appreciation in the exchange rate would once again be approximately 4 per cent. As the differential is 2 per cent in each period, from the UIP relationship, the expected depreciation in each would also be 2 per cent, justifying the initial appreciation of about 4 per cent. This is shown in Figure 11.13.

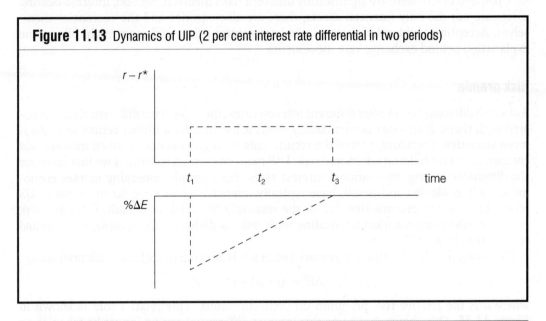

Figure 11.13 Dynamics of UIP (2 per cent interest rate differential in two periods)

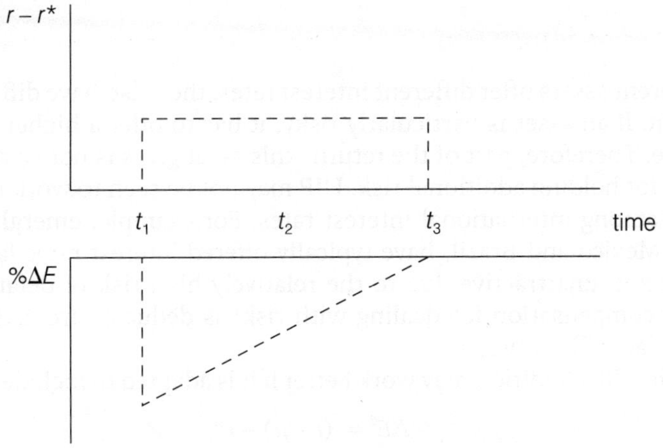

Figure 11.14 UIP in the £–$ exchange rate

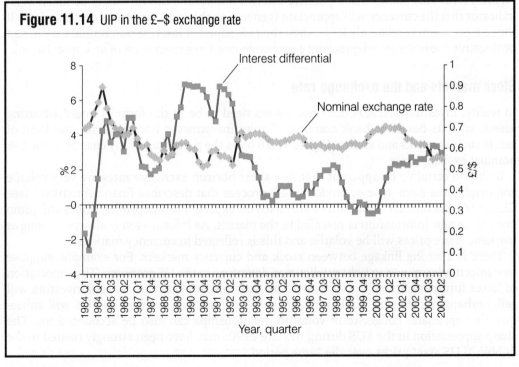

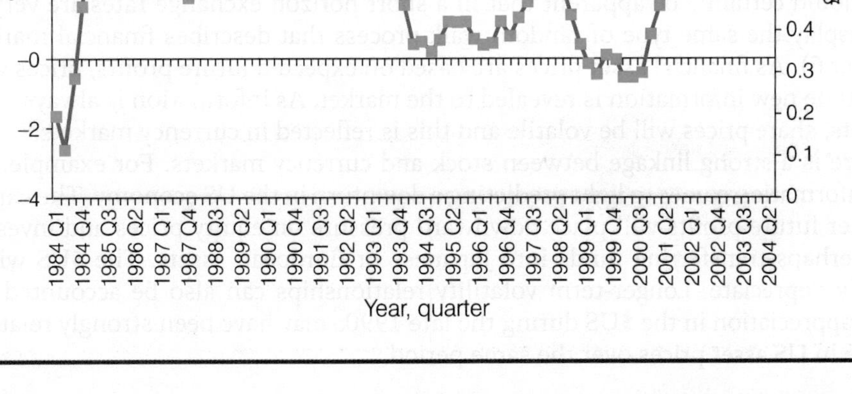

As a theory accounting for short-term movements in the exchange rate, UIP is important. Figure 11.14 plots evidence for the UK–US nominal exchange rate. There is cursory evidence to suggest that an appreciation in the exchange rate is associated with a positive interest differential. The fact that financial markets really do act to arbitrage the differences in international asset returns also means that UIP should be considered as more than just a theoretical curiosity, but as something that is widely applied throughout the world.

However, there are two extensions to the theory of UIP, which might break the relationship between short-term exchange rate movements and the interest differential. The first is the idea that there are different risks in investing in different assets. Even if two different assets offer the same rate of interest, international investors will still have a strong preference towards one if there are significantly different risks involved. Second, interest-bearing assets are not the only financial assets; there are also equities and the currencies themselves. Accepting a wider definition of what constitutes a financial asset might offer some explanation behind exchange rate movements.

Risk premia

Although different assets offer different interest rates, they also have different risks associated with them. If an asset is particularly risky, it has to offer a higher return to make it more attractive. Therefore, part of the returns this asset gives is not so much interest, but compensation for holding additional risk. UIP may not be seen to work if we just consider the difference among international interest rates. For example, emerging market economies, such as Mexico and Brazil, have typically offered interest rates far in excess of US levels, but are still unattractive due to the relatively high risk of default. Once the risk premium (the compensation for dealing with risk) is deducted from these, the residual returns may be actually very low.

Therefore, the UIP condition may work better if it is adapted to include a risk premium.

$$\Delta E^e = (r - \mu) - r^*$$

where μ is the relative risk premium on domestic assets. This relationship is shown in Figure 11.15. This shows that a positive interest differential can no longer be taken as an indicator that the currency will appreciate (generating the expectation of a depreciation). If the risk premium is relatively large, then the risk-adjusted interest differential may in fact be negative – leading to a depreciating exchange rate (an expectation of an appreciation).

11

Stock markets and the exchange rate

In reality, investing overseas does not always need to be in the form of interest-bearing assets, such as bonds or bank accounts. Equity investments normally take the form of assets such as stocks and shares. Figure 11.16 plots the percentage daily change in the £–$ nominal exchange rate.

It should certainly be apparent that in a short horizon exchange rates are very volatile and display the same type of random walk process that describes financial markets (see Chapter 6). As financial asset prices are based on expected future profits, prices will jump every time new information is revealed to the market. As information is always arriving at markets, share prices will be volatile and this is reflected in currency markets.

There is a strong linkage between stock and currency markets. For example, suppose new information comes to light predicting a downturn in the US economy. The expectation of lower future profits will place downward pressure on equity prices and investors will sell, perhaps transferring funds into Japanese or European assets. The $US will subsequently depreciate. Longer-term volatility relationships can also be accounted for. The sharp appreciation in the $US during the late 1990s may have been strongly related to the bubble in US asset prices over the same period.

The relationship between stock markets and currencies can also cloud the UIP relationship. Increases in interest rates need not always lead to an appreciation in the exchange rate. In fact, a rise in interest rates would be expected to lead to a fall in stock market prices and therefore may lead to a depreciation in the exchange rate.

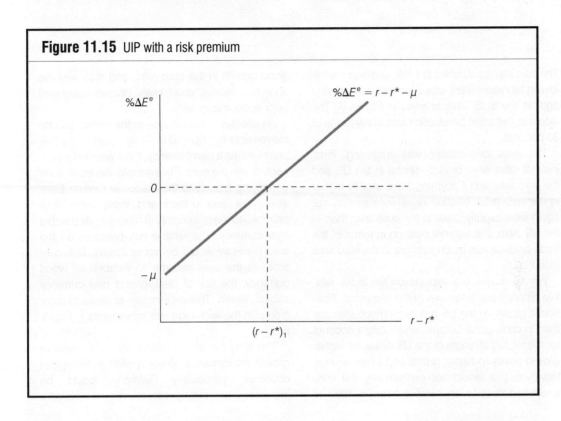

Figure 11.15 UIP with a risk premium

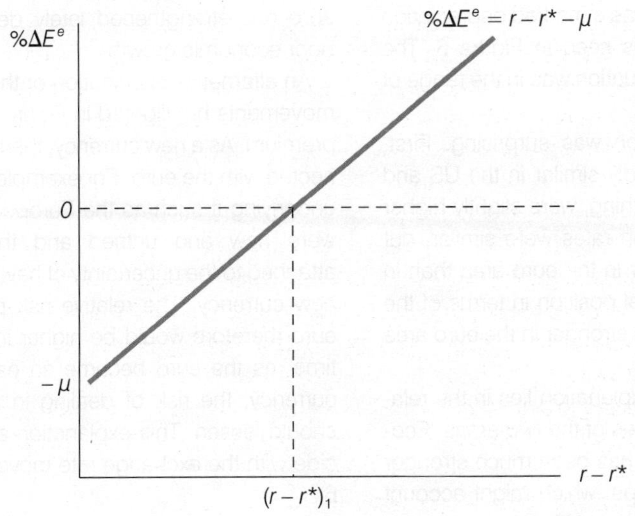

Figure 11.16 Daily £–$ exchange rate changes

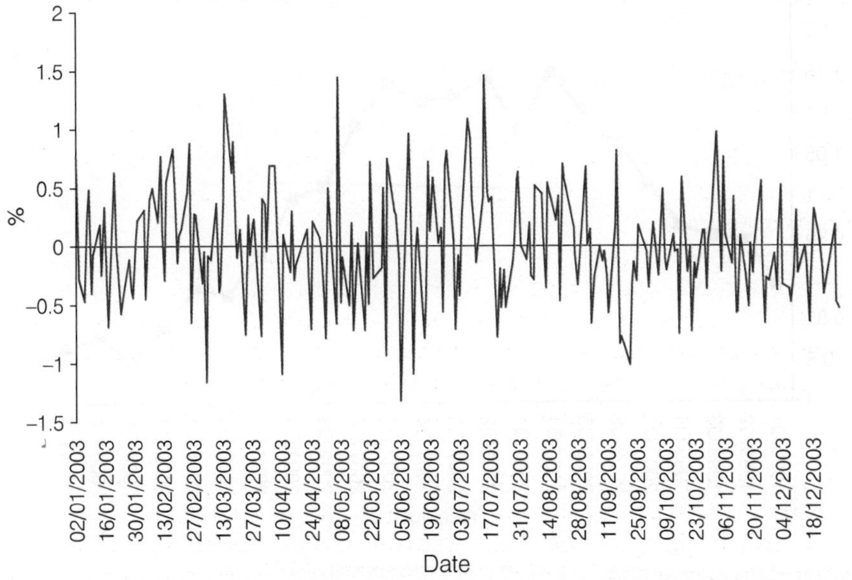

Global applications 11.6

Why was the euro so weak

The euro was established in 1999, and over the following two years there was a marked depreciation against the $US. This is seen in Figure 6. The extent of this initial devaluation was in the range of 30 per cent.

This initial depreciation was surprising. First, interest rates were broadly similar in the US and the euro area and if anything, were slightly higher in the euro area. Inflation rates were similar, but again were slightly lower in the euro area than in the US. Also, the external position in terms of the trade balance was much stronger in the euro area than the US.

With hindsight, one explanation lies in the relative different performances of the two areas. Economic growth in the US has been much stronger than in continental Europe, which might account for the relative strength of the US dollar, as higher growth points to higher profits and asset returns. However, this would not explain why the euro weakened despite an initial outlook in 1999 of good growth in the euro area, and also why the euro has strengthened lately despite continued poor economic growth.

An alternative explanation of the exchange rate movements highlighted in Figure 6 lies in the risk premium. As a new currency, there were risks connected with the euro. For example, the institutions underlying it such as the European Central Bank were new and untried and there were risks attached to the uncertainty of having to deal with a new currency. The relative risk premium on the euro therefore would be higher initially. But, over time, as the euro became an established world currency, the risk of dealing in a new currency should lessen. This explanation appears to coincide with the exchange rate movements in Figure 6.

This story can also be connected to the relative growth performance. Weak growth in European countries, particularly Germany, could be expected to put pressure on a nation's

Figure 6 €–$ exchange rate since 1999

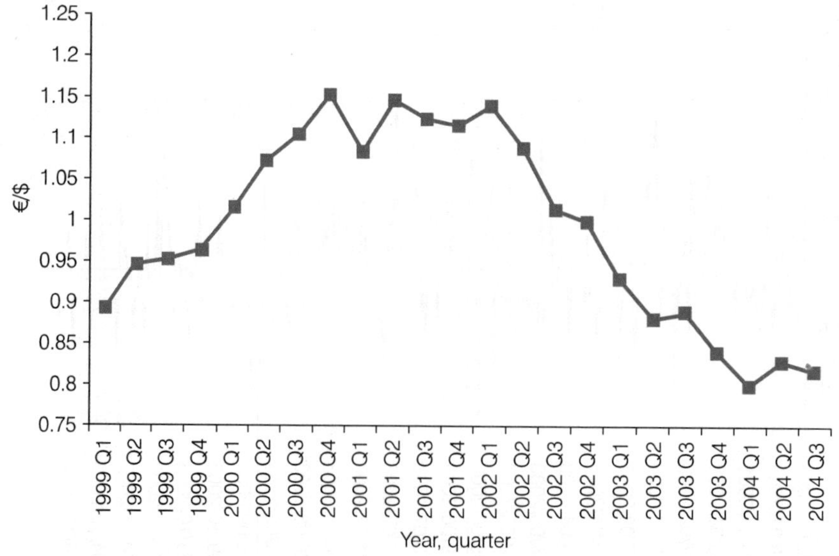

Global application 11.6 (continued)

commitment to euro membership. This is because leaving the single currency would give domestic policy makers more discretion to enact policies to deal with weak domestic growth. If international traders considered this to be a possibility, then it might explain why initial confidence in the euro was low. At the same time, though, continued membership of the single currency would be a sign of commitment, so confidence in the sustainability of European Monetary Union (EMU) and the euro itself would rise, reducing any associated risk premium.

Global application 11.7

Exchange rates and fundamentals

Asset prices are linked to the expected future earnings those assets produce. In turn, the demand for assets is likely to have similar implications for the exchange rate. Logically, there should be a direct relationship between the factors that drive asset prices and the exchange rate.

A recent working paper from the European Central Bank has investigated the relationship between US macroeconomic announcements and the exchange rate. These results are shown in Table 8.

An appreciation in the effective exchange rate is a downward movement (meaning, of course, that fewer dollars are required in order to purchase a unit of foreign currency). From Table 8, we can see that announcements of monetary policy expansions, higher expectations from a survey of purchasing managers (NAPM), higher GDP estimates, higher consumer confidence, higher non-farm payroll employment, higher average work weeks, lower unemployment, and lower consumer price inflation (CPI) will all generate significant appreciations in the US dollar. All these are indicators that the strength of the economy is improving, which would be expected to have a positive effect on asset prices.

Table 8 The significance of US announcement surprises on the effective dollar exchange rate (1993–2003)

	Coefficient	(t-statistic)
Monetary policy)	–1.616**	(–2.364)
NAPM	–0.526***	(–3.351)
Non-farm payrolls	–0.246**	(–2.485)
Industrial production	–0.212	(–1.348)
Advance GDP	–0.616**	(–2.427)
Consumer confidence	–0.652**	(–2.254)
Retail sales	–0.133	(–0.995)
CPI	0.198*	(1.561)
Unemployment rate	1.703**	(2.848)
Housing starts	0.009	(0.038)
PPI	0.041	(0.0472)
Trade balance	–0.348	(–1.133)
Average work-week	–0.338*	(–1.597)

Significance at the * 90%, ** 95% and the *** 99% levels
Source: Ehrmann and Fratzscher (2004)

11

Currency trading

Explaining exchange rate volatility is even easier once we allow for the fact that the exchange rate itself can be viewed as the price of a financial asset. This is because currency traders aim to make money by predicting the movements in the exchange rate. For example, at one moment in time, a trader could purchase on the spot market. If the domestic currency depreciates, then the domestic currency can be repurchased and a profit made.

When currencies themselves are viewed as financial assets, it means that they too can be subject to the same volatility as other financial assets. This is certainly true in the short run, but may also manifest itself in long-term volatility, such as bubbles. The long appreciation in the $US at the beginning of the 1980s is certainly an example of this.

11.4.3 The Dornbusch model of exchange rate overshooting

The two most common theories accounting for exchange rate movements have just been introduced. One of the most common observations regarding the exchange rate is its relative volatility in the short-run. This is a feature of Figure 11.9, where movements in the nominal exchange rate are large compared to those in relative prices. Explaining this short-run volatility is a challenge for the traditional models.

The Dornbusch overshooting model is one answer. It simply looks at how the PPP and UIP conditions interact, and predicts that the exchange rate might be quite volatile to changes in monetary policy. As will be seen, the important factor generating the exchange rate overshooting result is price rigidity.

To see why, consider what happens when prices adjust quickly to changes in the money supply. Figure 11.17 represents equilibrium in the money market. An increase in the money supply from M_1 to M_2 shifts the money supply curve to the right. However, because there are no price rigidities, the predictions of the quantity theory of money will conclude

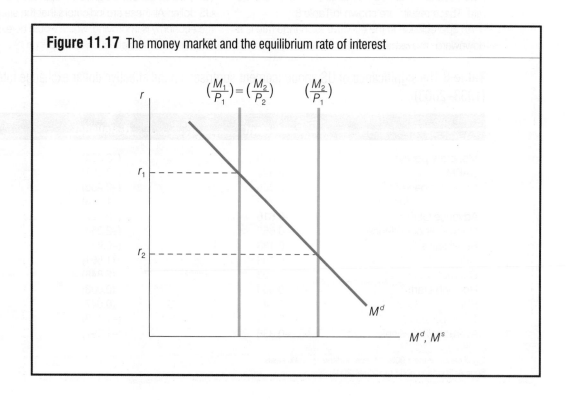

Figure 11.17 The money market and the equilibrium rate of interest

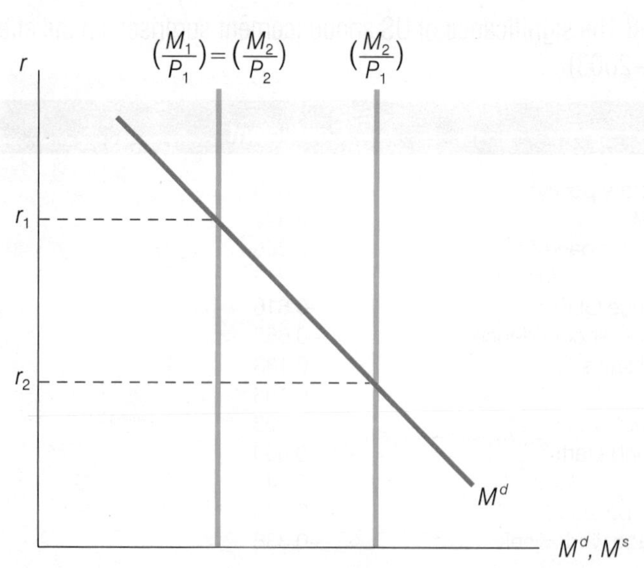

11

that prices will rise proportionately, P_1 to P_2, so that $\%\Delta M = \%\Delta P$. As a result, there will be no overall effect on the real money supply, which will leave the interest rate unchanged at r_1.

In the absence of price rigidities, this happens quickly. As interest rates do not change, the theory of UIP will not offer any prediction here as to how the exchange rate will change. Instead, movements in the exchange rate will be completely described by the monetary theory of the exchange rate, or PPP. This is shown in Figure 11.18.

The exchange rate will only move proportionately with the initial change in the money supply and prices (E_1 to E_2 in panel D of Figure 11.18). This is certainly at odds with Figure 11.9, which would indicate a more than proportional reaction of the exchange rate to fit in with empirical observation.

Suppose now that there are price rigidities. The same increase in the money supply will not be offset by a proportional rise in prices. This is shown in panel B of Figure 11.19, where it now takes time for prices to rise. What we are saying here is that, in the long run, the predictions of the quantity theory of money still apply, but price changes are not instantaneous and, in the short run, prices will rise proportionately less than the change in the money supply. In Chapter 9, there is a fair amount of discussion which offers justifications as to why prices should adjust slowly.

In this case, the real money supply is affected in the short run, which places downward pressure on the interest rate (r_1 to r_2 in Figure 11.17). According to the theory of UIP, this will lead to the expectation of an appreciation. However, in the long run, the predictions of PPP must still apply – which suggest a proportional depreciation in the currency.

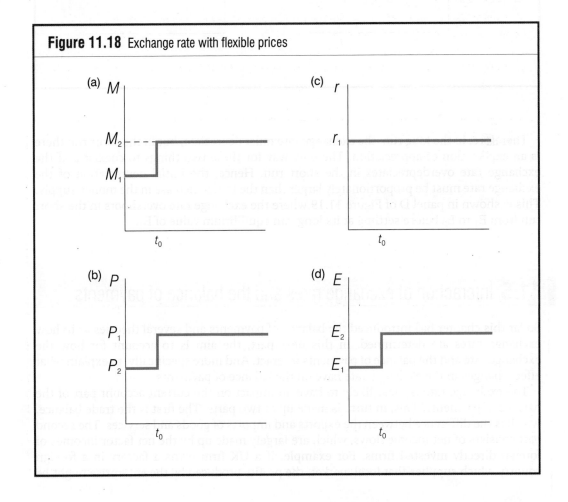

Figure 11.18 Exchange rate with flexible prices

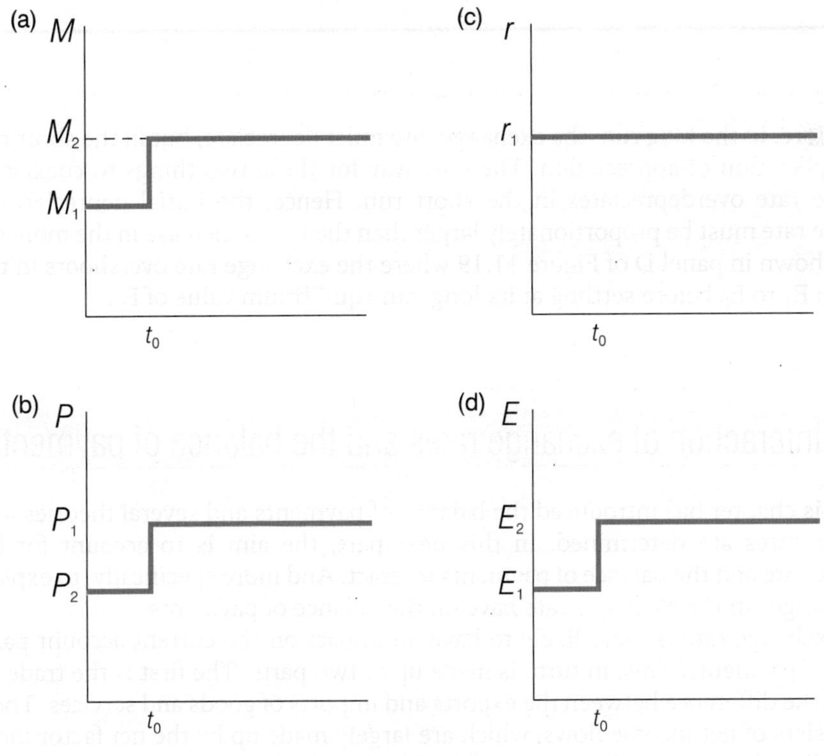

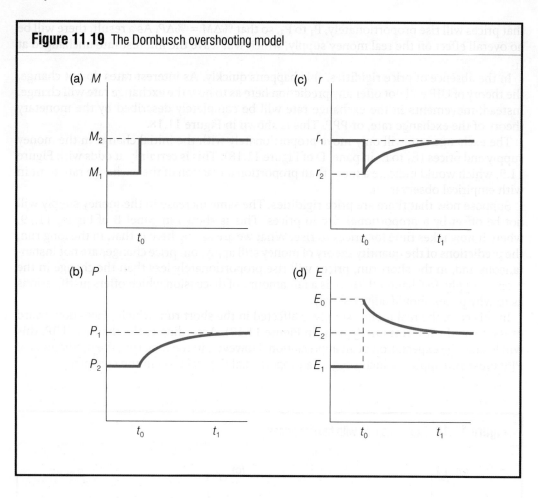

Figure 11.19 The Dornbusch overshooting model

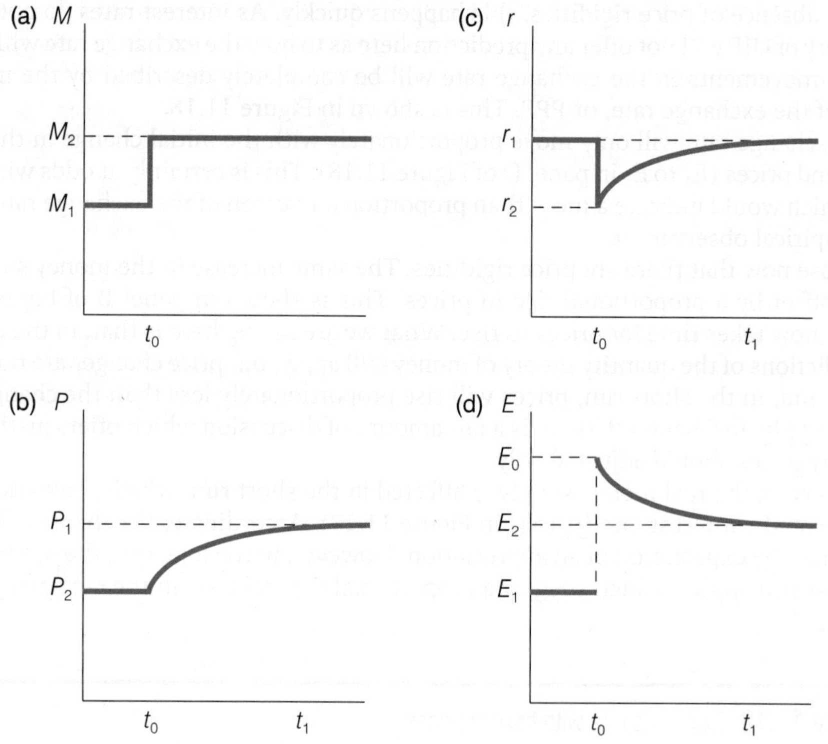

Therefore, in the long run, the exchange rate must depreciate, but in the short run there is an expectation of appreciation. The only way for these two things to coexist is if the exchange rate overdepreciates in the short run. Hence, the initial depreciation of the exchange rate must be proportionately larger than the initial increase in the money supply. This is shown in panel D of Figure 11.19 where the exchange rate overshoots in the short run from E_1 to E_0 before settling at its long-run equilibrium value of E_2.

11

11.5 Interaction of exchange rates and the balance of payments

So far this chapter has introduced the balance of payments and several theories as to how exchange rates are determined. In this next part, the aim is to account for how the exchange rate and the balance of payments interact. And more specifically, to explain what effect changes in the exchange rate have on the balance of payments.

The exchange rate is most likely to have an impact on the current account part of the balance of payments. This, in turn, is made up of two parts. The first is the trade balance, which is the difference between the exports and imports of goods and services. The second part consists of net income flows, which are largely made up by the net factor incomes of foreign directly invested firms. For example, if a UK firm owns a factory in a foreign country which supplies that local market, the profits produced by the enterprise might be repatriated to the UK. This would represent a positive income flow that improves the current account. However, the domestic currency value of the foreign earned income, and hence the size of the flow, will depend on the exchange rate.

Although the exchange rate will affect the size of these flows, the conventional approach is to assume that the exchange rate has the most significant effect on the trade balance. The position of the trade balance is determined by the net value of exports and imports, with the value being determined by price and volume. Movements in the exchange rate can be expected to have two effects on trade.

Competitiveness

A depreciation in the exchange rate makes foreign goods more expensive in terms of domestic currency, and domestic goods cheaper in foreign currency terms. Therefore, at both home and overseas, there should be substitution away from foreign to domestic goods. By making domestic goods more competitive in international markets, the trade balance should be expected to improve. An appreciation in the currency would, of course, have the opposite effect.

Terms of trade

This refers to the ratio of export to import prices. A depreciation in the exchange rate will increase import prices, worsening the terms of trade. This will deteriorate the trade balance, as for every unit imported, a greater number of exports would be required to balance trade. An exchange rate appreciation has the opposite effect – improving the terms of trade and making imports cheaper so fewer exports are required per unit of import to balance trade.

It should be apparent that these two effects work in opposite directions. An exchange rate depreciation makes domestic goods more competitive, in that exports are cheaper in the global market and imports are more expensive in the domestic market. However, the terms of trade effect means that in the case of domestic currency, imports are now more expensive so that making the same trades will result in deterioration in the current account. An appreciation would, of course, have the opposite effect.

Competitiveness and the trade balance

The price of exports in terms of the domestic currency is given by the domestic price level.

$$P_X = P$$

The price of foreign goods is given by the overseas price level and the nominal exchange rate.

$$P_M = EP^*$$

Competitiveness is the ratio of export and import prices or, alternatively, the real exchange rate. This can also be thought of the inverse of the terms of trade.

$$\theta = \frac{EP^*}{P}$$

The demand for exports (X) is a positive function of the level of competitiveness and overseas income.

$$X = x_{y^*}(\theta)Y^*, \quad \frac{\Delta x_{y^*}(\theta)}{\Delta \theta} > 0$$

Global application 11.8

Why are UK imports so cyclical?

Figure 7 plots the percentage change in domestic household consumption and imports in the UK economy since 1970.

Two things are noticeable. The first is that both follow cyclical trends; the second is that imports tend to be more cyclical than consumption. This implies that when the economy grows strongly consumption rises, but foreign goods make up an increasing proportion of this. Likewise, in a downturn, demand for imports falls faster than for domestic goods.

From Table 11.2, it is clear that the UK has a high income elasticity of demand. The conventional argument is that the UK economy has a small manufacturing sector, so when incomes and the demand for consumer goods rise, a disproportionate amount of this is met from foreign producers.

A slightly different (although mainly along similar lines) explanation is made by Valerie Herzberg, Maria Sebastia-Barriel and Simon Whitaker (*Bank of England Quarterly Bulletin*, Summer 2002). In Table 9, the import content of each component of domestic demand is reported. This shows that the import content of investment, particularly in inventories, is typically the greatest.

However, from Chapters 2, 3 and 4, we have seen that each of these demand components has a different degree of cyclicality. Cyclical movements in household and government (which has a very small import content, as most is on the procurement of domestically provided services) consumption tends to be lower than investment. Inventories (which consist of materials and fuel), work in progress and finished goods, are highly cyclical. The overall cyclical nature of imports might be accounted for partly by the fact that there is a high import content in the most cyclical components of aggregate demand. Imports are more cyclical than domestic demand, in part because domestic producers may face costs in rapid adjustments so increases in demand are met disproportionately from overseas suppliers.

Figure 7 UK consumption and imports

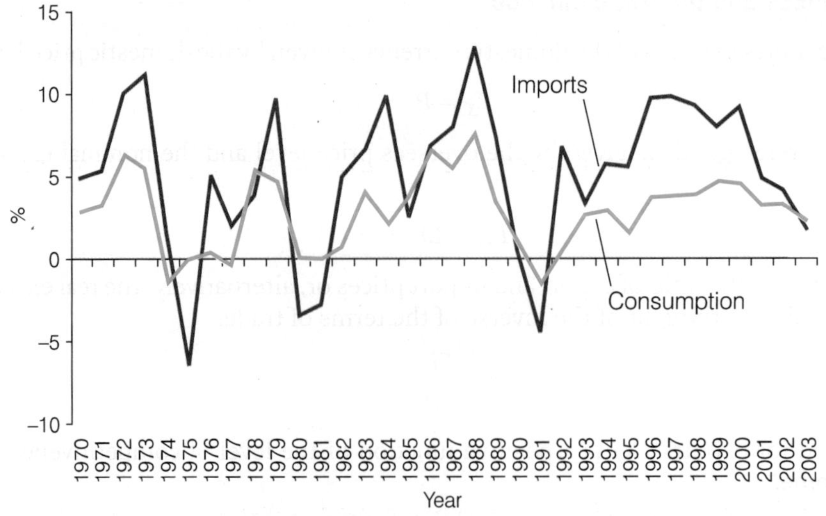

11

Global application 11.8 (continued)

Table 9 Import content of expenditures

Expenditure component	Import content 1990	Import content 1995
Household consumption	20.3	20.3
Government consumption	13.2	11.5
Whole economy investment	31.8	35.9
Changes in inventories	73.9	45.6
Domestic demand	20.9	21.3

Source: Herzberg, Sebastia-Barriel and Whitaker (2002)

Overseas income is represented by Y. The coefficient, $x_y{}^*(\theta)$, is the proportion of total foreign income that is spent on domestic goods. As the exchange rate depreciates (θ rises), domestic goods become cheaper, which encourages substitution towards them, so $xy^*(\theta)$ rises.

The demand for imports is a negative function of competitiveness and a positive function of domestic income.

$$M = m_y{}^*(\theta)Y, \qquad \frac{\Delta m_y{}^*(\theta)}{\Delta\theta} < 0$$

As income rises, households tend to consume more – a proportion of which will go on imported goods, so there is a positive relationship between imports and income. This proportion is governed by the marginal propensity to import, $m_y(\theta)$. This will be related negatively to the real exchange rate, as a depreciation will make domestic goods relatively cheaper encouraging substitution towards them. So, as θ rises (falls), $m_y(\theta)$ falls (rises).

The trade balance is the value of exports minus the value of imports. In terms of domestic currency, this is:

$$BT = Px_{y*}(\theta)Y^* - EP^* m_y(\theta)Y$$

The real value of the trade balance can be calculated by dividing by the domestic price level.

$$\frac{BT}{P} = x_{y*}(\theta)Y^* - \frac{EP^*}{P} m_Y(\theta)Y$$

$$\text{As } \theta = \frac{EP^*}{P}$$

$$\frac{BT}{P} = x_{y*}(\theta)Y^* - \theta m_y(\theta)Y$$

When trade is balanced, $BT = 0$, this can be rearranged to give:

$$x_y{}^*(\theta)Y = \theta m_y(\theta)Y \text{ or } X = M$$

11

Global application 11.9

Is an improvement in the terms of trade always bad?

An improvement in the terms of trade means that the price of domestically produced goods and services has risen relative to foreign goods and services. This could result through either an increase in relative prices (P/P^*) or an appreciation in the nominal exchange rate. An improvement in the terms of trade is the same as a real appreciation of the domestic currency.

In some of the analysis presented in this chapter, an upward movement in the terms of trade is bad. Because domestically produced goods are relatively more expensive than those produced overseas, there will be a substitution away from domestic to foreign goods and if the Marshall-Lerner conditions hold true, the current account will deteriorate. A real appreciation/improvement in the terms of trade will have a negative competitiveness effect.

There is, though, a potential benefit which should not be overlooked. A real appreciation means that one unit of the domestic currency can purchase a larger amount of goods and services from abroad. The budget constraint the household faces has therefore changed in a way that alters the welfare of consumers. In Chapter 2, we outlined the theory of choice behind intertemporal consumption; i.e., how much to consume today and how much to consume tomorrow. Using the same theory, we can analyse the effects of an improvement in the terms of trade.

There are two types of goods, C are domestic goods and C^* are foreign goods. A representative household has preferences between the two types of goods represented by a utility function $U(C,C^*)$ from which a set of convex indifference curves can be drawn, $u(C,C^*)$. The household has a fixed income of Y and the relative prices of the two goods are P and EP^*. The household utility maximization problem is:

$$\max U(C,C^*) \text{ subject to } PC + EP^*C^* \leq Y$$

The solution to this is shown in Figure 8, where the household chooses the optimal consumption bundle $(\hat{C}, \hat{C}^*)$ to maximize the utility (i.e., to move

Figure 8 Optimal consumption of domestic and foreign goods

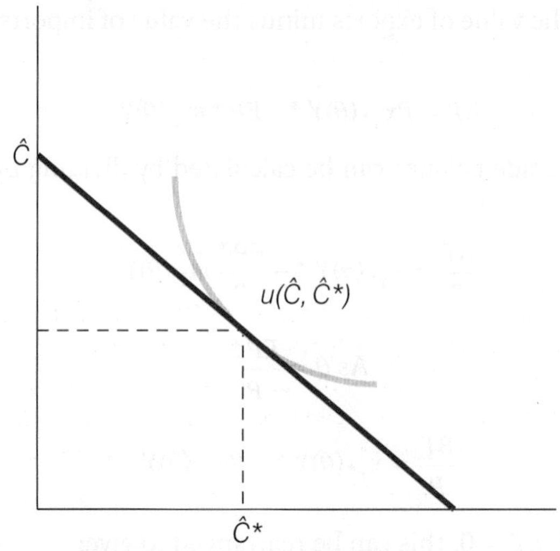

Global application 11.9 (continued)

Figure 9 Optimal consumption and welfare following a real appreciation

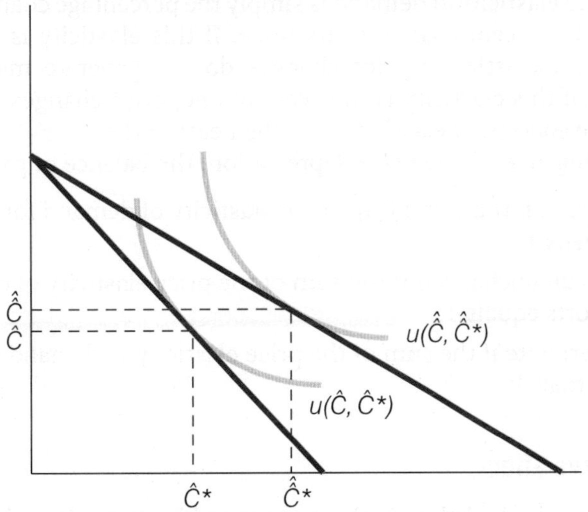

to the highest indifference curve) subject to the budget constraint. The slope of the budget constraint here is the price ratio between domestic and foreign goods: $-EP^*/P^*$.

If there were a real appreciation due to a fall in overseas prices ($P^*\downarrow$)or a nominal appreciation ($E\downarrow$), then the budget constraint will pivot outwards. As foreign goods are now cheaper, the purchasing power of domestic income over foreign goods and services is now greater. This is shown in Figure 9 where the optimal consumption bundle changes to $\left(\hat{\hat{C}}, \hat{\hat{C}}^*\right)$. Although the terms of trade effect elicits some substitution towards foreign goods, consumption of both goods actually rises and welfare rises as the household has moved on to a higher indifference curve. This is because the cheaper foreign goods generate a positive income effect.

Terms of trade effects do have an effect on domestic competitiveness, but they also have consequences for the purchasing power of domestically generated income. Although an improvement in the terms of trade will reduce competitiveness, it can also improve household welfare via positive income effects.

This equation aptly describes the effect of exchange rate movements on the trade balance. A depreciation in the currency will increase the volume of exports and reduce the volume of imports. However, it will also increase the price of imports, so the competitiveness and the terms of trade effects are working in opposite directions. The overall impact on the trade balance will depend on which effect is the greater.

An appreciating exchange rate has the opposite effect. The volume of exports will fall, and the volume of imports will rise. However, the price of imports will also fall. Although net exports have fallen in volume, the terms of trade have moved to counter this. Again, the overall impact will depend on which effect dominates.

Marshall-Lerner condition

For a depreciation to improve the trade balance, a necessary condition is that the competitiveness effect outweighs the terms of trade effect. For this to happen, the substitution towards domestic goods must be sufficiently strong, which will depend on the price elasticity of demand.

The price elasticity of demand is simply the percentage change in quantity demanded following a 1 per cent change in its price. If this elasticity is between zero and one, then demand is inelastic, so price changes do not generate much of a substitution effect. However, if this elasticity is in excess of one, price changes generate a large substitution effect. The concept of elasticity is at the heart of the **Marshall-Lerner condition**.

Following an exchange rate depreciation, the balance of payments will:

- Improve if the sum of the price elasticity of demand for exports and imports exceeds 1.
- Remain unchanged if the sum of the price elasticity of demand for exports and imports equals 1.
- Deteriorate if the sum of the price elasticity of demand for exports and imports is less than 1.

The J-curve effect

The conventional wisdom is that export and import prices elasticities are much greater in the longer rather than the shorter run. This is logical as it takes a while for consumers to discover and then adjust to new prices. Due to this time-delay pattern of elasticities, many prescribe to the idea that the balance of payments follows a J-type movement to depreciations (see Figure 11.20). In the short run, elasticities are low, the Marshall-Lerner condition is violated and the terms of trade effect of depreciations dominate. In the longer run, though, elasticities are greater, so the depreciation improves the balance of payments.

Some empirical evidence behind **the J-curve effect** is offered in Figure 11.21. This plots the US trade balance as a proportion of the GDP and the $ nominal effective exchange rate during the 1980s. In 1985, there was a fairly sharp devaluation in the $ exchange rate, reversing the strong appreciation during the first half of the decade. However, it is clear that net exports as a proportion of GDP responds with a two-year lag.

11

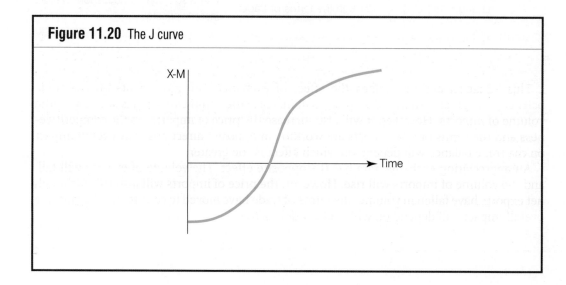

Figure 11.20 The J curve

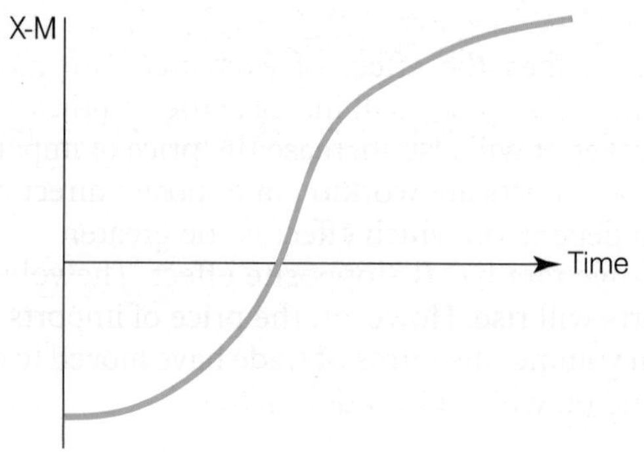

Figure 11.21 US trade balance and effective exchange rate

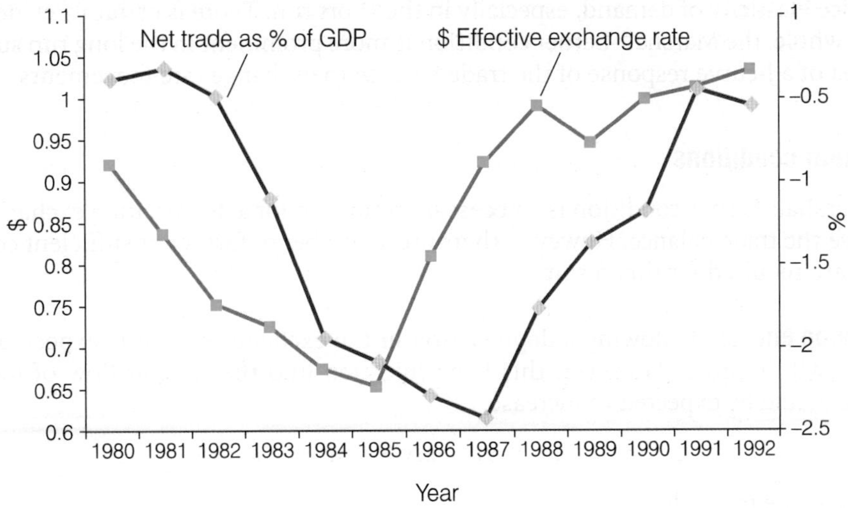

Table 11.2 Trade elasticities for G7 countries

	Long-run elasticities			
	Income		Price	
	Exports	Imports	Exports	Imports
Canada	1.1	1.4	–0.9	–0.9
France	1.5	1.6	–0.2	–0.4
Germany	1.4	1.5	–0.3	–0.06
Italy	1.6	1.4	–0.9	–0.4
Japan	1.1	0.9	–1.0	–0.3
UK	1.1	2.2	–1.6	–0.6
US	0.8	1.8	–1.5	–0.3

	Short-run elasticities			
	Income		Price	
	Exports	Imports	Exports	Imports
Canada	1.1	1.3	–0.5	–0.1
France	1.8	1.6	–0.1	–0.1
Germany	0.5	1.0	–0.1	–0.2
Italy	2.3	1.0	–0.3	–0.0
Japan	0.6	1.0	–0.5	–0.1
UK	1.1	1.0	–0.2	–0.0
US	1.8	1.0	–0.5	–0.1

Source: Hooper. Johnson, Marquez (1998)

11

Some calculations of the price elasticities of exports and imports in various countries for the short and long run are shown in Table 11.2. These elasticities are a little lower than reported in other studies because they include figures for oil, which tends to have a very low price elasticity of demand, especially in the short run. There is certainly evidence that, on the whole, the Marshall-Lerner condition is more prominent in the long run supporting the idea of a J-curve response of the trade balance to exchange rate movements.

Sufficient conditions

The Marshall-Lerner condition is a necessary condition for a depreciating exchange rate to improve the trade balance. However, there are a number of further or sufficient conditions which are required for this result.

Absorption effects Following a depreciation in the exchange rate, it is expected that net exports will improve. However, this is an injection into the circular flow of income, so income would be expected to increase.

$$\Delta Y = k\Delta(X - M)$$

where k is the multiplier.

Imports are a function of income, $M = mY$, where m is the marginal propensity to import. Hence, it must be the case that:

$$\Delta M = m\Delta k(X - M)$$

This is the absorption effect on the balance of payments. Taken together, the total change in the trade balance will be:

$$\Delta(X - M) - mk\Delta(X - M)$$
$$= (1 - mk)\Delta(X - M)$$

The trade balance will only improve if $1 > mk$. If m and k are sufficiently large, then an initial improvement in the trade balance will generate a large increase in income, of which a large proportion will be spent on imports.

11

Real wage resistance Competitiveness is given by the real exchange rate, θ.

$$\theta = \frac{EP^*}{P}$$

It is clear that a depreciation will lead to a rise in both E and θ.

The consumer price index (CPI) represents the cost of living. Some of the goods and services that make up household consumption will come from overseas; therefore, a depreciation will lead to an increase in the cost of living.

$$CPI = \alpha P + (1 - \alpha)EP^*$$

The value of wages is determined in part by the cost of living. This is the nominal wage divided by the CPI.

$$w = \frac{W}{CPI}$$

Hence, an exchange rate depreciation through the cost of imports, and then a depreciation of the overall price level, will lead to a fall in the real wage. In order to restore the value of the real wage, organized labour groups such as trade unions may push for a higher nominal wage (W).

However, if domestic prices are simply a mark-up over costs, then this will lead to an increase in domestic prices.

$$P = (1 + \mu)W$$

This will begin to reduce competitiveness. It will also lead to a further increase in the cost of living, leading to a wage-price spiral. In seeking to maintain the value of real wages (real wage resistance), the competitiveness effects of a depreciation may be reversed.

Pricing to market In a competitive industry, prices are set equal to marginal costs and normal profits are made. In an imperfectly competitive industry, firms have some market power and prices are a mark-up on marginal costs.

$$P = (1 + \mu)MC$$

$$P^* = (1 + \mu^*)MC^*$$

In this case, competitiveness is given by:

$$\theta = \frac{E(1+\mu^*)P^*}{(1+\mu)P}$$

It is perfectly conceivable that changes in the mark-up may cancel out any movements in the exchange rate, leaving θ and the trade balance unchanged.

If there is a depreciation (E rises), the effect on competition will be neutralized if:

- domestic firms increase their mark-ups, using the exchange rate depreciation as an opportunity to increase margins
- foreign firms reduce their mark-ups. Perhaps they are concerned about losing market share and therefore are prepared to sacrifice some margin in order to maintain competitiveness
- a combination of the two.

Current account deficits and surpluses: do they matter?

Why might large imbalances in the current account be of concern to policy makers? After all, we have already seen that the current account is offset by the capital account in the balance of payments.

11

Deficits This implies that exports exceed imports. From the national income identity:

$$Y = C + I + G + X - M$$

which can be rearranged to give:

$$X - M = Y - C - I - G$$

Therefore, a deficit indicates that the citizens of a country are consuming more than they are producing. This results in one of two things.

- Foreign currency reserves are being run down to fund the deficit. This, though, cannot be done forever due to the finiteness of reserves.
- If foreign reserves are exhausted, the deficit can be funded by borrowing from overseas. However, large and sustained deficits result in larger and larger foreign liabilities. These liabilities are subject to interest, and the rate tends to increase with the size of the debt. Foreign indebtedness means that a large future constraint

may be placed on the economy, which has to divert resources to meeting its debt requirements.

Surpluses When an economy is in equilibrium, it is the case that injections are equal to leakages:

$$I + G + X = S + T + M$$

which can be rearranged to give:

$$(X - M) = (S - I) + (T - G)$$

Running a surplus means that the economy is a net lender to the rest of the world. However, what is apparent is that these funds could be allocated to domestic usages, either in private investment or government spending. The question here is whether it is better for domestic residents to save in domestic or foreign assets.

Correcting a trade deficit

If a country is running a persistent deficit on the trade balance, there are generally two policy options that can be used to correct it.

Exchange rates Providing the Marshall-Lerner condition holds, a depreciation in the exchange rate will lead to an improvement in the trade balance. In this respect, trade deficits may be self-correcting. For example, suppose there is a large increase in imports which leads to a deterioration in the trade balance. However, this also increases the demand for foreign currency, and reduces the demand for domestic currency, so the exchange rate will depreciate any way. Therefore, automatic correction should result. See Global application 11.10.

Absorption approach From the national income identity, the trade balance is simply:

$$X - M = Y - C - I - G$$

For a given level of output, the trade balance can be improved by simply reducing domestic absorption, $(C + I + G)$. These are components of aggregate demand. If these exceed the level of domestically-produced output $(C + I + G > Y)$, then the demand for goods and services can only be met by imports. Likewise, if domestic absorption is less than domestic output $(C + I + G < Y)$, there is no need to import goods and the excess production can be exported. Any policy which controls the absorption factors – consumption, investment and government spending – will influence the trade balance.

Global application 11.10

What if the Marshall-Lerner condition does not hold?

One important implication of the Marshall-Lerner condition is that current account imbalances will be offset by movements in the exchange rate. Any imbalance in the current account will imply an imbalance between the demand and supply of domestic and foreign currencies. Both these imbalances will be corrected by the movement of exchange rates to their equilibrium levels.

Global application 11.10 (continued)

Figure 10 The Marshall-Lerner condition and equilibrium in the currency market

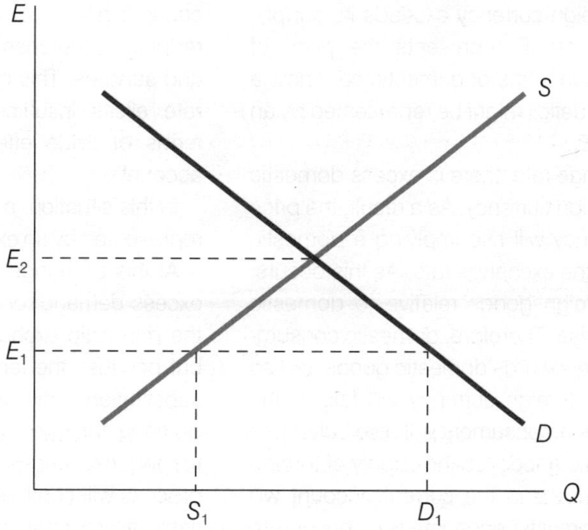

Figure 11 The failure of the Marshall-Lerner coalition and currency market disequilibrium

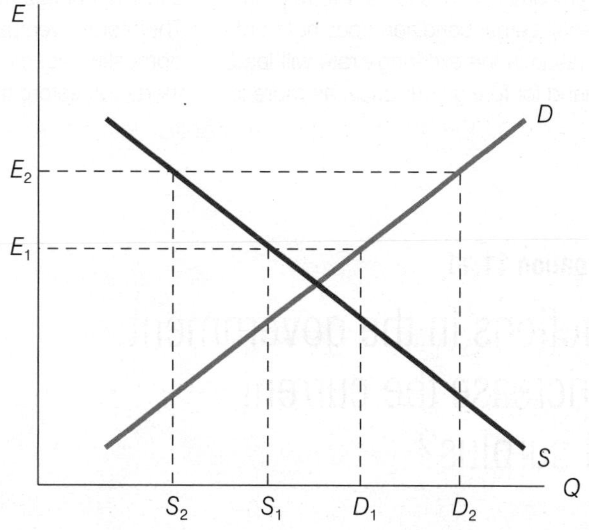

Global application 11.10 (continued)

Figure 10 is based on the same principle underlying Figure 11.5. If the economy is running a current account deficit, then it implies that the demand for foreign currency exceeds its supply. The exchange rate E represents the price of foreign currency in terms of domestic currency; a current account deficit might be represented by an exchange rate, E_1.

At this exchange rate, there is excess domestic demand for foreign currency. As a result, the price of foreign currency will rise implying a domestic depreciation in the exchange rate. As this occurs, the price of foreign goods relative to domestic goods will also rise. Therefore, domestic consumers will substitute towards domestic goods and so the demand for foreign currency will fall. At the same time, foreign consumers will also substitute towards domestic goods, so the supply of foreign currencies will rise and the current account will improve. The domestic economy will continue to depreciate until it reaches the level E_2, which is also consistent with current account equilibrium.

If the Marshall-Lerner condition fails to hold, this automatic correction procedure breaks down. Here, a depreciation in the currency actually leads to a deterioration in the current account. The effects can be shown by using an upward-sloping demand curve and a downward-sloping supply curve for foreign currency. This is easy to rationalize. If the Marshall-Lerner condition does not hold, then a depreciation in the exchange rate will lead to higher demand for foreign currency, as more is required to purchase the same goods from overseas. Likewise, the supply of foreign currency will fall because domestic goods and services are cheaper in terms of foreign currency, so less of it is required to purchase the same amount of goods and services. This occurs because the exchange rate elicits insufficient substitution leaving the terms of trade effect to dominate the current account.

In this situation, a current account deficit will be represented by an exchange rate of E_1 in Figure 11.

At this exchange rate, there will once again be excess demand for foreign currency. As a result, the domestic exchange will be depreciate to E_2, but because the terms of trade effect dominates substitution, this will only widen the excess demand for foreign currency. This will initiate a further exchange rate depreciation and the process will continue. The Marshall-Lerner condition is an important rule as without it exchange rate markets would be unstable.

There are, though, some limits to this instability. Figure 11 implies that the exchange rate will depreciate indefinitely and as a result the current account deficit will grow substantially. This, though, must be bounded by absorption effects. As the current account deficit grows, the trade sector subtracts from domestic output as it represents a leakage from the circular flow of income. Therefore, eventually imports will begin to fall as domestic income falls. Absorption effects will therefore restore the stability of the system.

Global application 11.11

Do reductions in the government deficit increase the current account surplus?

The identity surrounding national income flows suggests that the current account and the fiscal deficit are intrinsically related. Nations that run large government deficits also tend to run large

Global application 11.11 (continued)

current account deficits, commonly known as the 'twin deficits' problem. This view, however, tends to ignore another important factor.

$$(G-T) = (S-I) + (M-X)$$

The twin deficits approach implies that a reduction in the government deficit should increase the current account surplus. This, though, ignores the other part of the flow relationship – the difference between domestic saving and investment.

A reduction in the fiscal deficit will have limited effect on the current account if it is met by a reduction in domestic saving. Therefore, the fall in (G – T) is matched by a fall in (S – I), leaving (M – X) unchanged. The theory of Ricardian equivalence (as outlined in Chapter 3) is a powerful economic argument that would order this.

If households smooth consumption over their lifetime in line with utility maximizing behaviour, then an increase in taxes would be met by a fall in saving. Essentially, the public believes that the government will run a balanced budget, so the current surplus will be offset by future deficits, meaning that taxes in the future will fall. This would leave the value of expected present discounted value of lifetime income unchanged and therefore there would be no need to change consumption. Present consumption is sustained by running down saving or through borrowing, which is then repaid using the proceeds from future tax cuts.

As discussed earlier in this book, there are many reasons to suggest that Ricardian Equivalence does not hold exactly in practice. However, it certainly highlights that the 'twin deficits' line of thinking can be an incomplete description of how the economy works.

Summary

- The objective of this chapter was to introduce the important features of the open economy.
- First it explained how the balance of payments are constructed.
- Next, attention was turned to defining and describing exchange rates.
- Two main theories of exchange rate determination were introduced; these are purchasing power parity (PPP) and uncovered interest parity (UIP). The Dornbusch model of exchange rate overshooting was also examined.
- Finally, the important interactions between the exchange rate and the balance of payments were analysed.

Key terms

Balance of payments
Exchange rates
J-curve effect
Marshall-Lerner condition
Purchasing power parity (PPP)
Uncovered interest parity (UIP)

Review questions

1. Explain why the theory of purchasing power parity is often referred to as the law of one price.
2. According to the theory of PPP, what would happen to the nominal exchange rate in the following circumstances:
   a. an increase in the overseas money supply
   b. a reduction in the margins on domestic goods prices
   c. what would happen to the real exchange rate in each instance?
3. The domestic interest rate falls, so that it stands 3 per cent below the overseas interest rate. This interest differential is expected to remain for one year. According to the theory of uncovered interest parity, what would be the effect on the domestic exchange rate?
   What if:
   a. the interest differential was 6 per cent
   b. the 3 per cent interest differential lasted for two years
   c. there was a 5 per cent risk premium attached to domestic bonds?
4. In the *Financial Times,* you notice that interest rates in the UK are 6 per cent, whereas in the US they are currently only 3 per cent. A friend has proposed a 'get rich quick' scheme where you borrow from the US banks and reinvest in UK banks, and make a profit on the difference in interest rates. Is this plan likely to work?
5. Under what conditions will devaluation in the exchange rate improve the current account?

More advanced problems

6. 'Purchasing power parity (PPP) is a long-run theory of the exchange rate.' Discuss.
7. What factors might account for high exchange rate volatility in the short run?

For further resources, visit
http://www.thomsonlearning.co.uk/chamberlin_yueh

12 The IS-LM-BP model

Learning objectives

- Extend the traditional IS-LM model to incorporate open economy considerations
- Understand the open economy version of this model, the IS-LM-BP model. The BP schedule reflects equilibrium in the balance of payments
- Analyse the various applications of this model
- Evaluate a particular version of the IS-LM-BP model, known as the Mundell-Fleming model.
- Understand the impact of different exchange rate regimes on the IS-LM-BP model

12.1 Introduction

The basic version of the IS-LM model introduced in Chapter 7 is a closed economy model. When this model was first established, most economies traded a small proportion of GDP, meaning that it was empirically acceptable to study the effects of policy within this framework. Over the last 40 years, economies have become increasingly open to each other: trade is a higher proportion of GDP than before, and capital can flow across borders from one country to another more freely than ever.

The current account largely reflects the trade in goods and services between nations. As a proportion of GDP, exports and imports have risen fairly substantially in recent times. As exports are an injection into the circular flow of income and imports a leakage, it is clear that the determination of a particular nation's GDP cannot be made in isolation.

The capital account mainly consists of financial flows. Quantitatively, this is the major component of the balance of payments, with its growth reflecting the continued deregulation and increasing openness of international financial markets. These linkages are important because overseas investors can invest in the domestic economy, and domestic residents have the opportunity to invest abroad. Overall, it implies that the domestic availability and price of credit can be determined by overseas factors.

In this chapter, we extend the traditional IS-LM model to incorporate these open economy effects. The IS-LM model is a general equilibrium model, where the IS curve represents equilibrium in the goods market and the LM equilibrium in the money market. General equilibrium is where these two curves intersect, implying both real and monetary equilibrium in an economy. The open economy version of this model is the IS-LM-BP model. This adds a new line: the BP schedule, which reflects equilibrium in the balance of payments. Overall equilibrium will now exist where the economy is in real, monetary and external equilibrium.

The IS-LM-BP model has many applications. It can be used to analyse the effects of policy on the domestic economy, now taking into account the actions or reactions from overseas. It can also be used to analyse the effects of overseas shocks on the domestic economy. The aim of this chapter is to construct the IS-LM-BP model and then to demonstrate its applications.

There are many different variants of the IS-LM-BP model, all of which will be covered in this chapter. Different versions make different assumptions about the degree of capital mobility and the exchange rate regime. Capital mobility refers to the ease at which finance can move around the world. It is a given fact that with global financial deregulation, capital mobility has increased substantially. Bearing this in mind, a particular version of the IS-LM-BP model which definitely deserves attention is known as the Mundell-Fleming model. This is just the basic IS-LM-BP model with perfect capital mobility.

Spain has relied heavily on foreign direct investment for its growth, but trade is also expanding...

Source: Real image/Alamy

12

The second way in which different versions of the model may arise is through the type of exchange rate regime that is assumed. Under a floating regime, the exchange rate is market determined and can fluctuate accordingly. A fixed regime is where the policy maker acts to maintain the exchange rate at a particular level. In Chapter 14, the advantages and disadvantages of these different regimes are covered in detail. In this chapter, we will investigate what effects the regime has in the workings of the model. It will be seen that the effects of different policies is not independent of the exchange rate regime in place.

12.2 Constructing the IS-LM-BP model

Extending the basic IS-LM to the open economy requires two additions. First, the closed economy IS and LM curves need to be adapted to take into account the foreign influences on the domestic goods and money markets, respectively. Second, the **BP Curve** must be constructed. This represents the combination of income and interest rates where the balance of payments (or the external part of the economy) is in equilibrium.

12.2.1 The open economy IS curve (the ISXM schedule)

Extending the IS curve to the open economy simply requires the addition of the current account or net exports. The IS curve simply reflects equilibrium in the goods market, where the demand and supply of domestically produced output are equal to each other. In the open economy, some domestically produced output will be sold overseas as exports, and a portion of aggregate demand will be accounted for through the importing of goods and services from abroad. Demand will therefore equal supply when this national income identity holds.

$$Y = C + I + G + X - M \tag{12.1}$$

C represents domestic consumption, which is represented by a typical Keynesian consumption function of disposable income

$$C = a + c(Y - T)$$

where a is autonomous consumption, c the marginal propensity to consume, and T the size of lump sum taxes.

Investment is a negative function of the interest rate and also a set of exogenous factors Θ. These are discussed in detail in Chapter 3.

$$I = I(r,\Theta), \quad \frac{\Delta I}{\Delta r} < 0$$

Government spending is exogenously set:

$$G = \hat{G}$$

In the previous chapter, a simple functional form for the real value of net exports or the trade balance was given as follows:

$$X - M = x_y{}^*Y^* - \theta m_y\ (\theta)Y \tag{12.2}$$

where $\theta = \dfrac{EP^*}{P}$ is the real exchange rate and represents the competitiveness of domestically produced goods in world markets. E is the nominal exchange rate, P is the domestic price level, and P* is the price of foreign goods.

12

There are several parameters and factors here which determine the size of net exports. The first is the real exchange rate, θ. Providing the Marshall-Lerner condition holds, a depreciation in the real exchange rate will lead to an improvement in net exports, as consumers substitute away from foreign-produced goods to domestically produced goods.

Exports are determined by the level of overseas income Y^*, and the parameter $x_y^*(\theta)$, which is the proportion of foreign income spent on domestic goods. If foreign income rises, or foreigners develop a higher preference for domestic goods, then each of these and net exports will rise.

The total level of imports is the product of domestic income Y and the marginal propensity to import, $m_y(\theta)$. As income rises, consumers will tend to spend more – a proportion $(m_y(\theta))$ of which will be on foreign goods and services. Alternatively, if the preferences of domestic consumers were to switch towards foreign goods, then $m_y(\theta)$ and total imports will rise.

Hence, substituting this into (12.1) gives:

$$Y = a + c(Y - T) + I(r, \Theta) + \hat{G} + x_y{}^*(\theta)Y^* - \theta m_y(\theta)Y \tag{12.3}$$

Rearranging this, we can derive the equilibrium level of income as a function of all the parameters and variables.

$$Y = \frac{a - cT + I(r, \Theta) + \hat{G} + x_y{}^*(\theta)Y^*}{1 - c + \theta m_y(\theta)} \tag{12.4}$$

This is the open economy version of the IS curve. To differentiate this from the closed economy version, we can call it the **ISXM schedule**. In income (Y) and interest rate (r) space, this will also be a downward-sloping curve. But, as Figure 12.1 shows, there are differences compared to the closed economy IS curve.

The ISXM curve also slopes downwards, as a rise in interest rates will lead to a fall in investment, and then a multiplied fall in income. However, the slope of the ISXM curve will be steeper than that of the standard IS curve. This is because the multiplier is now smaller, following the addition of the *marginal propensity to import*.

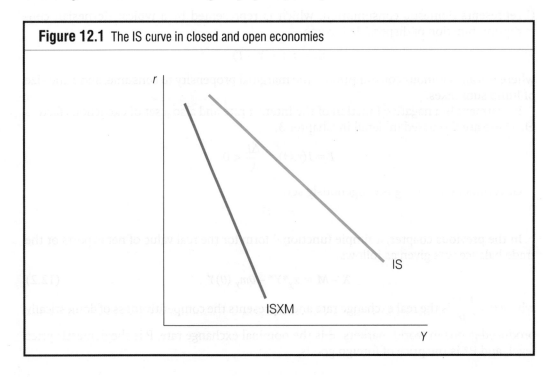

Figure 12.1 The IS curve in closed and open economies

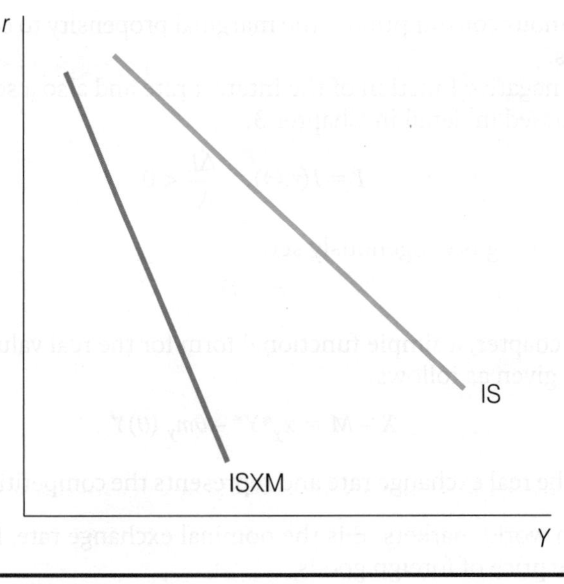

12

In the closed economy, the multiplier was $1/(1-c)$, where c is the marginal propensity to consume. This can be written as $1/s$, where s is the marginal propensity to save. In the open economy, the multiplier is $1/(1 - c + \theta m_{Y^*}(\theta))$ or $1/(s + \theta m_{Y^*}(\theta))$. It is easy to see that as long as the marginal propensity to import is positive, the multiplier will be smaller.

Imports are a leakage from the circular flow of income. As the marginal propensity of import increases, a higher proportion of any additional income will be spent overseas rather than on domestically produced goods and services. Consequently, the multiplier will be lower. In Chapter 7, we showed in some detail that the slope of the IS curve will fall as the multiplier increases.

Other than this, the ISXM schedule will behave in exactly the same way as the closed economy version. A change in anything other than the level of income or the interest rate will lead to a shift in the ISXM curve. Specifically, if exports rise because foreign income Y^* or the proportion dedicated to domestic goods and services x_{Y^*} increases; or imports fall due to a decline in the marginal propensity to import m_Y, then equilibrium output will rise and the ISXM curve will shift outwards.

An important feature of the ISXM curve is that it will be expected to shift if there is a change in the real exchange rate. Providing that the Marshall-Lerner condition holds, a real appreciation reduces the competitiveness of domestic goods and services. Exports will fall, and imports will rise and the ISXM curve will shift inwards. If there is a real depreciation, then the opposite holds true. The improved competitiveness of output produced at home will lead to a fall in imports and a rise in exports, and the ISXM curve will shift outwards. This is shown in Figure 12.2.

Strictly speaking, the ISXM curve should also pivot as the multiplier will change due to the exchange rate effect on the marginal propensity to import. However, for the sake of simplicity, we will abstract from this in developing and using the model further.

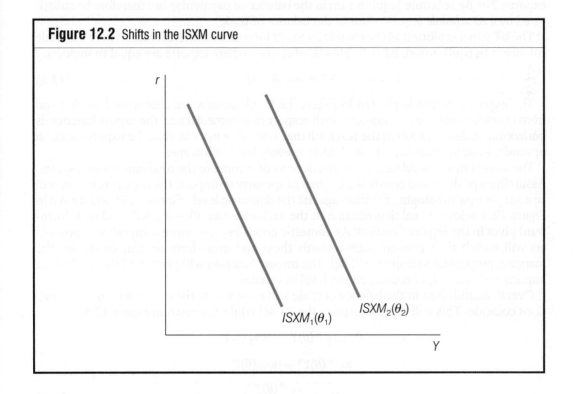

Figure 12.2 Shifts in the ISXM curve

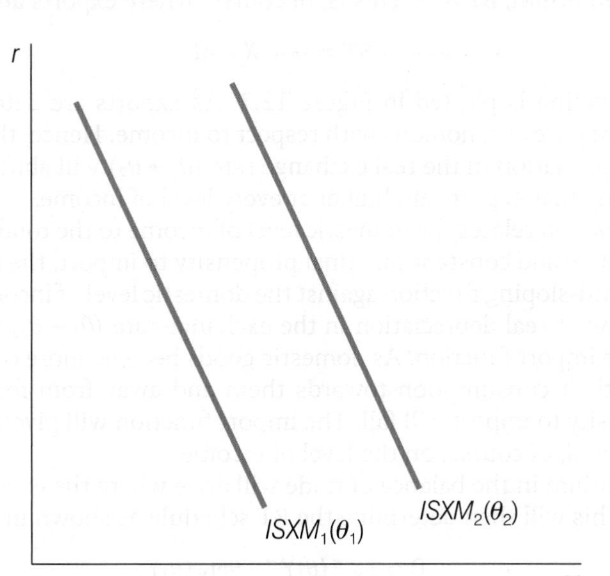

12.2.2 The BP curve

This represents equilibrium in the balance of payments. The BP schedule plots the combinations of income (Y) and interest rates (r) where total inflows and outflows to and from overseas are equal. In the previous chapter, we noted that the balance of payments consists of two main parts: the current and capital accounts.

The current account is mainly determined by the trade balance or the value of net exports (X–M). The capital account is largely driven by financial flows, where international investors move funds around the world in search of the highest returns. In the introduction, we noted that different versions of the IS-LM-BP model exist, and that making different assumptions about the degree of capital mobility is one way in which these different versions can be generated.

If there is no capital mobility, then finance cannot flow across borders and the capital account does not exist. The entire balance of payments position is set by the trade balance. As capital mobility increases, then cross-border flows of finance become larger and the capital account grows in size. Where there is perfect capital mobility, capital can flow freely with no restrictions. Given that capital flows are large in comparison to trade (exports and imports), the capital account will then tend to dominate the balance of payments position.

In constructing the BP curve, we allow for three different levels of capital mobility. The first is the case where there is no or zero capital mobility, and the second is the other extreme where capital mobility is perfect or completely unrestricted. The other is naturally the intermediate case, where capital mobility is neither zero nor perfect.

No capital mobility

The balance of payments is represented only by the trade balance or the value of net exports. The BP schedule (equilibrium in the balance of payments) can therefore be substituted by a *BT schedule* (equilibrium in the balance of trade).

The BT curve is plotted as the combinations of income and interest rates where the trade balance is in equilibrium, $BT = 0$. This is, of course, where exports are equal to imports.

$$BT = 0 = X - M \tag{12.5}$$

The export function is plotted in Figure 12.3. As exports are determined by demand from overseas, they are autonomous with respect to income. Hence, the export function is horizontal. A depreciation in the real exchange rate ($\theta_1 \rightarrow \theta_2$) will shift the export function upwards, meaning that exports are higher at every level of income.

12

The import function relates the domestic level of income to the total amount of imports. Assuming a positive and constant marginal propensity to import, the import function will be a simple upward-sloping function against the domestic level of income. This is shown in Figure 12.4 below. A real depreciation in the exchange rate ($\theta_1 \rightarrow \theta_2$) will lead to a downward pivot in the import function. As domestic goods become more competitive, consumers will switch their consumption towards them and away from foreign goods; so, the marginal propensity to import will fall. The import function will pivot, and the total fall in imports will depend, of course, on the level of income.

Overall equilibrium in the balance of trade will arise where the export and import functions coincide. This will then determine the BT schedule as shown in Figure 12.5.

$$0 = x_Y{}^*(\theta)Y^* - \theta m_Y(\theta)Y$$

$$x_Y{}^*(\theta)Y^* = \theta m_Y(\theta)Y$$

$$Y_{TB} = \frac{x_Y{}^*(\theta)Y^*}{\theta m_Y(\theta)} \tag{12.6}$$

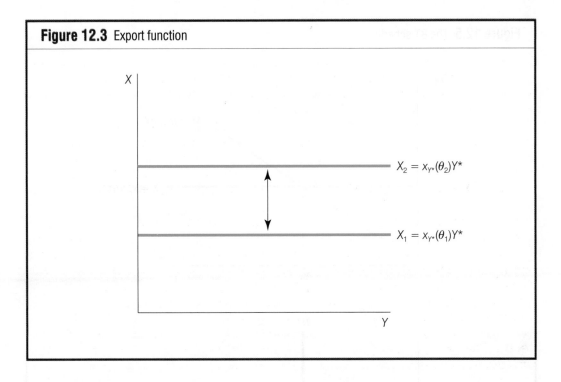

Figure 12.3 Export function

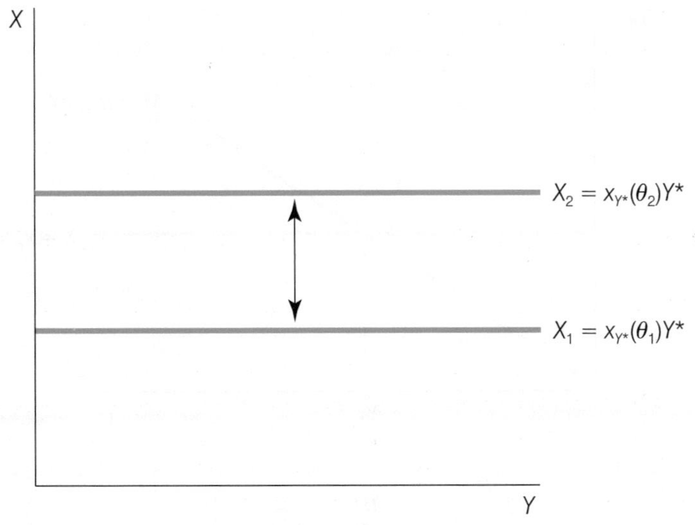

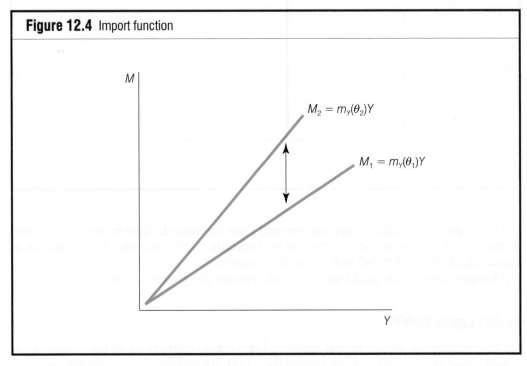

Figure 12.4 Import function

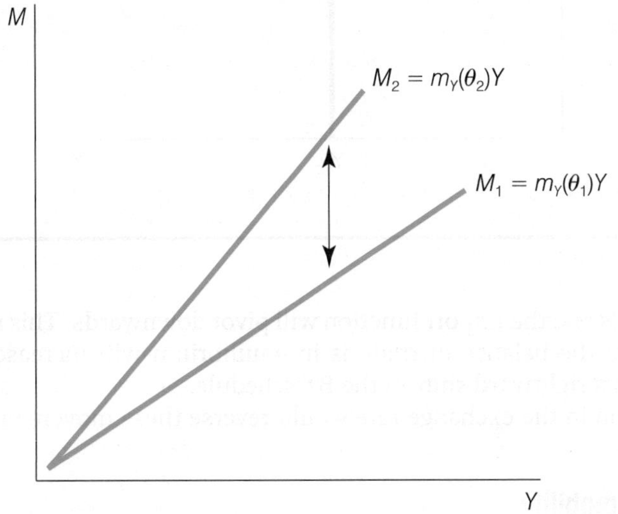

A position to the right of the BT schedule indicates a deficit in the balance of trade. Here, $Y > Y_{TB}$, so imports exceed exports. Likewise, a position to the left of the BT schedule represents a deficit, where $Y < Y_{TB}$ and exports exceed imports.

We have already seen that a change in the real exchange rate leads to a shift in the export function and a pivot in the import function. Following a real depreciation, domestic goods become more competitive vis-à-vis those produced abroad. As a result, the export function

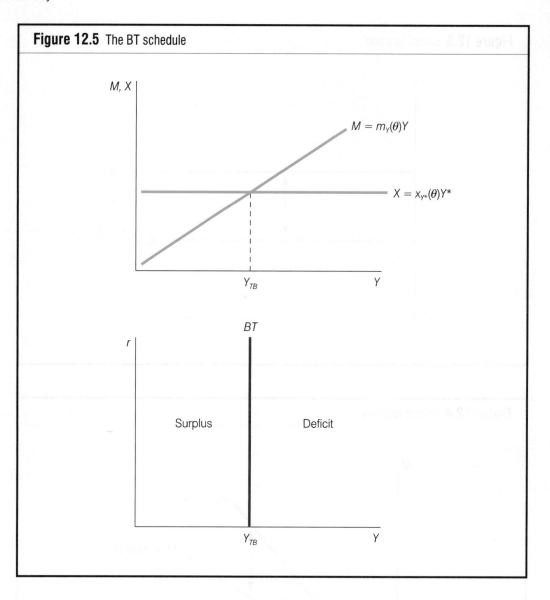

Figure 12.5 The BT schedule

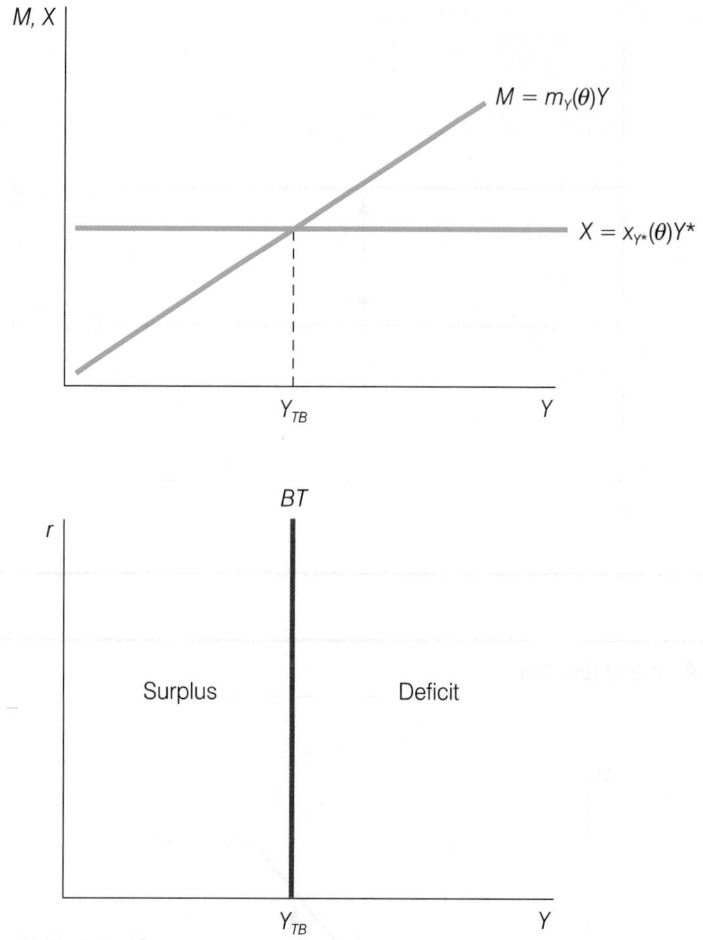

12

will shift upwards and the import function will pivot downwards. This means that the level of income where the balance of trade is in equilibrium will increase. This is shown in Figure 12.6 with a rightward shift in the BT schedule.

An appreciation in the exchange rate would reverse these movements.

Perfect capital mobility

Under conditions of perfect capital mobility, there are no restrictions on the movement of capital (most of it financial) from around the world. International investors are therefore not restricted to investing in their own country of origin, but can seek investment opportunities throughout the world. In this situation, the investor will seek the highest returns possible regardless of international borders.

As the scope of these financial flows is large relative to trade, then under the conditions of perfect capital mobility, the capital account position will tend to dominate the overall balance of payments position. Large inflows of capital will produce capital account and balance of payments surpluses, and outflows will equal deficits.

Figure 12.6 The BT schedule and exchange rate depreciation

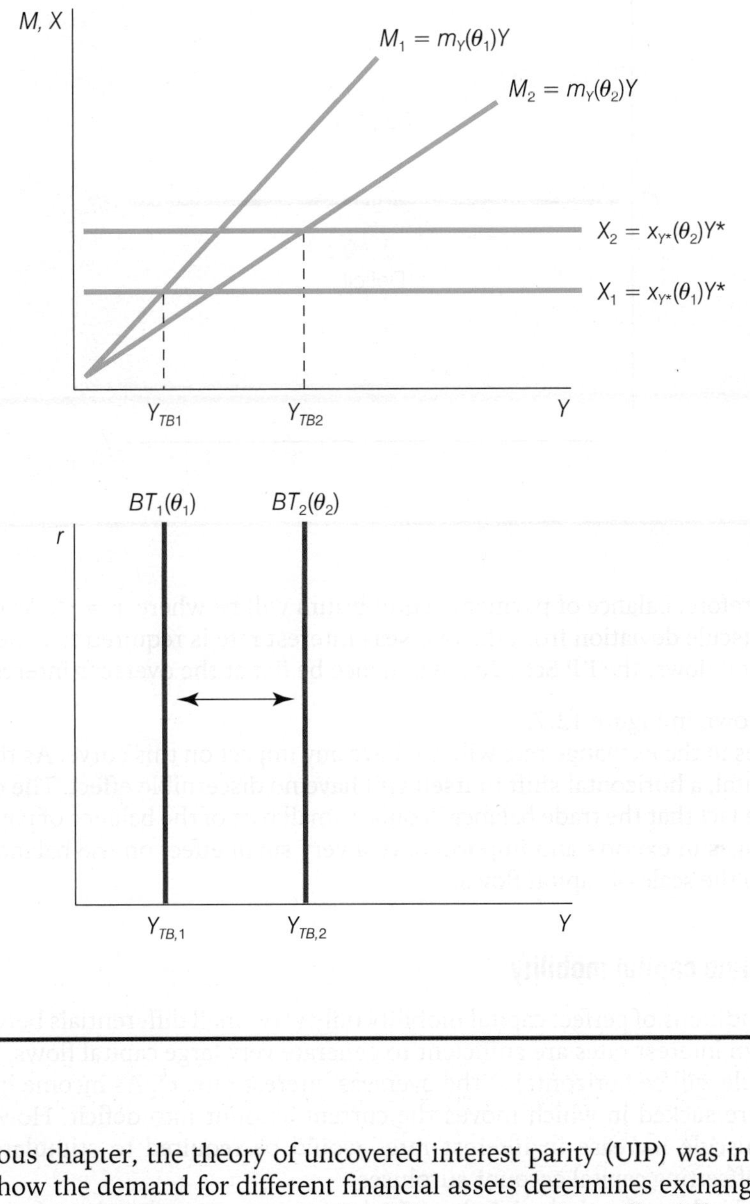

In the previous chapter, the theory of uncovered interest parity (UIP) was introduced. This explains how the demand for different financial assets determines exchange rates. If bonds denominated in different currencies (in different countries) offer different rates of interest, then investors will move into the bonds that offer the highest rates of return. Therefore, countries which offer higher interest rates will experience capital inflows, and capital account surpluses. Countries with low interest rates on bonds will face outflows and deficits.

Under conditions of perfect capital mobility, if r is the domestic interest rate and r* is the foreign rate, then the following holds true:

- If the domestic interest rate exceeds the foreign interest rate, $r > r^*$, then capital will flow into the country and the balance of payments will move into surplus.
- If the domestic interest rate is less than the foreign interest rate, $r < r^*$, then capital will flow out of the country and the balance of payments will move into deficit.

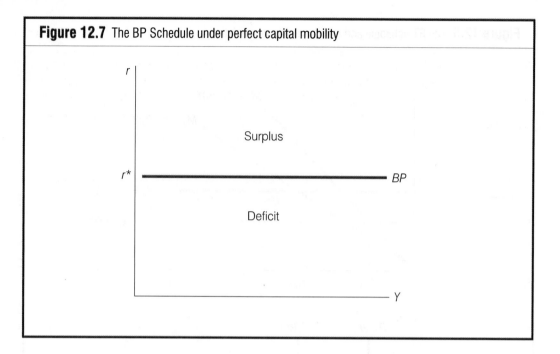

Figure 12.7 The BP Schedule under perfect capital mobility

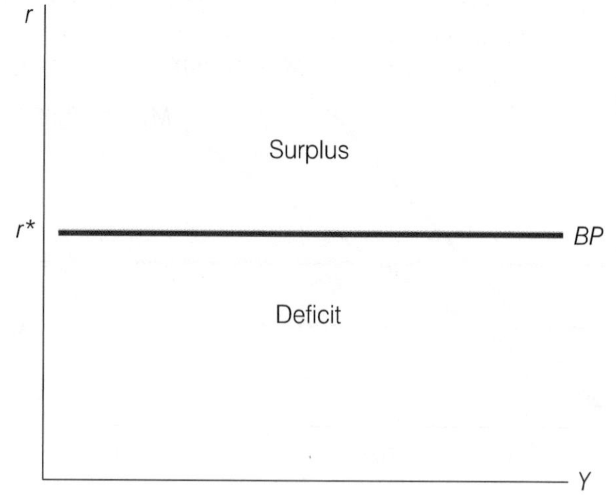

- Therefore, balance of payments equilibrium will be where $r = r^*$. As only a miniscule deviation from the overseas interest rate is required to generate large capital flows, the BP Schedule will hence be flat at the overseas interest rate.

This is shown in Figure 12.7.

Changes in the exchange rate will not have any impact on this curve. As the BP schedule is horizontal, a horizontal shift in itself will have no discernible effect. The other reason is due to the fact that the trade balance is only a small part of the balance of payments. Therefore, changes in exports and imports have a very small effect on the balance of payments relative to the scale of capital flows.

Intermediate capital mobility

12

Under conditions of perfect capital mobility only very small differentials between domestic and foreign interest rates are sufficient to generate very large capital flows. Therefore, the BP schedule will be horizontal at the overseas interest rate, r^*. As income increases, more imports are sucked in which moves the current account into deficit. However, only the most miniscule increase in interest rates would be required to stimulate inflows that produce offsetting capital account surpluses.

A typical inflow of capital might be the sale of a government bond to a foreigner. The foreigner purchases the bond with cash, and this represents a capital inflow. In return, the bond will pay the rate r at some specified time in the future. Therefore, these capital inflows can be considered as the rest of the world lending to the home country, which undertakes the interest burden.

If capital markets are perfect, then nations are assumed able to borrow as much as they like from international financial markets at a given rate of interest. If the government, though, is borrowing large sums over a long period of time, then it will be accepting an ever-increasing interest burden. If financial markets believe that the probability of default rises with the size of the loans, then they might consider loans to countries which are borrowing heavily as being more risky. Consequently, they will only be willing to lend if a risk premium in the form of a higher interest rate is offered on bonds.

This will imply that the BP curve is upward-sloping. As income rises, imports and the balance of trade deficit become greater. In turn, larger capital account surpluses will be required to offset this deficit. These capital account surpluses can be achieved by offering higher interest rates. If a country borrows heavily, however, the increased perception of default is likely to increase the risk premium. As a result, higher and higher interest rates would be required in order to attract the required capital inflows to maintain the balance of payments. This is shown in Figure 12.8.

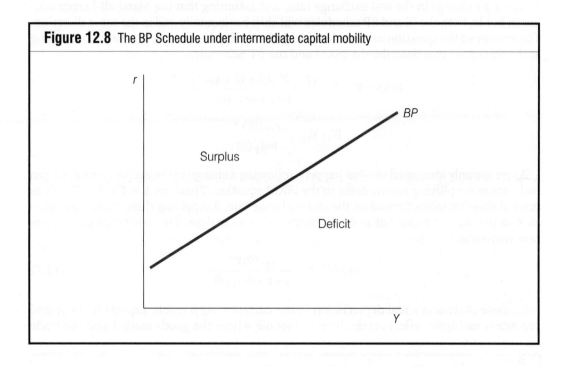

Figure 12.8 The BP Schedule under intermediate capital mobility

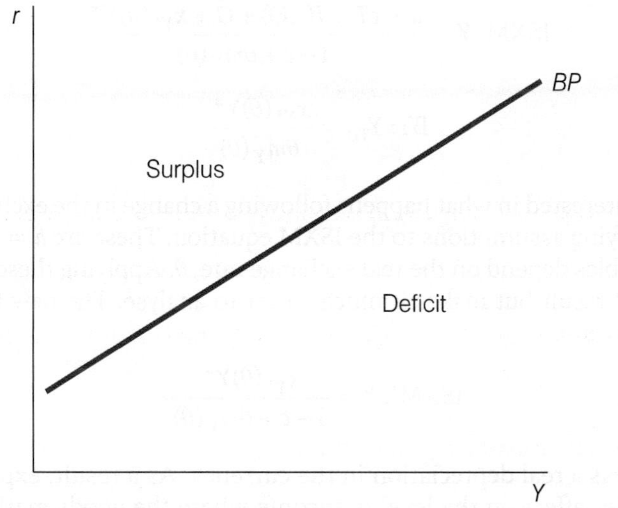

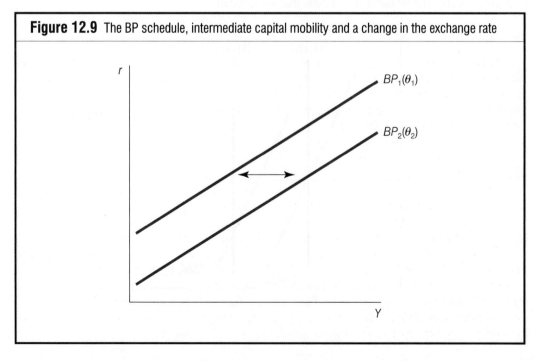

Figure 12.9 The BP schedule, intermediate capital mobility and a change in the exchange rate

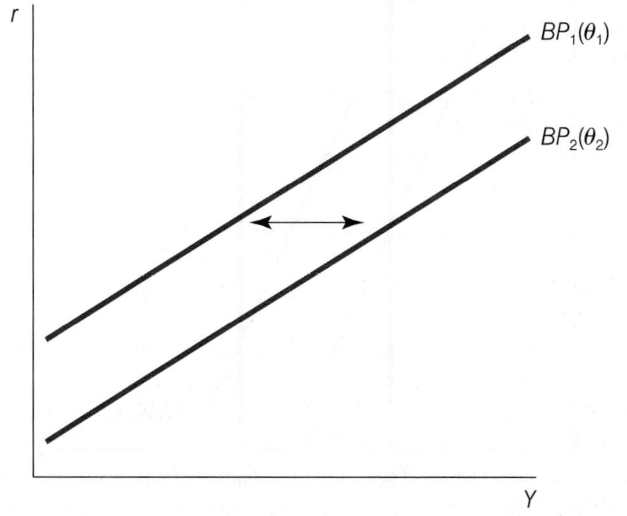

We have seen already that changes in competitiveness of the real exchange rate lead to horizontal movements in the BP schedule. The same holds true here. A real depreciation would reduce the trade deficit at each level of income, implying that a lower rate of interest would be required at each income level to attract the necessary capital inflows. This is shown in Figure 12.9.

What shifts the furthest: The IS or BP schedules?

Following a change in the real exchange rate, and assuming that the Marshall-Lerner condition holds, both the IS and BP schedules will shift horizontally and in the same direction. The answer to the question as to which one shifts the furthest can be answered by looking at the equations that describe the ISXM and the BT Schedules.

$$\text{ISXM: } Y = \frac{a - cT + I(r,\Theta) + \hat{G} + x_{Y^*}(\theta)Y^*}{1 - c + \theta m_Y(\theta)}$$

$$\text{BT: } Y_{TB} = \frac{x_{Y^*}(\theta)Y^*}{\theta m_Y(\theta)}$$

As we are only interested in what happens following a change in the exchange rate, we can make some simplifying assumptions to the ISXM equation. These are $a = T = I = G = 0$, as none of these variables depend on the real exchange rate, θ. Applying these makes no difference to the general result but makes it much easier to analyse. The new ISXM schedule is now written as:

$$\text{ISXM': } Y = \frac{x_{Y^*}(\theta)Y^*}{1 - c + \theta m_Y(\theta)} \tag{12.7}$$

Suppose there was a real depreciation in the currency. As a result, exports will rise and produce a multiplier effect on the level of income where the goods market and the trade

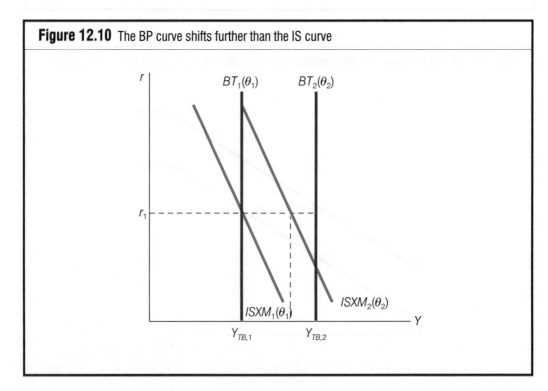

Figure 12.10 The BP curve shifts further than the IS curve

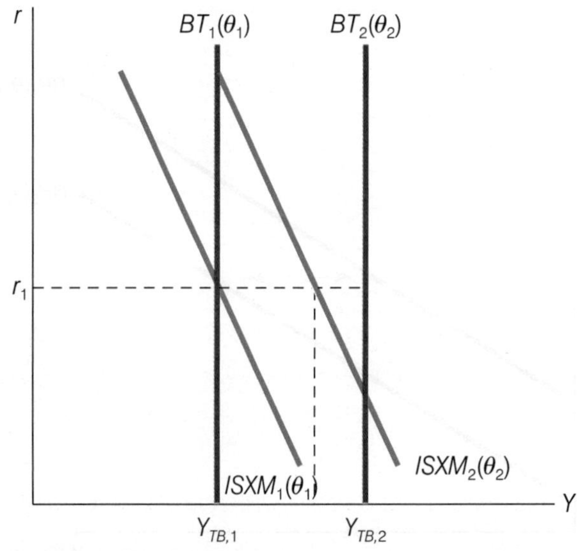

12

balance are in equilibrium. The only difference between the multipliers is the term $1 - c$ in the IS schedule. As long as this is greater than zero, the multiplier attached to the ISXM schedule will be smaller. Given that it is almost certainly the case that $1 - c > 0$, the ISXM schedule will shift by a smaller amount than the BT schedule.

The reason why this is so is quite intuitive. The injection of higher exports is the same in both cases, but as long as $1 - c > 0$, some of the additional income generated will be lost to saving. So, the presence of this additional leakage is sufficient to reduce the multiplier and therefore the relative size of the horizontal shift in the schedule.

12.2.3 The open economy LM curve

The LM curve in an open economy is exactly the same as its closed economy counterpart. It defines the combinations of income and interest rates where the demand and supply of money are equal to each other. As we have seen in Chapter 7, and again in Figure 12.11 below, this is an upward-sloping function. As income rises, the demand for money increases due to the transactions motive. By increasing interest rates, the excess demand for money is countered, as higher bond yields encourage people to hold less cash and move into bonds.

The open economy, though, can exert a powerful effect on the money market. The conventional closed economy LM curve is derived under the assumption that the money supply is fixed. In a closed economy, the government or the monetary authority is assumed to have complete control over the money supply. In an open economy, in contrast, this proposition is less likely. As we will see, there is a direct relationship between the money supply and the balance of payments position. The position of the LM curve is therefore linked to that of the BP schedule.

The factors determining the supply of money are covered in some detail in Chapter 5. In brief, the money supply is equal to a multiple of the high powered money stock (H), also

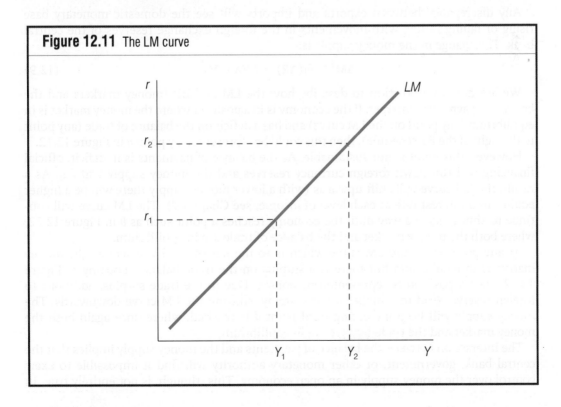

Figure 12.11 The LM curve

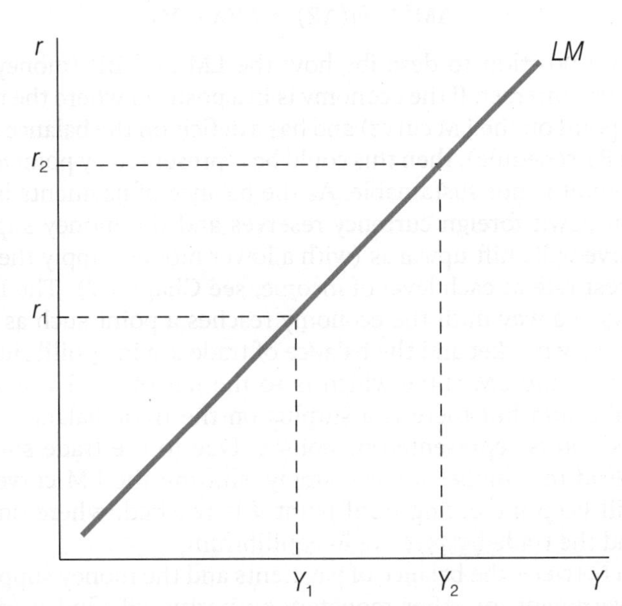

known as the monetary base. These are deposits on which banks and other financial institutions can create demand deposits. The money supply, including the demand deposits, will be a multiple of the monetary base. This multiple will be determined by the size of the money multiplier.

$$M^S = mH \tag{12.8}$$

In the closed economy, the change in the monetary base is equal to the public sector deficit (PSD) less government sales of bonds. This is essentially the government deficit that is paid for by cash (by printing money) rather than through bond sales.

$$\Delta H = PSD - bond\_sales$$

In an open economy, there will a further determinant to the stock of high powered money. This is the net purchase of foreign reserves (R) by the central bank.

$$\Delta H = PSD - bond\_sales + \Delta R$$

Assuming that the public deficit is entirely financed by bond sales, then in the open economy, the money supply is driven by central bank changes in reserves (foreign assets). The change in reserves now represents the official financing of the balance of payments. If the balance of payments position is in surplus, then the central bank is adding to the stocks of foreign assets and building reserves. These constitute part of the high powered money stock on which demand deposits can be produced.

When the balance of payments position moves to deficits, the official financing requires the running down of foreign reserves, reducing the size of the monetary stock. For the sake of simplicity, assume that there is no capital mobility, so that the balance of payments position and thus the size of official financing or the change in foreign reserves (ΔR) is determined by the trade balance ($X - M$). In this case, the high powered money stock can be described as follows:

$$\Delta H = \Delta R = X - M \tag{12.8}$$

Any discrepancy between exports and imports will see the domestic monetary base rising or falling in line with movements in the foreign exchange reserves of the central bank. The change in the money supply is:

$$\Delta M^S = m(\Delta R) = M(X - M) \tag{12.9}$$

We are now in a position to describe how the LM and BP (money markets and the balance of payments) interact. If the economy is in a position where the money market is in equilibrium (any point on the LM curve) and has a deficit on the balance of trade (any point to the right of the BT schedule), then this could be represented by point *a* in Figure 12.12.

12

However, this point is not sustainable. As the balance of payments is in deficit, official financing will run down foreign currency reserves and the money supply will fall. As a result, the LM curve will shift upwards (with a lower money supply there will be a higher equilibrium interest rate at each level of income, see Chapter 7). The LM curve will continue to shift in such a way until the economy reaches a point such as *b* in Figure 12.12, where both the money market and the balance of trade are in equilibrium.

At any position on the LM curve which is to the left of the BT schedule, the money market is in equilibrium but there is a surplus on the trade balance. Looking at Figure 12.12, such a position is represented by point *c*. Due to the trade surplus, additions to foreign reserves lead to a higher money supply, shifting the LM curve downwards. The money supply will keep increasing until point *d* is reached, where once again both the money market and the trade balance are in equilibrium.

The interaction between the balance of payments and the money supply implies that the central bank, government, or other monetary authority will find it impossible to exert control over the money supply in an open economy. This, though, is not entirely true. In

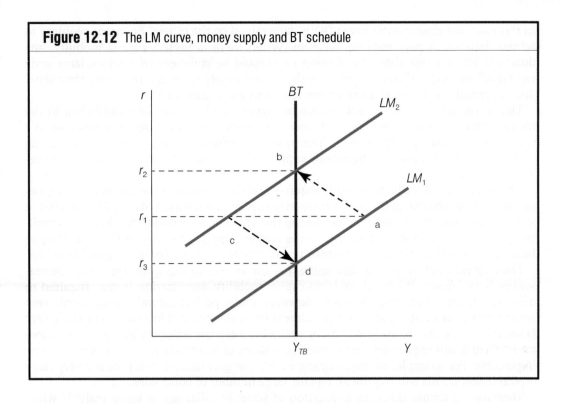

Figure 12.12 The LM curve, money supply and BT schedule

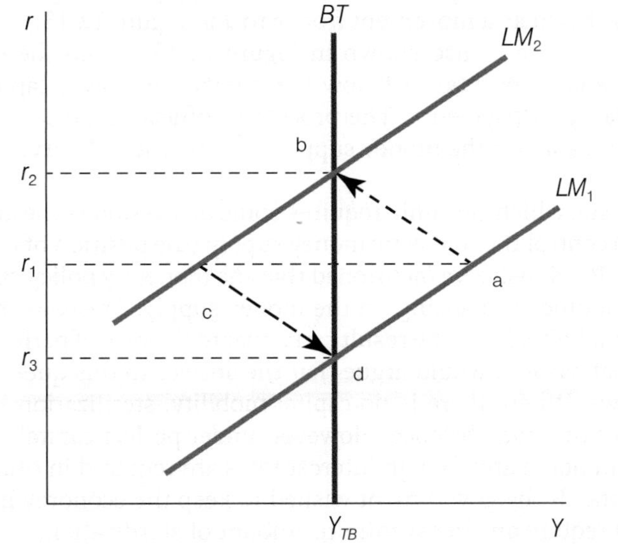

Figure 12.12 above, we suggested that points *a* and *c* are not sustainable because adjustments in the money supply will push the economy to a position where the balance of payments is equilibrated.

In an open economy, the money supply can be expressed as follows.

$$\Delta M^S = m(PSD - \Delta B + \Delta R) \tag{12.10}$$

In the above, we simply assumed that the public sector debt was funded entirely by bond sales ($PSD - \Delta B = 0$, leaving the money supply to be driven by the change in foreign reserves (ΔR). Bond sales in this case are just sufficient to stop any public sector surplus or deficit from affecting the money supply. However, in the same way, it is possible for bond sales to be used to prevent trade imbalances from affecting the domestic money supply. In this case, bond sales are set so that $PSD - \Delta B + \Delta R = 0$; this process of selling or purchasing excess bonds is known as *sterilization*.

If, in Figure 12.12, the economy at point *a* is running a trade deficit and the fall in foreign reserves reduces the stock of high powered money and the government purchases bonds (negative bond sales) from the private sector with cash, it can leave the overall money supply unchanged. The economy can remain at point *a*, as there is no change in the money supply.

In a similar manner, bond sales can be used to offset the increase in reserves that result from surpluses. In Figure 12.12, this would again keep the economy at a point, such as *c*. So, it can be seen that by making use of sterilized bond sales, the monetary authority in an economy can counteract the open economy determinants of the domestic money supply. This implies that the economy can move to a position away from the level of output where the trade balance is in equilibrium.

In a more general sense, the balance of payments consists not only of the trade balance (current account) but also the capital account, which records net capital flows.

$$BP = X - M + \text{net capital inflows}$$

In this case, the change in reserves (R) is determined by the official financing required to achieve balance of payments equilibrium. When there is perfect capital mobility, any domestic interest rate above the foreign rate would be sufficient to produce large-scale capital inflows and lead to an increase in the money supply as foreign reserves accumulate. Such a scenario is shown as a movement from *c* to *d* in Figure 12.13.

The corresponding case is also shown in Figure 12.13. When the equilibrium in the money market produces an interest below the foreign rate, large capital flows lead to a deficit on the balance of payments. The process of official financing will lead to falling foreign reserves and a fall in the money supply, shifting the LM curve upwards – a movement from *a* to *b*.

An important issue which certainly requires some discussion is the ability of the monetary authorities to control the domestic money supply (the position of the LM schedule) in an open economy. Previously, we mentioned that the monetary policy can do this by sterilizing the impact of official financing on the money supply. This was in the case of there being low capital mobility. Does the result carry over to the case of perfect capital mobility?

The conventional wisdom would argue that the answer to this question is no. The reasoning is as follows. Where there is no capital mobility, sterilization is only required to offset the effects of the trade balance. However, under perfect capital mobility, only very small differences in home and foreign interest rates are required in order to produce very large flows of capital. If the government wished to keep the economy in a position where $r \neq r^*$, then it will require an almost infinite amount of sterilization. This is deemed to be impossible. For example, by maintaining $r > r^*$, the government will produce very large capital inflows. This will require an equally large number of bond sales.

Therefore, it comes down to a question of scale. Sterilization is more realistic when dealing with relatively small levels of official financing. For this reason, it has become a well-established phenomenon that policy makers cannot hope to have high capital mobility and also the power to control the money supply (i.e to set the position of the LM curve). In fact, where capital is perfectly mobile, the LM curve effectively disappears, and the money supply is automatically determined so that $r = r^*$.

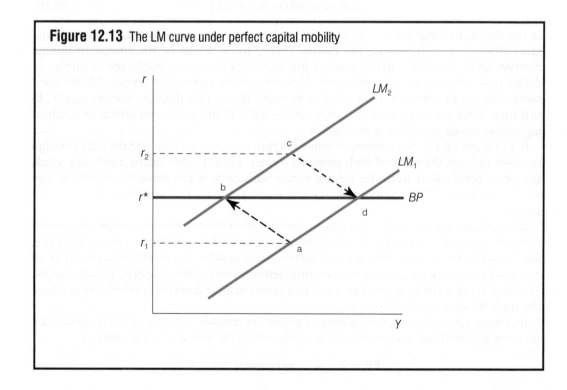

Figure 12.13 The LM curve under perfect capital mobility

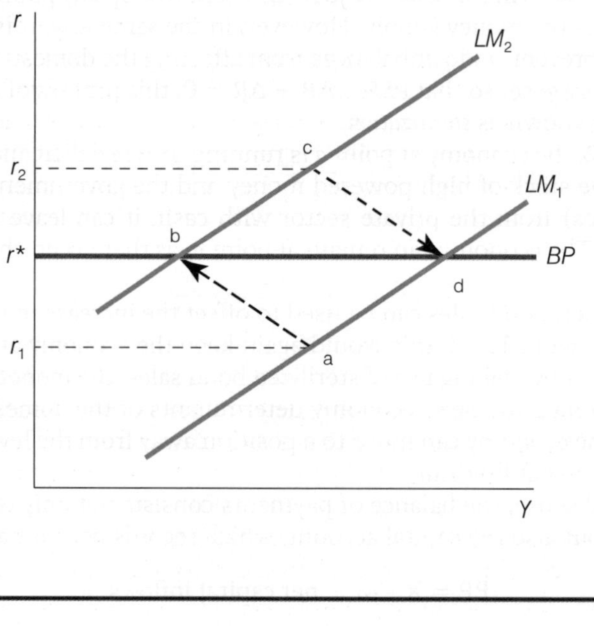

12

There are certainly advantages to controlling the money supply; it is a tool which can be used to manage the economy. However, there are also benefits from being open to international capital markets, which will be covered in more detail in Chapter 15. Open and competitive markets are adjudged to lead to efficiency and, therefore, an optimal allocation of resources. As we shall see, again in Chapter 15, this trade-off between capital mobility and monetary policy is certainly an issue of great importance for the world economy.

This trade-off is worth bearing in mind when considering intermediate levels of capital mobility. Positions of balance of payments deficit will lead to an outflow of foreign reserves, as will surpluses lead to inflows. However, as capital mobility increases, these flows will become larger and larger, making sterilization more and more difficult.

12.2.4 Exchange rate regimes

In the introduction, we mentioned that the type of exchange rate regime has an important bearing on the effectiveness of different policies in an open economy. There are essentially two different types of exchange rate regime: *floating* and *fixed*. A discussion of the relative advantages and disadvantages of these will be reserved for a later chapter, where each can be analysed in more depth. Here, we are concerned with describing what each type of regime is, how it works, and how it is modelled in the IS-LM-BP model.

In a floating regime, the exchange rate is market-determined. This means that the exchange rate is determined by demand and supply. The demand for a currency is of course derived, so the positions of excess demand and supply of a currency will relate to disequilibria in the balance of payments.

A balance of payments deficit is indicative of an excess supply of domestic currency. As a result, the currency would be expected to depreciate. A surplus shows excess demand, producing an anticipation of an appreciation. The strength of the currency is then related to the strength of the balance of payments position.

Under a fixed exchange rate regime, policy makers intervene in the exchange rate market in order to maintain the exchange rate at a target or par value. Given that movements in the exchange rate arise from balance of payments disequilibria, the key to fixing the exchange rate is to equilibrate the balance of payments. This is achieved predominately by using monetary policy.

This should not be too surprising, especially if we think about the interaction between the money supply and the balance of payments, which was described in the previous section. From a policy maker's perspective, though, it requires the facing of another trade-off. It is impossible to fix both the money supply and the exchange rate simultaneously. If the exchange rate is allowed to float, policy makers can exert influence over the money supply. However, if they wish to fix the exchange rate, monetary policy must become subservient to this goal and set in accordance with the fixed rate.

12.2.5 Equilibrium in the IS-LM-BP model

The IS-LM-BP model is a general equilibrium model. The point where the three schedules intersect represents the combination of income and interest rates where the goods market, the money market and the balance of payments are all in equilibrium. This is shown in Figure 12.14.

Having established this model, it can now be applied in a number of ways. The most obvious is to use it to describe the effects of different policies. Fiscal policy will shift the IS schedule, monetary policy the LM schedule, and exchange rate policy the BP schedule.

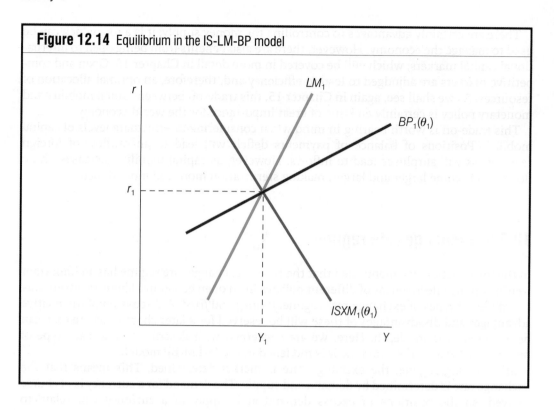

Figure 12.14 Equilibrium in the IS-LM-BP model

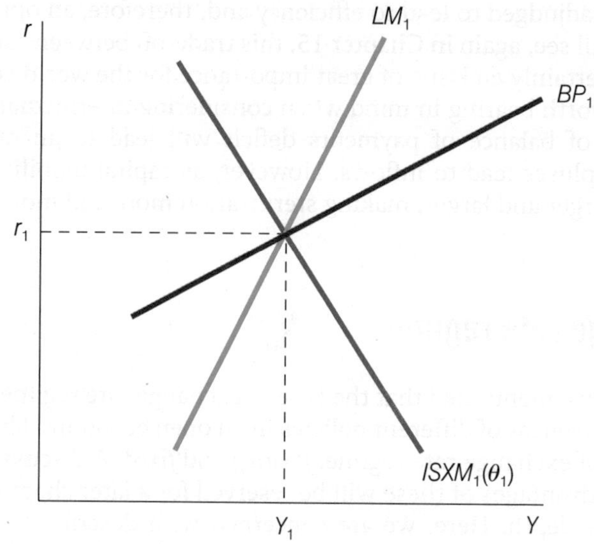

Naturally, shifts in these schedules could originate from a wide variety of sources. This point was made in Chapter 7 when using the closed economy version of the IS-LM model. For example, an increase in government spending will shift the IS schedule outwards, but the same movement could result from any factor other than income or interest rates that leads to an increase in consumption or investment.

In the previous sections, we have shown that there are two important features concerning the IS-LM-BP model that can affect the outcomes produced by the model. The first is the degree of capital mobility and the second the type of exchange rate regime. It is likely that different shocks or policies will have different effects under these different assumptions.

12

12.3 Comparative statics

In this section, we perform various comparative statics exercises using the IS-LM-BP model. The five we consider are as follows:

1. A fiscal expansion under a floating exchange rate regime
2. A monetary expansion under a floating exchange rate regime
3. A fiscal expansion under a fixed exchange rate regime
4. A monetary expansion under a fixed exchange rate regime
5. An exchange rate devaluation in a fixed exchange rate regime.

Exercises 1 and 3 are examples of a shift in the IS schedule, and 2 and 4 are examples of shifts in the LM schedule under different types of exchange rate regime. Exercise 5 reflects a shift in the BP schedule. A devaluation refers to a policy of moving from one fixed exchange rate to another lower one.

These different types of comparative statics exercises can be evaluated under different degrees of capital mobility. Initially, we plan to conduct these five exercises under three different levels of capital mobility.

The first is where there is zero capital mobility. Here, the balance of payments consists only of the trade balance, so the BP schedule can be replaced with a BT line. The second is referred to as low capital mobility. This is simply defined as a situation where the BP curve is steeper than the LM curve. Likewise, the third situation of high capital mobility is characteristic of where the BP curve is flatter than the LM curve. Both the BP and LM schedules are typically upward-sloping, but we will see that the relative slopes of the two may lead to the same policy having different effects.

Our description of low and high capital mobility must be taken therefore with a degree of caution. For example, capital mobility might be quite high, justifying a relatively flat BP schedule. However, as we saw from Chapter 7, the LM curve will tend towards horizontal when the elasticity of money demand becomes large. Alternatively, capital mobility may be low, but the LM curve could just be steeper due to a very low interest elasticity of money demand. The labels of high and low capital mobility are therefore just a description of the two relative slopes. Naturally, as capital mobility increases, the BP schedule will flatten, meaning that its gradient is likely to fall below that of the LM schedule. However, this generalization will not always apply.

The final situation which requires analysis is that of perfect capital mobility, where the BP curve becomes horizontal at the overseas interest rate. This version of the IS-LM-BP model is commonly referred to as the **Mundell-Fleming model**. We will also look at similar comparative statics in this version of the model, and there is an important empirical reason for doing so, as the high integration and liquidity of today's global financial markets suggests that countries and policy makers really do operate in a world of very high capital mobility. For this reason, we shall focus on this model in a little more detail.

Policy with zero or low capital mobility

In both these cases, the BP curve will be steeper than the LM schedule. As we will see, this means that the effects of different policies will have mainly the same effects on the economy. Therefore, to avoid repetition, we consider both these cases together.

Exercise 1: Fiscal expansion, flexible exchange rates, zero or low capital mobility Figure 12.15a depicts the case where there is no capital mobility, while Figure 12.15b describes the outcome where there is low capital mobility.

1. The economy starts off at point *a*, where income is Y_1 and the interest rate is r_1.
2. A fiscal expansion shifts the ISXM curve to the right, $(ISXM_1(\theta_1) \rightarrow ISXM_2(\theta_1))$. The economy moves to point *b*, where income rises to Y_2 and interest rates to r_2.
3. However, point *b* is to the right of the BP schedule, so the trade balance moves into deficit, as higher income leads to higher imports. This also means that the demand for foreign currency increases so the domestic exchange rate will depreciate, $(\theta_1 \rightarrow \theta_2)$.
4. Given that the Marshall-Lerner condition holds, the depreciation in the exchange rate will improve the relative competitiveness of domestic goods. As exports increase and imports fall, the ISXM curve will shift to the right $(ISXM_2(\theta_1) \rightarrow ISXM_3(\theta_2))$, as will the BP schedule $(BP_1(\theta_1) \rightarrow BP_2(\theta_2))$. As reasoned above, the horizontal shift in the BT schedule will be greater than that for the ISXM schedule.
5. The economy will reach a new equilibrium where the ISXM, LM and BP schedules intersect at point *c*. The new equilibrium levels of output and interest rates are Y_3 and r_3, respectively.

In this example, fiscal policy is highly effective in influencing output. An expansionary fiscal policy leads to depreciation in the exchange rate, which leads to a further expansion in output. Therefore, the exchange rate movements act to reinforce fiscal policy.

Figure 12.15a Fiscal expansion under floating exchange rates with no capital mobility

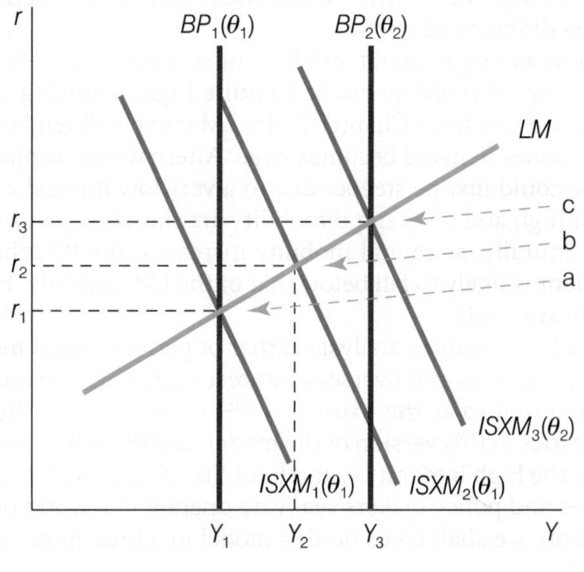

Figure 12.15b Fiscal expansion under floating exchange rates with low capital mobility

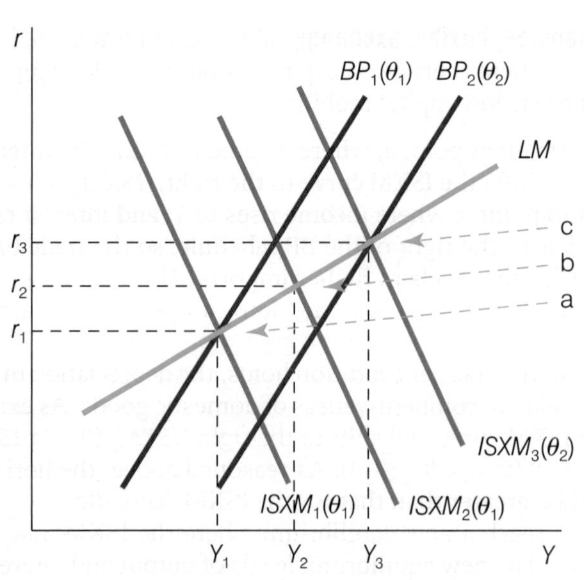

Exercise 2: Monetary expansion, flexible exchange rates, zero or low capital mobility
Figure 12.16a again depicts the case where there is no capital mobility, while Figure 12.16b describes the outcome where there is low capital mobility.

1. The economy starts off a point *a*, where income is Y_1 and interest rates are at r_1.
2. A monetary expansion shifts the LM curve to the right ($LM_1 \rightarrow LM_2$). As a result, the equilibrium rate of interest rates fall to r_2, which encourages investment and income rises to Y_2. This is shown as a movement from point *a* to *b*.

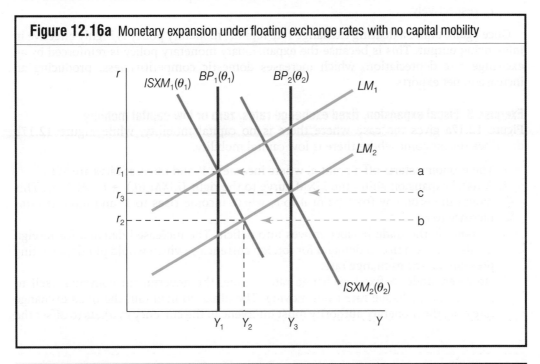

Figure 12.16a Monetary expansion under floating exchange rates with no capital mobility

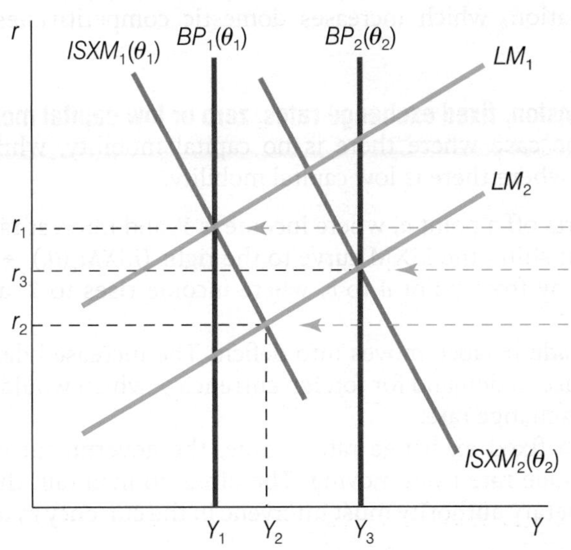

Figure 12.16b Monetary expansion under floating exchange rates with low capital mobility

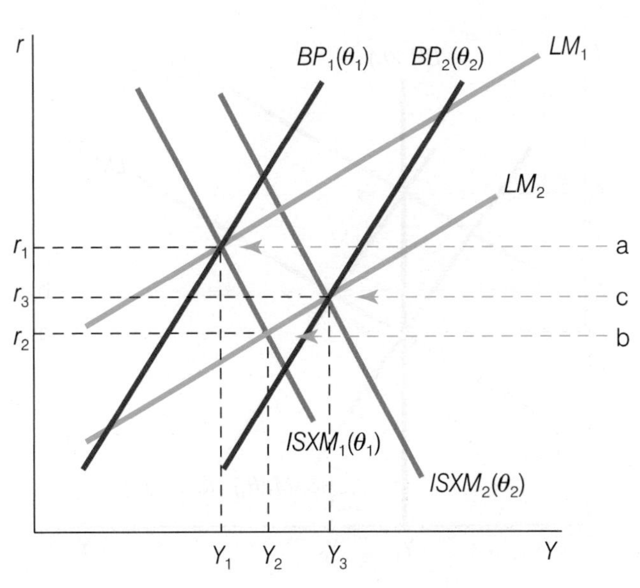

3. However, point *b* is to the right of the BP schedule, so the trade balance moves into deficit. This also means that the domestic exchange rate will depreciate ($\theta_1 \rightarrow \theta_2$).
4. Given that the Marshall-Lerner condition holds, the depreciation in the exchange rate will improve the relative competitiveness of domestic goods. As exports increase and imports fall, the ISXM curve will shift to the right ($ISXM_1(\theta_1) \rightarrow ISXM_2(\theta_2)$) as will the BP schedule ($BP_1(\theta_1) \rightarrow BP_2(\theta_2)$).
5. The economy will reach a new equilibrium where the ISXM, LM and BP schedules intersect at point *c*. The new equilibrium levels of output and interest rates are Y_3 and r_3, respectively.

Once again, under a floating exchange rate regime, monetary policy is highly effective in influencing output. This is because the expansionary monetary policy is reinforced by an exchange rate depreciation, which increases domestic competitiveness, producing an increase in net exports.

Exercise 3: Fiscal expansion, fixed exchange rates, zero or low capital mobility

Figure 12.17a gives the case where there is no capital mobility, while Figure 12.17b describes the outcome where there is low capital mobility.

1. The economy starts off a point *a*, where income is Y_1 and interest rates are at r_1.
2. A fiscal expansion shifts the ISXM curve to the right ($ISXM_1(\theta_1) \rightarrow ISXM_2(\theta_2)$). This moves the economy from point *a* to *b*, where income rises to Y_2 and interest rates increase to r_2.
3. At point *b*, the trade balance moves into deficit. The increased demand for foreign goods leads to a rise in demand for foreign currencies, which would put depreciating pressure on the exchange rate.
4. However, under a fixed exchange rate regime, the government commits itself to prevent the exchange rate from moving. Therefore, to maintain the fixed exchange rate at θ_1, the monetary authority must intervene in the currency markets to offset the

Figure 12.17a Fiscal expansion under fixed exchange rates with no capital mobility

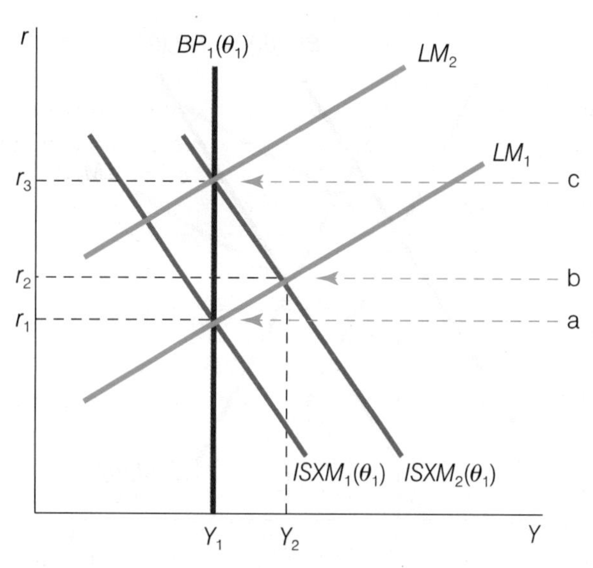

12

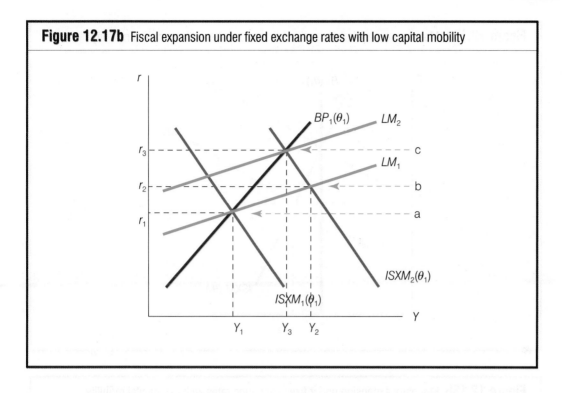

Figure 12.17b Fiscal expansion under fixed exchange rates with low capital mobility

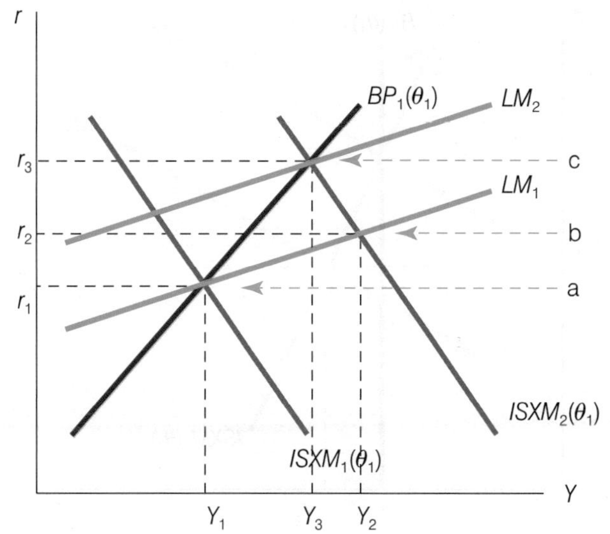

increased demand for foreign currencies. It can do this by using its reserves of foreign currency. By selling these and purchasing domestic currency in international currency markets, there will be a counteracting, upward pressure on the exchange rate.

5. By running down foreign currency reserves, the monetary authority is reducing the stock of high powered money and, therefore, the overall money supply. Consequently, the LM curve will shift upwards from LM_1 to LM_2.
6. The contraction in the money supply will put upward pressure on interest rates, leading to a fall in investment and output. The new equilibrium levels of output and interest rates are Y_3 and r_3, respectively, at point *c*.

In this case, there is a difference between the zero and low capital mobility cases. With zero capital mobility, there is no overall effect on output, although its composition has altered. There is now higher government spending, but this has generated higher equilibrium interest rates, which crowds out an equal amount of investment.

When there is some capital mobility, so that the BP curve is no longer vertical, there will be a permanent increase in output. This can be understood by thinking about the change in income which is required to keep the balance of payments in overall equilibrium. When there is no capital mobility, any increase in income will lead to higher imports and deterioration in the balance of payments. The only way this can be rebalanced is by driving income back to its original level. When there is some capital mobility, though, an increase in income will put upward pressure on interest rates, generating capital inflows. The improvement in the capital account therefore counters the need to lower income in order to correct the trade deficit. So, an overall balance of payments equilibrium can persist at a higher income level.

Under a fixed regime with no capital mobility, fiscal policy is ineffective. This is because as income moves away from the level where trade is balanced Y_1, maintaining the fixed exchange rate will require an offsetting change in monetary policy. When capital mobility is low, fiscal policy will have a limited effect, as it will be offset by accommodating monetary policy.

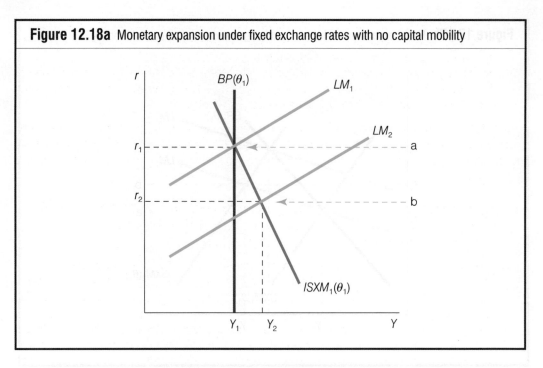

Figure 12.18a Monetary expansion under fixed exchange rates with no capital mobility

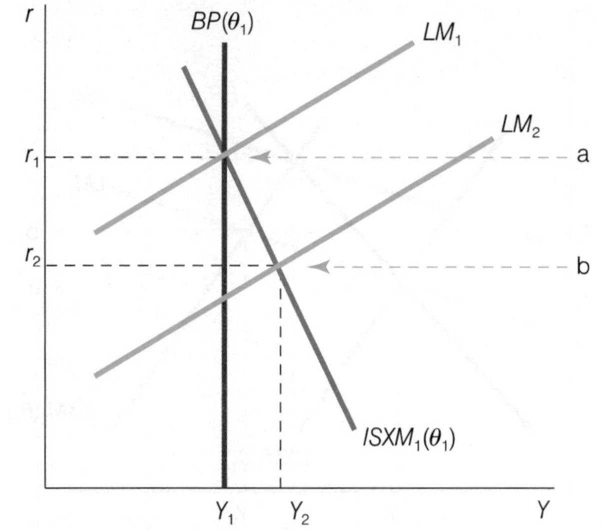

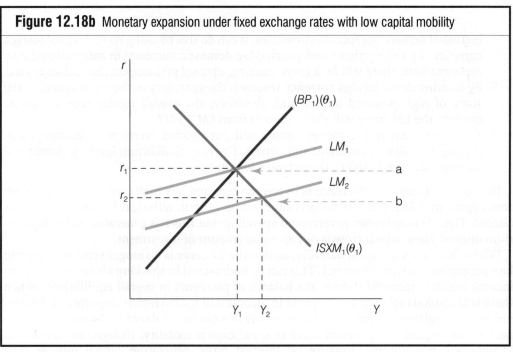

Figure 12.18b Monetary expansion under fixed exchange rates with low capital mobility

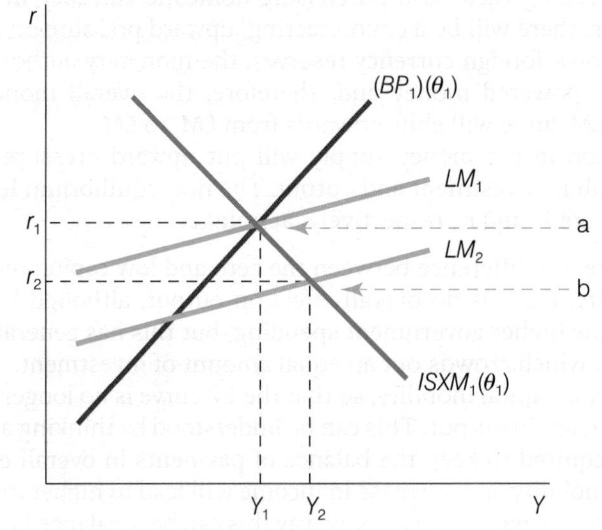

Exercise 4: Monetary expansion, fixed exchange rates, zero or low capital mobility Figure 12.18a gives the case where there is no capital mobility, while Figure 12.18b depicts the situation where there is low capital mobility.

1. The economy starts off at point *a*, where income is Y_1 and interest rates are at r_1.
2. An increase in the money supply shifts the LM curve downwards from LM_1 to LM_2. This puts downward pressure on interest rates to r_2, which would have increased investment and income to Y_2, moving the economy from point *a* to *b*.

3. Once again, fixing the exchange rate requires the demand and supply of domestic currency to remain unchanged. Therefore, foreign reserves are used to purchase domestic currency to prevent it from depreciating.
4. As foreign currency reserves are run down, the domestic money supply is contracted. This simply shifts the LM curve upwards in the direction from whence it came, LM_1 to LM_2. The economy will therefore move back to point *a*.

In this case, monetary policy will have no effect on output. Any change in monetary policy will have to be reserved in order to keep the exchange rate at its fixed value. This underlies the point that policy makers cannot control both the money supply and the exchange rate.

Exercise 5: Exchange rate devaluation, fixed exchange rates, zero or low capital mobility

Figure 12.19a gives the case where there is no capital mobility, while Figure 12.19b describes the outcome where there is low capital mobility.

1. The economy starts off at point *a*, where income is Y_1 and interest rates are at r_1.
2. The government is currently running a fixed exchange rate regime where the parity value of the real exchange rate is θ_1. The government, though, decides to boost the economy by devaluing the exchange rate to θ_2.
3. A depreciation in the exchange rate will, providing the Marshall-Lerner condition holds, improve the competitiveness of domestic goods and services, leading to a rise in exports and a fall in imports. As a result, the ISXM schedule will shift outwards ($ISXM_1(\theta_1) \rightarrow ISXM_2(\theta_2)$), as will the BP schedule ($BP_1(\theta_1) \rightarrow BP_2(\theta_2)$). The economy will therefore move from point *a* to *b*.
4. At point *b*, the economy is running a balance of trade surplus. Left unchecked, the exchange rate will start to appreciate and will reverse the effects of the devaluation. In order to keep the exchange rate constant, the monetary authorities will be forced to intervene in currency markets by buying foreign currency and selling domestic currency.

Figure 12.19a Exchange rate devaluation under fixed exchange rates with capital mobility

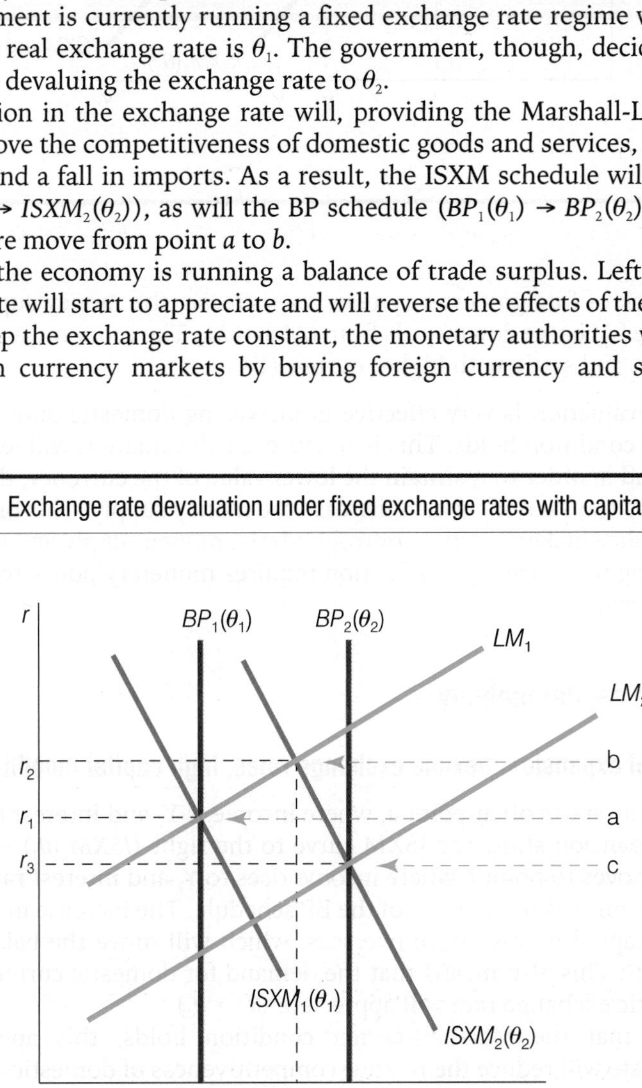

Figure 12.19b Exchange rate devaluation under fixed exchange rates with low capital mobility

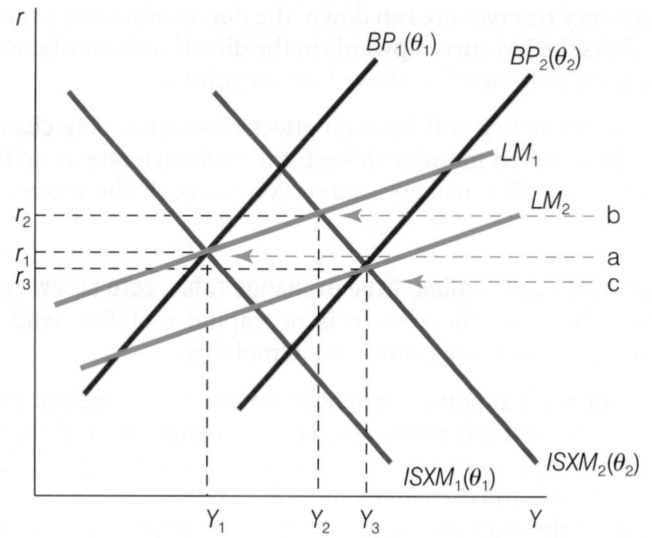

5. As the stock of foreign currency reserves increase, the money supply will increase, shifting the LM curve downwards from LM_1 to LM_2. The economy will then move from point *b* to *c*, and settle with higher output (Y_3).

A currency devaluation is very effective in increasing domestic output, but only if the Marshall-Lerner condition holds. This is because the devaluation will lead to a balance of trade surplus, and in order to maintain the lower value of the currency, this will have to be offset by currency transactions which increase the money supply. This once again exhibits the point that policy makers cannot control both the money supply and the exchange rate. Here, establishing the currency devaluation requires monetary policy to be accommodating to the new regime.

Policy with high capital mobility

Exercise 1: Fiscal expansion, flexible exchange rates, high capital mobility

1. The economy starts off at point *a*, where income is Y_1 and interest rates are at r_1.
2. A fiscal expansion shifts the ISXM curve to the right ($ISXM_1(\theta_1) \rightarrow ISXM_2(\theta_1)$). The economy moves to point *b* where income rises to Y_2 and interest rates increase to r_2.
3. However, point *b* is to the right of the BP schedule. The increase in interest rates will stimulate capital inflows from overseas, which will move the balance of payments into surplus. This also means that the demand for domestic currency increases and the domestic exchange rate will appreciate ($\theta_1 \rightarrow \theta_2$).
4. Assuming that the Marshall-Lerner condition holds, this appreciation in the exchange rate will reduce the relative competitiveness of domestic goods. As exports fall and imports rise, the ISXM curve will shift to the left ($ISXM_2(\theta_1) \rightarrow ISXM_3(\theta_2)$). The BP schedule will also shift to the left ($BP_1(\theta_1) \rightarrow BP_2(\theta_2)$). The horizontal shift in the BP schedule will be greater than that of ISXM.

Figure 12.20 Fiscal expansion under flexible exchange rates with high capital mobility

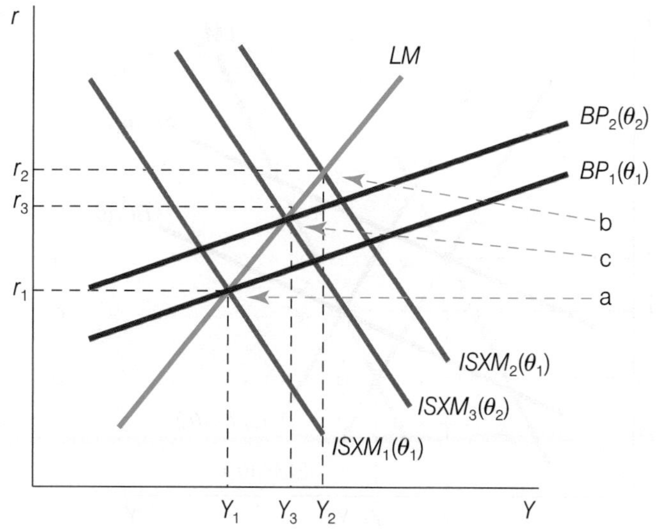

5. The economy will reach a new equilibrium where the ISXM, LM and BP schedules intersect at point *c*. The new equilibrium levels of output and interest rates are Y_3 and r_3, respectively.

In this example, fiscal expansion will increase output initially. When capital mobility was low, the rise in interest rates had a negligible effect on the balance of payments. However, the rise in income would generate increasing imports and move the balance of trade into deficit. This is not the case where capital mobility is high. Although imports will rise, this is more than countered by the capital inflows, so the balance of payments will move into surplus.

Consequently, the exchange rate will appreciate, and this will counteract the fiscal expansion. The ISXM and BP curves will shift in the opposite direction to the fiscal expansion. The overall effect on income will depend on how far these curves shift in response to the exchange rate appreciation. However, we can conclude that when capital mobility is high, fiscal policy under flexible exchange rate regimes is likely to be less effective than when capital mobility is low.

12

Exercise 2: Monetary expansion, flexible exchange rates, high capital mobility

1. The economy starts off a point *a*, where income is Y_1 and interest rates are at r_1.
2. A monetary expansion shifts the LM curve downwards ($LM_1 \rightarrow LM_2$). As a result, the equilibrium rate of interest rates fall to r_2, which encourages investment and income rises to Y_2. This is shown as a movement from point *a* to *b* in Figure 12.21.
3. At point *b*, the economy has moved to the right of the BP schedule. As income rises, imports increase, pushing the current account into deficit. The fall in the interest rate will produce capital outflows, moving the capital account into deficit. Overall, the balance of payments will move into deficit and demand for domestic currency will fall, leading to a depreciation of the exchange rate ($\theta_1 \rightarrow \theta_2$).
4. Following the exchange rate depreciation, the competitiveness of domestic goods and services will improve. The ISXM curve will shift to the right, ($ISXM_1(\theta_1) \rightarrow ISXM_2(\theta_2)$), as will the BP schedule, ($BP_1(\theta_1) \rightarrow BP_2(\theta_2)$).

Figure 12.21 Monetary expansion under flexible rates with high capital mobility

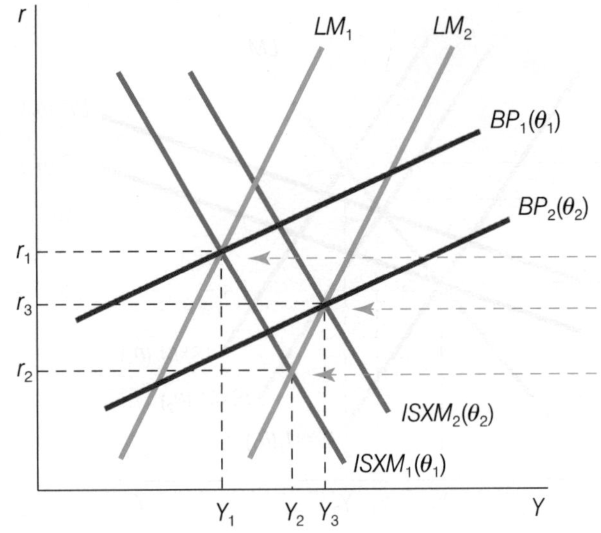

5. The horizontal shift in the BP schedule will be greater than that of the ISXM schedule. The economy will settle at a new equilibrium represented at point *c*, where income and interest rates are Y_3 and r_3, respectively.

When capital mobility is high, a monetary expansion under a floating exchange rate regime will be very successful in raising output. This is because the exchange rate movement reinforces the expansionary effects of the monetary policy.

Exercise 3: Fiscal expansion, fixed exchange rates, high capital mobility

1. The economy starts off a point *a*, where income is Y_1 and interest rates are at r_1 in Figure 12.22.
2. A fiscal expansion shifts the ISXM curve to the right ($ISXM_1(\theta_1) \rightarrow ISXM_2(\theta_1)$). This moves the economy from point *a* to *b*, where income rises to Y_2 and interest rates increase to r_2.
3. Higher interest rates will lead to capital inflows from overseas, putting upward pressure on the exchange rate. Under a fixed exchange rate regime, this cannot be allowed to happen. In order to maintain the fixed rate, the monetary authorities must expand the money supply (LM_1 to LM_2). This will put downward pressure on interest rates and counter the upward pressure on the exchange rate.
4. The new equilibrium levels of output and interest rates are Y_3 and r_3, respectively. At point *c*, output has increased. This will lead to higher imports, but this is offset by higher capital inflows as the equilibrium interest rate is also higher.

A fiscal expansion is very effective when capital mobility is high and the economy is operating under a fixed exchange rate regime. This is because any expansionary fiscal policy change will require an accommodating expansion in monetary policy. This once again demonstrates that in a fixed exchange rate regime, policy makers have no control over the money supply as it must passively adapt to maintain the fixed exchange rate.

12

Figure 12.22 Fiscal expansion under fixed exchange rates with high capital mobility

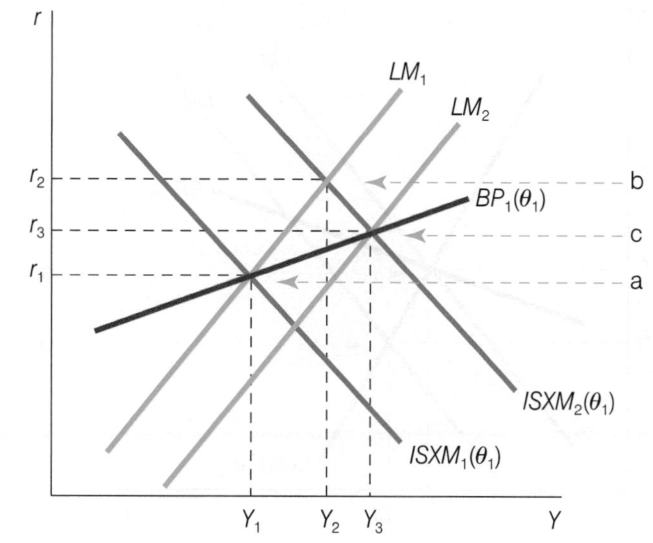

Exercise 4: Monetary expansion, fixed exchange rates, high capital mobility

1. The economy starts off at point *a*, where income is Y_1 and interest rates are at r_1 in Figure 12.23.
2. An increase in the money supply shifts the LM curve downwards from LM_1 to LM_2. This puts downward pressure on interest rates, which fall to r_2. This increases investment and income to Y_2, moving the economy from point *a* to *b*.
3. Once again, fixing the exchange rate requires the demand and supply of domestic currency to remain unchanged. Therefore, domestic interest rates must remain equal to the overseas rate to prevent a depreciation occuring.
4. Policy makers contract the domestic money supply to raise interest rates. This simply shifts the LM curve upwards, back to its original position, LM_2 to LM_1. The economy will therefore move back to point *a*.

In this case, monetary policy will have no effect on output. Any change in monetary policy will have to be reserved in order to keep the exchange rate at its fixed value. This underlies the point that policy makers cannot control both the money supply and the exchange rate.

Exercise 5: Exchange rate devaluation, fixed exchange rates, high capital mobility

1. The economy starts off at point *a*, where income is Y_1 and interest rates are at r_1.
2. The government is running a fixed exchange rate regime, where the parity value of the real exchange rate is θ_1. The government, though, decides to boost the economy by devaluing the exchange rate to θ_2.
3. A depreciation in the exchange rate will, providing the Marshall-Lerner condition holds, improve the competitiveness of domestic goods and services, leading to a rise in exports and a fall in imports. As a result, the ISXM schedule will shift outwards ($ISXM_1(\theta_1) \rightarrow ISXM_2(\theta_2)$), as will the BP schedule ($BP_1(\theta_1) \rightarrow BP_2(\theta_2)$). The economy therefore will move from point *a* to *b*.

12

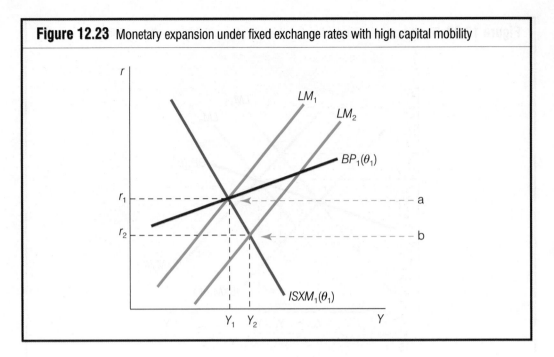

Figure 12.23 Monetary expansion under fixed exchange rates with high capital mobility

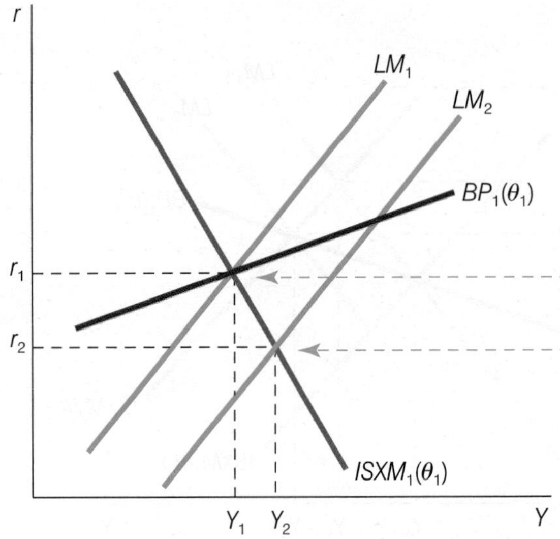

Figure 12.24 Exchange rate devaluation under fixed exchange rates with high capital mobility

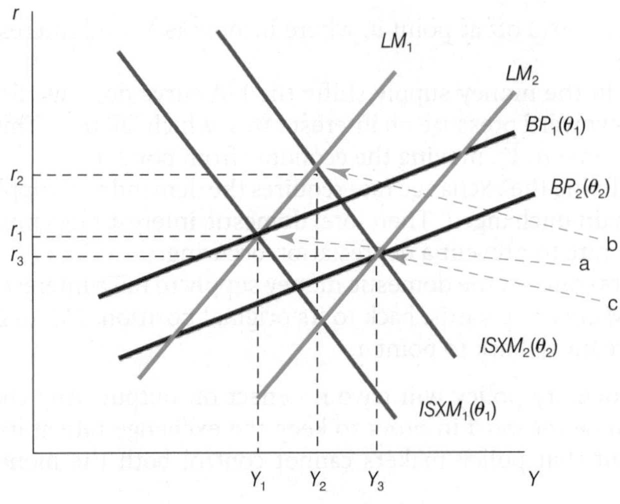

4. At point *b*, though, the economy is running a balance of trade surplus. Left unchecked, the exchange rate will start to appreciate and will reverse the effects of the devaluation. In order to keep the exchange rate constant, the monetary authorities will be forced to intervene in currency markets by reducing the domestic interest rate.
5. To lower domestic interest rates, the money supply is expanded shifting the LM curve downwards from LM_1 to LM_2. The economy will then move from point *b* to *c* and settle with higher output (Y_3).

A currency devaluation is very effective in increasing domestic output, but only if the Marshall-Lerner condition holds. This is because the devaluation will lead to a balance of trade surplus, and in order to maintain the lower value of the currency, domestic interest rates must fall. This once again exhibits the point that policy makers cannot control both the money supply and the exchange rate. Here, establishing the currency devaluation requires monetary policy to be accommodative.

12.4 The Mundell-Fleming model

The **Mundell-Fleming model** is just the IS-LM-BP model under the conditions of perfect capital mobility. If we consider the comparative statics exercises in the previous section, then the results under perfect capital mobility will be similar to those under high capital mobility. However, to add something further to the analysis, we can consider an extension of the model. As changes in the exchange rate will no longer lead to a shift in the BP curve (as it is horizontal), then the model is simpler to look at. This enables us to broaden the scope of the model without it becoming too complicated.

The IS-LM-BP model is a fixed price model; there is nothing that explains or accounts for price changes. In the closed economy version of the model, we addressed this through the Neoclassical IS-LM model and the same approach can be taken here.

It is assumed that prices are determined implicitly in this model. There is a full employment/natural level of output $\hat{Y}$ such that:

$$\dot{P} = \pi(Y - \hat{Y})$$

Prices will change in the same direction as the deviation of output from its natural level, and π determines the speed at which prices change in this case. Its size will be influenced by factors discussed previously in earlier chapters, such as expectations (adaptive or rational) and factors that cause sticky or rigid prices. If expectations are updated quickly, or there is little in the way of price rigidities, we would expect π to be correspondingly larger, so prices would respond faster to the deviation of output from the full employment level.

With the addition of this price adjustment feature, equilibrium in the Mundell-Fleming model is shown in Figure 12.25.

General equilibrium for an economy is thus where the goods market (ISXM curve), the money market (LM curve), and the balance of payments (BP curve) are all in equilibrium, and output is at its full employment level ($Y = \hat{Y}$).

12

Monetary and fiscal policy using the Mundell-Fleming model

The Mundell-Fleming model can be used to analyse the effects of monetary and fiscal policies in an open economy. Once again, the effects of policy will depend on the type of exchange rate that is implemented.

Monetary and fiscal policy under floating exchange rates In Figure 12.26, an expansionary monetary policy implies path a-b-c-a, whereas expansionary fiscal policy implies path a-d-a.

A monetary expansion shifts the LM curve downwards ($LM_1 \rightarrow LM_2$). As a result, the domestic interest rate falls below the overseas rate ($r_1 < r^*$). From the UIP condition, the nominal exchange rate will depreciate inducing a rise in competitiveness. The improvement in competitiveness shifts the ISXM curve to the right, ($ISXM_1 \rightarrow ISXM_2$), and the economy moves to a higher level of output ($Y_1 > \hat{Y}$). However, as output is now above the full employment level, prices will begin to rise, which has two effects. First, the real

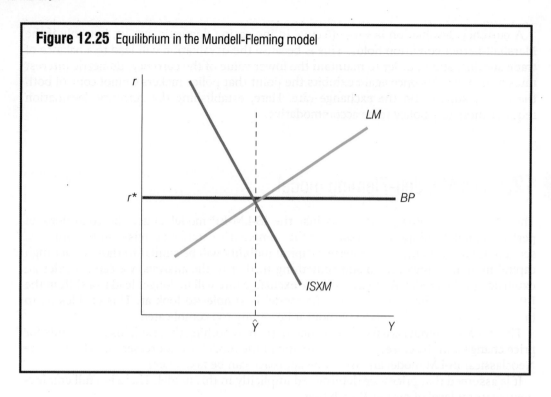

Figure 12.25 Equilibrium in the Mundell-Fleming model

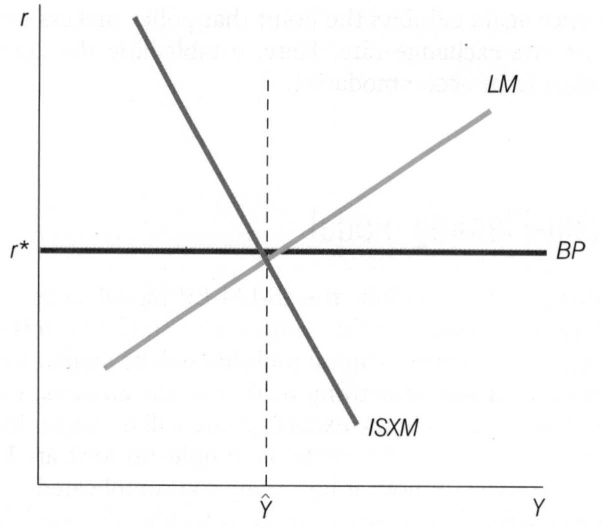

value of the money stock begins to fall, pushing the LM curve upwards ($LM_2 \rightarrow LM_1$). Also, rising prices begin to reduce competitiveness, pushing the ISXM curve backwards ($ISXM_2 \rightarrow ISXM_1$)and returning the economy back to the full employment level of output.

A fiscal expansion shifts the ISXM curve to the right, ($ISXM_1 \rightarrow ISXM_2$); however, the interest rate rises ($r_2 > r^*$)and the nominal exchange rate appreciates. As a result, competitiveness falls and the ISXM curve shifts back to the right ($ISXM_2 \rightarrow ISXM_1$).

In an open economy with floating exchange rates, it is clear that, in the long run, output will return to its natural level. But, in the short run, monetary policy expansions are more successful. Output will rise above its natural level for as long as it takes prices to adjust it back. Therefore, if π is quite small (implying slow adaptive expectations or significant price rigidities), then output will remain above the natural level for a considerable period of time. Fiscal policy, though, is ineffective in the short run as well as the long run. This is because the increase in government spending immediately crowds out net exports through a higher nominal exchange rate. The only impact is compositional, in that the share of government spending is higher and net exports lower.

12

Monetary and fiscal policy under fixed exchange rates This policy regime is very important, both historically (ERM) and hypothetically (EMU). These issues will be developed further in a later chapter. Figure 12.26 can be used here as well. An expansionary monetary policy will imply path a-b-a, whereas an expansionary fiscal policy will move the economy along the path a-d-c-a.

A monetary expansion shifts the LM curve downwards ($LM_1 \rightarrow LM_2$). As a result, the domestic interest rate falls below the overseas rate ($r_1 < r^*$). From UIP, this would place downward pressure on the nominal exchange rate. Therefore, policy makers must act to restore ($r = r^*$) by contracting the money supply, ($LM_2 \rightarrow LM_1$). As monetary policy changes must be reversed instantly to maintain the fixed exchange rate, there will be no effect on output.

Figure 12.26 Monetary and fiscal expansions in the Mundell-Fleming model

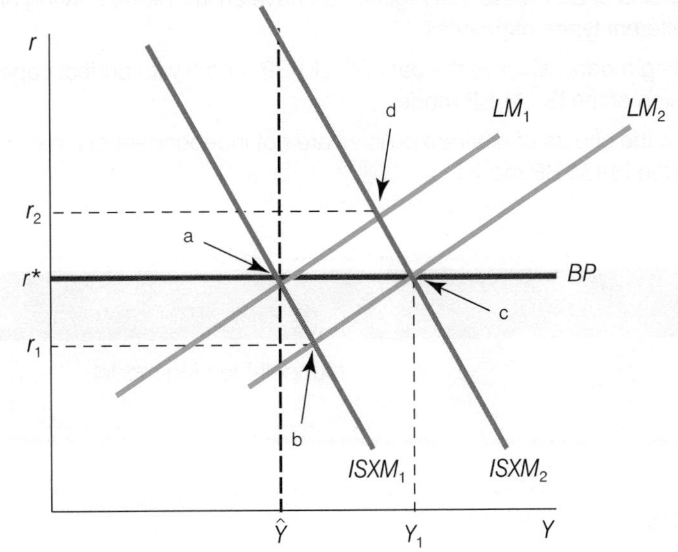

A fiscal expansion shifts the ISXM curve to the right, ($ISXM_1 \rightarrow ISXM_2$). However, the interest rate rises ($r_2 > r^*$), so monetary policy must also expand ($LM_1 \rightarrow LM_2$) in order that $r = r^*$. As a result, output will rise to $Y_1 > \hat{Y}$. However, as output is now above the natural level, prices will begin to rise, which has two effects. First, the real value of the money stock begins to fall, pushing the LM curve upwards ($LM_2 \rightarrow LM_1$). Also, rising prices begin to reduce competitiveness, pushing the ISXM curve backwards ($IS_2 \rightarrow IS_1$) and returning the economy back to the full employment level of output.

Under a fixed exchange rate system, monetary policy is ineffectual. Fiscal policy, in contrast, is very effective in changing output from its natural level in the short run. Once again, this deviation will depend on how quickly prices adjust. Also, there is a compositional element here as well. Higher government spending will eventually crowd out net exports even though the nominal exchange rate has not changed, as rising prices will reduce domestic competitiveness through an appreciation in the real exchange rate.

12

Summary

- In this chapter the IS-LM-BP model has been constructed and analysed in all its variety. This is a very useful model that can be applied widely in the analysis of an open economy and the impact of shocks and policies.
- We worked through the general equilibrium of the IS-LM-BP model, which includes a new BP schedule that reflects equilibrium in the balance of payments. Overall equilibrium will now show where the economy is in real, monetary and external equilibrium.

- There are many different variants of the IS-LM-BP model, which make different assumptions about the degree of capital mobility and the exchange rate regime. The degree of capital mobility and the choice of exchange rate regime can have an important bearing on the effectiveness of different types of process.
- The Mundell-Fleming model, which is the basic IS-LM-BP model with perfect capital mobility, is a widely used version of the IS-LM-BP model.
- Finally, we saw that the effects of different policies are not independent of the exchange rate regime in place in the IS-LM-BP model.

Key terms

BP curve
ISXM schedule
Mundell-Fleming model

Review questions

1. The IS-LM-BP model defines six regions, each corresponding to disequilibrium in the money market, goods market and/or the balance of payments. Identify each of these when capital is perfectly mobile, and when capital is perfectly immobile.
2. In a floating exchange rate regime, to what extent does the effectiveness of fiscal policy depend on the degree of capital mobility?
3. Using the IS-LM-BP model with a low degree of capital mobility, what will be the effects of the following:
   a. a deterioration in business optimism with fixed exchange rates
   b. an increase in the money supply with floating exchange rates
   c. a rise in taxes with floating exchange rates
   d. a fall in the money supply with fixed exchange rates?
4. Using the Mundell-Fleming model, what will be the effects of the following:
   a. a boom in stock market prices with fixed exchange rates
   b. an increase in ATM charges with floating exchange rates
   c. an increase in the money supply with fixed exchange rates
   d. a reduction in government spending with floating exchange rates?
5. An open economy with zero capital mobility consists of the following components:

   $C = 2000 + 0.6(Y - T)$

   $I = 300 - 3000r$

   $G = 300$

   $T = 300$

   $NX = 400 - 200S$

   $M = 500$

   $M_d = 0.2Y - 1000r$

   where Y is output, C is consumption, I is investment, r is the interest rate, T is the lump sum tax, G is government spending, NX is net exports, S is the nominal exchange rate (expressed in

12

Review questions (continued)

terms of foreign currency/domestic currency), M is the money supply and M_d is the demand for money.

a. For this economy, derive the IS, LM and BT schedules.
b. What are the equilibrium levels of income and interest rates?

6. How will a change in the world interest rate affect the equilibrium level of output when:
   a. capital mobility is low and exchange rates are fixed
   b. capital mobility is perfect and exchange rates are floating?

More advanced problems

7. Domestic demand (E) is determined in the following way:

   $E = 2000 + 0.75(Y–T) + G–2000r – 400S$

   where Y is output, T is lump sum tax, G is government spending, r is the interest rate and S is the nominal exchange rate (foreign currency/domestic currency).

   The money demand equation is $M_d = 0.5Y–3000r$.

   Initially, the government runs a balanced budget, so that $G = T = 200$.

   Finally, there is perfect capital mobility and world interest rates are $r^* = 0.1$.

   a. If the government decides to run a fixed exchange rate regime so that $S = 1$, what level of money supply is required?
   b. Using your answer in part (a), what will be the effects of an increase in government spending by 100? Will the effect on output be greater under the fixed exchange regime ($S=1$) or if the government allows the exchange rate to float? Explain your answer.
8. Some new empirical research has found that the demand for money is a better function of disposable income (Y–T) than actual income Y. What would be the consequences of a tax cut T, under fixed and floating exchange rate regimes?
9. Using the Mundell-Fleming model, examine the impact of an increase in the risk premium on domestic bonds on the level of output under fixed and floating exchange rate regimes. What factors are likely to influence the risk premium?
10. Using the Mundell-Fleming model, with fixed and floating exchange rates, describe the effects of an increase in the full employment level of output. What are the likely determinants of the full employment level of output?
11. If monetary policy is neutral, are there any costs in forsaking discretionary monetary policy to fix the exchange rate?
12. With the use of a conventional IS-LM-BP model (i.e. no price adjustment), identify the conditions where fiscal policy is most effective in influencing the level of output in the economy.
13. If exchange rates are free to float, under what conditions does an expansive monetary policy fail to increase the equilibrium level of output?

For further resources, visit
http://www.thomsonlearning.co.uk/chamberlin_yueh

13 Aggregate demand and aggregate supply in the open economy

Learning objectives

- Understand how to construct and use the AD-CCE-BT or Salter-Swan model to analyse an open economy
- Describe how prices and the NAIRU are determined in an open economy
- Identify the sustainable level of output for an economy

13.1 Introduction

In the previous chapter, we extended the traditional IS-LM model to the open economy. The aim of this chapter is to do the same with the aggregate demand-aggregate supply (AD-AS) model. This model not only enables us to analyse the potential effects of policy and other shocks on the domestic economy, but also helps us understand how prices are determined by giving a more thorough treatment of the supply side.

The non-accelerating inflation rate of unemployment or the NAIRU is the rate of unemployment where there is no pressure on inflation to accelerate or decelerate. Corresponding to this rate of unemployment is a level of output, which we referred to in Chapter 8 as the long-run equilibrium level of output, where inflation is also constant. This level of output determines the position of the economy's long-run aggregate supply curve. We will see in this chapter that in an open economy, there will be an overseas effect on the NAIRU and the shape of the long-run aggregate supply curve, which will have an important implication for the domestic economy's path in the medium to long run.

The open economy version of the AD-AS model is commonly known as the Salter-Swan model. It essentially consists of three lines, each representing the demand, supply and external parts of the economy, respectively. The aggregate demand schedule (AD) is essentially the same as that in the closed economy, except now of course with the addition of net exports. The aggregate supply schedule is once again derived from the equilibrium in the labour market.This is known as the competing claims equilibrium (CCE), as real wage bargaining seeks to divide output between firms, workers and foreigners. Finally, external equilibrium is represented by equilibrium in the balance of trade.This is exactly the same as the BT schedule derived in the previous chapter. A good account of this model has been developed by Layard, Nickell and Jackman (1991) and by Carlin and Soskice (1990).

13.2 The AD-CCE-BT (Salter-Swan) model

The **AD-CCE-BT** or **Salter-Swan model** can be used to analyse how aggregate demand and aggregate supply determine output and prices in an open economy. It consists of three equilibrium relationships examining the links between **competitiveness** and, in turn, the trade balance, aggregate demand and aggregate supply.

Competitiveness is determined by the real exchange rate, $\theta = \frac{EP^*}{P}$, which is the ratio of foreign to domestic prices in terms of the domestic currency. A real appreciation marks a fall in θ and competitiveness, which can arise through either a nominal appreciation (a fall in E), a fall in foreign prices (P^*) or an increase in domestic prices (P). All of these will lower foreign prices relative to domestic prices.

13

13.2.1 Competitiveness and the trade balance

From the previous two chapters, we have seen that the trade balance is the difference between exports and imports.

Exports reflect the demand for domestically produced goods from overseas residents and are a positive function of the level of competitiveness and the overseas level of income:

$$X = x_{Y^*}(\theta)Y^* \quad (13.1)$$

Floating market, Damnoen Saduak, near Bangkok, Thailand
Source: Getty Images

As before, Y^* is the overseas level of income and x_{Y^*} is the propensity to consume domestic goods, which is positively related to the real exchange rate. If the real exchange rate appreciates, then the relative price of foreign to domestic goods falls which would encourage substitution away from domestic and towards foreign goods.

Imports represent the demand from domestic firms and households for goods and services produced overseas and is determined by domestic income and the marginal propensity to import:

$$M = \theta m_Y(\theta)Y \tag{13.2}$$

Once again, the propensity to import ($m_Y(\theta)$) is a function – this time negative – of the real exchange rate. A real appreciation would encourage substitution towards foreign goods, so total imports will rise at every level of income. The relationship between imports and the real exchange rate is complicated slightly by terms of trade effects, which work in the opposite direction to the competitiveness effects. A real appreciation, by making foreign goods cheaper, would mean that the same quantity of goods and services could be imported at a lower cost.

The **trade balance (BT)** is therefore the value of real exports (13.1) minus the value of imports (13.2).

$$BT = x_{Y^*}(\theta)Y^* - \theta m_Y(\theta)Y \tag{13.3}$$

The trade balance is in equilibrium when $BT = 0$, or where exports are equal to imports. From (13.3), this implies:

$$x_{Y^*}(\theta)Y^* = \theta m_Y(\theta)Y \tag{13.4}$$

This relationship (13.4) can be rearranged to give the level of income where the trade balance is in equilibrium (Y_{TB}).

$$\frac{x_{Y^*}(\theta)Y^*}{\theta m_Y(\theta)} = Y_{TB} \tag{13.5}$$

The effect of the real exchange rate on the level of income when the trade balance is in equilibrium will depend on the relative strengths of the competitiveness and terms of trade effects. In Chapter 11, it was argued that the substitution effect will dominate when the Marshall-Lerner condition holds, that is, the price elasticity of exports and imports sum to greater than 1. Providing the Marshall-Lerner condition is satisfied, an improvement in competitiveness enables the trade balance to remain in equilibrium at higher levels of domestic income. Therefore, the BT curve will slope upwards as shown in Figure 13.1.

When income rises from Y_1 to Y_2, imports will rise. Therefore, the only way to keep the trade balance in equilibrium at this higher level of income would be to encourage

Figure 13.1 The BT schedule

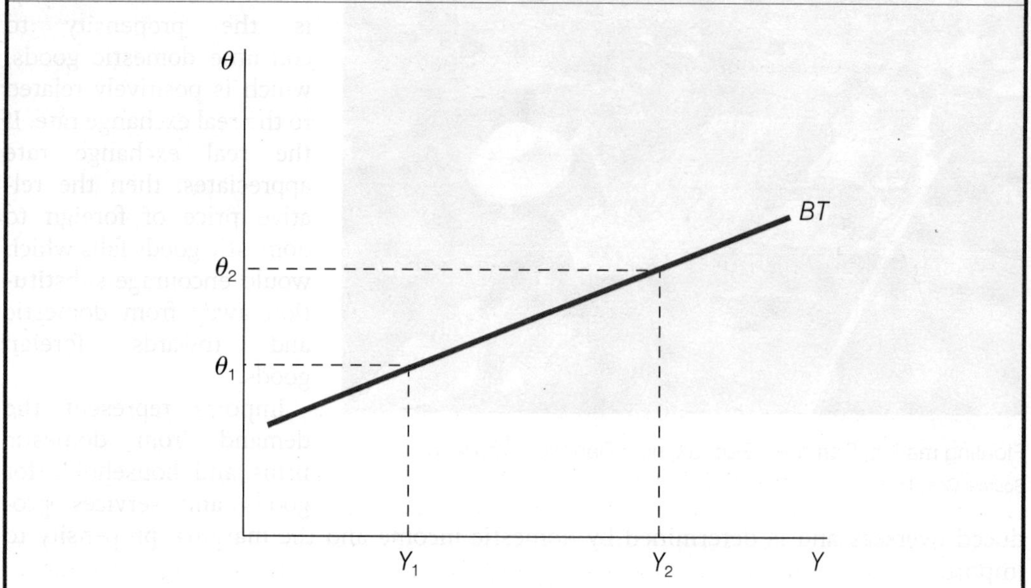

substitution towards domestic goods through an improvement in competitiveness. This will require a real depreciation from θ_1 to θ_2, accounting for the upward-sloping BT curve.

13.2.2 Aggregate demand and competitiveness

The aggregate demand (AD) schedule plots the combinations of real exchange rates and output where planned expenditures equal actual output. Essentially, it is telling us what the level of aggregate demand is when the economy is in goods market equilibrium. Total planned expenditures equals of the sum of consumption (C), investment (I), government spending (G) and net exports (X–M), so the AD curve can be written as:

$$Y_{AD} = C + I + G + X - M$$

Consumption is a function of autonomous consumption (a), the marginal propensity to consume (c), and personal disposable income (Y–T), where T is the level of lump sum taxes.

13

$$C = a + c(Y - T) \tag{13.6}$$

Investment is a function of autonomous factors (Θ) described in Chapters 3 and 7, such as expectations, taxes, credit restrictions, etc., and a negative function of the interest rate (r).

$$I = I(\Theta, r), \frac{\Delta I}{\Delta r} < 0 \tag{13.7}$$

Government spending and lump sum taxes are exogenously determined, being set by politicians.

$$G = \overline{G}$$

$$T = \overline{T}$$

And, net exports are calculated as the trade balance.

$$X - M = x_{Y^*}(\theta)Y^* - \theta m_Y(\theta)Y \tag{13.8}$$

Substituting these components into the AD Schedule gives:

$$Y = a + c\,(Y - \overline{T}) + I(\theta, r) + \overline{G} + x_{Y^*}(\theta)Y^* - \theta m_Y(\theta)Y \tag{13.9}$$

This can be rearranged by collecting terms in Y:

$$Y = a + I(\Theta, r) + \overline{G} - c\overline{T} + x_{Y^*}(\theta)Y^* + (c - \theta m_Y(\theta))Y \tag{13.10}$$

And simplified by moving the Y terms to the left-hand side,

$$Y_{AD} = \frac{a + I(\Theta, r) + \overline{G} - cT + x_{Y^*}(\theta)Y^*}{(1 - c + \theta m_{Y^*}(\theta))} \tag{13.11}$$

If the Marshall-Lerner condition holds, the AD schedule in 13.11 will also be upward sloping in $\theta - Y$ space, as shown in Figure 13.2.

This is not surprising because the AD schedule incorporates the trade balance, which is also an upward-sloping schedule. As long as the Marshall-Lerner condition holds, then a real depreciation will increase net exports and aggregate demand.

There are many things that may shift the AD schedule. In fact, anything that leads to a change in any of the parameters in (13.11) other than θ will lead to a shift in the schedule. For example, if government spending were to rise from G_1 to G_2, then aggregate demand would be higher at every level of θ, so the AD schedule will shift horizontally to the right. A shift in the AD Schedule is shown in Figure 13.3.

Why is the BT schedule flatter than the AD schedule?

Although both the BT and AD schedules are upward-sloping, it is generally accepted that the BT curve will be flatter than the AD curve. The explanation is the same as that given in

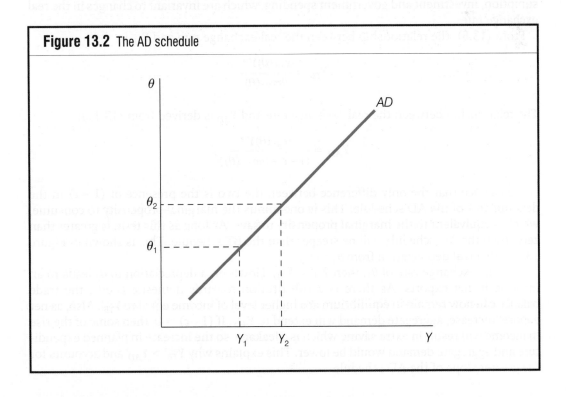

Figure 13.2 The AD schedule

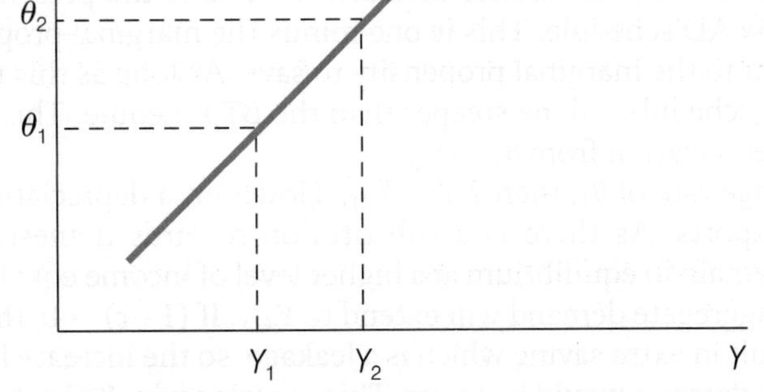

13

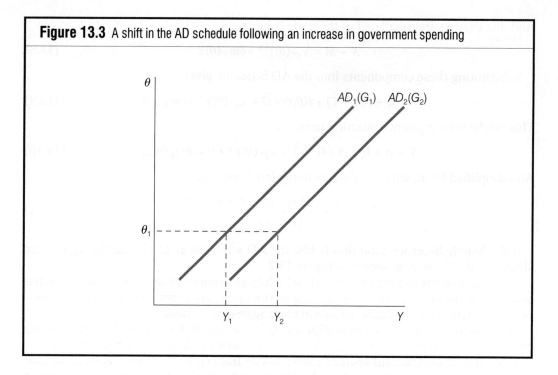

Figure 13.3 A shift in the AD schedule following an increase in government spending

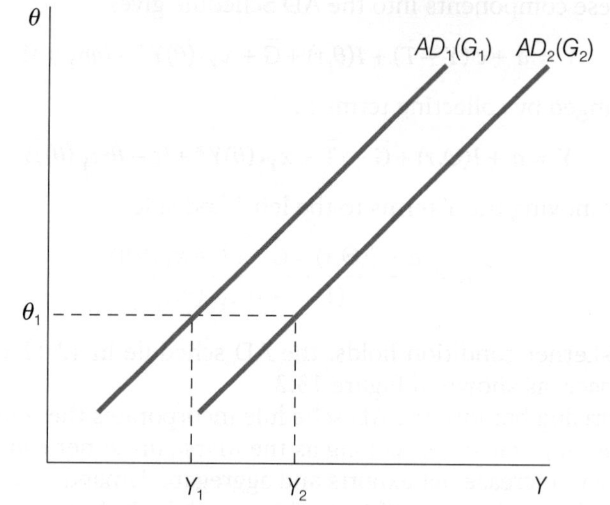

the previous chapter to explain why the BT schedule will shift further than the ISXM schedule following a change in the exchange rate.

If we look at the equations for the BT and the AD schedules, we can see what happens to Y_{TB} and Y_{AD} when the real exchange depreciates. To do this, we only need to think about the factors that depend on the real exchange rate in each equation. This will lead to no change for the BT schedule, but in the AD schedule, we can ignore factors such as consumption, investment and government spending, which are invariant to changes in the real exchange rate.

From (13.5), the relationship between the real exchange rate and Y_{TB} is:

$$Y_{TB} = \frac{x_{Y^*}(\theta)Y^*}{\theta m_{Y^*}(\theta)}$$

The relationship between the real exchange rate and Y_{AD} is derived from (13.11):

$$Y_{AD} = \frac{x_{Y^*}(\theta)Y^*}{(1 - c + \theta m_{Y^*}(\theta))}$$

13

We can see that the only difference between the two is the presence of $(1 - c)$ in the denominator of the AD schedule. This is one minus the marginal propensity to consume, which is equivalent to the marginal propensity to save. As long as this term is greater than zero, then the AD schedule will be steeper than the BT schedule. This is shown in Figure 13.4 with a real depreciation from θ_1 to θ_2.

At a real exchange rate of θ_1, then $Y_{TB} = Y_{AD}$. However, a depreciation to θ_2 leads to an increase in net exports. As there is a substitution towards domestic goods, the trade balance can now remain in equilibrium at a higher level of income equal to Y_{TB}'. Also, as net exports increase, aggregate demand will extend to Y_{AD}'. If $(1 - c) > 0$, then some of the rise in income will result in extra saving which is a leakage, so the increase in planned expenditure and aggregate demand would be lower. This explains why $Y_{TB}' > Y_{AD}'$ and accounts for the greater slope of the AD schedule.

Figure 13.4 Why the BT schedule is flatter than the AD schedule

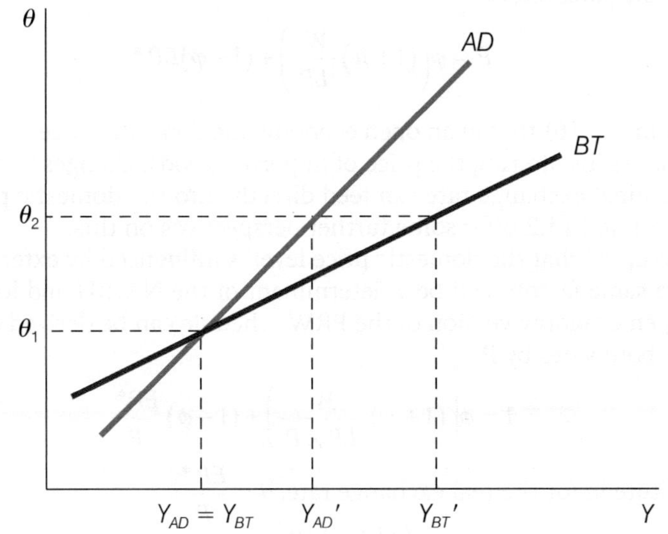

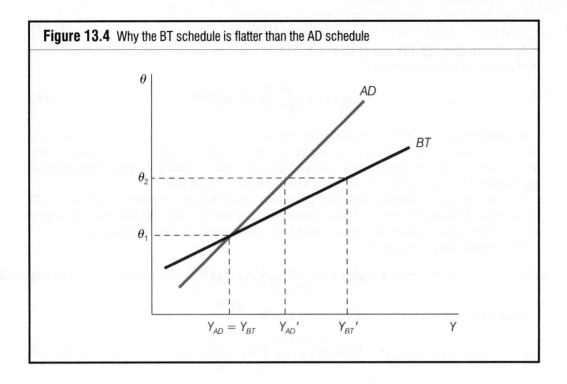

13.2.3 The NAIRU and long-run aggregate supply in the open economy

In a closed economy, we saw that the NAIRU and the associated long-run aggregate supply curve were determined by a bargaining equilibrium in the labour market. This is where the price-determined real wage (PRW) curve intersected the bargained real wage (BRW) curve, giving equilibrium levels of the real wage and unemployment. This model was outlined in some detail in Chapter 8.

The PRW curve is derived from a firm's price-setting relationship and describes how the price level is determined in the economy. In a closed economy, this was simply a mark-up over marginal costs. This can be considered as the price of domestic output (P_D), i.e., the price of output produced by domestic firms:

$$P_D = (1+\mu)\frac{W}{LP} \tag{13.12}$$

The mark-up is μ, and marginal costs are simply the ratio of nominal wages (W) and labour productivity (LP). This can be rearranged to give the PRW:

$$PRW\colon w = \frac{W}{P} = \frac{LP}{(1+\mu)} \tag{13.13}$$

As justified in Chapter 8, this can be plotted as a horizontal schedule.

In an open economy, however, the domestic price level, will not be determined solely by the price of domestic goods; it will also consist of the price of goods imported from overseas. The price of imported goods (P_M) will be determined by the foreign price level (P^*) and the nominal exchange rate (E).

$$P_M = EP^* \tag{13.14}$$

The overall price level (P) is then a weighted combination of domestic (P_D) and imported prices (P_M), where the respective weights ϕ and $(1 - \phi)$ reflect the proportion of domestic and foreign goods sold in the home market.

$$P = \phi P_D + (1-\phi)P_M \tag{13.15}$$

By substituting (13.13) and (13.14) into (13.15), we can express the domestic price level in terms of all the parameters.

$$P = \phi\left((1+\mu)\frac{W}{LP}\right) + (1-\phi)EP^* \tag{13.16}$$

It is clear from (13.16) that in an open economy the domestic price level will be affected by overseas factors. By altering the price of imported goods, changes in the overseas price level or the nominal exchange rate can feed directly into the domestic price level. Global applications 13.1 and 13.2 offer some further perspectives on this.

Once it is accepted that the domestic price level is influenced by external factors, it will follow that the same factors will be a determinant of the NAIRU and long-run aggregate supply. The open economy version of the PRW schedule can be derived from (13.16).

First, divide both sides by P,

$$1 = \phi\left((1+\mu)\frac{W}{LP \times P}\right) + (1-\phi)\frac{EP^*}{P} \tag{13.17}$$

Next, substitute in for the real exchange rate, $\theta = \dfrac{EP^*}{P}$:

$$1 = \phi\left(\frac{(1+\mu)}{LP}\frac{W}{P}\right) + (1-\phi)\theta \tag{13.18}$$

And finally rearrange,

$$1-(1-\phi)\theta = \phi\left(\frac{(1+\mu)}{LP}\right)\left(\frac{W}{P}\right) \tag{13.19}$$

$$\frac{1-(1-\phi)\theta}{\phi} = \left(\frac{(1+\mu)}{LP}\right)\left(\frac{W}{P}\right) \tag{13.20}$$

$$PRW: w = \frac{W}{P} = \frac{1-(1-\phi)\theta}{\phi}\left(\frac{LP}{(1+\mu)}\right) \tag{13.21}$$

The open economy price-determined real wage (PRW) schedule in (13.21) is an interesting relationship. The closed economy price-setting relationship in (13.12) will simply result if we set $\phi = 1$. However, as long as $\phi < 1$, foreign goods will constitute a positive proportion of the price level. In this case, the price level will be determined by the real exchange rate and, in particular, the nominal exchange rate and overseas price level. Changes in the real exchange rate will then change domestic prices and the price-determined real wage, as shown in Figure 13.5.

13

If the real exchange rate appreciates (θ falls from $\theta_1 \rightarrow \theta_2 \rightarrow \theta_3$), then foreign goods become cheaper so overall domestic prices will fall. As a result, the price determined real wage will rise, ($w_1 \rightarrow w_2 \rightarrow w_3$) shifting the PRW schedule upwards. Alternatively, a real exchange rate depreciation (θ rises) will make foreign goods more expensive and the domestic price level will rise, shifting the PRW schedule downwards.

The other side of the bargaining framework is the wage-setting relationship, which describes the real wage that workers will push for at each level of unemployment. In Chapter 8, we saw that this is a downward-sloping function because workers will moderate wage claims in times of high unemployment. The bargained real wage (BRW) can then be represented in the following way:

$$BRW: \frac{W}{P} = Z - \beta u \tag{13.22}$$

Global application 13.1

The pass through from the exchange rate to inflation

In an open economy, the domestic price level (P) is given by a combination of domestic (P_D) and import prices (P_M).

$$P = \phi P_D + (1-\phi)P_M$$

Import prices, in turn, are derived as foreign prices (P^*) in terms of domestic currency using the nominal exchange rate (E):

$$P_M = EP^*$$

It is assumed that the price of foreign goods is just a mark-up on the marginal cost of production.

$$P^* = (1-\mu)\, MC^*$$

Taken together, these three equations then can describe fully the external effects on the domestic price level.

$$P = \phi P_D + (1-\phi)E(1+\mu)MC^*$$

Any factor that changes import prices, whether it is the marginal cost of production, the mark-up or the nominal exchange rate, can have a bearing on the domestic price level. Out of these, the factor that has attracted the most interest is the nominal exchange rate. In Chapter 11, it was established that the nominal exchange is prone to relatively large and prolonged movements in the short run. As economies become more open and macroeconomic policy more fixated on controlling inflation, the pass through from the nominal exchange rate to domestic prices has become a significant issue.

It is clear that changes in the exchange rate have direct effects on the domestic price level through its impact on import prices.

$$\Delta P = (1-\phi)(1+\mu)MC^* \,\Delta E$$

Empirical evidence, though, shows that exchange rates are much more volatile than import prices. This implies that the pass through from exchange rate changes to the domestic price level is fairly weak.

One explanation is pricing to market by foreign firms. Foreign firms change their mark-up μ to offset the effects of exchange rates on their prices in foreign markets. Under imperfect competition, the price is often set strategically.

For example, if a foreign firm has invested substantially to build market share in a foreign country, then it would make sense to let the mark-up take the brunt rather than let this previous investment be undone by an exchange rate movement which reduces competitiveness.

An alternative explanation of weak pass through is that exchange rate movements tend to be temporary and largely offset each other. If firms face menu or other costs of changing prices, then it does not make sense to continuously change prices whereas changing the mark-up is a relatively costly procedure. This is particularly the case when exchange rate volatility is often short-lived.

Both these effects – strategy/pricing to market and costs of price adjustment – can explain why import price movements are less volatile than the exchange rate. Hence, the immediate pass through from the exchange rate to inflation is fairly small.

Again, following the notation in Chapter 8, Z represents a set of exogenous factors which determine the real wage, such as trade union power, minimum wage levels, etc., and β represents the sensitivity of the real wage to the rate of unemployment (u).

The non-accelerating inflation rate of unemployment (NAIRU) is determined by the intersection of the price-setting (13.21) and wage-setting schedules (13.22). In the open economy, though, we will see that there is no longer a unique NAIRU. In fact, the NAIRU will be different depending on the level of the real exchange rate. This is shown in Figure 13.6.

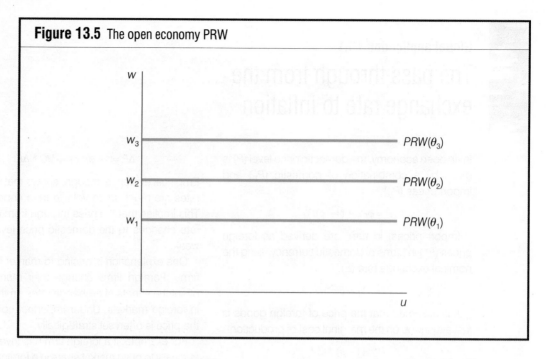

Figure 13.5 The open economy PRW

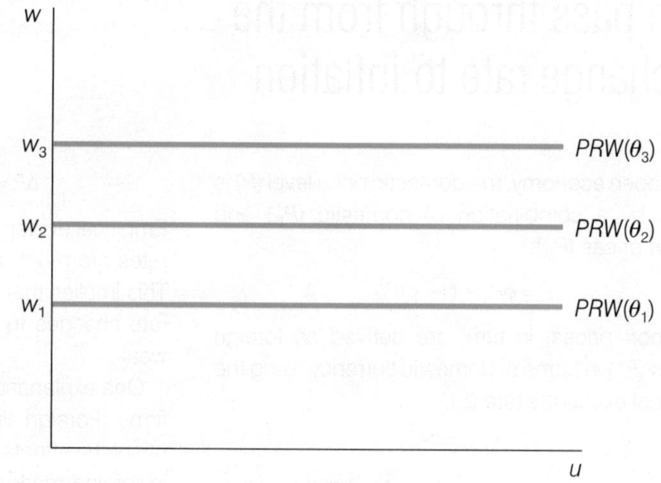

Figure 13.6 NAIRU in the open economy

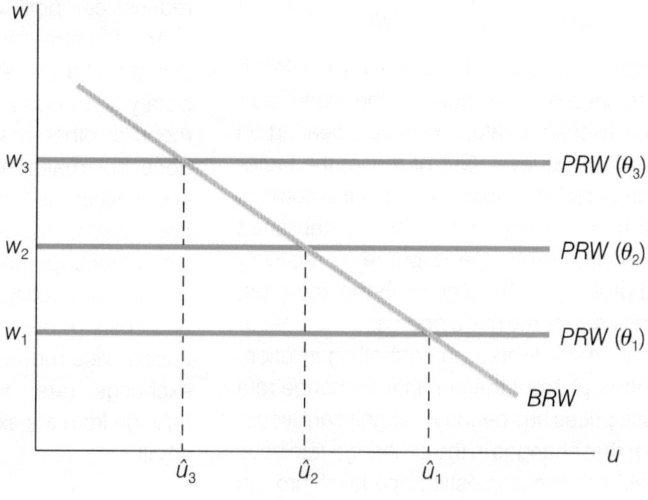

As the real exchange rate appreciates, the NAIRU falls – meaning that non-accelerating inflation is sustainable at a lower rate of unemployment. There is an intuitive reason why this would happen.

As unemployment falls, we would expect workers to push for higher wages. This will then raise the costs of firms, and lead to an upward pressure on prices. In the closed economy, the increase in prices would then act to reduce the real wage, meaning that it was impossible to depart from the NAIRU in the long run once wages and prices had fully adjusted.

Global application 13.2

Is China exporting deflation?

China's recent economic performance has been truly impressive, growing at an average rate of 9.8 per cent per year since 1978. During this time, China has become increasingly important in the global economy. Table 1 shows that a growing proportion of goods imported into the three main economic areas comes from China. This table slightly understates China's role, as over the last four decades imports themselves have become an increasing proportion of GDP.

Figure 1 shows that, at the same time, China's production has moved towards machinery, electronics and transportation equipment, and away from primary goods. This trend is concurred in Figure 2, which shows China's increasing importance in certain export markets.

The growth in demand for Chinese products is largely driven by their price competitiveness. China has a large, relatively skilled workforce, and labour costs are substantially less than in advanced countries. Therefore, China has recently been exporting a large number of cheap manufactured goods to the rest of the world. These cheap imports would then feed directly into the domestic price level.

Table 1 China's share in major export markets

	1960	1970	1980	1990	1995	2000	2001	2002
Japan	0.5	1.4	3.1	5.1	10.7	14.5	16.6	18.3
US	–	–	0.5	3.2	6.3	8.6	9.3	11.1
EU	0.8	0.6	0.7	2.0	3.7	6.2	6.7	7.5

Notes: EU figures are adjusted for intra-EU trade; imports from China as a percentage of total imports.
Source: IMF, Direction of Trade Statistics

Figure 1 Composition of output

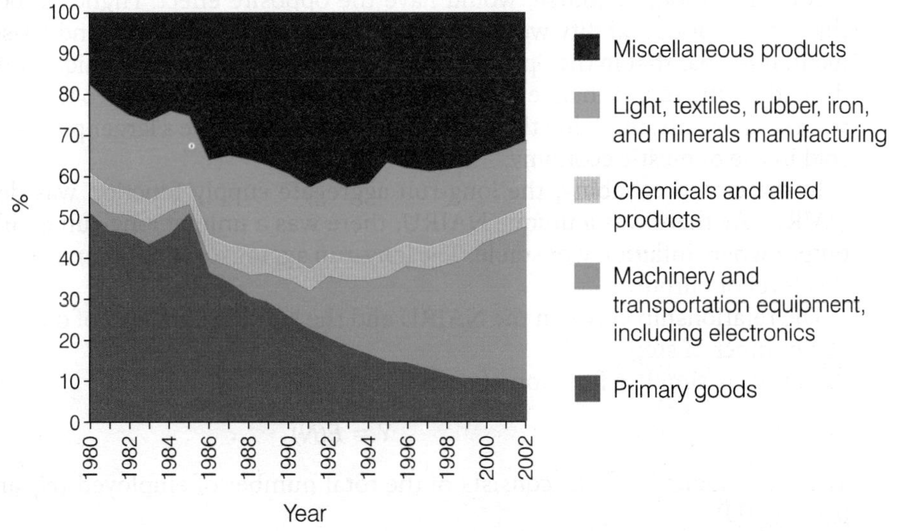

13

Global application 13.2 (continued)

Figure 2 China's share of world export markets Source: IMF

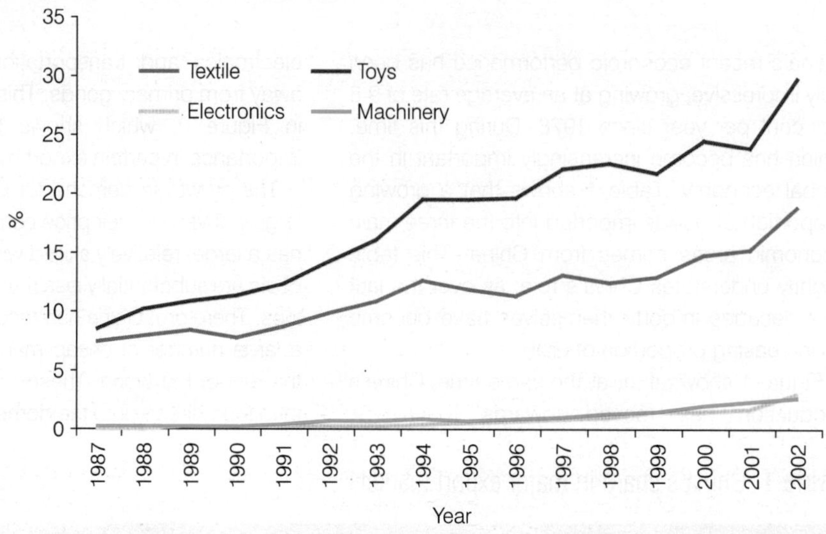

In an open economy, however, an appreciated exchange rate would give the economy an inflation subsidy. Falling import prices (P_M) would put downward pressure on the overall price level (P). If unemployment were then to fall, this would put upward pressure on domestic prices (P_D), but this would be offset by the fall in import prices – leaving the overall price level unchanged. Therefore, it can be seen that an exchange rate appreciation enables the economy to move to a lower level of unemployment while maintaining price stability.

A depreciation, of course, would have the opposite effect. Higher import prices mean that overall price stability would require a fall in domestic prices and a rise in unemployment. It is clear that in the open economy, the NAIRU will not be uniquely determined, but depend on the real exchange rate θ. The sensitivity of the NAIRU to the real exchange rate will rise as ϕ falls, implying that foreign imported goods are a larger proportion of all goods sold in the domestic economy.

13

In the closed economy, the long-run aggregate supply function was derived from the NAIRU. As there was a unique NAIRU, there was a unique long-run equilibrium level of output where inflation was stable. The long-run aggregate supply curve is simply vertical at this level of output.

The relationship between the NAIRU and the equilibrium level of output is determined in a number of steps.

Output is simply a function of employment (N).

$$Y = F(N)$$

The total labour force (L) consists of the total number of employed (N) and unemployed persons (U).

$$L = N + U$$

Dividing both sides by L enables us to see that the relative proportions of employed and unemployed workers in the economy add up to one.

$$1 = \frac{N}{L} + \frac{U}{L}$$

$$1 = \frac{N}{L} + u, \text{ as } u = \frac{U}{L} \text{ is the unemployment rate.}$$

Rearranging this, we can then express employment as a function of unemployment, i.e., employment is equal to the proportion of the labour force that is not unemployed.

$$N = L\ (1 - u)$$

If unemployment ($\hat{u}$) is at the NAIRU, then the long-run aggregate supply level of output ($\hat{Y}$) will be defined:

$$\hat{Y} = F(L(1 - \hat{u})) \tag{13.23}$$

There is an inverse relationship between the equilibrium level of output and the NAIRU. In an open economy, the long-run aggregate supply curve is referred to as the **competing claims equilibrium (CCE)**. This plots the relationship between the real exchange rate and the equilibrium level of output. Clearly from Figure 13.6 and equation (13.23), this will be a downward-sloping function, as shown in Figure 13.7.

As the exchange rate appreciates $\theta_1 \rightarrow \theta_2 \rightarrow \theta_3$, the equilibrium level of output (where inflation is constant) will rise, $Y_1 \rightarrow Y_2 \rightarrow Y_3$. Note that the slope of the CCE schedule depends on the size of the shifts in the PRW curve for a given change in competitiveness. This is largely determined by the parameter ϕ. If $\phi = 1$, then the foreign price effect on the PRW curve would disappear completely, as imports constitute no part of the domestic price level. In this instance, the NAIRU and the equilibrium level of output will once again be uniquely determined.

If this were the case, the CCE schedule would simply be like its closed economy counterpart and would be vertical at the equilibrium level of output. However, as $\phi \rightarrow 0$, foreign

Figure 13.7 The CCE schedule

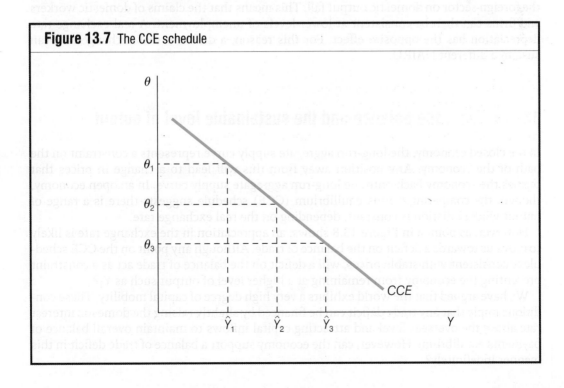

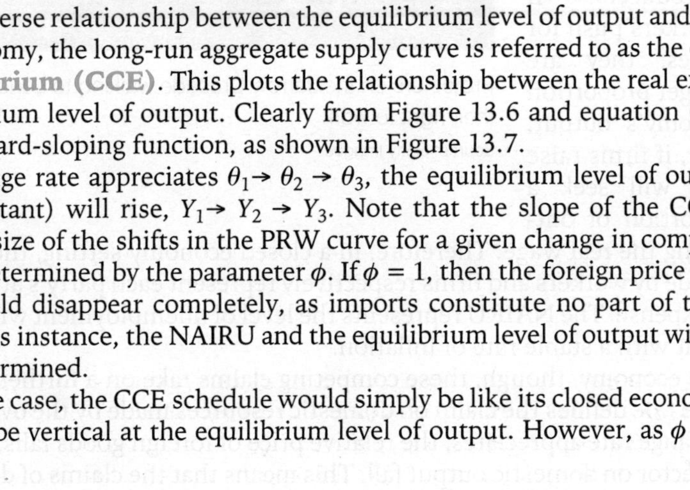

goods increasingly are a proportion of the domestic price level. As competitiveness falls, higher levels of output can be sustained without prices rising, so the CCE curve becomes flatter.

Protesters on the Jarrow Crusade walking to London to demand their right to work

Source: Getty Images

The term, competing claims equilibrium (CCE), arises because price inflation results from the competing claims of domestic workers and firms – and also, in the open economy, foreign producers. If domestic workers push for higher wages, they are seeking a larger proportion of the economy's output. Alternatively, if firms raise prices, they will seek a higher proportion of output by limiting the real wage. Therefore, in a closed economy setting, the wage and price demands made by workers and firms respectively represent each party's attempts to gain at the others' expense. The NAIRU represents the level of unemployment where these claims are consistent with a stable rate of inflation.

In an open economy, though, these competing claims take on a further dimension. The real exchange rate defines the claim on domestic resources made by the overseas sector. As the real exchange rate appreciates, the relative price of foreign goods falls, so the claims of the foreign sector on domestic output fall. This means that the claims of domestic workers and firms can then be consistent at lower levels of unemployment. A real exchange rate depreciation has the opposite effect. For this reason, a different real exchange rate can sustain a different NAIRU.

13.2.4 The trade balance and the sustainable level of output

13

In the closed economy, the long-run aggregate supply curve represents a constraint on the path of the economy. Any position away from this will lead to a change in prices that pushes the economy back onto the long-run aggregate supply curve. In an open economy, though, the competing claims equilibrium (CCE) schedule suggests there is a range of output where inflation is constant, depending on the real exchange rate.

However, as point *a* in Figure 13.8 shows, an appreciation in the exchange rate is likely to move us towards a deficit on the balance of trade. Although any point on the CCE schedule is consistent with stable prices, will a deficit on the balance of trade act as a constraint preventing the economy from remaining at a higher level of output such as Y_1?

We have argued that the world exhibits a very high degree of capital mobility. These conditions imply that any trade deficit can be financed by slightly raising the domestic interest rate above the overseas level and attracting capital inflows to maintain overall balance of payments equilibrium. However, can the economy support a balance of trade deficit in this manner indefinitely?

Figure 13.8 Sustainable level of output

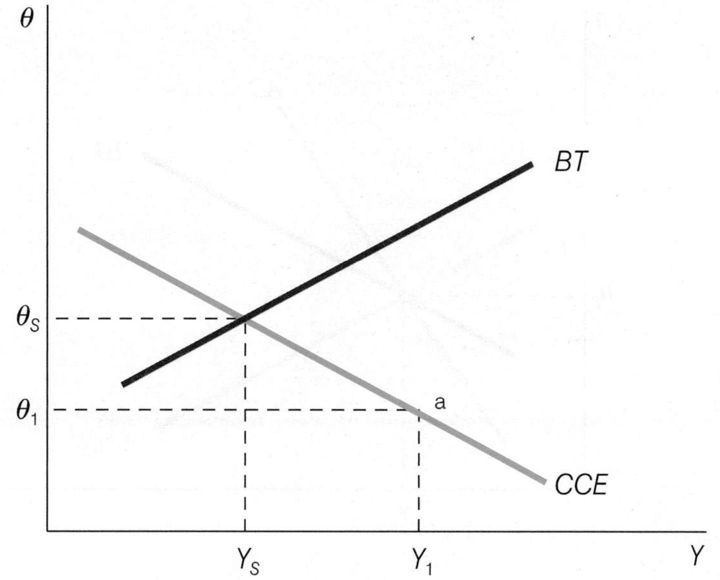

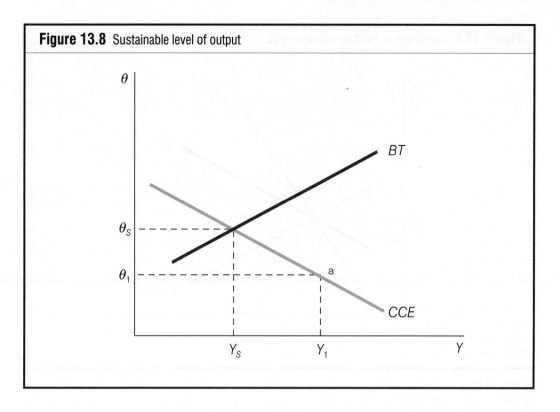

Persistent trade deficits will require persistent capital inflows, but interest must be paid on these. A balance of trade deficit is similar to borrowing from the rest of the world. If a deficit remains for a long period of time, the mounting interest rate payments place increasing pressure on the economy as the flow of interest payments overseas increases, which will require even more offsetting capital inflows.

Therefore, in the long run, the trade balance could well exert a constraint on the economy. Given that foreign borrowing cannot rise forever, and the burden of interest payments will become more and more acute, it is argued that eventually measures will have to be taken to restore the balance of trade. The obvious solution would be to simply let the exchange rate depreciate in order to improve competitiveness, but of course, this will lead to a movement along the CCE schedule, increasing the NAIRU.

The **sustainable level of output** is therefore where the CCE and BT curves intersect, shown by Y_S in Figure 13.8. This is regarded as a long-run point, where the economy is at its NAIRU, and the balance of trade is in equilibrium.

13

13.2.5 Equilibrium in the Salter-Swan model

Equilibrium in the open economy is where the AD, CCE and BT schedules intersect. This represents a position where the goods market is in equilibrium, output is at a level where unemployment is at the NAIRU and the trade balance is in equilibrium. This is shown in Figure 13.9, where the equilibrium level of output is Y_S and the equilibrium real exchange rate is θs.

The dynamics of this model are fairly simple. In the short run, the economy will always be on the AD schedule, which just represents a point where planned expenditures are equal to actual income.

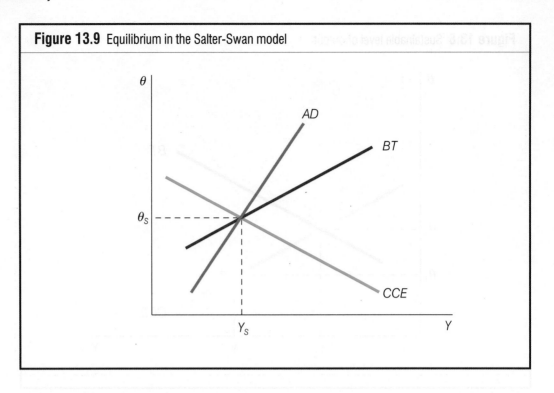

Figure 13.9 Equilibrium in the Salter-Swan model

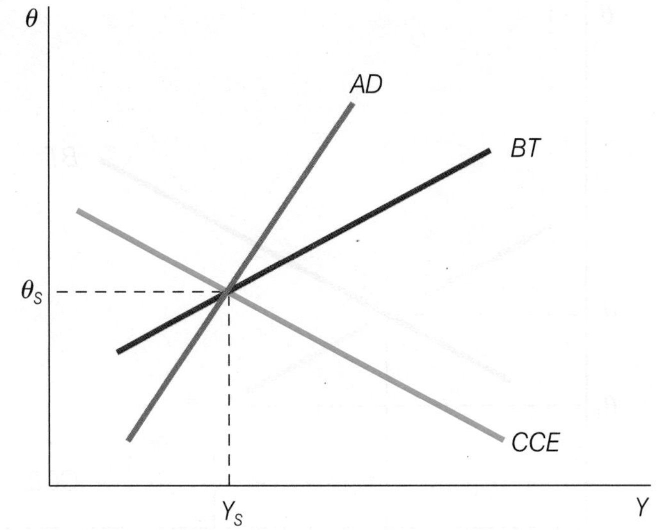

A position on the competing claims equilibrium (CCE) can be thought of as a long-run equilibrium point for the economy. In the short run, the economy can move off this schedule, but in the long run a movement in prices would be sufficient to push the economy back towards this schedule. If prices adjust slowly, then this might take some time.

In the very long run, the economy will also need to maintain the balance of trade equilibrium. If the economy is running a surplus or a deficit for a sustained period of time, it will either accumulate an increasing number of assets or liabilities, respectively, which are ultimately unsustainable. Therefore, the economy should end up on a position on the BT schedule.

Therefore, the long-run equilibrium of the economy is the sustainable level of output, Y_S.

13.3 Achieving a target level of output

13

Suppose the government had a target level of income such that $Y_T > Y_S$. In Figure 13.10, the government may aim to achieve this by a fiscal expansion, which will shift the AD schedule outwards ($AD_1 \rightarrow AD_2$) moving the economy from a to b.

At point b, though, the economy has moved to the right of the CCE schedule. This means that unemployment has been driven below the NAIRU, which will lead to upward pressure on both wages and prices. As prices begin to rise, the real exchange rate will begin to appreciate. As the adjustment in prices continues, the economy will move down the new AD schedule to point c. This is where AD_2 and the CCE schedules intersect.

Although output will fall as prices rise, output will still remain above its starting value. This implies that the fiscal expansion has led the economy to a position with higher output, but where unemployment is still at the NAIRU, so there is no suggestion that inflation will rise. However, the rise in income (by sucking in imports) and the real appreciation (by reducing competitiveness) will move the trade balance into deficit.

Figure 13.10 Achieving a target level of income

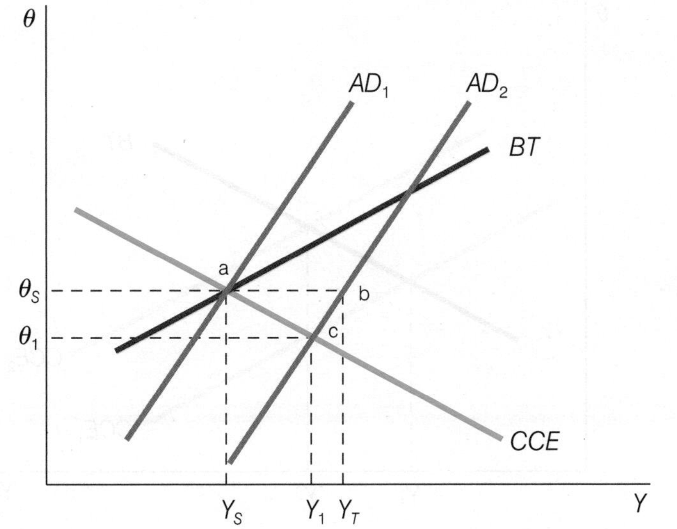

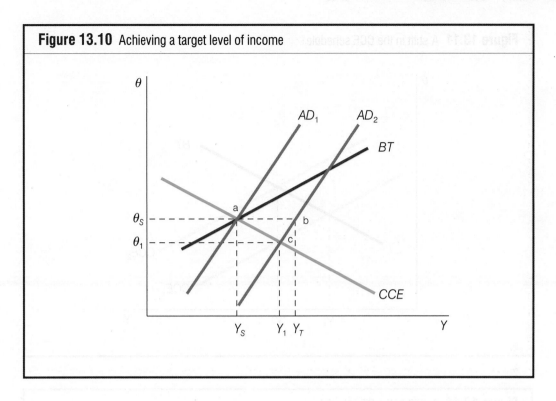

A deficit can be sustained for a considerable period of time by attracting capital inflows, so the fiscal expansion appears to have been successful in moving output towards a higher target. Over time, though, the economy will build up increasing foreign liabilities, which can only be stemmed by moving the trade balance back to equilibrium. Eventually, the exchange rate will have to depreciate to restore competitiveness, which will move the economy back along the CCE schedule to point a, where output is restored to the sustainable level, Y_S.

As the economy will always return to its sustainable level of output, it is clear that the only way to permanently achieve the target level of income would be through a shift in either or both the CCE and BT schedules, so that the sustainable level of output coincides with its target ($Y_S \rightarrow Y_T$).

Shifting the CCE schedule

Looking at Figure 13.11, if the CCE schedule shifts to the right ($CCE_1 \rightarrow CCE_2$), then a lower NAIRU results at each real exchange rate. The sustainable level of output will increase from Y_1^S to Y_2^S.

The same things which led to an outward shift in the long-run aggregate supply schedule will lead to an outward shift in the CCE. These were discussed in some detail in Chapter 8. Any policy that leads to an upward shift in the PRW schedule other than an exchange rate appreciation, or an inward shift in the BRW, would achieve a lower NAIRU. Long-run aggregate supply would therefore be greater at every exchange rate.

Shifting the BT schedule

If the BT schedule shifts to the right ($BT_1 \rightarrow BT_2$), then it implies that the trade balance will remain in equilibrium at an appreciated exchange rate. Therefore, the sustainable level of output will increase ($Y_1^S \rightarrow Y_2^S$), as shown in Figure 13.12.

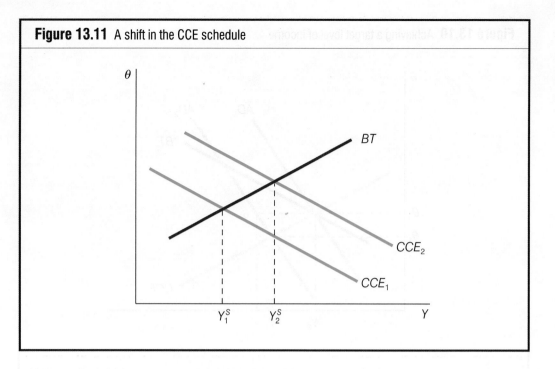

Figure 13.11 A shift in the CCE schedule

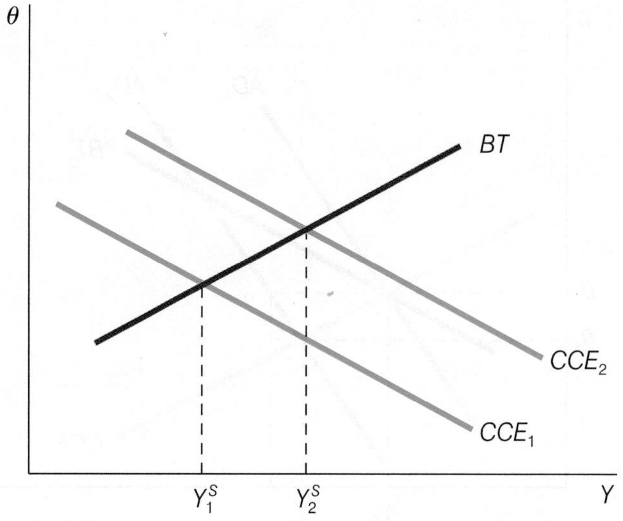

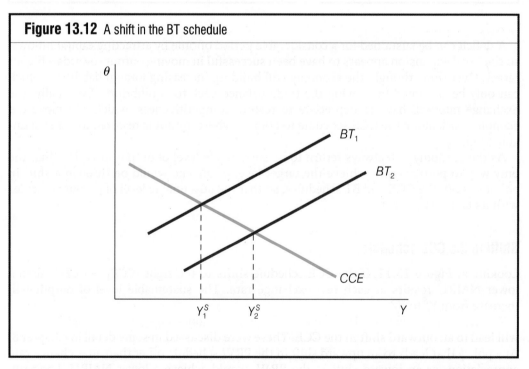

Figure 13.12 A shift in the BT schedule

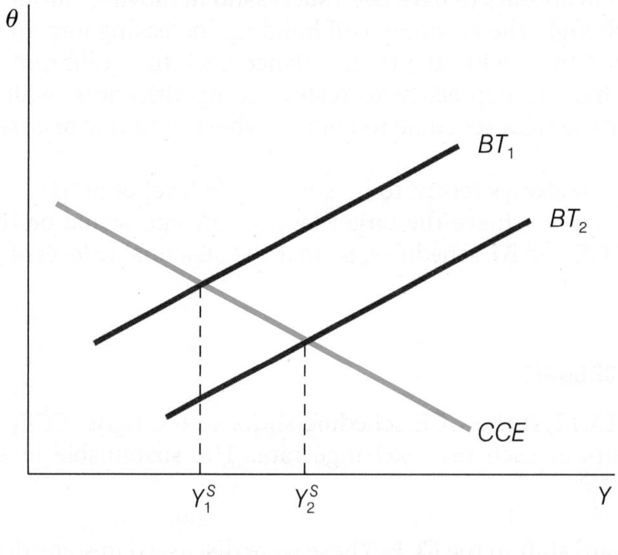

In the previous chapter, we have already investigated what factors might lead to a shift in the BT schedule. Such a shift will result from any factor other than a change in the real exchange rate, which leads to either a rise in exports or a fall in imports. One example might be an increase in foreign income, Y^*. Alternatively, a rising preference for domestic goods (increasing x_{Y^*} or a decreasing m_Y) will produce this shift. This could come through improving the non-price competitiveness of goods. For example by:

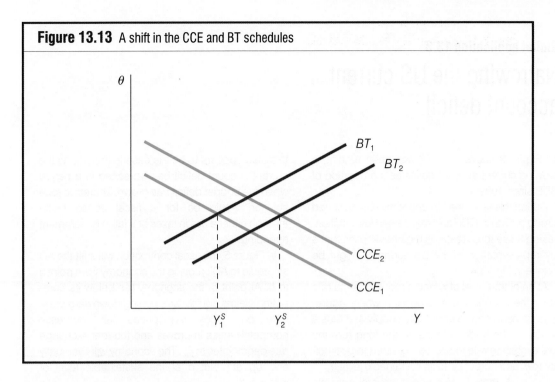

Figure 13.13 A shift in the CCE and BT schedules

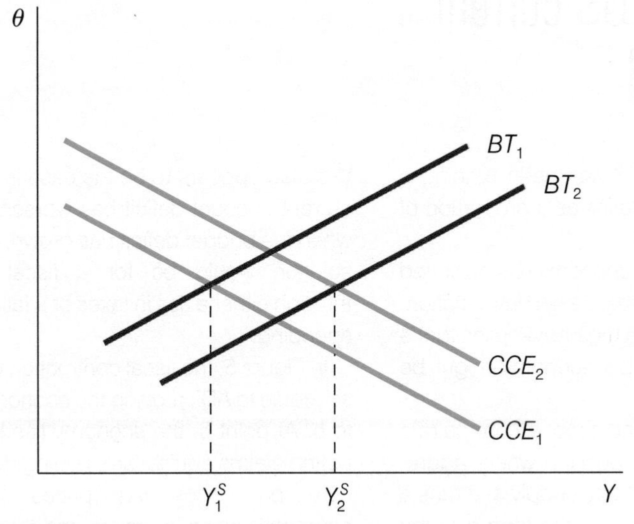

- better advertising of domestic products through trade fairs
- encouraging innovation to improve the quality and design of domestic goods
- improving after sales services.

Shifting the CCE and the BT schedules

As Figure 13.13 shows, an increase in the sustainable level of output will result if both curves shift accordingly. It could certainly be the case that policies aimed at shifting one curve could shift the other. For example, government spending on education and training may improve labour productivity (CCE shifts right), but also lead to the development of better designed products that are more competitive in world markets (BT shifts right).

Global application 13.3

Narrowing the US current account deficit

As Figure 3 shows, the US has been running a growing current account deficit as a proportion of GDP since 1992.

During this time, the US economy has exhibited strong growth in GDP and maintained low inflation. Taking these three features together implies that a fair representation of the US economy might be point *a* in Figure 4.

At an output level of Y_1 and a real exchange rate of θ_1, the economy is in a position where aggregate demand equals aggregate supply, but runs a deficit on the trade balance. In the long run, the real exchange rate would be expected to depreciate to θ_S and output fall to its sustainable level, Y_S.

Figure 4, though, also shows several possible options that US policy makers can implement to correct the trade deficit.

A fiscal consolidation

In Chapter 11, the concept of the 'twin deficits' implied that current account deficits were often synonymous with fiscal deficits. In recent times, this also appears to be the case in the US, as the current account deficit has worsened in a period when the budget deficit has grown. Therefore, one solution would be for a fiscal consolidation through either a rise in taxes or a fall in government spending.

In Figure 5, the fiscal contraction will shift the AD schedule to AD', moving the economy from point *a* to *b*. At point *b*, the economy lies below its competing claims equilibrium, putting downward pressure on prices. As prices fall, domestic competitiveness improves and the real exchange rate depreciates to θ_S. The economy will eventually end up at point *c* at the sustainable level of income, Y_S.

Shifting the BT schedule

As Figure 6 shows, an outward shift in the BT schedule enables the economy to remain at point *a* while improving its external position. This would obviously be the most preferable option as output is sustained at Y_1.

Figure 3 US current account deficit as a percentage of GDP

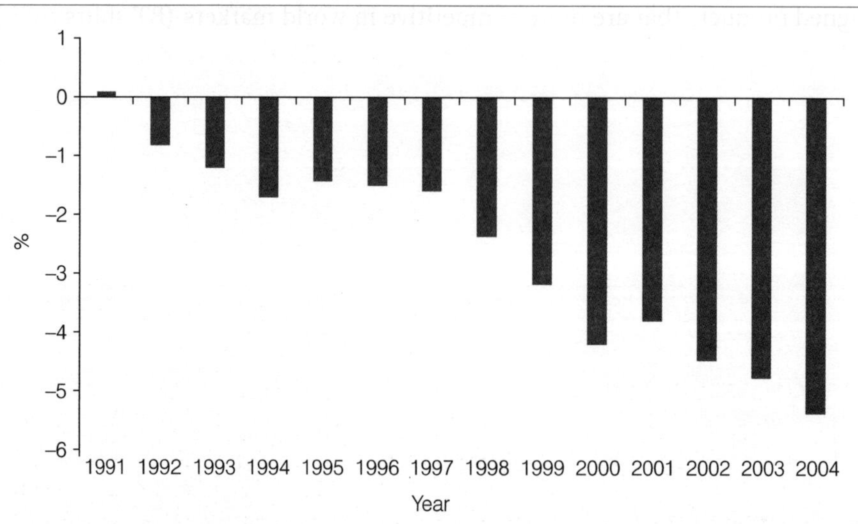

13

Global application 13.3 (continued)

Figure 4 Current and sustainable levels of output in the US economy

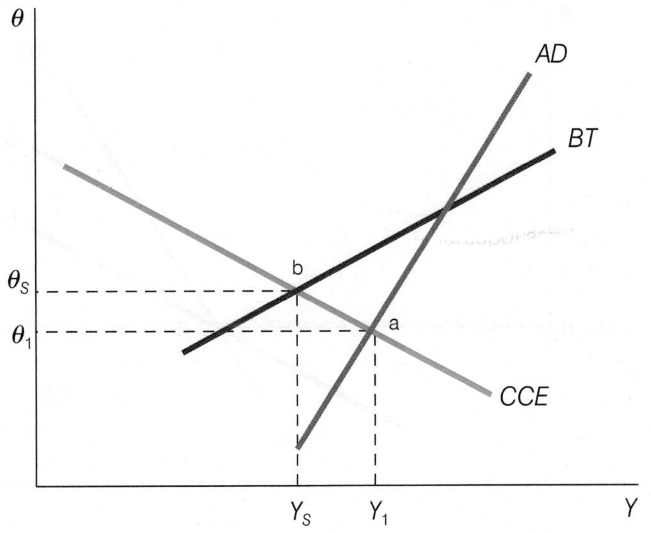

Figure 5 A fiscal consolidation

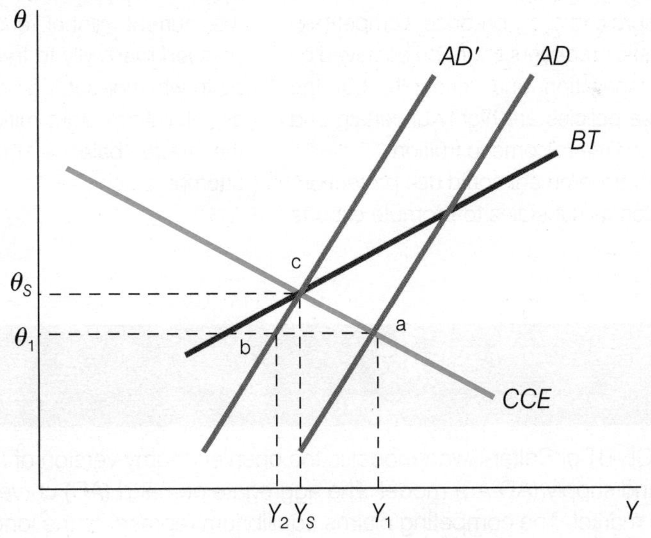

There are various ways in which this can be achieved. First, aggregate demand and economic growth in the major economies of Europe and Japan have been weak. If growth in these regions picks up, then the US would expect to see an increase in exports and an outward shift in the BT schedule. If policy makers in these nations were successful in improving economic growth, it would

Global application 13.3 (continued)

Figure 6 Shifting the BT schedule to correct a trade deficit

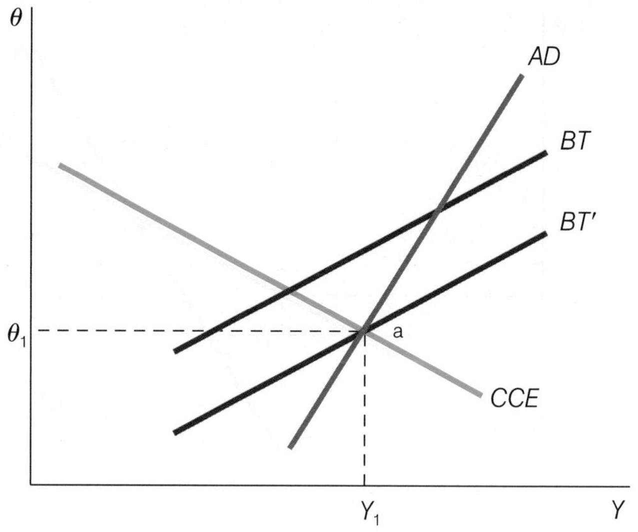

mitigate some of the need for action to correct the US trade deficit.

Second, improving the non-price competitiveness of domestic producers might be achieved by encouraging innovation and research, but the results of these policies are highly uncertain and may take a long time to come to fruition.

Third, the US government could use protectionist policies, such as subsidies to promote exports or tariffs and quotas to reduce imports. It is unlikely that such a policy could be seriously considered in the current global economy, which has progressed markedly to freer trade. It is also unclear as to whether such a policy could be successful, as retaliation might mitigate any improvement to the trade balance that protectionist policies attempt to achieve.

Summary

- The AD-CCE-BT or Salter-Swan model is the open economy version of the traditional aggregate demand and supply (AD-AS) model. The aggregate demand (AD) curve reflects equilibrium in the goods market. The competing claims equilibrium represents the long-run aggregate supply curve consistent with the NAIRU and with the BT schedule, when the trade balance is in equilibrium.
- In an open economy, the domestic price level will consist of goods and services imported from overseas. Therefore, foreign goods prices and changes in the nominal exchange rate can pass through into the domestic price level.

- In an open economy, the NAIRU is not unique but depends on the prevailing real exchange rate. A real exchange rate appreciation lowers the cost of foreign goods and puts downward pressure on the domestic exchange rate. This enables a lower rate of domestic unemployment to be achieved while maintaining overall price stability.
- The trade balance forms a long-run constraint on the level of output. The sustainable level of output is where the BT and CCE schedules intersect. Maintaining a target level of income requires either a shift in the CCE, BT or both schedules.

Key terms

Aggregate demand (AD) schedule
Aggregate supply (AS) schedule
Balance of trade/trade balance (BT)
Competing claims equilibrium (CCE)
Competitiveness
Salter-Swan (AD-CCE-BT) model
Sustainable level of output

Review questions

1. How is the NAIRU determined in an open economy?
2. What factors determine the slope of the long-run aggregate supply curve?
3. Can shifts in aggregate demand permanently alter the NAIRU?
4. An economy is currently in a position characterized by stable prices and a trade surplus.
   a. Use the AD-CCE-BT model to represent this economy.
   b. What is the long-run sustainable level of output in this economy? Explain how the economy might move to this level of output.
5. Using the AD-CCE-BT model, what would be the short-run and long-run effects of the following:
   a. an increase in consumer confidence
   b. a positive productivity shock
   c. a tariff on all imports
   d. an increase in the domestic money supply
   e. an increase in global demand
   f. a fall in the level of the workforce?
6. Under what conditions will movements in the exchange rate have a large effect on the domestic price level?

More advanced problems

7. Is there a three-way trade-off between unemployment, inflation and the trade balance?
8. 'Whether an economy is open or closed, the gap between actual and equilibrium unemployment can be inferred from the change in inflation.' Discuss.
9. Explain how temporary movements in the real exchange rate might generate permanent effects on the trade balance. Using the AD-CCE-BT model, explain what implications this effect will have on the sustainable level of output following a fiscal expansion.

For further resources, visit
http://www.thomsonlearning.co.uk/chamberlin_yueh

Part VII

International financial architecture

Continuing from the previous part, the focus in this part is on several extensions of the empirical analysis of open economies. The choice of exchange rate regimes and international policy coordination are covered. This is followed by an analysis of the developments in international financial markets and models of currency crises.

14 Exchange rate regimes and international policy coordination

Learning objectives

- Determine the advantages and disadvantages of different exchange rate regimes; namely, fixed and floating
- Investigate the subject of international policy coordination, for in an open economy, policies or shocks specific to one country can be transmitted to others
- Understand the concept of optimal currency areas (OCA) and recent examples such as the European Monetary Union (EMU), and the establishment of a single currency in Europe (the euro)

14.1 Introduction

This chapter investigates three topics on how policy makers manage the international aspects of their economy. These are: the type of exchange rate regime, international policy coordination and monetary union. Over the last 25 years, each of these has been an important consideration for most developed nations.

There are effectively two types of exchange rate regime: fixed and floating. In previous chapters, we have discussed what each involves. Each offers advantages and disadvantages in terms of enabling policy makers to reach their goals. The choice of regime has been an ongoing issue for the past century.

The subject of international policy coordination has become increasingly important. In an open economy it is clear that policies or shocks specific to one country can be transmitted to others. One possible channel is through exchange rate movements. Also, as economies become more open, they become more dependent on the state of global demand. A phrase that is often heard is, 'if America sneezes, the rest of the world catches a cold'. This reflects the importance of a large, economically developed country like the US in global terms. A weak US economy will have external effects on other countries.

Finally, the topic of optimal currency areas (OCA) is covered. With the recent development of European Monetary Union (EMU) and the establishment of a single currency in Europe (the euro) this has been important. There are several remaining issues that deserve investigation. EMU represents one of the final steps to completing a single market in Europe. However, the federal structure of the US has effectively experienced a monetary union among its states for centuries. It will be interesting to see if the euro can be as successful as the dollar in this manner. In addition, several nations – most notably the UK – have abstained from participating in EMU. For these countries, the theory of optimal currency areas is particularly important.

14.2 The choice of exchange rate regime

What factors might determine whether or not policy makers opt to fix the exchange rate at a given level against another currency, or let it float, allowing its value to be determined by market forces? The answer is essentially the regime that policy makers feel will most realistically achieve their economic goals.

Historically, the main goal of governments has been to achieve high and stable economic growth. It is from high, long-term economic growth that living standards are improved. The role of government therefore is to manage the economy in order to engineer the conditions that will best achieve this.

Exchange rate stability

It has already been shown that in the short run, there is substantial volatility in the nominal exchange rate. This could act as an impediment to the cross-border movement of goods and services, and of capital. If exchange rates are continuously changing, then there are risks and uncertainties when undertaking contracts that involve a foreign exchange transaction. This might be sufficient to prevent otherwise valuable trade from occurring. Also, exchange rate instability poses high search costs on consumers, who must not only learn to reckon with prices being quoted in different currencies but also that the rate of exchange between these currencies is constantly in flux. These high search costs also might prevent trade and lower consumer welfare.

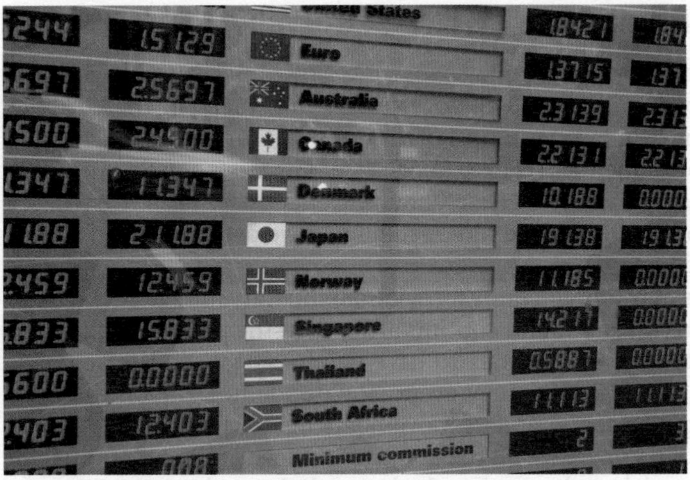

Exchange rates Sterling: will EMU increase stability?
Source: Dominc Burke/Alamy

Exchange rate instability therefore is a possible impediment preventing the welfare gains from trade from being realized. It is argued that every 1 per cent increase in trade leads to 1/3 per cent increase in output (HM Treasury assessment on the euro). Therefore, exchange rate stability is seen as an important element of promoting trade-related growth.

Price (inflation) stability

Conventionally, long-term economic growth requires long-term productivity growth, which in turn relies on long-term investment. In order to calculate the returns to an investment, the value of future expected cash flows must be evaluated, and this becomes very difficult when prices are constantly changing. For this reason, price stability is deemed to be necessary for long-term investments, as costs and revenues have to be accurately measured over a long-time horizon.

Over the last 30 years, the control of inflation typically has been the overarching objective of economic policy. During this period, economic growth has been continually interrupted by spates of inflation and this has led to less stability, stop-go economic policy and, arguably, lower trend growth.

Output (business cycle) stability

Economic fluctuations in themselves can be painful, particularly the welfare costs associated with high unemployment. Therefore, maintaining output at its full employment level is often thought to be desirable. In addition, short-term output instability can be very persistent and detrimental to long-term growth. The process by which short-term shocks are propagated into the long run is known as hysteresis. For example, in a recession, unemployed labour loses skills and firms cut back on investment – both of which will have an effect on the long-term growth path of the economy. Therefore, short-run output instability is painful in its own right, but could also provoke more severe long-term consequences for economic growth.

It is likely that different policy makers will attach a different degree of relative importance to each of these. The type of exchange rate regime adopted therefore may be the one that is most likely to be successful in meeting the policy maker's priorities. An evaluation of the advantages and disadvantages of each type of exchange rate regime can be couched in terms of its ability to meet the three objectives of exchange rate stability, price (inflation) stability and output (business cycle) stability.

Exchange rate stability and regime choice

The question of regime choice with respect to exchange rate volatility is fairly trivial; it is obvious that a fixed regime will win here. The government intervenes in the currency markets to offset changes in the demand and supply of the domestic currency, which would otherwise lead to significant movements in the exchange rate. There is, though, one qualification to this. In the next chapter, when analysing how currency crises form, we will see that some of the largest episodes of exchange rate instability have occurred when a fixed exchange rate regime breaks down.

Fixed exchange rate regimes may therefore only provide a temporary mirage of exchange rate stability. If pressures on a currency build continuously, then the policies required to maintain a fixed exchange rate regime may start to have painful effects on the domestic economy. In such situations, policy makers may eventually decide to abandon the fixed regime, at which point there can be very dramatic movements in the currency.

What effect will the choice of regime have on the ability to achieve price and output stability? The Mundell-Fleming model can be used to shed some light on this question.

Price stability and regime choice

A traditional reason for maintaining a fixed exchange rate is in order to control inflation. UK membership of the exchange rate mechanism (ERM) basically involved fixing the pound against the Deutschmark (DM), but was solely motivated to try and import low levels of West German inflation. Mexico has recently tried to fix the value of the peso against the US dollar, the aim of which is to demonstrate a commitment to low inflation. There are two reasons why this is the case.

First, and most obviously, once a country commits to fixing its exchange rate it gives up control of monetary policy. The quantity theory of money argues that:

$$Mv = PY$$

where M is the money stock, v the velocity of circulation, P the price level, and Y the level of output. It is assumed that the velocity of circulation is fixed, and that output is always at its equilibrium of full employment level. In this case, it stands that:

$$\%\Delta M = \%\Delta P$$

Changes in the money supply will have directly proportional effects on prices.

Under a floating exchange rate regime, policy makers may undertake a monetary expansion in order to stimulate the economy. If there are some price rigidities, they may be successful in raising output in the short run, but ultimately the predictions of the quantity theory of money hold true in that output stays at the natural level and prices rise.

This is shown in Figure 14.1. The economy starts off at point *a*. Following a monetary expansion, the LM curve will shift downwards from LM_1 to LM_2, moving the economy to point *b* where the interest rate has fallen to r_1. The lower interest rate will encourage investment and output will improve to Y_1. However, because the domestic interest rate has fallen below the overseas rate, capital outflows will depreciate the nominal (E) and real (θ) exchange rate, improving competitiveness and shifting the ISXM schedule outwards as net exports improve. The economy will move to *c*, where output is now substantially higher at Y_2.

However, this point is unsustainable. As output has moved above the full employment level, there will be upward pressure on prices (P). As a result, the real money supply will fall, shifting the LM schedule back to LM_1. Rising prices will also diminish competitiveness through a real exchange rate appreciation shifting the ISXM schedule backwards. Eventually, as prices increase, the economy will move back to point *a* where it started.

Figure 14.1a Monetary policy with a floating exchange rate

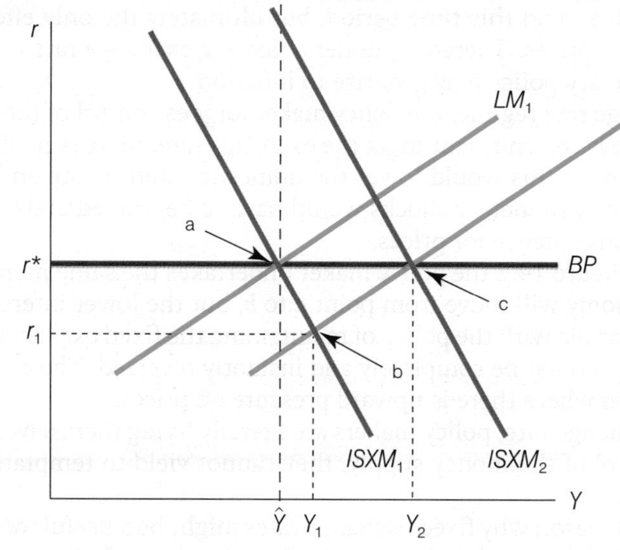

Figure 14.1b Dynamics

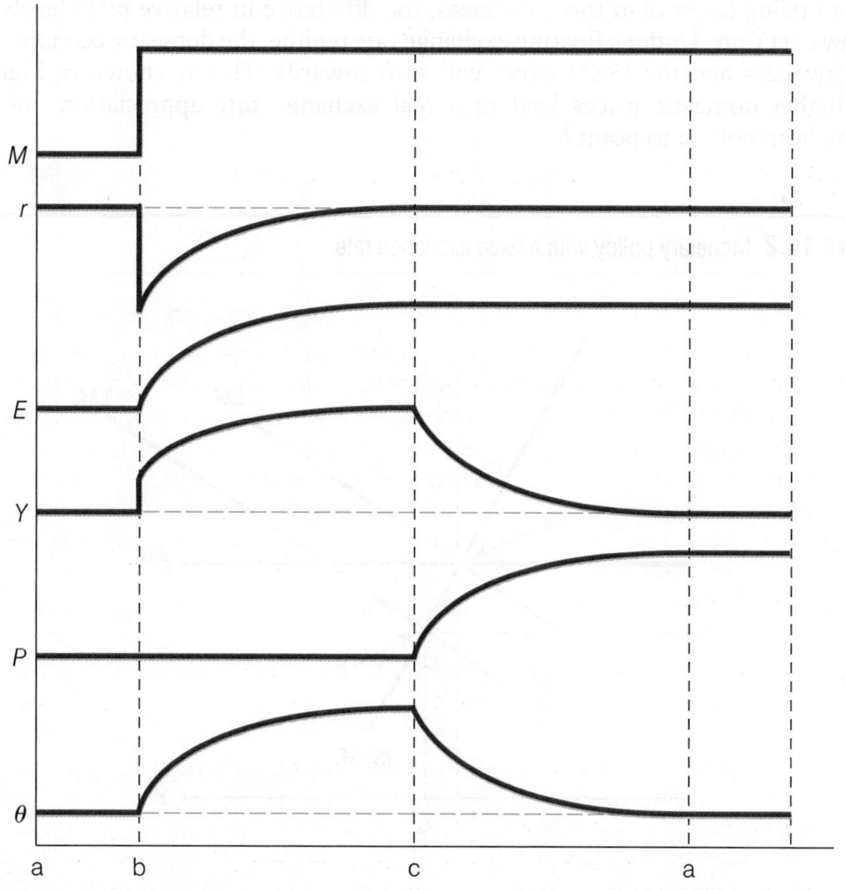

If prices adjust quickly, then the economy will move rapidly through points *b* and *c*, and output will only deviate from its full employment level for a short while. Slower movements in prices will extend this time period, but ultimately the only effect of the money expansion will be on prices. Therefore, under a floating exchange rate regime, the discretionary use of monetary policy may give rise to inflation.

In a fixed exchange rate regime, the policy maker forgoes control of the domestic money supply. While there is commitment to fix the exchange rate, there is no liberty to launch a monetary expansion, as this would lower the domestic interest rate and then depreciate the exchange rate. Any monetary shocks would have to be immediately offset, and therefore will have no consequence for prices.

For example, in Figure 14.2 the policy maker undertakes the same monetary expansion. As before, the economy will move from point *a* to *b*, but the lower interest rate at point *b* would not be compatible with the policy of maintaining the fixed exchange rate. Therefore, the money expansion must be completely and instantly reversed. The economy will never move into a position where there is upward pressure on prices.

By fixing the exchange rate, policy makers are literally 'tying themselves to the mast'. By giving up the control of the money supply, they cannot yield to temptation and generate inflationary shocks.

There is a second reason why fixed exchange rates might be a useful tool for establishing low inflation. This is connected with the general maxim that inflation rates cannot permanently differ between two nations who have fixed their exchange rates. This will give the high inflation country an opportunity to import the low inflation from the country with lower inflation.

For example, suppose domestic inflation exceeded that from overseas. As domestic prices are rising faster than those overseas, the difference in relative price levels ($P - P^*$) will grow over time. Under a floating exchange rate regime, the domestic economy will lose competitiveness and the ISXM curve will shift inwards. This is shown in Figure 14.3, where higher domestic prices lead to a real exchange rate appreciation, moving the economy from point *a* to point *b*.

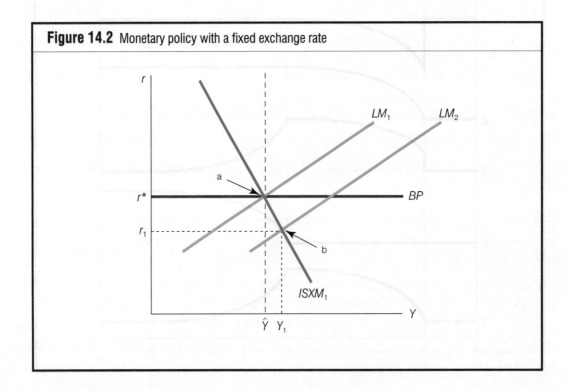

Figure 14.2 Monetary policy with a fixed exchange rate

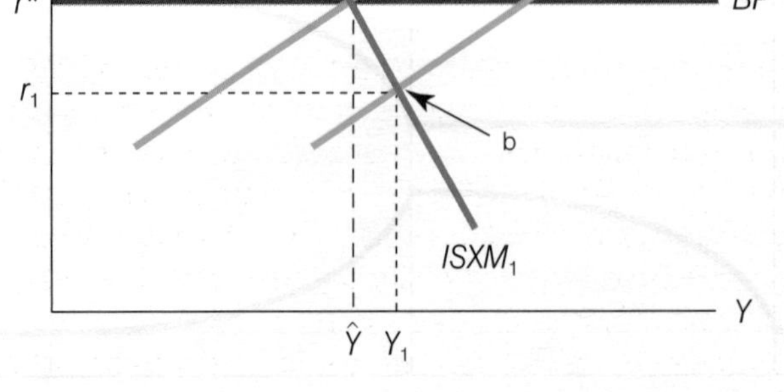

14

Figure 14.3 Differential inflation rates and flexible exchange rates

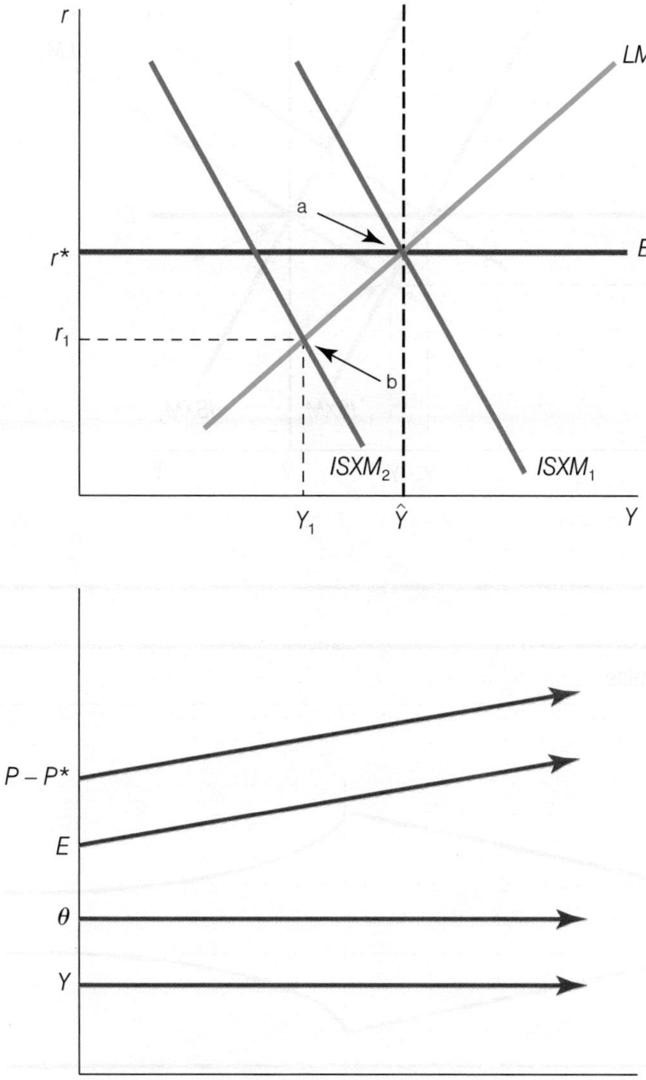

However, as the ISXM schedule shifts inwards, the domestic interest rate falls below the foreign interest rate. As a result, the domestic currency will depreciate and competitiveness will be restored. The economy will then move back to point *a*. It is clear that in a floating exchange rate system, domestic inflation can remain permanently above overseas inflation without any adverse effect on domestic output. This is because domestic competitiveness is continually restored by a depreciating currency. The real exchange rate and output level will be insulated from the inflation differential.

Under a fixed exchange rate regime, though, could a persistent inflation differential be maintained? This is investigated in Figure 14.4. Once again, if domestic inflation exceeded that overseas, then competitiveness would fall, shifting the ISXM curve inwards. However,

Figure 14.4a Inflation differences in a fixed exchange regime

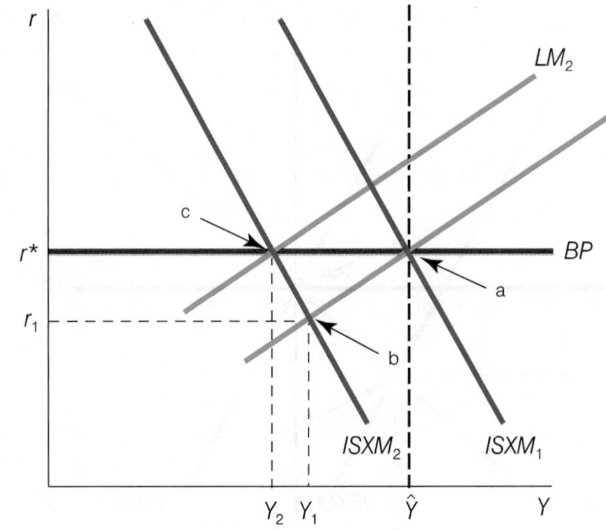

Figure 14.4b Dynamics

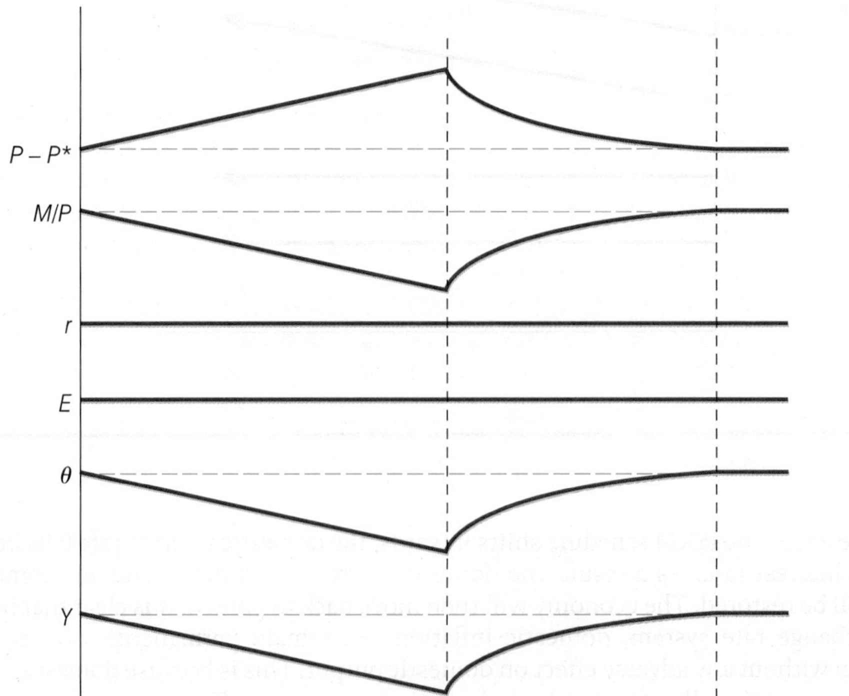

this would put downward pressure on the domestic interest rate leading to an exchange rate depreciation. Maintaining a fixed exchange rate would require a monetary contraction, the LM curve would shift upwards as well restore the domestic interest rate to r^*. The overall impact would be that the economy moves quickly through point *b* to point *c*, where output has fallen below its full employment level.

When output falls below its natural/full employment level, the economy enters a recession. Firms will accumulate unsold stocks of goods and, in order to clear these, will cut prices. Workers fearful of losing their jobs will be willing to accept lower wage awards. This has a knock-on effect on firm costs and then consumer prices. The domestic recession will therefore put downward pressure on domestic inflation. As prices fall, domestic competitiveness will be restored, shifting the ISXM curve outwards and the real money stock will begin to rise, pushing the LM schedule downwards. Overall, the economy will move from point *c* back towards point *a*. The recession in output will continue until there is price level convergence, at which point competitiveness is fully restored.

Membership of a fixed exchange rate regime can create and enforce inflation discipline. Firms are unlikely to increase prices if they know that the exchange rate will not depreciate in order to restore their competitiveness and workers are unlikely to push for higher wages if they know that the result of this will be lower competitiveness and higher unemployment. Therefore, by fixing the exchange rate against a low inflation country, the aim is simply to import that country's lower inflation into the domestic economy. As long as domestic inflation exceeds that from overseas, the domestic economy will suffer a loss in competitiveness that pushes output below its natural level.

Foreign price shocks

Suppose, though, that there is a price shock overseas. What would be the prediction for domestic inflation under both types of exchange rate regimes? A foreign price shock would improve the relative competitiveness of domestic products, shifting the ISXM schedule outwards.

The effects of this under a floating regime are shown in Figure 14.5. Here, the outward shift in the ISXM schedule would put upward pressure on the domestic interest rate leading to an exchange rate appreciation. This will then offset the shift in the ISXM schedule, returning the economy to its full employment level. In Figure 14.5, the economy will move from point *a* to *b*, but return to *a* almost immediately following the domestic exchange rate appreciation.

Essentially, what is happening here is that the exchange rate moves to insulate domestic inflation from the overseas price shock.

Remember from the theory of purchasing power parity (PPP):

$$\%\Delta P \approx \%\Delta E + \%\Delta P^*$$

The change in the domestic price level is approximately equal to the change in the foreign price level and the change in the nominal exchange rate.

Hence, if $-\%\Delta E = \%\Delta P^*$, then $\%\Delta P = 0$. The exchange rate appreciation is sufficient to offset the higher overseas price level.

Under a fixed regime, the economy will not experience the insulating effect of exchange rate movements. Instead, the foreign price shock would have to be accommodated by an expansionary monetary policy and would be transmitted directly into domestic prices. This is shown in Figure 14.6.

The foreign price shock would improve domestic competitiveness and shift the ISXM schedule outwards, pushing up the domestic interest rate. To prevent the exchange rate from appreciating, the monetary authority would need to expand the domestic money supply in order to return the domestic interest rate to the overseas rate. The consequence

14

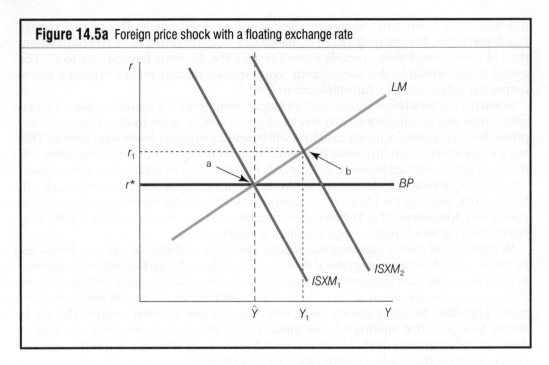

Figure 14.5a Foreign price shock with a floating exchange rate

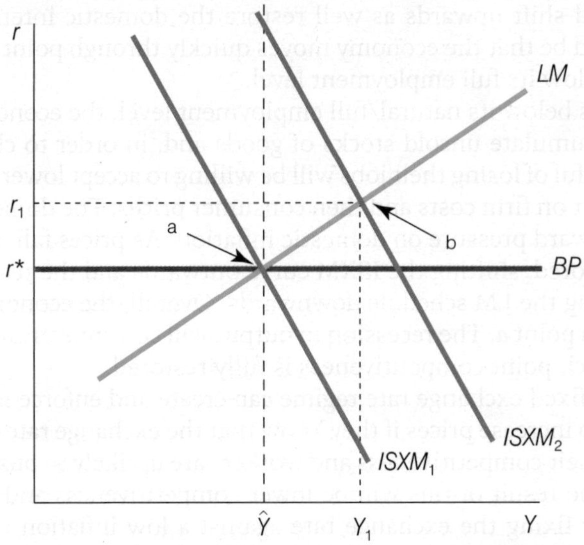

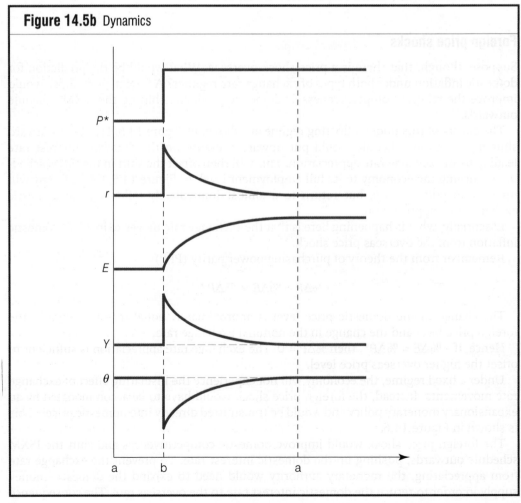

Figure 14.5b Dynamics

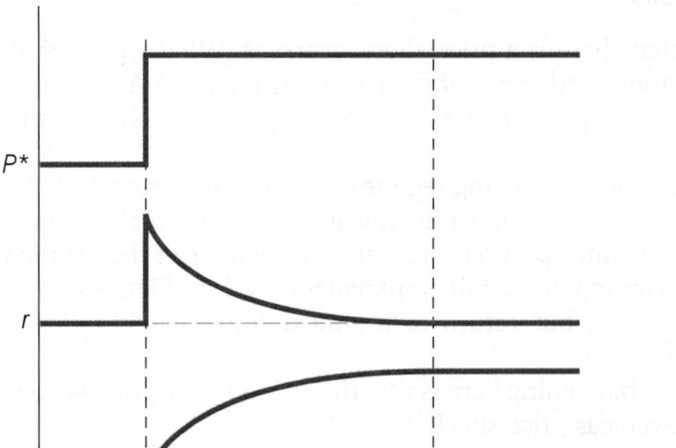

Global application 14.1

Why did Britain join the ERM?

The decision to join the European exchange rate mechanism (ERM) in 1990 put exchange rate targeting at the centre of monetary policy. In the years preceding entry, the rate of inflation had steadily risen in the UK economy. This had been fuelled by a rapid expansion in aggregate demand through falling unemployment, rising house prices, income tax cuts and the greater availability of credit. This had been allowed to go unchecked due to the belief that supply side reforms would enable the economy to operate at higher levels of output without producing inflationary pressures. However, during 1990, inflation reached double digits and it was clear that economic policy would have to respond to an overheating economy.

The decision to join the ERM represented the necessary policy response to control inflation. The UK pound was fixed against the German Deutschmark, with central banks obliged to intervene in the currency markets to keep the exchange rate within the bounds, £1:DM 2.77 and £1:DM 3.13. This was to control inflation in three ways.

1. Under the ERM, monetary policy was required in order to maintain the fixed exchange rate against the DM. As long as the private sector believed that membership of the ERM was credible, it implied that the government was unlikely to use monetary policy in order to inflate the economy. Therefore, government announcements of low policy inflation gained credibility because reneging would compromise ERM membership, and given that the government had put this as the cornerstone of its monetary policy, the government would face a high political and reputation cost. The time inconsistency problems that hindered monetary policy in the early 1980s could be avoided and low inflation expectations maintained.
2. The German Bundesbank had a strong reputation for being tough on inflation, and German inflation rates had been, on average, significantly lower than those in the UK. Fixing the £–DM exchange rate then allowed the UK government to gain some of the Bundesbank's low inflation credibility. If UK inflation rates exceeded those in Germany, then pressure would mount for a sterling depreciation, which the UK government would be obliged to offset using tighter monetary policy (higher interest rates). As long as the private sector was aware of this, inflation expectations would be anchored to German levels.
3. The above two mechanisms both work by manipulating expectations of inflation, which would then feed into wage bargains and actual inflation. There was, however, also a direct effect of ERM entry on prices. The rate of exchange that the UK entered at was widely considered to be at a high or appreciated level. One effect of this is that imported goods would be cheaper, and as a consequence, the overall inflation rate in the economy would fall. Second, the appreciated exchange rate would put domestic firms at a competitive disadvantage vis-à-vis European firms. As a result, they would be forced to cut costs and margins in order to remain competitive, which would also lower inflation. In addition, knowing that domestic firms were under strong competitive pressures would put pressure on workers to restrain wage demands.

Looking at Figure 1, the empirical evidence is clear that ERM membership coincided with a reduction in UK inflation. However, membership also brought other pressures on the economy that would ultimately make continued membership unsustainable. This story is continued in the next chapter where the reasons underlying the pound's exit from the ERM in September 1992, on a day known as 'Black Wednesday', is covered in detail.

Global application 14.1 (continued)

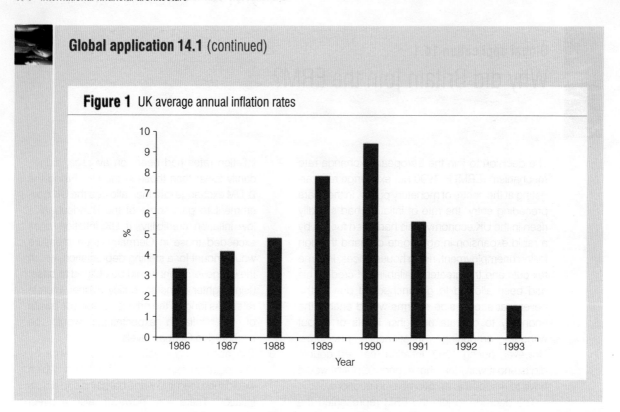

Figure 1 UK average annual inflation rates

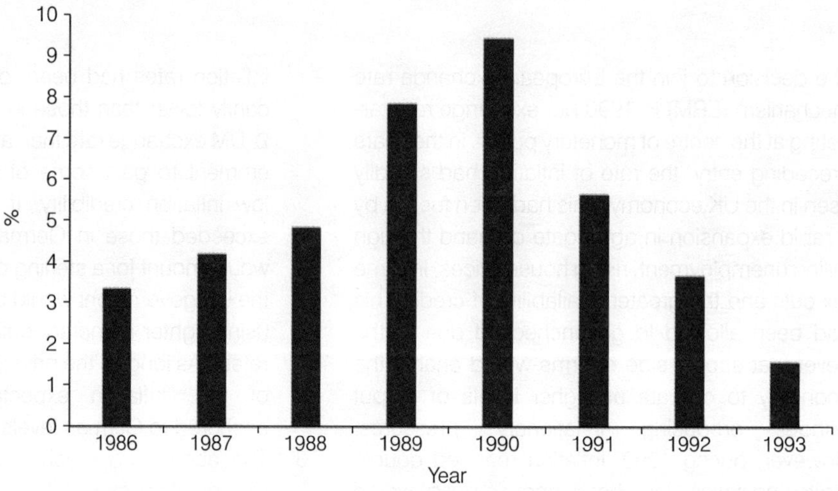

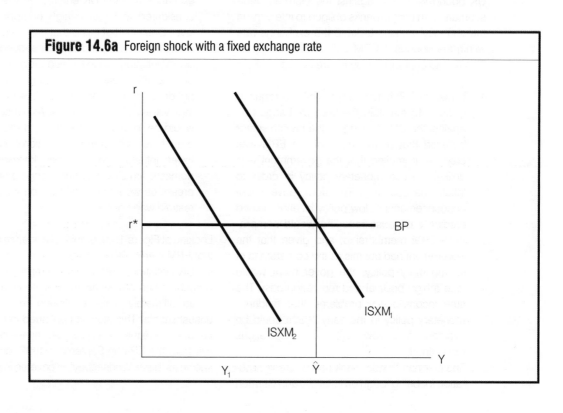

Figure 14.6a Foreign shock with a fixed exchange rate

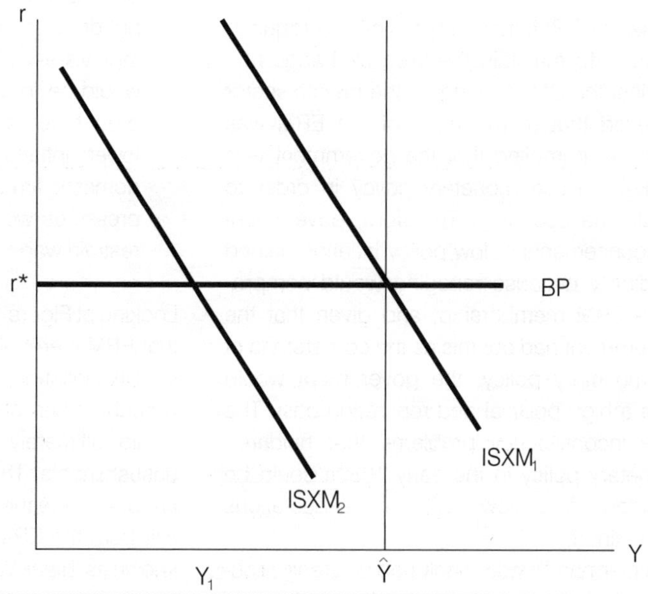

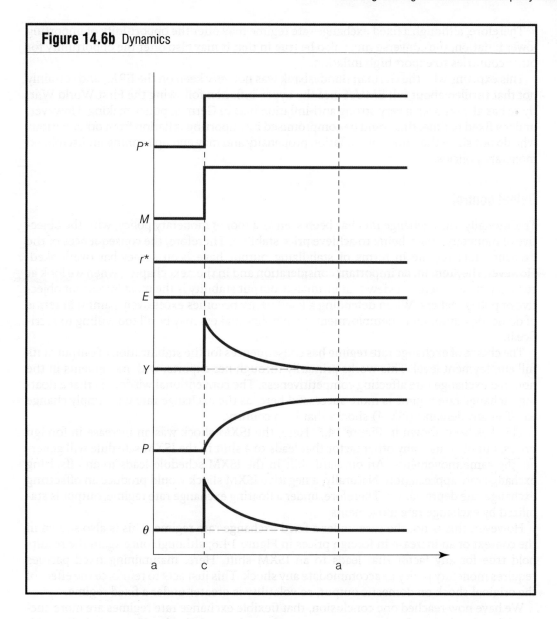

Figure 14.6b Dynamics

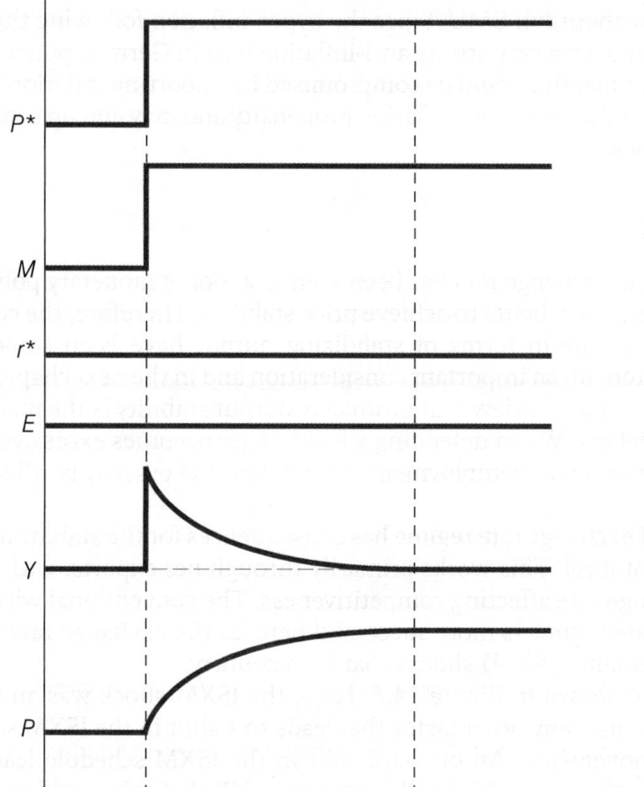

of these actions is that the economy will move quickly from point *a* to point *c* and output will expand in the short run to Y_1 and then Y_2.

As output now lies above its natural level, there will be upward pressure on prices which over time, by reducing competitiveness and the real money stock, will move the economy back to its initial starting point *a*. The only long-run difference is that the overseas price shock has been absorbed into the domestic price level.

This can once again be seen by looking at the relative PPP equation.

$$\text{If } \%\Delta P \approx \%\Delta E + \%\Delta P^*$$

then under a fixed regime, it must be the case that $\%\Delta E = 0$,
and

$$\%\Delta P \approx \%\Delta P^*$$

Therefore, although a fixed exchange rate regime may offer the opportunity of importing lower inflation, the converse must also be true in that it may also offer the opportunity for other countries to export high inflation.

This explains why the German Bundesbank was not very keen on the ERM, and certainly not that thrilled about full EMU. Since the hyper-inflation following the First World War, there has always been a very strong anti-inflation bias in German policy making. However, under a fixed regime, this could be compromised by importing inflation from other nations who do not share the same anti-inflation propensity and may end up running undisciplined monetary policies.

Output control

Traditionally, the exchange rate has been seen as a tool of monetary policy, with the objective of monetary policy being to achieve price stability. Therefore, the consequences of the exchange rate regime in terms of stabilizing output have been somewhat overlooked. However, they remain an important consideration and in the next chapter, when we look at currency crises, there is a view that ultimately output stability is the most important objective of policy makers. When defending a fixed parity becomes excessively painful in terms of domestic output and unemployment, then policy makers may be all too willing to sacrifice it.

The choice of exchange rate regime has consequences for the stabilization of output at its full employment level. This works primarily through net exports, with movements in the nominal exchange rate affecting competitiveness. The conventional wisdom is that a floating exchange rate regime is more successful here, as the exchange rate will simply change to offset any demand (ISXM) shocks that hit a country.

This has been shown in Figure 14.5. Here, the ISXM shock was an increase in foreign prices, but obviously any other factor that leads to a shift in the ISXM schedule will generate the same movements. An outward shift in the ISXM schedule leads to an offsetting exchange rate appreciation. Naturally, a negative ISXM shock would produce an offsetting exchange rate depreciation. Therefore, under a floating exchange rate regime, output is stabilized by exchange rate movements.

However, this is not the case under a fixed exchange rate regime. This is also shown in the context of an increase in foreign prices in Figure 14.6, although once again the results hold true for any factor that leads to an ISXM shift. Here, maintaining fixed parities requires monetary policy to accommodate any shock. This just acts to reinforce the effect of the original shock on domestic output, so volatility is greater under a fixed regime.

We have now reached one conclusion, that flexible exchange rate regimes are more successful at insulating the domestic economy from demand shocks. However, it is worth bearing in mind that not all shocks affecting output are necessarily demand shocks; although it is reasonable to argue that these are the most important. A monetary shock will lead to a shift in the LM schedule, which via its effect on the domestic interest rate, can have implications for output.

Figure 14.1 mapped out the path the economy takes when there is a monetary shock under a floating exchange rate regime. The expansion in the domestic money supply lowered the domestic rate of interest and increased output by stimulating investment. In addition, the corresponding exchange rate depreciation then amplified this initial increase in output. Under a fixed regime though, as shown in Figure 14.2, this monetary shock would be offset completely by the actions of the monetary authority.

Therefore, it appears that a second valid conclusion is that countries which are prone to monetary (LM) shocks are more likely to be successful in stabilizing output with a fixed exchange rate regime.

Global application 14.2

Historical examples of fixed exchange rate regimes

Gold Standard: 1870–1914

The Gold Standard was a mechanism for ensuring that exchange rates remained fixed.

Under the Gold Standard, each central bank acted to fix its currency in terms of gold; i.e., a unit of currency would purchase a number of grams of gold. This meant that all currency was fully convertible into gold and all currency in circulation was backed by gold reserves held at the central bank.

As the world supply of gold is fixed, it would constrain monetary policy. A government that printed money would no longer be able to maintain its parity. Because all currencies were fixed against a certain amount of gold, exchange rates between the currencies were de facto fixed. As long as the gold parity was maintained, the rate of exchange between two currencies would remain constant.

The main threat to the operation of the Gold Standard would arise when there were balance of payments disequilibria. No adjustment would result from a movement in the nominal exchange rate, so a country running a deficit would see a large outflow of gold and would have no choice but to devalue its exchange rate. However, the Gold Standard contained a mechanism that was supposed to prevent persistent balance of permanents disequilibria from occurring. This was known as the *price-specie flow* mechanism.

A deficit on the balance of payments would imply outflows of gold. This would lower the monetary base and put downward pressure on the domestic inflation rate. This, in turn, would restore competitiveness and correct the deficit. Likewise, a balance of payments surplus implies gold inflows, higher prices and lower competitiveness. Although the nominal exchange rate remained fixed, movements in the price level enabled flexibility in the real exchange rate through changes in the price level that acted to restore external balance.

The price-specie flow mechanism was speeded up by the central bank who applied what came to be known as the 'rules of the game'. A deficit country, which was losing gold, faced the risk of becoming unable to meet its obligation to redeem currency notes. It was therefore motivated to push interest rates upwards in order to attract inflows from abroad. The rise in interest rates would contract domestic demand and put downward pressure on prices. The opposite case would arise in surplus nations. Because the accumulated gold reserves earned no interest, the central bank would use gold reserves to purchase domestic financial assets, and in turn this would lower domestic interest rates and drive gold abroad. Lower interest rates would also stimulate domestic demand, putting upward pressure on the price level.

The Gold Standard was tremendously successful and, by the late nineteenth century, all the major world currencies were tied to gold and no country was ever forced to devalue its currency. The end came for the Gold Standard in 1914 with the outbreak of the First World War. Governments faced with a sudden need to increase expenditure dramatically, funded mainly by borrowing, could no longer maintain the parity of their currency against gold.

Bretton Woods: 1944–1973

In July 1944, the Articles of Agreement of the International Monetary Fund were established. The overarching aim was to provide an international framework for maintaining stability and growth in the post-Second World War era. Growth in international trade was central, and this in turn would be enhanced by a fixed exchange rate regime.

The Bretton Woods system was a reserve currency system. All currencies were fixed to one, namely, the US dollar. The reserve currency was then fixed to gold, at the rate $35 per ounce of gold. Like the Gold Standard before it, one of the central tenets was to impose inflation discipline on countries. Any expanding country would generate inflation creating pressure for an exchange rate depreciation.

Another central tenet was currency convertibility. A convertible currency is one that can be exchanged freely for foreign currencies. Currencies, however, were made only partially

Global application 14.2 (continued)

convertible. There was free movement for currency transactions on the current account, but not on the capital or financial account. This was so as to allow trade while restricting destabilizing short-term hot money flows linked to speculation.

The reserve currency enjoys a privileged position in the system. As it is the designated *n*th currency, it is up to the *n-1* other governments to use monetary policy in order to fix their currencies against the $US. Therefore, it can enjoy the benefits of the fixed exchange rate system while at the same time maintaining autonomy over its own monetary policy.

Realizing that commitment to fixed exchange rate regimes might lead to the sacrifice of internal for external objectives, the system was designed to incorporate some flexibility. Protection against speculative attacks and short-term balance of payments disequilibria was supported by IMF lending facilities and special drawing rights, each subject to IMF conditionality. Special drawing rights referred to the access to a special pool of reserves (to which each country paid a quota). These could be used to defend the currency against a speculative attack or to fund short-term balance of payments deficits. Conditionality refers to the surveillance of the policies of the member countries, so loans were only advanced if the country involved undertook the necessary corrective policies.

Adjustable parities meant that devaluations or revaluations were designed to deal with fundamental disequilibrium. These might arise from permanent adverse shifts in the demand for a country's products. With slow adjustment in prices, a country may otherwise face a sustained deficit and unemployment.

Decline of the Bretton Woods system

As the US committed more reserves to the Vietnam War, government spending rose dramatically. At the same time, the Great Society programmes of spending also increased. These spending hikes were not matched by tax rises, meaning of course that the US budget deficit moved significantly into debt. The fiscal expansion levered up US prices, putting pressure on the dollar–gold parity.

The first indication of the demise in the Bretton Woods system arose in late 1967/early 1968 in the gold market, where speculators started to buy gold under the assumption that a devaluation might happen. After large interventions by the US Federal Reserve Bank and European central banks failed to stem the speculation, a two-tier gold market was established. One tier was private; the other official. Private gold traders would have the price of gold determined by market forces, whereas central banks would continue to trade at the official gold price of $35 per ounce.

This effectively ended the gold standard/low inflation commitment of the system. A deterioration in the US current account in 1971 generated huge purchases of German Deutschmarks motivated by the feeling that the DM would be revalued against the dollar. The Bundesbank had to purchase dollars, but ultimately would not compromise its monetary policy and thus it allowed its exchange rate to float. It was then evitable that the dollar would require a devaluation against other European currencies.

In August 1971, the US ended convertibility against gold and devalued against all countries by an average of 8 per cent. Then, the beginning of the official end came in February 1973 when a massive speculative attack on the dollar led to a further 10 per cent devaluation. A shutdown in the foreign exchange market could not prevent further speculation against the US dollar. When markets reopened, Japan and the European nations floated their currencies against the dollar. By March 1973, it was all over.

Brief summary

The advantages and disadvantages of each type of regime have been vigorously discussed over the years. Conventionally, it is argued that fixed regimes are best at achieving nominal (exchange rate and price) stability, whereas floating regimes are better at dealing with real (output, employment) disturbances.

14.3 International policy coordination

So far the analysis of open economies has implied a small country assumption. That is, each nation is, in fact, too small to have any impact on the rest of the world. Analytically this is convenient because it means that policy actions can be viewed in relative isolation and without regard to any feedback or reactions that arise from the effects of policy changes on other countries.

The small country assumption, though, appears to be at odds with the real world. Few would deny that US economic policy will have a substantial impact on the rest of the world. This impact could then, of course, feed back into the US economy. The same is true of Germany within the European Union, or Japan (and now increasingly China) on the rest of Asia.

As countries become increasingly more open with respect to international trade and capital flows, the linkages among these countries will strengthen. This will reinforce the spillover and feedback effects of shocks and policies in domestic economies. There are principally two mechanisms through which these work. The first is through exchange rate movements, and the second is through aggregate demand.

Exchange rate externalities

This can be seen using the Mundell-Fleming model where policy changes through the impact on the exchange rate have a clear effect on other countries.

Figure 14.7 represents the case when a large country unleashes a fiscal expansion. Panel (a) represents the domestic economy, whereas panel (b) represents the rest of the world. The effect of the fiscal expansion is to shift the ISXM schedules outwards from $ISXM_1$ to $ISXM_2$. Consequently, the economy moves from point *a* to point *b*.

If this were a small country, then as the domestic interest rate has risen above the overseas interest rate, the exchange rate will appreciate and crowd out the fiscal expansion. If

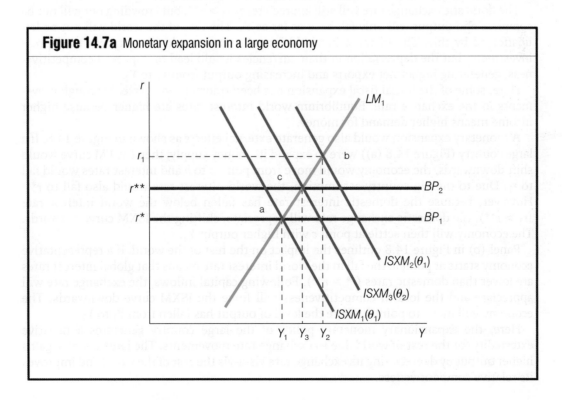

Figure 14.7a Monetary expansion in a large economy

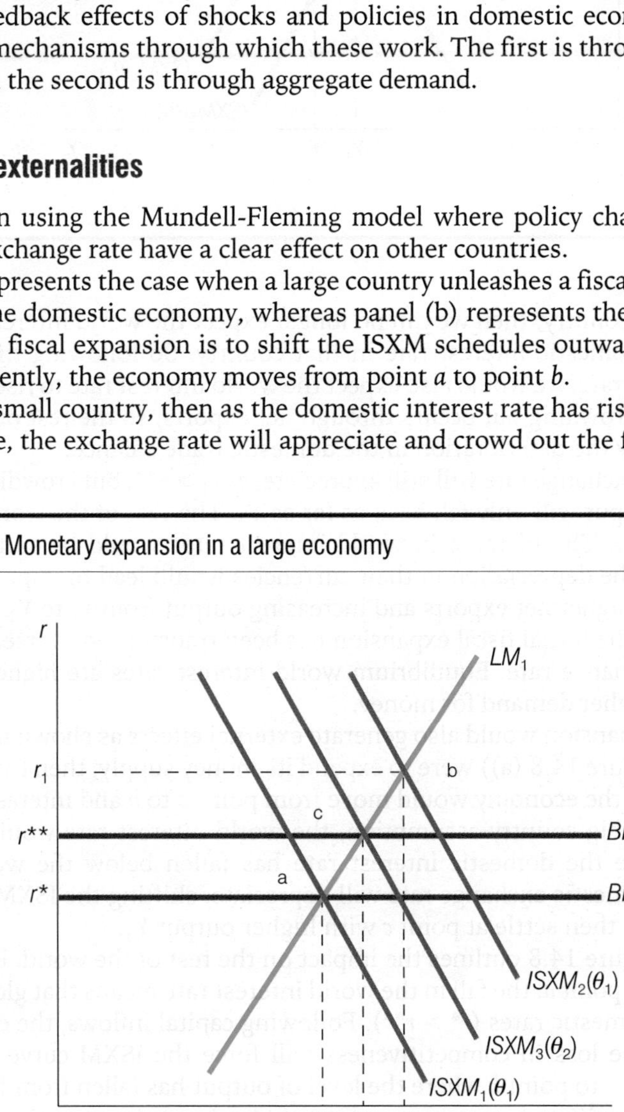

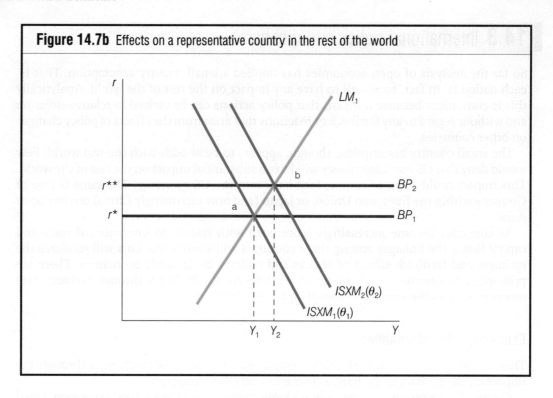

Figure 14.7b Effects on a representative country in the rest of the world

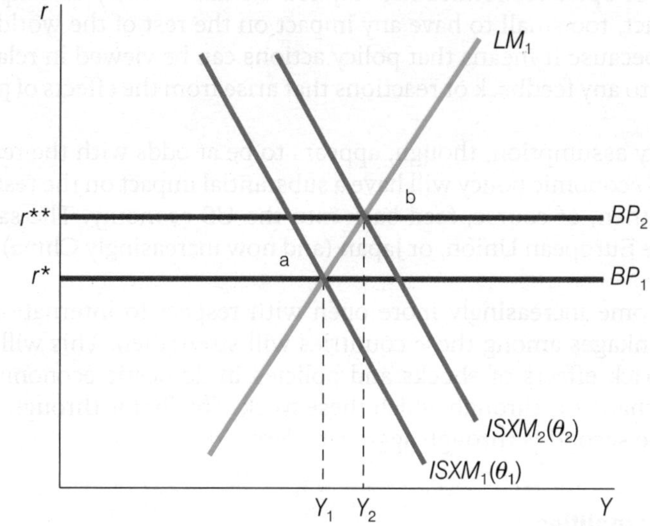

this were a large country, then we can no longer expect the world interest rate to be independent of the domestic interest rate in that country. So following the increase in the domestic interest rate, we would also expect the world interest rate to rise to a level such as r^{**}. In addition, crowding out occurs through net exports, so the rest of the world would also be affected by the deterioration in the domestic trade balance.

The domestic exchange rate will still appreciate, as $r_1 > r^{**}$, but crowding out will not be complete and output will only fall back as far as Y_3. The rest of the world will not be left unaffected by this. The increase in world interest rates would be sufficient to depress investment, but the depreciation in their currencies would lead to improved competitiveness, generating higher net exports and increasing output from Y_1 to Y_2.

Here, some of the initial fiscal expansion has been transmitted overseas through movements in the exchange rate. Equilibrium world interest rates are higher because higher income means higher demand for money.

A monetary expansion would also generate external effects as shown in Figure 14.8. If a large country (Figure 14.8 (a)) were to expand its money supply, then the LM curve would shift downwards, the economy would move from point *a* to *b* and interest rates would fall to r_1. Due to the big country assumption, the world interest rate would also fall to r^{**}. However, because the domestic interest rate has fallen below the world interest rate ($r_1 > r^{**}$), the domestic exchange rate will depreciate, shifting the ISXM curve outwards. The economy will then settle at point *c* with higher output Y_3.

Panel (b) in Figure 14.8 outlines the impact on the rest of the world. If a representative economy starts at point *a*, the fall in the world interest rate means that global interest rates are lower than domestic rates ($r^* > r^{**}$). Following capital inflows, the exchange rate will appreciate and the loss in competitiveness will force the ISXM curve downwards. The economy will move to point *b* where the level of output has fallen from Y_1 to Y_2.

Here, the expansionary monetary policy of the large country generates a negative externality for the rest of world due to exchange rate movements. The large country gains higher output by depreciating its exchange rate vis-à-vis the rest of the world and improves its relative competitiveness.

Figure 14.8a Monetary expansion in a large economy

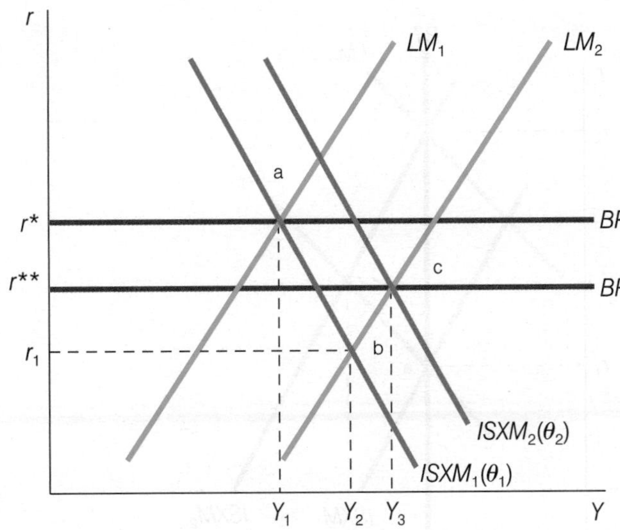

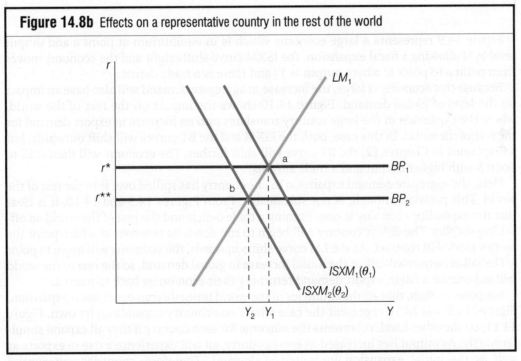

Figure 14.8b Effects on a representative country in the rest of the world

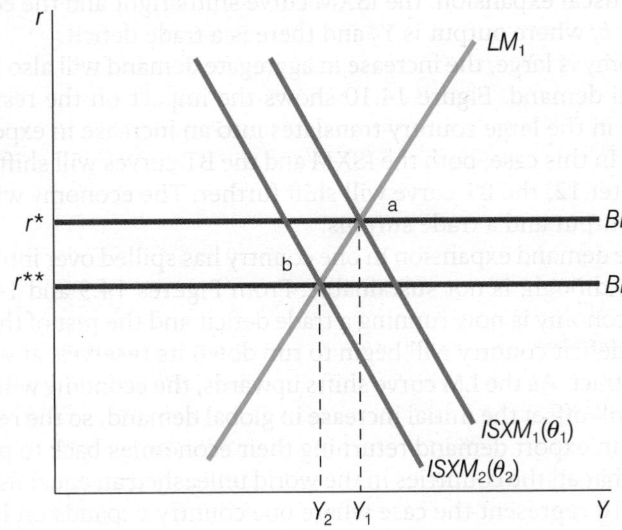

Aggregate demand externalities

Policy in one country can also directly spill over into others through aggregate demand externalities. When capital mobility is high, as in the Mundell-Fleming model, the exchange rate is the main source of externality because it reacts quickly and spontaneously to changes in interest rates. For this reason, it is easier to discern the effects of aggregate demand externalities by assuming no capital mobility.

14

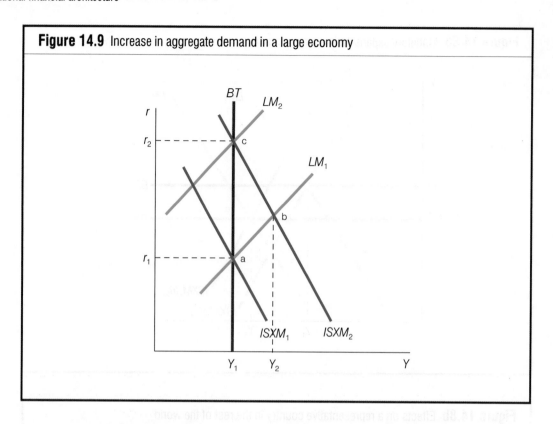

Figure 14.9 Increase in aggregate demand in a large economy

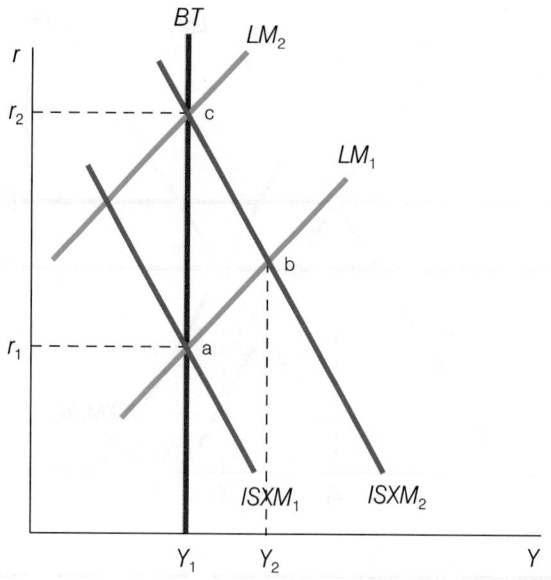

Figure 14.9 represents a large economy which is in equilibrium at point *a* and output level Y_1. Following a fiscal expansion, the ISXM curve shifts right and the economy moves from point *a* to point *b*, where output is Y_2 and there is a trade deficit.

Because this economy is large, the increase in aggregate demand will also have an impact on the level of global demand. Figure 14.10 shows the impact on the rest of the world, where the expansion in the large country translates into an increase in export demand for the rest of the world. In this case, both the ISXM and the BT curves will shift outwards, but as explained in Chapter 12, the BT curve will shift further. The economy will then shift to point *b* with higher output and a trade surplus.

Here, the aggregate demand expansion in one country has spilled over into the rest of the world. This position, though, is not sustainable. From Figures 14.9 and 14.10, it is clear that the expanding economy is now running a trade deficit and the rest of the world an offsetting surplus. The deficit country will begin to run down its reserves, at which point the money stock will contract. As the LM curve shifts upwards, the economy will move to point *c*. The fall in output will offset the initial increase in global demand, so the rest of the world will experience a fall in export demand returning their economies back to point *a*.

Suppose, though, that all the countries in the world unleashed an equal fiscal expansion. Figures 14.9 and 14.10 represent the case where one country expands on its own. Figure 14.11, on the other hand, represents the outcome for each country if they all expand simultaneously. As output has increased in every country, all will experience a rise in exports as well as the initial expansion in aggregate demand. Therefore, countries can expand without running into trade deficits as before, making the increase in output more sustainable.

This is an example of how coordinating policy can deliver a mutually preferable outcome. As there are potentially very important spillovers among different economies, it is obvious that there might be some benefits from coordinating economic policies. Global applications 14.4 and 14.5 describe two policy games where coordinating international policy can deliver mutual gains.

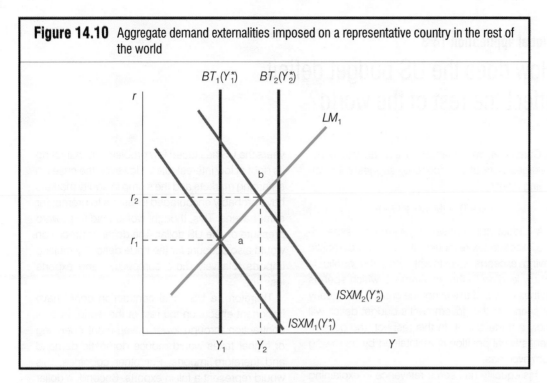

Figure 14.10 Aggregate demand externalities imposed on a representative country in the rest of the world

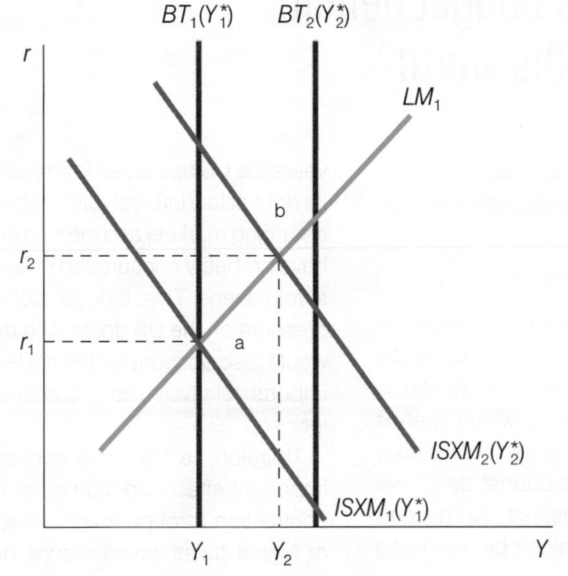

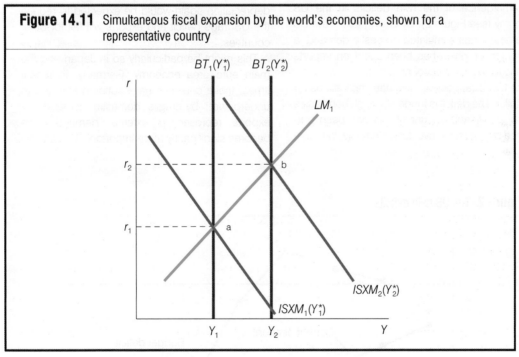

Figure 14.11 Simultaneous fiscal expansion by the world's economies, shown for a representative country

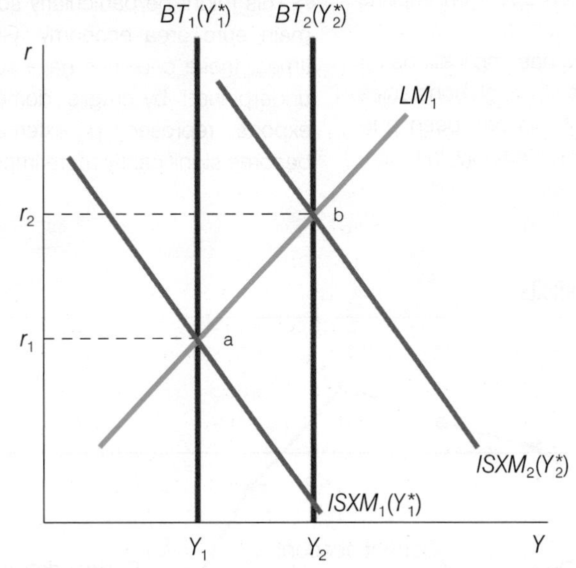

History has provided several examples where nations have sought to coordinate policies. The Bretton Woods Agreement described in Global application 14.2 is one such example, which was originally designed to help the global economy recover from the ravages of the Second World War. Global application 14.6 gives another example where the main G7 countries coordinated their actions to correct a misalignment in the currency markets. In the next section, we turn our attention to a more formal example of international policy coordination by analysing the effects of monetary unions.

Global application 14.3

How does the US budget deficit affect the rest of the world?

In Chapter 4, we established that an injections-leakages view of the economy suggests the following identity.

$$(G - T) = (M - X) + (S - I)$$

A budget deficit arises if government expenditure exceeds tax revenues. If, however, domestic saving exceeds investment, then the public is simply lending to the government, which spends on their behalf. If this is not the case, it can clearly be seen that the government's budget deficit will imply a trade deficit. In this respect, the government's fiscal position is maintained by borrowing from overseas.

This equality has some relevance in explaining the emergence of the twin deficits in the US economy (see Figure 2). By cutting taxes, the US government has stimulated domestic demand, a proportion of which has been spent on imports leading to a current account deficit.

The US fiscal position also has implications for the dollar. The deficit is funded through bond sales and a significant amount of this has been purchased by overseas investors. Certainly, in recent years the US has faced few problems in marketing its debt at low interest rates. However, the crises in emerging markets and the slump in equity markets have probably encouraged investors to prompt for safer havens. This, though, would lead to upward pressure on the US dollar. The dollar appreciation would also account for the trade deficit by making imports relatively more competitive and exports less so.

Therefore, a US fiscal contraction could have important effects on the rest of the world. First, a contraction through lower government spending or higher taxes would reduce domestic demand and therefore imports. For other countries, this would represent a fall in exports. Second, a dollar depreciation again would be expected to reduce the US trade deficit and exports will fall for other countries.

This might be particularly so in Japan and the main euro area economy, Germany. In recent times, these countries have suffered low growth underpinned by fragile domestic demand, so exports representing external demand have become significantly more important. This can be

Figure 2 The US twin deficits

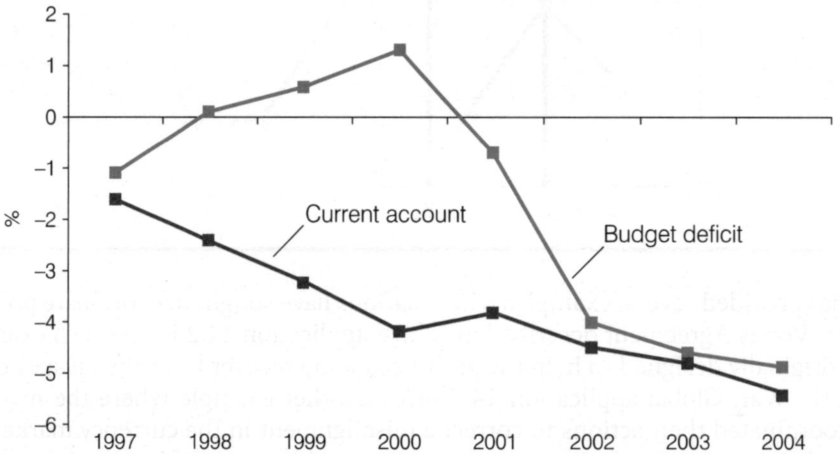

14

Global application 14.3 (continued)

Figure 3 Current account as a proportion of GDP

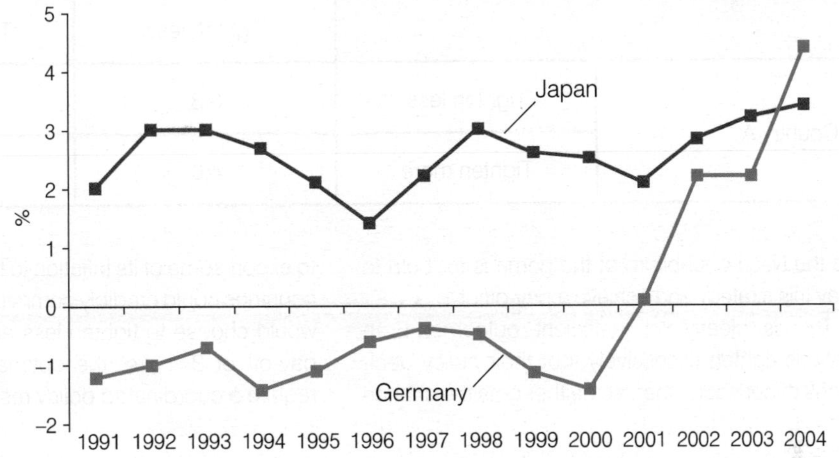

seen in Figure 3, where the current account as a proportion of GDP has risen in both countries in recent years, particularly in Germany. A US contraction therefore would be especially significant for these countries which have recently relied on export-orientated growth.

Global application 14.4

Exporting inflation

Consider two countries, A and B, which both face a common negative productivity shock. With unchanged domestic policies, this increases inflation in each country. Each country's logical response is to tighten monetary policy in order to control domestic inflation.

However, both countries have an incentive to tighten monetary policy more than the other. The nation that tightens the most will be able to appreciate its exchange rate against the other and export some of its inflation to the other. This could lead to an outcome where both countries tighten policy too much.

This game can be formalized as a typical prisoners' dilemma game, where each nation must decide whether to tighten less, or tighten more. The pay-off matrix from each course of action is shown overleaf.

The first number in any pair is the pay-off to country A. If A believes that country B will tighten less, it will have an incentive to tighten more and deliver lower domestic inflation through the exchange rate appreciation, achieving a pay-off of 4 compared to 0 for country B. If country A believes that country B will tighten more, its optimal response is also to tighten more so as to avoid a relative depreciation in its currency and import inflation. For each country, 'tighten more' is a dominant strategy,

Global application 14.4 (continued)

		Country B	
		Tighten less	Tighten more
Country A	Tighten less	3,3	0,4
	Tighten more	4,0	1,1

so the Nash equilibrium of the game is for both to play this strategy and achieve a pay-off of 1.

This is clearly an inefficient outcome. Both nations tighten excessively, but their policy decisions offset each other, so neither gets the chance to export some of its inflation to the other. If the two countries could credibly commit their policies, they would choose to tighten less and each receive a pay-off of 3. Here, the optimal outcome would require a coordinated policy response.

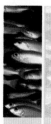

Global application 14.5

Coordinated policies in international output

This simple game formalizes the aggregate demand game described in the text. A unilateral expansion in fiscal policy will generate current account deficits making the policy's effect on domestic output unsustainable. However, if all countries expand together in a coordinated fashion, then each can achieve higher output while maintaining a steady external position.

Assume that there are two countries with output in each given by Y and Y^* such that:

$$Y = cY + G + X - mY$$

$$Y^* = cY^* + G^* + X^* - mY^*$$

The two countries have a symmetric structure. Output depends on domestic demand given by consumption (cY) and government spending (G), and external demand given by net trade ($X - mY$). The parameters c and m are the marginal propensity to consume and import respectively, and due to symmetry, are the same in each country.

If these are the only two countries in the world economy, then the exports of one would equate to the imports of the other.

$$X = mY^*$$

$$X^* = mY$$

Essentially, the output of one country depends on the level of demand in the other through trade.

$$Y = cY + G + mY^* - mY$$

This can be simplified to:

$$Y = \frac{G + mY^*}{(1 - c + m)}$$

And, because of symmetry, the same relationship would apply in the other country.

$$Y^* = \frac{G^* + mY}{(1 - c + m)}$$

These two relationships for a given level of government spending are plotted in Figure 4. So long

Global application 14.5 (continued)

Figure 4 Aggregate demand externalities and international policy coordination

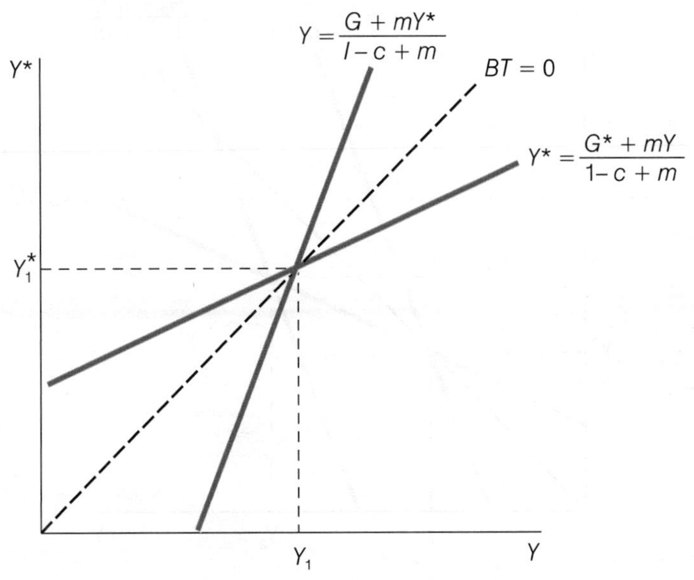

as $Y = Y^*$, then each nation would be in equilibrium on the balance of trade, which is plotted as the 45-degree line in Figure 4.

Any position on the 45-degree line represents a sustainable position in output. This is because it is assumed that each nation cannot run a balance of trade deficit ad infinitum, as this would represent an increasing stock of borrowed liabilities.

The policy choice that each country has is the level of government spending. However, there is a clear coordination game here because one nation's attempt to increase output will only be sustainable if it is reciprocated in the other.

For example, in Figure 5, one country unleashes a fiscal expansion ($G_1 \rightarrow G_2$) while the other does not. As a result, the demand function of this country shifts outwards and the global economy moves from position *a* to *b*. Output in both countries increases because the domestic expansion will spill over into the other through trade. However, output in the expanding country ($Y_1 \rightarrow Y_2$) will increase the furthest. Because of this, the expanding country starts to run a trade deficit and the unexpanded country a trade surplus. This outcome, though, is unsustainable in the long run and will require a reversal in the fiscal expansion in order to restore trade balance equilibrium.

If, however, both countries unleash the same fiscal expansion ($G_1 \rightarrow G_2$) and ($G_1^* \rightarrow G_2^*$), then the same shift in demand function occurs as shown in Figure 6.

In figure 6, a common fiscal expansion moves the economy from point *a* to *b*. However, in this case because there has been a coordinated expansion, output in each country increases by the same magnitude. Therefore, each country enjoys higher sustainable output as the trade balance remains in equilibrium.

Global application 14.5 (continued)

Figure 5 Unilateral fiscal expansion

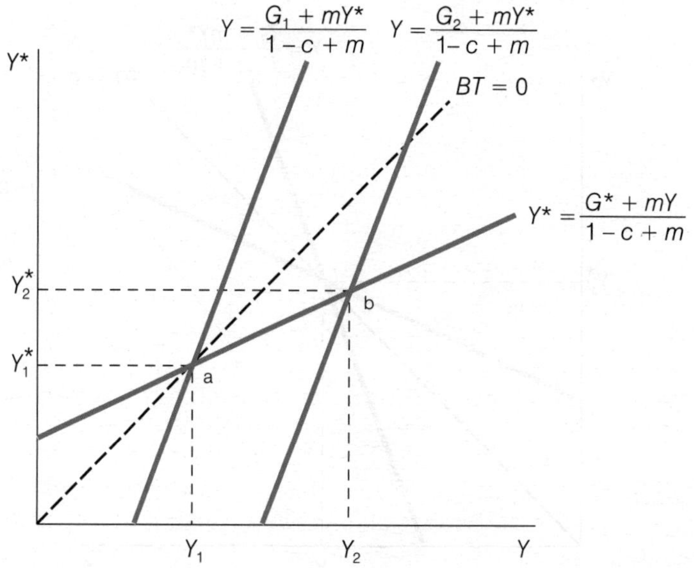

Figure 6 Coordinated fiscal expansion

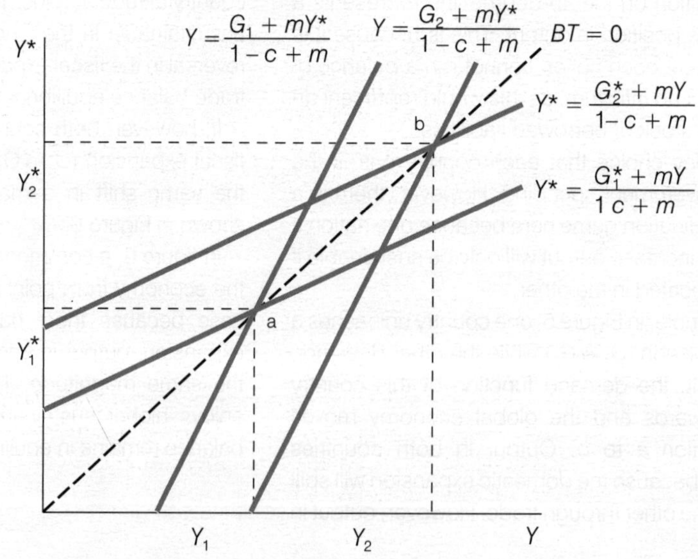

Global application 14.6

The Plaza and Louvre Accords

The first half of the 1980s saw a large and prolonged appreciation of the US dollar against the world's currencies. Given that the $US was central to the world trading system, with many emerging market economies operating fixed rate regimes against it, the significant movement in the exchange rate created fears of large external balances and the threat of protectionist measures. Concern also existed in the US that the dollar's strength was creating problems for the manufacturing industry.

The G5 represents the group of the five most important developed economies (US, Japan, Germany, UK and France), which emerged after the breakdown of the Bretton Woods system in 1973. Later, this was to become the G7 by incorporating Canada and Italy. It was, in effect, a group of the world's richest countries consisting of a specialized circle of finance ministers and economic diplomats and experts.

The conventional wisdom at the time was against intervention in the currency markets. However, in February 1985, the G5 moved into action, launching a programme of large-scale dollar sales by the major central banks. Following the announcement, the dollar immediately dropped by around 6 per cent. It also created a new view in the market, which had until then placed little weight on the power of the G5 and central banks to intervene in markets, and also which could no longer see the dollar as a one-way bet. This action, though, failed to push the dollar down to levels that were considered reasonable.

In September 1985, at the Plaza hotel in New York, a new concerted attempt was made by the G5 participants to bring about an orderly depreciation of the dollar. Central banks showed they were serious by selling the dollar and by the end of October more than $10 billion had been expended on the policy. The Plaza agreement was a critical event ushering in a new spirit of international economic cooperation. The G5 met regularly during 1986 and was expanded to become the G7 in 1987. The Louvre Accord of February 1987 continued the theme of coordination, but this time the focus was to stabilize the dollar once it had fallen to a sustainable level.

The common thrust of these agreed policies was to moderate domestic demand growth in the US and to accelerate it in Europe and particularly in Japan. Bond markets, though, did not share the optimism of the Louvre Accord, which saw inflationary pressures as likely to push up global interest rates. The German Bundesbank was always unlikely to compromise German inflationary performance in support of international objectives and tightened monetary policy. The brief era of international policy cooperation was now over.

14.4 Optimal currency areas

The logic behind the theory of **optimal currency areas (OCA)** is very simple – it just implies that an economic region is an optimal currency area if the advantages of adopting a single currency outweigh the disadvantages. A basic cost-benefit analysis can help find the answer to whether a country should join an OCA or not.

Benefits: the GG Schedule

The most obvious benefits are the monetary efficiency gains of a single currency. Trade can now occur without the transactions costs and uncertainty of dealing in different currencies. A single currency also makes it easier to compare prices in different countries; the fact

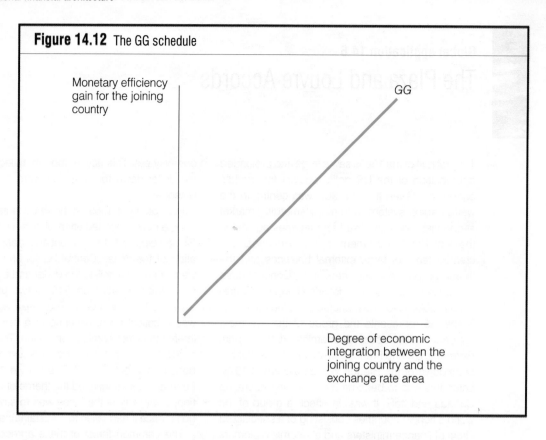

Figure 14.12 The GG schedule

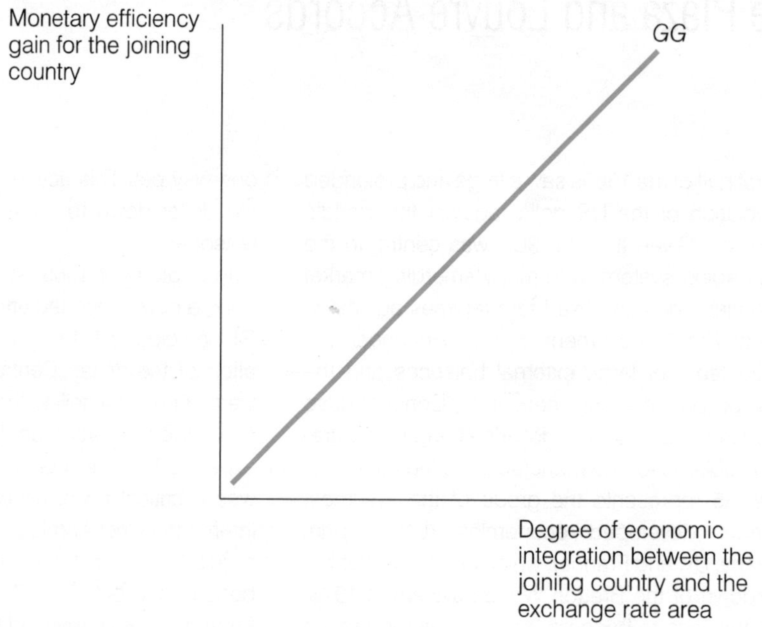

that markets will then be more competitive would be expected to result in higher welfare. It is difficult to quantify the exact size of these benefits, but it seems plausible to argue that the gains to a country from joining a monetary union will depend on the degree of economic integration (trading links) that country has with the area. The GG schedule is drawn in Figure 14.12 as an upward-sloping schedule, where the monetary efficiency gains from joining a single currency area rises with the degree of economic integration.

Costs: the LL schedule

Once a country signs up to a single currency, it loses the ability to use monetary policy and the exchange rate to control the economy. This could result in an economic stability loss. As all the countries in a single currency must have a common interest rate and exchange rate, asymmetric shocks become very difficult to correct. If a shock is symmetric – so that it affects all countries equally – then a common policy response may be sufficient. However, if a shock only hits one country, then it will require a policy response that the other countries do not, and as it will be in the minority, it will have little ability to enforce it. In this situation, the inability to allow the exchange rate to change, or for monetary policy to be used, means the shock remains uncorrected.

These losses are likely to fall as the degree of economic integration rises. The more closely integrated two economies are, the more likely that the shocks affecting one country will spill over into another, and therefore a common policy response would be required. Also, the greater the regional mobility of labour the better, as following a shock, unemployed workers can simply migrate to areas with jobs. In this case, the costs of not being able to use a unique policy are diminished. The LL schedule in Figure 14.13 is a downward-sloping function, which shows that the economic stability loss of joining a single currency falls with the degree of integration.

Figure 14.13 The LL schedule

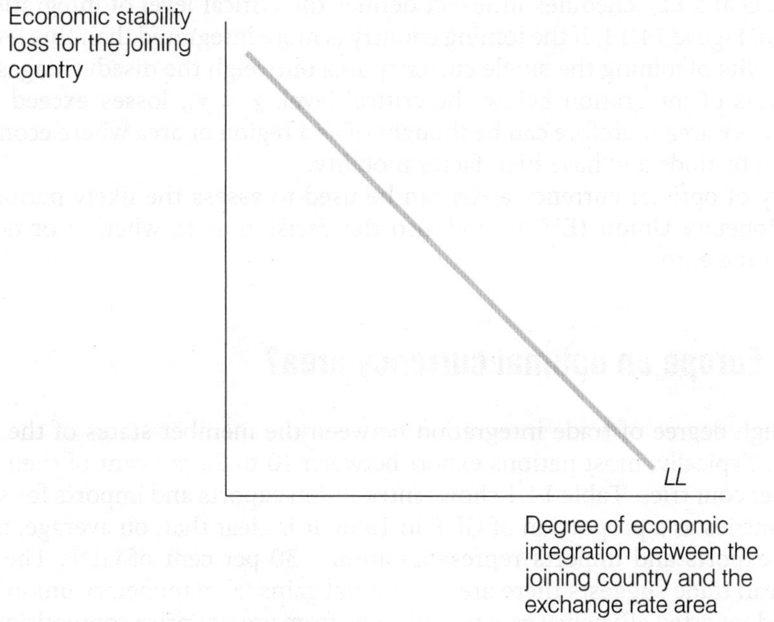

Figure 14.14 An optimal currency area

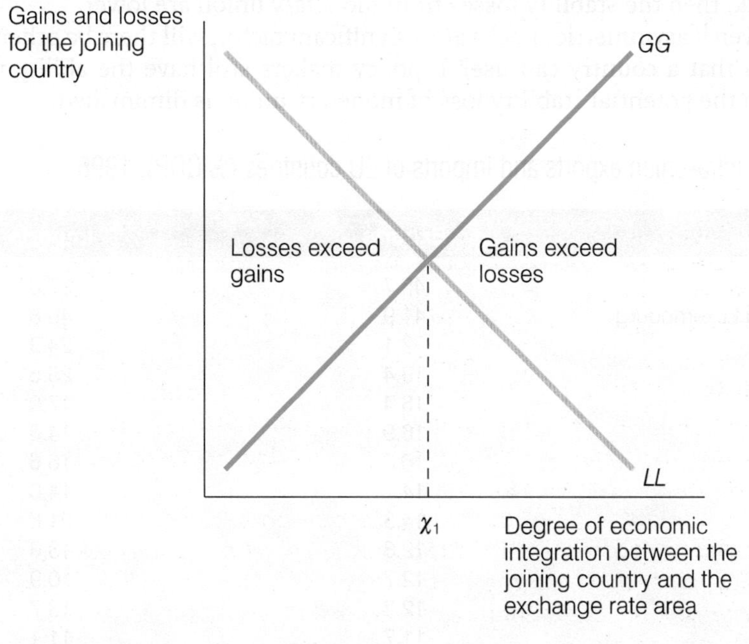

Optimal currency area or not?

The answer, as already alluded to, is simply to see whether the costs outweigh the benefits. Where the GG and LL schedules intersect defines the critical level of integration: this is shown as χ_1 in Figure 14.14. If the joining country is more integrated than this level, $\chi > \chi_1$, then the benefits of joining the single currency area outweigh the disadvantages. Alternatively, at levels of integration below the critical level, $\chi < \chi_1$, losses exceed gains. An optimal currency area therefore can be thought of as a region or area where economies are closely linked by trade and have high factor mobility.

The theory of optimal currency areas can be used to assess the likely performance of European Monetary Union (EMU), and also the decision as to whether or not the UK should adopt the euro.

14.4.1 Is Europe an optimal currency area?

There is a high degree of trade integration between the member states of the European Union (EU). Typically, most nations export between 10 to 20 per cent of their output to other member countries. Table 14.1 shows intra-union exports and imports for several EU member countries as a proportion of GDP in 1996. It is clear that, on average, the sum of intra-union exports and imports represents around 30 per cent of GDP. The extent of intra-European trade suggests there are substantial gains from monetary union.

The second reported efficiency gain would come from greater price competition, benefiting European consumers. Once all prices are quoted in the same currency, it should be easier for consumers to buy goods and services where they are cheapest.

The main debate, though, on whether or not the euro area constitutes an OCA centres on the cost side. The true costs of giving up control of monetary policy and an independent exchange rate will depend upon two factors.

First, how likely are asymmetric shocks? If there is little chance of a country suffering a unique shock, then the stability losses from monetary union are lower.

Second, even if asymmetric shocks are a significant factor, will there be other adjustment mechanisms that a country can use? If policy makers still have the ability to deal with shocks, then the potential stability loss of monetary union is diminished.

Table 14.1 Intra-union exports and imports of EU countries (% GDP), 1996

Country	Exports	Imports
Ireland	45.7	27.8
Belgium and Luxembourg	41.9	40.8
Netherlands	32.1	24.9
Portugal	19.4	25.5
Sweden	18.4	17.0
Finland	16.9	14.3
Denmark	16.3	16.6
EU-15	14.7	14.0
Austria	14.3	21.6
UK	12.8	13.3
Germany	12.7	10.9
Spain	12.2	13.7
France	11.7	11.1
Italy	11.0	10.0
Greece	5.7	16.1

Source: EC Commission

Figure 14.15 High stabilization costs

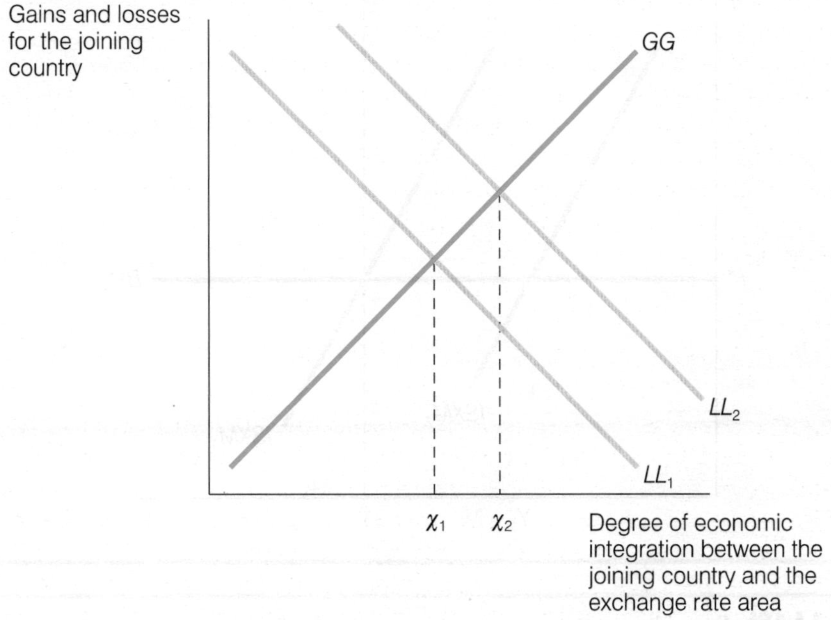

These two considerations will determine the position of the LL schedule. If both are significant factors, then for every level of economic integration the stabilization costs of a single currency will be higher and the LL schedule will shift upwards. As a result, the area is less likely to be an OCA, even with a relatively high level of economic integration. In Figure 14.15, the critical degree of integration depends on the position of the LL schedule.

Therefore, much of the debate on whether or not Europe is an OCA lies in the likelihood of different shocks, or the lack of flexibility to deal with them.

Asymmetric shocks

An asymmetric shock is a shock that has a disproportionate impact on one particular country or region. These types of shocks are more likely when a region or a country has a high concentration of a particular industry, so anything that hits that industry has a large impact on that region, and that region alone.

In this respect, the euro area would actually be expected to be less prone to asymmetric shocks than the regions of the US. The euro area is a group of sovereign nations, each with a well-diversified production sector. The US, however, has been a single market for a considerable period of time during which a more acute degree of regional specialization has occurred.

It is difficult to find much evidence that one country will be subject to an asymmetric shock. This is the finding of Blanchard and Wolfers (2000). They attempt to explain national differences in unemployment – the hypothesis being that differences must be accounted for by specific shocks to certain countries. However, their findings did not reach these conclusions. There simply were not enough different shocks of a sufficient size to explain the differences in unemployment. Instead, it is argued that all nations face roughly the same shocks, but differences in labour market institutions propagate these shocks differently, creating different effects on unemployment.

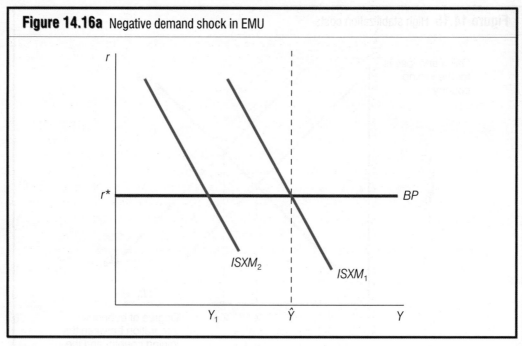

Figure 14.16a Negative demand shock in EMU

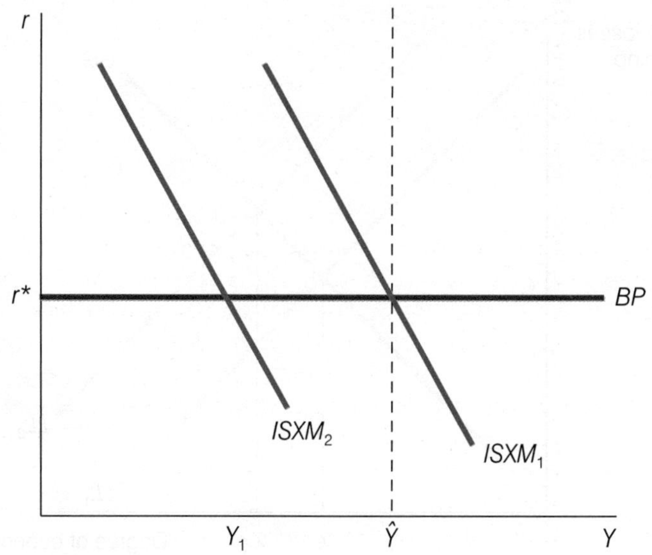

Figure 14.16b Dynamics

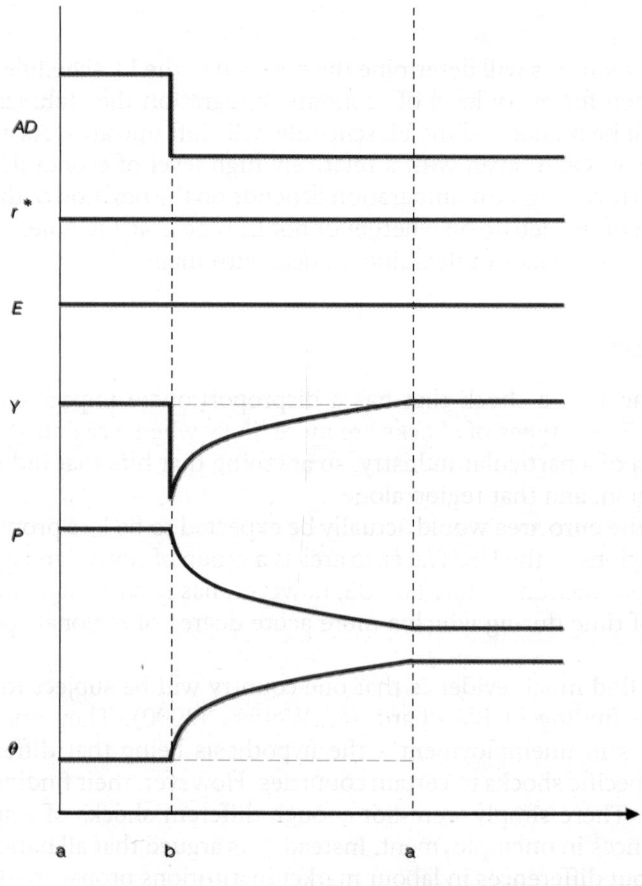

Correction mechanisms: flexibility

Asymmetric shocks are not a problem so long as there is sufficient flexibility to deal with them if and when they occur.

Wage and price flexibility Using the Mundell-Fleming model in Figure 14.16, we can see why high wage and price flexibility may be important in the EMU. In a monetary union, there is perfect capital mobility and a common interest rate (r^*). As there is no independent monetary policy, there is no LM curve. Equilibrium is where the horizontal BP curve intersects the ISXM schedule at the full employment level of output ($\hat{Y}$).

Suppose a country suffers a negative aggregate demand shock, as a result the ISXM curve shifts inwards ($ISXM_1 \rightarrow ISXM_2$) and the equilibrium level of output falls below the full employment level ($Y_1 < \hat{Y}$). This would put downward pressure on wages and prices, which would improve competitiveness and lead to an improvement in output. Eventually, it is the adjustment of prices and wages that restores output to the full employment level. However, the speed at which this happens is crucial, and obviously depends on the flexibility of labour and goods markets. If these are inflexible, then correction will be very slow, implying that a shock can have long-lasting effects on output.

Figure 14.17 shows an index of labour market flexibility in several countries, a lower value implies a more flexible institutional environment.

It is clear that the EMU member countries tend to perform very badly on this scale, especially in comparison to the US which is deemed to have a very flexible labour market. In Figure 14.18, overall product market regulation is reported and the same conclusions reached. The higher value of the index implies a higher level of regulation, and an expected lower level of flexibility. It is again clear that EMU member states perform relatively badly, which raises fears of inadequate flexibility.

Low nominal flexibility increases the stability costs associated with a joining a monetary union. The LL Schedule in Figure 14.15 would shift outwards, so even at high levels of integration, the EU may fail to be an optimal currency area.

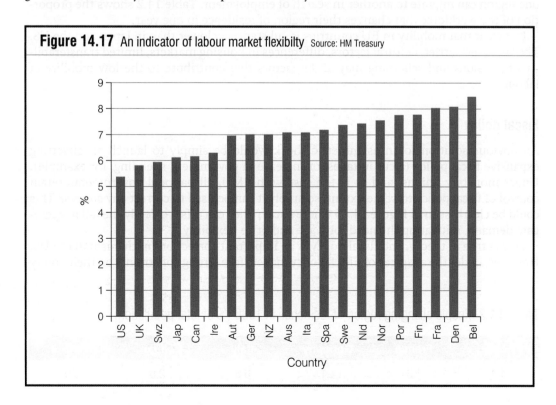

Figure 14.17 An indicator of labour market flexibilty Source: HM Treasury

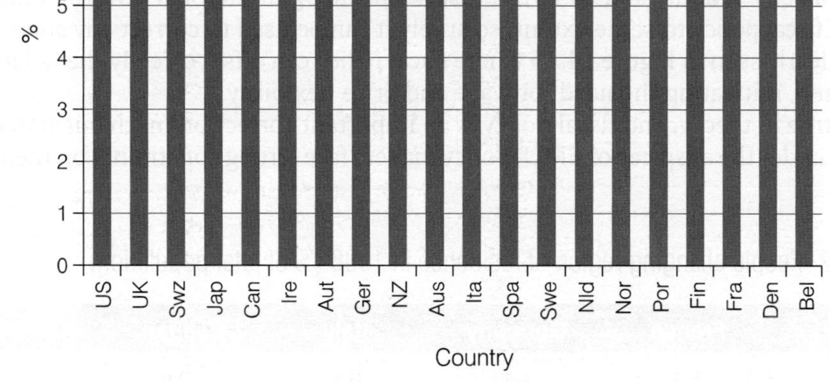

14

Figure 14.18 Overall product market regulation Source: HM Treasury

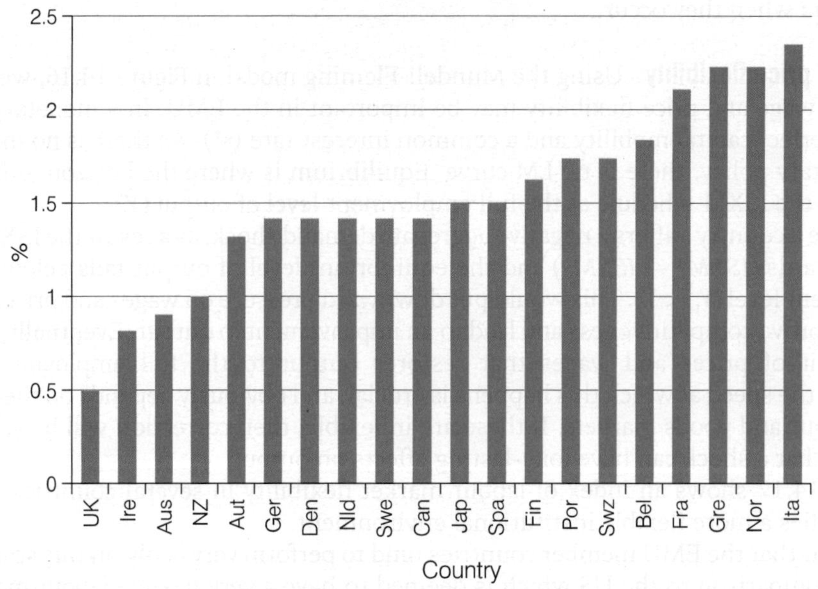

Factor mobility

Even if wage and price flexibility are poor, problems can be mitigated if the mobility of the factors of production, and in particular labour, is high. In this case, unemployed workers in one region can migrate to another in search of employment. Table 14.2 shows the proportion of the workforce that changes their region of residence in one year.

It is clear that mobility in EU countries is substantially lower than in Japan and the US. The language barrier, cultural factors, differences in housing markets, limited transferability of pensions and schooling may all be factors that contribute to the low mobility of labour.

Fiscal policy

An obvious solution to an asymmetric shock would be simply to launch an offsetting expansive fiscal policy (a cut in taxes, or increase in government spending, for example). Under monetary unions, and as is the case with EMU, all national governments retain control of fiscal policy to some extent, so surely it can be used to correct any shocks? This could be clearly seen in Figure 14.16 where fiscal policy can offset directly the fall in aggregate demand, mitigating the need for wage and price flexibility.

This is true in theory, and fiscal policy is an important correction mechanism in the US. However, under the auspices of EMU, policy makers face strong constraints on their ability

Table 14.2 People changing region of residence in 1986 (% of total population)

UK	France	Germany	Italy	Japan	US
1.1	1.3	1.1	0.6	2.6	3.0

14

to use fiscal policy, which will obviously hinder its ability to act as a correcting mechanism. Part of the EMU treaty is the Stability and Growth Pact (SGP). This requires government deficits to not exceed 3 per cent of GDP, and the total national debt not to exceed 60 per cent of GDP. Repeated failure to comply could result in a fine of up to 0.5 per cent of GDP.

The rationale behind the SGP is due to the fear that under a monetary union, there is an incentive for fiscal indiscipline, which can interfere in the efficient operation of monetary policy. When a government is running large deficits, they have to borrow a great deal. In order to effectively market this debt (by selling bonds), they may have to offer a higher interest rate. Also, as government debt rises, there are increasing fears that a government may go bankrupt and default on the debt. Any bonds that are issued will therefore be regarded as more risky, and will require a higher interest rate to be levied which incorporates the risk premium (ρ).

In a monetary union, there is only one interest rate. All government bonds, wherever they are issued are denominated in euros and there is one euro interest rate. In this case, if one nation runs an unsustainable debt, its risk premium will be spread over the bonds issued by the n members of the single currency, which would put upward pressure on the union interest rate. As the effects of a fiscal expansion will be localized in the country it was undertaken whereas the interest rate effects will be shared around the union, there is an incentive to run excessive deficits. This situation is shown in panels (a) and (b) of Figure 14.19.

In Figure 14.19(a), a nation using expansionary fiscal policy sees the ISXM schedule shift outwards and the equilibrium interest rate rises to $r^* + \rho/n$. The overall effect is that output increases to Y_2. The higher interest rate, though, would weigh on the rest of the EMU members, which would see output fall to Y_1 in Figure 14.19(b).

A counter argument to the SGP is that financial markets should be efficient and sophisticated enough to deal with the excessive deficits problem. If one country is running large deficits, then the interest rate penalty should only apply to the bonds which that country issues. Even though there is only one euro interest rate, the risk premium on top of this

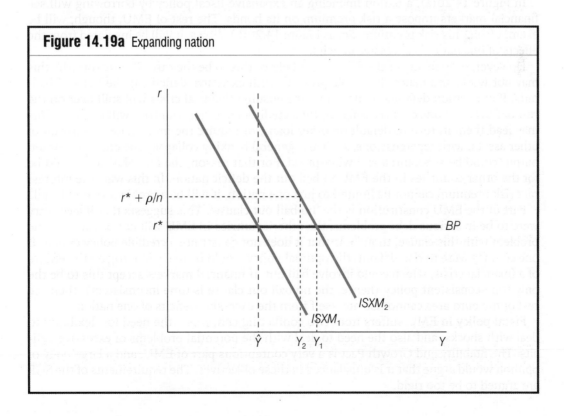

Figure 14.19a Expanding nation

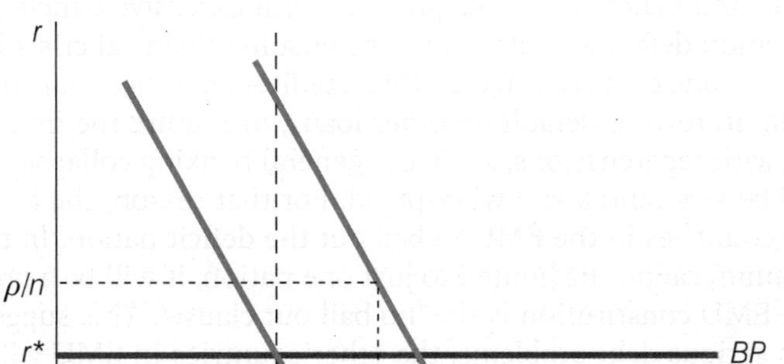

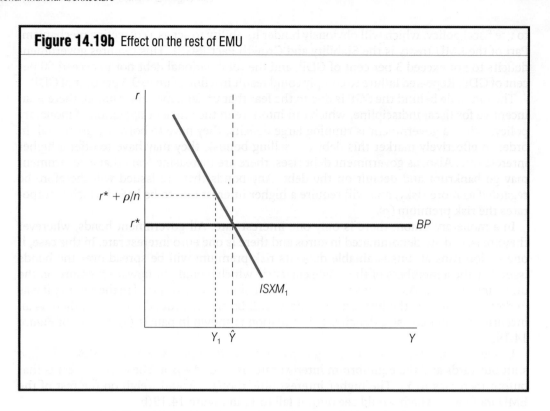

Figure 14.19b Effect on the rest of EMU

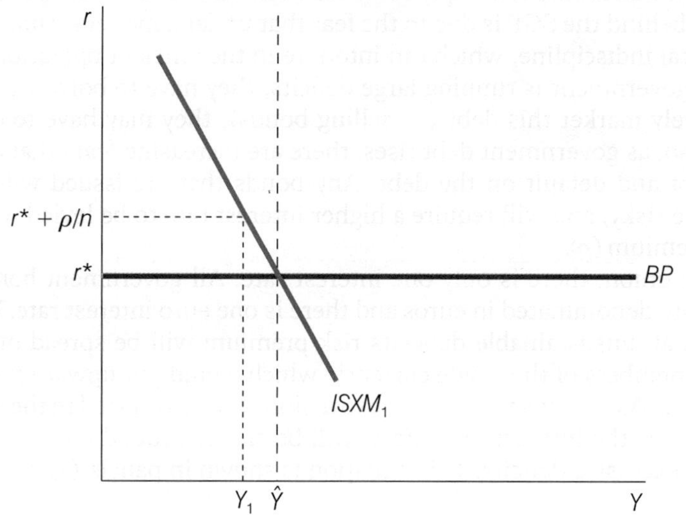

could still vary from country to country. If this were to happen, the rest of EMU would be isolated from the fiscal complacency of one country. This situation is depicted in Figure 14.20.

In Figure 14.20(a), a nation financing an expansive fiscal policy by borrowing will see financial markets impose a risk premium on its bonds. The rest of EMU, though, will be exempt from this risk premium. So, as Figure 14.20(b) shows, it will be insulated from the effects of one nation's excessive deficits.

However, proponents of the SGP do not believe this to be the case. The reason why this may not work, and hence the whole problem with excessive deficits, is the issue of bail-outs. If one nation defaults on its debts, the ensuing financial crisis will spill over on the rest of Europe. If one country defaults, then creditors in other countries will lose out. This may lead them in turn to default on other loans, or require the immediate liquidation of other assets, with repercussions, such as a general banking collapse. The effects on union output could be substantial and widespread. For that reason, the logical action would be for the other countries in the EMU to bail out the deficit nation. In this way, the interest rate risk premium cannot be limited to just one nation, it will be a problem shared by all.

Part of the EMU constitution is the 'no bail out clause'. This suggests that if a country were to be in serious debt problems, the other countries in EMU will not bail it out. The problem with this clause, though, is that it does not constitute a credible policy *ex post*. If one country were to risk default, the optimal policy would be to try to mitigate the effects of a financial crisis, which could involve bail out. If financial markets accept this to be the only time-consistent policy (hence, the no bail out clause is time inconsistent), then the rest of the euro area cannot isolate itself from the excessive deficits of one nation.

Fiscal policy in EMU suffers from two conflicting concerns – the need for flexibility to deal with shocks, and also the need to deal with the potential problems of excessive deficits. The Stability and Growth Pact is a very contentious part of EMU, and a large body of opinion would argue that it is unbalanced in these objectives. The requirements of the SGP are argued to be too rigid.

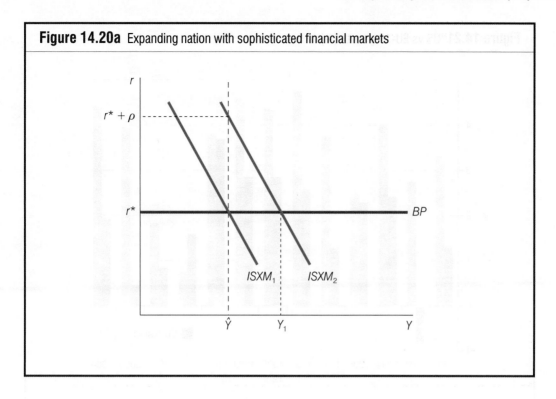

Figure 14.20a Expanding nation with sophisticated financial markets

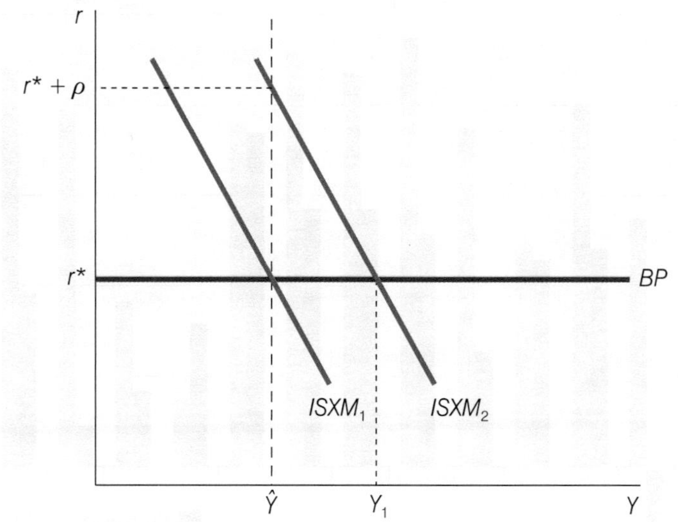

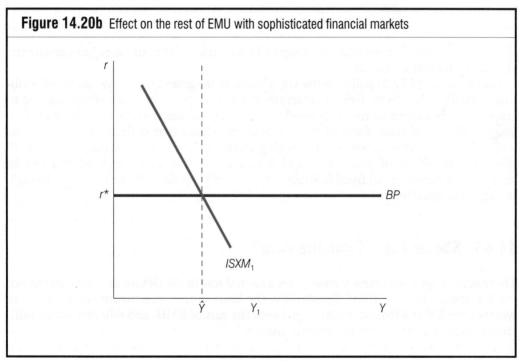

Figure 14.20b Effect on the rest of EMU with sophisticated financial markets

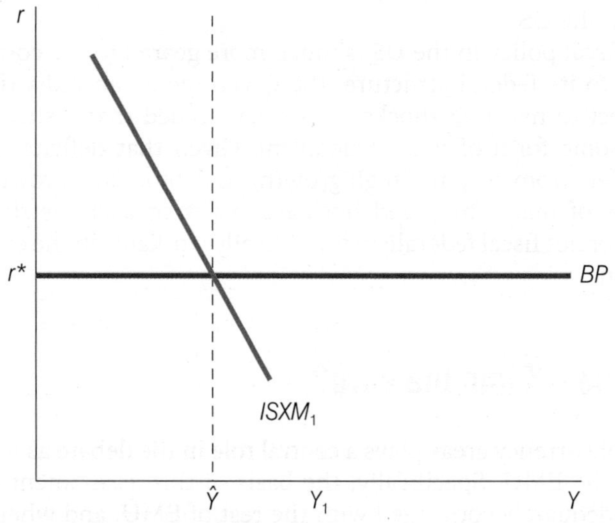

In Chapter 4, we saw that government deficits are likely to be cyclical due to automatic stabilizers. In a recession, the government budget moves towards deficit (as benefit spending increases and tax revenues fall), meaning that fiscal policy becomes most constrained at precisely the point it is most needed. The SGP, therefore, imposes a heavy deflationary burden on Europe because policy must tighten in times of low growth. Figure 14.21 shows

Figure 14.21 US vs EU-11 growth (%)

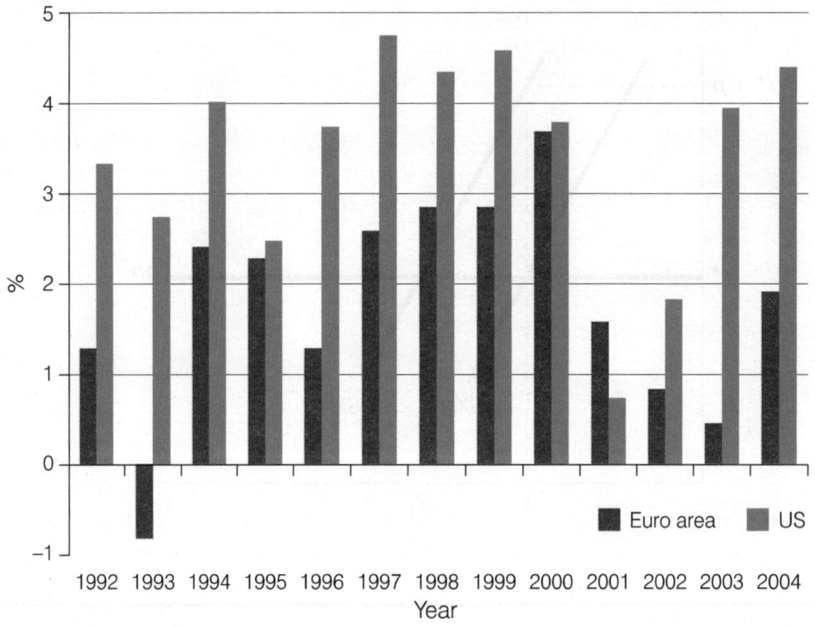

that recent economic growth in the group of 11 countries in the euro area has persistently lagged behind that in the US

The operation of fiscal policy in the US is much more geared to the correction of asymmetric shocks. Due to its federal structure, the government can redistribute income to states that are subject to negative shocks. It is often argued that a successful monetary union will require some form of fiscal federalism. Given that deficits are cyclical, this would involve transfers from surplus (high growth) to debtor (low growth) countries. In this way, the effects of unsynchronized business cycles or asymmetric shocks can be smoothed. Whether or not fiscal federalism is politically workable in the euro area, though, is a separate question.

14.4.2 Should the UK join the euro?

The theory of optimal currency areas plays a central role in the debate as to whether or not the UK should join the EMU. Specifically, the basis of this assessment comes down to whether the UK is adequately converged with the rest of EMU, and whether it has sufficient flexibility to deal with asymmetric shocks.

14

Convergence

Adopting a single currency implies the sacrificing of monetary policy autonomy. Exchange rates disappear and a one-size-fits-all interest rate is applied across the entire monetary union. For a single monetary policy to be universally appropriate, it must be the case that economies have achieved an adequate degree of convergence. There are two strands to the convergence issue: convergence in cycles and convergence in structures.

Convergence in cycles refers to the synchronization of business cycles. A one-size-fits-all interest rate will be problematic if different countries are in different stages of the economic cycle. A nation experiencing slow growth would require a loosening of policy, whereas those growing strongly might require higher rates to control inflation. Under these conditions, it would be impossible for one monetary policy to satisfy the differing needs of each economy simultaneously. Stability losses could be reduced by reasserting autonomy over monetary policy.

Table 14.3 shows the business cycle correlation between the UK and various regions. It appears to be the case that, historically, the UK business cycle is more strongly correlated with the US than the euro area. As such, European levels of interest rates may be inappropriate for the UK economy.

There appears to be sufficient evidence to conclude that the UK and Euro-11 business cycles are not sufficiently convergent to make UK entry into EMU feasible. However, even if an adequate degree of cyclical convergence is achieved, and the business cycles move more harmoniously, the convergence test can still be subject to failure. This is because there would be significant structural differences between the UK and the rest of EMU to make the possibility of future asymmetric shocks a major cause for concern.

Convergence in structures relates to the idea that economies may have structural differences that will make a common monetary policy infeasible. If different economies are subject to different shocks, or react in different ways to the same shocks, then a different monetary policy would become optimal. In addition, different economies might have different monetary policy transmission mechanisms. This describes how a change in interest rates feeds through to the level of output. In this case, the common monetary policy itself can be the cause of asymmetric shocks.

Table 14.3 Correlations of business cycles over time

Correlations	UK/EU15	UK/EMU	UK/Ger	UK/US	Ger/EMU
1970–2002	0.66	0.45	0.12	0.78	0.84
1976–1986	0.77	0.61	0.62	0.78	0.98
1986–1997	0.43	0.11	–0.58	0.93	0.72
1997–2002	0.66	0.64	0.79	0.73	0.96

Source: European Commission

Table 14.4 Key features of housing markets

	UK	Germany	France	Italy
House price inflation (% per year, 1971–2001)	2.4	0.0	0.8	1.2
Value of mortgage debt (% GDP, 2001)	59	55	19	10
Variable rate mortgages (% of total, 2001)	64	0	5	34
Owner occupation rate (%, 2000)	69	42	55	68
Mortgage equity withdrawal (% disposable income, 1979–1999)	2.6	–5.7	–6.3	–6.1

Source: HM Treasury

Empirical evidence indicates that the monetary policy transmission mechanism is much stronger in the UK than the rest of Europe due to the structure of its housing market. Table 14.4 compares the key features of different housing markets in the four major European economies. The two most important features are the relatively high proportion of owner-occupied housing in the UK, and also the high proportion of owners that hold flexible rate mortgages.

The evidence in Table 14.4 suggest that interest rate changes will have a much more profound effect on UK aggregate demand than in the rest of Europe (i.e., the transmission mechanism is much stronger). Flexible rate mortgages imply that changes in interest rates will have direct effects on mortgage rates. Given that mortgage debt represents a relatively large proportion of GDP, interest rate changes will generate significant income effects and large changes in consumption (see Chapter 2). This almost certainly means that even if the UK achieves convergence in cycles with the rest of Europe, it would still stand to benefit strongly by maintaining autonomy over monetary policy.

Flexibility

There is little doubt that on almost all measures the UK exhibits higher nominal flexibility than Europe (see Figures 14.16 and 14.17). This would imply that the UK is relatively well positioned to adjust to asymmetric shocks and so the stability costs of adopting a single currency are correspondingly lower.

However, this may be a problem as the UK's flexibility does not appear to be mirrored in the major EMU member states. Work by Blanchard and Wolfers (2000) argues that differences in unemployment are not accounted for by asymmetric shocks, but by asymmetric responses to common or symmetric shocks. This is explained by differences in labour market institutions.

For example, if a common negative shock hit all of Europe, then unemployment will rise. However, labour market flexibility in the UK might be expected to offset some of the negative shock, implying that the fall in unemployment will be lower. Therefore, the UK will find itself in a position where it requires less of a stimulus than other EMU states in order to reinstall full employment. This issue points to a lack of structural convergence in labour market institutions. Again, there are clear benefits of maintaining policy discretion by remaining outside of EMU.

The dynamic nature of optimal currency areas

A valid criticism of the OCA theory and evidence presented so far is that it is very static. The costs and benefits of being in a monetary union are simply calculated at one point in time. In assessing entry to a monetary union, it is also necessary to consider the dynamics that might result from the entry decision.

A simple way of analysing this was devised by Frankel who derived the OCA line (Figure 14.22). Countries that are highly integrated and have high income correlations are more likely to develop and maintain an OCA successfully. Strong trade links increase the monetary benefits of a single currency, whereas high correlation of incomes represents convergence and lower stability losses. The OCA line in Figure 14.22 is the marginal case, where the advantages of a common currency and the advantages of monetary independence are equal. Groups of countries to the right of the OCA line are where the benefits of a single currency dominate, and groups to the left are where advantages of monetary independence dominate.

The OCA line essentially compares the costs and benefits of adopting a single currency. However, it cannot be ignored that these may change over time, especially once a monetary union has been established and a single currency adopted. For example, once a single currency has been established, the nature of trade and income convergence might change.

Figure 14.22 Two key OCA properties

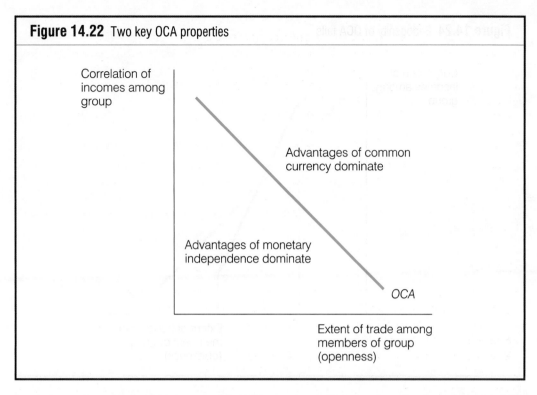

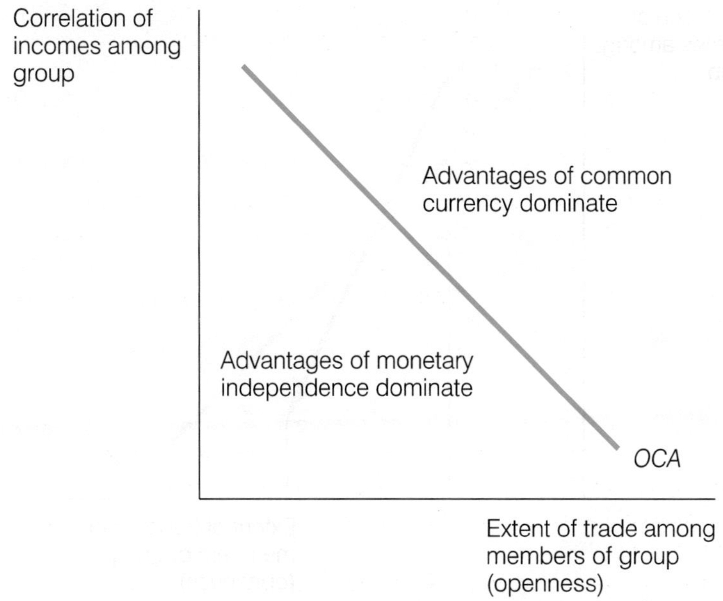

Figure 14.23 Endogeneity of OCAs dominate

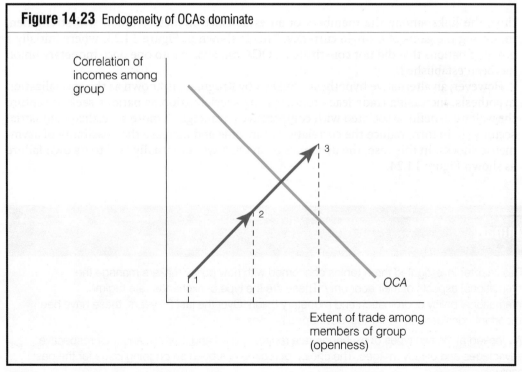

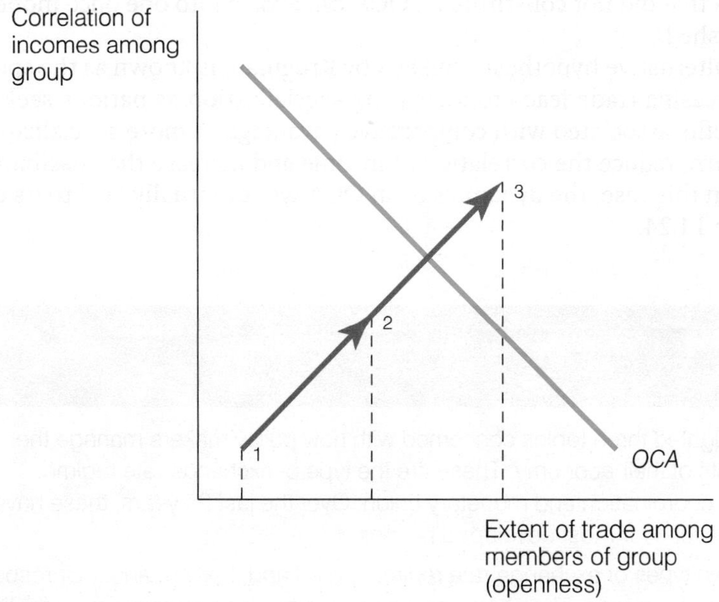

Almost certainly, a single currency will increase the extent of trade among the members of the single currency as transactions costs are reduced. Whether or not this makes an OCA more or less likely depends on the effect increasing openness has on income correlation.

One view by McCallum is that increasing openness leads to more significant spillovers between countries and therefore a higher degree of income correlation. Therefore, over

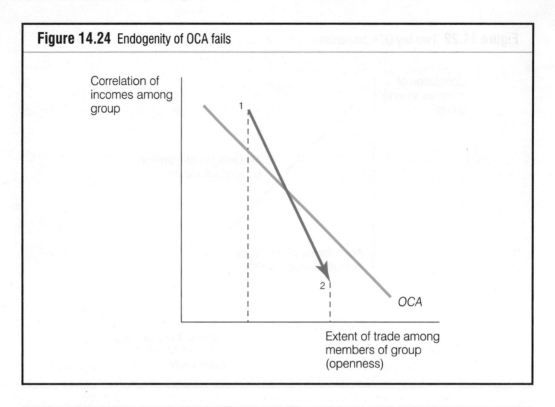

Figure 14.24 Endogenity of OCA fails

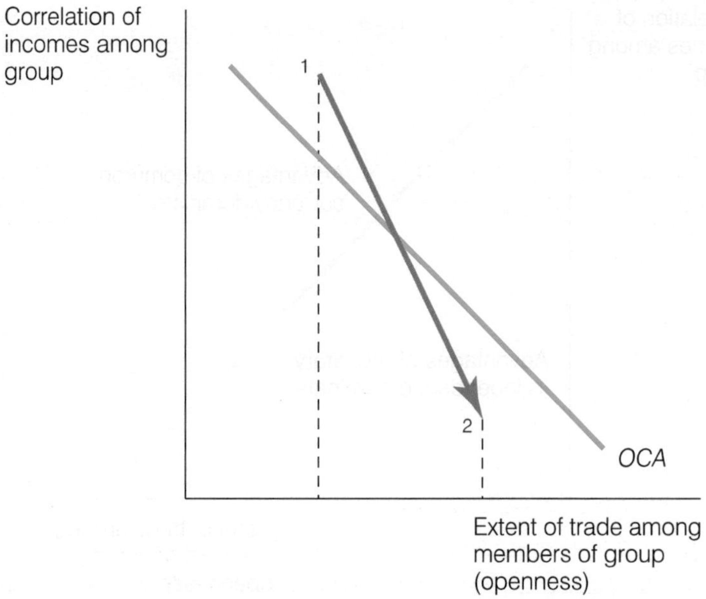

time, the links among the members of an established monetary union will strengthen, increasing the gains of a single currency. This is shown in Figure 14.23, where initially a group of nations that did not constitute an OCA can evolve into one once monetary union has been established.

However, an alternative hypothesis, pushed by Krugman, is known as the specialization hypothesis. Increasing trade leads to increasing specialization as nations seek to capture the welfare benefits associated with comparative advantage. A more specialized industrial sector will, in turn, reduce the correlation of income and increase the possibility of asymmetric shocks. In this case, the dynamics of an OCA will eventually lead to its own failure as shown Figure 14.24.

Summary

- This chapter investigated three topics concerned with how policy makers manage the international aspects of their economy. These are the type of exchange rate regime, international policy coordination and monetary union. Over the last 25 years, these have been important considerations for most developed nations.
- We looked at the two types of exchange rate regimes, fixed and floating, and their respective advantages and disadvantages. The choice of regime has been an ongoing issue for the past century.
- We also considered the subject of international policy coordination in terms of transmission of shocks and the impact of global demand. The role of the US in the global economy was analysed.

- Finally, we covered optimal currency areas (OCA). With the recent development of European Monetary Union (EMU) and the establishment of a single currency in Europe (the euro), this has become increasingly important.
- We examined several outstanding issues for OCAs, including the single market in Europe and whether the UK should adopt the euro.

Key term

Optimal currency areas (OCA)

Review questions

1. Using the Mundell-Fleming model, show why it is impossible to fix the exchange rate and exercise autonomy over monetary policy.
2. Briefly explain the advantages and disadvantages of fixed and floating exchange rate regimes.
3. Under conditions of perfect capital mobility, what would be the effect in Europe of a substantial tax cut in the US? (Assume that the US is a large country.) How might the European Central Bank or the national governments of Europe respond? What impact would this have on the US?
4. What are the main characteristics of an optimal currency area (OCA)?
5. Is convergence a necessary requirement before adopting a single currency?

More advanced problems

6. 'Fixed exchange rate regimes deliver price stability; floating exchange rate regimes maintain output stability.' Is this a fair statement? Explain your answer.
7. What is more relevant for the sustainability of EMU: asymmetric shocks, or asymmetric responses to symmetric shocks?
8. The problem of time inconsistency suggests that government announcements of low inflation lack credibility. Why should government announcements of maintaining a fixed exchange rate be more credible?
9. Are single currency areas unsustainable?

For further resources, visit
http://www.thomsonlearning.co.uk/chamberlin_yueh

15 International financial markets and currency crises

Learning objectives

- Learn about the internationalization of financial markets
- Determine the causes of currency crises around the world
- Assess policy options to combat currency crises

15.1 Introduction

Over the last two decades, there has been a tremendous change in the nature and the scale of financial markets. Previously, most financial activity was purely domestic with financial institutions acting as an intermediary between domestic savers and borrowers. Most countries had imposed exchange controls, which restricted the access of households and firms to foreign currency. These exchange controls meant that international capital mobility was low, and with only limited availability to obtain foreign currency, the opportunity for international trades was low.

Since the 1980s, though, there has been a dramatic reduction in exchange controls throughout the world, leading to a large rise in international capital mobility. This has helped to promote more trade between countries, and particularly so in financial assets. Domestic households and firms are no longer limited to borrowing and saving in the domestic financial market but have access to those overseas. The consequence being that financial markets in different countries have become increasingly interlinked, giving rise to what can be described as an international financial market. In addition, the scale of international trading has risen dramatically. The majority of this is short term and highly liquid, known as 'hot money', which can move quickly in and out of different markets in different countries.

In Chapter 6, we saw that financial markets can play an important role in the economy, offering the opportunity to diversify risks and allocate resources efficiently. By being able to trade in an international, rather than just a domestic market, these efficiencies should be enhanced. However, we also saw in Chapter 6 that financial markets can be prone to excessive volatility, which also appears to be a feature of the international financial market.

During the last few decades, there have been various episodes of high volatility in currency markets. A currency crisis arises when a currency comes under huge selling pressure forcing a very large and dramatic devaluation. Developing and transition countries have traditionally been the victims, especially in Latin America and more recently in Asia. However, the collapse of the Exchange Rate Mechanism (ERM) in the early 1990s aptly demonstrates that developed nations can also be prone to these crises.

Currency crises can be extremely damaging to developing and transition economies. Increasing openness has meant that shocks that happen in one country can quickly spread around the world; so, the economic progress of one country can be affected adversely by developments in another country. The process by which shocks can be transmitted across countries is known as *contagion*. One solution would be to reimpose capital controls, but this would also make the advantages of international financial markets unattainable. Therefore, policy makers have become increasingly concerned with designing the international financial architecture to maintain high capital mobility, while at the same time dealing with these instabilities.

The aim of this chapter is to introduce briefly the international financial market, and then concentrate on explaining why currency crises might arise, and what policies could be implemented to prevent them.

15.2 The internationalization of financial markets

International capital mobility has increased substantially. Since the 1970s, the growth in international financial transactions has far outstripped that of GDP. This feature is clearly seen in Chapter 11, where we saw the growing importance of the capital account in the balance of payments. There are three main reasons which have promoted the development of the international financial market. We have termed these as the historical change in exchange rate regimes; the growth in offshore banking and currency trading; and a change in ideology.

Changing exchange rate regimes

From the end of the Second World War to the early 1970s, most countries operated a fixed exchange rate policy as part of the Bretton Woods Agreement. A description of this was given in the previous chapter. In maintaining the fixed parity against the $US, central banks were inclined to intervene in currency markets to offset any change in the exchange rate. This, though, presented policy makers with restrictions elsewhere in managing the economy.

By intervening in currency markets, policy makers will have to either relinquish control of monetary policy, or impose capital controls. We explained the reasons for this in some detail in Chapter 12. By intervening in currency markets, the central bank will add to or decrease its foreign reserves, which constitute part of the monetary base and therefore the money supply. The effects of these interventions can be offset by sterilization, so it is possible to operate monetary policy under a fixed exchange rate.

The effective use of sterilization, though, depends on the degree of capital mobility. When this is high, capital flows will be large, so sterilization is hard to use. This presents a dilemma, which has come to be known as the *trilemma of policy* in open economies. The government can choose only two of the following: fixed exchange rates, control of monetary policy, or capital mobility.

Under a fixed exchange rate regime, policy makers must choose to control monetary policy or to impose exchange controls. However, with the abolition of Bretton Woods and the movement to floating rates, the choice changes to one where control over both monetary policy and openness in financial markets are possible. Therefore, the abolition of exchange controls may be driven partly by the fact that they are no longer needed to maintain monetary policy autonomy under a floating exchange rate regime.

Offshore banking and currency trading

In the previous chapter, it was shown that one of the developments leading to the collapse of the Bretton Woods system was the development of the Eurodollar market. This meant

Global application 15.1

Eurocurrency markets

The growth in offshore currency trading has gone hand-in-hand with that of offshore banking. Offshore currency deposits are usually referred to as Eurocurrencies, which is bit of a misnomer as much of this occurs in non-European centres, such as Singapore and Hong Kong. Dollar deposits located outside the US are referred to as Eurodollars. Banks that accept deposits of Eurocurrencies are called Eurobanks.

Several factors have been proposed to account for the rise in offshore banking and currency trading. The rise of the multinational firm and increasing world trade would increase the demand for overseas financial services. However, as

Global application 15.1 (continued)

mentioned in previous chapters, the growth in currency trading has far outstripped the growth in trade, so other factors must be relevant. These can be illustrated by looking at the growth of Eurocurrency trading.

Eurodollars were born in the 1950s in response to growing world trade. European firms involved in world trade frequently wished to hold dollar balances, but found it cheaper to obtain or borrow these from local banks rather than from the US itself. As other currencies became convertible, offshore markets also sprang up.

Two other factors contributing to the growth of Eurocurrency trading were official regulations and political concerns. During the 1957 balance of payments crisis in the UK, British banks were subject to strong exchange controls which prevented them from lending pounds to finance non-UK trade. This had been a highly profitable source of trade. Banks, though, could continue to profit by borrowing and lending dollars instead of sterling. This was generally free from exchange controls.

The Cold War was also a reason prompting the growth in Eurodollars. The USSR held dollar reserves in order to purchase grain from Western economies, but feared that depositing them in US banks might lead to confiscation if political events became more sensitive. Therefore, the USSR placed its dollar deposits in European banks.

Growth continued sharply during the 1960s. Severe restrictions on capital flows and banking regulation encouraged the creation of Eurodollars, which managed to circumvent these rules. This accelerated further with the collapse of the Bretton Woods Agreement, which diluted the need to restrict capital mobility to maintain the fixed exchange rate parity. In addition, the large oil price rises during the 1970s led to a large build up of dollar assets which Arab nations preferred not to hold in US accounts. They, too, worried about confiscation if the political climate became sensitive.

The growth in Eurocurrencies has been partially due to increasing world trade, but also as a result of great improvements in capital mobility through more liberalized financial markets. Freedom from reserve asset requirements was probably the most important of these. However, political effects have also played an important role in the past.

that the value of the dollar was determined in currency trading outside of the boundaries of the US. Consequently, any attempt made by the US Federal Reserve to assert exchange rate control could be circumvented by trading in the Eurodollar market, as this lies outside of the jurisdiction of the US and therefore cannot be subject to such restrictions.

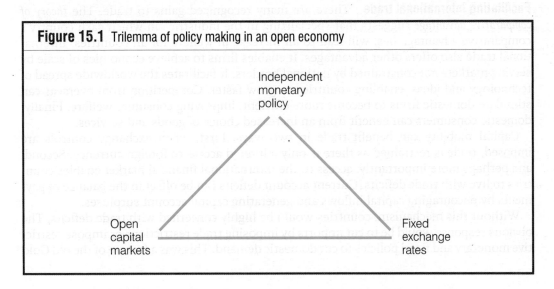

Figure 15.1 Trilemma of policy making in an open economy

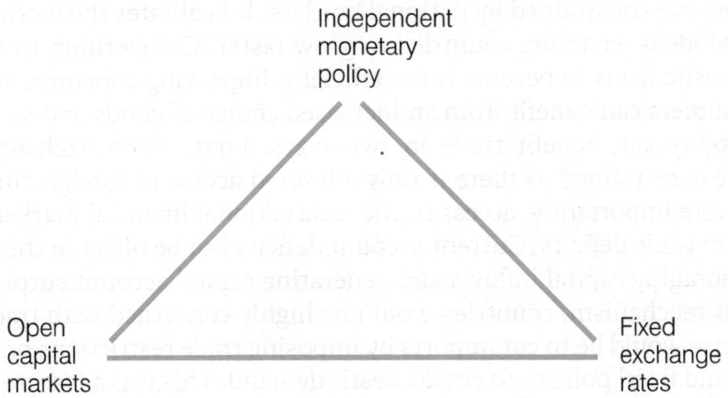

Offshore banking refers to the business that banks undertake in their foreign offices. Offshore currency trading has grown hand-in-hand with this, enabling people to trade a nation's currency outside of that country. This has steadily reduced the effectiveness of exchange controls and has also been an important factor in accounting for their demise. If capital controls can be easily circumvented, then they essentially become useless.

Stock exchange, Bangkok, Thailand
Source: Time Life Pictures/Getty Images

Changing ideology

The abolition of exchange controls and the increasing freedom to make international financial transactions have often mirrored the deregulation in domestic financial markets. The previous arguments are somewhat negative. They suggest that increasing capital mobility is simply a consequence of no longer needing controls to help maintain a fixed exchange rate, or that they are becoming increasingly irrelevant due to the scale of currency trading taking place outside of a nation's borders. However, a positive argument is that openness in financial markets might be something that is demanded in its own right.

As mentioned in the introduction, which also referred to some of the content in Chapter 6, there are potential benefits to integrating with the international financial market. In the next section, we aim to give a brief description to what some of these may be.

An international financial market: the advantages

There are several clear advantages to engaging with an international financial market.

Facilitating international trade There are many recognized gains to trade. The *theory of comparative advantage* suggests that specializing in the industries in which each country's comparative advantage lies, will lead to an increase in welfare for all countries. International trade also offers other advantages. It enables firms to achieve economies of scale by serving markets not constrained by national borders. It facilitates the worldwide spread of technology and ideas, enabling countries to grow faster. Competition from overseas can stimulate domestic firms to become more efficient, improving consumer welfare. Finally, domestic consumers can benefit from an increased choice of goods and services.

Capital mobility can benefit trade in two ways. First, when exchange controls are imposed, trade is restrained as there is only a limited access to foreign currency. Second, and perhaps more importantly, access to the international financial market enables countries to live with trade deficits. Current account deficits can be offset in the balance of payments by encouraging capital inflows and generating capital account surpluses.

Without this mechanism, countries would be highly concerned with trade deficits. The obvious response would be to cut imports by imposing trade restrictions or impose restrictive monetary and fiscal policies to cut domestic demand. This was a feature of the old Gold

Global application 15.2

The Feldstein-Horioka debate

If global financial markets are truly globalized, then investors will seek the highest possible returns regardless of national borders. Feldstein and Horioka argue that if this is the case, the link between domestic saving and investment should be small, but this is at odds with empirical evidence.

In a regression of domestic investment on domestic saving:

$$I_t = \alpha + \beta S_t$$

acceptance of the Feldstein-Horioka hypothesis requires $\beta \approx 0$. Empirical evidence, though, finds that β is significantly different from zero. This relationship is shown in Figure 1, where there is a clear positive relationship between the investment and saving proportions of GDP.

All this suggests that saving does not flow easily across national borders, and most investors lend to borrowers in the same country. One explanation might be that there is an endemic 'home bias'. If information is limited, then more risk-averse investors would be less willing to invest overseas. The effects of protecting trade would also increase the size of β, as domestic investors are prevented from moving funds overseas.

Figure 1 National savings and national investment

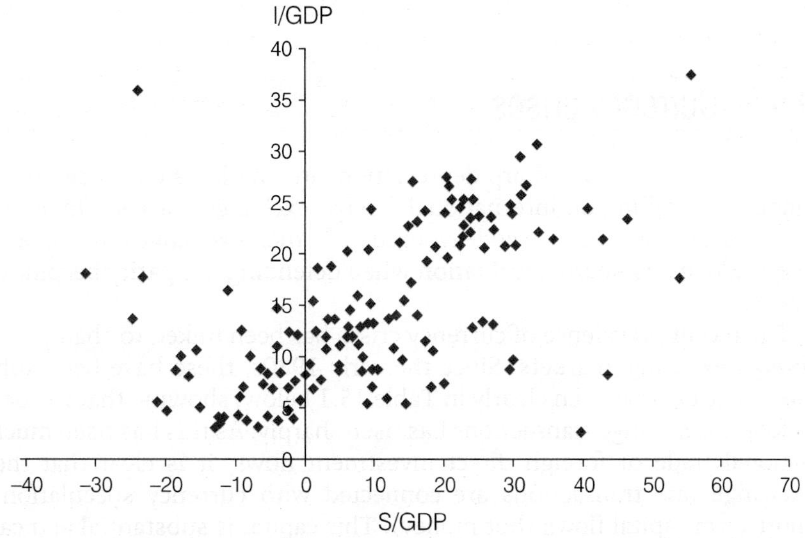

Standard system, where countries were hesitant to trade with each other due to the difficulties involved with correcting external deficits.

Portfolio diversification In Chapter 6, we saw that financial markets enable investors to diversify risk. If these investors are risk averse, then this achieves higher welfare. Portfolio diversification is a way of diversifying risks by investing in a range of different assets. This will limit the exposure of the investor to the poor performance of any particular asset. In an international financial market, the opportunities for doing this are much greater.

By investing solely in the assets of one country, the investor is still open to systemic risks, even if their portfolios are well diversified. This is because it might be expected that all the assets in one country might react in the same way if that country is subject to a specific shock or policy. Naturally, exposure to these risks can be limited by investing in the assets of several different countries.

Promoting an efficient allocation of resources An international financial market enables savers and borrowers to invest anywhere in the world. As a result, investors will move their funds in order to achieve the highest return possible, wherever that is in the world. The projects offering the highest returns will be those that are actually undertaken, meaning that world output will increase. Competition in international financial markets can also have strong dynamic effects. In order to achieve the highest rate of return, firms will be encouraged to minimize costs and only undertake investment projects that yield positive returns.

A disciplining device on policy making

In the same way that international capital markets encourage firms to behave efficiently, they can have a similar disciplining device on policy makers. Poor policy is likely to be punished with capital outflows. For example, if a country is running excessive fiscal deficits, then the increasing risk of default will lead to higher risk premiums being imposed on that nation's debt. Therefore, poor policy produces an interest rate penalty for the economy.

15.3 Currency crises

Currency crises are sharp depreciations in a nation's currency brought about by large amounts of selling on international foreign exchange markets. In almost all instances, it involves nations that have endeavoured to fix their exchange rate, but are then forced into a very sudden and sharp devaluation when defending the parity becomes impossible or too costly.

The recent prevalence of currency crises has been linked to changes in the international foreign exchange markets. Since the early 1980s, these have been substantially deregulated. The effect is seen clearly in Table 15.1 below, showing that the daily global turnover of foreign exchange transactions has risen sharply. As this has risen much faster than international trade or foreign direct investment flows, it is clear that the vast majority of exchange rate transactions are connected with currency speculation or in facilitating short-term capital flows (hot money). This capital is substantial and can flow around the world exceptionally fast.

A policy maker can protect a fixed exchange rate by using foreign currency and gold reserves to intervene in the market. However, given the large increase in turnover, the heavy selling required to force a devaluation is now much more plausible.

15

Recent currency crises of note that will be discussed are:

- The Latin American crisis, 1981–1982
- The ERM crisis, 1992
- The Mexican crisis, 1994–1995
- The Asian crisis, 1997–1998

Table 15.1 Aggregate reserves and currency trading, 1977–1998

Year	(1) Official reserves	(2) Official reserves and gold	(3) Daily global turnover	(4) Reserves/ turnover (1)/(3)	(5) Reserves and gold/ turnover (2)/(3)
1977	265.8	296.6	18.3	14.5	16.2
1980	386.6	468.9	82.5	4.7	5.7
1983	339.7	494.6	119.0	2.8	4.2
1986	456.0	540.0	270.0	1.7	2.0
1989	722.3	826.8	590.0	1.2	1.4
1992	910.8	1022.5	820.0	1.1	1.2
1995	1347.3	1450.0	1190.0	1.1	1.2
1998	1636.1	1972.0	1500.0	1.0	1.3

Source: Bank of International Settlements (BIS)

Why attack a currency: how do speculators make money from devaluations?

If a speculator thinks that a currency will devalue, then he can submit an order to the markets to sell the currency now and buy it back at a later date. If, in the meantime, the exchange rate depreciates, it means that the speculator is selling the currency for far more than for which it is being bought back, representing in many cases a sizeable trading profit. For example, if the currency devalues by 50 per cent, then this is the size of the capital gain that the speculator will make.

To maintain a fixed exchange rate, the government must use its gold and foreign exchange reserves to intervene in the currency markets. If a speculator tries to sell the currency, then the government must use some of its reserves to buy the currency and prevent downward pressure being placed on the exchange rate. If a devaluation occurs, then the source of speculator profit will be the capital losses that governments make on their interventions (i.e., a devaluation would mean that they are buying the currency now for more than they could sell it for later).

Conventional models argue that a currency crisis will emerge when the government runs out of reserves and is no longer able to defend the fixed exchange rate against heavy selling by speculators. The heavy selling by speculators is a vital part of the anatomy of a crisis. Remember that speculators can profit from a devaluation, and that by their selling actions, they can help create this by exhausting the government's reserves. Therefore, speculators know that when the government is low on reserves, they may be able to force a devaluation and profit from their own actions.

Example The theory behind this is best represented by an example which is taken from Obstfeld and Rogoff (1995). Suppose there are two traders, 1 and 2, who can either sell or hold their currency holdings, each having six units. The cost of undertaking a sell order is 1, whereas holding costs are 0.

Suppose the government has reserves of 20 with which to defend the currency. If a devaluation is forced, then the exchange rate will depreciate by 50 per cent. In this case, the pay-off each trader receives given the action of the other can be represented in Figure 15.2.

The equilibrium in this game is for both traders to hold, no matter what the other does. This is because, individually or together, the speculators cannot exert enough pressure to overwhelm the government, so any action would be unsuccessful and cost 1 unit.

However, suppose the government's reserves are low, and are only 6. In this case, either speculator has the ability to force a devaluation since they can completely exhaust the government's reserves by their selling actions. The pay-off matrix in Figure 15.3 will result.

15

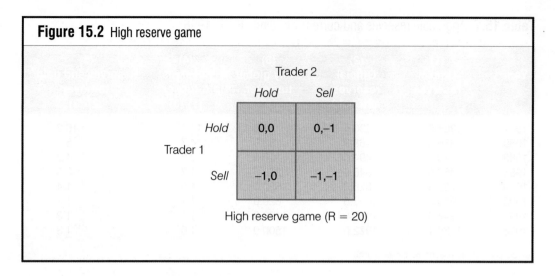

Figure 15.2 High reserve game

Trader 1 \ Trader 2	*Hold*	*Sell*
Hold	0,0	0,–1
Sell	–1,0	–1,–1

High reserve game (R = 20)

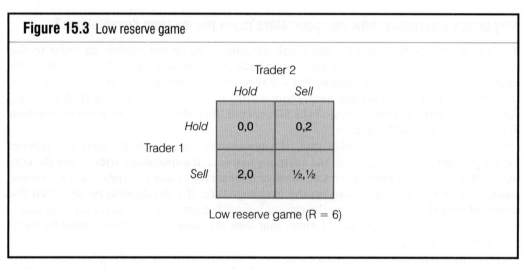

Figure 15.3 Low reserve game

Trader 1 \ Trader 2	*Hold*	*Sell*
Hold	0,0	0,2
Sell	2,0	½,½

Low reserve game (R = 6)

If one trader sold while the other did not, a profit of 2 will be made. This is because the government would commit its assets of 6, but these can be exhausted by an individual trader causing a 50 per cent devaluation. This transfers trading revenue of 3 to the trader, who then pays the trading cost to end up with a positive profit of 2.

If both traders sell, then the trading revenue of 3 is shared between them, each receiving 1.5 units each. They then both pay the transaction charge of 1 to leave a possible profit of 0.5. Therefore, as any sell action would yield a profit, no trader would ever wish to hold, so both traders selling would be the equilibrium of the game.

Whether or not a speculative attack occurs depends on it having a good chance of succeeding, and this is most likely to occur when the government has few resources with which to defend the currency. Under what conditions then is a currency likely to come under attack?

1. **Balance of payments crisis**: the government runs down its reserves in the official financing of current account deficits. However, because reserves are limited, official financing cannot sustain deficits forever. Eventually, the balance of payments deficit will require an exchange rate devaluation.
2. **Inflation**: in a fixed exchange rate regime, runaway inflation will erode competitiveness, as there will be no offsetting exchange rate depreciations. This will lead to the

actual exchange rate being overvalued compared to its PPP level, and the erosion of competitiveness would be expected to put pressure on the current account.

3. **Government deficits**: a government running a substantial debt may be encouraged to produce some inflation (seigniorage revenues) in order to reduce the real value of its debt. Therefore, large deficits may be seen as inflationary, with consequences for competitiveness and the balance of payments.

15.3.1 First generation models

The first generation of currency crises models links the onset of the crisis to one of these problems. All of them are expected to lead to a demise in the external competitiveness of the nation and in a fall in reserves. The eventual exhaustion of reserves would lead to a collapse in the fixed rate.

The timing of the crisis will be as soon as speculators believe that it will be successful to attack and this is when the government is down to a critical level of reserves. Heavy selling will then just exhaust the remaining reserves. The fixed rate is ultimately unsustainable because of fundamental factors; the actions of speculators just bring its eventual demise forward.

Latin America, 1981–1982

This is a conventional example of a first generation currency crisis. The economies of Chile, Brazil, Mexico and Argentina were operating a fixed exchange rate against the $US. These were collectively known as the Tablitas, which was a pre-announced schedule of depreciations against the US dollar known as a crawling peg. However, a substantial inflation differential between these Latin American nations and the US meant that inflation rose in excess of the currency depreciations, which eroded their competitiveness and put pressure on their balance of payments.

15.3.2 Second generation models: ERM, 1992; Mexico, 1994–1995

An extension to the game introduced above is the following, where the government has resources of 10. The pay-offs are shown in Figure 15.4 below.

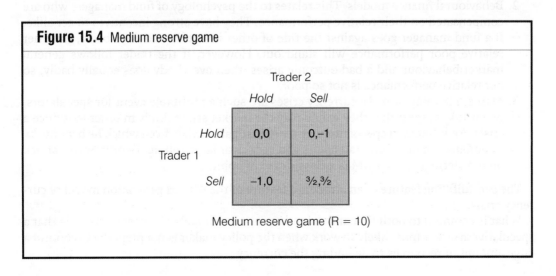

Figure 15.4 Medium reserve game

		Trader 2: *Hold*	Trader 2: *Sell*
Trader 1	*Hold*	0,0	0,−1
	Sell	−1,0	$3/2$,$3/2$

Medium reserve game (R = 10)

The feature of this game is that no trader on his own can initiate a crisis, but both working together can. If both hold, then the pay-offs are obviously zero. If one held and one sold, the seller would lose 1 unit. However, if both sold, then the government would commit its reserves and make a 50 per cent loss, so the trading revenue would be 5, or 2.5 each. After paying the trading fee, residual profits are 1.5 each.

As each trader's optimal decision is to do what the other does, this game has two solutions. Either both will sell, or both will hold. The interesting feature of this game is that a currency crisis may hit one nation, whereas a similar country can escape such a situation. If speculators decide to attack and can coordinate their actions, then the attack will be successful in forcing a devaluation. In this case, there is a degree of arbitrariness about a speculative attack. Attacks are self-fulfilling, in the sense that once they start they will ultimately succeed, but otherwise a country that is not subject to attack can continue to maintain the fixed parity.

Self-fulfilling crises

The end of the peg is not preordained. There may be no worsening trend in fundamentals, and no reason as to why a currency should necessarily be subject to attack. However, the possibility can still exist that a large attack may be impossible to defend should it happen. There is a range of fundamentals where a crisis may happen, but not necessarily must do. In such a situation, a crisis can become a self-fulfilling event. A strong degree of coordination among speculators is required for pessimism to become self-confirming.

The situation in which a crisis could happen, but need not, presents speculators with a one-way bet. They will reap a huge capital gain by selling currency if the exchange rate regime collapses, but will make no losses (apart from transaction costs) if the collapse fails to materialize. If self-fulfilling crises are a possibility, then what can create the coordination dynamics that can set them off?

'Herding' is the simple idea that speculators will all move in the same direction because the behaviour of one will influence the behaviour of others in the same direction. There are several explanations as to why this might happen.

1. A *bandwagon effect* induced by the presumption that an investor has private information. These bandwagon effects create hot money that destabilizes markets and causes an overreaction. When one speculator sees the actions of another, he may conclude that the behaviour of that speculator is based on some private information that he does not know about. As a result, thinking that another speculator is more informed than he is, he is inclined to copy the speculator's actions.
2. Behavioural finance models. This relates to the psychology of fund managers who are compensated on their relative performance. They have strong incentives to act alike. If a fund manager goes against the tide of other investors and does badly, then her relative poor performance will stand out. However, if the trader follows general market behaviour and a bad outcome arises, then everybody does equally badly, so her relative performance is not so poor.
3. Market manipulation. As currency crises are such a profitable event for speculators, one would suspect that they would play the market strategically in order to induce a crisis. An influential speculator may try to instigate a crisis from which he benefits by a combination of public statements and very clear large selling. George Soros' attack on the sterling in the ERM is a classic case in point.

The self-fulfilling feature of an attack is a feature of the second generation model of currency crisis.

What is common to both first and second generation models of currency crises is that a speculative attack is most likely to work when the policy maker is not prepared to commit a large amount of resources to defending the currency.

In the first generation model, this is because something fundamental about the economy ultimately makes the fixed parity unsustainable. A speculative attack just brings forward the inevitable.

In the second generation model, a speculative attack may or may not happen, but what is likely to make speculators attack a particular country? This will happen, as in the above example, when the policy maker may be unwilling to defend the parity of the currency. This is most likely to be the case (as we will see with the ERM and Mexican crises) when such a commitment would require measures that the policy maker would rather not take.

Why might the exchange rate be so hard to peg?

Capital market deregulation has led to an explosion in hot money flows (see Table 15.1). A common misconception is that daily trading of currencies is too large – exceeding $1 trillion per day – and that no government could hope to defend their currency against such an attack. The largest individual hedge funds command enough resources to wipe out the foreign exchange reserves of all but 20 central banks.

For example, in 1994, Soros Management reported investment capital of $11 billion and Tiger Management of more than $6 billion. An estimate of total hedge fund reserves was $75–100 billion. Despite the existence of these large funds, there is no insurmountable obstacle to fixing the exchange rate.

This is simply because a monetary authority can use the interest rate to defend the currency. From UIP, we know that the exchange rate will change unless:

$$r = r^* + \rho \tag{15.1}$$

So, this has to be the minimum interest rate that the government can offer. ρ reflects the relative risk premium of domestic and foreign assets. The risk premium largely reflects the probability of a devaluation (as a devaluation will result in capital losses for foreign investors). Consequently, as the expectation of a devaluation becomes larger, the risk premium rises, which requires a larger interest rate to attract the necessary inflows.

However, high interest rates will have an adverse impact on the rest of the economy. The government is then faced with a choice: it can either accept the higher rate with its effects on the domestic economy, or it can abandon the fixed rate and let the currency depreciate.

The government's resolve to defend the currency will be influenced by its ability to accept higher interest rates. Under what conditions might the rise in interest rates required be intolerable?

1. Unemployment – significant unemployment will make rises in interest rates more unbearable.
2. Public debt – highly indebted countries with short-term debt will find the chances of fiscal insolvency are greatly increased if the threat of devaluation drives up interest rates (as was the case in Italy in 1992).
3. Banks – higher interest rates may lead to corporate and personal bankruptcies which will increase the number of non-performing loans held by creditors, perhaps precipitating a banking crisis.

Therefore, there are three ingredients which lead to a potential crisis:

1. a reason as to why the government may wish to abandon the fixed exchange rate
2. a reason as to why the government would wish to defend the exchange rate; so there is a degree of conflict between its objectives
3. the cost of defending a currency must increase when people expect that the rate might be abandoned.

These three factors taken together are all that is required to generate a conventional model of a currency crisis.

A nation may have reasons to defend the currency:

- a fixed exchange rate is important for facilitating international trade and investment
- as a way of introducing inflation discipline/credibility into the economy.

However, if under pressure of a devaluation, the cost of defending the currency becomes too great, the policy maker may be prepared to let go of the fixed parity. A speculative attack on the currency may then become likely as speculators are prepared to gamble on the resolve of the policy maker to sustain the high interest rates necessary to defend the currency.

ERM crisis, 1992

In 1992, massive speculation led to the exit of Britain, Spain and Italy from the ERM. All these countries fit the second generation model well, but the UK example is particularly illuminating.

The UK's decision to join the ERM (exchange rate mechanism) was the cornerstone of its anti-inflation policy. By fixing the pound (£) against the German Deutschmark (DM), Germany's low inflation discipline could be imported and, for a time, it worked as UK inflation came under control from its peak in 1990. Therefore, there was a clear reason as to why the UK would wish to maintain the fixed exchange rate.

However, maintaining the fixed exchange rate against the DM required UK interest rates to follow German levels, and they were particularly high. German reunification was largely paid for by borrowing rather than tax cuts, and in order to prevent inflation, the German Bundesbank substantially increased German interest rates. If the UK wished to keep its fixed parity, then obviously it would need to follow suit.

Figure 15.5 UK interest rates, 1980–2002 Source: ONS

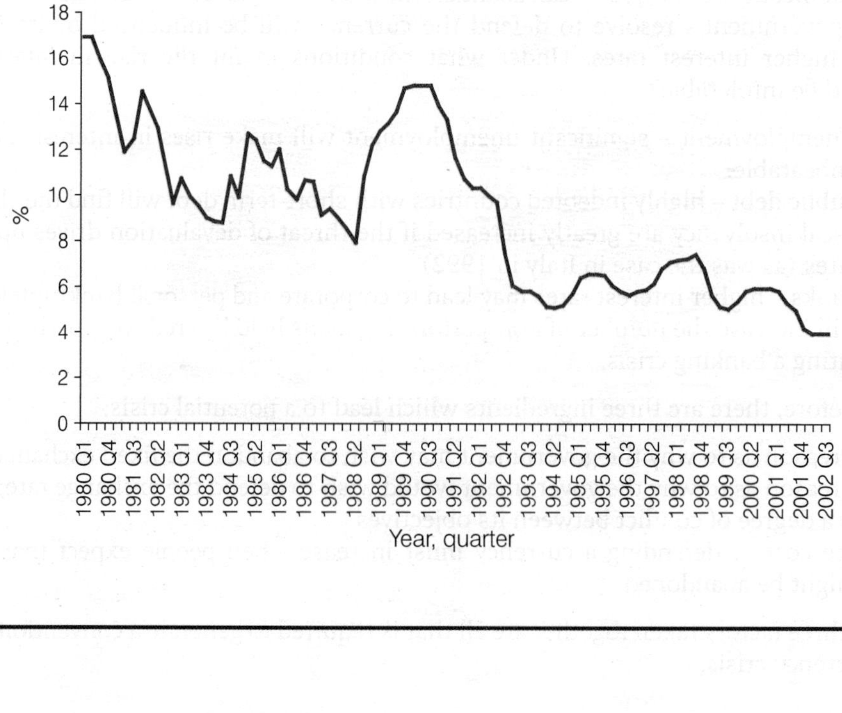

Figure 15.6 UK unemployment, 1980–2002 Source: ONS

Figure 15.5 shows the path of UK interest rates; the upward push in 1990–1991 is clearly observable.

However, operating high interest rates put other pressures on the UK economy. At the time, the UK was in a severe recession and suffering high unemployment, as Figure 15.6 will testify.

If anything, the UK needed lower interest rates in order to try to invigorate the economy and reduce unemployment. As this was impossible for as long the UK belonged to the ERM and there was no movement in German interest rates, there was a clear argument for abandoning the fixed exchange rate.

Speculative pressure on the pound arose simply because of this conflict of policy objectives. If the pound came under heavy selling pressure, it would seem a very reasonable policy for the UK to simply let the pound devalue and sacrifice ERM membership. This is because defending the pound would require higher and higher interest rates, which would be intolerable for domestic reasons.

George Soros accumulated a $15 billion short position against the pound. However, the UK could easily have defended the fixed rate if it so desired. On Black Wednesday, after renewed heavy selling, a brief defence of the pound was undertaken: interest rates rose from 10 per cent to 12 per cent, and then further to 15 per cent. This did not avert the attack, but still the UK could have imposed higher interest rates if it really wanted to. (For example, Swedish overnight interest rates jumped to 500 per cent at one point.) However, when 15 per cent did not work, the UK government gave up the parity, prompting a collapse in the £ against the DM, as Figure 15.7 shows.

However, exit from the ERM was not necessarily such bad news. First, it enabled UK interest rates to come down quite sharply (Figure 15.5) and the depreciation in the exchange rate (Figure 15.7) boosted UK competitiveness. The result was that the UK economy began to grow, and the fall in unemployment is easily observed in Figure 15.6.

Figure 15.7 The DM–£ exchange rate, 1992

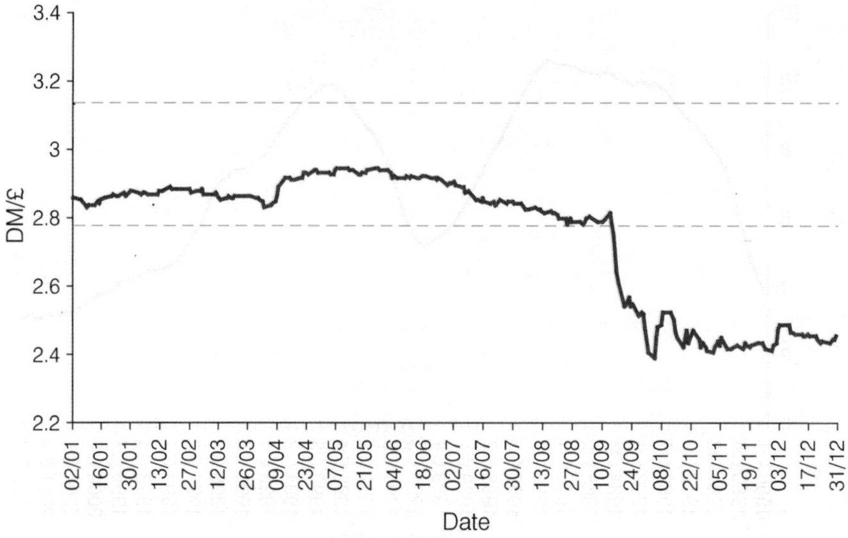

For this reason, there are many who refer to Black Wednesday as White Wednesday. The day after Black Wednesday much of the British press attacked George Soros who personally made £1 billion from the pound devaluation. However, given the UK's economic performance subsequently, there have even been calls to put up a statue of him in Trafalgar Square!

The anatomy of the ERM crisis is shown in Figure 15.8. The high German interest rate meant that the interest rate required to maintain the fixed exchange rate (r^*) was above the interest rate (r_1) that maintains full employment output (Y^*). As a result, maintaining membership of the ERM required a tight monetary policy ($LM_1 \rightarrow LM_2$), forcing output below its full employment level ($Y_1 < Y^*$). This led to the conflict which is at the centre of the second generation model. The UK government had an incentive to raise interest rates so as to preserve membership of the ERM, but also an incentive to leave in order to relax monetary policy and lower unemployment. The third feature of the crisis is that the costs of defending the fixed exchange rate must increase as it becomes increasingly expected that the parity will be abandoned.

This is also shown in Figure 15.8. As the belief rises, that the government would be prepared to abandon the fixed parity to reduce unemployment, the expectation of a currency depreciation becomes greater. As a result, this adds extra risk to holding sterling denominated assets, so interest rates must rise further to maintain the ERM membership. This is shown as the restrictive monetary policy ($LM_2 \rightarrow LM_3$), which increases the interest rate to $r^* + \rho_1$, where ρ_1 is the risk premium reflecting the probability of devaluation.

However, this action will simply exasperate the situation. Income will be reduced even further to Y_2, pushing unemployment higher. As the domestic situation becomes more acute, then the expectation of a devaluation will increase, requiring a further contraction in monetary policy ($LM_3 \rightarrow LM_4$), higher interest rates $r^* + \rho_2$, and a fall in income to Y_3. This reaffirms the predictions of the second generation model. The government can defend the exchange rate by tightening monetary policy, but the domestic costs of doing so can rise to the extent that this becomes a fruitless exercise. By abandoning the policy, the liberation of monetary policy would enable interest rates to be lowered to r_1 and restore full employment.

Figure 15.8 The anatomy of the UK ERM crisis

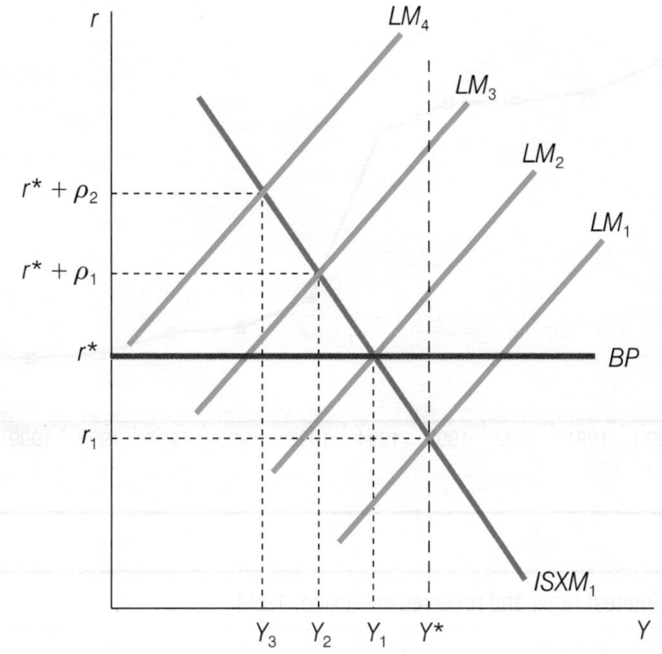

Mexico crisis, 1994–1995

The collapse of the Mexican peso against the $US in 1994 is shown in Figure 15.9.

Prior to the collapse, the Mexican peso had been operating a fixed parity against the $US. However, leading up to the end of 1994, there were several underlying weaknesses in the Mexican economy which led speculators to question the sustainability of the peg.

1. Concerns originated from PPP calculations, which indicated that prices/costs had risen in excess of trading partners, implying that the fixed exchange rate was overvalued. This was indicated as the cause of a growing current account deficit, which rose to 7 per cent of GDP in 1993 and 8 per cent in 1994.
2. Central bank reserves were running down and defending the currency was requiring higher interest rates. This was a time when Mexico was suffering high unemployment.
3. There was a lot of political pressure for a devaluation. Mexico had a history of devaluing in election years. Civil unrest at the hard economic conditions culminated in the assassination of Luis Donaldo Colosio, the ruling party's presidential candidate. Monetary policy was relaxed in the build-up to elections and, at the same time, the election year rise in public spending had weakened the government's fiscal position.

The growing need for a devaluation, though, was ignored initially by policy makers. Even if it made sense to devalue, the cost in terms of credibility would be high. The fixed exchange rate regime and price stability would, if the present difficulties could be tolerated, yield the conditions that are favourable to long-term investment – a due consideration for an emerging market economy that is largely dependent on outside investment.

Faced with mounting external pressure, Mexico decided to devalue the peso, but in many respects this was botched. The initial devaluation of 15 per cent was widely perceived

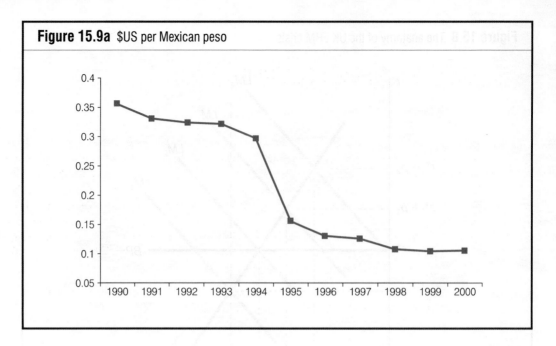

Figure 15.9a $US per Mexican peso

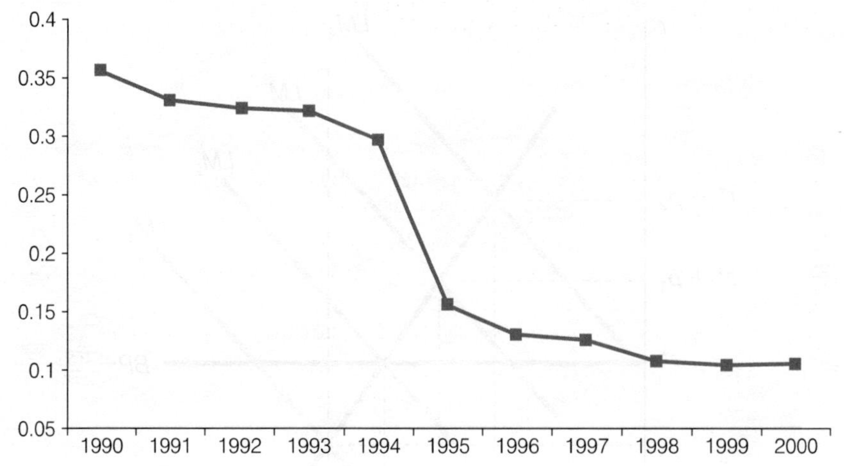

Figure 15.9b Interest rates and reserves in Mexico, 1994

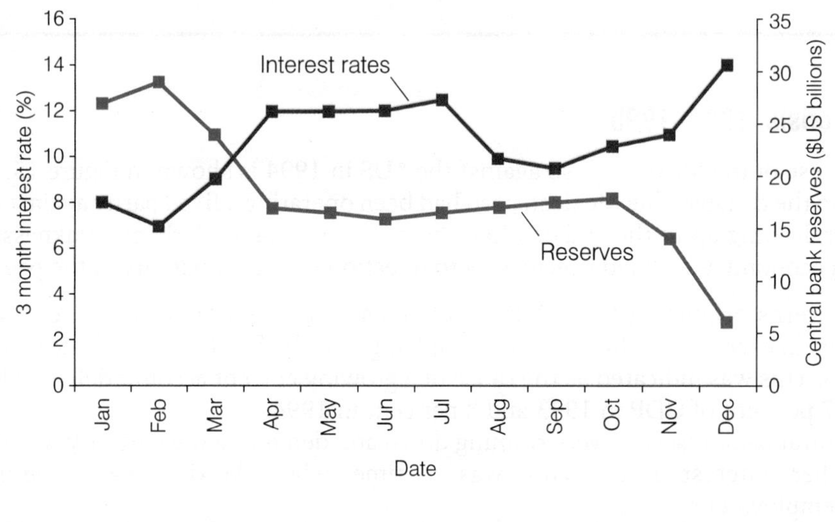

as being inadequate, so the government had compromised its credibility for no real gain in competitiveness. Second, by consulting Mexican business leaders about the plan, a large group of insiders stood ready to capitalize on the devaluation at the expense of the uninformed foreign investors. Therefore, the small initial devaluation was quickly followed by a complete loss of confidence. The falling peso threatened to create a large spike in inflation (due to more expensive imports), requiring a very large increase in short-term interest rates and leading to a substantial fall in aggregate demand and output. GDP fell by 7 per cent.

The general principle behind attacks seems to be inconsistency in policy making and the fact that ultimately governments are prepared to forsake long-term political or inflation credibility for a short-run economic expansion.

Global application 15.3

Chile and capital controls

During the 1990s, Chile was not subjected to the type of destabilizing capital outflows that beset much of Latin America. Therefore, its economy remained intact and between 1991 and 1997, GDP growth averaged in excess of 8 per cent (see Figure 2 for a comparison of Chile with Mexico). The reason for this is that financial markets, including the banking sector, were not completely open. All capital inflows other than equity purchases had to be accompanied by a one-year non-interest bearing deposit account equal to as much as 30 per cent of the transaction. This penalized short-term capital flows and removed the likelihood of crisis provoked by rapid withdrawal of capital.

Figure 2 GDP growth in Chile and Mexico, 1991–1998

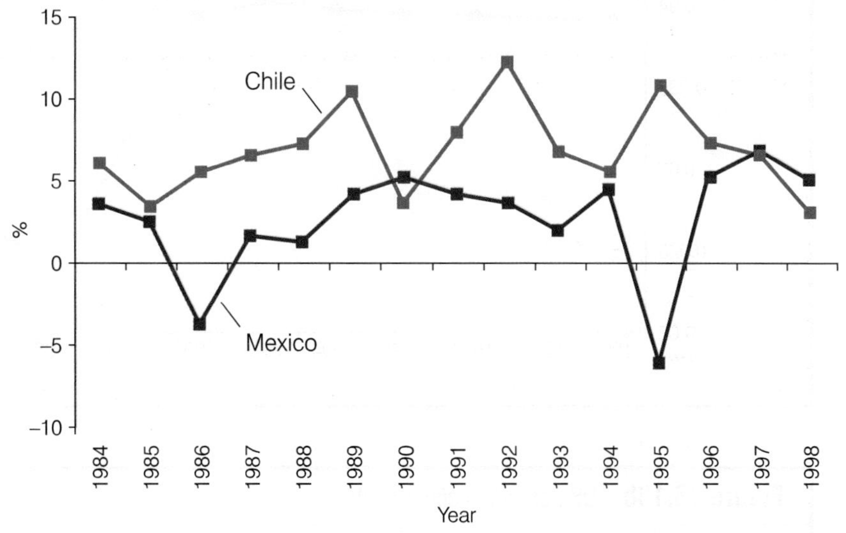

The Latin American crisis shares some common features with the ERM collapse, but the most striking difference was in the aftermath. The countries that were forced to parachute out of the ERM performed well; the depreciation injected competitiveness, and the freedom to reduce interest rates was exercised. However, the Mexican economy suffered severe downturns following devaluation.

Why did Latin America do so badly in the aftermath compared to Europe? Well, a UK devaluation may erode the credibility of the Chancellor, but will not shake confidence in UK institutions in general. A free market economy will continue to operate, debts will be honoured, and the Bank of England will continue to care about inflation. However, in Mexico a large devaluation raises all these questions. Will there be a backlash against reformist policy makers? All these issues may precipitate further capital outflows, deepening the crisis. This may explain why Mexican interest rates went up, and UK rates fell, following the crisis.

15.3.3 Third generation models: Asian crisis, 1997–1998

Figure 15.10 highlights the currency crisis that manifested itself in Asia during the end of 1997 and the beginning of 1998. The Asian five – Thailand, Malaysia, South Korea, Indonesia and the Philippines – all suffered from a collapse in the currency brought on by large-scale outflows of financial capital. Up until this time, these currencies were held relatively fixed against the $US. It is clear that the rapid drop in the exchange rate is a similar feature to the crises already described, but this is where the comparisons finish.

Although there were those who questioned the extent of Asia's economic miracle, it was largely unthinkable that the region would suffer the crisis that it did. True, current account

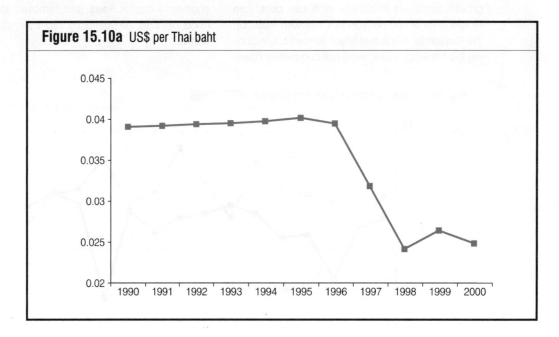

Figure 15.10a US$ per Thai baht

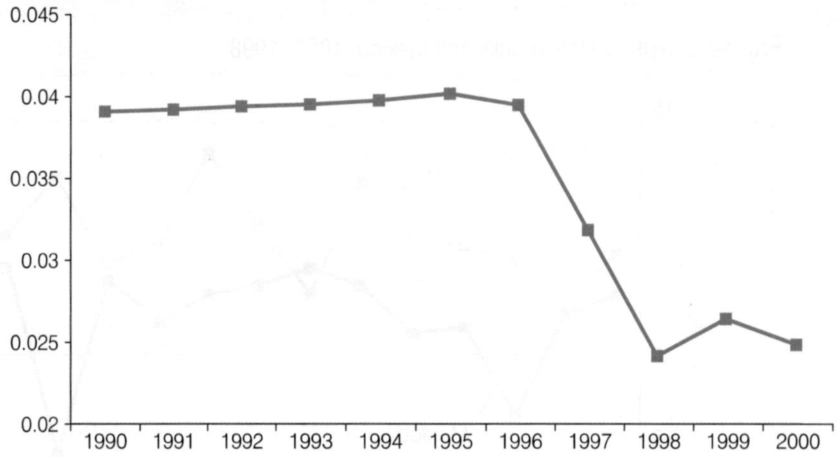

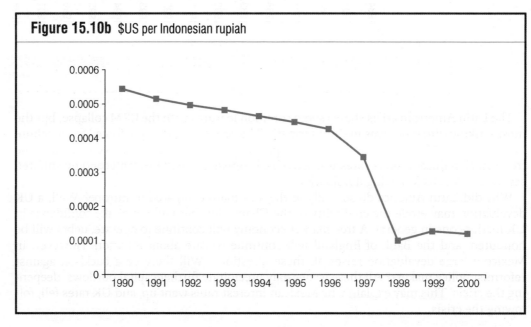

Figure 15.10b $US per Indonesian rupiah

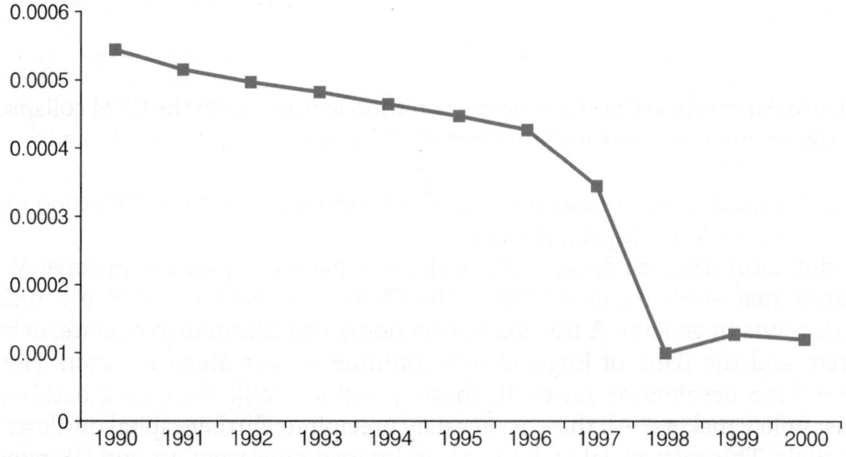

15

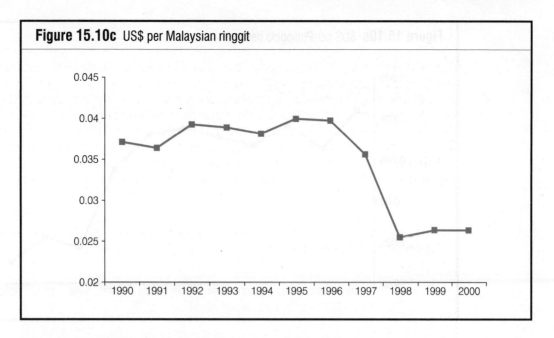

Figure 15.10c US$ per Malaysian ringgit

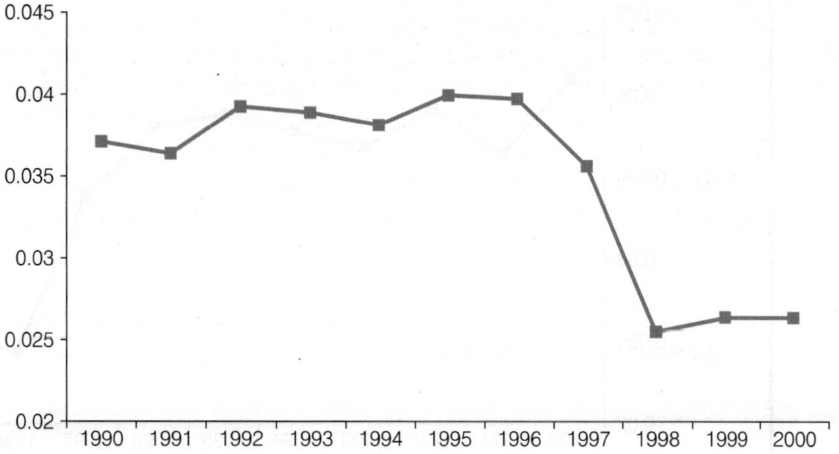

Figure 15.10d $US per Korean won

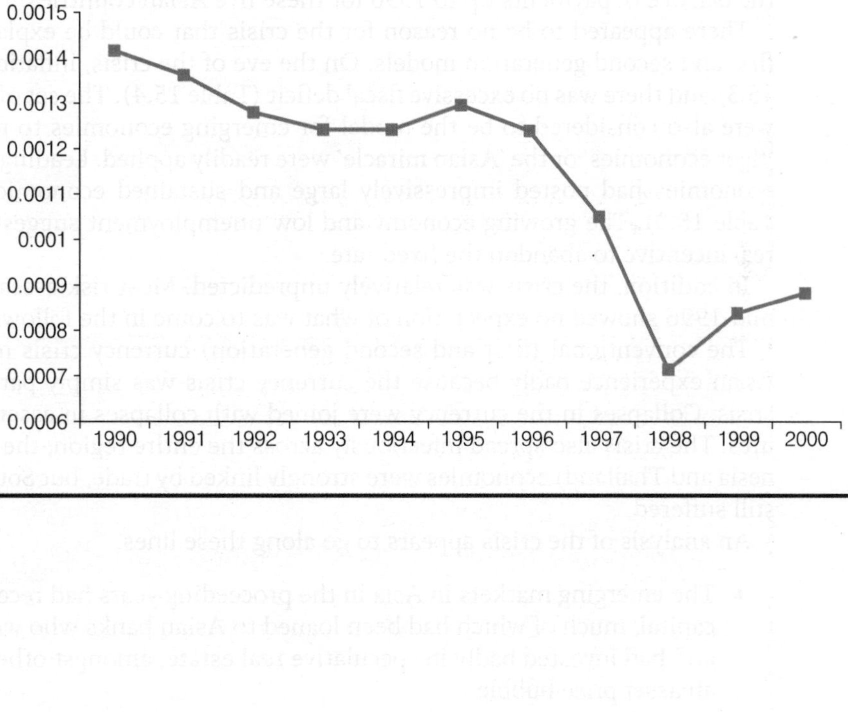

15

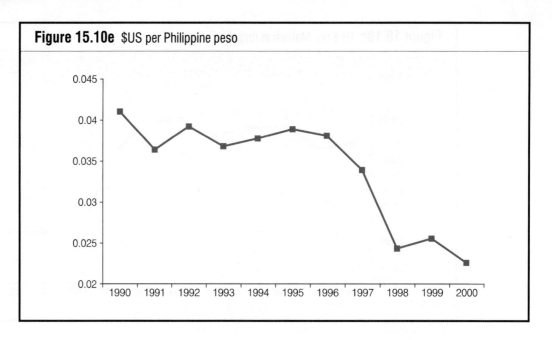

Figure 15.10e $US per Philippine peso

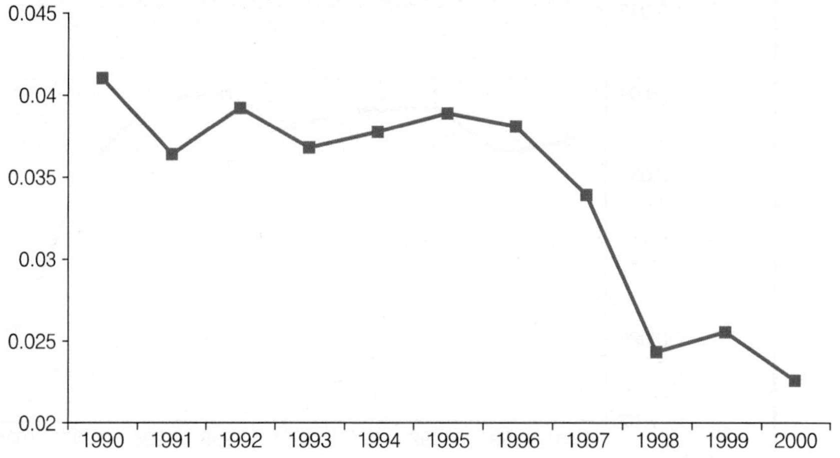

deficits were rising, but these were offset by a healthy capital account. Table 15.2 shows the balance of payments up to 1996 for these five Asian countries.

There appeared to be no reason for the crisis that could be explained by conventional first and second generation models. On the eve of the crisis, inflation was low (see Table 15.3) and there was no excessive fiscal deficit (Table 15.4). The set of five Asian economies were also considered to be the model for emerging economies to follow. Terms such as 'tiger economies' or the 'Asian miracle' were readily applied. Leading up to the crisis, these economies had posted impressively large and sustained economic growth figures (see Table 15.5). The growing economy and low unemployment suggested that there was no real incentive to abandon the fixed rate.

In addition, the crisis was relatively unpredicted. Most risk assessments of the area in mid-1996 showed no expectation of what was to come in the following months.

The conventional (first and second generation) currency crisis models tend to fit the Asian experience badly because the currency crisis was simply part of a larger financial crisis. Collapses in the currency were joined with collapses in asset prices and bank failures. The crisis also spread infectiously across the entire region, the MIT (Malaysia, Indonesia and Thailand) economies were strongly linked by trade, but South Korea was not and still suffered.

An analysis of the crisis appears to go along these lines:

- The emerging markets in Asia in the proceeding years had received large inflows of capital, much of which had been loaned to Asian banks who were poorly regulated and had invested badly in speculative real estate, amongst other things. This led to an asset price bubble.
- Therefore, the impressive growth figures masked deep underlying fragilities. This was particularly true in the banking system where the bubble in domestic asset prices and overexposure to foreign creditors made the economy vulnerable to a financial panic.
- In general terms, a panic arises when short-term debts exceed short-term assets. If a run starts, investors know that there are insufficient funds to pay all creditors. This encourages quick liquidation in order to avoid losses.

Table 15.2 Balance of payments 1990–1996 (% of GDP)

	Korea	Indonesia	Malaysia	Philippines	Thailand
Current account	–1.7	–2.5	–5.6	–3.3	–6.8
Capital account	2.5	4.1	9.6	5.5	10.2
Reserve assets	–0.6	–1.1	–5.0	–1.8	–3.6

Source: IMF

Table 15.3 Average inflation rate (%), 1980–1995

Indonesia	9.3
South Korea	7.7
Malaysia	3.7
Thailand	5.5
Philippines	13.1
Mexico	50.5
Brazil	740.0
Argentina	514.9

Source: IMF World Economic Outlook

Table 15.4 Overall central government budget balance (% of GDP)

Year	Indonesia	Malaysia	Philippines	Thailand	Korea
1990	0.4	–3.0	–3.5	4.5	–0.7
1991	0.4	–2.0	–2.1	4.7	–1.6
1992	–0.4	–0.8	–1.2	2.8	–0.5
1993	0.6	0.2	–1.5	2.1	0.6
1994	0.9	2.3	1.1	1.9	0.3
1995	2.2	0.9	0.5	2.9	0.3
1996	1.2	0.7	0.3	2.3	–0.1

Source: IMF World Economic Outlook

Table 15.5 Average annual growth rates (%), 1985–1995

US	2.8
Germany	2.1
Japan	3.1
Argentina	1.3
Brazil	2.6
Mexico	2.3
Malaysia	7.2
South Korea	7.8
Thailand	8.0
Indonesia	6.3
Philippines	2.1

Source: IMF World Economic Outlook

- Several triggering factors led to a quick withdrawal of investor funds in the region. The main element of the currency crisis was the sudden reversal of the large private capital flows that had previously flowed into the region.
- The problem with such panics is that they may involve some degree of *disorderly workout*. This is when an insolvent or an illiquid borrower provokes a creditor grab even though the borrower is worth more as an ongoing enterprise.

Let's analyse this basic story in a little more detail.

Capital flows into and out of the Asian five

From Table 15.6, it can be seen that preceding the crisis the Asian Five experienced strong inflows. In 1996, private net flows into these economies were $93 billion. The majority of this was accounted for by private creditors and portfolio investment. Direct physical investment (factories, etc.) made up a very small part of the inflow. Therefore, the vast majority ($86 billion = 92 per cent) of the private capital flowing into the region was paper and lent on a short-term basis.

These large-scale inflows were encouraged by several factors:

- continuing and high economic growth gave confidence to foreign investors
- wide-ranging deregulation enabled banks and domestic corporations to tap into foreign finance for domestic investments
- nominal exchange rates were pegged to the $US and hence the removal of exchange rate uncertainty encouraged inward investment
- governments gave special incentives that encouraged foreign borrowing, e.g., no reserve requirements for foreign exchange rate loans.

The crisis was brought on by the sudden reversal of a long and sustained period of inflows. In 1997, net inflows into the Asian five (Indonesia, Korea, Malaysia, Philippines and Thailand) dropped from $93 billion to –$12 billion, a swing of $105 billion which is

Table 15.6 Five Asian economies: external financing (All figures in $US billions)

	1994	1995	1996	1997	1998
Current account balance	–24.6	–41.3	–54.9	–26.0	17.6
External financing net	47.4	80.9	92.8	15.2	15.2
Private flows net	40.5	77.4	93.0	–12.1	–9.4
Equity investment	12.2	15.5	19.1	–4.5	7.9
Direct	4.7	4.9	7.0	7.2	9.8
Portfolio	7.6	10.6	12.1	–11.6	–1.9
Private creditors	28.2	61.8	74.0	–7.6	–17.3
Commercial banks	24.0	49.5	55.5	–21.3	–14.1
Non-bank	4.2	12.4	18.4	13.7	–3.2
Official flows net	7.0	3.6	–0.2	27.2	24.6
Resident lending	–17.5	–25.9	–19.6	–11.9	–5.7
Reserves	–5.4	–13.7	–18.3	22.7	–27.1

Source: Institute of International Finance

about 11 per cent of collective GDP. Foreign direct investment remained constant at about $7 billion, so most of the decline came from these private short-term paper money flows or 'hot money'.

But why did this sudden reversal take place? This involves an analysis of how the large inflows led to increasing fragility, and then consideration of the triggering factors that resulted in financial panic and large outflows.

Moral hazard and increasing economic risk

Given the boom-bust behaviour in asset prices and the general banking collapse which were the striking features of the Asian crisis, it appears that the financial intermediaries may have been central players. In Thailand, finance companies borrowed short-term money (often in $US) and then lent to long-term speculative investors, particularly in real estate. The problem with these intermediaries, though, was that they were seen to have a government guarantee, a problem known as *moral hazard*.

The banking system in many Asian countries was somewhat murky. Although there were no explicit government guarantees, most banks had strong political connections and there was a belief that if there was a default, the government would bail them out to prevent a banking collapse. Experience also vindicated this. Such a system is likely to lead to risky investments, which offer the opportunity (although perhaps with small probability) to make large returns.

The logic of moral hazard can be demonstrated by a simple numerical example taken from Krugman. Table 15.7 shows the options facing the owner of a financial intermediary who raised $100 million from creditors. No capital of his own needs to have been put up, and bankruptcy has no personal cost.

There are two investments options: one yields a certain outcome of $107 million, whereas the other yields a 50:50 gamble between £120 million and $80 million, depending on whether conditions are good or bad. In this case, this risky investment has expected returns of $100 million.

The financial intermediary sees these options and knows that if the good state arises, then the investment will yield a $20 million profit. However, in the bad state, it is not the case that a $20 million loss is made, as the intermediary can just walk away without any cost – the return is hence just $0.

Given this state of affairs, the risky investment yields an expected return of $10 million, whereas the safe investment delivers just $7 million. Therefore, moral hazard leads to a distortion in investment. Riskier projects are undertaken, and the inefficient choice is taken.

Risky bank lending led to an asset price boom, particularly in real estate and share prices. High asset prices and high equity values meant that property companies and the corporate sector could use these highly valued assets as collateral on further loans. Therefore, the banking system was prepared to borrow from overseas and provide further loans. The extent of bank lending meant that the real estate and corporate sectors became increasingly

Table 15.7 Example of moral hazard

	Safe	Risky
Return in good state	107	120
Return in bad state	107	80
Expected return	107	100
Expected return to owner	7	10

15

Table 15.8 Increasing scale of financial institution claims on the corporate sector

Country	Financial institution claims on private sector/GDP (%)		Short-term debt/reserves	
	1990	1996	June 1994	June 1997
Argentina	15.6	18.4	1.3	1.2
Brazil	40.8	30.7	0.7	0.8
Chile	47.0	57.0	0.5	0.4
Indonesia	50.6	55.4	1.7	1.7
Korea	56.8	65.7	1.6	2.1
Malaysia	71.4	144.6	0.3	0.6
Mexico	22.7	21.6	1.7	1.2
Philippines	19.3	48.4	0.4	0.8
Thailand	83.1	141.9	1.0	1.5

Source: Bank for International Settlements

indebted to banks who were themselves increasingly indebted to foreign creditors. However, the fragility was masked by these high asset prices giving a sense that all loans were collateralized and that even if anything did go wrong there would be a government rescue package.

The increasing scale of financial institution claims on the corporate sector is shown in Table 15.8.

The fragility of the banking sector became apparent with the bursting of the asset price bubble. The bursting of the bubble then brought to light the true fragility of these economies. Banks had advanced many loans on what they perceived to be good collateral, but with falling prices this meant that the collateral disappeared and banks ended up holding loans with little security. These banks had also borrowed substantially from overseas, so the reserves to short-term debt ratio had risen.

Now everything was set up for a potential crisis. If foreign investors had a loss of confidence, they would call in the loans made to Asian banks. With short-term debt being relatively high compared to reserves, the banking sector would have to liquidate some of its loans but the security supporting these loans no longer existed. Therefore, any attempt by the banking sector to liquidate firm assets would lead to a succession of corporate bankruptcies and non-performing loans (as the value of these loans is greater than the collateral/assets used to secure them). Worried that loans may be defaulted upon, foreign creditors would panic and attempt to salvage as much as possible by withdrawing as quickly as possible – an action which would then lead to a quick downward spiral of bankruptcies, default and further panic.

Triggering events

The triggering events are factors that would lead to a loss of foreign investor confidence, which when combined with the fragile economic conditions, will lead to panic and large outflows. There may be several examples of specific triggering factors.

15

In Korea, it appeared to be increasing incidents of corporate failure. In early 1997, Hanbo Steel collapsed under $6 billion in debts. This was the first Korean bankruptcy of a chaebol in a decade. Sammi Steel and Kia Motors suffered a similar fate. This put merchant banks under chronic pressure.

In Thailand, Samprasong Land missed payments on its foreign debts, signalling the demise of the property market and the beginning of the end for the Thai finance companies that lent heavily to property investors. In June 1997, the Thai government removed support from a major finance company, Finance One, and announced that creditors –

domestic and foreign – would have to incur losses. Therefore, the collapse of the property market and resulting bank failures appear to be important here.

In addition, there was political uncertainty with elections in Korea, Thailand and the Philippines.

The Asian crisis also shows a substantial degree of contagion, particularly with regards to how the Thai baht devaluation triggered outflows from the rest of Asia. Creditors appeared to treat the region as a whole, which meant that the collapse of the Thai baht was the spark for the crisis in Malaysia, Philippines and Indonesia.

Global application 15.4

Why did China escape the Asian financial crisis?

When the Asian financial crisis hit in 1997–1998, successfully growing economies, such as Indonesia, Thailand, Malaysia, and South Korea, went into a meltdown. China, in contrast, was relatively insulated from the crisis except for experiencing some deflationary effects. How did this happen? To explore this question, we must first take a look at the traits that characterized the Asian financial crisis. This crisis is considered to be a third generation model of currency crisis in that domestic financial sector weaknesses can transform a currency crisis to a financial crisis.

What has emerged from this model is the importance of the soundness of financial markets. Even though firms in emerging markets do not always meet the accounting or transparency requirements of developed markets, they are able to obtain credit. Part of the assessment of the riskiness of lending capital to these firms involves an assessment of the firms' relationship with the government so that 'crony capitalism' suggests that the government will not allow these firms to become bankrupt. Thus, when debt levels become unsustainable for these firms, they begin to default but are not necessarily put into orderly bankruptcy proceedings. Foreign lenders react by calling in short-term loans. As some do so, others will act similarly. As vast amounts of capital flow out of a country, the exchange rate, trade and investment are all affected. With aggregate demand falling, the economy is in a downward spiral. As trade is integrated among nations in a region, there is a possible contagion effect, although this Asian crisis spread beyond trading partners to other emerging markets, increasing the likelihood of a financial panic model in explaining the collective withdrawal of funds.

For China, the lack of liberalization of the external and financial sector may have insulated it from the destabilizing effects in the region. Specifically, the lack of privatization, exchange rate controls and limited commercial credit denominated in foreign currencies all contributed to relative insulation. Since China was not a member of the World Trade Organization in 1997–1998, it had not undertaken significant financial liberalization. In fact, China had currency controls in place, which prevented large exchange rate fluctuations. It also had limited capital convertibility, which prevented the movement of capital in and out of the economy. Although China has poor regulatory oversight and a high degree of perceived crony capitalism as most enterprises are state-owned, in the late 1990s its firms had minimal exposure to foreign currency liabilities and strict capital controls meant little foreign lending except for foreign direct investment, which is more stable than short-term capital flows or 'hot money'. Therefore, the traits of the third generation model did not fit China, and it did not experience the 'twin crises' in the currency and banking sector.

However, China was not immune from the deflationary stance of the region, and this is likely to become more characteristic as it becomes a more open economy. Macroeconomic instability will be one of the main concerns of China as it increasingly liberalizes its financial sector with this experience in mind.

Table 15.9 Growth rates (%) and current account (% GDP) of the Asian Five in the aftermath of the Asian crisis

	Growth	Current account
1996	7.0	–5.1
1997	4.5	–2.7
1998	–8.1	10.5
1999	6.9	7.6
2000	7.0	5.1
2001	1.6	3.9

Source: IMF

Effects on economic growth

Table 15.9 shows the economic growth and current accounts of the five Asian economies post-1996.

It is clear that the financial crisis had a stinging effect on growth in 1998. Much of this demise came through a very large number of bankruptcies. Firms were made insolvent in two ways. First, offshore creditors were more nervous about rolling over debts. Second, given that a large number of debts were in $US, the large devaluations substantially increased the value of these debts creating additional bankruptcies.

It is also clear that a lack of bankruptcy laws created disorderly workout problems. In the panic to salvage bad loans, many viable firms were probably forced to close.

However, it appears that the crisis was certainly V-shaped, in that from 1999, positive growth re-emerged. The source of this should be fairly obvious. The large currency depreciations greatly increased the export competitiveness of these nations, and Table 15.9 clearly shows the large improvement in the current account following the crisis.

Global application 15.5

Argentinian crisis, 2001–2002

Following the turmoil of the late 1990s in Russia and Asia, several countries in Latin America, including Brazil, Chile and Mexico, moved to flexible exchange rate regimes. Argentina, though, continued to fix the peso against the dollar. During the second half of the 1990s, the US dollar appreciated strongly, owing to a strong domestic economy, high equity prices and low confidence in emerging markets. The sharp rise in the dollar meant that this policy became increasingly painful for Argentina. As the real exchange rate increased, competitiveness fell, putting substantial pressure on the current account. Maintaining the fixed rate required contractionary monetary policy, generating high unemployment. The weak domestic economy saw worsening fiscal deficits and sky-rocketing foreign borrowing.

It was clear that the policies required to maintain the fixed rate against the dollar imparted very high costs for the domestic economy. Speculation against the peso began to increase, which meant that increasingly drastic policies were required to maintain the fixed peg. Late in 2001, the government restricted residents' withdrawals from banks to stem the run on the peso and the government stopped payments on its foreign debts.

Following the nearly $100 billion default on repaying its loans, the government established a dual exchange rate system in 2002 with controls on capital outflows and different exchange rates

Global application 15.5 (continued)

for current and capital account transactions. The rate for the current account was devalued to 1.4 pesos per US dollar, while the floating financial rate quickly headed to two pesos per dollar. A month later, a single floating rate was established for the peso which depreciated to four pesos per dollar. Growth recovered but Argentina was still negotiating with creditors four years on.

Figure 3 Comparative growth rates

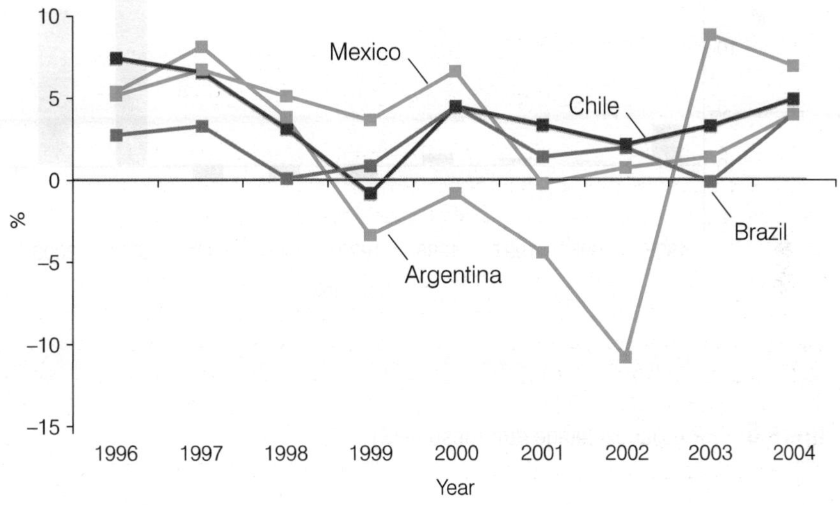

Figure 4 Current account balance for Argentina: % of GDP

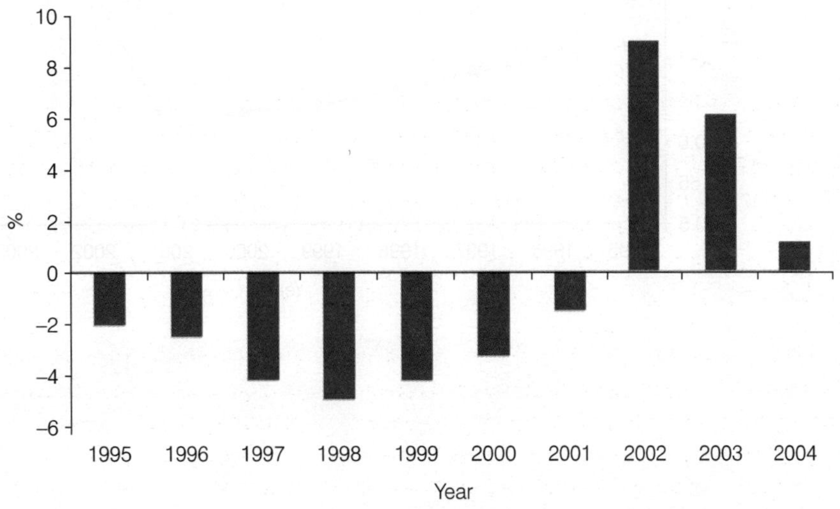

Global application 15.5 (continued)

Figure 5 Inflation in Argentina

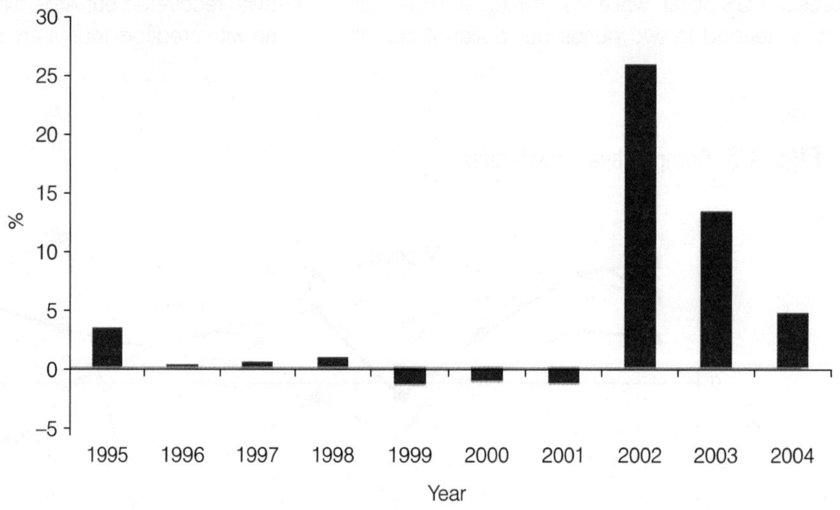

Figure 6 PPP dollar exchange rate (peso/$US)

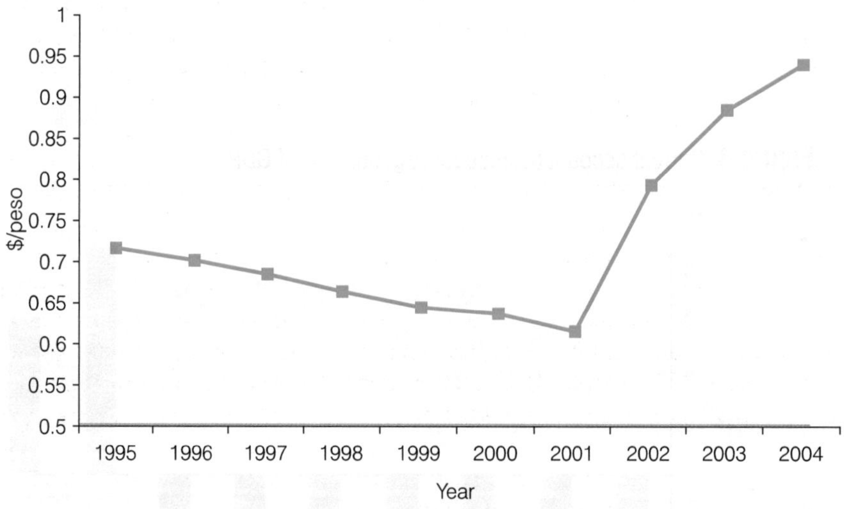

Global application 15.6

Contagion

Throughout history, it appears that the incidence of a currency crisis is rarely limited to just one country. In fact, as seen in Latin America and Asia, when one country becomes subject to attack, its neighbours often share the same fate. Contagion refers to the process whereby a shock or a crisis that originates in one country can spread to others.

The regional nature of a currency crisis might be accounted for by the fact that countries that are close to each other geographically are often integrated with each other through trade. Therefore, if a crisis were to develop in one country leading to a large and rapid devaluation in the exchange rate, this might have strong adverse consequences for the competitiveness of neighbour countries. As nations that are close together geographically tend to export similar goods and services, they tend to be competitors in global markets. A large devaluation in one might lead to speculation that similar devaluations will be required in the others, in order to maintain the competitiveness of exports in global markets.

Also, neighbouring countries may share similar cultures and languages, which might point to similar economic structures, institutions and policies. In this event, speculators and investors might hypothesize that the economies may also share similar weaknesses. When a crisis develops in one country, it simply highlights that neighbouring countries might be subjected to the same events. The financial crisis in East Asia may have spread due to a perceived general lack of confidence in the banking sector in all countries in the region.

However, two countries that are close geographically need not suffer from the same fundamental problems, so there is not always an obvious reason why a crisis in one should spread readily to another. In fact, the incidence can spread far and wide between very disparate economies. The collapse in Russia in late 1998 generated large-scale capital outflows from South America, even though the economies were very different structurally, geographically far apart and exhibited few trade or financial links.

Although trade effects have been shown to be significant, these effects tend to be gradual and protracted. Explaining the rapid transmission of crises requires a different explanation. A currency crisis usually results when investors rapidly move their funds out of assets (such as bonds, banks, equities or even just currency itself) denominated in a certain currency through fear of devaluation or default. How, though, can a crisis in one country necessarily lead to these large movements out of other currencies?

One explanation is that investors' appetites for risk may also diminish in times of market stress and increased uncertainty. Emerging market economies can grow strongly, but this growth is fragile as a lack of formal institutions makes the economies more prone to shocks. Therefore, assets in emerging markets may offer higher returns but at the cost of more risk. Advanced economies might offer a slightly different type of portfolio. As these are large, wealthy and mature economies, assets are less risky, but the relative return will also be lower (as the market risk premium will be so).

In Chapter 6, we presented a brief model that might account for the risk-return features of the portfolio an investor will hold. The market price of risk means that portfolios which involve more risk will offer higher returns. Looking at Figure 7, a stylized example might be that assets in emerging market economies offer the risk-return combination of (r_2, σ_2), whereas the assets of a developed country offer the lower risk and return combination of (r_1, σ_1). If investor preferences are represented by indifference curve I_A, then it is optimal to hold emerging market assets.

However, a crisis in one emerging market might lead to a change in investor preferences. As investors become risk averse, their indifference curves will change to perhaps I_B, meaning that the optimal risk-return portfolio is now one that involves less risk. Such a result would see investors transfer their funds out of emerging market economies into safer havens, such as US Treasury bills.

Global application 15.6 (continued)

Figure 7 Portfolio selection and changing attitudes to risk and return

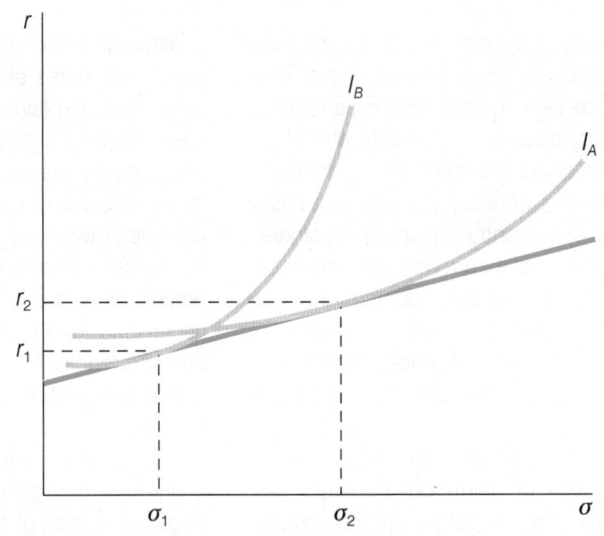

Although emerging markets may share different fundamentals, they all might be affected by a general increase in risk aversion. This increased risk aversion may also be centred on a particular region. It is clear that emerging market crises become more likely as more and more investors become risk averse. If a crisis were to emerge, no investor would wish to be at the back of the stampede to exit the currency since default might occur before they could liquidate their positions. Therefore, the nervousness of investors can be infectious, in that some investors will naturally become more nervous simply because others already are. This type of reaction could be sufficient to generate the coordination or 'herding' among investors required to precipitate a currency crisis.

15.4 Preventing currency crises

Currency crises appear to be a significant worry for emerging markets. Many have attempted to operate a fixed exchange rate regime against the $US. According to the IMF and World Bank, this is good policy, as it creates an inflation discipline and removes exchange rate uncertainty, thus encouraging the capital inflows these nations typically need to invest in their continuing development.

When a crisis strikes an emerging market, the consequences for output tend to be rather severe. We have seen this with Mexico and the suite of Asian economies, but we could also draw similar conclusions from the events in Russia and Argentina, to name but a few. When a crisis strikes, the usual defence is to tighten monetary policy, which has strong implications for the domestic economy, and for there to be some reversal of capital inflows. The result is usually a number of bankruptcies with a strong degree of disorderly workout.

So, how can a currency crisis be prevented?

15

The lender of last resort

In all three generations of currency crisis model, a speculative attack on a fixed exchange rate will occur when the policy maker has few reserves to defend the currency.

In the first generation model, a crisis arises when the policy maker runs low on reserves, mainly due to the official financing of current account deficits.

In the second generation model, a policy maker could defend the currency, but the cost of doing so proves detrimental to other conflicting objectives. Therefore, the policy maker is unwilling to commit a large amount of resources to the defence.

In the third generation model describing Asia, the crisis appears to be a feature of a financial panic because short-term debts exceed short-term reserves.

In each of these cases, when the currency comes under selling pressure, the policy maker finds it either impossible or just too costly to defend the parity. If there were, though, a cheap and plentiful source of currency reserves that could be mobilized to the defence, then the high reserve game (Figure 15.2) should always be the outcome.

This source of reserves could come from an international lender of last resort. This is the role played by the IMF in the post-war period under the Bretton Woods Agreement (1950–1973). Each nation commits reserves to a pool, and if an attack were to arise, then sufficient resources could be borrowed from the fund. These funds are then repaid after the crisis has abated and normal economic conditions ensue.

An international lender of last resort will obviously help in defending an exchange rate. However, there are several issues that need to be considered. First, if governments know that an international bailout will come to the rescue, then it may encourage them to do little to prevent the crisis in the first place. In fact, the prospect of a rescue may encourage them to undertake overly risky policies in the first place; this is an obvious example of moral hazard. To prevent this, any loans may be made at a penal rate of interest, so that there remains some incentive not to undertake undisciplined policy making.

Second, a crisis is harmful if it evokes disorderly workout, that is, the forced bankruptcy of firms that would still be valuable as a going concern. However, should funds be mobilized to rescue firms that are economically inefficient? Therefore, a second requirement for any loan would be that it is made on good collateral. It would be inefficient to maintain firms that have no positive value as a going concern.

Capital controls

From Table 15.1, the evidence indicates that the increasing prevalence of currency crises has gone hand-in-hand with the large increase in currency trading. The fact that a large volume of currency can move around the world economy very quickly means that the heavy selling required to start a crisis is a possibility. All this has arisen from continued deregulation and liberalization of international financial markets.

Reimposing capital controls could rule out the bad equilibrium in Figure 15.2 by *force majeur*. Extensive capital controls would prevent large flows of hot money. This, though, invokes a debate about the pros and cons of re-establishing capital controls.

On the pro side, obviously capital controls will prevent instability brought on by hot money flows. It will also give policy makers more influence over their domestic monetary policy, and a greater ability to set interest rates. However, on the con side, interrupting the flow of international capital could result in problems and inefficiencies. Policy makers would find it harder to deal with balance of payments problems brought on by current account shocks, if offsetting capital account transactions are limited. Second, it is argued that capital flows act as a good disciplining device on policy making; bad policies resulting in current account deficits, inflation or fiscal deficits will be punished by outflows of capital. Finally, capital should be free to move to where it can achieve the highest possible return, imposing such limits on its mobility may well result in a sub-optimal worldwide allocation of capital.

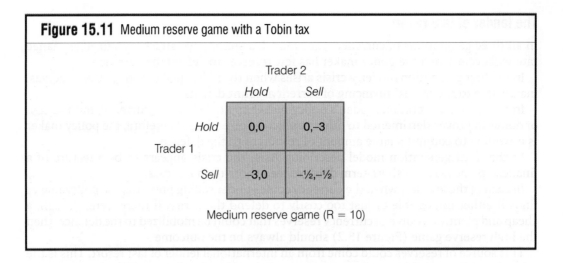

Figure 15.11 Medium reserve game with a Tobin tax

		Trader 2	
		Hold	*Sell*
Trader 1	*Hold*	0,0	0,–3
	Sell	–3,0	–½,–½

Medium reserve game (R = 10)

Therefore, imposing capital controls may help prevent crises, but also introduces a myriad of other considerations.

Tobin taxes

Tobin argued that short-term capital movements (hot money) is the main culprit in injecting volatility into foreign exchange markets. Long-term capital movements are less volatile. The solution, to reduce hot money flows without unduly affecting longer-term foreign direct investment, is a tax on any short-term international transactions. This would discourage active speculation against a currency.

To see why, reconsider the game outlined in Figure 15.4. This time, making a transaction again costs 1 unit, but is now also subject to a tax of 2 units. Therefore, selling costs a total of 3 units whereas holding continues to be free. Making these changes leads to a new pay-off matrix shown in Figure 15.11.

It is clear that the only solution to this game is now for both traders to hold. Previously, a speculative attack would have worked if coordinated, but this simple tax is sufficient to now rule out this possibility.

A **Tobin tax** seems like a simple effective solution to the increasing volatility of international foreign exchange markets without adversely affecting foreign direct capital. However, there are problems with its implementation in complex financial markets, which has led many to believe that it could never work in practice.

Exchange rate regimes

A fixed exchange rate regime is regarded by many as being ultimately unsustainable. As speculators are offered a one-way bet, an attack is always an eventual outcome. In this respect, there are two alternatives for policy makers.

1. **Floating exchange rate regimes**: obviously the exchange rate is market-determined, hence the opportunities for speculators to mount an attack is diminished. The floating versus fixed debate, though, then arises.
2. **Monetary union**: if fixed rates are irrevocably unworkable, then full monetary union would see a single currency and the abolition of exchange rates. The overall debate must be analysed in the context of optimal currency area theory.

Banking regulation

The fractional reserve banking system described in Chapter 5 shows how financial institutions can create deposits to a multiple of reserves. In doing so, there is an implicit assumption that all the depositors will not withdraw their funds at once. Therefore, financial institutions are free to use their assets to advance profitable loans. The stability of the banking system is reliant on the confidence that depositors can withdraw cash on demand. When this confidence disappears, a sudden rush to withdraw funds is likely to lead to bank failure as the bank's assets are illiquid and cannot be dissolved to meet the depositor's claims for cash.

Bank failures can become self-fulfilling prophecies, where the expectation of a bank run is enough to start one. This is exactly like the second generation currency crisis in that the banking system can have multiple equilibriums which are reinforced by coordination amongst the public. From the perspective of an individual depositor, knowing that the bank only has limited assets, the withdrawal by some depositors should be sufficient to convince other investors to do so. Therefore, when confidence is fragile, a relatively small amount of withdrawals might be enough to spark outright panic.

Bank runs can have strong macroeconomic consequences. The failure of one bank can lead to a general banking collapse as confidence in other banks collapses, especially if they have lent to the bank that collapsed. There can also be disorderly workouts, where otherwise profitable investments are liquidated in order to try to satisfy short-term demands for cash. Bank failures can then lead to corporate bankruptcies, collapses in investment and the capital stock, and also unemployment (see a paper by Ben Bernanke on the Great Depression and credit crunches). The experience of the Asian countries in the late 1990s links currency crises to a general financial collapse.

Possible solutions

1. **Reserve requirements**: in Chapter 5, it was described how these could be used to control the money supply. However, it is not just a tool of monetary policy but a means of ensuring that banks hold sufficient deposits to meet demands for cash.
2. **Lender of last resort**: the banking system is most fragile when it has little liquidity. As the collapse of one bank can have large externalities such as disorderly workout, an important remedy is for an organization such as the central bank to provide liquidity in times of crisis.
3. **Capital requirements and asset restrictions**: a bank's capital is the difference between its assets and liabilities. A highly capitalized bank is less likely to default as it can always draw on its own capital. This could be achieved by placing minimum capital requirements on the banking system.
4. **Banking supervision**: regulators would check the banks' books, ensure capital compliance, prevent risky loans and undiversified loan structures, and so on.
5. **Deposit insurance**: a bank run arises when depositors feel that they are in a race to withdraw funds. By insuring small depositors against bank default, they would no longer have an incentive to precipitate a banking crisis. This type of insurance, though, does raise moral hazard issues.

Difficulties in regulating international banking

In an international setting, banks can shift their business among different regulatory jurisdictions, so supervising and regulating banks can be difficult. For example, should the Madrid branch of a British bank be subject to Bank of England or Bank of Espana's supervision? We have also seen the rise in offshore banking where there is generally no jurisdiction. Also, competition for banking business tends to push towards the limit of low regulation, perhaps sub-optimally low. Therefore, banking supervision is harder to carry out and enforce in an international setting. It requires international regulatory cooperation among different central banks and supranational bodies. The establishment of the Basel Committee in 1974 by ten central bank governors is an example of such cooperation.

Basel Committee (1974)

A sequence of measures was undertaken by the Basel Committee as follows:

- 1975 (revised 1983): 'The Concordat' or principles for the supervision of banks' foreign establishments allocated responsibility for supervising multinational banking establishments between parent and host countries. This prompted the sharing of information between host and parent regulators, and action to locate and shut down loopholes in the supervision of international banks.
- 1988: Basel Committee set up common standards for assessing banks' capital adequacy. Banks must hold capital equal to 8 per cent of their risk-weighted assets plus off-sheet balance commitments.
- 1997: in the 1990s, there were several episodes of crises in emerging markets, where the banking system was much weaker than in industrialized countries. In response, the Basel Committee issued the *Core Principles for Effective Banking Supervision*. This extended the principles to new, emerging market economies regarding banking supervision and implementation.
- 2004: The 'Basel II Framework' is announced that adds more risk considerations to the minimum capital requirements of Basel I, and also supervisory and public disclosure requirements for banks.

Currency boards

A currency board is where the monetary base is backed 100 per cent by foreign currency. In this case, the central bank holds no domestic assets. This places a tough constraint on fiscal policy, but means that in the event of a speculative attack on the currency, the central bank can never run out of foreign currency reserves.

Under a currency board, the central bank announces an exchange rate against some foreign currency and simply carries out any trades of domestic currency notes against the foreign currency that the public initiates. The currency board is prohibited by law against obtaining domestic assets, so all the currency it issues is automatically fully backed against the foreign currency. In most cases, the note issuing authority does not need to be a central bank and only performs the role of a vending machine.

In this way, a currency board, like a fixed exchange rate, allows a country to import inflation credibility from overseas (as was the case in Argentina in 1991). This is because the country is effectively allowing its monetary policy to be run from overseas and cannot profit from seignorage revenues. Hence, monetary policy is removed from those that otherwise might abuse the discretion. The central bank can no longer freely lend currency to banks in times of panic. However, there are the obvious disadvantages of completely losing control of monetary policy. In addition, like a fixed exchange rate, currency boards can become subject to speculative attack, as devaluations will be seen as a loss in credibility.

Global application 15.7

The pros and cons of dollarization

Dollarization is the adoption of the US dollar as the domestic legal tender. Essentially, the government uses its own reserves and borrows funds to buy back its entire money stock from the public and at the same time replace it with US dollars. In doing so, the country involved is essentially joining a single currency area with the US.

The reasons for doing this are partly similar to those that underlie the adoption of a single currency in Europe. We have seen that fixed exchange rate regimes have a tendency to breakdown eventually. This is usually when speculators believe that commitment to the fixed parity is no longer credible and that domestic policy objectives will override it. This was certainly the case with the ERM and pointed to full monetary union as the only long-term way of sustaining fixed exchange rates.

There are many reasons why emerging market economies may wish to adopt a fixed rate against the US dollar. If the fixed rate is credible, then it can encourage low domestic inflation. In addition, stable exchange rates and prices would encourage capital inflows and trade – all potentially valuable things for a nation looking to promote long-run growth. However, if commitment to the fixed rate requires the imposition of painful domestic policies, then speculators may be only too willing to test the resolve of governments.

However, dollarization is an ultimate form of a fixed exchange rate. A fixed exchange rate regime can be abandoned relatively easily when the going gets tough, either by resorting to floating rates or through a devaluation. Once the domestic currency has been replaced, these easy exit options are no longer available, which arguably makes the regime more credible and then less likely to be attacked. The required exit action here would require the restoration of the domestic currency, not an easy thing to do when the public also have the option of holding a strong, fully convertible foreign currency. In this situation, it is likely that there would be little confidence in any new currency that was introduced. Dollarization is therefore an attempt to introduce extra credibility into a nation's monetary and exchange rate policy. There are, though, other issues that stem from this.

Risk premiums

As the domestic currency no longer exists, the risk associated with devaluation should disappear. As a result, an immediate reduction in the risk premium will lead to lower domestic interest rates, which could stimulate investment and lower the cost of servicing public debt. However, although the part of the risk premium attributed to devaluation risk would disappear, the part associated with sovereign risk would not.

There is reason to believe that devaluation and default risks are positively related, so a reduction in one will reduce the other. First, governments attempting to avoid currency runs may impose currency controls that force a suspension of payments on foreign debt. Without the need to defend the currency, governments would no longer need to place moratoriums on debt repayments in order to stem capital outflows. Second, as seen in Asia, default risks could rise with a devaluation, owing to the higher costs of servicing dollar-denominated debts. Third, a currency crisis may produce heavy losses in the financial sector, which might require costly government bail outs in order to prevent total meltdown. Despite these reasons, it must also be accepted that not all default risks necessarily arise from the risk of currency crises. Dollarization certainly cannot prevent risks associated with political turmoil or an unsustainable fiscal position.

Stability and integration

Speculative attacks can have dire effects on the domestic economy, such as bankruptcies and disorderly workout. Dollarization offers no guarantees, but could certainly diminish the threat of attacks. It can also promote trade integration with the US.

Global application 15.7 (continued)

Seigniorage

The adopting country will lose seigniorage revenues as it is no longer in a position to obtain real resources by printing money. In developing countries, seignorage can be an important source of revenue. With dollarization, any seignorage revenues would simply accrue to the US.

Exit option

Under a floating regime, the exchange rate will automatically offset any external imbalances. However, a dollarized economy acts exactly like a fixed exchange rate or a monetary union in that any adjustment would need to come through nominal wages and prices in the domestic economy. Any rigidity here will have implications for output and unemployment, as adjustments come in real and not just nominal variables. We have seen that most monetary unions throughout history have broken down due to shocks that ultimately have required countries to obtain greater flexibility with respect to domestic policy.

A currency board still has some flexibility here. The domestic currency is backed by dollars, so could, in principle, be devalued by simply changing the conversion rate. Under dollarization, though, the economy has converted all domestic currency into dollars; as mentioned above, reintroducing the new currency along side a strong fully convertible foreign one would be hard since confidence and acceptability would be low. Therefore, the exit option is substantially reduced. But, as mentioned already, the lack of an exit position may help to achieve greater credibility.

Lender of last resort

Central banks operating in this role can provide liquidity to markets in the event of runs. This is an important function as a general banking collapse can lead to disorderly workout, where otherwise solvent firms are forced into bankruptcy. Under a currency board, this option is restricted, as all money created must be backed by reserves. However, by altering the ratio of the monetary base that must be backed by reserves, there is still an ability to create some extra liquidity if needed. Full dollarization, though, is completely restrictive.

However, once again there may be advantages to giving up this discretion with the aim of enhancing credibility of domestic policy, making a bank run less likely in the first place. The whole process of dollarization may actually improve confidence in the banking system. In addition, it could encourage more large foreign banks into the banking sector, diminishing the need for a lender of last resort.

Summary

- We have seen how a dramatic reduction in exchange controls throughout the world has led to a large rise in international capital mobility. The consequence is that financial markets in different countries have become increasingly interlinked, giving rise to what can be described as an international financial market.
- In addition, the scale of international trading has risen dramatically. The majority of this is short term and highly liquid, known as 'hot money', which can move quickly in and out of different markets in different countries.
- We reviewed various episodes of high volatility in currency markets, where traditionally developing and transition countries have been the victims, especially in Latin America and more recently in Asia. However, the collapse of the exchange rate mechanism (ERM) in the early 1990s demonstrates that developed nations can also be prone to these crises.

- Increasing openness has meant that shocks that happen in one country can quickly spread around the world, so the economic progress of one country can be adversely affected by a development in another country. We learned that the process by which shocks can be transmitted across countries is known as contagion.
- We investigated solutions, such as imposing capital controls, but discovered that this would also make the advantages of international financial markets unattainable. Therefore, policy makers have become increasingly concerned with designing the international financial architecture to maintain high capital mobility while at the same time dealing with these instabilities.

Key terms

Currency crises

Tobin tax

Review questions

1. What are the benefits of a global financial market?
2. Are currency crises self-fulfilling?
3. Why are emerging market economies particularly vulnerable to currency crises?

More advanced problems

4. 'Exchange rate volatility is the symptom of poor domestic macroeconomic policies.' Discuss.
5. Capital controls give policy makers an extra degree of freedom. Is this a decisive argument in favour of their implementation? What other policies can policy makers use to prevent currency crises?
6. Should a small country print its own money or adopt that of a large established economy? How might the relative political stability of the two countries play a role in this decision?

For further resources, visit
http://www.thomsonlearning.co.uk/chamberlin_yueh

Part VIII

Economic growth in the long run

Chapter 16 Models of long-run growth

The final section of the book focuses on the long-run models of economic growth and the empirical approaches to growth undertaken by countries.

16 Models of long-run growth

Learning objectives

- Understand the drivers of long-term growth
- Use the neoclassical model of growth to assess changes in growth rates
- Introduce human capital into growth models
- Assess the contribution of endogenous growth theories
- Gain perspective into why countries grow at different rates

16.1 Introduction

The question of why some economies grow faster than others is one of the most important questions in economics. Economic growth leads to higher standards of living, more technological progress, advancements in knowledge and a better quality of life, for the most part. In other words, it is difficult to think about anything else once we start thinking about growth, paraphrasing Nobel Laureate Robert Lucas. This leads us to first define economic growth. What is it?

Economic growth is the change in GDP on an annual basis. Therefore, a growth rate of one per cent indicates that GDP has increased by one per cent from the previous year. A useful way to interpret growth rates was offered by Robert Lucas, in a paper, 'On the Mechanics of Economic Development,' in 1988. A rule of thumb is that a country growing at g per cent per year will double its per capita GDP every $70/g$ years. To see this, let $Y(t)$ be per capita GDP at time t and let Y_0 be the initial value of per capita GDP. Then, $Y(t) = Y_0 e^{gt}$. Therefore, per capita GDP will double when $Y(t) = 2Y_0$. The rule of thumb can be worked out as follows. First, $2Y_0 = Y_0 e^{gt}$. Then, solving for t, $t = \frac{\log 2}{g}$. We get the rule of thumb by noting: $\log 2 \approx 0.7$.

Therefore, if the US grew at 3 per cent per annum for the past 30 years while China grew at 8 per cent per annum, then GDP per capita will double approximately every 23 years in the US and every nine years in China. Within a generation, the average American will be three times as rich as his grandparents, while a Chinese person would be more than 18 times richer. Over a fairly short period of time, small differences in compound growth rates can lead to large differences in per capita incomes.

When we discuss economic growth, economists are also referring to the **long-run growth** of an economy. In other words, the rate of growth that is consistent with an economy's natural rate of output and the position of the long-run aggregate supply curve seen in earlier chapters. Therefore, when policy makers are interested in improving the long-run potential of an economy and economists are attempting to understand why countries grow at different rates, these are the models that are relevant.

In this chapter, we will explore the models of long-run growth starting with the classic Solow model. We will then turn to models where human capital is included to try and understand another reason why countries may exhibit different growth rates over time. We conclude with looking at the theory and evidence surrounding endogenous growth, where the main drivers of growth are considered to be determined within the model. Finally, we conclude the chapter by focusing on the numerous factors that are important to contemplate when trying to understand long-run economic growth.

16.2 The neoclassical model of growth

16.2.1 The Solow model

The neoclassical framework for long-run growth is the **Solow model**. The Solow model is comprised of a production function and a capital accumulation function. The production function refers to the inputs of capital (K) and labour (L) necessary to produce output (Y). It is assumed to have the Cobb-Douglas form and is given by:

$$Y = F(K,L) = K^{a} L^{1-a} \tag{16.1}$$

where α is a number between 0 and 1. This production function exhibits constant returns to scale, so that if all inputs are doubled, then output will double. We are interested in finding output per worker or per capita output, so we write the production in terms of output per worker and capital per worker, which are given respectively by:

$$y \equiv \frac{Y}{L}$$

$$k \equiv \frac{K}{L}$$

which gives $y = k$. With more capital per worker, firms produce more output per worker. But, there are diminishing returns to capital per worker, so each additional unit of capital increases the output per worker by less than the previous unit of capital.

The second equation of the Solow model is an equation that explains how capital is accumulated in the economy. The capital accumulation equation is given by:

$$\dot{K} = sY - dK \tag{16.2}$$

According to (16.2), the change in the capital stock, $\dot{K}$, is equal to the gross investment, sY, minus depreciation, dK. The change in capital stock is given by the variable differentiated with respect to time, so $\dot{K} \equiv \frac{dK}{dt}$. The notation simply denotes the change in capital stock per period, so it is the continuous time version of $K_{t+1} - K_t$. We will see the notation again, so it is worth bearing in mind!

But how is gross investment determined in the Solow model? Well, it is simply investment. The model assumes that workers save a constant fraction, s, of their combined wage and rental income. Because the economy is closed, savings equals investment and investment is used solely to accumulate capital. The other assumption relates to the depreciation of the capital stock that occurs during production, which is a constant fraction, d, of the capital stock. Depreciation happens every period regardless of how much output is produced.

Now, we have the capital accumulation equation in per worker terms: $\dot{k} = sy - (n + d)k$. This equation says that capital per worker in each period is determined by three factors. The first is that investment per worker, sy, increases capital, k, while depreciation per worker, dk, reduces k. There is also a reduction in k because of population growth, the nk term. Each period there are nL new workers since the model assumes a constant growth rate of n in the population, which is also assumed to have a 100 per cent labour force participation rate. So, if there were no new investment and no depreciation, capital per worker would decline because of the increase in the labour force. Because k is known as capital per worker, it is also referred to as the capital-labour ratio. (See the Appendix for the derivation.)

To solve the Solow model, we take the production function and capital accumulation equation together. The production function in terms of output per worker is given by: $y = k^{\alpha}$. The capital accumulation function in terms of capital per worker is: $\dot{k} = sy - (n + d)k$. The equilibrium is found where the two curves meet. To find this point, which is the **steady state** of the economy, we use the **Solow diagram** to first find the steady-state value of capital per worker and then the steady-state value of output per worker.

In Figure 16.1, the Solow diagram consists of two curves, which are functions of k, capital per person or the capital–labour ratio. The first depicts the amount of investment per person, $sy = sk^{\alpha}$. The curve has the same shape as the production function but is translated in terms of the function s. The second curve is the amount of new investment per person required to keep the amount of capital per worker constant, $(n + d)k$. Population growth and depreciation will both reduce the amount of capital per person, which is captured here.

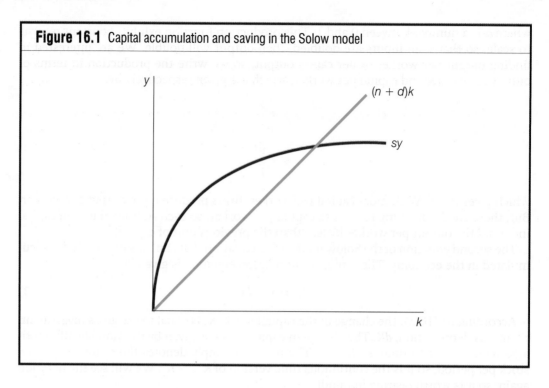

Figure 16.1 Capital accumulation and saving in the Solow model

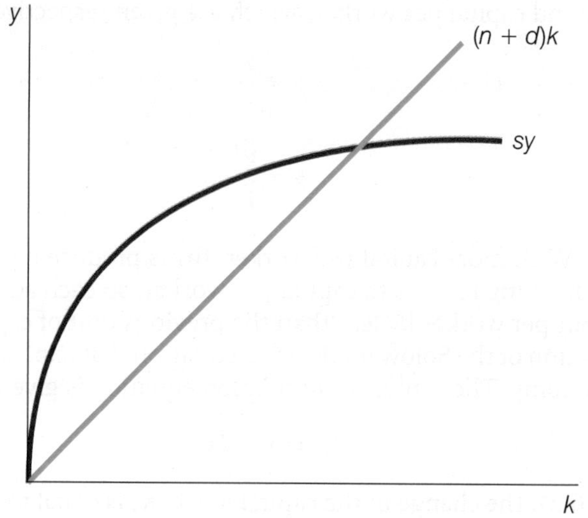

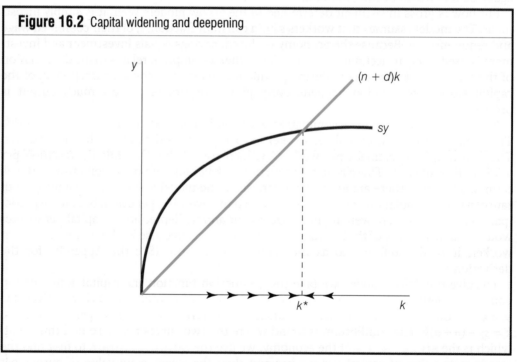

Figure 16.2 Capital widening and deepening

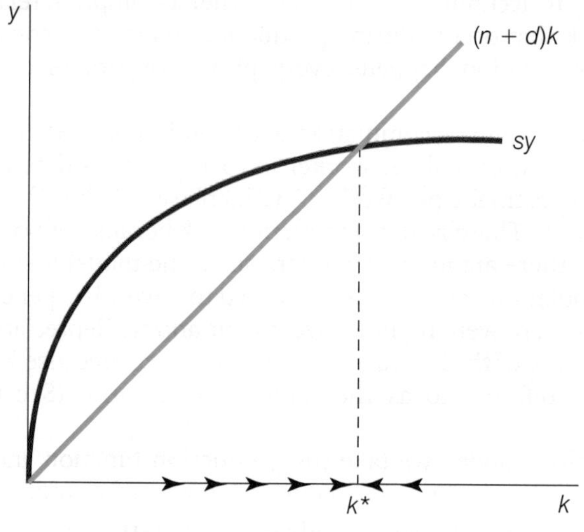

Figure 16.2 shows what happens when the economy is away from equilibrium. When the economy is below k^* and say capital per worker is increasing, then **capital deepening** occurs. Below k^*, the amount of investment per worker exceeds the amount needed to keep capital per worker constant, so k increases over time. Capital deepening will continue until $k = k^*$, at which point $sy = (n + d)k$ and $\dot{k} = 0$. At k^*, the amount of capital per worker is constant and the economy has reached a steady state. If the economy, on the other hand,

began with a capital stock per worker that was larger than k^*, then we would be to the right of k^*. The amount of investment per worker provided by the economy is less than the amount needed to keep the capital–labour ratio constant. The term $\dot{k}$ is negative and thus the amount of capital per worker will decline. This decline will cease when the amount of capital per worker falls to k^*. This is known as **capital widening**.

Therefore, the Solow diagram determines the steady-state value of capital per worker. We now add the production function to find the steady-state value of output per worker in Figure 16.3. At k^*, the steady-state output of the economy is at y^*. If different countries have different values of y^*, then some will be richer and some will be poorer. So, we need to do one more thing which is to solve the model and find out what determines y^*. We can do this by finding the steady-state quantities of capital per worker and output per worker.

Recall that the steady-state quantity of capital per worker is determined by the condition, $\dot{k} = 0$. This means that there is no change in the capital–labour ratio over time so that the economy is at its steady state. We also need the two key equations of the Solow model, the production function and capital accumulation function. The first equation is output per worker which is given by $y = k^{\alpha}$. The second is capital per worker which is given by $\dot{k} = sy - (n + d)k$. Substitute the first equation into the second and we get $\dot{k} = sk^{\alpha} - (n + d)k$. Setting this equation to zero yields the steady-state quantity of capital per worker, as follows:

$$k^* = \left(\frac{s}{n+d}\right)^{1/1-\alpha} \qquad (16.3)$$

We now need to find the steady-state output per worker, which is found by substituting (16.3) into the production function (16.1). So, y^* is given by:

$$y^* = \left(\frac{s}{n+d}\right)^{1/1-\alpha} \qquad (16.4)$$

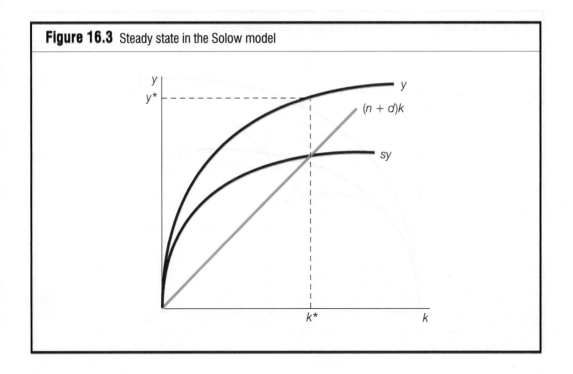

Figure 16.3 Steady state in the Solow model

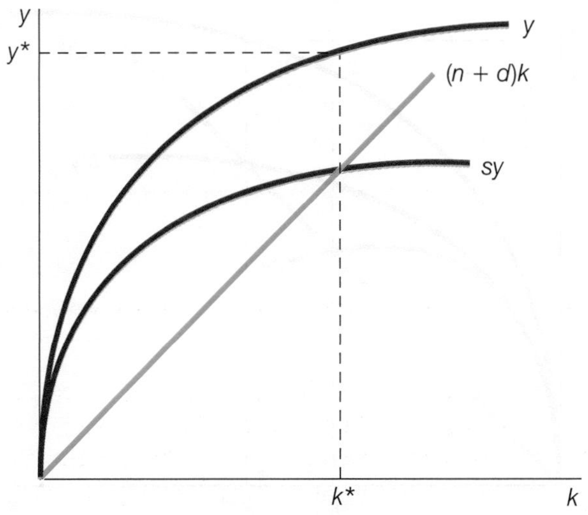

Therefore, y^* is now written in terms of the parameters of the model and we have a solution, seen in Figure 16.3. It follows from this solution that countries which have higher savings and investment rates will tend to be richer than those who do not. These countries accumulate more capital per worker and thus more output per worker. In contrast, countries which have high population growth will be poorer. And, in these countries, a larger portion of savings will be required to keep the capital–labour ratio constant. The tendency for capital widening will make capital deepening more difficult and these countries will tend to accumulate less capital per worker.

Changing the steady state

So, how do we use the model to show when steady states differ for countries? Let's examine what happens when there is an increase in the investment rate and in the population growth rate. When the economy is in steady state, it can still experience 'shocks' along these lines where key parameters like savings rates and population change.

We start with an increase in the investment rate. Say that the consumers in this economy decide to save more and there is a permanent increase from s to s'. Figure 16.4 shows what happens in this case.

In Figure 16.4, an increase in the investment rate shifts the sy curve upward to $s'y$. At the current value of k^*, investment per worker exceeds the amount required to keep capital per worker constant. So, the economy starts to undertake capital deepening. This continues until $s'y = (n + d)k$. Capital stock per worker now reaches a higher value of k^{**}. The economy is now richer than it was before since the higher level of capital per worker will be associated with a higher level of output per worker, y^{**}.

But, what happens if there is an increase in the population growth rate? Suppose an economy has reached its steady state, but population growth increases such as the 'baby boom' after the Second World War. Figure 16.5 shows the effects.

The $(n + d)k$ curve shifts left and the new curve is given by $(n' + d)k$ as n has increased to n'. At the current value of the capital stock, k^*, investment per worker is no longer high

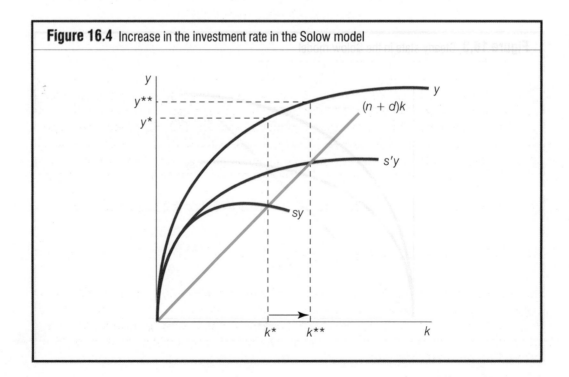

Figure 16.4 Increase in the investment rate in the Solow model

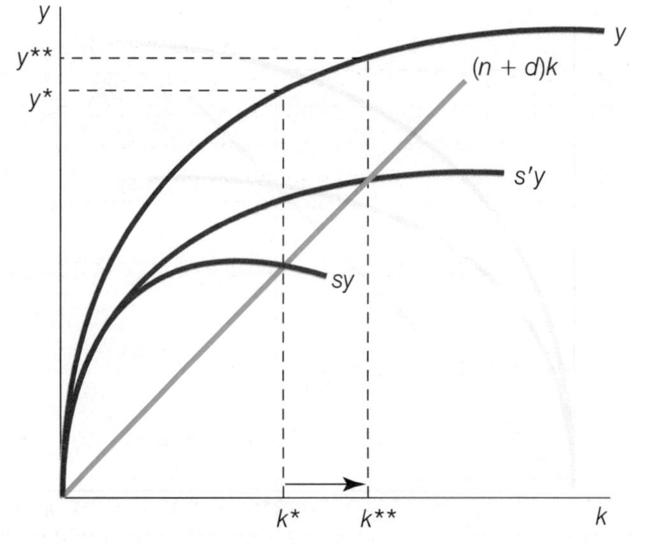

Figure 16.5 Increase in population growth in the Solow model

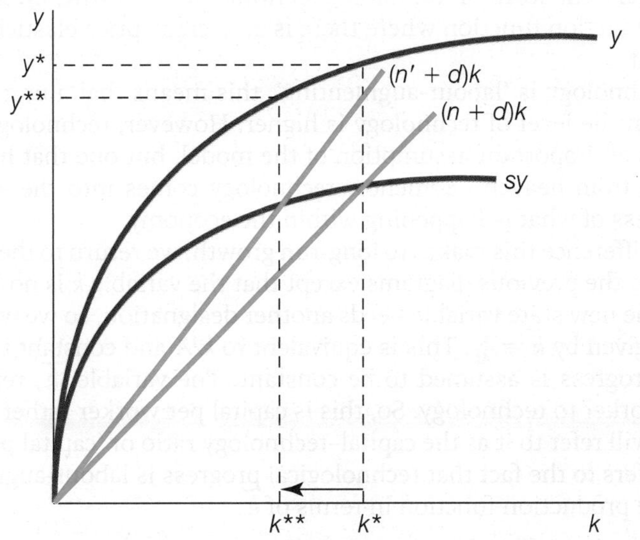

enough to keep the capital–labour ratio constant with a growing population. The capital–labour ratio begins to fall. It continues to fall until $sy = (n' + d)k$. At this point, the capital stock is k^{**} and the economy also has a lower value of output per worker, y^{**}. The economy is poorer now than it was before!

This explains and fits the empirical fact that countries have different levels of per capita income. The steady state will differ for countries depending on the level of savings, investment, population growth, labour force participation, etc. This is why countries try hard to increase savings while attempting to control population growth.

Rate of economic growth

In the simple version of the Solow model, there is no per capita growth when the economy is at its steady state. The model generates a constant capital–output ratio because both k and y are constant, implying that K/Y is constant. It also generates a constant interest rate, which is the marginal product of capital. Workers (who are also consumers) save a constant fraction of their wage and rental income, $Y = wL + rK$. Output per worker, which is the same as output per person, is thus constant in the steady state. Output, Y, is growing but only at the rate of population growth. This can be seen if we recall that $y \equiv \frac{Y}{L}$. (See the Appendix for the derivation.) In the simple Solow model, this means that economies will grow until they reach their steady state and eventually growth will stop altogether!

16.2.2 Solow model with technology

So, although the outcome of the Solow model fits the empirical observation that countries have different per capita incomes, it does not explain why economies grow persistently over long periods of time. To generate sustained growth in per capita income, we have to introduce **technological progress**. Thus, we include a technology variable, A, to the production function:

$$Y = F(K, AL) = K^{\alpha} (AL)^{1-\alpha} \quad (16.5)$$

The technology variable is viewed as 'labour-augmenting' in this formulation. Alternatively, it could take the form of 'capital-augmenting' or $Y = F(AK, L)$. In a Cobb-Douglas form for the production function where there is zero cross-price elasticity, the distinction is not significant.

So, where technology is 'labour-augmenting', this means that a unit of labour is more productive when the level of technology is higher. However, technology in this model is exogenous. It is an important assumption of the model, but one that has been viewed as akin to 'manna from heaven'. Somehow technology comes into the economy from the outside regardless of what is happening within the economy.

To see what difference this makes to long-run growth, we return to the Solow diagram. It is very similar to the previous diagrams except that the variable k is no longer constant in the long run. The new state variable needs another designation, so we will call it $\tilde{k}$ and it is approximately given by $\tilde{k} \equiv \frac{K}{AL}$. This is equivalent to k/A and constant because the rate of technological progress is assumed to be constant. The variable, $\tilde{k}$, represents the ratio of capital per worker to technology. So, this is capital per worker rather than total level of capital and we will refer to it as the capital–technology ratio or 'capital per effective unit of labour'. This refers to the fact that technological progress is labour-augmenting.

Rewriting the production function in terms of $\tilde{k}$.

$$\tilde{y} = \tilde{k}^{\alpha} \quad (16.6)$$

where $\tilde{y} = \frac{Y}{AL} = \frac{y}{A}$. We will now refer to $\tilde{y}$ as the output–technology ratio or 'output per effective unit of labour'. Again, this is because technology is labour–augmenting and AL is the 'effective' amount of labour used in production.

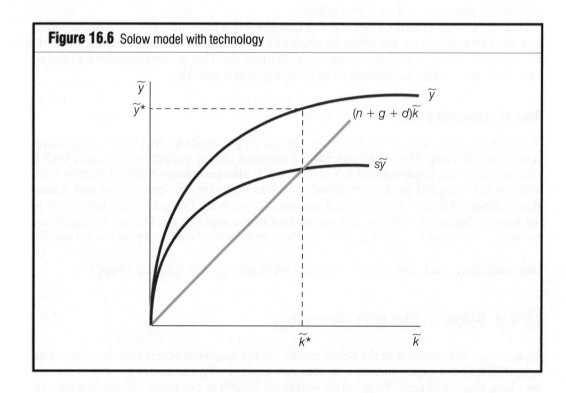

Figure 16.6 Solow model with technology

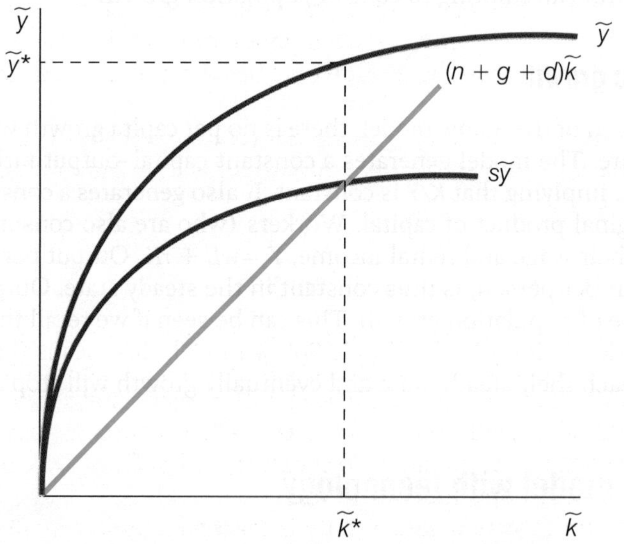

We also need to rewrite the capital accumulation function in terms of $\tilde{k}$. This is given by $\dot{\tilde{k}} = s\tilde{y} - (n + g + d)\tilde{k}$.[1] Combining the new versions of the production function and capital accumulation function, we have the Solow diagram with technological progress in Figure 16.6.

If an economy is below its steady state, then the capital–technology ratio or capital per effective unit of labour will rise over time because the amount of investment undertaken exceeds the amount needed to keep the capital–technology ratio constant. Similarly, if the capital per effective unit of labour is above the steady state, then the amount of investment undertaken is less than the amount needed to keep the capital–technology ratio constant. This will be true in both cases until $s\tilde{y} = (n + g + d)\tilde{k}$, at point $\tilde{k}$ *. The economy is in steady state and grows at the rate of technological progress, g. This also implies that capital, output, consumption and population are growing at constant rates as a result, and so the economy is said to be growing along a **balanced growth path**.

We will now work out the steady state in the Solow model with technology. Recall that the steady-state output per effective unit of labour is determined by the production function and the condition that $\dot{\tilde{k}} = 0$. First, similar to the simple Solow model, we find that

$$\tilde{k}^* = \left(\frac{s}{n+g+d}\right)^{1/1-\alpha} \tag{16.7}$$

Substituting into the production function yields

$$\tilde{y}^* = \left(\frac{s}{n+g+d}\right)^{\alpha/1-\alpha} \tag{16.8}$$

In terms of output per worker, we rewrite the above as

$$y^*(t) = A(t)\left(\frac{s}{n+g+d}\right)^{\alpha/1-\alpha} \tag{16.9}$$

What is notable and different here is that output y^* and A both depend on time, so an economy can grow at the rate of technological progress. So, output per worker is determined by technology, the investment rate and population growth rate. Figure 16.6 shows the outcome. Now, if $g = 0$, then the result would be identical to the Solow model without technology.

Another interesting result from this is that changes in the investment rate and population growth rate affect the long-run *level* of output per worker but not the long-run *growth rate* of output per worker!

Changing the long-run level of output per worker

To illustrate how the long-run level of output per worker can be changed in the Solow model, we will suppose that there is a permanent increase in the saving rate from s to s'. Figure 16.7 looks very much like the result seen in the Solow model with no technological progress. At the initial capital–technology ratio, $\tilde{k}$ *, investment exceeds the amount needed to keep the capital–technology ratio constant, so $\tilde{k}$ begins to rise until a new steady state of $\tilde{k}$ ** is reached. An upward shift in the $s\tilde{y}$ curve, therefore, speeds up the rate of growth temporarily until the new steady state is reached. Fundamentally, however, g has

---

1 The derivation is the same as the Solow model without technology. We instead derive it from

$$\frac{\dot{\tilde{k}}}{\tilde{k}} = \frac{\dot{K}}{K} - \frac{\dot{A}}{A} - \frac{\dot{L}}{L}$$

16

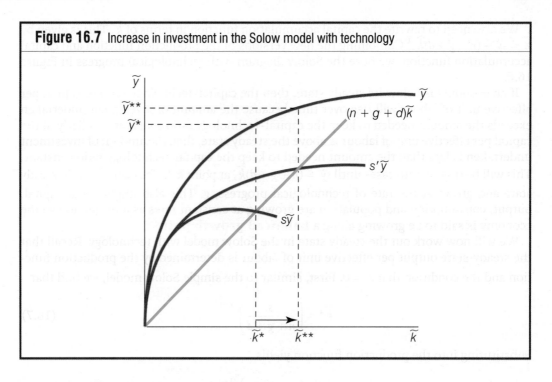

Figure 16.7 Increase in investment in the Solow model with technology

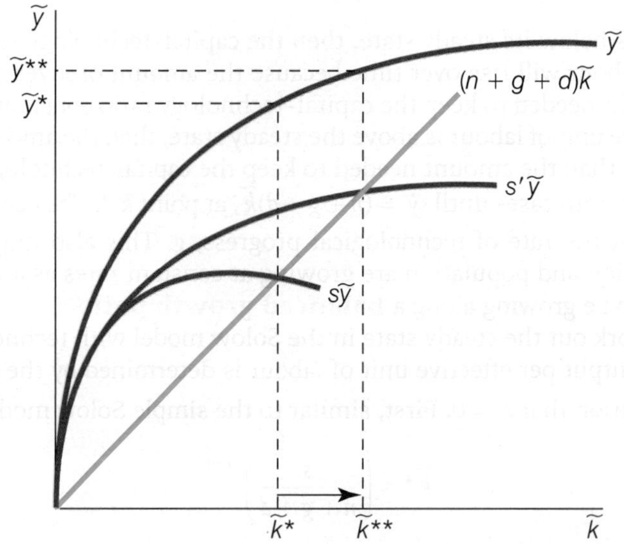

not been affected and thus the rate of economic growth remains the same as before. Therefore, policies that, say, permanently increase the rate of investment will push the economy to a higher steady-state *level* of income, but will not increase its long-run rate of growth.

16.2.3 Long-run growth in the Solow model

The Solow model shows that sustained economic growth occurs only in the presence of technological progress. Without technological progress, capital accumulation will encounter diminishing returns. However, if there were improvement in technology, then labour productivity will grow and capital accumulation will also increase because it slows down the diminishing returns to capital. Figure 16.8 shows long-run growth in the Solow model when there is a technological improvement.

In Figure 16.8, technological progress has allowed the existing inputs to be used more efficiently, so the production function has shifted upwards. At the initial capital–technology ratio $\widetilde{k}^*$, there is now a higher level of steady state output, $\widetilde{y}^{**}$. Part of this increase in output is due to productivity advancement or **total factor productivity** (TFP) and the other part is ensuing capital accumulation.

The difficulty of the Solow model is that seemingly it cannot account for differences in growth rates across countries except by appealing to technological progress, which is not modelled in this framework. Table 16.1 shows the importance of technological progress as suggested by the Solow model.

There are two things to note here. First, there is a clear association between periods of high output growth and high technological progress. Second, these developed nations follow similar experiences with much better performance over 1950–1973 than 1974–1987, implying that all the most significant developed economies are subject to similar technology shocks.

Figure 16.8 Technological progress in the Solow model

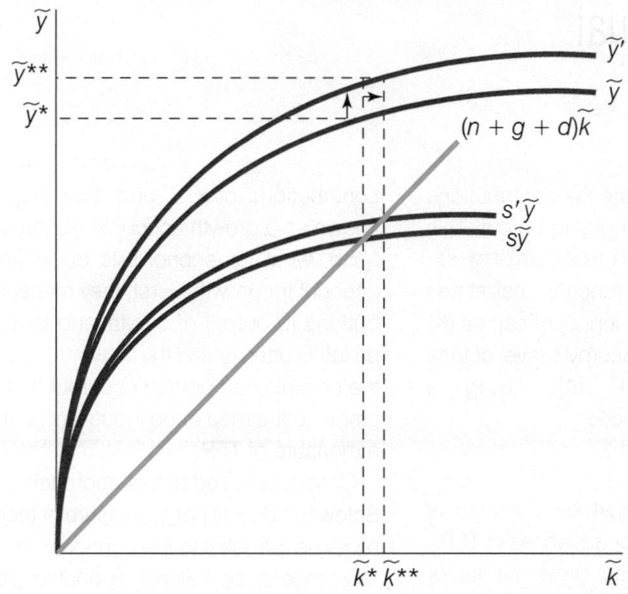

16.2.4 The convergence hypothesis

We have highlighted the difficulty of the Solow model in explaining long-run rates of economic growth, but it does seem to explain why countries have different levels of per capita income. In this section, we will examine the suggestion that growth should speed up if an economy is below its steady-state level of output. Consider the key equation from the Solow model again,

$$\frac{\dot{\tilde{k}}}{\tilde{k}} = s\frac{\tilde{y}}{\tilde{k}} - (n+g+d)$$

This means that output per effective unit of labour will decline as $\tilde{k}$ rises because of diminishing returns to capital. Therefore, if, for example, an economy is beginning to develop and has low levels of capital stock, then it should realize higher returns to its capital than a country which is developed and has had a lot of capital accumulation. If these economies have the same levels of technology, investment rate and population growth, then the developing country will grow faster than the developed economy because of diminishing returns to capital. The output per worker gap between these countries will narrow over time as both economies approach the steady state. Therefore, an important prediction of the neoclassical model is a **convergence hypothesis**. This hypothesis predicts that developing countries will grow faster than developed countries, if they have the same steady state.

Does this bear out empirically? Tables 16.2 and 16.3 give some indication of the growth rates of rich countries since 1950. In terms of annual growth rates, it is clear that Japan, which started at a much lower level of development at the start of this period, grew faster than other more developed economies. Several observations can be made. First, growth rates were much higher between 1950–1973 than 1974–2000. Second, the ratio of real per capita output between 2000 and 1950 shows that, in the space of 50 years, the size of these

Global application 16.1

The Solow residual

Suppose we wanted to estimate the contributions of inputs and productivity changes to output. This approach is known as **growth accounting**.

We start with a production function that states that output (Y) is produced by inputs of capital (K) and labour (L), and by the economy's level of total factor productivity or TFP (A). Using a Cobb-Douglas production function:

$$Y = AK^{\alpha}L^{1-\alpha}$$

If output changes, then it must be because of changes in capital or labour, or advances in TFP.

Therefore, an economy can grow via factor accumulation, which refers to increasing the inputs of labour and capital, or by increases in total factor productivity, which refers to productivity advances or technological progress. The former would lead to an increase in the level of growth, if it were say investment in the neoclassical model, while the latter could generate an increase in the rate of economic growth. Computing the different contributions of *K*, *L* and *A* to output growth is known as a growth accounting exercise.

So, what do economists do when they try to account for growth? First, they measure the contributions to output of capital and labour. What will be left is often called the **Solow residual**. This is the unexplained portion of output that is not attributable to the measured inputs and is thought to be a measure of TFP.

Criticisms levied at this approach argue that the Solow residual is not a measure of technology, but picks up 'shocks' to the economy, such as monetary shocks or military spending, for example. Essentially, the critique is that the Solow residual just captures growth that is not explained by the growth in inputs because of measurement problems, and therefore, we cannot assume that these are productivity advances. Another difficulty is getting the right measures of capital stock. This has proved to be tricky, so always read the estimates carefully before drawing conclusions.

Table 16.1 Annual growth rates of output per capita and of technological progress, 1950–1987

	Rates of growth of output per capita (%)			Rates of technological progress (%)		
Country	**1950–1973**	**1974–1987**	**Change**	**1950–1973**	**1974–1987**	**Change**
France	4.0	1.8	–2.2	4.9	2.3	–2.6
Germany	4.9	2.1	–2.8	5.6	1.9	–3.7
Japan	8.0	3.1	–4.9	6.4	1.7	–4.7
UK	2.5	1.8	–0.7	2.3	1.7	–0.6
US	2.2	1.6	–0.6	2.6	0.6	–2.0
Average	4.3	2.1	–2.2	4.4	1.6	–2.8

Source: IMF. International Financial Statistics

economies has increased substantially from 2.6 times for the US economy to 11.4 times for Japan. Table 16.3 makes the same observation, but over a longer period of time. It is clear from these tables that even slight differences in growth performance, when compounded over a long time, can result in remarkably different levels of output.

If there is convergence, then there should be an inverse relationship between a nation's starting level of income and subsequent growth. Cursory evidence has already been

Table 16.2 The evolution of output per capita in five rich countries since 1950

	Annual growth rate output per capita (%)		Real output per capita (1996 $US)		
	1950–1973	1974–2000	1950	2000	2000/1950
France	4.1	1.6	5489	21 282	3.9
Germany	4.8	1.7	4642	21 910	4.7
Japan	7.8	2.4	1940	22 039	11.4
UK	2.5	1.9	7321	21 645	3.4
US	2.2	1.7	11 903	30 637	2.6
Average	4.3	1.8	6259	23 503	3.7

Source: Penn World Tables

Table 16.3 Per capita real GDP

Country	Ratio of 2000 to 1870	Annual growth (%)
Japan	27	2.7
US	10	1.8
France	10	1.9
UK	5	1.3

Source: IMF, International Financial Statistics

provided in Table 16.3, where we can see that Japan being the poorest country in 1950 experiences phenomenal growth up to the year 2000, which is on average five times greater than that experienced by the US, which was the richest nation in 1950.

Figure 16.9 shows a clear negative relationship between initial level of per capita income and growth rate for countries between 1880 and 1973. However, if we look at a more recent period (1960–1995) there is no clear relationship, as seen in Figure 16.10. You would have noticed that there were fewer observations in the 1880 chart than in the later one. This is precisely the critique levied by DeLong (1988), who argued that results found by Baumol (1986) relied too much on the countries which were industrialized and therefore had data which was available from the earlier period. We will return to these rich countries to see what has happened in the past few decades.

Conditional convergence

Another inference that can be drawn from the Solow model is that countries will converge in growth rates conditioned on differences in steady states. This means that countries are converging to their own steady states. This is known as **conditional convergence** or sigma convergence. This concept tests for convergence by looking at the actual distribution of world income levels. If convergence is to be observed, then the variance of income levels should be falling over time. Table 16.4 looks at the comparative growth performance of poor and middle income countries compared to the industrialized nations in the OECD.

What is apparent from Table 16.4 is that some poor and middle income countries (particularly China and Korea) have a tendency to grow faster, and catch up with the richer nations, whereas there are many other poor countries that actually record growth rates that are lower than those in the OECD. In terms of the world income distribution, this implies that instead of seeing convergence, you may actually observe polarization between rich and poor nations. Figure 16.11 gives the growth rates plotted against initial income levels in the OECD countries from 1960–1995. The negative relationship looks like there is conditional convergence among these nations, the world's richest countries, in this later period as well as in the earlier period.

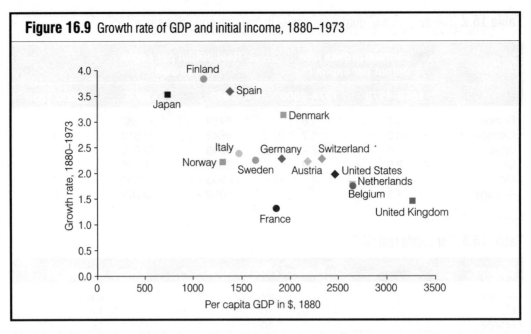

Figure 16.9 Growth rate of GDP and initial income, 1880–1973

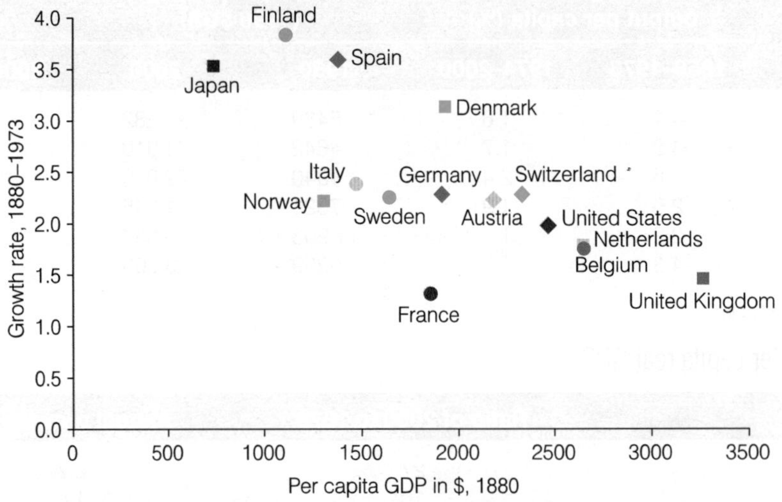

Figure 16.10 Growth rate of GDP and initial income, 1960–1995

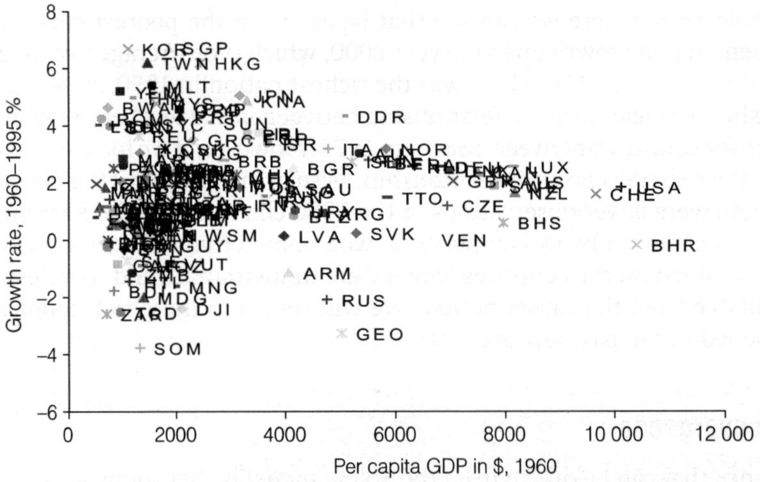

Table 16.4 Per capita GNP and annual growth rates

Poor and middle income countries	1997 level ($US)	1980–1997 growth (%)	OECD countries	1997 level ($US)	1980–1997 growth (%)
Mozambique	100	−1.2	Portugal	10 500	2.9
Bangladesh	300	2.3	Spain	14 500	2.0
Nigeria	300	−1.2	Ireland	18 300	4.2
China	800	11.0	Italy	20 100	1.4
Indonesia	1100	5.5	UK	20 700	2.0
Philippines	1200	1.1	France	26 500	2.0
Turkey	3100	1.7	US	28 700	1.7
Korea	10 500	7.8	Switzerland	44 300	1.6

Source: World Bank, World Development Report

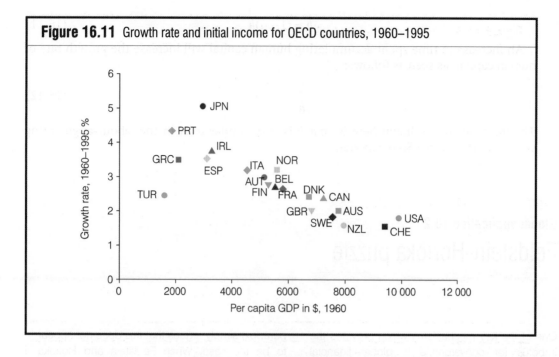

Figure 16.11 Growth rate and initial income for OECD countries, 1960–1995

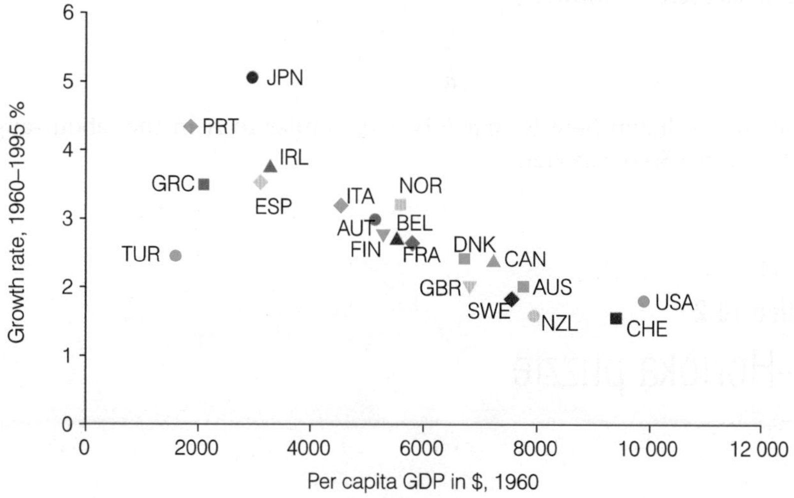

16.3 Growth models with human capital

We will conclude this section of neoclassical growth by examining one of the extensions of the Solow model. The simple assumptions surrounding labour in the Solow model can be revised to include **human capital**, that is, workers with skills and education; so growth could be driven by human capital instead of 'manna from heaven'.

In 1988, Lucas extended the neoclassical model by assuming that individuals spend time accumulating skills, such as by going to school. Mankiw, Romer and Weil (1992) thought of human capital accumulation in the same way as physical capital accumulation by forgoing consumption. We will now incorporate human capital into the Solow model by introducing a concept of labour that includes human capital.

Output, Y, is produced by physical capital, K, labour, L, and h which is human capital per person, in a Cobb-Douglas production function. This can be seen as:

$$Y = K^{\alpha}(hL)^{1-\alpha} \qquad (16.10)$$

Technology is still assumed to grow exogenously at rate, g. However, individuals in this economy accumulate human capital by spending time learning new skills instead of working. So, if an individual $1-\mu$ devotes fraction of time learning (and μ amount of time working), then

Pudong area of Shanghai, China

Source: Getty Images

16

$$\dot{h} = (1 - \mu)h \tag{16.11}$$

An increase in time spent accumulating human capital will increase the growth rate of human capital, as seen as follows:

$$\frac{\dot{h}}{h} = 1 - \mu \tag{16.12}$$

The inference to be drawn here is that h is very similar to A in the labour-augmenting version of the simple Solow model.

Global application 16.2

Feldstein-Horioka puzzle

One of the key mechanisms which provides the impetus for convergence is global financial markets that transfer savings to where they can achieve the highest return, which according to the Solow model is in the poorer nations. But what if markets do not behave in this way? If savings will move to where they can receive the highest return regardless of national boundaries, then there should be no relationship between national savings and national investment. The Feldstein-Horioka puzzle (probably more of a paradox) simply argues that this does not appear to be the case. When Feldstein and Horioka looked at average saving and investment rates for 25 countries between 1990–1997, they found a strong positive correlation between the two. Figure 1 gives a picture of this relationship for some industrialized countries. Thus, a key mechanism for convergence simply does not bear out empirically, and perhaps we should not be surprised about the lack of convergence in growth rates among the world's economies.

Figure 1 National savings versus national investment, for industrialized countries

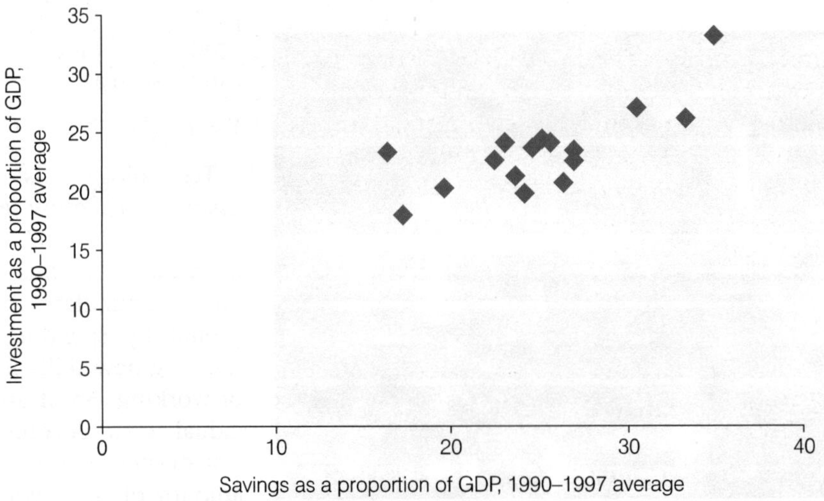

Source: Penn World Tables

The solution to the neoclassical model with human capital in steady state is virtually identical to the simple version of the Solow model. We start by writing the production function in terms of output per worker:

$$y = k^{\alpha} (hl)^{1-\alpha} \tag{16.13}$$

The parameter $1-\mu$ is assumed to be constant and exogenously determined, so individuals accumulate human capital at a constant rate. Since it is constant, the equation should look very similar to the Solow model from before. So, y and k will grow at the constant rate, g, the rate of technological progress, which is now determined by human capital accumulation, so that $g = 1-\mu$.

Since $1-\mu$ is constant, the output per worker equation is still given by:

$$\tilde{y} = \tilde{k}^{\alpha} \tag{16.14}$$

The capital accumulation equation can be written similarly as:

$$\dot{\tilde{k}} = s\tilde{y} - (n+g+d)\tilde{k} \tag{16.15}$$

These are exactly the same equations as in the simple Solow model! Adding human capital does not change the basic predictions of the model. To finish the solution, we first set $\dot{\tilde{k}} = 0$ and find $\frac{\tilde{k}}{\tilde{y}} = \frac{s}{n+g+d}$. Substituting this condition into the output per worker equation gives the steady-state value of $\tilde{y}$. This is given by

$$\tilde{y}^{*} = \left(\frac{s}{n+g+d}\right)^{\alpha/1-\alpha} \tag{16.16}$$

Rewriting this in terms of output per worker,

$$y^{*}(t) = \left(\frac{s}{n+g+d}\right)^{\alpha/1-\alpha} h(t) \tag{16.17}$$

This shows that y^* should grow at the same rate as $1-\mu$. This solution suggests that the extended Solow model sheds some additional light on why some countries are rich and others are poor. Some countries do well because they have high investment rates in physical capital, low population growth, high levels of technology and spend a large fraction of time accumulating human capital. In steady state, though, do not forget that this extended Solow model still predicts that per capita output grows at the rate of technological progress, g, as in the simple model. It is clear, therefore, that the main determinant of long-run growth is technological progress. Yet, this is the one variable that is determined outside of the neoclassical models.

16.4 Endogenous growth theories

This section covers a newer strand of models, known as **endogenous growth theory**, which attempt to incorporate the determinants of the main engine of growth, technology, into the framework. If we can understand what determines A, then we can explain the growth rate of y^*. This is what endogenous growth theories try to do.

16.4.1 The AK model

The simplest version of this strand of theories is the **AK model**. Let us start with a modified Solow-type production function where $\alpha = 1$. The production function is now given by:

$$Y = AK \tag{16.18}$$

where A is a positive constant and K is **broad capital**. Broad capital represents physical capital, but also human capital. Though it is a notion of broad capital, we simplify the analysis to say that capital is accumulated as individuals save in the economy rather than consume. This is given by

$$\dot{K} = sY - dK \tag{16.19}$$

where s is the investment rate and d is the rate of depreciation, both are assumed to be constant. We assume that no population growth occurs and treat these as per capita variables for simplicity. Now consider the Solow diagram for this production function in Figure 16.12.

There are two curves in the diagram, where the dK line represents the amount of investment needed to replace the depreciation of the capital stock. The sY curve is the total investment in the economy as a function of the capital stock. Because Y is a linear function of K, this is a straight line.

When we assume that total investment is larger than depreciation, the capital stock will grow. This is the key feature of the AK model. In Figure 16.12, we illustrate this by having the economy start at point K_0. At every point to the right of K_0, the investment exceeds depreciation so the economy continues to grow. In fact, the capital stock is always growing and growth never stops in this model.

The key difference between the AK model and the Solow model is that this model assumes constant returns to capital, while the Solow model assumed diminishing returns, so that each unit of capital was less productive than the previous unit. The marginal product in the AK model, in contrast, is always A. This means that growth can continue

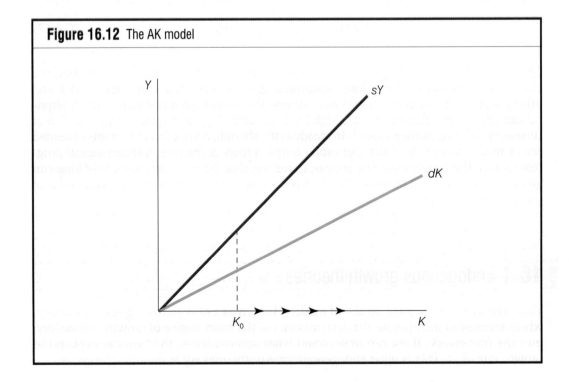

Figure 16.12 The AK model

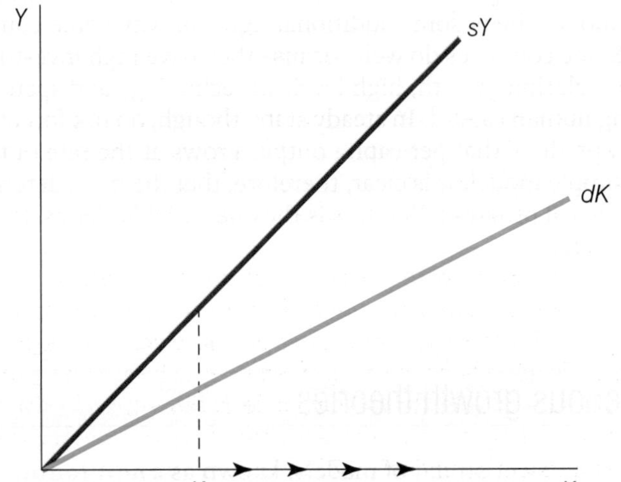

perpetually. And it means that the growth rate of output is equal to the growth rate of capital because A is constant. This implies that the growth rate of the economy is an increasing function of the investment rate, as seen in Figure 16.12. See the Appendix for the derivation.

However, a failing is that the AK model does not provide an explanation as to why constant returns to scale are achievable with broad capital. For instance, if the capital had positive spill-over effects so that it made other capital productive, then we might not expect diminishing returns to set in. This explanation is provided by the next set of models.

16.4.2 The Romer model

The endogenous growth model developed by Romer endogenizes technological progress by introducing researchers who invent new ideas and spur on technological advancement. In these types of models, technological progress is driven by R&D (research and development) and can explain why rich countries experience persistent growth. It also goes to show why technology transfer is so important for developing countries and why poor countries have lower levels of technology if they do not have much R&D.

Similar to the Solow model, the Romer model has two main elements representing the production function and a set of equations explaining how the inputs into production evolve over time. The key point is that technology can be thought of as ideas, which are generated by researchers. So, similar to the neoclassical models, for a given level of technology, A, the production function exhibits constant returns to scale. But, because ideas are also an input into production, the production function exhibits increasing returns with respect to technology. This derives from the non-rivalrous nature of ideas. Ideas can benefit many and not just the inventor. We are all better off because Edison invented the light bulb.

The accumulation equations for capital and labour are identical to the Solow model in the Romer model. The only difference is the treatment of technological progress, which is now not assumed to be driven by factors outside of the model. Instead, Romer introduces a production function for ideas. The Romer model offers $A(t)$ as the stock of knowledge or ideas that have been invented through history up to time t. Then, $\dot{A}$ is the number of new ideas produced at any given time. So, it is equal to the number of people inventing new ideas, L_A, multiplied by the rate at which they discover these new ideas, $\bar{\delta}$. The production function for A is thus given by:

$$\dot{A} = \bar{\delta} L_A \tag{16.20}$$

where the discovery rate, $\bar{\delta}$, could be constant or could be an increasing or decreasing function of A. There are essentially three possibilities. One is a non-changing rate of invention, so it is simply a constant stream of inventions. The second is a 'standing on shoulders of giants' notion where current ideas are easier to uncover because of the wealth of past knowledge. Ideas of the past increase the productivity of current researchers. So, the invention of lasers makes the invention of surgical tools much easier. Conversely, a third possibility is a 'crowding out' effect where researchers duplicate each other's work, so having more people does not increase the rate of scientific discovery. Also, the most obvious inventions would have already been undertaken so it is increasingly more difficult to discover new ideas. These would lead $\bar{\delta}$ to being a decreasing function of A.

This framework also suggests that there are two types of workers in this model, those who produce L_Y and those who invent L_A. This implies that $L_Y + L_A = L$. This brings us back to the realization that the set-up is similar to the Solow model except that there are two types of workers and there is also an ideas equation. In addition, in this model, the rate of technological progress is generated by workers, L_A, and does not rely on exogenous shocks.

So long as inventive activities continue, the economy will grow and A is now determined within the model.

16.4.3 Evidence of growth

The Romer model is actually quite testable. For instance, would increasing the number of researchers increase the rate of invention? Would investing more in R&D prompt technological progress? Can countries therefore increase the long-run rate of economic growth in their economies through implementing these types of policies?

Jones (1995) evaluated the evidence for endogenous growth theory by reference to the US which has had persistent growth in the last century. Jones finds that since 1950, the fraction of the labour force that consists of scientists and engineers engaged in R&D had increased threefold. However, average growth rates in the US are no higher today than they were from 1870 to 1929.

What about the evidence concerning investment, for instance, which is thought to be a driver of long-run growth in the AK model of endogenous growth? Well, Jones again finds that investment rates in the US also increased greatly since 1950 without similar evidence of an increase in growth rates.

Finally, what about human capital? Now, educational attainment has increased tremendously in the US in the past century. In 1940, fewer than one in four adults had completed secondary school. By 1995, more than 80 per cent of adults had a completion diploma. Despite this investment in human capital, Jones finds that the US, Bolivia and Malawi all grew at around the same rate despite significant differences in the level of human capital, investment and also R&D personnel. Table 16.5 gives further evidence along these lines.

In the first grouping of four countries in Table 16.5, we see that the US, New Zealand, Greece and Ethiopia have very different levels of educational enrolment. However, they grew at around the same rate of 2 per cent between 1990 and 2002. The second group of countries all have almost the same rate of educational enrolment, but have vastly different growth rates. Ireland and South Korea are fast growing exceeding 6 per cent and 4 per cent, respectively, while Brazil and Spain grew much more slowly at around 2 per cent. Finally,

Table 16.5 International comparisons

Country	Real GDP per capita, 1990 ($)	Real GDP per capita growth, 1990–2002 (%)	Educational enrolment (gross for all levels combined), 2002 (%)
US	18 054	2.0	92
New Zealand	11 513	2.1	101
Greece	6768	2.2	86
Ethiopia	312	2.3	34
Spain	9583	2.3	92
Ireland	9274	6.8	90
Brazil	4042	1.3	92
Korea	6673	4.7	92
Netherlands	13 029	2.2	99
France	13 904	1.6	91
Belgium	13 232	1.8	111
United Kingdom	13 297	2.4	113

Sources: World Bank, World Development Report; UNDP Human Development Indicators; Penn World Tables

16

the third group of countries all have approximately the same level of initial income in 1990, and they possess roughly equivalent growth rates with some notable differences in educational enrolment. From a cursory examination of the evidence, the rate of growth seems to be more closely related to initial levels of income than education.

Global application 16.3

Does the 'new economy' measure up to the inventions of the past?

Is the 'new economy', characterized by advances in computing and information technology such as the Internet, as important for productivity growth as the past great inventions of electricity and the internal combustion engine?

The first industrial revolution largely began in the UK in 1760 and lasted to about 1830. However, despite the innovations of this period, which included the steam engine, productivity growth was rather slow. The second industrial revolution occurred simultaneously in the US and Europe around 1860 to 1900. This witnessed the invention of electricity, the internal combustion engine, and so forth, which together led to the golden age of productivity between 1913–1972.

The late 1990s witnessed a period of rapid advances in productivity that has led many to believe that the 'new economy' has resulted in permanently higher levels of labour productivity. The rate of total factor productivity growth between 1995 and 1999 in the US was 1.79 per cent, as compared with 0.62 per cent from 1972-1995, 1.60 per cent between 1913–1972 and 0.77 per cent between 1870–1913. It therefore looks like the current rate of productivity growth exceeds even the golden era of 1913–1972. Will the 'new economy' comprise a third industrial revolution with lasting productivity gains?

First, the total factor productivity growth appears to exist only in the part of the economy engaged in producing computers and peripherals as well as the durable manufacturing sector. This comprises 12 per cent of the economy, which raises the question of how far the 'new economy' reaches into the rest of the 88 per cent. The evidence thus far is that three-quarters of all computer investment has been in industries with no perceptible trend increase in productivity. In fact, there has been a measured deceleration of productivity growth in the bulk of the economy outside of durable manufacturing. This has been called the Solow computer paradox where Solow declared in 1987 that the computer age appears to be everywhere except in the productivity statistics. Also, the current period of measured productivity advances is a relatively short period of time as compared with the estimates for the earlier periods. In fact, if output was growing faster than trend, then productivity was also growing faster than trend. Some part of the productivity gain would be transitory rather than permanent, and there is some evidence of this as well. Third, it does not matter how powerful the computer and how user-friendly the software, humans are required to make computers productive. This would lead to diminishing returns for the productivity impact of computers. Finally, although the Internet has undoubtedly increased consumer welfare, e-commerce consists of a number of duplicative activities by competing businesses and, in the end, it still requires human input. Therefore, the jury is still out as to whether the Internet and computing can measure up to the great inventions of the past, such as electricity extending the working day, electric motors that transformed manufacturing, the saving of time achieved by the automobile, the accessibility of travel through air travel, and the dissemination of information through the telephone, radio and television.

Technology transfers

One of the main implications from the neoclassical model is the convergence hypothesis that we reviewed earlier. Countries at low levels of development should have low levels of investment, which means that capital will not yet reach diminishing returns and poorer countries should grow faster than rich countries. With free capital markets, in fact, capital should move to countries with higher returns thereby facilitating capital accumulation in developing countries and helping them grow more quickly. In this way, countries can 'catch up' in the growth process and we should see a convergence in worldwide incomes.

Endogenous growth theory adds to this by saying that technology is determined within the model and produced by having researchers. If poorer countries do not have investment funds for R&D facilities and personnel, then they will have a lower level of technology than rich countries. This main driver of growth is not exogenously given but very much related to the factors within the model, such as the level of development, capital stock, human capital, etc. These theories suggest that developing countries can catch up by imitating the technology in developed countries rather than re-invent the wheel, as the saying goes.

Technology transfers can come in two forms, indirect or direct. Indirect transfers are things like 'learning by doing', a concept developed by Arrow. So, a German firm that sets up a factory in China will hire Chinese workers who will learn skills on the job based on more advanced German technology. Examples of direct transfers would be if the German company licensed its technology for use by a Chinese firm. Of course, technology transfers of this latter type will be costly. And, there is no guarantee that the Chinese firm will have the absorptive capacity to be able to use the more advanced technology. For these reasons, the 'catch up' process is probably both more costly and complex than the models indicate.

Threshold effects and general purpose technologies

On a similar point, the growth of most modern nations is actually built upon significant breakthroughs in technology. These having been established, they then support further growth through the continual development of secondary innovations, but these all stem from the original breakthrough technology which is often regarded as a general purpose technology (GPT). It is often noted that Britain's Industrial Revolution stemmed from two major developments in the spinning of cotton and smelting of iron ore. The whole concept of GPTs is that they are inventions that drive growth across the entire economy. The

Table 16.6 The making of Western Europe

Date	Per capita income (1990 prices)	Inventions
1000	400	Watermills
1100	430	Padded horse collar
1200	480	Windmills
1300	510	Compass
1400	600	Blast furnace
1500	660	Gutenburg printing press
1600	780	Telescope
1700	880	Pendulum
1800	1280	Steam engine, spinning and weaving machines, cast iron, electric battery
1900	3400	Telegraph, telephone, electric light, wireless
2000	17 400	Steel, cars, planes, computers, nuclear energy

Source: *The Economist*, December 1999

electrification of factories is an important example and, in more recent times, the microprocessor and information technology. Table 16.6 identifies some of the key inventions in the historical development of Western Europe. Therefore, growth may depend largely on the ready development or adoption of these important technologies.

16.4.4 Evaluation of endogenous growth theories

Endogenous growth theories attempt to understand the driver of growth in neoclassical models within the parameters of the model itself. In this way, these models seek to explain how persistent growth can occur and why countries grow at consistently different rates. However, once these models move away from the highly stylized and simple framework of the Solow model and its extensions, they move into a murkier realm. We have looked closely at technology and increasing returns. The AK model made some simple assumptions and seemed to predict a long-run growth rate for an economy. However, the main driver of growth remains elusive. As for the more complicated models, such as the Romer model, it has not yet borne out well. Crucially, the driver of growth in this type of model is a constant rate of invention that may vary positively or negatively with the number of researchers in the economy. Rate of invention and innovation appear to be exogenous to the model. So, although endogenous growth models go further than neoclassical models in trying to explain how technological progress (the driver of long-run growth) occurs, it still leaves many questions unanswered.

Moreover, once we start looking, there are a lot of other factors that seem to be important too. Insofar as the endogenous growth models are an attempt to understand why industrialized countries persistently grew so well, the newer growth literature tries to explain why some countries persistently lag behind. The poor countries in the world have had negative average growth rates over the past three decades. Sub-Saharan Africa, which includes some of the world's poorest countries, grew at a negative 0.8 per cent between 1972–2002, while the rich OECD countries grew at 2.0 per cent on average per annum over the same period.

The new growth literature, however, lacks a ready framework because the numerous relevant factors affecting growth include institutions, infrastructure, health, social capital, legal contracting regimes, political instability, conflict and war, among many others. These factors appear to be important in determining the growth prospects of a country, but are not easy to fit within a stylized framework. Although there are a number of empirical studies primarily using cross-country regressions to gauge the significance of various factors, there are conceptual difficulties. For instance, there are likely to be systematic differences across countries.

This emerging literature also has to contend with the question as to whether these types of factors are those which will drive long-run growth or fall within the category of changing the steady-state level of an economy.

Telecommunications, Congo

Source: Getty Images

Summary

- In this chapter, we have covered the main models of long-run economic growth.
- We started with neoclassical growth models, namely the Solow model.
- We also considered an extended version of the Solow model that included human capital, known as the Lucas formulation.
- After discussing the limitations of the Solow model, we moved to consider endogenous growth theories or new growth theories.
- The simplest formulation of an endogenous growth model is the AK model, which could explain persistent growth by modifying the assumption of constant returns in the neoclassical framework.
- Then, we considered the Romer model, which introduced a new production equation for ideas into the mix. Ideas and inventions can generate increasing returns, thus providing for persistent growth of an economy.
- We also examined the notion of technology transfers in versions of the convergence hypothesis.
- We concluded with an assessment of endogenous growth theories and how they still leave key factors unanswered, such as what drives innovation.
- We also looked briefly at new growth theories which attempt to understand why some countries seem persistently to lag behind. The evidence suggests that there are numerous factors, such as differing types of institutions and levels of political stability, which seem to contribute to developing countries falling further behind.

Key terms

AK model
Balanced growth path
Broad capital
Capital deepening
Capital widening
Conditional convergence
Convergence hypothesis
Economic growth
Endogenous growth theories
Growth accounting
Human capital
Long-run growth
Solow diagram
Solow model
Solow residual
Steady state
Technological progress
Technology transfer
Total factor productivity (TFP)

Review questions

1. After decades of exhorting, Americans are finally saving more. What will be the effects of this permanent change in behaviour in a simple Solow model without technology? What is the marginal product of capital in this new steady state? Is it possible to save too much?
2. Suppose there is free migration throughout the European Union, and many workers immigrated into Germany. Graph the effects of this policy in the Solow model with and without human capital. Will this affect the level or the rate of economic growth?

Review questions (continued)

3. To what extent does the Romer model depend on ideas being non-rivalrous? What would happen to the rate of economic growth if ideas were freely disseminated?
4. Is it possible for a developing country to 'catch up' just by receiving technology transfers from developed countries?

More advanced problems

5. The Solow model is as follows: $Y = Af(K,L)$, where $f(\cdot)$ is a Cobb-Douglas production function and K and L respectively represent capital and labour. The Solow residual is given by A. The model can be rewritten as $Y = AK^bL^{1-b}$, where b lies between 1 and 0 and $A > 0$.
   a. Show that Y is increasing in K.
   b. What is the marginal product of labour if $K = 25$, $L = 10$, and $b = 0.5$?
   c. What is the value of the Solow residual if $Y = 30$, $\dot{Y} = 64.5$, $\dot{K} = 20$, $\dot{L} = 5$?
6. Using the Solow model with human capital, assess the effects of the following factors:
   a. the rate of technological progress is permanently doubled
   b. the rate of population growth permanently halves
   c. the average educational attainment of the labour force increases by two years.
7. Sketch what happens in the AK model when the rate of investment permanently increases threefold.
8. Which of these economies will become the largest in the world and why?

Country	GDP per capita ($)	Growth rate (%)	TFP growth (%)
US	36 006	2.0	4.0
Japan	31 407	2.6	3.0
Germany	24 051	2.0	1.5
China	989	8.2	1.5
India	487	3.3	1.5
Brazil	2593	0.8	0.8

For further resources, visit
http://www.thomsonlearning.co.uk/chamberlin_yueh

Appendix

Deriving the Solow model

To derive output per person, we first assume that the labour force participation rate is 100 per cent so that every person is a worker. Then, we rewrite the capital accumulation equation in terms of capital per person, which will then give us the amount of output per person for the given level of capital stock per person in the economy. First, we take the logarithms as follows:

$$k = \frac{K}{L}$$

$$\log k = \log K - \log L$$

Then, we take the derivatives: $\frac{\dot{k}}{K} = \frac{\dot{K}}{K} - \frac{\dot{L}}{L}$

Similarly, we rewrite the production function by first taking logs:

$$y = k^{\alpha}$$

$$\log y = \alpha \log k$$

And then, taking the derivatives: $\frac{\dot{y}}{y} = \alpha \frac{\dot{k}}{k}$

Finally, let us consider the growth rate of the labour force, $\frac{\dot{L}}{L}$. The Solow model assumes that the labour force participation rate is constant and that population growth is given by n. This implies that the labour force participation rate is also given by n. Alternatively, we can infer the exponential growth of the labour force as follows:

$$L(t) = L_0 e^{nt}$$

Taking the logs and differentiating once again gives n as the growth rate.

Combining the capital accumulation equation with the above gives:

$$\frac{\dot{k}}{k} = \frac{sY}{K} - n - d \Rightarrow \frac{sy}{k} - n - d$$

This now gives the capital accumulation equation in per worker terms:

$$\dot{k} = sy - (n + d)k$$

Deriving the rate of growth in the Solow model

To work out the rate of economic growth in the model, we start with $Y = K^{\alpha} L^{1-\alpha}$. If we take the logs of both sides:

$$\log Y = \log K^{\alpha} + \log L^{1-\alpha}$$

This can be rewritten as:

$$\log Y = \alpha \log K + (1 - \alpha) \log L$$

Taking the derivatives of both sides with respect to time, we see how the rate of growth of output is related to the rate of growth of inputs in the model. This is seen as follows:

$$\frac{d \log Y}{dt} = \alpha \frac{d \log K}{dt} + (1-\alpha)\frac{d \log L}{dt}$$

This implies that:

$$\frac{\dot{Y}}{Y} = \alpha \frac{\dot{K}}{K} + (1-\alpha)\frac{\dot{L}}{L}$$

This means that the rate of growth of output in the Solow model is a weighted average of the growth rates of capital and labour. Since the rate of growth of capital per worker is constant in the steady state, then output only grows in the economy at the rate of growth of labour. Since there is an assumed constant rate of labour force participation, the rate of growth of labour is the same as the rate of population growth, *n*. Thus, in steady state, there is only economic growth at the rate of increase in population in the Solow model.

Deriving the rate of growth in the Solow model with technology

The Solow model proceeds by acknowledging that there is technological progress and makes the further assumption that *A* is growing at a constant rate:

$$\frac{\dot{A}}{A} = g$$

This can be rewritten as: $A = A_0 e^{gt}$. The parameter *g* is the growth rate of technology. The capital accumulation equation in the Solow model with technology is given as:

$$\frac{\dot{K}}{K} = s\frac{Y}{K} - d$$

This implies that the growth rate of *K* is constant if and only if *Y/K* is constant. If that holds, then *y/k* is also constant, which further means that *y* and *k* are growing at the same rate. When capital, output, consumption and population are growing at constant rates, it is known as a balanced growth path. We then rewrite the production function in terms of output per worker:

$$y = k^{\alpha} A^{1-\alpha}$$

Taking logs and differentiating,

$$\frac{\dot{y}}{y} = \alpha \frac{\dot{k}}{k} + (1-\alpha)\frac{\dot{A}}{A}$$

Recall that $\frac{\dot{A}}{A} = g$, so substituting this into the above equation will give a constant rate of growth of output per worker and capital per worker at the rate of exogenous technological change, *g*.

Deriving the rate of growth in the AK model

Rewrite the capital accumulation equation in the AK model as:

$$\frac{\dot{K}}{K} = s\frac{Y}{K} - d$$

From the production function, we know that $\frac{Y}{K} = A$. So

$$\frac{\dot{K}}{K} = sA - d$$

For the production function, we first take logs which gives

$$\log Y = \log A + \log K$$

Then, taking the derivatives,

$$\frac{\dot{Y}}{Y} = \frac{\dot{A}}{A} + \frac{\dot{K}}{K}$$

Since technology is exogenously determined in the model, $g = \frac{\dot{A}}{A} = 0$. We can now see that the growth rate of output is equal to the growth rate of capital, as follows:

$$g = \frac{\dot{Y}}{Y} = sA - d$$

The key result is that the growth rate is an increasing function of the rate of investment in an economy.

Index